THE STATE, LAW AND DEVELOPMENT

ROBERT B. SEIDMAN

CROOM HELM LONDON

©1978 Robert B. Seidman
Croom Helm Ltd, 2-10 St John's Road, London SW11

British Library Cataloguing in Publication Data

Seidman, Robert Benjamin
    The state, law and development.
    1. Africa – Economic conditions – 1945 –
    2. Economic development 3. Law – Africa
    4. Law
    I. Title
    330.9'6   HC515

    ISBN 0-85664-630-X

Excerpts from this book have appeared in the *Wisconsin Law Review*, the *Journal of Economic Issues*, the *Eastern African Law Journal*, the *East African Law Review*, the *Zambian Law Review*, the *Law and Society Review*, *Contemporary Crises*, the *British Journal of the Sociology of Law*, the *Journal of Modern African Studies* and the *Journal of African Law*.

FOR JONATHAN, JUDY, KATHA, NEVA, GAY, AND ESPECIALLY ANN

Printed in Great Britain by offset lithography by
Billing & Sons Ltd, Guildford, London and Worcester

CONTENTS

PREFACE

This book sets forth a theory about the relationship between the state, the legal order, and social, political and economic development. Because it concerns theory, I explicate in some detail the methodology, perspectives and categories I think useful in generating middle level hypotheses. Good theory never arises in a vacuum; it *necessarily* arises to explain existential problems. Here I use the African experience as the historical matrix from which to derive theoretical propositions. Whether they can be useful only in explaining the state, law and development in Africa, or whether they have more general applications, each reader will answer from his own knowledge and experience. To avoid the obscurity that too frequently marks lawyers' theory, I usually set out each chapter's contributions to theory as a set of numbered sentences that, hopefully, hang together logically. It is not original to say that while I may be clearly wrong, I hope that I will at least be wrong clearly. The danger, of course, exists that the attempt to catch theory in so structured a form makes it static. I trust that I have avoided that danger, but of course the reader must judge for himself.

I owe a great many debts in connection with this book. I had practised law in Connecticut for fourteen years until, like Melville's Ishmael, boredom snatched me from my usual pursuits. In 1962, I found myself teaching law in Nkrumah's Ghana, trying to understand that strange world with only the usual philosophical and technical accoutrements of a practising lawyer of my generation – that is, not very much that helped.

Ghana in 1962 had a long suit in the rhetoric of development, and only a short one in action, a phenomenon that in this book I call 'soft development'. William B. Harvey, then Dean of the Faculty of Law at the University of Ghana, suggested that I try to put on paper my discontents. I tried to use Pound's schema of jural postulates to explain soft development, and discovered that it did not work very well.

In 1966, I took up a teaching post at the University of Wisconsin. There, J. Willard Hurst and the late Jacob Beuscher taught doctrines of the relationship between law and society that I found very exciting. A number of agricultural economists, sociologists and a few lawyers connected with the Land Tenure Center carried on the tradition of John R. Commons in institutional economics, and applied it to deve-

lopment problems — Raymond Penn, Peter Dorner, Herman
Felstenhausen, Joseph R. Thome, Marion Brown and Eugene Havens
were among them. In particular, they exposed me to a seminar in the
philosophy of John Dewey, led by Carl Boegholt, which opened up
fascinating paths that I have yet to explore fully, but whose influence
appears on every page of this volume. My law school colleagues at
Wisconsin too helped enormously: Zigurds Zile, William C. Whitford,
Joel Handler and Robert Shapiro, among many others.

I returned to Africa for two-year stints in Tanzania (1968-70) and
Zambia (1972-4). In Tanzania, I learned a great deal from Y.P. Ghai,
Aki Sawyerr, Rudy James, Lionel Cliffe and Tamas Szentes; in Zambia,
particularly from B.O. Nwabueze, then the Dean of the Law School at
the University of Zambia, and from Simbi Mubako.

By the time I left Zambia to take up a new post at Boston University, I had about half the MS for this book in draft. William B. Harvey,
who by chance found himself on the same fac⋯¹ᵗʸ ᵍᵉⁿᵉrously organized
a staff seminar on the draft MS. I owe a particular debt to him and all
the participants in that seminar, among them Robert Kent, Gilbert
Verbit, Charles Smith, Stanley Fisher, Robert Chin, Alan Hoben, David
Phillips and John Harris.

A number of people read the MS at various stages and gave time and
effort to help me: Joel Samoff, who with William J. Chambliss introduced me to the problems of methodology, Lawrence Church and J.
Willard Hurst, who not only read the MS but supplied six single-spaced
typewritten pages of critique. How can one adequately express grati-
tude for that?

A veritable host of research assistants have made my task easier,
William Tam, Richard Bourgeois, Richard Nelson, Kamau Williams and
Thomas Russell among many. John Allison cleaned up my awkward
prose, simplifying, querying, spearing the passive form and annihilating
the verb to be.

Nor can I really do justice to the many men and women who helped
with the technical aspects of producing this MS. Janice Lahey especially
proved a real rock, infinitely reliable, efficient and good-humoured.

I owe many more generalized debts. James C.N. Paul provided
continuous support, encouragement and advice. William J. Chambliss
taught me sociology by osmosis. Alan Feld and Tamar Frankel, the
kindest and most helpful colleagues, bore the burden of my incessant
talking about this material and always added fresh insights. My children
only complained mildly at debating epistemology at the breakfast table.
All of them have argued with me at length about this book — and I

learned from that. Many students in many countries taught me more by half than I taught them.

Most of all, of course, I am indebted to my wife, Ann Seidman, as my reliance on many of her writings demonstrates. If I were to do her justice, I would include her as co-author, for we have taught law and development so often, at so many different universities and elsewhere in Africa and the United States, and discussed every notion in this book at such length, that I am no longer sure where my ideas leave off and hers begin. Every author-husband of course owes a debt to his wife's patience, fortitude and good humour, and so do I; very few can owe as much as I do to his wife as scholar, teacher and colleague.

Finally, I must say my thanks to the various agencies that generously provided support and financial assistance: The International Legal Center, and especially John Bainbridge, who directed its SAILER programmes for years; the Ford Foundation, who supported me in Zambia; the University of Wisconsin and the Russell Sage Foundation, who supported me for a year in Tanzania; and the National Science Foundation, who supported me one summer when I wrote Part Four of the MS.

Obviously, none of these kind people made any of the errors which I am sure critics will find here; they are mine alone.

Robert B. Seidman

Cambridge, Massachusetts
June, 1977.

Part One

THE DOMAIN OF STUDY

1 THE DOMAIN OF STUDY

The torment of the Third World is the great issue of the age. Two thirds of the human race suffers in abject poverty. Hunger haunts their days, disease tortures their lives, death lurks in their doorways. Trussed in ancient bonds not of their own making, they do not control their resources or destinies.

Today all the world plucks at the sleeves of the academy, asking, What do you know? What are you good for?[1] Any answer must include a statement of the discipline's response to the Third World's torment. How lawyers respond ought to define the domain of the study of law and development. Lawyers, however, march to a discordant beat, suggesting at least three different definitions of that domain: conflict amelioration, law and society studies and problem solving.

I Conflict Amelioration; Law and Society Studies

The dominant Western jurisprudential and sociological tradition assumes that conflict amelioration is the law's basic function.[2] Law is an 'integrative' mechanism.[3] 'The function of the law is the orderly resolution of disputes. As this implies, "the law" (the clearest model of which I shall take to be the court system) is brought into operation after there has been a conflict. The court's task is to render a decision that will prevent the conflict – and all potential conflicts like it – from disrupting productive co-operation.'[4] This tradition celebrates the law as a great wall against Hobbesian anarchy.

Some modern writers on law in the less developed countries (the 'LDCs') have assumed that law functions in the LDCs just as they think it does in the metropolis. That function is 'to create a milieu in which social and cultural diversities are harmonized, values essential to societal and governmental purposes are unified (and others left alone), and tensions resolved . . . to maintain stability within a climate of desired, necessary and inevitable change'.[5] The Third World's imperative is social transformation, a painful, tension-ridden, conflict-plagued, inescapable middle passage. Avoiding tension and conflict in that passage too easily becomes an excuse for supporting the *status quo*. Conflict amelioration as a domain of study responds to the uncertainties of power, not the pain of poverty.

Other lawyer-academics have not responded to the cries of the Third

World, but to the more muted whimpers of the US academic community. These scholars have defined the domain of study for law and
development as 'the general connections between law, culture and
development'.[6] 'The basic goal', writes David M. Trubek, 'is to understand "law" as a social phenomenon.'[7] They assume that law and social
change in conditions of development is not different from law and
social change generally. They begin with variables derived from studies
of law and society in the Western developed world — 'universalistic
rules' or 'the legal culture' or 'the autonomous legal system'. They
study the Third World and its legal order not in order to ameliorate the
torment of the LDCs, but as an exotic laboratory in which to test the
chosen variables.

II Problem Solving

Another method of selecting the domain of study requires the researcher
to begin with difficulties faced by real people — poverty, pain, suffering,
conflict, vulnerability, power — rather than variables of academic
interest. 'Good research should scratch where people itch.'[8] The
pervasive troubles of the poor countries are poverty and oppression.
How are lawyers and the law engaged with these troubles? The answer
to that question defines our domain of study. I examine first, the
function of law in development and, second, the role of lawyers in that
process.

A. The Function of Law in Development

Modern social science conceives that each society is defined by the
repetitive interactions between its members. Nigeria differs from the
United States because its members interact differently than do
Americans. To say that a society changes is to say that these repetitive
interactions change. Social change can therefore be defined as a change
in repetitive patterns of behaviour. Development is a form of social
change.

Repetitive patterns of human behaviour are defined by norms,
supported by sanctions, expressing how the members of society are
expected to behave. State officials promulgate, communicate and
sanction a few of these norms. I shall use the words 'law' and 'the legal
order' interchangeably to mean all or any part of the normative system
in which the State has a finger. It includes the rules themselves, and the
processes by which they are promulgated, communicated or sanctioned
by officials. D.J. Black similarly defines the law as 'governmental social
control'.[9]

Law enters into the processes of development in two ways. First, today the state usually has the burden of trying purposely to induce social change. Only the state ordinarily has sufficient capacity, resources or legitimacy to undertake such a formidable task. Typically, the state tries to induce development by changing the rules defining repetitive patterns of behaviour, and by directing its officials to act in new ways — that is, by changing the legal order. Demands for development therefore appear as demands for new law: new rules of land tenure, marketing boards, planning machinery, electoral politics, educational institutions, monetary systems, taxation. The International Congress of Jurists in 1959 modified its definition of 'The Rule of Law'. That concept, they said, 'should be employed not only to safeguard and advance the civil and political rights of the individual in a free society, but also to establish social, political, educational and cultural conditions under which his legitimate aspirations and dignity may be realized'.[10]

Circumstances thrust this function of the legal order upon the governors. The patterns of behaviour that define society are in constant flux. Society ever changes. However little a government changes its law, vast upheavals inevitably erupt: wars, revolutions, famines, new philosophies, cash cropping, industrialization, foreign or domestic investment. The romantic vision of a never-changing tropical society — poor, to be sure, but in the unhurried idyll of its days blessedly free of future shock — is a lie. Since societies change even within the constraints of their legal order, a decision to induce new patterns of behaviour by changing the law is not, as is frequently thought, a decision to introduce change into an otherwise static world. Rather, it is an attempt to deflect existing processes of change into channels thought more desirable. To maintain existing law is a decision to accept whatever changes social processes themselves induce.

Besides being an instrument for channelling social change, the legal order enters into development processes in another, perhaps even more fundamental way. The nation-state today mainly determines the course of social change, rather than church, family or village. That reflects the great transformation from kin-oriented, village, agricultural subsistence communities into societies with a high degree of specialization and exchange. In such societies, the shoemaker must know not only that others will supply him with leather, but that some will keep a monetary system going, and others will create and maintain markets where he can purchase food and sell his shoes. 'Modernization requires a whole range of new, specialized roles. This can only succeed if the persons who

occupy them mesh their activities with each other. This requires a high
degree of co-ordination.'[11] Hence the long-term trend in Western
Europe was 'toward the perfection of systems of obligations and their
transformation from a network of individual relationships into obligations to the community'.[12] Law is the most available instrument to
define, create, enforce and co-ordinate these obligations. In conditions
of development, the problem posed for social control is not merely to
restrain deviance from the old order and to restore the *status quo ante*,
but to induce change. Most non-governmental social control agencies
are not designed as change mechanisms. They function to meliorate
conflict. Law has significance for development not because law
influences behaviour significantly – in many, perhaps most cases its
actual influence on behaviour is peripheral – but because, in spite of its
manifest limitations, it is the most available instrument to induce social
change.

It is a common dirge the world around, however, that too frequently
law fails to induce the prescribed behaviour. Development programmes
remain on paper, plans die in parturition, policies remain unimplemen-
ted. Myrdal has denoted the consequences 'soft development'; that
is,

> a general lack of social discipline in underdeveloped countries,
> signified by many weaknesses: deficiencies in their legislation and,
> in particular, in law observance and enforcement; lack of obedience
> to rules and directives handed down to public officials on various
> levels; frequent collusion of these officials with powerful persons or
> groups of persons whose conduct they should regulate; and, at
> bottom, a general inclination of people in all strata to resist public
> controls and their implementation. Also within the concept of the
> soft state is corruption, a phenomenon which seems to be generally
> on the increase in underdeveloped countries.[13]

To explain the soft state is to discover the limits on law as a tool of
social change in conditions of development.

B. The Roles at the Interface of Means and Ends

It is sometimes argued that all this does not concern lawyers. The
content of law comes from policy-makers – politicians, Cabinet, Revolutionary Councils. While of course lawyers draft the rules relating to
development, some (frequently lawyers) argue that they are mere
scriveners who translate programmes of others into the obscurantist

language of the law. Similarly, some argue that the policy-makers have nothing to do with the law itself — that is the concern of the lawyers, civil servants, bureaucrats and other technicians who draft and implement the rules. So do we all: when asked what we do, we respond with only an idealized part of what we are *supposed* to do. 'It is as if a policeman were to describe his role by saying that he catches criminals; as if a businessman were to say, he makes soap; . . . a priest . . . [that] he celebrates mass; . . . a congressman, [that] he passes laws.'[14] Separating 'technical' from 'policy' roles insulates both technicians and policy-makers from moral and political responsibility for their actions. 'To limit judgment solely to "autonomous" technical criteria is in effect not only to permit but to require men to be moral cretins in their technical roles.'[15] To formulate 'policy' while disregarding implementation effectively assumes that the chosen ends will justify any means — a proposition no less morally cretinous.

Every government includes some actors whose roles place them at the interface between ends and means, between policy formulation and implementation. There are many actors at that interface, drafting legislation, structuring options, raising questions and reviewing drafts, as well as some who finally decide yea or nay. Their titles vary: Permanent Secretary, Ministerial Counsel, consultant, Civil Servant, Parliamentary Draftsman, Solicitor General, and so on. In every country that I know, some of those actors are lawyers. Unless these lawyers, and the other actors at the interface, fully understand the policy implications of their actions, the ultimate policy may be pragmatically and morally indefensible.

C. A Case Study of the Formulation of Legislation

The history of Tanzania's Range Management and Development Act exemplifies the way decisions about the details of legislation affect the substance of policy. The Act created a programme to introduce a new way of life to the Masai, who drift with their herds across vast arid plains in northern Tanzania. It purported to transform their nomadic, cattle-centred economy and culture, organized in clan and family, into a society of permanent villages, producing cattle for the cash market. That programme was born out of a concern for conservation. The present revolutionary thrust of the statute came about mainly during its drafting. The continual exhaustion of the Masai ranges concerned the colonial rulers. The Ministry of Agriculture in independent Tanzania inherited the problem. Typically the initiative for the new legislation came not from the Cabinet, who in constitutional myth are the policy-makers, but from ministerial bureaucrats. A memorandum in 1963[16] defined its objectives as a phased plan covering control over stock movements and members, the prevention of further indiscriminate and unprofitable land use, and the development of a selected area of Masailand. The authors suggested doing this by (1) dividing the district into zones based so far as possible on traditional Masai social patterns; (2) declaring the maximum number of stock that might use each zone; (3) branding or marking all stock with at least a zonal identification mark; and (4) prohibiting cultivation without permission. Legislation would create an Authority, charged with defining the various areas, branding stock, setting stock limits, and enforcement. In special Development Areas, the statute would establish an appropriate system of land tenure, control water supplies and determine the location of buildings, roads and other works. The plan would cover all Masailand, but intensive development would occur only in the Development Areas. An inter-ministerial Co-ordinating Committee received instructions to pursue the matter. Following the usual procedure, the Committee submitted the memorandum to the Law Officers. 'This is necessary to ensure, first, that the proposed legislation is in line with Government policy; second, whether the new activity can be undertaken administratively, without requiring new legislation; and last, to determine whether it is mere tidying up of existing legislation, or involves a change in policy.'[17]

Obviously when a Law Officer decides whether a proposal is 'in line' with government policy, he must interpret that policy. Policy is usually vague. In many cases, the decision that a programme conforms to existing policy, itself defines the policy. In Tanzania, the Law Officers asked only two questions: whether the legislation would permit growing food crops (it would) and whether the proposed restraints on the movement of cattle followed Ministerial policy (it did). Even as early as 1963, the Government – or at least President Nyerere – had expressed a strong policy against class stratification,[18] and a socialist rhetoric. The Law Officers did not mention any issues concerning those policies. The matter then went to a meeting of the Legislation Committee of the Cabinet, which requested a paper for Cabinet consideration, 'stating the policy which the Bill is to implement'.[19] It took a year to shake that memorandum out of the Ministry.

In the meantime, however, Ministerial thinking about the proposed new legislation underwent re-examination. In the first place, the United States Agency for International Development agreed to supply technical assistance. Its report [20] developed a method of measuring the number of cattle using a range, equating one bull with two heifers or five goats, etc. It suggested that the Masai be organized into 'Ranching Associations Ltd', with whom the Government could deal and in whom title to land could be vested. This was the earliest mention of plans for the radical transformation of Masai society. Secondly, an intra-ministerial memorandum suggested that the legislation's emphasis shift from conservation to increased productivity. An essential object of the new legislation was to form new ranching organizations, probably co-operative in form, based upon the traditional Masai social unit, the extended family.

After a year, a cabinet paper emerged. The minute asking for it had required that it concern itself 'with principles, not with legislative detail'. The cabinet paper[21] obliged. It returned to the earlier definition of the problem, that is, overstocking and poor animal husbandry. It did not discuss the broader issues of incorporating the Masai in the money economy. It viewed the proposed ranching corporations only as handy title-holders to the range, so that their members' cattle could be restricted to it. If a majority of family heads in a proposed range wished to join a corporation they could form one in which 'all the heads of families would be eligible to join subject to their limiting their herds to an *appropriate proportion* of the assessed capacity' [emphasis added].

The cabinet memorandum said nothing specific about the form of the Ranching Associations, nor about the formula for reducing the size of the permissible herd. These questions, however, were critical. Masai society today contains gross inequities. The family herd varies from two thousand or more down to a handful. The new 'Ranching Associations Ltd' might become mere forms through which traditional practices would continue and the existing wide disparities in cattle holding remain. They might instead move Masai society toward egalitarian producer co-operatives, increasingly involved in the money economy. On these issues, however, the cabinet paper was silent.

No one faced them until the bill's drafting. The drafting procedure, common in Anglophonic Africa, only crudely resembled British practice. In Britain, each department had its own solicitor, who reduced departmental policy into detailed Instructions for Parliamentary Counsel. The administrators of the department concerned scrutinized these before sending them to the draftsmen. The Treasury Centre for Administrative Studies in London even had a training programme, to train young administrators in the drafting process.[22] In Africa, this detailed departmental consideration of the instructions usually did not occur. Instead, in Tanzania the very general cabinet memorandum went directly to the Parliamentary draftsman.

The draft Bill that emerged in Tanzania decided the form of the Ranching Associations, and the method for reducing the number of cattle. It endowed the Minister with power through subsidiary legislation to write the constitutions and by-laws of the Associations. By so doing, the Bill abdicated that decision to future Ministry officials. By stipulating a pro rata reduction of cattle, it continued existing Masai stratification, and reinforced individual ownership.[23]

These decisions developed in the course of the drafting process. They did not come from politicians or 'policy-makers', but from 'mere technicians', concerned with 'legislative details'. These discretionary choices, however, in fact defined the central thrust of the programmes under the Act. The 1972 Development Plan proposed to establish some seventy-two of these ranching associations, thus profoundly and probably irrevocably changing the course of Masai society. If implemented these changes will follow a course plainly contrary to Tanzania's egalitarian and socialist orientation.

Conclusion

John Dewey distinguishes the 'end' of policy, and the 'end-in-view'. If I want to build a house, the house is the 'end'. The actual house plans are the 'end-in-view'. Until detailed plans are drawn, it is impossible to discern what concrete meaning to give to the word 'house'. In the same way, no one could define Tanzanian policy concerning the Masai until the detailed legislation and rules emerged which concretely defined that policy. It is immaterial whether the lawyers made these decisions on their own, or in conjunction with Ministry officials. The lawyer's specific contribution to any bill, of course, varies with circumstance. Bills that directly touch elite interests undoubtedly receive sharper scrutiny by politicians than do other bills. Zambia's Leadership Code, which cut very close to elite bone, endured four successive detailed amendments.[24] As time presses, so do the temptations to draftsmen to decide policy themselves, rather than referring back to the initiating Ministry. The more complex the legal issues, the more technical the legal jargon and the greater the draftsman's policy-making power.

Detailing specific rules is a complex process, in which many different people with different titles participate. Until these details emerge, however, it is impossible to specify the actual content of 'policy'. When lawyer or civil servant insists upon a sharp division between 'policy' and 'law', he ensures that nobody raises those crucial questions which are indispensable if the end-in-view is to be effective, and consistent with broader perspectives.

Lawyers in the developing world increasingly deal with 'the scope and formulation of policies . . . the exercise of legal powers constructively establishing or altering the relations between private legal parties inter se, between public authorities and private parties, between government and foreign investors, and the like'.[25] Such lawyers must understand the uses and limits of governmental power to influence the direction and intensity of social change, because they are involved in devising the appropriate structures of government and the state to induce the sorts of change denoted as developmental.

Scholars have not addressed these issues extensively. 'The view that government is an integral part of the social structure, but may have the capacity of altering it significantly, is not in the mainstream of social theory. The opposite view is more common: that the formal government and its actions are epiphenomena, the product of forces arising from the social and economic structure of society.'[26]

'Mainstream' social science lags behind. Every government today perceives one of its functions to be the channelling of on-going change into desirable directions. The study of 'soft' development ought to lead to knowledge likely to improve that function. Such studies should lead to considering the proper uses for state power — that is, into the nature and meaning of development, and the interests it does and should serve. It is a study at once pragmatic and theoretical, specific and general, professional and academic. It aims at discovering the sorts of knowledge that professionals need at the interface between policy and implementation. Their tasks require them to understand the uses and limits of the legal order in initiating and regulating change. Instead of law being a brake on change, the actors at the interface invoke it as change's very engine. A brake specialist is not necessarily knowledgeable about engines.

The study of the legal order as the initiator of development, therefore, will lead us far from our usual ideas about law. My concern is with how the legal order affects behaviour. The legal order, as I have defined it, is, as Kelsen taught,[27] one side of the coin whose reverse is the state. The study of the legal order in development requires that we examine how state power is and how it ought to be organized to alleviate the twin horrors of poverty and oppression. Because that domain of study is relatively unploughed, conventional methodologies, perspectives and categories of legal or social science research frequently do not work well. I discuss these in Part II. In Part III, I begin developing some general propositions explaining why people respond as as they do to rules of law. In Part IV, I discuss implementing, and Part V, law-making institutions. That is to say, in Parts II and III, I propose a paradigm how to go about studying law and development; in Parts IV and V, I attempt to use that paradigm to study the structure of the state in conditions of development in Africa.

Before we embark on that study, however, I must first examine two positions that deprecate its utility. One asserts that good law in one place is good law anyplace; the other asserts that good men (and not good institutions) make good government.

Notes

1. R. Lynd, *Knowledge for What?* (Princeton: Princeton UP, 1945), p. 7.
2. C.J. Friedrich, *Constitutional Government and Democracy,* rev. ed. (New York: Blaisdell, 1950), p. 102.
3. T. Parsons, 'The Law and Social Control', in W.M. Evan (ed.), *Law and Sociology* (New York: The Free Press of Glencoe, 1962), pp. 56, 58.
4. H.C. Bredemeier, 'Law as an Integrative Mechanism', in Evan, ibid., pp. 72, 74.
5. P. Proehl, 'Book Review', *Indiana L.J.,* 42, 277 (1967).
6. L. Friedman, 'Legal Culture and Social Development', *Law and Society Rev.,* 4, 29 (1969).
7. D.M. Trubek, 'Toward a Social Theory of Law: An Essay on Law and Development', *Yale L.J.,* 82, 1 (1972).
8. I regret that I have lost the source of this quotation.
9. D.J. Black, 'The Boundaries of Legal Sociology', *Yale L.J.,* 81 1086, 1096, (1972).
10. International Commission of Jurists, *The Rule of Law and Human Rights: Principles and Definition* (Geneva: International Commission of Jurists, 1966), p. 66 (The Declaration of Delhi).
11. F.W. Riggs, 'Modernization and Political Problems: Some Developmental Prerequisites' in W.A. Beling and G.O. Totten (eds), *Developing Nations: Quest for a Model* (New York: Van Nostrand Reinhold, 1970), p. 11.
12. G. Myrdal, *Asian Drama: An Inquiry into the Poverty of Nations,* (New York: Pantheon, 1968), p. 896.
13. G. Myrdal, 'The "Soft State" in Underdeveloped Countries', *UCLA L. Rev.,* 15, 1118, 1120 (1968).
14. A.W. Gouldner, *The Coming Crisis of Western Sociology* (New York: Avon Books, 1970), p. 25.
15. Ibid., p. 13.
16. Dated 2.2.63, in the Ministry files.
17. Zambia: Cabinet Office Circular No. 72 of 1969.
18. J. Nyerere, *Ujaama – The Basis of African Socialism* (Dar es Salaam mimeo, 1962).
19. Tanzania: Ministry of Agriculture Memorandum, dated 16 May 1963.
20. The Fallon Report (USAID Mission to Kenya) 25 May 1963. See also *Parliamentary Debates of the National Assembly of Republic of Tanganyika and Zanzibar,* (Dar es Salaam: Gov't Printer, 1964), pp. 33, 43-6, 74.

25

21. Tanzania: Cabinet Paper No. 65 of 1964.
22. A. Kean, 'Drafting a Bill in Britain', *Harv. J. of Legis.*, 5, 253, 255-8 (1968).
23. Range Management and Development Act: Draft Bill (1964) sec. 24(5).
24. Zambia Statutory Instruments, Nos. 249 and 288 of 1973, Nos. 47 and 108 of 1974.
25. W. Friedman, 'The Role of Law and the Function of the Lawyer in Developing Countries', *Vanderbilt L. Rev.*, 17, 181, 186-7 (1963); see also J.D. Nyquist, 'The Role of Law in Economic Development', *Sud. L. J.R.*, 394, 404-10 (1962).
26. R. Bendix, 'What is Modernization?', in Beling and Tottem, *Developing Nations*, n. 11, p. 3.
27. H. Kelsen, *General Theory of Law and State* (A. Wedburg, tr, N.Y.: Russell, 1961).

Part Two

METHODOLOGY, PERSPECTIVES AND VOCABULARY

Part One

EPIDEMIOLOGY: PERSPECTIVES AND DEVELOPING

2 THE LAW OF NON-TRANSFERABILITY OF LAW AND THE LAW OF THE REPRODUCTION OF INSTITUTIONS

There are two common notions about how to change the legal order. One argues that good law in one place is good law anyplace else. It advises the lawmaker to copy the legal order of developed countries in order to achieve development. The other advises that laws make little difference in people's behaviour. Good men, not good laws, make good government. These notions dominated colonial thinking about law. They persisted in modern Africa. As a result either (1) laws were mechanically copied from other contexts, and did not work; or (2) governments did little to change inherited legal order, but instead 'explained' poverty by the 'innate character' of the poor. This chapter examines each of these notions in turn.

I The Non-Transferability of Law

A. *The Reception of English Law*

Upon asserting sovereignty over a new territory, the metropolitan power had to decide what law to introduce. In 1874, the principal legal officer of the Gold Coast requested some textbooks and other legal materials so that he might draft a suitable statute defining the laws for the courts to apply.[1] The Colonial Office responded with the Gold Coast reception statute (so called because it 'received' English law for the Gold Coast). It provided that the courts of the Colony should apply the common law of England, the doctrines of equity and 'statutes of general application', reserving, however, to Africans rights they might have under customary law.[2] The statute was the prototype for the reception statutes of all the British African dependencies, with only minor changes.

The reception statutes buttressed a divided society. Customary law applied to Africans, who lived and worked almost entirely in the sub-sistence sector of the economy. It was appropriate for that sector, since it responded to the needs of rural societies dominated by low technologies. English law mainly applied to Europeans. It provided an appropriate legal framework for developing export-oriented relatively modern extractive industries and plantation farming, for purchasing African-

grown export crops, and for selling imported manufactured goods. The
criminal law supposedly provided the overall framework for law and
order. A variety of legal compulsions, direct and indirect, drove
Africans into European employment.

Plainly, the imposition of English law on Africa did not recreate
Africa in England's image. In every way colonial Africa exhibited a
special sort of dualism. Impoverished black workers in an export enclave produced raw materials for metropolitan markets. Most blacks
lived in the hinterlands, farming for subsistence.

Within the export enclave, expatriates (and, as Independence approached, a few Africans), the managers and captains of both private
and public sectors, lived very high on the hog. In Kenya in 1962 the per
capita income of non-Africans was £400. Most Africans, however, lived
in dreadful poverty, with an average income in the same year (including
an estimate for subsistence farming) of only £14.9 per annum.[3]

The dual economy, however, did not, as is sometimes supposed,
allow Africans to live as they had before, with a new, one-way flow
from the 'backward' hinterland into the 'modern' export enclave.
Colonialism brought massive destruction to traditional economies.
Sometimes this was done by raiding and burning huts and villages.
Mainly, however, a variety of legal compulsions made the hinterland
unlivable for the black labour force needed by European employers: a
poll tax, to be paid only in cash; restrictions on African land ownership;
prohibitions on African cash cropping; and others.[4]

Multiple dependencies marked the colonial economy. The hinterland
came to depend on the export sector. The country as a whole depended
on the markets of the capitalist world. The importation of manufactured goods reinforced that dependency. The economic surpluses from
African productive enterprise and the sale of imported goods, instead
of being invested in Africa, were shipped overseas to enrich investors in
the home countries. The banks which 'managed' the economies invested
their funds in the home countries, bolstering the economies of England
and France, not Africa. Marketing boards used their surpluses to
stabilize the pound, not African monetary systems.[5] 'Invisibles' —
mainly insurance and shipping costs — drained off additional sums. All
these far exceeded any money flowing into Africa from 1880 until the
end of Empire. England always had a trade deficit, but a balance of
payments surplus with her dependencies.

The foreign firms of course made their economic decisions in their
own interests, not those of their African hosts. They developed almost
no local processing or manufacturing. The Gold Coast, the largest cocoa

producer in the world, did not process cocoa. A consumer there had to
purchase processed cocoa from Europe or the United States. Northern
Rhodesia, a principal world supplier of copper, had no plant to fabricate
copper goods. Countries that exported sugar, cotton, sisal, coffee,
vegetable oil and a dozen other commodities engaged at most in
primary stage processing. Lumber companies did not even square off
logs of rare tropical timber, but shipped them overseas in their raw
form.

Land use patterns marched with the dual economies. Most Africans
lived in the countryside. The settler colonies sharply separated them
physically from whites. Kenya, for example, reserved the highlands —
the best agricultural land in the country — for white settlement.
Africans lived in terribly over-populated reserves with very low agricultural potential. The imperial power enforced even sharper divisions
in the urban areas between whites and blacks. Every city in Africa had
its exclusively white residential areas, off-limits to Africans: Ikoyi in
Lagos, Oyster Bay in Dar-es-Salaam. Many countries imposed various
sorts of pass laws to prevent African influx into white cities. Northern
Rhodesia forbade Africans without a pass to walk on the main street
of Lusaka, its capital city.

The government of these two areas also differed. The colonial
administration governed the export enclaves directly, but nominally
left blacks in the hinterland to their traditional institutions. Colonial
officials in fact controlled them under the rubric of 'indirect rule'. The
local traditional authority continued to rule as before, but now maintained law and order and collected taxes not in its own right, but in
the right of the imperial government. Socially, the split between
African and white communities was complete. Clubs, schools and social
organizations were all segregated. Whites and Africans rubbed elbows in
productive enterprises, and as masters and servants in homes and clubs,
but lived a world apart.

English law in Africa plainly did not induce behaviour which re-
shaped Africa to the English pattern. In the next section I attempt to
explain why the British introduced it into Africa, and why it did not
reproduce English institutions there.

B. The Impact of Analytical Positivism

The colonial decision to impose English law on Africa was rooted in
part in the perception of Colonial Office lawyers of the function of
law in society. That perception stemmed largely from the then dominant jurisprudential theory, analytical positivism. Theories that purport

to explain the world inevitably become the rationale for policy. Peter Dorner distinguished two such explanations. 'Organized systems of thought are results of man's efforts to cope with experienced difficulties. The configurations of such a system of thought will be different if establishment of basic institutions is a key issue, in contrast to the system of thought that emerges from inquiry into policy issues that arise within an established and accepted institutional framework.'[6] Analytical positivism arose to guide investigations within the legal framework of nineteenth-century England. It became, however, the philosophical guide for structuring the legal order of tropical Africa.

Max Weber argued that the principal capitalist legal requirement was predictability.[7] Entrepreneurs must so far as possible reduce their risk. Lawyers can advise their business clients only if they can calculate how the state will act towards their clients' activities.[8] Predictability, lawyers believed, required that the legal order minimize official discretion, and that 'independent' courts decide, as it were, like computers, whether state power should be applied in specific cases. Predictability was impossible if the judge might decide the case according to his subjective ethical notions. Weber said that predictability in law demanded 'logical formal rationality', that is, decisions in particular cases that relied exclusively for their justification upon materials drawn from the legal order itself, derived by a specialized deductive mode of legal thought. Positivism therefore purported to limit the courts' function to law-finding, not law-making. This system implies a model of the legal order that has been denoted as 'legalism'. That model defines the law as a 'logically consistent set of rules constructed in a specialized fashion', which are the exclusive rules for settling disputes. There must be a 'clear differentiation of law from other sources of normative ordering. Law must become both autonomous and supreme.'[9] A system of law enforced through courts appears autonomous par excellence.

The school of jurisprudence called analytical positivism met these requirements. John Austin, its nineteenth-century author, announced a single, thundering proposition. All law, he said, was the command of the sovereign. His system limited the function of the lawyer to determining not what the law ought to be, but what it is.[10] It confined the study of law to examining the universe of legal rules, to harmonizing and elucidating them. As an empirically grounded hypothesis, Austin's major affirmation was nonsense. As an intellectual construct, it matched all the demands made upon the lawyer. It explained to him why he directed his attention not to how the rules worked in society, but to the rules as guides to judicial decisions.[11] The legal order became

not a normative system ordering social life, but the rules of the litigation game. Positivism directed the lawyer's attention towards what
Austin called the Province of Jurisprudence, and away from the Province of Legislation. Analytical positivism pretended that the corpus of
the law was a gapless web. If a gap appeared, one could deduce from
legal materials and logic alone, what the law covering the supposed gap
had to be. Analytical positivism therefore directed attention to the
internal elegance and logical consistency of the rules, not to the relative
desirability of the behaviour the rules prescribed. If its internal elegance
and consistency, rather than its consequences for society, defines good
law, then good law in one time and place must be equally good in other
times and places.

The Colonial Office imposed English law on Africa without considering what sort of society the new law would mould. In all the
correspondence, internal memoranda and bureaucratic minutes that
preceded the Gold Coast reception statute, nothing suggests that its
authors addressed the question of how the legal order they were proposing would affect Gold Coast society.[12] British lawyers imposed the
law they knew, and therefore, the law they believed to be 'good'. In
fact, the reception statutes facilitated imperial exploitation of Africa.

The myth of Empire was robustly stated by Joseph Chamberlain:
'We develop new territory as Trustees for civilization, for the
Commerce of the world.'[13] Harry Johnstone, one of the great British
pro-consuls in East Africa, explained how this was to be done: 'All . . .
things are possible', he wrote in 1918, 'if the European capitalist can be
induced by proper security to invest his money in Africa and if native
labour can be obtained by the requisite guarantees of fairplay towards
native rights.'[14] Lord Lugard, the greatest of them all, concurred. The
commercial imperative of the Dual Mandate 'is for the most part undertaken with avidity by private enterprise, and the function of the Power
in control is limited to providing the main essentials, such as railways
and harbours, to seeing that the natives have their fair share and that
material development does not injuriously affect the fulfillment of the
second mandate . . .'[15]

An attractive investment climate is a necessary condition to capitalist investment. The government can, as a minimum, supply law and
order, and a judicial system to protect property and enforce contracts.
The colonial powers everywhere imposed a centralized bureaucracy and
courts upon their dependent territories. The mere existence of courts
and law became a hallmark of 'development'.

English law apparently came to Africa, however, not out of deep laid plots by imperialists intent on Africa's exploitation, but out of the pervasive insularity of analytical positivism. Nevertheless, English law in Africa as in England nicely served the interests of British entrepreneurs, now at the expense of African peasants. Where necessary to advance English interests, the colonial power readily changed it; but the fact that English law in its larger outlines remained largely unchanged down to independence demonstrates its effectiveness in serving English rather than African concerns.

Analytical positivism, although powerfully challenged, remained the dominant jurisprudence for practising lawyers in independent Africa. It remained concerned with legal elegance, not legal content.[16] When drafting a new law, African lawyers and their expatriate advisers all but invariably copied the laws of the former metropole. For example, Lesotho recently borrowed the highway traffic act of South Africa.[17] It included a provision that forbade lorries above a specified weight from travelling on Lesotho's roads. Lesotho had no weighbridge. A second example: Every African country after Independence entered into double-taxation treaties similar to those in force before independence. Those treaties taxed income mainly in the country of domicile of the tax-payer, rather than the country of the origin of the income.[18] Transnational corporations operating in Africa frequently paid more income tax to their home governments on their African income than they did to the African country where they made it. A third example: The penal laws of Anglophonic Africa were all modelled after English law.[19] They all contained a provision, following an eighteenth-century English statute aimed at highwaymen and footpads, forbidding wandering about at night with intent to commit a felony with one's face blackened.[20]

C. The Law of Non-Transferability of Law

Legal transplants practically never work.[21] Attaturk introduced the French Civil Code into Turkey: Turkey does not resemble France. Anglophonic Africa, despite the reception of English law, did not develop as did England. Why this nearly universal failure of transferred law to induce behaviour in its new home similar to that which it induced in its original site?

The anthropologist Fredrik Barth has suggested that 'The most simple and general model [of man in society] is one of an aggregate of people exercising choice while influenced by certain constraints and incentives ... Our central problem becomes what are the constraints and incentives that canalize choice.' Patterns of social form — i.e. of the repetitive actions of people — can be explained through the assumption that they are 'generated through processes of interaction and in their form reflect the constraints and incentives under which people act'.[22]

Law affects the choices of individuals in two ways. In the first place, each actor perceives the commands of the law as constraints or incentives which he must take into account, either because he believes that it is right and proper that he obey them or, like Holmes's 'bad man', he obeys the law only because of its threats. To each actor, 'the law appears as a factor which affects his decisions but over which he has no control'.[23]

The law also affects the choices of individuals indirectly. We make our choices about what to do in the light of the repetitive patterns of behaviour of others — i.e. the institutions of the society. I drive on the left hand side of the road not merely because the law commands me to do so, but because I know that others will drive on the left, and therefore I drive there for my own safety. Just as much of my own behaviour is in part a function of the law's commands to me, so is the institutionalized behaviour of others, that so powerfully affects my own behaviour, in part a function of the law's commands to them.

Most of the constraints and resources within which individuals choose, however, are of course not a function of the law. Custom, geography, history, technology and a host of other non-legal factors affect my behaviour directly and indirectly by structuring the choice and thus channelling the behaviour of others. These other, non-legal constraints and resources are the reason for the failure of legal transplants. It is as though two hikers were making their way through different forests, each with thickly set underbrush, rocks, swamps, streams, lakes and ravines, and also glades of soft grass, flat places with easy walking, and frequently a well-defined path. The course that each takes through the woods results from his constantly choosing the easiest way to go. Were a forester to transport some of the trees from one forest into the other, the path taken by the hiker in that forest might change somewhat, even radically, to avoid the new trees. It could never, however, resemble the path in that other forest from which the trees were transplanted. The rocks, swamps, streams, and other determinants of the hikers' routes are too different.

So with the transplantation of law. In acting, individuals take some account of the constraints and incentives offered by the law. They also take into account a host of non-legal factors. A particular law in two places with different social, political, economic and other circumstances can therefore only by coincidence induce similar behaviour in both places.

English law failed to recreate in Africa anything resembling English
society and the English economy because of the vast difference
between all the other, non-legal institutions of England and of Africa.
English law's principal economic institution was contract. Contract
law assumes that each actor seeks his individual advantage. Nineteenth-
century English society as a whole embodied such constraints and
resources that its entrepreneurs made choices that produced history's
most rapid economic development. In Africa, British entrepreneurs
faced quite different institutions, posing a different set of constraints
and rewards. When England was undergoing development, the local
English market offered the greatest rewards for the entrepreneur.
When Africa was being developed, England, not the local, African
market, offered the greatest rewards. The export-oriented, dual
economies of tropical Africa resulted from English entrepreneurs
seizing that advantage.

To summarize:

1. Laws are addressed to addressees (here called 'role-occupants'),
   prescribing their behaviour.

2. How a role-occupant acts in response to rules of law is a function
   not only of their prescriptions but also of his physical environment and of the complex of social, political, economic and other
   institutions within which he makes his choices about how to
   behave.

3. The physical and institutional environments of different sets of
   role-occupants differ from time to time and place to place.

4. Therefore, the activity induced by rules of law is usually specific
   to time and place.

5. Therefore, the same rules of law and their sanctions in different
   times and places, with different physical and institutional environments will not induce the same behaviour in role-occupants
   in different times and places.[24]

This I denote the Law of Non-Transferability of Law.

II The Law of the Reproduction of Institutions

Analytical positivism does not attempt to explain how law induces
social change, because in effect it denies any causal connection between

them. Most African leaders since independence did not consciously try
to use the legal order to induce development. This section examines why
they did not, and its consequences. I first sketch the legal order of post-
independence Africa and its failure to induce much change; second,
the Colonial Service explanation for the failure of social change; and
third, an alternative explanation that argues that, other things remaining the same, unless the legal order is changed institutions will not
change.

A. *The Legal Order of Post-Independence Africa*

At Independence, the constitutional documents of every African
country or their earliest statutes, provided that until amended all
existing laws would remain in effect. Save for constitutional provisions the legal order at Independence remained unchanged. In most
African countries to a very great extent it remained unchanged.
Blatantly discriminatory statutes were repealed. But the courts of
Africa as a matter of course habitually deferred to English precedents
in most private law areas, such as torts, property, contracts, insurance
and commercial law. More statutes by far remained unchanged, than
were amended. The Penal Codes remained all but untouched. Zambia's
Price Control Ordinance[25] except for details, was a colonial left-over.

Plainly, this generalization does not perfectly describe every country,
particularly not Tanzania. Every country had some programmes where
the legal order tried to change particular institutions, sometimes quite
radically. In its million-acre scheme, for example, Kenya distributed
more than a million acres of the best agricultural land in the former
White Highlands to 35,000 Africans. However, most large farms in the
Kenya Highlands remained intact. By 1964, when the Government
had already taken over about three-fourths of all the acreage it
intended to take over from the Europeans, '2,958 of the large farms
remain[ed] holding a total of 6,797,000 acres, or an average of 2,298
acres each; this compared to 3,609 large farms with an average of 2,142
acres each which had existed in 1960'.[26] Two hundred and forty-nine
of the largest of these had an average size of 25.7 square miles. Whites
still owned most of them, although wealthy Africans had purchased a
few. These owners held their land under property laws that were
mainly a colonial legacy.

Many aspects of African society continued to resemble the colonial
situation. A small handful lived very well in the urban centres, mainly
employed in senior government posts or by firms that still dominated
the economy. The majority of the population still lived in poverty in

the countryside. Some governments notably increased social services. By 1974, Zambian roads were much better than in colonial times. Educational programmes brought primary school education to most young Zambians, and a national university to a very few. Hospitals and clinics abounded. But the basic structures of the colonial situation remained: Society and economy bifurcated between export enclave and immiserated hinterland, subject to the vagaries of world markets and the interests of multinational corporations.

The major change after independence in most of Africa substituted black faces for white in the seats of power. Black, not white, officials in most of Anglophonic Africa made the great political decisions. (In these former colonies, which had a very low educational base at independence, even this change was long in coming. In 1973 it was still difficult to discover a black face in the Zambian Ministries between Permanent Secretary and stenographer.) An African sat as a director of Anglo-American, one of the two great mining firms that dominated the Zambian copper industry. African lawyers and doctors increasingly replaced expatriates. Black politicians and civil servants slowly but inexorably bought out the large line-of-rail farms, once exclusively white.

A change in the colour of the faces of those on top, without significant change in institutions did not improve the standard of living in the hinterland, the mines or the plantations. In the main, governments failed to alleviate poverty and oppression, despite their rhetoric.

B. Good Government and Good Men

Why do some governments succeed in inducing desirable change, and others do not? The two most common explanations are poles apart. One looks to the character of the governors. The other looks to the character of the institutions.

The process of transfer of power from the Colonial Service to Africans is a useful body of data to test the first of these propositions. I examine, first, the Colonial Service explanations for good government; and, second, the policy they built on that explanation.

1. The Colonial Service. Systems of thought explain phenomena as perceived by their proponents. The conditions of the Colonial Service led to explanations for social change that depended on men, not institutions.

The colonial system of government was thoroughly authoritarian. It had no representative institutions. The Administration not only

implemented policy, but made it as well.[27] The authoritarian principle
of colonial government matched its theory of the exercise of power:
trust 'the man on the spot'.[28] The Colonial Service was dominated by a
conviction that affairs of state were 'handled in a more efficient manner
if standards of administration were set by the collective wisdom of
those responsible, not by a legal code or a court of judges. The kind of
men who were recruited from Britain for service in the colonies
appeared to believe that the official class constituted the state.'[29]

Authoritarian government everywhere expresses its character in giving
broad discretion to 'the man on the spot'. The colonial governors received
grants of virtually unbounded discretion. The East Africa Order in
Council, 1902, gave the Commissioner power 'to make Ordinances for
the administration of justice, the raising of revenue, and generally for
the peace, good order and good government of all persons in East
Africa'. The Ordinances issued under these grants in turn granted great
discretion to lower officials.[30] Few controls limited these broad grants
of discretion, despite the nominal reception of English administrative
law and the doctrine of judicial review.[31] The Colonial Service developed
an explanation for the absence of rules. Good government, it said,
depends not upon good rules and institutions, but upon good men.[32]
The public schools, it turned out, bred almost all the 'good men'.
Lugard wrote:[33]

> The District Officer comes of the class which has made and main-
> tained the British Empire. That Britain has never lacked a super-
> abundance of such men is in part due to the national character, in
> part perhaps to our law of primogeniture, which compels the
> younger son to carve out his career. His assets are usually a public
> school, and probably a university education, neither of which have
> hitherto furnished him with an appreciable amount of positive know-
> ledge especially adapted to his work. But they had produced an
> English gentleman with an almost passionate conception of fair play,
> of protection for the weak, and of 'playing the game'. They have
> taught him personal initiative and resource, and how to command
> and obey. There is no danger of such men falling prey to the subtle
> moral deterioration which the exercise of power over inferior races
> produces in men of a different type, and which finds its expression
> in cruelty.

The selection system ensured that practically every member of the
Colonial Service would come from a public school — Oxbridge back-

ground, with an impeccable family tree (and probably with a Blue in athletics[34] — although how that was related to the job of a colonial bureaucrat was never precisely explained).

For more than thirty of the fifty years of the life of the Colonial Service, one officer, Sir Ralph Furse, handpicked every recruit — applicants took no examinations.[35] He developed 'a secret list of Oxford and Cambridge tutors in order of reliability of their reports on undergraduates, and a close connection with headmasters of [public] schools . . . Our methods were mole-like, quiet, persistent and indirect.'[36] Family, public school, senior prefectship, university and a 'cut of the jib' that Furse liked: these were the requirements for employment in the Colonial Service.[37] The rigid selection system produced officials with a narrow public school ethic. Authoritarian, paternalistic, formally incorruptible, an underlying spirit of duty coupled with a calm assumption of superiority,[38] that ethic formed a kind of surrogate for detailed rules. It filled two of Etzioni's hypotheses: the more effective the selection, the less need for socialization; the more effective the socialization, the less need for supervision.[39]

The homogeneity of the service produced a remarkable amount of in-service camaraderie. When Lugard arrived in Lagos to assume the governor-generalship of Nigeria, an official held aloft a hand-painted signs, 'floreat Rosalli' (Lugard was an old boy of Rossall School). For the new recruit to the Colonial Service,

> there would be no jarring surprises in learning what one was expected to do. One's superiors from the Governor down to the DC were all alike, like oneself, products of the same system. By the age of 21 the basic assumptions were so deeply engrained that everyone knew what to expect. Few written rules were necessary. Everyone was an Old Boy . . . The level of consensus among officials was an essential ingredient of stability in the colonies and of such uniformity as there was.[40]

This solidarity also derived from the romantic conditions of the service, a 'thin red line' holding together the far-flung marches of the Empire. In every organization, 'functionaries have a sense of common destiny'.[41] Inevitably, so did colonial civil servants.

Every condition of the Colonial Service strengthened the officers' conviction that they were an unusual breed of men. Positivist legal philosophy had its corollary: institutions and rules do not make good government; good men do. The Colonial Service had no doubt about who were the good men. A colonial under-secretary, the Duke of Devonshire, said in 1923, 'The code which must guide the [colonial] administrator is to be found in no book of regulations. It demands that in every circumstance and under all conditions, he shall act in accordance with the traditions of an English gentleman.'[42]

Explanations identify causes. Inevitably, they become the basis of policy, for policy always attempts to address the causes of problems. When times change, and the Colonial Service had to vacate the seats of power, they based their policies in preparing their successors upon their explanation for what they believed were their own unbounded successes.

2. Creating the 'Good Men'. Following the Second World War, the inexorable dictate of history plainly put self-government and independence on the agenda. France and Portugal, aided by the United States, chose to oppose the tide, and reaped the bonfires of Algeria, Angola, Mozambique and Vietnam. Britain accepted the inevitable, and charged the Colonial Service with preparing the African dependencies for self-government.

In 1957, Sir Alan Burns, a long-serving high-level colonial official laid down the conditions for self-government. He did not mention political or social institutions. He did specify, however, 'there must be a sufficient number of trustworthy and well educated inhabitants capable of assuming the responsibilities of administration; and a reasonable level of general education and understanding to ensure that "self-government" does not merely mean the exploitation of the masses by the few behind the façade of a democracy'.[43] The Colonial Office suggested a programme to create these 'good men'. 'First, local government institutions gave training in administration; second, educational institutions were charged with the modernization of the traditional culture; third, co-operatives provided experience in community living and fourth, trade unions were the basis of a craft apprenticeship into the complexities of modern society.'[44] The British diligently moved ahead on all four fronts.

They made considerable efforts to educate a governing elite. The governing principle was that the educational system should produce men as much like the colonial administrators as possible. The colonial administrators therefore created out of whole cloth an educational system that aped that which they had attended. Secondary schools sprouted, surrounded by all the trappings of the English public school: boarding pupils, masters, prefects, hazing, high-table, cricket. In Ghana, Achimota old boys dominated the senior civil service. The colonial old boy network replicated itself.

University education, too, followed the English upper-class model. After repeated study commissions[45] the Asquith Commission[46] reported in 1954 that:

> The main consideration in our minds is that His Majesty's Government has entered upon a programme of social and economic development for the Colonies which is not merely the outcome of a desire to fulfill our moral obligations as trustees of the welfare of Colonial peoples, but it also designed to lead to the exercise of self-government by them. In the stage preparatory to self-government, universities have an important part to play; indeed they may be said to be indispensable. To them we must look for the production of men and women with the standards of public service and capacity for leadership which self-rule requires.

These new Universities — Ibadan in Nigeria, Legon in Ghana and Makerere in Uganda — attempted to accomplish this ideal. They were residential universities, for 'a university which has as its prime function education for leadership has an easier task if it is a residential society'.[47] With it went all the paraphernalia of Oxbridge: student gowns; grace before meals; high table, with Fellows solemnly filing in wearing their gowns while the student body stood at attention as the Fellows sat down at table set on a platform six inches above the common clay. As late as 1963, during the 'socialist' Nkrumah regime, the University of Ghana employed stewards to clean students' rooms, servants to wait on tables and to shine students' shoes. In the Oxbridge style, the university caterer was called the Manciple, and the university grocery store was called the Buttery. (Oxford kept the butts of wine there many centuries ago.) To receive degrees in law, the first graduating class in the University College in Tanzania had to attend classes in horsemanship.

The curriculum also aimed to produce 'leaders'. The Asquith Commission explicitly denigrated 'professional' studies in favour of 'liberal' ones. All three early African universities had a chair in Classics but not in engineering. The Universities followed what Ashby, perhaps satirically, suggests was the British ideal:

> The flower of the English Universities was . . . of two kinds: one, the Oxford Greats man with a rowing blue who governed a province, or silently controlled the treasury, or sat on a front bench in the House of Commons; the other, the man with a 'first' in natural science who

became a professor and, in the German tradition, assembled disciples around him and made his laboratory in Cambridge or Manchester a world-centre for research.[48]

The British succeeded in producing successors in their own image. Anyone who has met African Permanent Secretaries in Ghana or Nigeria educated under this system cannot but marvel at the Colonial Service's success. It did not, however, build institutions apt to bring about democracy or development. 'The gift of England to her former dependencies was a mixture of authoritarian spirit and machinery plus democratic ideals — not, as is sometimes imagined, a set of democratic ideals and institutions.'[49]

The Colonial Service policy in preparing for self-government conformed to long-standing imperial interests. To leave a legacy of authoritarian institutions in charge of men moulded as closely as possible to the image of the departing rulers ensured that social radicals would not likely grasp the levers of power. It ensured that the new rulers would not likely change institutions. Not to change its institutions ensured that Africa would continue to grind out surpluses for the benefit of owners in the former metropole, continue to supply the raw materials for the factories of England and guarantee a market for her manufactured goods.

Summary. The Colonial Service used as a basis for their policies in preparing Africa for independence an explanation derived from their own authoritarian rule:

1. Societies consist in governors and governed.

2. The character of the governors (rather than the institutions of the society) determine the choices made by the governors.

3. Therefore, the sort of social change that ensues depends upon the character of the governors.

This explanation, like analytical positivism, denied the efficacy of law to change society. The critical variable lay elsewhere.

That explanation is non-falsifiable. If a government is unsuccessful, one can always say that the governors were simply not good enough. The sort of society they produce measures the 'goodness' of the governors although the sort of society they produce is precisely the phenomenon the 'goodness' of the governors is supposed to explain. The explanation is circular.

Assuming that one can define an independent measure of the competence and morality of the governors, the Colonial Service did everything
possible to train competent successors. Their failure, of course, may not
prove that their theory was false. It may only prove that the problems
of government in Africa were insuperable, no matter how 'good' the
governors. Rejecting that give-it-up philosophy, the failure of development in most of Africa is inconsistent with the positivist explanation.
The massive effort made by the British to train good men is probably
as good a case study of policy stemming from that explanation as any.

C. The Reproduction of Institutions

An alternative explanation suggests that so long as institutions do not
change, society does not change. This explanation, too, runs in circles.
The repetitive patterns of behaviour of its members — i.e. its institutions — define society. The proposition says only that society does not
change unless it changes.

In fact, of course, societies constantly change. Institutions in consequences constantly change. Change comes from sources as manifold
as life itself: changing climate, technologies, populations, ideologies and
individual innovation, war, pestilence, disease and natural disaster.
Developing nations must guide that inevitable change into desired
channels.

What can those in control of state power do to induce desirable
social change? If 'good' men, inserted into existing institutions, cannot
succeed, what alternatives are there? The obvious alternative invokes
the legal order and the state to change behaviour and hence to change
institutions. No forester can raze the forest flat, and create a new forest
and new paths. He can at most plant new trees here and there at critical
points, or cut down old trees, to induce the hiker to follow a new path,
determined by all of the trees and shrubs in the forest — those older
ones that remain and the few new ones planted by the foresters. The
forester cannot determine the new path absolutely. He can, however,
induce desirable change within existing constraints.

Following Robert Lee Hale, Warren J. Samuels has proposed a distinction between 'voluntary freedom' and 'volitional freedom'. 'Voluntary freedom' implies 'complete autonomy with the absence of constrained choice or limits to choice or behavior, in effect, choice
governing the range of alternatives which one will choose'. 'Volitional
freedom' is the 'circumstantially limited exercise of choice between
alternatives or behavour'.[50] Obviously, these ideal types occupy the

ends of a continuum. Circumstances constrain all choice. Asked by a robber, 'Your money or your life', the victim has a very narrow volitional freedom. Robinson Crusoe comes as close as anyone to 'voluntary freedom'. At any point, one must choose the path from among those few alternatives that the various obstacles permit.

In any given set of social, economic and political circumstances, no doubt the social choices of well trained, technically competent and dedicated leaders will serve society better than those of stupid, incompetent crooks. To that extent, the 'good man' theory is valid. Because it accepts existing institutions, however, it, like analytical positivism, at best explains policy-choice within a given institutional structure.[51] Continuing existing social institutions limits the possible choices to those already in existence — in Africa, to those that maintained the colonial situation. Our domain of study demands a theory for changing institutions, rather than a theory of choice within existing ones.

Theories of change begin by explicating causes. What are the causes for the continuation of the colonial situation in Africa, in terms of the legal order? I suggest that:

1. Societies consist of sets of repetitive behaviour by their members, i.e. their institutions.

2. Unless the legal order that defines the principal institutions of the society changes, institutions change, but not through affirmative governmental action.

3. Conversely, other things remaining the same, unless the legal order changes, institutions remain the same.

Conclusion

Neo-colonialism continued because the colonial legacy continued. Institutions continued to perpetuate dependency. The basic structure of the legal order, which buttressed and defined these institutions, likewise continued. In Africa the continuing dominance of the notion that good men, not good laws, make good government, and its corollary, that the legal order and the state cannot change society, contributed to prevalent stagnation.

Two general propositions oppose these notions. The first I denoted the law of non-transferability of law: the same rules of law and sanctions in different times and places, cannot induce the same behaviour by the role occupant as they did in their time and place of origin. The

second I denoted the law of the reproduction of institutions: other
things remaining the same, unless the legal order is changed, institutions
will continue as they are.

These two 'laws' say that unless policy-makers initiate change
through the legal order, change will nevertheless take place, but it will
arise through other agencies than the conscious action of government.
If he does not desire that change, the law-maker must intervene to
deflect the processes of history. He cannot merely seek out laws which
seem to induce desirable activity elsewhere, and copy them blindly in
his own polity. He must identify the specific problems that confront
him, and seek out appropriate solutions for them in his country's concrete historical situation. That self-reliant imperative is not imposed by
demands of nationalist ideology, of philosophical notions of the sacred-
ness of the indigenous *Volksgeist,* of negritude or of the African
personality, but by the nature of societies and social change.

Without self-reliant problem-solving, government cannot change
institutions except marginally. Without fundamental institutional
changes, Africa will remain dependent upon the metropolitan powers,
economically, politically, socially, culturally and intellectually, despite
the forms and rhetoric of independence. Without changes in the legal
order — that is, in the structure of the state — institutions change, but
not as the consequence of conscious direction. Without changes in the
legal order, Africa stagnated.

Changing institutions requires a theory about how to acquire knowledge relevant to that task, and institutions capable of making decisions
related to those changes, and implementing them. That is to say,
development requires a theory of how to change institutions, and a
state structure efficient to do so.

Notes

1. See generally R.B. Seidman, 'A Note on the Gold Coast Reception Statute',
   J. Afr. L., 13, 45 (1969).
2. Gold Coast: Supreme Court Ordinance, 1876.
3. A. Seidman, *Comparative Development Strategies in East Africa* (Nairobi:
   East African Publishing House, 1972), p. 53.
4. See Chap. 5.
5. B. Finch and M. Oppenheimer, *Ghana: End of an Illusion* (New York:
   Monthly Review Press, 1966).
6. P. Dorner, 'Needed Redirections in Economic Analysis for Agricultural
   Development Policy', in P. Dorner (ed.), *Land Reform in Latin America*
   (Madison, Wisconsin: Land Economics, 1972), p. 5.
7. D. Trubek, 'Max Weber on Law and the Rise of Capitalism', *Wis. L. Rev.,*

270, 730 (1972).

8. W. Friedmann, 'The Role of Law and the Function of the Lawyer in Developing Countries', *Vand. L. Rev.*, 17, 181, 186-97.

9. Trubek, 'Max Weber on Law', p. 736.

10. J. Austin, in H.L.A. Hart (ed.), *The Province of Jurisprudence Determined* (London: Oxford University Press, 1958).

11. R. Pound, 'The Limits of Effective Legal Action', *ABAJ*, 3, 55 (1917).

12. A. Seidman, *Comparative Development Strategies*.

13. Lord Lugard used it as the theme of his influential book. F. Lugard, *The Dual Mandate in British Tropical Africa* (London: Frank Cass, 1922), frontispiece.

14. F. Lugard, 'The White Man's Task in Tropical Africa', reprinted in W. Quigg (ed.), *Africa, A Foreign Affairs Reader* (New York: Praeger, 1964), p. 5.

15. H. Johnstone, 'The Importance of Africa', *J. African Society*, 17, 179 (1918).

16. See e.g., H.M. Marshall, *The Changes and Adjustments which should be made to the Present Legal Systems of Africa to Permit them to Respond More Effectively to the Requirements of Development* (Paris: Librairie Dalloz, 1966), p. 75; A. Allott, 'Legal Development and Economic Growth in Africa', in J.N.D. Anderson (ed.), *Changing Law in Developing Countries* (London: George Allen and Unwin, 1963), p. 194; A. Allott, 'The Future of African Law', in L. Kuper and H. Kuper, *African Law: Adaption and Development* (Los Angeles: University of California Press, 1965), p. 216; R. David, 'A Civil Code for Ethiopia', *Tulane L. Rev.*, 37, 187 (1966).

17. Lesotho: Highway Traffic Act, 1972.

18. C. Irish, 'Double Taxation Treaties and Income Taxation at Source', *Int. & Comp. L.Q.*, 23, 292 (1974).

19. J. Read, 'Criminal Law in Africa of Today and Tomorrow', *J. Afr. L.*, 5, (1963).

20. See, e.g., Zambia: Penal Code (Cap. 146) Sec. 305 (e).

21. R.S. Jordan and J.P. Renninger, 'The New Environment of Nation-Building', *J. Mod. Af. Stud.*, 13, 187, 190 (1975) ('naive' and 'hopelessly romantic' to assume that institutional transfer would work.)

22. F. Barth, 'Models of Social Organization', *Royal Anthropological Institute Occasional Paper No. 23* (Glasgow: The University Press, 1966); see also F.S. Nadel, 'Social Control and Self-Regulation', *Social Forces*, 31, 265 (1953).

23. M. Tushnet, 'Lumber and the Legal Process', *Wisc. L. Rev.* 114, 116-117 (1972).

24. J.J. Spengler says the same thing in the vocabulary peculiar to economies: 'suppose we are in advanced country A and wish to transfer to underdeveloped county U a given institution I. I is embedded in a loosely or tightly integrated culture complex Ca and there performs a set of functions Fa. If the culture complex CU of a country U is not very different from Ca and the objective is the performance of the same kind of function Fu (Fa), we can speak of transfer. But as we depart from these conditions Fu differs somewhat from Fa (because some are otherwise performed), we have a transfer problem. We have a transformation indicated. It is essential, therefore, to contrast Ca and Cu and Fu and determine when it is transfer that suffices and when it is more.' Quoted in D. Lerner, 'The Transformation of Institutions', in W.B. Hamilton (ed.), *The Transfer of Institutions* (Durham, N.C.: Duke University Press, 1964), p. 9, n. 7. President Kaunda put it more pithily: 'A tree that flourishes and is evergreen by the riverside will not survive and be evergreen by the desert.' K.K. Kaunda 'Mulungushi Speech',

Zambia Daily Mail (Lusaka) 1 July 1975.
25. Zambia: Cap. 690.
26. A. Seidman, *Comparative Development Strategies*, p. 166.
27. E.W. Evans, 'Principles and Methods of Administration in the British Colonial Empire', in *Principles and Methods of Colonial Administration* (London: Butterworth Scientific Publications, 1950), pp. 9, 13.
28. C.H. Stigand, *Administration in Tropical Africa* (London: Constable 1914), p. 45.
29. R. Lee, *Colonial Government and Good Government* (London: Oxford University Press, 1967), p. 39.
30. R.B. Seidman, 'Administrative Law and Legitimacy on Anglophonic Africa. A Problem in the Reception of Foreign Law', *Law and Society Review,* 161 (1970).
31. See Chap. 13.
32. *The Colonial Service as a Career* (London: HMSO, 1950), p. 24.
33. Lugard, *Dual Mandate*, pp. 131-2.
34. R. Heussler, *Yesterday's Rulers: The Making of the British Colonial Service* (London: Oxford University Press, 1963).
35. Ibid.
36. R. Furse, *Acuparius: Recollections of a Recruiting Officer* (London: Oxford University Press, 1962), p. 223.
37. Heussler, *Yesterday's Rulers.*
38. R. Kipling, *Stalky & Co.* (London: MacMillan, 1899), is a collection of stories describing life at a public school most of whose students ended in the Army, or the Indian or Colonial Service.
39. A. Etzioni, 'Organizational Control and Structure', in J.G. March (ed.), *Handbook for Organizations* (Chicago: Rand McNally, 1965), pp. 650, 657.
40. Heussler, *Yesterday's Rulers*, pp. 102-3.
41. R.K. Merton, *Social Theory and Social Structure* (New York: Free Press, 1957), pp. 195-206.
42. Heussler, *Yesterday's Rulers*, p. 60.
43. A. Burns, *In Defence of Colonies: British Colonial Territories in International Affairs* (London: George Allen & Unwin, 1957), pp. 190 et seq.
44. Lee, *Colonial Government*, p. 148.
45. E. Ashby, *Universities British, Indian, Africa: A Study in the Ecology of Higher Education* (London: Weidenfield and Nicolson, 1966), pp. 190 *et seq.*
46. *Report of the Commission on Higher Education in the Colonies* [The Asquith Report] *(London: HMSO 1945), p. 10.*
47. Ashby, *Universities*, p. 127.
48. Ibid, p. 277.
49. Heussler, *Yesterday's Rulers*, p. 237.
50. W.J. Samuels, 'The Economy as a System of Power and its Legal Bases: The Legal Economics of Robert Lee Hale', *U. Miami L. Rev.*, 27, 261, 277 (1973).
51. Dorner, *Land Reform*, p. 6.

3 METHODOLOGY, PERSPECTIVES AND THE DEFINITION OF 'DEVELOPMENT' *

Development requires a legal order adapted to solving the difficulties of poverty and oppression. That requires a theory of knowledge, providing an agenda of steps to take in order to decide what is a good (wise, useful) rule.[1] Such rules must be based upon knowledge of the 'limits of law',[2] that is, the limits that society imposes upon the legal order's capacity to induce changed behaviour. Propositions expressing that knowledge require a methodology, perspectives and a vocabulary adapted to the task of generating them. Methodology provides an agenda of procedures that likely result in propositions expressing reliable knowledge. Those procedures require a variety of discretionary choices; perspectives guide that discretion. Finally, research requires data. Our vocabulary (or set of categories) determines what we see and therefore what data we take into account. In this chapter, I discuss methodology and perspectives, and, in Chapter 4, vocabulary.

I. Methodology
Western social scientists commonly prescribed an ends-means schema for deciding what government ought to do. Policy-makers first decide upon their ends, and social scientists then determine through research how they might economically achieve them.[3] That system rests upon the common notion (ultimately deriving from David Hume) that the Is of the existential world bears no continuous relationship with the Oughts of the normative universe.[4] In this view, a policy-maker can only justify his choices by the assertion that that is the sort of man he is.[5] Justice becomes 'an irrational ideal'.[6]

That justification will hardly suffice for public policy. An alternative methodology, resting upon such disparate philosophers as Dewey,[7] Popper,[8] and Sartre[9] and Marx,[10] may supply the deficiency. It consists of four steps: selecting a troubled situation; explaining it; proposing a solution; and implementing, monitoring and evaluating that solution.[11]

Law and development research by lawyers usually begins not with a variable to be tested, or an interest in developing general theory, but

* I am indebted to Judy Seidman, Banks McDowell and Robert Liberman, among others, for useful criticism of earlier drafts of this chapter.

with an existential problem that causes someone a difficulty: public corporations do not operate very well, existing land tenures block agricultural development, tax laws prevent new investment that requires a preliminary selection of what existential problem to investigate. That in turn comes down to the question of *whose* trouble to examine. Secondly, having defined a specific trouble, one must propose alternative explanations for it. Explanations identify causes. Unless solutions address causes, frequently they do no more than poultice symptoms. The researcher must generate as many such causal explanations as possible, and then make a sensible choice between them. The most important of the criteria for choosing between various candidate explanations, I believe, consists of falsifiability and empirical falsification. First, an explanation which in principle one could not falsify entails only a definition (that is, it merely restates the trouble or it rests upon mysticism and intuition). One cannot use experience to ascertain its validity. Secondly, an explanation that experience in fact falsifies cannot provide a reliable basis upon which to build a solution for the original difficulty. The falsification teaches that the supposed cause does not in fact constitute a cause. Thirdly, having eliminated most of the candidate explanations and thus identified the 'causes' of the original trouble, one can propose alternative solutions addressed to those causes. The choice between those alternative solutions depends upon the constraints and resources of the situation, and notions of their probable consequences. Finally, the research requires implementation, monitoring and evaluation of the selected solution. Any failure of the action taken to resolve the original difficulty (and no solution ever works completely) falsifies to that extent all the previous steps. The failure in any particular of the bridge falsifies to that extent both the design and the theoretical physics upon which it rests. Thus we learn by doing (Dewey). Marx and Sartre called it *praxis*. [12]

In this agenda, the law-in-the-books constitutes a proposal for solution. The law-in-action constitutes its implementation. A systematic variance exists between the law-in-the-books and the activity it induces. [13] That gap constitutes a new trouble, requiring in turn explanation and solution. Life consists of one trouble after another.

In the course of proposing explanations, we must articulate major premises, in the form of general propositions. If they work in one case, these propositions have some status as knowledge — i.e. as useful guides (or heurisms) to further research. The principle task in the generation of knowledge constitutes the effort to falsify these general propositions, and to amend them or propose new ones. The general stock of knowledge consists in the main of these 'middle level' propositions or theories,[14] all of them heurisms, and (because they always hold the possibility of falsification when new data comes to light) none of them ever more than problematical. 'Policy', 'instrumental' or 'problem-solving' research and 'academic' or 'theoretical' research in this view constitute the same enterprise.

II The Intellectual Control over Value Choice

'Problem-solving' too easily becomes a blind instrumentalism that supposes that muddling through can substitute for methodology.[15] The then Paramount Chief of Basutoland (now the King of Lesotho) in 1962 complained

> that decisions are taken on purely short-term grounds, without any clear perception of their long-run implications . . . Policy is made hand-to-mouth; and where there are no agreed views about the general principles of public policy, the proper role of various organizations and institutions, or the ultimate shape of social and economic relations, these piecemeal decisions are apt to make two malcontents for every citizen . . . One empirical, ready-made, 'commonsense' decision after another, taken to deal with situations that are seldom foreseen, and carrying consequences which are equally full of surprises; until all too often a once-popular government finds itself grown authoritarian but to no particular purpose presiding over a stagnant economy, no longer expecting any enthusiasm among the people, or having any power to mold the future.[16]

'Muddling through' always happens unless there is intellectual control over values. Problem-solving enquiry requires many discretionary choices. The human condition requires choice. Even with computers, man cannot consider all the troubles, explanations and proposals for solution. The process of enquiry always entails filters. They make possible enquiry itself.

These filters differ, some practical, some institutional. Some, however, seem personal to the decision-maker. They may arise out of mere self-interest, or they may reflect those dark, irrational 'drives' or 'residues' of which social scientists warn us. These personal values sometimes get so deeply embedded that the researcher or decision-maker does not even know they exist. Hence the common prescription that the conscientious researcher must at least declare his values, and, by declaring them, confront them. That does not suffice with problems of public policy, because public policy requires public justification. If intellect and science can ever enlarge their control over public decision-making, public justification must rely upon appeals to them, not to unreason.

In this and the succeeding sections, I propose a general paradigm for increasing intellectual control over the choice of value-filters to use in problem-solving. I then attempt to articulate the value-filters possibly appropriate for the study of law and development, and conclude by defining 'development'. By intellectual control over value-judgements I mean using experience to justify proposed courses of action. That means that we must find a way to invoke experience to control the discretionary choices that arise in the course of problem-solving.

The ends-means methodology holds that having defined the ends, the search for means is a matter for social science. The usual concept of ends defines them as a state of affairs, and the more precise, the better. When the difficulty of defining precise ends reveals itself, end-means methodologists then urge that the ends be stated as consummatory 'interests' — freedom, prosperity, order, equality.[17] Such generalized ends, however, only state the obverse of perceived troubles — oppression, poverty, disorder, inequity. In decision-making, they serve not as goals of policy but to exclude some alternatives from consideration. The value of 'freedom', for example, likely excludes programmes to recruit a labour force by coercion.[18] That is to say, such consummatory values serve not as ends, but to guide discretionary choices in problem-solving. In practice, such values, so broad and vacuous that everyone gives them verbal support, give no guide to the solution of concrete problems.

The problem remains: how to specify the value-filters that ought to control decision-making? Some avoid the normative issue, since (they say) in this brute world the values of the decision-makers will inevitably control.[19] Others purport to find authoritative values in religion (as in some notions of natural law), or in the inherent nature of man-in-society.[20] Roscoe Pound suggested that the significant value acceptances in a democratic polity ought to be those of the subjects of the law (on which he assumed essentially a consensus). Such 'jural postulates', he thought, might emerge through examining the claims and demands the citizenry make upon the legal order.[21]

In the final analysis, all such schemes come aground on methodological problems. To tell the decision-makers that their values will control decision does not tell them how to control their values. Natural law (as Pareto has warned us) teaches us not *why* men made the claims and demand they did, but *what* claims they made.[22] Religious affirmations derive from faith, not data. Speculation, not science, defines the characteristics of man-in-society. (Every interest-jurisprudent advances a different list of immutable interests).[23] Even if one could uncover jural postulates from the subjects or the law, so long as social conflict exists, those postulates must differ between classes and strata.

I suggest another account, which offers the possibility of using empirical data to ground these discretionary choices in the course of problem-solving, policy-oriented enquiry. Those choices can be guided by unarticulated 'values' or domain assumptions; or by ideal-typical models (or 'paradigms'); or by large-scale explanations (or 'grand theory'). My account depends upon the functional equivalence in problem-solving of these three very different sorts of guides to discretion.

A. Values and Ideal-Typical Models

Ordinarily, values comprise a mishmash of sentiments, feelings and vague beliefs, inarticulate and unexamined. They guide research, but unconsciously. Unless the researcher 'delivers his domain assumptions from the dim realm of subsidiary awareness into the clearer realm of focal awareness, where they can be held firmly in view, they can never be brought before the bar of reason or submitted to the test of evidence'.[24] One must begin by articulating one's domain assumptions, and thus confronting them. These domain assumptions take many forms. They may describe prizings, or desired state of affairs; tastes; broad goals ('freedom' or 'justice'); or perceived reality ('all peasants are fatalistic'). Most cannot be tested by evidence, for most do not purport to describe what is the case, but what ought to be the case.

Stating one's values as domain assumptions, however, inevitably leads to attempts at rationalizing and harmonizing them. Together, they become the researcher's ideal-typical 'model of society and man',[25] or paradigm. The neo-classical model of capitalist society,[26] various utopian socialist constructs,[27] and Professors Trubek and Galanter's model of 'legal liberalism'[28] are examples. Such ideal-typical models perform the same function in problem-solving enquiry as do values: they guide discretionary choice. A researcher with a 'value' of free enterprise will likely select similar subjects for research, and similar explanations for testing, as one wed to the neo-classical model. One with a 'value' of socialism will do the same research as one who has a well-defined model of utopian socialism.

B.   Ideal-Typical Models and Large-scale Explanations

Ideal-typical models frequently embody proposals for solutions, for they put forward what their authors think desirable. Like all proposals for solutions, they nevertheless state or imply explanations to which they are addressed. Instead of writing a tract exalting free enterprise, or describing a capitalist utopia, Adam Smith wrote a scientific treatise *explaining* mercantilist society and the wealth of nations. So also Marx: *Das Kapital* did not propagandize for a socialist society (I am told that the word 'socialism' does not appear in its four long volumes). Rather, he *explained* mid-century English capitalism.

In principle, every end or value is a proposal for solution. Every proposal for solution implies an explanation. The great trick in policy-oriented research is to convert propositions for solutions, themselves not testable, into their correlative explanations, which are. Every over-arching end implies a correlative over-arching explanation — some call such explanations 'grand theory'. Using grand theory to guide discretionary choices in research should, therefore, result in the same results as using either its correlative ideal-typical model, or the unexpressed values upon which the ideal-typical model was built. It would at first blush seem that in principle, one could appraise even very grand theory by the same criteria as any other explanation: falsifiability, consistency with known data and so forth. In fact, however, one cannot do so, for two reasons. First, grand theory purports to explain human society. Human society is too complex; there is too much data to order. Second, grand theory is an explanation for over-arching difficulties. Like any explanation, its articulation too requires discretionary choices. If the purpose of grand theory is to guide such discretionary choices, what guides those choices in generating grand theory itself?

The test for grand theory ultimately lies in praxis, in learning-through-doing. The process of problem-solving enquiry includes the implementation and monitoring of solutions. Implementation generates data to test the entire preceding process. Just as building a bridge tests not only its particular design, but the general theoretical principles that underlie it, the successes or failures of particular social interventions may test the grand theories on which they were based. Ultimately, however, even that answer is unsatisfactory. What, or whose, standards measure the success or failure of development programmes? That question demands from the researcher an affirmation, itself incapable of control by data, about whose troubles he wants to alleviate. I return to this issue in the conclusion of this chapter. Given such an affirmation, however, alternative explanations for underdevelopment in principal lend themselves to comparative assessment,[29] although obviously the path is strewn with bear traps and land mines. History generates the necessary data.

III The Value Frameworks of Law and Development

For two-thirds of the human race, the ageless cry for justice manifests itself today in demands for development and modernization. The guiding values of the legal order in the new states ought to find their principal well-spring in the concept of development. Most definitions of 'development' or 'modernization' stated these as a prized state of affairs: increased per capita income, or that plus a distribution function, or both plus increased employment.[30] For Western observers, frequently 'development' meant to be like *us*.[31] Western law became the model for African polities.[32] Some invoked natural law to justify such values as 'the respect and dignity accorded to individuals, and the opportunities for each to realize his potentiality'.[33] Other scholars borrowed their definitions from the political or other pronouncements of African leaders or political parties, which were just as vague as most other statements of generalized ends.[34] Ends so vague that they have no perceptible content until we examine the actual activity of implementation[35] have no use as explicit problem-solving criteria.

Most of these definitions of 'development' or 'modernization' as prizings only reflect the intuitive value-sets of their authors. A researcher who invoked them to justify his proposals for new law would end by saying merely that he makes his proposals because that is the sort of man he is. Since there is no commonly agreed defintion, the best I can do is to stipulate what I mean by the word 'development'. My definition, of course, must be useful to the present enquiry. Like other 'big words' ('freedom', 'prosperity', 'equality') 'development' guides discretionary choices in the process of social enquiry. It serves the same function therefore, as ideal-typical models of the process of development, or large-scale explanations of underdevelopment. To define the word 'development' requires that we first try to explain poverty and oppression.

A. The Troubled Situation

What troubled situation falls for explanation? The absence of industry? Low technology? The relative absence of freedom of choice for the consumer? Lack of effective guarantees for individual liberty? The slow rate of growth of per capita GNP?

The question, of course, becomes *whose* trouble? Most people in the

Third World plainly complain mainly of poverty. The so-called developed countries have per capita incomes of $1,500 or more. The less developed countries have per capita incomes as low as $50 per annum. Life expectancy in the developed countries is sixty-five or seventy years. In most LDCs it is about thirty-two years or less. In the developed world, only a few infants die; in many LDCs, 50 per cent or more do. Disease — cholera, typhus, syphilis, river blindness, malaria, kwashiokor (severe malnutrition), leprosy, tuberculosis — stalk every man his life long. At the door of every hut stands always the spectre of famine. Whatever the deficiencies in housing in the developed countries, housing there serves better than a mud hut with a thatched roof, interminably dripping during the rains. Illiteracy is not exceptional but usual. Closely-knit, kin-oriented folk societies no doubt provide valued psychological supports for their members, but they are poor. Our definition of 'development' starts with the trouble which affects most people in the world: poverty. Many years ago men might argue that if they were poor, they did not know that. The winds of change blew away that state of innocence. Across the world, the people of the less developed countries know about hospitals, bicycles, radios, motor cars, decent housing and an abundance of food. They realize, too, the impotence that is handmaiden to their poverty.[36]

Values of course decide whose troubles to explain. Why choose to study the problems of the masses, rather than of the classes? For the vast majority of mankind, that question answers itself. They themselves are poor. For the researcher, himself usually well-paid and well-fed, and frequently expatriate, the answer becomes more problematic. I choose to start with the trouble that afflicts the vast majority of mankind. Why the poverty of nations?

B. Explanations and Solutions

Obviously, at best I can here suggest only a barebones outline to that question. I begin with two propositions on which practically all social scientists today, I think, agree:

1. The total consumption of a society cannot over a long period of time exceed its total production.
2. An improvement in technology is a necessary but not sufficient condition for an increase in production.

This explanation reflects our own epoch. In the mercantilist age, the then current explanation for poverty differed: poor countries lacked money — gold and silver. Whatever one country gained in wealth, another lost. The modern explanation for poverty in terms of production could not arise until the advent of technological innovation. The modern explanation for poverty urges that the existing technology of African economies must vastly improve in order to eliminate poverty. Does this imply a necessary change in law and institutions?

a. Status and the Subsistence Economy. With low technology, ownership of the tools and land required for production becomes closely tied to labour. Only one man at a time can use a simple hoe. Machinery, however, requires many people to operate it. The individual owner of machinery must employ others to work on it. The very existence of a high technology raises questions of the relationship between ownership and labour that do not exist in a society with simple technology, such as the distribution of income between owners and workers, and the location of decision-making power concerning investment and the use of the means of production.

A low technology economy typically approaches subsistence. Increased technology leads to specialization and exchange. Subsistence economies are poor, and have a central jural theme of status:

1. Traditional societies have low levels of technology.

2. Having low levels of technology, the ownership of productive assets (especially land) and the labour on those assets are closely integrated.

3. Having low levels of technology, such societies are geographically static.

4. Such societies have social orders that depend primarily upon kinship ties for social solidarity, rather than the social solidarity that arises from the interchange of goods and services (i.e. mechanical rather than organic solidarity).

5. Such societies are relatively impoverished, and population tends to be low in relation to available land.

6. Given these propositions, no market for the interchange of factors of production exists.

7. Without such a market, the norms defining right to land define it in terms of membership in a kinship group, i.e. of status.

The transition from economies marked by low technology, unity of ownership and labour and low levels of specialization and exchange to economies with a sophisticated technology, dichotomies between ownership and labour, and a high degree of specialization and exchange, has received a variety of names: from status to contract (Maine); from *Gemeinschaft* to *Gesellschaft* (Tönnies); from folk to urban societies (Redfield); from mechanical to organic solidarity (Durkheim); from sacred to secular societies (Weber); from patriarchal to industrial societies (Stalin).[37] Some definitions of 'development' or 'modernization' only describe that same transition.[38] They tell us nothing about how to get those processes underway, or in what general direction one should try to move.

b. Contract. How ought societies move away from a regime of status to a regime of high specialization and exchange? The many explanations of poverty lead to quite different prescriptions for action. Most of these fall into one of two categories. A typical example of the first sort is Paul Samuelson's:[39]

1. The poor countries lack the four 'economic fundamentals', viz., population, natural resources, capital formation and technology.

2. Absent these economic fundamentals, neither opportunities for profitable investment, nor investors with capital can easily develop.

3. Absent opportunities for investment, and investors with capital, investment cannot occur.

4. Absent investment, the productive capacity of a country remains low.

5. Poverty exists where the productive capacity of a country remains low.

Lurking behind this explanation lies an important unstated assumption put nicely by Herbert A. Simon. He distinguishes between the 'inner' and 'outer' environment of a system, between the substance and organization of the system itself, and the surroundings in which it works. Since any given system adjusts somehow to its environment, a small change in the environment will produce a corresponding adaptive change in the system. Thus, 'we can often predict behaviour from knowledge of the system's goals and its outer environment, with only minimal assumptions about the inner environment'.[40]

Samuelson makes an analogous assumption. Given a change in the climate of investment entrepreneurs will invest and there will be a corresponding change in output. His explanation therefore need not examine closely the 'black box' — that is, the institutional arrangements of the economy. His explanation directs attention away from institutional explanations for poverty. As a consequence of Samuelson's implicit acceptance of the notion of system adaptability, his proposals for governmental action in aid of development would not change the institutions of the inner environment (the economic system itself). Rather, they only go to provide conditions for private entrepreneurial investment. Government must reform those institutions which inhibit individual entrepreneurship: tax systems, land tenures and systems of private commercial law. In addition, the state can help private entrepreneurs directly by providing cheap risk capital or soft loans through Development Finance Corporations. Many states seek to create entrepreneurial spirit and skills through Institutes of Business Administration and the like. Most theorists today, like Samuelson, go somewhat further. Classical *laisser-faire,* like the old soldier in the song, may not yet have died, but it has long since faded away. Despite commitment to the premiss, that the initiative for development can come only from private entrepreneurs, Samuelson recognizes practical difficulties. Certain sorts of socially desirable enterprises are not profitable. The profit motive can sometimes lead to undesirable uses of capital, such as speculative real estate ventures. Hence he urges that the state undertake 'social overhead' projects which, while 'extremely valuable . . . create intangible benefits that cannot be expected to yield pecuniary profits to private investors'.

Samuelson's economics resonates easily with the pluralist political paradigm.[41] Because Samuelson excludes economic institutions as possible causes of poverty he necessarily excludes them from state control. He thus places them — especially the institutions of productive enterprise — in a completely different arena from politics. He bifurcates the polity between economics and government. That sharply confines the functions of government. It must maintain the conditions for economic functioning; and it must extract enough taxes to maintain itself. To meet the rhetoric of the welfare state, governments must also build schools, roads, hospitals, better housing, water supplies. What government may not do is to engage in productive enterprise.

Following Samuelson's explanation of underdevelopment, the main political problems become twofold: first, to insulate the economic system against tinkering by social radicals; and second, to ensure that the government remains honest and competent. His model thus implies a neutral state within which social conflict can take place — the model of interest-group pluralism.

Samuelson's explanation focuses in part on insufficient development capital. After all, capitalism cannot succeed without capitalists, by definition, those who have accumulated capital. Samuelson's explanation *requires* sharp differentials in income, so that capital will accumulate in private hands. He therefore ignores distribution in his definition of 'underdevelopment':

> An underdeveloped nation is simply one with real per capita income that is low relative to the present day per capita income of such nations as Canada, the United States, Great Britain, France, and Western Europe generally. Usually an underdeveloped nation is one regarded as capable of substantial improvement in its income level . . .[42]

What legal order does this explanation and set of proposals imply? Mainly, it must ensure that private entrepreneurs can function as such; that requires the legalistic model:[43]

1. Specialization and exchange require a high degree of co-ordination between economic units.

2. That co-ordination will come from entrepreneurs if the law grants them this power.

3. The institutions of private property, and contract, and other regimes of facilitative law, enforced by autonomous courts, delegate such power to entrepreneurs.

The agenda for law-makers that the regime of contract demands seems reasonably clear. It consists of the conventional Western wisdom for legal development. They must supply legal devices to facilitate entrepreneurial activity, principally property and contract law in all their ramifications. They must provide facilitative forms for capitalists to organize the economy, such as corporation law. Finally, some states may decide to delegate law-making power directly to entrepreneurs by creating official cartels: Industry Boards, parastatal corporations and the like. The legal order can encourage private capital by providing an hospitable investment climate: easy tax laws, an educated labour force, research institutes, law and order, a well-developed infrastructure generally. In political affairs, the law can provide clear lines of demarcation between administrative power and individual rights, prevent official corruption, collect taxes and preserve law and order. State planning of productive enterprise, and legal forms that might undermine individual ownership, such as producer's co-operatives however, fall outside the pale of permissible governmental activity.

c. Plan. A book by Ann Seidman exemplifies an alternative set of explanations.[44] Her explanation of the poverty of nations differs markedly from Samuelson's:

1. The way that members of a society interact with each other in the material conditions of a particular society determines how material resources are created and allocated in that society.

2. How members of a society interact with each other is a function of the institutions of the country.

3. In every modern polity, the state possesses the best organized and most powerful instruments to change institutions.

4. In every society, the classes or groups that have economic power and privilege tend to control the machinery of the state in their own interests.

5. In every Anglophonic African state, the formal and informal institutional structures existing on the emergence from the imperial era consisted of the following:

   a. An export enclave, consisting of a few foreign firms, local entrepreneurs, managers and bureaucrats with high incomes; wage workers and cash crop peasants with low incomes; and an economy with a high degree of specialization and exchange, mainly producing raw materials for export overseas to developed countries, and draining surpluses by that trade to the metropolitan countries as profits, interest, dividends and remitted expatriate salaries;

   b. A hinterland, consisting of the great mass of peasants engaged in subsistence farming with low technology in conditions of poverty;

   c. A set of institutions supported by state power that drives peasants from the subsistence sector to work at low wages in the export enclave.

6. The political elite and the economic ruling class in the export enclave continue their power and privilege by continuing the existing set of institutions, making incremental changes only where necessary to maintain stability and equilibrium, and to increase their own power and privilege.

7. In most countries, foreign and local entrepreneurs, managers and bureaucrats in the export enclave have effective control of the state machinery.

This explanation points to significantly different variables than does Samuelson's. Rather than asserting that only private entrepreneurs can provide the indispensable engine of development, it suggests that the state itself inevitably determines the shape of development. It does not ignore the institutional structure embodied in the dual economy, but defines it as the cause of the poverty of the great mass of the population. Since the African polities' present deplorable economic conditions result from a colonial regime which made contract its central jural theme, her explanation suggests that contract, far from a solution for the troubled situation, is its cause. If the legal order remains as received it will tend to reproduce itself. Unless it changes, her explanation suggests that poverty will continue.

This model does not sharply distinguish between economics and politics as Samuelson's does. Precisely because it insists that the explanation for poverty lies in the institutions of the economy, it explains poverty in part by what the state does. She suggests that the appropriate role of the state includes doing whatever is necessary, particularly in productive sectors, to induce development. She looks to major changes in the institutional structure, and suggests that until the elites who control the machinery of the state change, the existing relationships will change, if at all, only incrementally. She argues that because the existing institutional structure will necessarily provide greater profits to entrepreneurs dealing in overseas markets, the state must restructure existing institutions to provide a balanced nationally integrated economy with a strong internal market. Most important, so long as particular classes have radically disproportionate shares of power and privilege, those with the larger shares will likely control the political machinery in their own interest. Therefore, she advocates solutions that look towards equitable shareouts of income and greater participation in decision-making by wage earners and peasants.

It follows, therefore, that her definition of 'development' differs markedly from Samuelson's: 'The goal of development explicitly stated, is attainment of increased specialization and exchange leading to increased productivity directed to raising the level of living of the entire population as rapidly as existing material constraints permit'.[45] The regime of law that this explanation and definition suggest is completely different from that flowing from Samuelson's model. The legal order, far from merely providing facilitative forms for private economic actors, must induce new, desired behaviour. Rather than constituting separate, seemingly autonomous systems, law, government and the economic order become a continuum. We can state this as the Law of the Plan:

1. Specialization and exchange required a high degree of co-ordination between economic units.

2. How members of a society interact with each other depends on the normative system defining their roles and applying related sanctions.

3. The state can and does determine the content of this normative system.

4. The state should use this power to define institutions which will lead away from the dual economy towards a nationally unified and integrated economy, expressed in national plans.

5. The political structure of the state must provide the maximum feasible participation of the large masses in decision-making processes.

The Law of the Plan is obviously very different to the Law of Contract. Many of the conceptual difficulties that have plagued the study of law and development have arisen from an insistence that somewhere, somehow lay a magic formula to dictate the appropriate law for every sort of economy.[46] The chase for that ideal law became the hunt for the chimera. I explore the difference between the Law of the Plan and the Law of Contract throughout this volume.

C. The Choice Between Alternatives

The different definitions of development of these two writers arise out of their explanations of underdevelopment. The choice of definition does not involve merely an exercise in taste or values. It flows from these different explanations. We can learn which of these inconsistent explanations is 'false', by discovering which of them better generates solutions for the difficulties they try to solve, that is, by asking which of them more likely leads to a reduction of poverty and oppression. For this test we have an embarrassingly large mass of data to examine, far beyond the scope of this book. Analyses such as Samuelson's dominated the policy of most LDCs in the nominally 'free' world. Everywhere, these states sought to attract foreign capital, improve infrastructure, encourage export crops, and generally follow Samuelson's recommendations. In Africa at least, these programmes did not differ radically from those of the last decades of colonialism, and they did not usually significantly increase the pace of development. The principal investment opportunities for short-term profit in the LDCs, as during the colonial era, lay in the export of raw materials and the sale of imported manufactured goods, not in creating local industry. Entrepreneurs took advantage of these opportunities: cocoa in Ghana, coffee and tea in Kenya, copper in Zambia. That process, however, led mainly to growth without development.[47] The institutions of the colonial situation replicated themselves. External dependency continued or increased; economic independence remained a dream. Internal specialization and exchange eluded the economic planners in Africa. Samuelson's solutions led not to change, but rather to institutionalized poverty and oppression.

In Anglophonic Africa, only Tanzania's policies approximate those that Ann Seidman's explanation suggests. Tanzania 'seized the commanding heights', and nationalized export-import and internal wholesale trade, important industry and financial institutions. Rather than relying upon private enterprise, it consciously sought to change economic institutions through planning. It explicitly tried to develop new sorts of participatory institutions.[48] The relative success of these different policies cannot sustain analysis in gross, but only through detailed case studies. In fact, these exist in many different countries, although those in English dwell more on the 'free world' countries. Their examination is beyond my scope here.

Conclusion

History leaves policy-makers no easy exit from self-reliant problem-solving. The methodology of problem-solving proposed in the preceding chapter contains a number of discretionary choices. How to control these choices by intelligence and experience, rather than sentiments and 'values'? In this chapter I have suggested that such intellectual controls are possible because of the functional equivalence of values, ideal-typical models and large-scale explanations, or grand theory. It is possible to test the last of these in the fire of practical work; and, as a result, amend our theories (or change them completely) as experience teaches. Of course, this agenda does not completely succeed in replacing personal values with testable propositions at every stage. It purports to show how to impose intellectual controls over every discretionary choice in research, except one: *which* over-arching trouble requires immediate explanation and solution? But, the same facts constitute different sorts of troubles for different people. To the rich, poverty means the threat of unrest and riot; to the poor, hungry bellies. Research on threats to elite rule will produce different explanations and different solutions to research on hunger of the immiserated. The question for the researcher is not *which* problem, but whose?

Most Africans worry about hunger, disease, brutality, vulnerability, early death. To do meaningful research on these issues requires us to adopt their point of view. That calls, not for cold-blooded objectivity, but for commitment, engagement, empathy and concern — in short, for passion. A familiar folk song puts it directly: Which side are you on? To say that all research requires commitment in this sense does not say that the researcher can therefore ignore intellectual controls in favour of the interests of those to whom he feels committed. Rather, intellectual controls must govern every stage of enquiry except for the decision with whom to empathize. The 'researcher' who ignores the controls of social science becomes not a researcher but a propagandist, and likely a sycophant for the authorities. As such, he is useless both to his employers, and those for whom he declares commitment.

Most of us, of course, have a much simpler question. Its answer comes from the rhetoric of every government and every constitution. Today they all claim to represent 'the masses'. The *ancien régime* has long since expired. Given agreement that government should resolve the difficulties of the many, what it ought to do in principle can result from problem-solving enquiry coming ultimately not from 'values' but experience. Patently, no real-life law-maker is so completely rational or scientific. Decision-makers have their own agendas, and those of the powerful and the privileged to contend with. So long as government responds to troubles through measures based not on reason but on parochial or class interest, prejudice, myth, legend or blind chance, their 'solutions' will only compound the trouble. Irrationality excites the raw assertion of force; force saps legitimacy.

Edward Levi once called for an epistemology or methodology for determining how to improve the law,[49] that is to say, for a theory of justice that was not a blueprint of the Good, but a process which made it likely that just law would emerge. In that sense, justice rests upon a set of propositions that instruct us how to go about solving the troubles that plague the human condition. A decision can claim to embody justice to the extent that it persuades all men who abide by reason and science and the arguments of data. If it be true, as I have argued, that that persuasion occurs only in so far as men have a common commitment, then justice in the sense that I use it here must always be relative. Given that commitment, what is just is that which emerges from a rational enquiry process. That process is justice itself.

Notes

1. E.H. Levi, 'An Approach to Law', speech to the entering class of the University of Chicago Law School, 2 October 1974, p. 13 (mimeo).
2. J.A. Robertson and P. Teitlebaum, 'Optimizing Legal Impact: A Case Study in Search of a Theory', *Wisconsin Law Review,* 663 (1973).
3. See e.g. V. Pareto, *Mind and Society* (N.Y.: Harcourt, Brace, 1935); M. Weber, *Max Weber on the Methodology of the Social Sciences* (E.A. Shils and H.A. Finch, eds. trs.; Glencoe: The Free Press, 1949); A. Podgerecki and R. Schulze, 'Socio-Technique', *Soc. Sci. Info.,* 7, 135, 149 (1968); J.J. Spengler, 'Bureaucracy and Economic Development', in J. LaPalombara, *Bureaucracy and Political Development* (Princeton: Princeton UP, 1963), p. 199.
4. See, e.g., D. Hume, *A Treatise of Human Nature* (London: Everyman's Library, 1972), p. 127; G.A. Moore, *Principia Ethica* (Cambridge: University Press, 1903); A.J. Ayer, *Language, Truth and Logic* (N.Y.: Oxford University Press, 1936); C.L. Stevenson, *Ethics and Language* (New Haven: Yale University Press, 1944); T.D. Weldon, *The Language of Politics* (London: Penguin, 1953); P.H. Nowell-Smith, *Ethics* (Middlesex: Penguin, 1954), p. 13.
5. Weber, *Methodology of the Social Sciences,* p. 54; see also D.J. Black, 'The Boundaries of Legal Sociology', *Yale L.J.,* 81, 1086 (1972).
6. H. Kelsen, 'The Pure Theory of Law' (C.H. Wilson, tr.), *L.Q.R.,* 50, 474, 502 (1930).
7. J. Dewey, *Theory of Valuation* (Chicago: University of Chicago Press, 1939); J. Dewey, *Logic: The Art of Inquiry* (N.Y.: Holt, Rinehart and Winston, 1938).
8. K. Popper, *The Logic of Scientific Discovery* (New York: Harper and Row, 1968).
9. J.P. Sartre, *Search for a Method,* H.E. Barnes, ed. (New York: Knopf 1963).
10. K. Marx, *Writings of a Young Marx on Philosophy and Science* (L.D. Easton and K.H. Guddat, eds.; New York: Doubleday, 1967).
11. See generally, R.B. Seidman, 'The Lessons of Self-Estrangement: On the Methodology of Law and Development', forthcoming in R. Simon (ed.), *Yearbook of the Sociology of Law* (Greenwich, Conn: Johnson Associates, 1977).
12. R.L. Bernstein, *Praxis and Action* (Philadelphia: University of Pennsylvania Press 1971). Professor Robert Liberman points out that the methodology suggested in the text correlates with the familiar *Rule in Heydon's Case* 3 Co. Rep. 7b (1584). (In construing a statute a court should consider four

things: '1st. What was the common law before the making of the act. 2nd. What was the mischief and defect for which the common law did not provide. 3rd. What remedy hath the Parliament resolved and appointed to cure the disease of the commonwealth. And, 4th. The true reason for the remedy.')

13. The categories, 'law-in-the-books' and 'law-in-action' come from the legal realist school of jurisprudence. See K. Llewellyn, 'Some Realism about Realism', *Harvard L. Rev.*, 44, 1222 (1935).

14. A.W Gouldner, *The Coming Crisis of Western Sociology* (New York: Avon Books, 1970).

15. A. Hirschmann, *Journeys to Progress: Studies of Economic Policy-Making in Latin America* (New York: Twentieth Century Fund, 1963); F. Braybrooke and C.E. Lindblom, *A Strategy of Decision: Policy Evaluation as a Social Process* (New York: The Free Press, 1963); C. Leys, 'The Analysis of Planning', in C. Leys (ed.), *Politics and Change in Developing Countries* (Cambridge: The University Press, 1969).

16. Quoted in R.P. Stevens, *Lesotho, Botswana and Swaziland* (London: Pall Mall Press, 1967), pp. 71-2.

17. W.B. Harvey, 'The Challenge of the Rule of Law', *Mich. L. Rev.*, 59, 603, 606-7 (1961); A. Poderecki and R. Schulze, 'Socio-technique', *Soc. Sci. Info.*, 7, 135 (1968).

18. M.D. Bayles, 'A Concept of Coercion' in J.R. Pennock and J.W. Chapman (eds.), *Coercion, Nomus XIV*, (Chicago: Aldine Atherton, 1972), pp. 16, 22; B. Gert, 'Coercion and Freedom' in *Coercion*, pp. 30, 32; A.P. Wertheimer, 'Political Coercion and Political Obligation', ibid., pp. 213, 222; but see V. Held, 'Coercion and Coercive Offers', ibid., pp. 49, 51 and D. MacIntosh, 'Coercion and International Politics', ibid., pp. 243, 244-5.

19. Weber, *Methodology of the Social Sciences*.

20. See H.L.A. Hart, *The Concept of Law* (Oxford: Clarendon, 1962); W.G. Runciman, *Social Science and Political Theory* (Cambridge: The University Press 1965).

21. R. Pound, *Social Control Through Law* (New Haven: Yale University Press 1942).

22. Pareto, *Mind and Society*.

23. Compare, e.g., M.S. McDougal, 'The Comparative Study of Law for Policy Purposes', *Yale L.J.*, 61, 915 (1952) with C.A. Auerbach, W.Hurst, L. Garrison, and S. Mermin, *The Legal Process: An Introduction to Decision-Making by Judicial, Legislative, Executive and Administrative Agencies* (San Francisco: Chandler, 1961), p. 661; and compare D. Trubek and M. Galanter, 'Scholars in Self-Estrangement: Reflections on the Crisis in Law and Development Studies in the United States', *Wisc. L. Rev.* 1062 (1974) ('greater equality, enhanced freedom, and fuller participation in the community') with D. Trubek and M. Galanter, 'Scholars in the Funhouse: A Reply to Professor Seidman', forthcoming in R. Simon (ed.), *Yearbook of the Sociology of Law* (Greenwich, Conn: Johnson Associates 1977) ('increased equality, enhanced participation in public life, and greater mastery of natural and social forces') and with D. Trubek, 'Complexity and Contradiction in the Legal Order: Balbus and the Challenge of Critical Social Thought of Law', *Law and Soc. Rev.*, 11, 529, 546 (1977) ('equality, individuality and community').

24. Gouldner, *Coming Crisis*, p. 35.

25. A. Inkeles, *What is Sociology?* (Englewood Cliffs, N.J.: Prentice-Hall, 1964), pp. 28, 29.

26. See, e.g., E. Bellamy, *Looking Backward* (Boston & New York: Houghton Mifflin, 1929).

27. See, e.g. J. Gilson, *The Soviet Image of Utopias* (Baltimore & London: John Hopkins, 1975), Chapters 1 and 3.
28. Trubek and Galanter, 'Scholars in the Funhouse'; cf. Seidman, 'Lessons of Self-Estrangement'.
29. But cf. T.S. Kuhn, *The Structure of Scientific Revolutions* (University of Chicago Press 1964); compare D.L. Phillips, 'Paradigms and Incommensurability', *Theory and Society*, 2, 37 (1975).
30. D. Seers, 'The Meaning of Development', *International Development Review*, 11, 2 (1969).
31. See, e.g., J.P. Nettl, 'Strategies in the Study of Political Development', in C. Leys (ed.), *Politics and Change*, p. 13; B. Higgins, *Economic Development: Principles, Problems and Policies* (New York: Norton, 1959); P.T. Bauer and B.S. Yamey, *The Economies of Underdeveloped Countries* (London: Nisbet, 1957); R. Bendix, *Nation-Building and Citizenship* (New York: Harpers, 1961), R. Holt and J. Turner, *The Political Basis of Economic Underdevelopment* (New York: Van Nostrand, 1966); S.P. Huntington, *Political Order in Changing Societies* (New Haven: Yale University Press, 1968), G. Almond and W. Powell, *Comparative Politics: A Developmental Approach* (Boston: Little, Brown, 1966).
32. K. Roberts-Wray, 'The Adaptation of Imported Law in Africa', *J. Af. L.*, 4, 66 (1960); A. Allott, 'The Changing Law in a Changing Africa', *Sociologus*, 11, 115 (1961); M. Gallanter, 'The Modernization of Law', in M. Weiner (ed.), *Modernization: The Dynamics of Growth* (New York: Basic Books, 1966).
33. D. Apter, *The Politics of Modernization* (Chicago: University of Chicago Press, 1965).
34. C. Leys, 'The Limits of African Capitalism: The Formation of the Monopolistic Petty-Bourgeois in Kenya' (Cyclostyle: n.d.); compare A.J. Gregor, 'African Socialism, Socialism and Fascism: An Appraisal', *Rev. of Politics*, 29, 324 (1967) with J. Mohan, 'Varieties of African Socialism', *Socialist Register*, 220 (1966); cf. E. Shils, *Political Development in the New States, 11 Comparative Studies in Society and History* (The Hague: Mouton, 1959).
35. Cf. W.B. Harvey, *Law and Change in Ghana* (Princeton: Princeton University Press, 1966).
36. D. Goulet, *The Cruel Choice* (New York: Atheneum, 1973).
37. M. Gluckman, *Politics, Law and Ritual in Tribal Society* (Oxford: Basil Blackwell, 1965), p. 213.
38. See, e.g., M. Kilson, 'African Political Change and the Modernization Process', *J. Mod. Af. Studies*, 1, 425 (1963).
39. P. Samuelson, *Economics, An Introductory Analysis*, 4th ed. (New York: McGraw-Hill, 1958), pp. 758-68.
40. H. Simon, *The Sciences of the Artificial* (Cambridge, Mass.: MIT Press, 1969), p. 8.
41. See Almond and Powell, *Comparative Politics*.
42. P. Samuelson, *Economics, an Introductory Analysis*, 6th ed. (New York: McGraw-Hill, 1964), p. 755.
43. Trubek and Galanter, 'Scholars in the Funhouse'.
44. A. Seidman, *Comparative Development Strategies in East Africa* (Nairobi: East Af. Pub. House, 1972).
45. Ibid., p. 5.
46. See Chap. 2.
47. See R.W. Clower, G. Dalton, M. Horwitz and A.A. Walters, *Growth without Development: An Economic Survey of Liberia* (Evanston: Northwestern University Press, 1966).
48. See generally L. Cliffe and J. Saul, *Socialism in Tanzania: An Interdisciplinary Reader* (Nairobi: East Af. Pub. House, 1972).
49. Levi, 'An Approach to Law'.

4 THE VOCABULARY FOR A THEORY OF LAW AND DEVELOPMENT

The final element in an adequate theory of law and development is a set of categories to guide investigation. Explanations point to causes, the variables that make social intervention possible (or impossible). These categories form the vocabulary of theory. Any such choice of categories (or vocabulary) entails an evaluation. It judges the category important for explaining the phenomenon under investigation. Words identify *what counts as belonging to the world.*[1]

To select these categories consciously, rather than permitting linguistic history to do it for us, one must in general terms explain the phenomenon under study. Paradoxically, that explanation must precede the research. Without a word for something, we do not see it. The Eskimos have over thirty words for different sorts of snow. In English we have only a few. The Eskimo sees more sorts of snow. Without a vocabulary, research cannot advance, for we do not know what data to gather. How to explain phenomena, before doing research concerning them?

The ideal-type functions to formulate such categories. It is in this sense neo-Kantian. It expresses what the theorist, based on his present knowledge, views as the key variables. Not neophytes but scholars deep in their subject matter create great intellectual constructs. Such an ideal-type frequently begins as a statement of Utopia; but it is invariably based implictly or explicitly on an explanation. It must therefore meet our criteria for explanations. The wide-ranging explanations that constitute these ideal-types address the general range of difficulties included in the domain of study. Our concern lies in the phenomenon of soft development, that is, the frequent failure of law to induce the behaviour seemingly demanded to accomplish development. Rather than review the jurisprudential and sociological literature concerning the issue, I shall directly put forward the model that underlies this book.

I The Structure of Choice

Human history, as contrasted, say, with geology, concerns acts, not events.[2] Acts imply choice.[3] The simplest and most general model of society consists of people and collectivities making choices among the

constraints and resources of their environments as they perceive them.[4]
A science of law and development must begin with categories useful in
explaining choice.

One can ask two questions about choice. First, within what arena of
choice — i.e. what rewards and punishments, resources and constraints
— must the actor choose his course? Second, within that arena, why
does he choose as he does?[5] These questions deny any contest between
determinism and freedom. Both are always present. The environment
imposes constraints. Within those constraints there always lies some
potential for choice.[6] All the social and physical forces of the world
combine to lay out alternative potential courses of action: technology,
geography, the behaviour of others. In a society built upon human
interdependence the expected behaviour of others plays the most
pervasive function. For example, if a farmer requires credit, and only a
village money lender charging extortionate rates of interest will lend
him money, the farmer's choice depends on the money lender: he can
either borrow money at the extortionate rate and continue farming,
or he can cease farming.

Within the arena of choice people do make choices. People act in
repetitive patterns. That fact defines society, as opposed to anarchy.
Why do people make *repetitive* choices? Role-theory suggests an
answer: 'Individuals in society occupy positions, and their role performance in these positions is determined by social norms, demands
and rules; by the role performances of others in their respective
positions; by those who observe and react to the performance; and by
the individual's capabilities and personality.'[7] Norms prescribe expected behaviour. The attendant sanctioning statements prescribe the
consequences to be expected from breach. The individual's arena of
choice includes the behaviour of others that his knowledge of social
norms leads him to expect, both as they occupy their own positions,
and as they respond directly to his own behaviour. The concept of
norm bridges the internal world of the actor, and social reality. To
explain why a person makes the particular choices he does, we must
take into account his notions of what he ought to do, and of what
circumstances compel and his interests induce him to do. Although
both human and animal colonies exhibit a high degree of regularity of
behaviour, the human condition is distinguished from that of the
lower orders by the normative system. 'By contrast, the intricate interactions of an ant colony or a beehive, like those of a prairie dog village,
are governed mainly by the instinctive reactions of natural and social
stimuli.'[8] Human beings possess consciousness, and hence to some

extent respond to changes in prescriptive rules. That raises the possibility for consciously induced social change by consciously changing those rules.

The categories of role-theory thus became important building blocks for a theory of controlling behaviour through law. By 'norm' I mean a prescriptive rule; by 'role', its addressee. 'Role-occupant' denotes any particular person or collectivity that fills a role. Instead of the more usual 'sanction', i.e. punishment for breach of a norm, I use the phrase 'conformity inducing measures', to denote all the different activities that government does to induce obedience.[9] I represent this model of man-in-society by a simple diagram:

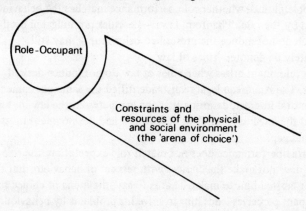

The behaviour of any role occupant can be explained by the range of constraints and resources thrown up by his physical and social environment within which he chooses, and how he views that arena of choice, that is, his perceptions, tastes, domain assumptions, internalized norms and so forth. The model directs attention to the two sorts of causal explanations for human behaviour: propositions describing the role-occupant's arena of choice, and propositions explaining why the role-occupant chooses among that range.[10] The problem is to identify those tools which government has available to change the behaviour these propositions explain. I turn now to that question.

II The Tools of Legal Engineering

What is law? poses the oldest chestnut in jurisprudence. Physicists do not debate with each other over what is physics. Plumbers do not worry about what is plumbing. Lawyers concern themselves about the 'nature' or 'essence' of law because they constitute so generalist a profession. By defining law, an author states only what he believes are the proper concerns of lawyers. My definition of law reflects my concern with the uses of law to change society.

Every rule of law is a norm, as John Austin grasped when he defined law as a 'command'. It is a rule prescribing the behaviour of the role-occupants. One can divide all norms between law and custom. By custom I mean any norm which people come to hold or to follow without its having been promulgated by an agency of the state. By 'a law' or 'a rule of law', I mean any norm so promulgated. A custom becomes a law when it is so promulgated. This definition ignores the question, whether a role-occupant has internalized a rule of law.[11] It leaves problematical, whether role performance matches the behaviour prescribed by the rule. 'Phantom' laws — i.e. rules promulgated by the state which do not induce the prescribed behaviour — may still appropriately be denoted 'rules of law'.

Soft development arises when rules of law do not induce desired behaviour. The American legal realists identified the same phenomenon as their central interest, denoting it as the gap between the law-in-the-books and the law-in-action. A model for law and development must explain that gap.

When role-performance does not match role-expectation, the role-occupant does not make the choices with respect of behaviour that the law-maker desired him to make. That is to say, the arena of choice the role-occupant perceives leads him to solve his problems by behaviour different from that prescribed by the rule of law. He disobeys.

Within that arena, governors believe themselves to have the greatest control over the behaviour of state officials. Hans Kelsen's ideal-typical model of the legal order suggests the relationship between rules of law and behaviour-inducing activity by state officials. He taught that 'the legal norm does not, like the moral norm, refer to the behaviour of one individual only, but to the behaviour of two individuals at least: the individual who commits or may commit the delict, the delinquent, and the individual who ought to execute the sanction'.[12] The law that adjures a role-occupant not to commit murder, simultaneously instructs the judge to convict him of the crime if he disobeys, and to sentence him to punishment. The former norm (the 'secondary' norm), addressed to the role-occupant is only an epiphenomenon of the primary norm addressed to the judge. He conceded, however, that 'the representation of law is greatly facilitated if we allow ourselves to assume also the existence of the first norm'.[13] We can represent the form of the legal order thus postulated:

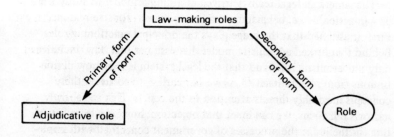

I have already argued that a role-occupant makes choices within his arena of choice. The rules of law, and the behaviour of officials in sanctioning them, are part of that arena. Law affects behaviour by structuring the choices of role-occupants through rules and through sanctioning processes. It does so, in Kelsen's model, (1) by stating a rule which the role-occupant may feel obligated to obey, or (2) by instructing the judge to act in such a way that the benefits and rewards offered the role-occupant in consequence of his behaviour will be altered. 'The secondary norm stipulates the behaviour which the legal order endeavours to bring about by stipulating the sanction.'[14]

III A Model of Law and Development

Kelsen's model states only relationships between rules of law and roles. If for the abstraction 'role' we substitute people — role-occupants — each of whom acts within his own arena of choice, we can assimilate our two diagrams:

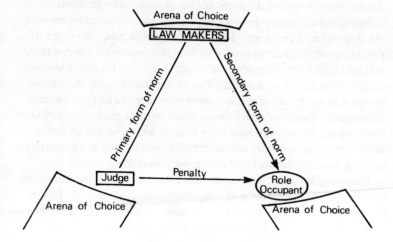

The American legal realists arrived at a similar model to study the 'law-in-action' — i.e. behaviour. It failed, however, for five reasons. First, it assumed that the judge plays the principal sanctioning roles. Behind that lurked a legalistic model that assumes that 'law' includes only universalistic rules and that the legal system is somehow discontinuous from society itself.[15] As we saw earlier, to focus on these concepts inevitably directs attention to the courts. This too sharply narrows our focus. We can meet that objection, however, by substituting for the judge the processes of government concerned with implementation, that is, with inducing desired activity (the bureaucracy, the police, state corporations and so forth).

Second, the realist model directed attention only to explicit *laws* addressed by law-makers to role-occupants for the breach of which there is a stipulated sanction. It did not address the question, whether a particular law or set of behaviour-inducing activities achieves conformity to less formally articulated *policy*. An example may help. A US state wished to induce citizens to hunt and kill coyotes (a wolf-like predator in the American West). It offered a reward or bounty for each one killed, contained in a law directing county agricultural extension agents to pay one dollar for each pair of coyote's ears presented to them. The realist model directed attention to the county agent's behaviour under the law — a relatively trivial issue. It ignored the important question — whether the law induced citizens to kill more coyotes. (In fact, farmers raised coyotes for the bounty.)

The realist model did not accomodate the study of how well law implemented government policy. We can adapt it to that study if we broaden the concept of the norm addressed to the role-occupant to include exhortation or other sort of prescription, indicated by a wavy line. A government may wish to induce farmers to grow cash crops. If it enacts a statute (such as existed in Tanzania) making it a crime to fail to grow a stipulated acreage of cash crops, I indicate the rule addressed to the role-occupant by a straight line. If it merely exhorts the role-occupant to grow cash crops, and seeks to induce the activity by rules addressed to bureaucrats (to provide credit, seed or marketing facilities) I indicate the exhortation by a wavy line. As amended, the model directs attention not to success in providing credit, seed and marketing facilities, but in inducing farmers to grow cash crops.

Third, any law, once passed, changes from the day of passage, either by formal amendment, or by the way the bureaucracy acts. It changes because the arena of choice changes. Feedback constitutes the most important explanation of those changes. Citizens express their reactions to a particular law or programme to law-makers or to bureaucrats, who in turn communicate to law-makers. In addition, various sorts of formal and informal monitoring devices teach law-makers and bureaucrats about the rule's relative success, thus affecting decisions about the law.

Fourth, laws are not generated by a single law-maker. They arise out of a process of law-making involving many roles in complex relationships. Sanctions are not applied by individuals; they are the consequences of complex sanctioning processes. The categories 'law-makers' and 'judge' must be replaced by 'law-making processes' and 'law-implementing processes'.

Finally, conformity-inducing measures may be aimed directly at the role-occupant, at changing the constraints and resources of the environment, or at changing the perceptions of the role-occupant through education or moral suasion. 'Sanctions' is too limited; our diagram must indicate a broader category. We can complete our proposed model thus:

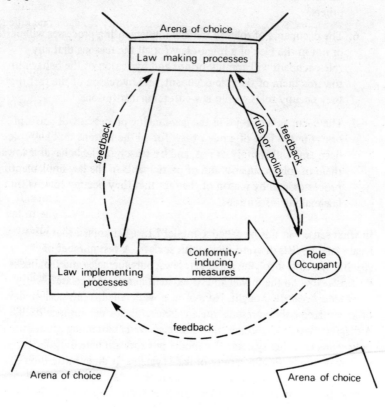

I can now state, in very general terms, why role-occupants behave as they do in the face of a particular norm addressed to them by law-makers:

1. Role-occupants act pursuant to choices they make among their arenas of choice, as they perceive them.

2. The anticipated behaviour of others makes up part of each role-occupant's arena of choice, including the behaviour of role-occupants in the law-enforcing and law-making processes.

3. Role expectations are defined by norms.

4. Rules of law are norms promulgated by the state.

5. Every rule of law or government programme looking to changed behaviour by the role-occupant changes his arena of choice by the changed rule itself, and by changed anticipated behaviour by others.

6. The occupants of roles in the law implementing processes will perform or not in the face of a rule of law for all the reasons that any role-occupant will comply or not and by reason of the behaviour towards them of the role-occupant, and by reason of the fact that they occupy roles within law-enforcing institutions.

7. The occupants of roles in the law-making processes will perform or not in the face of a rule of law for all the reasons that any role-occupant will comply or not, and by reason of the behaviour towards them of role-occupants and of participants in the law-implementing processes, and by reason of the fact that they occupy roles within law-making institutions.

In what sense can this be called a 'model'? I earlier argued that no legal system exists discontinuous with society. A vast number of specific systems, involving particular laws, bureaucracies and feedbacks do exist. How do the model and its existential referents relate?

Models organize thought. No matter how detailed, a physical model of an airplane only represents the airplane. It is not the airplane itself. A diagrammatic representation of the legal system affecting agriculture only represents that system. The model put forward here only represents the form of a variety of legal systems. It directs attention to particular categories of data for investigation — that is, it constitutes a perspective to guide discretionary choice in social enquiry. *It is an agenda for research.* In principle it can be falsified, however, by the discovery of instances in which significant variables not subsumed by the model do affect behaviour in response to a rule of law´ — or at least, that might become possible after closing the vague boxes labelled 'arenas of choice'. Finally, this model implies a definition of law, that addresses law's function in channelling behaviour. *Law is a process by which government structures choice.* Law as a device to structure choice expresses at once law's usual marginality in influencing behaviour, and its importance as the principal instrument that government has to influence behaviour. Since society itself determines the arena of choice in most respects, society determines the limits on law. We can understand law only by understanding it as part of society.

Conclusion

Analytical positivism asserted the independence of law from society. In response, sociological jurisprudence and some crude versions of Marxist jurisprudence claimed that law was society's mere epiphenomenon. Neither proposition matched reality. The legal order structures society simultaneously with society's structuring of the legal order. The model advanced purports to explicate this complex relationship, by examining how the various actors in the system behave, and analyzing that behaviour in terms of constrained choice. The constraints that limit choice represent the influence of society on the legal order; the fact of choice represents the legal order's potential for influencing society.

The model depicts a deeply authoritarian legal order, where law-makers promulgate law, enforcers implement it, and the rest of us obey it. It assumes that the governors remain distinct from the masses of the people. That matches the situation in every African state today. I argue below that the broadest explanation for soft development lies in that authoritarian structure. Its solution must be found in erasing the sharp difference between elites and mass, that is, in some sort of participatory state. The process of development in this view must include the change from authoritarianism to participation. An adequate model of law and development must direct attention to critical variables in that transformation. The model advanced here purports to do this by its specific inclusion of feedback channels. To the extent that people provide inputs to decision-making, they participate in it. To the extent that feedback channels become stronger, to that extent does the separation between governors and governed tend to disappear. When it does, the model I have suggested will of course become useless, and new perspectives will become required.

The model's weakness obviously lies in the ambiguity of the arrows that represent the arenas of choice of the several actors. So open a set of residuary categories must render a model non-falsifiable. Most of the remainder of this book is an attempt to close these open boxes, and thus to subject this model to test.

Preliminarily, I examine a set of rules that the model at first glance does not seem to accommodate. The model seems adapted only to rules or policies directly addressed to the role-occupant as imperative commands: the 'shall nots' of criminal law, tort law and the like. How do the propositions of facilitative law — contract law, corporation law and so forth — fit the model? It is to that question that I turn in the next chapter.

Notes

1. W.C. Runciman, *Social Science and Political Theory* (Cambridge: University Press, 1965), p. 166; P. Winch, *The Idea of a Social Science and its Relation to Philosophy* (London: Routledge and Kegan Paul, 1958); B.A. Malinowski, *A Scientific Theory of Culture* (Chapel Hill: University of N. Carolina Press, 1944), p. 15.
2. W.G. Runciman, *Social Science and Political Theory* (Cambridge: University Press, 1965), p. 8, citing R.G. Collingwood, *The Idea of History* (London: Oxford University Press, 1946), p. 115.
3. A. MacIntyre, 'A Mistake About Causality in the Social Sciences', in P. Laslett and W.G. Runciman (eds.), *Philosophy, Politics and Society*, Second Series (Oxford: Basil Blackwell, 1962), p. 48.
4. See above, Chap. 2.
5. MacIntyre, 'Causality in the Social Sciences', p. 48.
6. A. Guerreirro-Ramos, 'Towards a Possibility Model', in W.A. Beling and G.A. Totting (eds.), *Developing Nations: Quest for a Model* (New York: Van Nostrand, 1970), p. 26.
7. B.J. Biddle and E.J. Thomas (eds.), *Role Theory: Concepts and Research* (New York: John Wiley, 1966), p. 4.
8. J. Blake and K. Davis, 'Norms, Values and Sanctions' in R. Faris (ed.), *Handbook of Modern Sociology* (Chicago: Rand, McNally, 1964), pp. 456, 457.
9. See below, Chap. 9.
10. MacIntyre, 'Causality in the Social Sciences', p. 48.
11. H.L.A. Hart argues that a legal system operates because its officials recognize and accept it as operative. H.L.A. Hart, *The Concept of Law* (Oxford: Clarendon Press, 1962) 117. He asserts that they do so because they have internalized the norm — i.e., they feel *obliged* to do so. Why they feel obliged to conform is, however, a problematical question in any given case. Perhaps they have internalized the norm. Perhaps they are afraid of losing their jobs.
12. H. Kelsen, *General Theory of Law and State* (tr. A. Wedburg; New York: Russell, 1961), p. 58.
13. Ibid., p. 61.
14. Ibid.

15. See D.M. Trubek, 'Max Weber on Law and the Rise of Capitalism', *Wisc. L. Rev.*, 720 (1972); D.M. Trubek and M. Galanter, 'Scholars in Self-Estrangement: Reflections on the Crisis in Law and Development Studies in the United States', *Wisc. L. Rev.*, 1062 (1974).

5 CONTRACT LAW, THE FREE MARKET AND STATE INTERVENTION

The preceding chapter's model radiates authoritarianism. Law-makers promulgate commands; law-implementers enforce them through sanctions applied to subjects. Criminal and tort law fit this model nicely. Other sorts of rules, however, seem cut from a different bolt of cloth. Contract law, for example, does not prescribe any behaviour although it requires the courts to levy a sanction if a party breaks an agreement. Such laws do not require anyone to form a corporation or a co-operative, or to buy property or insurance; they only provide facilitative forms. The facilitative form therefore seems to free the role occupant from the coercion of state power. Just as to some political scientists the market economy seems necessary to a free society, so too, does its legal expression, the law of contract. To the extent that facilitative law defeats authoritarianism, it falsifies the earlier model. But does facilitative law free the role occupant from coercion? I denote two opposite answers to this question as the classical and the anti-classical views.

I Facilitative Law: Alternative Explanations

A. *Classical Perspectives*

Contract promotes social co-operation. The division of labour requires manufacturers to buy from suppliers, employ labour and sell to customers; landlords, to rent to tenants; wholesalers and retailers and consumers, to buy and to sell goods. Without planned organization of these exchanges, every man must seize his own opportunity. Through contract, the parties create their private rules of law, exercising personal freedom to conduct their own affairs.

Contract law only embodies 'freedom' if the market matches its *laissez-faire* ideal-type. If perfect competition prevails, then by definition no individual can affect market price. Other potential bargaining partners, offering their services or goods on terms set by the invisible hand of the market, protect each party from another's arbitrary power. What ideal type of legal order will achieve this ideal economic order?[1] A customer will not buy goods unless his ownership will be exclusive. Property and tort law purportedly guarantee rights of peaceful possession, and the law of contract purports to ensure that promises, once made, will be kept.[2]

The classical view of contract does not describe or explain reality. Instead, it prescribes two principal conditions necessary to accomplish its objectives; the market, an invisible hand to protect everyman, and the state, a value-neutral framework. These imply dual discontinuities: the legal order, sharply discontinuous from the private sphere; and state action, clearly distinct from state non-action. If a genuinely free market and a genuinely neutral state existed, then facilitative law would ensure voluntariness and freedom, not manipulation and coercion.

B. The Anti-Classical Perspective

The anti-classical perspective argues that these oughts of the classical model cannot be achieved. Both perceptions agree that facilitative law permits the parties to a transaction to determine for themselves the norms defining their interchange, and provides coercive state machinery to enforce them. 'From this point of view, the law of contract may be viewed as a subsidiary branch of public law, as a body of rules according to which the sovereign power of the state will be exercised in accordance to the rules agreed upon between the parties to a more or less voluntary transaction.'[3] In terms of our earlier general model the contracting parties participate in law-making. Facilitative law delegates state power to them.

Parties to bargains seldom bargain from equal strength. To the extent of this inequality, the contract process is inherently coercive. Is it significantly different to say to a man, 'I will pay you a wage if you will work for me,' rather than, 'You will get no wage unless you work for me'? Two hundred years ago Lord Chancellor Northington expressed it succinctly: 'Necessitous men are not, truly speaking, free men.'

At law, to give unequals equal legal rights against each other ensures domination by the stronger. No equality exists between an African labourer and the giant Anglo-American copper complex in Zambia, or Lonhro's sugar plantation in Malawi. An African who must either pay a poll tax or go to jail cannot freely decline wage employment. Facilitative law in a society of unequals transfers sovereign power to make and enforce law to the economically strong. In this view, facilitative law as between unequals may be as authoritarian as any other law.

Classical theory relies upon the invisible hand of the market to determine 'objectively' the terms of any particular interchange, and thus avoid coercion by the powerful. The anti-classical model argues not only that the perfectly free market never appears in the real world, but that its existence is theoretically impossible. The model of perfect competition assumes that all preferences can and must find expression through the market. 'Before the principle of marginal utility nothing is sacred.'[4] If the price does not include some costs ('externalities'), how-ever, to that extent the market mechanism does not function.

All laws and customs are externalities in this sense.[5] They impose constraints on bargaining, constraints that do *not* fall before the principle of marginal utility, for they receive support from police, judges, bailiffs, sheriffs, jailers and, ultimately, the army. Willard Hurst made that proposition central to his jurisprudence.

> Law influences the decisions made by 'private orders' . . . Every entrepreneur, in deciding how to invest his time, energy and money, calculates the profits expected from the course open to him. Every calculation includes an assessment of the law's impact on profits: subsidies make some investments more attractive while laws that force the entrepreneur to absorb the 'external' costs of an activity make that activity less attractive. To each entrepreneur, then, the law appears as a factor which affects his decisions but over which he has no control.[6]

Theorists define society in terms of its normative (or institutional) system.[7] All norms assume the forms of contract, law or custom; and the norms embodied in contracts depend for enforcement on law or custom. Since all law and custom are externalities, all society must also be external to the ideal-type construct of the free market. Just when the ideal market becomes possible, society intrudes to make it im-possible. Far from maintaining a neutral, 'objective' invisible hand, the market incorporates the biasses of law and custom.

In a society of unequals, law cannot be 'neutral'. General rules affect different interests differently. The laws of land ownership, for example, determine credit, hiring, marketing. If I own no land, I cannot pledge it for a loan, nor hire anyone to work it, nor grow crops on it to sell.[8] The sorts of power delegated by such laws secretes itself in their details, as they affect different interests in particular situations. So long as people are differently situated, *any* law must advantage some more than others: buyers as against sellers, employers as against employees, landlords as against tenants. *Cui bono*? That question can be asked of every law, because no law hits everyone the same. The legal order takes sides in the perpetual warfare of inegalitarian society not because evil men will it so, but because law cannot be neutral. No more can the state avoid taking sides. The law defines law-making and law-implemen-ting processes. Since law can never be value-neutral, the state it defines cannot be value-neutral.[9]

In short, the anti-classical view holds that outside of economic theory, neither a free market nor a value-neutral state can ever exist. Behind the invisible hand, the state cannot avoid putting a thumb on the scales. Gunnar Myrdal makes the same point: 'Prices are manipulated. They are not the outcome only of the forces in the market; they are in a sense "political prices", depending also on the regulating activity of the state, of quasi-public and private organizations and of private busi-nesses. The state interferences in the price system are, in a sense, the ultimate ones . . .'[10]

II A Case Study: Colonial Anglophonic Africa, East and West

The two theories suggest alternative uses of facilitative law in shaping society. To test them, I explore a comparative case study: Colonial Kenya and the Gold Coast (now Ghana). Kenya was settler country. Whites dominated its economy, taking up land in the fertile White High-lands for commercial farming. The Gold Coast was African territory. Practically the only whites were state officials. In Kenya, the govern-ment coerced Africans to work for white employers, but not in the Gold Coast. In Kenya, a host of laws organized a command economy, in the Gold Coast, contract law reigned. How to account for these differen-ces?

A. *The Colonial Kenyan Economy*

The highlands of Kenya became the locus of British colonialism in East Africa. During the long period of colonial control, Africans hardly participated in government. The state systematically organized the economy favourably to settler interests.[11] Land, labour, the corporate organization of the economy – the state assumed direct control over each.

1. *Land.* In 1895 the British government amended the Foreign Juris-diction Act of 1843, and declared a protectorate over all the East African territory formerly administered by the British East Africa Company. In effect, that act gave the crown the same jurisdiction in a protectorate as if it had acquired the territory not by consent but by conquest.[12] Beginning in 1902, the government reserved the most beautiful and fertile lands in Kenya (some say the most beautiful in the world) for Europeans. By 1915, it had promulgated rules for herding

Africans into reserves. By the early 1920s it had firmly established the pattern of colonial agrarian development: whites farming spacious estates in the White Highlands, Africans crowded into native reserves. State intervention, not market forces created that pattern.

2. *Labour.*[13] Kenya attracted white settlers not only by its abundant, fertile and breathtaking land, but also by its cheap black labour. In the earliest days, however, Africans lived in their own communities, teasing subsistence out of low-technology agriculture or nomadic cattle herding. Government had to transform them into a labour force for whites. The eternal colonialist myth claimed that the 'natives' were not economically rational.[14] Lugard said,

> Since . . . the wants of the African peasant are few and are not
> necessities, and since he can generally obtain sufficient cash to pur-
> chase them and pay his small tax . . . by the sale of a little produce,
> there is . . . but little incentive to earn wages, and it may often
> happen that as soon as the small sum he requires has been obtained
> he will cease to work. The higher the wages in such a case the less the
> work, as the Indian industrial report says is the case with the Indian
> coolie.[15]

Theories of the backward-sloping labour supply curve and African eco-nomic irrationality have long since been exploded.[16] The remarkable African transformations in response to economic incentives for cocoa in Ghana and cotton and coffee in Uganda and Tanzania, the complex and vigorous trading economies of West Africa, and African entre-preneurship in Nigeria, among many examples, destroyed them long ago.

Nevertheless, those theories became a principal ideology of colonial-ists in Africa. Whites sought to drum up a labour force while paying only a starvation wage. They could not get away with slavery or forced labour, because British officials felt bound by the classical ideology of freedom. Opening a conference in 1928 on forced and contract labour, the Secretary of State for the Colonies´stated: 'We are all equally con-vinced that the only possible solution [for Africa] is a civilization based on work, as all civilization must be, but based on free work of men who give their labour because they desire the fruits of their labour . . .'[17]

A former Secretary for Native Affairs to the Government of Northern Rhodesia stated the classical view even more explicitly:

The first essential for the successful working of the labour contract is that its terms should be fair and reasonable and within the capacity of the parties of carry out; the second that there should subsist between the parties that *consensus ad idem* — to use the legal phrase — that understanding and agreement to the same thing, which is the basis of all contracts; and the third, that the agreement should be faithfully carried out on both sides. That is the agreement should be voluntarily entered into goes without saying.[18]

How to ensure a plentiful supply of labour without raising wages or violating the principle of 'voluntary' agreement? As a solution the government levied a poll or head tax upon every African male. An early Governor of Kenya said: 'We consider that taxation is the only possible method of compelling the native to leave his Reserve for the purpose of seeking work. Only in this way can the cost of living be increased for the native, and . . . it is on this that the supply of labour and the price of labour depends. To raise the rate of wages would not increase but would diminish the supply of labour. A rise in the rate of wages would enable the hut or poll tax of a family sub-tribe to be earned by fewer external workers.'[19] Sir Harry Johnstone spoke with feeling: 'A gentle insistence that the Native should contribute his fair share to the revenue of the country by paying his tax is all that is necessary on our part to ensure his taking a share in life's labour which no human being should avoid.'[20]

Beginning in 1908, therefore, the British imposed poll taxes. They remained the principal device for exciting in the African peasant that ardent lust for wages that the settlers wished to induce. To each African the law imposing the poll tax appeared 'as a factor which affect[ed] his decisions but over which he ha[d] no control'. The poll tax worked as a labour recruitment device. In Tanganyika, the district officials made regular rounds of their villages, recording their experiences in a safari book. The 1936 safari book for Iringa tells how the official would trek during the morning to a new village, stopping at any European farms on the way. Each farmer would tell him how many 'boys' he needed. At the next village, the official would have the village headman arraign the tax defaulters. The district official would order them to work off the tax, usually with the European farmer, or; if the African preferred, with the road gang. Village tours became blackbirding trips. Most Africans, of course, preferred to enter European employment 'voluntarily', thus choosing their employer and the time for wage labour.

A variety of other laws tended in the same direction. The land areas where Africans had to live cramped their populations unmercifully. African soldiers in the army consumed 2,843 calories per day, about the level recommended by medical authorities.[21] Other Africans consumed only 1,471 calories each per day. On existing levels of African food production, for a family of five the medically recommended diet required 27.5 areas of arable land. That would allow a density of 116 people per square mile. In the Kiambu, Fort Hall and Nyeri Districts, African densities were 283 per square mile; in South Nyeri in 1944 they rose to 542 per square mile; at Buntore 1,200 per square mile. During this period the density of the white population in the White Highlands averaged 16 per square mile. Land law so structured choice for Africans that hunger drove them into white employment.

Despite the prevailing official ideology of 'voluntary' labour, government required compulsory labour for community projects by able-bodied adult males aged 18 to 45. The law exempted Africans employed by Europeans, or who for three months out of the preceding twelve had worked for them. The unexempt faced the labour draft for sixty days out of the year. To avoid it most Africans preferred to work for Europeans at their own time and place. During both world wars the state enforced direct compulsory labour for private employers.[22] In order to ensure that Africans continued to work for their European employers, government went beyond ordinary contract remedies and enacted various criminal ordinances. Leaving employment without permission of the employer became a crime; being intoxicated during working hours became a crime; neglecting 'to perform any work which it was his duty to have performed', or 'carelessly or improperly' performing 'any work which from its nature it was his duty under his [employment] contract to have performed carefully and properly' became a crime; using abusive or insulting language to his employer became a crime; refusing 'to obey any command of his employer or of any person lawfully placed by his employer in authority over him, which command it was his duty to obey' became a crime.[23] To keep track of the African population, government imposed pass laws.[24] Every African had to carry with him a registration certificate in which his present and past employment for Europeans was entered. All endorsements in the pass were in English, so that usually the servant could not know the content of the employer's endorsement. Finally, the law excluded Africans from the cash crop market by a variety of devices, examined in the following section.

These measures generated a cheap labour force for white settlers. In 1944 the average wage was 15 shillings per month.[25] At rock-bottom, a single man in Mombassa in 1944 could not live on less than 29.05 shillings per month. A government scientist estimated that a married man and two children residing in a town needed 56.60 shillings per month. By contrast, in mining in 1938 the average European worker received a monthly wage of 612.90 shillings per month; the average African worker, 11.65 shillings per month.[24] Average per capita income for whites in Kenya in 1962 reached £400 per year; for Africans, including an estimate for subsistence crops, £14.9 per year.[27]

3. *Organization of the Economy.* The Kenya government overtly intervened in the economy in many ways. Direct government expenditure subsidized the settler economy, £13 million for building a railway to the sea. Government-set freight charges on the railway favoured the settlers. The better the growing year, the higher the production of agricultural crops, and the greater the deficit of the railways, and the greater the required government subsidy. Other governmental infrastructural expenditures aided the settlers: roads, easy credit and direct price supports. The government established marketing boards for most cash crops, that paid settlers more than the market price. Between 1931 and 1946 government spent almost four times as much for 2,000 white settler families as for several million African farmers.

Beginning with the Great Depression, government organized every branch of settler-dominated industry through an industry board – tea, coffee, sisal, pyrethrum, pigs, maize, cotton and others. The Tea Ordinance of 1960 followed the general pattern. It granted power to the Board to license tea growers and tea factories, to regulate, control and improve the cultivation and processing of tea, and to control the export of tea.[28] It became criminal for a person to grow or manufacture tea except as stipulated in his license.[29] The Board had power 'to issue a planting license subject to such terms and conditions as it may think fit, or . . . [it] may refuse to issue a planting license on any ground which may appear to the Board to be sufficient'.[30] With the approval of the Board,[31] the Minister of Agriculture might make regulations governing every aspect of tea culture, down to giving 'directions to any planter as to the method of sowing, planting and cultivation of tea and the harvesting, collection, movement, processing and storage of tea leaf . . .'[32]

The white settler producers elected most of the various industry boards. Until 1960, the settler Kenya Tea Growers' Association elected the Tea Board.[33] In that year European growers selected all the members of industry boards in coffee, tea, sisal, cereal, maize marketing, pigs, the Uplands Bacon Factory and horticultural products. Others had a minority of African members appointed by the government. These boards manipulated the economy to suit the interests of their white constituencies, effectively barring Africans from major cash crop markets until just before independence.[34]

B. *The Gold Coast and the 'Free Market'*

The non-settler territories of West Africa and of Uganda seemed completely different. For reasons that need not detain us, indigenous African production of cash crops for export flourished there: cocoa in the Gold Coast; oil palm, cocoa and groundnuts in Nigeria; cotton in Uganda. Few forces pressed government to allocate land to settler agriculture or to generate a labour force for settlers. I trace, first, the history of the cocoa industry in the Gold Coast, and, second, government response to its emergent problems.

1. *The Cocoa Industry*.[35] The Basel Missionaries imported cocoa seedlings into the Gold Coast in 1857. Despite very little overt government help the industry grew amazingly, entirely on the initiative of African growers,[36] indicated in Table 1.

Table 1: Cocoa Industry in the Gold Coast

Years	Five-year average tons
1891-1895	5
1896-1900	230
1901-1905	3,472
1906-1910	14,784
1911-1915	51,819
1916-1920	106,072
1921-1925	186,329
1926-1930	218,895

A handful of European factors, however, controlled marketing. During the period after 1920, thirteen firms purchased almost the entire crop. Four dominated the field: United Africa Company, a subsidiary of Unilever, one of England's greatest corporations; G.B. Ollivant Ltd; CFAO, a Swiss firm; and Cadbury and Fry, the great chocolate houses. These giants either absorbed or drove out their smaller competitors. The same firms imported manufactures into the Gold Coast. Their activities touched every aspect of cocoa belt life: financing, crops, purchasing and shipping cocoa, and importing manufactured goods. A parliamentary Under-Secretary of State for Colonies wrote: 'British West

Africa, in contrast to East, is a country where large firms or combinations of firms have become established. As a result, there is a danger that in some places active competition which is the life blood of progressive commercial enterprise may be restricted. Rings and monopolies in regard to the purchase of native produce always tend to restrict development . . .'[37]

These firms from time to time conspired to fix cocoa prices, and to divide the market.[38] Such an agreement in 1937 put the producers once again at the mercy of the factors. Cocoa can be stored only in costly, atmospherically controlled warehouses, none of which existed on the Gold Coast. As a consequence of the price-fixing agreement each producer faced only a single buyer. A farmer had Hobson's choice: sell to that buyer at the fixed price, or let the cocoa rot. The farmers responded at various times by attempts at boycott. In 1930, when the offered price fell precipitously to about 10 shillings a head-load (about 60 pounds), against demands for 25 shillings, they conducted a serious strike. In 1937 the buyers' agreement again precipitated a nationwide strike. The advent of World War II, however, radically changed the situation, and led to overt government intervention.

2. *Government Response.* Until World War II, explicit, visible government response to all this economic activity seemed minimal. It made only minuscule efforts at research and agricultural extension. Serious cocoa tree diseases appeared, but the state did nothing. In 1936 a colonial office expert reported that 'the Gold Coast with the largest cocoa industry in the world is still content with the present and is taking no steps to safeguard the future'.[39] Two years later the first cocoa research station opened. Government did build a railroad from Kumasi, in the centre of the main cocoa producing area, to an artificial port constructed in Takoradi, but precious little else. It did not even build feeder roads to move the cocoa from farm to collecting point.

Beyond these flimsy efforts, until the outbreak of World War II, the Gold Coast followed the *laissez-faire* model. In 1930, when the cocoa farmers held up deliveries to the companies, the governor refused to interfere. 'In the controversy as to what is, and what is not, a fair price for the cocoa farmer at this time, Government can take no position . . . One thing is certain: Government cannot fix prices and compel buyers to pay those prices. However, Government may deplore the present low prices, it is not practical politics to improve them by legislative or other means.'[40]

The government took the same position in 1937. A different

governor again declined to intervene. (He rather unhelpfully urged that the producers give the plan a one-year trial. The producers did not take up the offer.) A parliamentary commission (the Nowell Commission) negotiated a peace which lasted until World War II.

Otherwise Government did very little explicitly to help the producers. Money lenders (mainly brokers for the factors) held most growers hopelessly in debt. The land tenure system followed customary law. It made sense for shifting agriculture, not for cash cropping from trees with a fifty-year productive life. Endless disputes over land ensued, impairing its mortgageability and marketability. Government introduced no legislation to help the industry, but abided gradual changes in the rules through long, costly private adjudication.[41] Without much research or agricultural extension work, technology remained labour-intensive.

Although the state seemingly held aloof, its strong hand nevertheless shaped the Gold Coast economy. The reception statute imposed the common law, the doctrines of equity and the so-called statutes of general application on the Gold Coast. These comprised the 'general' law of the country. Africans retained certain rights arising under customary law, including rights in land. English law, however, controlled their relationships with non-Africans, supported by the coercive paraphenalia of the state: prisons,[42] army and police.

The law defined the property rights of the various economic actors. As a result, farmers had certain powers to grow cocoa on their land and to sell it. The legal order protected the factor's property rights to storage yards, transport facilities, docks, warehouses, shipping and liquid capital. These rights of ownership, protected by property and criminal law and enforced ultimately by courts, police, army and prisons, clothed the factors with the power to structure the very limited freedom of the cocoa producers: sell to us, or do not sell at all.

Cocoa farmers necessarily perceived these laws as constraints on decisions. No doubt they had 'freedom' to bargain within them, but the law determined the relative power of the participants and therefore determined the range of bargaining outcomes. The principle of marginal utility operated *within* the framework imposed by the law.

3. *Consequences.* The principal consequences of these market constraints manifested themselves in terms of power and price. Prior to the creation of the Cocoa Control Board during World War II, decision-making power about the cocoa industry lay with the great English firms. It became more or less equalized only momentarily when farmers

struck in 1937. The average per capita income in the Gold Coast, for all its 'free market' form, did not differ significantly from Kenya. In 1936-7 the average per capita income for cocoa farmers was about £5 16s. per year[43] much less than a shilling per day. The profits of the cocoa industry, like the profits of Kenya industry, went not to the Africans who worked, but to the expatriate firms which bought and sold.

Conclusion

In East Africa the law delegated to various government officials and boards power to structure choice for Africans in ways favourable to the settlers. In West Africa an analogous result obtained, but indirectly. There, the law commanded officials to protect property ownership and to enforce contracts. The great factoring firms then exercised the power delegated to them through property and contract law to structure choice for Africans. The two techniques of structuring choice differed as did the two core myths of what Francis X. Sutton calls the American business creed:

> The classical strand centers upon the model of a decentralized, private, competitive capitalism in which the forces of supply and demand, operating through the price mechanism, regulate the economy in detail and in aggregate. The managerial strand differs chiefly in the emphasis it places on the role of professional managers in the large business firms who continuously direct economic forces for the common good.[44]

Kenya operated in accordance with the managerial strand, the Gold Coast, the classical strand. In both cases, the law delegated power to the entrepreneurial class, which exercised it by limiting the choices of Africans. The imperial government was not schizophrenic. In each case, it invoked the legal order to lodge control with English entrepreneurs, using forms appropriate for each case. Facilitative law does not avoid authoritarian relationships, because it delegates authority to the economically powerful. Our case study falsifies the classical model. These propositions carry implications for the questions of state action and non-action, and of conflict or consensus models of society.

A. State Action and Non-Action

Solutions hinge on explanations. If the legal order (that is, state action) did not explain troublesome behaviour then one could not devise a 'legal' solution for it. In that case, a meaningful science of directed social change through law, a discipline of law and development, becomes impossible. The classical assumption of discontinuities between the legal order and the private sector, and between state action and non-action, by instructing the policy-maker to look for *non*-legal explanations for behaviour, also instructs him to look for solutions that do not depend upon the state for their execution, to *laissez-faire* and Contract, not to Plan.

That positive law directly affects a particular subject clearly evidences State action with respect to it. In what sense can one argue that a seeming *absence* of positive law also evidences State action? In the United States, a line of cases involving racial discrimination raised the same question. The Constitution of the United States does not prohibit discrimination by private individuals, but does prohibit discriminatory *state* action. A private covenant prohibited sale of a tract of land to non-Caucasians. The Supreme Court held[45] that for a court to enforce that covenant was sufficient state action to invoke constitutional protections. Carl Auerbach and others have asked: 'Shall we say, then, that when the state chooses not to exercise its power to prohibit racial discrimination, it is sanctioning such discrimination and such inaction constitutes state action subject to constitutional commands?'[46]

State action through the legal order consists of sets of instructions addressed to role-occupants, and to the variety of state employees who implement the laws. Those employees must have their instructions about how to deal with any situation that comes to their attention, even if (as in most cases) the rule states only that what is not forbidden is permitted. Frequently, the rules addressed to law-implementers have embodied themselves so deeply in our culture that they seem hardly visible, as did contract and property law in the Gold Coast. What appears to be state inaction permits existing rules to govern relationships. When the Governor of the Gold Coast decided not to intervene in 1937, he actually decided to continue state intervention through existing property and contract laws.

For another example, population growth depends upon innumerable decisions of men and women in the most intimate of relationships. But, all over the world there are now laws and public policies concerning population control.[47] Those programmes must rest on propositions that explain human fertility by the legal order. If (as is usual) no laws regulating family size appear on the statute books, in effect the state delegates power to determine the number of children to married couples. To structure that choice, Kenya attempted a programme of birth control clinics to provide information and hardware,[48] based implicitly on this explanation: Property and contract law grants power over the sale and distribution of birth control devices to private entrepreneurs; they find it profitable to sell only to elite women at high prices; birth control clinics could provide both advice and hardware at no cost to all women. The Kenya planned parenthood programme, like many development programmes, rested on an explanation that perceived state non-action as a form of state action.

B. *Conflict or Consensus*

Ralph Dahrendorff has posited two alternative perspectives of society, consensus and conflict.[49] The former assumes that every society rests on the consensus of its members; the latter, that every society rests on constraints by some of its members by others. But, the state and the legal order *cannot* act 'neutrally'. They *cannot* in a society of unequals treat everyone alike. They cannot even fulfil an 'objective', peace-keeping, society-preserving role; they must favour one or another.

The state does not exist by accident. It exists because at particular historical times particular groups or strata summoned it into being, and because at other times — including our own — particular groups and classes continue it in being. They continue it in being, obviously, not absent mindedly, but because it serves particular interests.

Even when the Gold Coast Government did its best to be 'neutral' during the cocoa hold-up, it in fact intervened pursuant to the dictates of property and contract law. The state exists precisely because it cannot be neutral. It exists because the contending classes and strata have different values and interests. Consensus differs from the values or interests of a shifting majority that in particular stages of history on particular issues may be quite widely shared. Axiomatically, the state has a monopoly of legitimate violence. That monopoly exists because it serves the interests of those who keep the state in existence. If consensus actually existed, why the need to threaten violence against those who disagree? The state and the legal order exist because those who rule need them to coerce others.

There are some who profess that the state and the legal order reflect the underlying consensus of society itself. On the contrary, the Gold Coast and Kenya experiences argue that the state and the legal order can never be neutral; and that therefore, they reflect not consensus, but conflict.[50]

Notes

1. See, generally, D.M. Trubek, 'Max Weber on Law and the Rise of Capitalism', *Wisc. L. Rev.,* 720 (1972).

2. See *Dartmouth College* v. *Woodward,* 4 Wheat. 518, 4 L. ed. 629 (US Supreme Court, 1819).

3. M.R. Cohen, *Law and the Social Order* (New Haven: Yale UP, 1964), p. 69.

4. L. Fuller, *The Morality of Law* (New Haven: Yale UP, 1964), p. 28.

5. But see R.H. Coase, 'The Problem of Social Cost', *J. of Law and Econ.* 3, 1 (1960).

6. M. Tushnet, 'Lumber and the Legal Process', *Wisc. L. Rev.,* 114 (1972). See also W.J. Samuels, 'The Economy as a System of Power and Its Legal Bases: The Legal Economics of Robert Lee Hale', *Miami L. Rev.,* 27, 261 (1973); see R.L. Hale, *Freedom Through Law* (New York: Columbia UP, 1952); W.J. Samuels, 'Inter-relations Between Legal and Economic Processes', *Journal of Law and Economics,* 14, 435 (1971).

7. J. Blake and K. Davis, 'Norms, Values, Sanctions', in R. Faris (ed.), *Handbook of Modern Sociology* (Chicago: Rand, McNally, 1964), p. 456.

8. See P. Dorner, *Land Reform and Economic Development* (Harmondsworth: Penguin, 1972).

9. K. Renner, *Institutions of Private Law and Their Social Functions,* (O. Kahn-Freund, ed. and tr.), (London: Routledge & Kegan Paul, 1949).

10. G. Myrdal, *Economic Theory and Under-Developed Regions* (London: Metliner, 1967), p. 49. The alternative to the value-neutral state is not, as is sometimes argued, a conceptualization of the state as an evil cabal of a few powerful men. There is no evidence, for example, that the Colonial Office legal advisers who wrote the initial reception statute which imposed English law on Africa had anything in mind except to do what was 'fair', to devise a set of laws that would guide the courts in Africa in dispute-settlement, and which were within their bureaucratic means. See Chap. 2, above.

11. See generally, Y.P. Ghai and J.P.W.B. McAuslan, *Public Law and Political Change in Kenya* (Nairobi: Oxford UP, 1970); S. and M. Aaronovitch, *Crisis in Kenya* (London: Laurence and Wishart, 1947); Lord Hailey, *African Survey Revised 1956* (London: Oxford UP, 1957); E. Huxley and M. Perham, *Race and Politics in Kenya* (London: Faber and Faber, 1944).

12. Full jurisdiction was asserted in the East African Order in Council 1902 S.R.O. 661, secs. 12(t) and 15(10)), by treaties of questionable validity (see, for example, the Masai Case, *Ole Njogo* v. *A.G. of the East African Protectorate,* 5 EALR 70 (1914), and by statute and rule (see, for example, the East African (Lands) Order in Council, 1901, S.R.O. 661). By the Crown Lands Ordinance, 1912, the government asserted power to sell land outright or on very long term leases (ultimately 999 years) to Europeans. As reinforced by the Crown Lands Ordinance, 1915, even land held by Africans in customary tenure had radical title in the Crown.

13. See, generally, E. Berg, 'The Development of a Labor Force in Sub-Saharan Africa', *Economic Development and Cultural Change,* 18, 394 (1965).

14. J.H. Boeke, *Economics and Economic Policy in Dual Societies* (New York: Institute of Pacific Relations, 1953).

15. F. Lugard, *The Dual Mandate in British Tropical Africa* (London: Frank Cass, 1922), pp. 404-5.

16. G. Hunter, *The New Societies of Tropical Africa* (London: Oxford UP, 1962), pp. 81-2; W.O. Jones, 'Economic Man in Africa', *Food Research Institute Studies* (May 1960), 1.

17. The Conference on Forced and Contract Labour, *Journal of the African*

   Society, 28, 281 (1928-9).
18. Ibid.
19. Quoted in N. Leys, *Kenya* (London: Leonard and Virginia Woolf, 1924), p. 186.
20. Sir H. Johnston, *Trade and General Conditions Report, Nyasaland 1895-96* (London: HMSO, 1897), p. 96.
21. Aaronovitch and Aaronovitch, *Crisis in Kenya*, p. 42.
22. The Defence Regulations, 1944 (Kenya). The regulations even imposed hardships on Europeans. Male personal servants were limited from three in the household of a single adult to five for two adults and two children. There was no limit on female servants. Defence (Limitation of Labour) Regulations, 1944 (Orders applicable to Nairobi Municipality).
23. Kenya: Employment of Servants Ordinance, 1937.
24. Kenya: The Native Registration Ordinance, 1919.
25. Aaronovitch and Aaronovitch, *Crisis in Kenya*, p. 112.
26. Ibid.
27. D. Ghai, 'Some Aspects of Income Distribution in East Africa' (Nairobi: Makerere University, 1962) (cyclostyle).
28. Kenya: Tea Ordinance, 1960, para. 4(2).
29. Ibid. para. 9(1).
30. Ibid., para. 8.
31. Ibid., para. 13.
32. Para. 25(2).
33. *Report of the Committee on the Organization of Agriculture (Colony and Protectorate of Kenya)* (Nairobi: Government Printer, 1960).
34. Regulations forbidding Africans to grow coffee ultimately were declared discriminatory and hence invalid under the Royal Instructions. *Koinage Mubi v. Rex*, 24(2) K.L.R. 130 (1950).
35. See, generally F.M. Bourret, *The Gold Coast: A Survey of the Gold Coast and British Togoland, 1919-1946* (Palo Alto: Stanford UP, 1949); F.M. Bourret, *Ghana, The Road to Independence* (London: Oxford UP, 1949); p. 163; G. Padmore, *The Gold Coast Revolution: The Struggle of an African People from Slavery to Freedom* (London: Dennis Dobson, 1953); G. Metcalfe, *Great Britain and Ghana: Documents of History 1807-1957* (Legon: The University of Ghana, 1964); R. Szerszewski, *Structural Changes in the Economy of Ghana, 1891-1911* (London: Weidenfeld and Nicholson, 1965).
36. Bourret, *The Gold Coast.*
37. Quoted in Padmore, *Gold Coast Revolution.*
38. Nowell Commission Report, 1938, quoted in Metcalfe, *Great Britain and Ghana*, p. 652.
39. Quoted in Bourret, *Ghana.*
40. Speech to the Legislative Council, 4 December 1930, quoted in Metcalfe, *Great Britain and Ghana*, p. 626.
41. S.K.B. Asante, 'Interests in Land in the Customary Law of Ghana: A New Appraisal', *Yale L.J.*, 74, 848 (1964).
42. R.B. Seidman, 'The Ghana Prison System: An Historical Perspective', in A. Milner (ed.), *African Penal Systems* (London: Routledge and Kegan Paul, 1969), p. 429.
43. Metcalfe, *Great Britain and Ghana*, p. 653.
44. F.X. Sutton *et al., The American Business Creed* (Cambridge, Mass: Harvard UP, 1956), pp. 33-4.
45. *Shelley v. Kramer*, 334 U.S. 1 (1948), see also J. Tussman (ed.), *The Supreme Court and Racial Discrimination* (New York: Oxford UP, 1963),

Introduction; *Steele* v. *L. and N.R. Company,* 323 U.S. 192 (1944); *Moose Lodge No. 107* v. *Irvis,* 92 Sup. Ct. 1965 (1972); *Jackson* v. *Metropolitan Edison Co.,* 419 U.S. 345 (1974).

46. C. Auerbach, L. Garrison, J.W. Hurst, and A. Mermin, *The Legal Process: An Introduction to Decision-Making by Judicial, Legislative, Executive and Administrative Agencies* (San Francisco: Chandler Publishing Co., 1961).
47. The literature is voluminous. For Africa, see U.U. Uche (ed.), *Law and Population Change in Africa* (Nairobi: East Af. Literature Bureau, 1976).
48. See U.U. Uche, 'Law and Population Growth in Kenya', in Uche, ibid., p. 68.
49. R. Dahrendorf, 'Toward a Theory of Social Conflict', *J. of Peace and Conflict Resolution,* 11, 170 (1958).
50. See V.I. Lenin, *State and Revolution: Marxist Teaching about the Theory of the State and the Tasks of the Proletariat in the Revolution* (New York: International, 1932).

Part Three

OBEDIENCE TO LAW

6 OBEDIENCE TO LAW: A GENERAL THEORY

The model advanced in Chapter 4 had vague categories comprising the various arenas of choice — that is, the social, political and economic forces acting upon role-occupants and implementing and law-making processes. A model with such vague categories cannot well fulfil its function of providing relevant criteria. To close the model, I begin by asking why some role-occupants obey some laws, and some do not. Most sociologists have not asked that question. Mainstream criminology focused on the issue of *deviance* — that is, behaviour inconsistent with socially derived and socially approved norms.[1] In development, however, governments proposed to induce new behaviour through positive law.[2] That new behaviour frequently differed sharply from existing behaviour, and the associated domain assumptions ('values') that explained and justified it. In conditions of development governments sought to *induce* deviance. Not deviance, but disobedience became the problem. Therefore, as Malinowski said long ago, 'questions about the limits of legislative action, about its ability to create new types of man and types of culture are as practically cogent as they are theoretically illuminating'.[3]

Models of deviance commonly made three assumptions.[4] First, they assumed that most people obeyed socially approved norms; only the rare deviant disobeyed.[5] Analytical jurisprudence similarly ignored the question of efficacy, because it assumed it.[6] It defined the common law as the 'custom of the country'. It assumed that the judges determined the law by observing how most people behaved over very long periods — that defined a 'custom'.[7] Even today most writers deny the independent efficacy of law to change behaviour.[8] Second, deviance theories relied on a consensus version of society, that the legal order itself demonstrated was invalid.[9] Third, those theories assumed that people do not reason in deciding whether or not to obey the law. They act pursuant to programmed values and instincts.[10] Given these three assumptions, disobedience to law can never become an issue. Everyone will disobey positive law which does not match the consensus. *Deviance* becomes the key: why do the values and attitudes of a few individuals differ from everybody else's? Sociologists inevitably explained this by psychology, not institutions.[11]

Legal tradition favoured a contrary model. 'A person weighs the benefits to him of the prohibited conduct against all the costs and the chances that he will have to pay those costs.'[12] Two arguments contradicted that proposition. First, critics charged that lawyers assume that actors take only 'legal' considerations into account in calculating.[13] The commands and sanctions of the law of course make up only part of the constraints and resources of the environment. Second, some argued that the ordinary functioning of society shows that we do not make conscious choices to obey or disobey the law. Most people go to their jobs, return to the family, engage in their everyday activities without consciously 'choosing' to do so. I do not calculate my advantage by the minute. Even criminals frequently do not do so.[14]

That objection correctly described obedience to some law. Any society becomes a *society* because of its repetitive patterns of behaviour. However well it responds to social claims and demands, at whatever level it functions, still, it does function, because the total set of norms roles, statuses, value sets, rewards and penalties, in short, the entire culture, form a more or less integral whole. If they did not, the society would become an anarchy. Laws more or less consistent with the existing social order need not rely upon the threat of legal sanction to induce obedience. The surrounding institutional matrix structures rewards and punishments, constraints and resources so that the role-occupant usually makes a personally advantageous decision — at least in the short run — when he chooses to conform. So obvious is the choice, that likely he does not make it consciously — that is, his behaviour has become institutionalized.

In many situations, however, even in highly institutionalized societies, choice does occur. Businesses calculate the consequences of tax and anti-trust law. My decision about where to park my car frequently depends upon the chances of getting a ticket.[15] As Lemert puts it, 'the captured positions of individuals in modern, pluralistic society sheds light on the choice of ends and means. One general consequence of this position is the increase in calculational behaviour and a heightened awareness of alternatives, a necessary willingness to consider a wide variety of values and norms as functional alternatives to ends.'[16] Many legal rules require or permit doing what one ordinarily would not do if the rules did not exist. Since these rules have a high nuisance value or offer great advantages, most people calculate extensively.[17]

Laws concerned with development usually conflict with institutionalized ways of doing things. They look to change present behaviour. They require the role-occupant to choose between norms, a condition that Durkheim called 'anomie'. That calls for calculational behaviour. A farmer does not lightly change to a new cash crop from the subsistence crop that has for generations sustained his family. He calculates. Developmental rules require whole sets of acts done 'on purpose'.[18] Reality falsifies the proposition that *all* behaviour depends on calculation. But, laws looking to changed behaviour do induce calculated responses.

The sociologists' model provided no useful guides for law and development. If both law and behaviour merely reflect values and attitudes, then neither will change until values and attitudes change first, at best a slow process. Development runs afoul of the 'common paradox' of the sociologists: 'If a law is not supported by the mores of the community, it is ineffectual; if it is, the law is unnecessary.'[19] That governments do seek to use law to induce change falsifies that proposition. Do they all act in vain? Ought they be told to abandon their efforts to improve man's lot?

A Theory of Obedience to New Law

If the law reflects our common values, deviance becomes a surprising event. If a law seeks to induce new behaviour, however, it seems odd that anyone should obey it at all. Obedience becomes the event requiring explanation. What are the necessary and sufficient causes of obedience to new law? In the first place, a person who obeys the law must have occasion to choose to do so. Second, he must perceive that to obey supports his interests. That thrusts a dual task on law-makers. They must accurately predict that the role-occupant will confront the necessity of choice, whether or not to obey, and that he will choose obedience. They must ask the anthropologists' question: How would a person in that culture respond?[20]

We can unpack these two requirements. Before a role-occupant has to choose to obey or not, he must know what the law requires of him. That calls first, for a rule or policy that defines and prescribes the required activity. If rule or policy wallows in ambiguity or vagueness, its addressee must behave as he thinks best; that is, ambiguity amplifies the influence of training, socialization and subjective factors.

Secondly, the role-occupant must receive notice of the rule in a way that will spark his obedient behaviour.[21] I discuss this second requirement in the following chapter.

In addition, the role-occupant must have opportunity and capacity to obey the law. ' "Ought" presupposes "can".'[22] Unless one *can* obey, he *will* not. Thus, physical impossibility provides a complete defence to a charge of crime.[23] Want of opportunity or capacity also prevents obedience to non-criminal rules. For example, the Prisons

Ordinance in Ghana since 1886 required that wardens keep prisoners
separate at night. The prison officials disobeyed the law every night
since its enactment because Ghanaian prisons never had sufficient cells
to permit obedience.[24] The great Groundnuts Scheme to transform
Tanganyika into the Commonwealth's chief source of vegetable oils
came a cropper largely because it lacked manpower, appropriate
machines or usable soil.[25]

Opportunity sometimes depends upon factors that others should
supply. The farmer cannot comply with a policy to grow a new crop
unless someone supplies necessary seed, credit and extension services.
Capacity sometimes concerns the sufficiency of the role-occupant's
qualifications for the job at hand. A law requiring an official to translate from French to English cannot be obeyed unless he is bilingual. An
hierarchical decision-making structure likely lacks capacity to make
change-oriented decisions. Conversely, opportunity and capacity to disobey increases the potential for violation. Laws prohibit the possession
of burglar's tools in part because they have a high potential for burg-
lary. Bankers commit embezzlement more often than do bricklayers.

Besides creating the necessity for choice, law-makers must ensure
that role-occupants will choose to obey. To do that, addressees must
perceive the desired behaviour as in their interest, taking into account
not only the legal sanctions but all the rewards and punishments of the
larger environment. Three elements bear upon that perception: (1)
the rewards and punishments the role-occupant will earn as a result of
obedience or disobediance; (2) the way in which the domain (value)
assumptions of role occupants filter reality; and (3) the process by
which role-occupants decide to obey. Do they choose publicly, or in
secret? By consulting an oracle, or the local party leadership? By
authoritarian command, or by participatory discussion?

Conclusion

The legal order necessarily commands its targets to do what otherwise
they might not. Especially in conditions of development, it prescribes
behaviour that goes against existing patterns and the domain assumptions that support them. The critical question is, Why do people obey
such law? I propose the following hypothesis: people will obey a law
requiring them to change their present behaviour if, but only if, it
meets the following conditions:

1. Its prescriptions are precise, and defined by rule or policy;
2. The rule or policy is communicated to its addressees;

3. They have opportunity to obey it;
4. They have capacity to obey it;
5. It is in their interests to obey it;
6. They perceive that it is in their interests to obey it; and
7. The process by which they come to decide, whether or not to obey, conduces towards obedience.

Ambiguity still shrouds these categories. I try to give them greater specificity in the following chapters.

Notes

1. H.M. Johnson, *Sociology: A Systematic Introduction* (New York: Harcourt, Brace & World, 1960), p. 552.
2. S.P. Huntington, *Political Order in Developing Societies* (New Haven: Yale UP, 1968), p. 59.
3. B. Malinowski, 'A New Instrument for the Interpretation of Law – Especially Primitive', *Yale L.J.*, 51, 1237 (1941).
4. J. Blake and K. Davis, 'Norms, Values and Sanctions' in R. Faris (ed.), *Handbook of Modern Sociology* (Chicago: Rand, McNally, 1964), pp. 456, 482.
5. W.E. Moore, *Social Change* (Englewood Cliffs: Prentice Hall, 1963), p. 19.
6. R. Pound, 'The Limits of Effective Legal Action', *ABAJ*, 3, 55, 62-3 (1917).
7. At common law the custom must have existed since 'time immemorial', quaintly defined as since the year 1189. *Simpson* v. *Wells* (1872) L.R. 2 Q. B. 214.
8. L. Friedman, 'On Legal Development', *Rutgers L. Rev.*, 24, 11 (1969); J.P. Roche and M.M. Gordon, 'Can Morality be Regulated?', *N.Y. Times Magazine*, 22 May 1955, p. 10.
9. See Chap. 5.
10. C. Kluckhorn, 'Values and Value-Orientations in the Theory of Action', in T. Parsons and E.A. Shills (eds.), *Toward a General Theory of Action: Theoretical Foundations for the Social Sciences* (New York: Harper and Row, 1962), p. 396.
11. A. Cohen, *Deviance and Control* (Englewood Cliffs, N.J.: Prentice Hall, 1966), pp. 41-5.
12. L. Berkowitz and N. Walker, 'Laws and Moral Judgments', Sociometry, 30, 410 (1967), reprinted in L. Friedman and S. Macauley, *Law and the Behavioural Sciences* (Indianapolis: Bobbs-Merill, 1969), pp. 198, 200 n.9.
13. Ibid., p. 200.
14. G. Gardiner, 'The Purposes of Criminal Punishment', *Mod. L. Rev.*, 21, 117, 122 (1958).
15. W.J. Chambliss, 'Types of Deviance and the Effectiveness of Legal Sanctions', *Wisconsin L. Rev.*, 703 (1967).
16. E. Lemert, *Human Deviance, Social Problems, and Special Control* (Englewood Cliffs, N.J.: Prentice Hall, 1967), p. 10.
17. Blake and Davis, 'Norms, Values and Sanctions'.
18. R.G. Collingwood, *The Idea of History* (London: Oxford UP, 1946).

19. R.A. Dahl and C.E. Lindblom, *Politics, Economics and Welfare* (New York: Harper and Row, 1953), p. 107.

20. F. Barth, 'Models for Social Organization', *Royal Anthropological Institute Occasional Paper No. 23* (Glasgow: The University Press, 1966).

21. H.W. Jones, *The Efficacy of Law* (Evanston, Ill.: Northwestern UP, 1969).

22. J. Hall, *General Principles of Criminal Law*, 2nd ed. (Indianapolis: Bobbs-Merrill, 1960), p. 425; see R. v. Bromley, (1955) S.R. 90.

23. Hall, ibid., p. 425.

24. R.B. Seidman, 'The Ghana Prison System: an Historical Perspective', *U. of Ghana L.J.*, 3, 89 (1966).

25. S. Frankel, *The Economic Impact on Underdeveloped Societies* (Cambridge: Mass.: Harvard UP, 1954) pp. 141-53.

7 THE COMMUNICATION OF LAW AND THE PROCESS OF DEVELOPMENT*

A law cannot induce consciously changed behaviour unless it is communicated to role-occupants. Self evidently, a role-occupant unaware of new rules will comply only accidentally, if at all. Development depends upon effective communication. To achieve higher levels of production and living new ideas must continuously enter the social order.[1] That particularly requires specific information about how government expects citizens and officials to behave. To induce new behaviour, law-makers must first communicate their expectations to bureaucrats and citizens. Because of communication gaps, some laws remain paper tigers. Peasants frequently did not know about agricultural credit programmes, just as in the United States, welfare clients did not know their entitlements. The first efforts to abolish *nyarubanja* tenancies (a form of feudal landholding) in western Tanzania ran aground in part because those affected lacked precise information about the new law.[2]

Every polity has formal rules for the communication of new laws. This chapter first describes these laws-in-the-books, both in their original English form and as received in Africa. Second, it looks at how government in fact communicated law. Finally, we examine the consequences for development of present African communications systems.

I. The Law Concerning the Communication of Law

The formal rules for the promulgation of law in Africa reflected the English rules. They responded to the perception of the situation that seized policy-makers in England and Africa during most of the colonial period.

A. Communication Rules in England

England and the United States employed state power massively to induce economic development. Government investment and subsidies induced and channelled private investment; special and local laws

*I am indebted to Aki Sawyer, Y.P. Ghai, Herman Felstehausen, William Thiesenheusen, Jean Zorn and Jay Himes for helpful suggestions made on an earlier draft of this chapter, although mistakes are, of course, mine. I am especially indebted to Jean Zorn for creative editing.

favoured corporations and productive use of resources.[3] This use of the
legal order to bring about directed change, however, hid behind an
ideology that denied either its desirability or possibility. The myths of
free enterprise stated that development will arise without state activity
as private individuals seize advantages for profit. Governments officially
exuded indifference. In those myths, law and state power should not
favour one class against another, but merely provide facilitative forms
through which individuals can accomplish the purposes that seem
economically desirable to them. The laws of corporations, of contract,
of property, of partnership and of commerce generally reflected this
ideology. So did the processes of the common law, whose judges
seemingly only gave the force of law to existing custom or private
agreement.

In modern times, the ideology of free enterprise had to accommodate itself to the welfare state. Regulatory laws – tax laws, planning
laws, food and drug laws, insurance and health programmes, for
example – increasingly occupied the statute books. Those laws involved
explicit government interventions in the economic system, but like the
Victorian virgin tubbing under her nightie,[4] the law-makers accomplished that while all the while denying it.

This situation produced two official rules for the communication of
law in England: *Ignorantia juris* and publication. In a few exceptional
situations, when government affirmatively required citizens to change
their activity, the state devised specific communication channels for the
law in question.

1. Ignorantia Juris. If laws merely restate social norms, every properly
raised person will know the law.[5] The criminal law particularly
supposedly only codifies established community mores.[6] An early
judge wrote, '[e]very one is bound to know what is done in Parliament
even though it has not been proclaimed in the country; as soon as
Parliament has concluded any matter, the law presumes that every
person has cognizance of it, for Parliament represents the body of the
realm'.[7] If every properly socialized person knows the law, its
communication becomes unnecessary.[8] Ignorance or mistake of law
cannot be a defence to a criminal charge, for such a plea implies that
the accused had not accepted community mores. Such a plea confesses
deviance. It cannot exonerate, for the criminal law aims precisely at the
deviant.[9]

In many cases, the *ignorantia juris* rule can create injustice. Scholars
have justified it, however, as a spur to communication.[10] It compels

'people to learn the standard of conduct expected of them . . . The rule is a useful weapon where the legislature intends to change the social mores, for the most effective way of bringing the new rule to the public is by convictions reported in the public press'.[11]

2. Publication. In the nineteenth century, cognoscibility[12] warred with *ignorantia juris.* Citizens demanded that the law be knowable before they acted. Entrepreneurs particularly must know the legal consequences before hazarding capital. In a compromise between the requirement of knowledge of the law, and the myth that government remains aloof, most modern capitalist states chose to make the law available to interested citizens, without requiring actual knowledge of it. Conforming to notions of *laissez-faire,* citizens have the burden of learning the law, while the state only accepts responsibility to make it available. With respect to case law, until recently private law reporters substituted for the British state. Government has printed statutes officially since approximately 1705. In 1893, statutes became effective only after publication.[13] In the United States, administrative rules follow the same requirement.

In Africa, as in England, criminal defendants invoked the publication rules as a defence. In *Mwangi s/o Githigi* v. *Rex*[14] for example, the price controller published an order in the *Gazette* establishing the price of haircuts by African barbers. When he amended his order, reducing the price, he did not publish in the *Gazette,* since no requirement of publication of subsidiary legislation existed. The Supreme Court of Kenya reversed a conviction for overcharging, construing the applicable statutes to mean that any revocation or variation in an order or rule required publication in the same manner as the original order.

3. Exceptions. Regulatory law attempts to change behaviour, but the rules did not ordinarily require the state to communicate the law to those it affected. The government did not, for example, promulgate anti-trust laws among businessmen. An entrepreneur had to discover the law himself. Public welfare and social security laws, too, operated as facilitative, requiring the affected individual to unearth them on his own.

Nevertheless, sometimes government cared whether citizens changed their behaviour to match new rules. Then the statute usually required its publication in newspapers or elsewhere. Internal revenue officials mailed tax forms and instructions to every tax-payer. Immigration authorities published widely the requirement that aliens register.

B. Communication Rules in Africa

The African states received formal rules for the communication of law similar to those of the mother country. The ideology of turn-of-the-century colonialism ensured that Africa would rely upon *ignorantia juris* and official gazettes to carry English common and local statutory law to an unlettered, African, non-English speaking population.

1. Trusteeship. Colonialist ideology rested upon the concept of Trusteeship.[15] Private (English) enterprise would perform its obligations.[16] 'The function of the Power in control is limited to providing the main essentials, such as railways and harbours, to seeing that the natives have their fair share, and that material development does not injuriously affect the fulfillment of the second mandate.'[17]

This perception of the function of government matched the then fashionable ideology: the colonial government should provide facilitative law that white entrepreneurs might utilize to exploit African resources. Government did not expect Africans to participate in economic development, except as hewers of wood and drawers of water. Of the laws that the central government enacted, only tax and criminal codes hit them directly. Beyond these, the state had little need to communicate with Africans. The colonialists therefore needed only the English rules for the promulgation of law. *Ignorantia juris*, justified by the assumption that the criminal law represents the common morality, however, led to weird results in Africa. In 1913, a serious epidemic broke out among the Kenya Kikuyu. The frightened villagers charged two men with witchcraft. Pursuant to customary law, the tribal council tried, convicted and executed the alleged witches. The fifty-four council members did not know that the colonial government had withdrawn their jurisdiction over capital offenses. The colonial court nevertheless convicted the entire council of culpable homicide, although the councillors had acted to preserve their people in the face of terrible supernatural threats. (It imposed mercifully light sentences — one day's imprisonment and a fine of 50 rupees each.[18]) The second formal rule of communication of law, publication in an official register, also travelled to a new African home. Tanganyika, for example, required that any formal rule having legislative effect be published in the Government *Gazette.*[19] In addition, a few regulatory rules, particularly in East Africa, affected Africans directly, especially those directly or indirectly requiring that Africans labour for Europeans. Although these rules had to reach Africans in the hinterland, under the publication rules government needed only to make information about them available.

Ignorance of even those laws did not excuse their violation.

2. *Colonial Development.* In 1946, a new philosophy of colonial
government accompanied the Labour Party to power. Colonial development advocated direct state intervention into African life to induce
rapid social, political and economic development. Lord Listowel, Minister of State for the Colonies, wrote in 1949: 'The administrative
machinery of Government [heretofore in Africa] was . . . a means of
establishing those orderly and static conditions which enabled social
evolution in Africa to take its normal course. It was a sort of midwife
attending a delivery to prevent interference, skilled or unskilled, with
the beneficent processes of nature.'[20] This would do no longer. The
colonial governments 'must accept direct responsibility for promoting
changes in the economic, social and political fields, which will enable
the traditional tribal societies to develop progressively on modern
lines'.[21]

Lord Listowel echoed the rhetoric of the welfare state. It called for
vastly increased efforts at development through direct state economic
intervention, particularly in the hinterland where Africans lived. The
colonial governments conceived and implemented these programmes
in a thoroughly authoritarian temper. In Tanzania, local colonial
administrators had broad powers to issue any orders and rules necessary 'for the peace, good order and welfare of the Natives'.[22] Resultant orders covered everything from 'improving beeswax and honey
production in Central Province'[23] to 'the control and eradication of the
banana weevil' around Lake Victoria.[24] The Gold Coast issued analogous orders, notably those designed to eradicate disease from cocoa
trees.

> Administrative ordinances were considered the proper instrument to
> get peasant development. Local authorities were instructed to issue
> agricultural regulations. The implementation of such regulations was
> supervised by officers of the Agricultural Department. Cases of non-
> observance were reported and punished by the Local Authorities.
> The increasing activity of the Department of Agriculture conse-
> quently meant more ordinances and more controls.[25]

Authoritarian communication rules inevitably accompanied so authoritarian a mode of changing behaviour. The official definition of the
situation matched Schramm's description: 'On the surface at least, it
seems that a very large part of development communications flows

from a leadership bent upon modernizing and a reluctant, if not resistant mass.'[26]

This definition flowed inevitably from the official ideology. Colonial development was at best a phantom glimmer at the tunnel's end. The central myth justifying trusteeship described Africans as primitives, a millenium behind Europeans in genetic development.[27] Most of the civil servants who designed and executed colonial development still believed this vicious nonsense, and differed from their predecessors only in their perception of how best to change the African personality. Where Lord Lugard patiently awaited the glacially slow evolution of African genes (meanwhile exploiting African resources) the new bureaucrats expected by direct intervention to achieve development within a generation. In both cases, racism inevitably bred paternalism.[28] Since interactions between whites and blacks were authoritarian, the resulting communications system too became one-way and hierarchical. Colonial development almost uniformly failed. Far from institutionalizing the desired new behaviour, the rules embodying it blew up a storm of opposition.[29] Africans had no institutionalized channels to tell administrators when and why they rejected new regulations. Again and again, colonial administrators saw no alternative to raw force.

Every communications transaction embodies a personal interaction.[30] The process and content of one conditions the other. Colonial development teaches that a communications system locked into a rigidly hierarchical social system must fail to transmit messages so as to induce voluntary change. First, such a system lacks an adequate feedback system. Erroneous decisions likely result.[31] When peasants ignored their orders, colonial administrators explained that Africans lacked economic rationality, or stagnated in conservatism and fatalism. Closer examination often proved the peasants right in their estimates of agricultural and economic policies, and the administrators wrong. Second, development required that individuals solve new problems. The authoritarian communications structure of colonial development destroyed peasant capacity to solve problems.[32] Finally, planned change required collaboration between change agent and client system, between administrators and peasants; minimally, that called for message flows in both directions. When colonial development failed to induce desired activity, government abandoned its programmes. The fault, however, lay not in the programmes alone, but also in a communications system that flowed in only one direction.

3. Independence. The independent African states looked to explicit government intervention in the economy as the principal vehicle for accomplishing economic and social development. Thus, the new governments followed the pattern of colonial development in enacting extensive regulatory laws. But, the formal rules for communication of law in every African country remained those of trusteeship. The obligation of governments to disseminate new laws remained limited to publishing in the gazettes.

II Communication Laws in Action

However well the British system for communicating laws worked in England, it failed miserably in Africa, another example of the Law of Non-Transferability of Law.[33] This failure reflected the different communication systems in the two places.

Lucien Pye suggested three models of communications systems — those of traditional, modern and transitional societies.[34] In traditional societies, the system reflects their status-oriented relationships. The communications system of a modern society operates on at least two levels, the highly structured communications flow of the media and the informal, face-to-face communications between opinion leaders and their followers. The two levels interact, so that the media adjust to feedback from informal controllers and vice versa.[35] The communications system in a transitional society both reflects and structures its dualistic characteristics. In the modernizing sector, the communications system approximates the modern society model. The communications system for the rural hinterland, however, approximates that of traditional society.[36]

A. England and the United States

In England and the United States, government announced a rule but made little effort to ensure its communication. Government met its formal duty when it published the new rule in a gazette or the Federal Register. The official publication, however, triggered a widespread, unofficial communications network. The mass media noted the publication and re-broadcast it. If they did not, government took pains to alert them to it, sometimes by the ceremonial and highly publicized signing of new statutes by the President.

In addition, official publication set off specialized legal information systems that communicated new laws to lawyers, the legal information brokers to government agencies and private clients, especially businessmen. Large businesses had their own house counsel. Smaller ones frequently had lawyers on retainer to advise them of changes in the law.

Vast and rapidly accumulating law reports and periodicals kept the profession up to date on the current state of law. Specialized reporting services proliferated. United States lawyers could subscribe to periodicals on federal taxation, state taxation, money and banking law, negligence law and trade regulation. In addition, a gaggle of law reviews listed recent legislation and reviewed recent cases. Services collected, indexed and annotated statutes, regulations and court decisions, so that lawyers could readily find the law. It matched the pattern of the two-step communications system with lawyers functioning as opinion leaders.

The structure of legal communications adhered to the official definition of the situation. The state only made the law available. Private entrepreneurs then republished it, mainly for the use of lawyer-information brokers, who serviced those who could afford them. This structure could communicate any law, but whether it did communicate any particular law depended, not upon official activity but upon the informal infrastructure.

The formal communications system appeared as a one-way flow: government published; lawyers and ultimately clients, learned. In fact, the system flowed both ways, since interest groups and parties had lobbyists and other informal channels to transmit their demands to the political leadership. Whether information moved down or up, the official communications system depended upon private informal institutions.[37] The necessary legal information came only to those who met preconditions. Lawyers cost money. Even where potential beneficiaries had free legal services available, many did not know of them or think to ask about new laws. Many persons eligible for welfare did not know it. Similarly, a system of feedbacks that depended upon private interest groups ensured the influence of the wealthy in policy-making. As a result, in recent years new roles developed to reach people otherwise outside the legal communications system. Legal aid and store-front lawyers became a significant source of information about the law. Moral entrepreneurs, such as welfare rights organizations, the NAACP, or the American Civil Liberties Union took the initiative to inform the ignorant of their legal entitlements and to communicate the demands of otherwise disenfranchised people to law-makers.

The liberal state confined its social engineering to formal rules requiring merely publication of its laws. In England and the United States, these limited formal rules for the publication of law nevertheless provided real communication to certain publics, because of a private, informal communications channel with lawyers as information brokers.

It reinforced the power of those with the money and sophistication to make use of it, and made unlikely successful social engineering through law aimed at the mass. In Africa, though the needs of society differed, the rules remained the same.

B. Africa

Developmental laws by definition prescribed new ways of doing things. They contradicted the myth that law merely embalms the customs of the people. Government had to do more than make the law cognoscible; it had to ensure that role-occupants knew the law, and acted on it. African communication rules, however, only made the law available to those who searched for it — arduously. Private communication channels relating to law barely existed. Official publication of the law triggered practically nothing, in either the modernizing or the traditional sectors.

1. The Modernizing Enclave. Pye's model suggested that within the modernizing enclave existing communications channels adequately served to communicate law. Members of the elite at least all spoke and read English. The official gazettes carried messages to upper bureaucratic levels. Intra-governmental communication lines brought new laws, more or less, to lower levels. In Tanzania in 1966 the newsletter of the Permanent Secretary of the Prime Minister's Office went to regional administrative secretaries, and another from the Prime Minister, to central offices; it dealt mainly with matters of political importance. In addition, face-to-face communications channels carried the message into the bureaucracy. For example, the Tanzanian permanent secretaries discussed new rules at weekly meetings.[38] Informal discussions helped to circulate the message through all the governmental structure.

Communication within change agencies themselves sometimes poses greater problems than communication with their clients. Often the change agent's behaviour alters less readily than the client's.[39] Nevertheless, probably African governments had institutions that might adequately serve as an intra-bureaucracy communications system. Outside government, such institutions hardly existed.

In Africa, as in England, communication of law to private entrepreneurs depended upon the legal profession. Africa, however, had few lawyers. England had in 1960 about 23,000 solicitors and 2,000 barristers for a population of 55 million. At independence Nigeria had 800 lawyers for a population about as large. Ghana in 1957 had, perhaps, 300 lawyers for nine million people. East Africa (Kenya, Tanganyika and Uganda) with perhaps 30 million, had at independence practically no African lawyers, although it had a small but active Asian and a still smaller European bar.[40] Of course, even these few lawyers did not equitably service the populace. Lawyers in Africa almost exclusively took as clients members of the elite in the small modernizing enclaves. Relatively few governmental agencies had their own lawyers. Instead, the Attorney General's Chambers bore an additional burden. They had to provide detailed legal opinions to the ministries, as well as performing all the other manifold tasks their counterparts elsewhere perform. Despite the need for lawyers, however, Nigeria and Kenya had by the early 1970s more lawyers than job openings.

Moreover, almost every West African lawyer, and most in East Africa, trained as a barrister, not a solicitor. Prior to the establishment of new law faculties, lawyers had to go to England for training. (In the post-war years, the London Inns of Court had far more black and brown than white students.) They could get barrister's qualifications more cheaply and quicker than solicitor's. As a result, many lawyers in Africa fancied themselves as litigators, not counsellors or advisers.[41]

Africa had few of the specialized legal services that supported the lawyer's information broker role in England and the United States, such as periodical loose-leaf reports of current changes in the law. Even law reports frequently became randomly episodic. As of 1969, the latest volume of the *Ghana Law Reports* printed and bound was that for 1960.[42]

Although new law reviews emerged with new university law faculties in Ghana, Nigeria and East Africa, they mainly served private practitioners. Of a total of sixty-two articles in the *East African Law Journal*, the *East African Law Review* and the *University of Ghana Law Journal*, only eleven concerned new problems and issues relating to development. Newspapers played an important role in communicating law within the modernizing sector. Enactments of new laws and regulations appeared prominently in every African newspaper. For example, when Tanzania decided to purchase vehicles for civil servants, Tanzania's two English language newspapers carried the story, and public outcry reversed the policy.[43]

Whatever the difficulties of communicating law within the modernizing sector, however, compared with the difficulties of communication from the centre to the periphery, it ran marvellously well. Most Africans lived in the countryside. How to bring the norms of development to them?

2. Crossing the Gap. Rules to induce development do not pretend

merely to reflect the customs or mores of the community. They intend
to change behaviour. The communications system, therefore, must
deliver communications so as to prompt the desired changes.

Messages of that sort differ from ones that merely expose the
receiver to information. In development, whether a law has regulatory
or facilitative form policy-makers adopt it because they want the
citizenry to behave differently. When Tanzania first promulgated its
ujamaa village programme, it let the individual decide whether to join.
In fact, however, government urgently wanted peasants to do so. The
communicator had to inform them about the new norms in a way
likely to induce them to enter the programme.

In Africa, four constraints limited that sort of communication:
language, style, media ineffectiveness and the absence of generalized
communication channels between centre and periphery. Only Tanzania
had an African language,[44] Swahili, shared by enough people to serve as
a second official language. Elsewhere, English remained the only official
one. In those countries, where statutes, regulations and law reports
appeared only in English, the communications system bore great
strains. Most peasants, even those literate in their own language, could
not read laws written in English. The lack of common language required
face-to-face legal information brokers.

Tanzania had to promulgate laws in two languages. Many of the
lowest level courts used Swahili, and the magistracy became almost
completely Africanized. But, all legislation, subsidiary regulations,
government gazettes, and administrative documents first appeared in
English. Many departments conducted business in English. A law professor compiled an English-Swahili legal dictionary.[45] The task required
great creativity, because almost half the common vocabulary of English
law had no Swahili equivalent. Difficult linguistic and jurisprudential
problems arose. Words usually translated as equivalents – e.g. 'trust'
and 'wakf' – frequently had quite different connotations to native
speakers of each language. Moreover, simply to translate English terms
into Swahili equivalents ran the considerable risk of imposing English
legal concepts upon Tanzania. For example, in Swahili the same word
described adultery and fornication, because Bantu culture did not
distinguish between them. Should the state manufacture a new Swahili
word to conform to the dual English concepts? Statutory interpretation
presented another problem: does a statute's plain meaning come from its
English or Swahili version? Moreover, translators with legal training did
not come in droves. In Tanzania, the attorney general's chambers
would, on request from official agencies, translate particular statutes

into Swahili. It took more than six months of steady reminders from the Ministry of Agriculture to obtain a Swahili copy of the Range Management and Development Act.

Language barriers aside, styles of legislative drafting tended to block government's communication to citizens. Statutory language 'has been sharpened and made precise as a means of communication within the legal profession. It has developed as a means to the goal of resolving legal conflicts through the intervention of judges and lawyers.'[46] Most development rules ideally operated without that intervention. The rules aimed at influencing the behaviour of a lay audience. Their interpretation fell mainly on bureaucrats not legally trained, and ordinary people. Lawyers' language — 'legalese' — differed sharply from the appropriate language for communicating prescriptions for behaviour to a lay audience. For example, the Co-operative Societies Ordinance 1948, of Zambia[47] provided as follows: 'In order to be qualified for membership of a co-operative society, a person other than a registered society, company or other association of persons, corporate or unincorporate, must have attained the age of sixteen years.' Translation: 'Anyone older than sixteen years may join a co-operative.' It further provided that:

> The minority or nonage of any person duly admitted as a member of any registered society shall not debar that person from executing any instrument or of giving any acquittance necessary to be executed or given under this Ordinance or the rules made thereunder, and shall not be ground for invalidating or avoiding any contract entered into by any such person, whether as principal or as surety, shall be enforceable at or against such person notwithstanding his minority or nonage.'

Translation: 'Members of co-operatives who are minors are liable upon their agreements with their co-operative.' As Aubert has remarked about legalese, 'A social mechanism which has achieved its form when fulfilling one function, remains unaltered when faced with an entirely different function, and fails accordingly.'[48]

Mass media scarcely penetrated the African countryside. In Buhaya, Tanzania, in the mid-1960s for example, Goren Hyden found that only 8.5 per cent of the population owned a radio,[49] and one-third had never even heard one. In a study in eastern Nigeria, though 62 of the 128 subjects claimed to listen to radio irregularly and 21 regularly, only 31 actually did so at all in a 26-week period.[50] 57.5 per cent of Hyden's sample never read a newspaper. In a Ugandan rural sample including 99 influential community members and 317 others, 63 per cent of the influentials, but only 37 per cent of the others, read a newspaper at least once a week.[51] In Nigeria, total radio and reading time of the entire population of the survey averaged only 3.4 per cent of the daylight hours.[52] Nevertheless, African countries made what use they could of the media to disseminate legal rules. The Tanzania Price Control Ordinance, for example, provided that the Price Controller might use gazettes, newspapers, public notices or letters to communicate any order or notice to its addressees.[53] Low literacy frequently made radio seem the most useful method of reaching the population. Government sometimes used it effectively to create a mood, to explain governmental programmes, to teach new techniques, as in Premier Castro's famous marathon speeches, or President Nkrumah's 'Dawn Broadcast', a famous attack on corruption.

Most people's information came not from the media but from face-to-face communication.[54] The impact of radio or newspapers depended upon the existence of the two-step communication system. As a result, reliance upon the media to reach the peasantry likely enhanced the power of existing elites. In Uganda, influentials listened to the radio and read newspapers far more than the rest of the population. Influentials included mainly chiefs, teachers and traders, whereas cultivators, carpenters, builders of all sorts, tailors, drivers, fishermen, potters and labourers of all kinds made up two-thirds of the rank and file.[55] Thus, those who already held power and privilege had the best position not only to relay information, but to choose what to relay, strengthening further their power and privilege in the countryside.

Absent lawyers and private non-professionals acting as legal information brokers to the peasantry, governments tended either not to communicate with the hinterlands at all or to use their own officials as a communications channel. The safari books of the Iringa District in Tanzania during the 1930s, for example, offer a colonial example. District officials tried to visit every village in the district biennially. Most of these safaris had to be on foot, for few roads existed. In 1936, one district officer covered 1,200 miles by foot safari. In each village the touring district officer would attend to tax defaulters (i.e. recruit labour), settle disputes and hold a general meeting. At these meetings, he explained government's current programme — the introduction of cash crops, the necessity for tie-ridging, or the importance of growing a root crop as famine protection. Sometimes he answered questions about legal matters; in one village, the district officer explained master and servant law, describing the rights and duties of the employee under it.

118   *The Communication of Law and the Process of Development*

3. New Institutions. Precisely because African governments tried to promote development, and thus used law to change society, they had to devise new institutions to communicate from the centre to the periphery. These communications systems fall into four categories: the bureaucracy, the Party, the Commission of Enquiry and quasi-governmental organizations.

a. The Bureaucracy. African governments discovered that the most important communication networks between the centre and the rural regions lay within government itself, rather than in private and unofficial communications channels. Area, regional and district commissioners, agricultural extension officers, community welfare officers, local planning agencies, the officers of co-operatives and of the ministry of co-operatives, and the police all served as information sources about their special areas of competence. In the villages of Buhaya, Hyden's respondents received much of their information about agricultural problems from government agents.[56] The government agencies that penetrated the countryside specialized. The legal communications system, therefore, depended upon each of the various agencies promulgating their own rules. No general system for the communication of law existed.

Table 7.1: Sources of Information

Buyombe Village Extension Office of Village District Committee	Kuyombe	Kitdagulo	Bwatangabo	Kabaganda	Kisuruma
Committee	31	37.5	49	71	82
Co-op leaders	31	34	19	12.5	12
Extension Officer	28	21	28	10	4
No information	10	7.5	4	6.5	2

Source: Hyden, Tanu Yajeng: Nethi: Political Development in Rural Tanzania (Nairobi: East Africa Pub. House, 1968), p. 192.

The Range Management and Development Act[57] exemplified the specificity problem. So grandiose a scheme for social change required knowledge of the Act by people involved. Officials in the Ministry of Agriculture pestered the Attorney General for a Swahili translation. They later produced an information booklet in the vernacular and obtained a mobile film unit. Officials visited the various Masai settlements, showing films and outlining the project. When the minister went on safari, he attended a meeting of Masai who had shown interest in the proposed ranching association. At the meeting, a loudspeaker system broadcast prepared tapes explaining details of the proposals.

The Ministry had to create its own channels to promulgate the new law, because no other agency in Masailand had a stake in the project, and no generalized infrastructure for the dissemination of law into the countryside existed. Only the Party and the Permanent Commission of Enquiries emerged as candidates for such an infrastructure.

b. The Party. Political parties served as a channel of communication from the political leadership to the mass.

> People are not highly dependent on mass media for information about government and politics and they show on the whole greater trust in direct face-to-face communication with friends, or in official government documents. This emphasizes the crucial role that the political organization play in the developmental process in the countryside.[58]

The early typologies of African parties tried to distinguish between 'mobilizing parties' and 'consociational' types.[59] The mobilizing polity supposedly reached people through a hierarchical political party.[60] It concerned itself with communicating messages from the top down, not from the bottom up. That system failed.

> The dynamic parties were not getting their programs across. Growth rates were not rising precipitously in Mali, Ghana, Guinea or Tanganyika. The Ivory Coast economy was growing faster. And as research was done outside the capital cities, it also became clear that the one-party revolutionary systems were not managing affairs well at local levels either. Central party organs were not exacting the responses they wanted from regional and district bodies. Plans and commands made at the centre did not get implemented.[61]

Rather than one-party states, these countries became 'no party states'.[62] Speaking of Tanzania as of 1965, Bienen concluded: 'The center does not propose and the district and village organizations obey. Neither does it propose and they deliberately disobey. More accurately, the center had ideas and programs which reach the territorial organizations in different forms from the original plans.'[63]

A third category appeared: the revolutionary party, forged in struggle — typically a guerilla war, either for independence or for social revolution. Its conduct and policies reflected the lessons of that struggle. Its archetype, of course, became the Chinese Communist Party, the product of a generation of armed struggle. African examples included regimes in Mozambique, Angola and Guinea Bissau. In their long struggles, the revolutionary parties relied heavily on popular rural support and learned to communicate effectively with that population. Because no Anglophonic sub-Saharan states won their independence through protracted armed struggle, no revolutionary party emerged there. Parties, like people, learn through experience. The revolutionary parties but not the mobilizing parties transmitted messages both ways, from government to mass, and vice versa. Without the guerilla experience, Tanzania uniquely attempted to forge such a party.[64]

c. The Permanent Commission of Enquiries. Its originators intended Tanzania's Permanent Commission of Enquiries to operate as an ombudsman to correct administrative irregularities. It had another, probably unintended function, to communicate and explain the law to the masses, and the lower ranks of the bureaucracy. In 1966-7, commission members travelled 16,096 miles and addressed 64,065 people, holding public meetings where members answered questions and received specific complaints.[65] The complaints and questions covered a broad spectrum. In England most of them would require a lawyer.[66] It did not, however, become a poor man's advocate, for the commission, unlike the private attorney, remained part of the bureaucracy. Three examples of the commission's work illustrated its position.

In one case the complainant alleged that he had applied to register his co-operative society, but had not received a reply. The commission investigated and advised the complainant that he had not amassed the requisite capital.[67] A complainant had been dismissed from his job as a government driver. The commissioner explained that he had violated regulations by taking on passengers.[68] A divisional executive officer had refused the complainant a licence to brew and sell liquor. Determining that the refusal violated the law, the commission obtained a licence for the complainant.[69]

In each case, the commission, like a lawyer, communicated the law to an interested party. To the extent that people used it, the commission filled a void in Tanzania's system for communicating legal information. But like a private attorney, the commission required its clients to trigger its activity.

d. Trade Unions. In developed countries, private associations of many sorts constitute important communications channels. In the United States many trade unions advise their members about minimum wage laws, workmen's compensation and the like. Co-operatives inform their members of marketing, tax and agricultural law. Manufacturers associations systematically call members' attention to new tax laws, anti-trust rulings, corporation laws and administrative rulings. Such non-governmental agencies can avoid the authoritarian overtones of bureaucratic communication channels. To what extent did similar channels exist in Africa?

After the Labour Party election victory in 1946, colonial trade union policy suffered schizophrenia. Only those territories having legislation protecting the rights of trade unions could receive aid under the Colonial Development and Welfare Act.[70] But, colonial governments saw trade unions as a threat to expatriate employers and British rule generally, and therefore rigidly controlled African unions. The laws regulating unions, though copies of English law, contained one significant difference: they required trade unions to register with government, but gave government discretion to refuse registration.[71] As a consequence, bureaucrats dominated trade unions during the later colonial period, and hence they could not serve very well as a private, non-official communications channel.

For a brief period during the struggle for independence, unions in many parts of Africa shook off bureaucratic domination. Soon after, however, the new governments that trade unions earlier had strongly supported first forced them into opposition and then again put them under bureaucratic control. Because of the unions' high level of organization some new governments believed that they threatened to gulp too large a share of the developmental pie. In Tanganyika at Independence, for example, unions demanded wage increases that would have absorbed almost all the aid granted by Britain.[72]

More and more African governments resurrected authoritarian controls over unions. In Nkrumah's Ghana, the Trades Union Congress became an integral wing of the ruling party.[73] Tanzania established by statute a new National Union of Tanganyikan Workers,[74] whose principal officers the President appointed. Increasingly, African governments tried to manipulate trade unions as top-down mobilization institutions, thus undercutting them as organizations to serve their members. The trade union leadership slipped quickly into the bureaucratic mould.

e. Co-operatives. At best, unions reached only the small group of

wage earners in the export enclave. The vast majority of Africans lived
on the land, frequently organized into marketing co-operatives.
(Tanzania again uniquely in its *ujamaa* village programme emphasized
producer co-operatives.) The co-operative movement might have
offered a viable communications system free of bureaucratic constraints. Speaking of Uganda, for example, Okore Okereke wrote that
co-operatives 'provide a useful channel for propagating ideas for the
improvement of methods of cultivation and marketing'.[75] In Tanzania,
Government Paper No. 4 of 1967 stated:

> There is no other type of organization [besides co-operatives] which
> is so suited to the problems and concepts of rural development . . .
> It would be impossible for the Government administrative
> machinery to deal with numerous individuals requiring Government
> assistance and services . . . Without the use of co-operatives the num-
> ber of people wanting Government help will make dissemination of
> Government services and assistance financially very expensive and
> administratively almost impossible. Self-help will be difficult to
> organize, and changes in attitudes so essential for bringing about
> required structural changes are likely to take much longer than if
> co-operatives are effectively organized, emphasizing production.[76]

However, if co-operatives were to develop as two-way communication
channels, they had to be shed of official domination, and become
genuinely participatory. But, even 'democratic' institutions in stratified
societies tend to reflect social inequality. Genuine participation
required that members determine their own affairs. Too often those
who already held wealth and status in the community dominated the
councils of the group. Information on new laws reached most co-
operative members through this self-interested layer. Conversely,
government heard not the response of the masses, but the wishes of the
privileged few. Without an informed and politically educated membership, domination of the co-operative movement by richer peasants and
mismanagement and corruption by staff became endemic. China perhaps reversed this tendency by guaranteeing a disproportionate share of
power over the co-operative's affairs to its poorer members. In Africa,
however, governments reacted to domination and mismanagement by
intervening. Co-operatives became another bureaucratic agency of the
central government, unable to function as independent communications
channels.

Nevertheless, co-operatives probably had potential for bridging the

gap between the countryside and the centre without massive bureaucratic involvement. Tanzania moved towards a total transformation of
peasant life into *ujamaa* villages. Its success will measure government
success in developing genuine communication channels to and from the
peasantry.

III The Consequences of the Sub-System for the Communication of Legal Norms in Africa

Form determines content. By defining and limiting ways of communicating norms, institutions determine what norms they will transmit.
Thus, the rules of the communications sub-system channel and constrain any country's potential for development.[77]

A. Mistaken Responses

Ill-defined channels for legal information lead to confusion and mis-
information. Hearing vague reports of government policy or intention,
the people may assume that the policy has become law. Iringa,
Tanzania, for example, had an active land market among maize farmers.
From speeches by President Nyerere and other officials, they believed,
incorrectly, that government had outlawed buying and selling land.
Feeling insecure in their titles, they did not build the fences, irrigation,
fertilizer and drainage that good agricultural practice required. The land
deteriorated, and sales — *sub rosa* — multiplied.

Another tragic example of mistaken response occurred in 1969, also
in Tanzania. Kasella Bantu, a member of Parliament, much disturbed
by repeated cattle thefts in his district, reported to a mass meeting of
his constituents that he proposed to introduce a bill in the National
Assembly,

> that since cattle raiders always went with arms that permission
> should be given that when cattle is stolen and an alarm raised, all the
> people who go to follow these cattle thieves who were defending
> themselves with arms were beaten badly and killed and the fact that
> the thieves were armed was proved, the people should be exempted
> from being tried.[78]

A hue and cry arose the next day.[79] Following local custom, all adult
males armed themselves and ran to help.[80] When people joined the
group, they heard that the MP for Nzoga East had said that 'when
cattle thieves were arrested, they should be killed'.[81] A peasant testified
he heard the group of armed men saying 'that they had been told by

Kasella Bantu to kill all cattle thieves'.[82] That day, five suspected cattle thieves died. A witness testified: 'In the morning of 21 September, my cattle were stolen, and as a result of . . . [the] meeting held by Kasella Bantu, I and others killed the thieves who were found with my cattle and as people heard what was announced at the meeting . . . people did not hesitate in killing the five thieves.'[83] The court sentenced eleven defendants to death for murder. Kasella Bantu himself was acquitted.

B. The Choice of Development Strategy

Insufficient communications had a second impact upon development. Available communications channels determined the kinds of laws government could communicate and try to implement and thus determined the course of development.

Government attempts to influence change — that is, development — require much more formal law than does *laissez-faire*, and Plan more than Contract.[84] Plan implementation especially requires communicating the details of expected behaviour to a host of addressees. For effective, democratic development, the communications system must provide for responses to the planning agencies from those affected. Development, especially planned development, involved two-way communications on every level, from investment decisions in heavy industry to specific peasant farming techniques. Frequently, developing nations evaded the problems of insufficient communications to the citizenry by disguising the regulatory or planning legislation as facilitative law, and addressing law to bureaucrats rather than citizens. Because African governments recognized that peasants received the law corrupted if at all, development programmes addressed to peasants rarely required or commanded them to do anything. Government instead exhorted, urged, and cajoled them to change their ways. That rarely persuaded anyone to make different choices, since exhortation and cajolery did not significantly change the peasants' arena of choice.

In lieu of direct commands likely to die in transit, sometimes government required civil servants to provide new constraints and resources for farmers — that is, to change their arena of choice. When Tanzania embarked on its *ujamaa* village programme, it did not at first require peasants to join it. It urged them to do so, and provided inducements — land, credit, extension services. That did not solve the underlying communications problem. In 1968, only 41 per cent of the farmers in a stratified sample had even heard of the *ujamaa* programme, and only 20 per cent could describe it.[85]

Communication systems, like other institutions, arise to solve particular problems. For example, the United States' communications system arose in response to the demands of a nominally *laissez-faire* economy. After World War II, even economic planners joined the call for a return for competitive pricing after wartime experience with price controls. They believed that 'hierarchical control of a national economy imposes such a staggering burden on communications that the dilemma of central co-ordination versus decentralized discretion is never satisfactorily resolved'.[86] In Africa, the existing communications systems arose in response to colonial requirements. They broke down when loaded with the new burdens of development. It seemed to many African governments, as it did to economic planners in the United States, that existing communications channels required the continuation of the existing situation, with incremental changes nibbling only at the edges.

Paradoxically, however, existing communications channels frequently coerced governments into placing specific programmes in the public rather than the private sector. One can more easily send messages to bureaucrats than to the citizenry at large. If, for example, government wants lorries to stop at a particular lorry park before leaving Accra to go to Kumasi, it might more easily create a government bus service to make the necessary stops than communicate the need to private lorry operators and induce compliance.[87]

Communication channels impose their own tyrannies. African governments inherited weak circuits to the peasantry, and therefore found it difficult to affect their behaviour. Increasingly, they lodged responsibility to solve emergent problems of development with the public, not the private sector. Whatever their nominal ideology, whether military or civilian regime, African governments moved rapidly towards state capitalism. The constraints of communication greased that track.

C. Communications, Bureaucracy and Power

Thus, every African country emphasized the bureaucratic input into development. In many cases this proved counter-productive.[88] Communicating a new rule to a bureaucrat may have led to new bureaucratic behaviour, but it did not often lead to new behaviour by the population at large. It did ensure enhanced bureaucratic power. Information and knowledge create power. A communications system that produces only top-down flows enhances the power of those on top, without increasing the potential of change by the citizenry at large upon whom development rests. Changed behaviour requires two-way communication flows. Communications channels pattern themselves on the inter-personal relationships of which they form a part. African bureau-cracies were hierarchical and authoritarian; so were their communications channels.

Existing communication systems, designed and adapted for colonial economies, served poorly the uses of development. Africa relied upon a communications network where official publication triggered nothing, rather than setting off the informal lawyer-client network that played so important a function in the developed, Western world. The inade-quacy of their channels for communicating law silently coerced African governments towards incremental changes, enlargement of the public sector and enhanced bureaucratic power. Development could succeed only if governments forged new systems between the centre and the periphery that made possible two-way, participatory communications.

Conclusion

I proposed an explanation for the failure of many development rules to induce their prescribed behaviour in Africa:

1. Unless role-occupants learn norms addressed to them, they will not consciously conform to them.
2. Because the norms of development require new sorts of activity by role-occupants, they do not learn of the norm through existing social-ization processes; those norms must be specifically communicated to them
3. The institutions of the communications system determine the messages that will be accepted and transmitted, and the likelihood that addres-sees will change behaviour in conformity with the messages.
4. Role-occupants will not obey norms prescribing new behaviour unless they learn of them in the context of a two-way communications channel.
5. Neither formal nor informal communications channels existed in Africa for the general communication of rules from the centre to the periphery.
6. As a consequence,
   a. Government frequently phrased its expectations of new behaviour as exhortation and cajolery, sometimes but not always supported by bureaucratic activity to change the arenas of choice of the addres-sees of the new norms; and
   b. Government used bureaucracy to communicate new rules to the citizenry at large; and
   c. Government lodged new development programmes as much as possible in the public sector.

7. As a consequence of (6).

   a. Legal rules frequently spread in a confused and imprecise way;

   b. Communications addressed to the citizenry were delivered if at all by a top-down communication channel;

   c. The power of the bureaucracy over the citizenry was enhanced.

This explanation can be subsumed under more general propositions. Every communication system is more or less limited. It accepts some messages and rejects others. It transmits some without distortion, and changes others in the course of transmission. It empowers those who control it, and subordinates those who do not. It admits some into participation and not others and will accordingly induce changed behaviour.

The characteristics of any set of communication institutions depend upon its social milieu. The system that serves an agrarian, subsistence, status-oriented, kin-connected society probably will not adequately serve an advanced capitalist industrial society, nor will the communications system of a colonial society directed at maintaining law and order and collecting taxes serve the imperatives of development. Faced by communications systems appropriate for a colonial order, African governments either cut their programmes to fit the communications system, or lapsed into rhetoric and soft development.

Every communications system, however, necessarily bolsters the power structure of its society. To entrust a communication system that bolsters hierarchical, bureaucratic superiors with messages aimed at helping the poor will end by enhancing still further the power of the bureaucracy. Too frequently, while trying to help the poor and the defenceless, African governments created development programmes which enlarged the power of the administrators, and increased the vulnerability of the clients.

Four prescriptions flow from this analysis. First, the draftsman of a statute or programme cannot assume, as he too easily might in England or the United States, that he can rely upon an existing infrastructure for the dissemination of law. Publishing the law in a gazette does not trigger a waiting informal communication system. The draftsman must write provisions into the law requiring particular officials to communicate the law to those who need to know, and prescribing the circumstances.

Secondly, analytical positivism teaches that laws simultaneously address role-occupants and enforcement officials. The colonial agricultural rules, commanding peasants to act in particular ways on pain of criminal sanction, exemplified that model. If the communication channels to role-occupants seem weak, however, law makers frequently address only exhortations to the role-occupants, and command civil servants to provide inducements for the desired behaviour. Rather than ordering peasants to grow cash crops most African governments only cajole him, and direct the civil service to provide credit, marketing and extension services. The exhortation to the peasant becomes the functional equivalent to the command to grow cash crops, the activity of the bureaucrats, the functional equivalent of the criminal sanction. One can easily forget that the new rules aimed at the bureaucracy cannot succeed in changing peasant behaviour unless the government transmits the new programme to the peasantry. A draftsman must therefore provide for its communication, just as he must provide for communication of a rule of law.

Third, we must enlarge our concept of legal actors. Where mainly bureaucrats communicate law, especially laws peculiar to development, the legal system includes many more roles besides lawyers and judges. It includes all official roles functionally related to making, communicating or implementing government programmes and rules.

Finally, communication systems relate to power. The legal draftsman cannot avoid making policy in designing communications for the rule at hand. If he makes the law available but does not ensure its communication he favours private interests with the resources and sophistication to enquire. If he tolerates a one-way flow from the centre to the periphery, he enhances the power of the bureaucracy and fosters authoritarianism. Only where government conscientiously designs a two-way communication system, guaranteeing both that addressees will learn the law and that government will receive meaningful feedback can it undercut elitism and accomplish change.

Society influences the legal order, the legal order influences society. Society creates communication systems, and in turn they limit the effectiveness of law. Since governments will not usually enact or implement laws, they cannot communicate; communication systems constitute one vehicle by which society shapes the legal order. Communication systems result from the repetitive behaviour of many people; that is, they constitute institutions. The legal order can change institutions. A government seriously bent on development must as an urgent priority transform the system of communicating law.

Notes

1. See E. Rogers, 'Communication Research and Rural Development', *Rural Africana*, 5, 3 (1968).
2. R. James, 'All Land to the Tillers' (unpublished manuscript).
3. See generally, J.W. Hurst, *The Growth of American Law: The Law Makers* (Boston: Little, Brown, 1950).
4. I borrow this image from K. Lewellyn, *The Common Law Tradition: Deciding Appeals* (Boston: Little, Brown, 1960).
5. J. Hall, *General Principles of Criminal Law*, 2nd ed. (Indianapolis: Bobbs-Merrill, 1960), pp. 163-70.
6. Ibid., pp. 382-7.
7. *Regina v. Bishop of Chichester*, Y.B. 59 Edw. III, 7 (1365), quoted in C. Allen, *Law in the Making*, 6th ed. (London: Oxford UP, 1958), p. 455.
8. L. Fuller, *The Morality of Law* (New Haven: Yale UP, 1964), p. 63.
9. *Regina v. Kemp* (1957) 1 Q.B. 399, 408 (insanity defence not available where claim is bad upbringing); but cf. *Lambert v. California*, 355 U.S. 255 1957 (unconstitutional to convict of crime of not registering as felon where accused unlikely to learn of requirement).
10. O.W. Holmes, *The Common Law* (Boston: Little, Brown, 1881), p. 48.
11. G. Williams, *The Criminal Law: The General Part*, 2nd ed. (London: Stevens, 1961), p. 289
12. See J. Bentham, *Theory of Legislation*, R. Hildreth, tr. (Boston: Weeks, Jordan, 1840).
13. Rules Publication Act, 1893, 56 & 57 Vict., c. 66; see also Statutory Instruments Act, 1946, 9 & 10 Geo. 6, c. 36.
14. 24(1) Kenya L.R. 72 (1950).
15. See F. Lugard, *The Dual Mandate in British Tropical Africa*, 5th ed. (London: Cass, 1965).
16. F. Lugard, 'The White Man's Task in Tropical Africa', in P.W. Quiggs (ed.), *Africa, A Foreign Affairs Reader* (N.Y.: Praeger, 1964), p. 5.
17. Ibid. Parallels between Lugard and Adam Smith's *Wealth of Nations* are not accidental. Cf. H. Johnstone, *Trade and General Conditions Report, Nyasaland* (London: HMSO, 1896), p. 189.
18. 5 E. Afr. L.R. 50 (East African Protectorate, 1913).
19. Interpretation and General Clauses Ordinance (Cap. 1) s 7; see also Uganda: Interpretation Act (Cap. 17) s s 19-24.
20. [Lord] Listowel, 'The Modern Conception of Government in British Africa', *J. African Administration*, 1, 99 (1949).
21. Ibid.
22. Native Authorities Ordinance, 1927 s9, 16.
23. Ibid.
24. L. Cliffe, 'Nationalism and the Reaction to Enforced Agricultural Improvement During the Colonial Period' (cyclostyle MS, 1965).
25. H. Rutherberg, *Agricultural Development in Tanganyika* (Berlin: Springer, 1964), p. 50.
26. W. Schramm, 'Communication and Change', in D. Lerner (ed.), *Communication and Change in the Developing Countries* (Honolulu: East-West Center P., 1967), pp. 5, 16.
27. F. Lugard, *Dual Mandate*, p. 69.
28. S. Makings, *Agricultural Problems of Developing Countries in Africa* (Nairobi: Oxford UP, 1967), p. 63.
29. L. Cliffe, 'Nationalism', p. 31.
30. See L. Pye (ed.), *Communication and Political Development* (Princeton:

(Princeton UP, 1963).
31. G. Almond and G. Powell, *Comparative Politics: A Developmental Approach* (Boston: Little, Brown, 1966), p. 178.
32. P. Blau and W. Scott, *Formal Organizations: A Comparative Approach* (San Francisco: Chandler, 1962), pp. 119 *et seq.*
33. See Chap. 2.
34. Pye, *Communication and Political Development*, pp. 24-7.
35. This two-step communication flow theory stemmed from the 1940 presidential election in the United States. P. Lazerfeld, B. Berelson & H. Gaudet, *The People's Choice: How the Voter Makes up his Mind in a Presidential Campaign*, 2nd ed. (N.Y.: Columbia UP, 1948). As Lloyd R. Bostian has pointed out, while the data there did not demonstrate the two-step theory, it did disprove a one-step theory. The two-step theory has never gained satisfactory proof. L. Bostian, 'The Two-Step Flow Theory: Cross Cultural Implications', *Journalism Q.*, 47, 109-17 (1970).
36. Pye, *Communication and Political Development*, pp. 24-7.
37. Almond and Powell, *Comparative Politics*, p. 168.
38. W. Tordoff, *Government and Politics in Tanzania* (Nairobi: East Africa Pub. House, 1967), p. 63.
39. Rogers, 'Communication Research'.
40. L.C.B. Gower, *Independent Africa: The Challenge to the Legal Profession* (Cambridge, Mass.: Harvard UP, 1967), p. 108. New law faculties now exist in almost every Anglophonic African country; Nigeria alone in 1970 had four.
41. Ibid.
42. East Africa was rather more up-to-date, thanks to a private British publisher. Malawi and Zambia lagged far behind.
43. For a discussion of the hire purchase act in Tanzania, see S. Picciotto and C. Whitford, 'The Impact of the Tanzania Hire Purchase Act', *East Afr. L. Rev.*, 2, 11 (1969).
44. Amharic is Ethiopia's official language, although it is spoken by only about 15 per cent of the population. The elite commonly speak English and French.
45. A.B. Weston, 'Law in Swahili – Problems in Developing the National Language', *East Afr. L.J.*, 1, 60 (1965).
46. V. Aubert, 'Some Social Functions of Legislation', *Acta Sociological*, 10, 99 (1966), reprinted in V. Aubert (ed.), *Sociology of Law* (Harmondsworth: Penguin Books, 1969), pp. 116, 123.
47. Zambia: laws 1961, Cap. 217, Art. 21.
48. Aubert, 'Social Functions of Legislation', p. 124.
49. G. Hyden, *Tanu Yajenga Nethi: Political Development in Rural Tanzania* (Nairobi: East Afr. Pub. House, 1968), p. 192.
50. G.H. Axinn and N.W. Axinn, 'Communication Among the Nsukka Igbo: A Folk-Village Society', Journalism Q., 46, 320, 324 (1969).
51. Oberschall, 'Communications, Information and Aspirations in Rural Uganda', *J. Asian and African Studies*, 4, 30 (1969).
52. Axinn & Axinn, 'Communication Among the Nsukka Igbo', p. 324.
53. Tanzania: Cap. 309, s23.
54. Axinn & Axinn, 'Communication Among the Nsukka Igbo', p. 406.
55. Oberschall, 'Communications, Information and Aspirations'.
56. G. Hyden, *Tanu Yajenga Nethi*, p. 195. The accompanying table is taken from the same source.
57. Tanzania: Law No. 51 of 1964; supra, Chap. 1.
58. Hyden, *Tanu Yajenga Nethi*, p. 107.
59. H. Bienen, 'The Ruling Party in the African One-Party States, TANU in Tanzania', *J. Comm. Pol. Studies*, 5, 214 (1966), reprinted in M.E. Doro and

N.M. Stultz (eds.), *Governing Black Africa: Perspectives on New States* (Englewood Cliffs: Prentice Hall, 1970), pp. 68, 69.

60. D. Apter, *The Political Kingdom in Uganda: A Study in Bureaucratic Nationalism* (Princeton: Princeton UP, 1964), p. 22.
61. Bienen, 'TANU in Tanzania', p. 69.
62. Ibid., p. 71.
63. Ibid., pp. 108-12; cf. D. Austin, *Politics in Ghana 1946-1960* (London: Oxford UP, 1964); see S.K.B. Asante, 'Law and Society in Ghana', *Wisc. L. Rev.*, 1113 (1966).
64. See Chap. 21, below.
65. *Annual Report of the Permanent Commission of Enquiry, June 1966-June 1967* (Dar es Salaam: Gov't. Printer, 1968).
66. Ibid.
67. Ibid, case no. 82 (1966-67).
68. Ibid., case no. 468 (1966-67).
69. Ibid., case no. 52 (1966-67).
70. See I. Davies, *African Trade Unions* (Harmondsworth: Penguin, 1966).
71. Ibid.
72. Ibid., p. 11.
73. Ibid., pp. 108-12.
74. Ibid.
75. O. Okereke, 'The Place of Marketing Co-operatives in the Economy of Uganda', in C.E. Widstrand (ed.), *Co-operatives and Rural Development in East Africa* (N.Y.: Africana, 1970), pp. 153, 154.
76. *Wages, Incomes Rural Development, Investment and Price Policy* (Dar es Salaam, Tanzania, Government Printer, 1967), p. 61.
77. H. Felstehausen, 'Conceptual Limits of Development Communications Theory' (paper presented at the 54th Annual Convention of Association for Education in Journalism, Columbia, South Carolina, 22-25 August 1971).
78. Record on appeal, *Republic* v. *Kasella Bantu,* Crim. Sess. No. 47 (Ct. of App. for E. Africa, 1969), p. 4.
79. Ibid., p. 17.
80. Ibid.
81. Ibid.
82. Ibid.
83. Ibid., pp. 18-19.
84. Cf. D.J. Giford, 'Communication of Legal Standards Policy Development and effective conduct Regulation', *Cornell L.Q.,* 56, 409 (1970-71) (legal system that services as 'a primary institutional force' imposes greater strain on communicaions processes than legal order in which moral standards serve that function).
85. Seminar by Belle Harris, Dar es Salaam, Tanzania, 1969.
86. R. Dahl and C. Lindblom, *Politics, Economics and Welfare: Planning and Politico-Economic Systems Resolved into Basic Social Processes* (N.Y.: Harper, 1953), pp. 97-115.
87. W.B. Harvey, 'Democratic Values, Social Change and Legal Institutions in the Development Process', in A. Rivkin (ed.), *Nations by Design* (Garden City, N.Y.: Anchor 1968), p. 62.
88. L. Cliffe and G. Cunningham, 'Ideology, Organization and the Settlement Experience in Tanzania' in L. Cliffe and J. Saul (eds.), *Socialism in Tanzania: An Interdisciplinary Reader* (Dar es Salaam: East Afr. Pub. House, 1973), p. 131.

8 THE CHOICE TO OBEY*

Presented by the necessity of choice, a citizen will probably obey a new law if the benefits of obedience in his view outweigh its costs. This chapter discusses the factors involved in that decision: the costs and benefits of obedience; the actor's assumptions, perceptions and other subjective factors; and the processes by which the role-occupant decides whether to obey. Since a sensible draftsman must try to predict how its addressees will react to his new law, he must determine the factors that comprise their arenas of choice.

I Interest

Soft development results from disobedience to law or policy. Presented with choice, the addressee disobeyed. He must have done so because he saw obedience as against his interest. People always obey a few laws in institutionalized societies that superficially seem against their interest. Such rare laws occasion wonder at obedience: the payment of high taxes or compulsory military service, for example. People obey most laws because obedience in the ordinary course of social events results in premiums and penalties, considering all the responses of law-enforcement officials, administrators and private individuals. Such laws are *working* rules. They both prescribe and describe behaviour. Any radical change in a working rule, if obeyed, triggers penalties for the actor from the existing social surroundings, not merely formal legal sanctions.

Many rules in development require radical changes in behaviour. Even where law-makers intend the rule to benefit the role-occupant it may not do so in the existing milieu. For example, David Feldman studied thirty-seven small tobacco farms near Iringa, Tanzania.[1] Prior to 1962, a licensing system practically barred African production of tobacco in the area. In that year, twenty Africans established the first African production co-operative. By 1967, aided by the boycott of Rhodesian tobacco and some governmental aid and credit, some 600 Africans farmed tobacco there, about two-thirds of them strangers. Despite a strong government policy favouring co-operatives, the Iringa farming groups became smaller, or changed to individually-owned enterprises. Why this tendency to fission?

* I have been particularly helped in revising this chapter by criticisms from W.J. Chambliss.

Feldman examined a number of variables. The technology of tobacco curing required one barn for every four acres of tobacco under
cultivation. An inexperienced farmer could not farm four acres; when
he became experienced he could farm many more. The co-operating
groups had no legitimate internal hierarchy of decision-making, and no
institutions to resolve internal disputes. Traditional notions of their
appropriate roles and fear of abandoning subsistence food plots until
the tobacco ventures proved successful kept female members of the
co-operators' families from participating, and prevented integrating
staples farming into the general co-operative scheme. Existing legal
rules added their own rewards and penalties. The credit system permitted government agencies to extend credit only to co-operatives. These,
however, included mere marketing co-operatives as well as producer
co-operatives. The applicable land tenure statute required government
to grant land only to co-operative societies, but expressly permitted
co-operatives to divide amongst their members the land they received.
Contract and labour law permitted hiring labour for cash wages, and a
plentiful labour supply existed. Cheap wage labour created high profits.
At the peak labour period, the thirty-seven farms averaged about nine
labourers per farmer; at lowest ebb, three.

Soon farmers found it advantageous to leave the co-operatives.
Technology, institutions for resolving internal conflict, credit and land
tenure rules, and cheap hired labour all contributed to this result,
despite strong governmental policies favouring co-operatives. Where the
total environment rewards disobedience and penalizes conformity, of
course disobedience will result. These premiums and penalties include
other interests besides economic ones: power, esteem, security, political
advantage and so forth. People supply most of them, including officials,
antagonistic interest groups, and members of one's economic class.

Official Activity. In weighing the costs and benefits of obedience,
official activity must be cast into the accounts. The actor, of course,
calculates official action, not *de jure* but *de facto*. Whether I violate
the speed limit depends in part on my estimate of the likelihood of
arrest and conviction and of the probable sentence, not the traffic
ordinance's paper sanctions.

Role-occupants' calculations of anticipated official action sometimes created bizarre results. In the early years of independence,
Zambia made lavish grants to agricultural co-operatives, hoping to
stimulate increased agricultural production. These grants included funds
for clearing and stumping fields. Government did not, however, provide

adequate marketing or transport. The villagers quickly learned that they could earn more by stumping fields than by growing crops. In 1974, Zambia had many fields quietly returning to the bush, that peasants never sowed although the government paid for clearing them.[2]

Disobedient sub-groups, generally. Another set of premiums and penalties resulted from various sub-groups who disapproved of the law. We all find ourselves 'captured' by various groups.[3] Where their informal norms conflict with the official rule of law, the role-occupant must violate the one norm or the other, and thereby incur some sanction, official or informal. It becomes a case of damned-if-you-do, damned-if-you-don't.

If a society changes relatively slowly, such conflicts exist, but with muted dissonance. Unless time or space insulated antagonistic roles from each other, confrontation would resolve their conflicts. What I do in the office may conflict with what I do as a member of my church, or as a parent. The conflict rarely manifests itself because these different activities usually involve different sets of actors. A corporate official can violate the anti-trust laws in his downtown office, while simultaneously earning respect as a conscientious and ethical vestryman of his suburban church, with neither his corporate nor his church colleagues aware of his other role.

Where law induces change, however, the situation differs. Many such rules contradict the older working rules. The older rules, however, retain their own sanctions enforced by unofficial but powerful actors. The new rules of development frequently arise without temporal and spatial insulation. Role conflict, unmuted, may lead to disobedience.

Coercive antagonistic interest groups. Antagonistic interest groups sometimes use private violence to prevent obedience to the new rules. For example, in the United States the Ku Klux Klan and White Citizens Councils lynched and beat blacks who complied with court orders for school integration. Soviet efforts in the early 1920s in Central Asia to induce Moslem women to assert their independence of male domination whipped up counter-revolutionary bands, who murdered some of the women who obeyed the new rules.[4]

Dependency upon antagonistic interest groups. Actors occasionally depend upon people whose interests a new rule adversely affects. Frequently this occurs in bureaucracies, where the reputation, advancement and status of the bureau chief depends upon the behaviour of his subordinates. In order to 'buy' their co-operation, he overlooks their misbehaviour, and himself disobeys the rule or policy. In the 'Society of Captives' (a maximum security prison), authorities evaluated the guards by the conduct of the men in his charge. He could not keep his charges in order, however, by naked force, and higher authority frowned upon constant appeals for help in maintaining discipline. 'The guard, then is under pressure to achieve a smoothly running cell-block not with the stick but with the carrot, but . . . his stock of rewards is limited. One of the best "offers" he can make is ignoring minor offences or making sure that he never places himself in a position to discover infractions of the rules.'[5]

Disobedient reference group. By the term 'reference group' I mean a group which a person desires to join and by whose standards he measures his own behaviour. The most common reference group constitutes the group to which the actor belongs. In development, the village becomes the main reference group for rural people. Bound by ties of kinship and custom, they look to it for emotional and economic security. The village normative structure usually focuses on status. Such a group would likely punish a member who obeyed the achievement-oriented norms of a legal system based on either Contract or Plan. The claims of family, clan or tribe upon civil servants or politicians frequently bred nepotism.[6] Such role conflicts sometimes had striking manifestations. Individuals who became wealthy as Ghana developed came to fear charges of witchcraft from more traditional elements. Margaret Field explained many of the colourful slogans on Ghana's 'mammy lorries' ('Still the same old Bob', or 'All is well') as efforts to ward off such informal sanctions.[7]

Class or strata. In any society, sets of people have broadly similar economic interests arising mainly out of similar roles in production: Entrepreneurs, high-level managers and high civil servants; peasants; wage workers. A host of constraints and resources affected role-occupants within each of these sets more or less equally. They had roughly equal access to communication channels and analogous opportunities and capacities. Thus their advantages or disadvantages of obeying tended to lead to similar behaviour. Common interests tended towards social cohesiveness, creating classes or strata.

II. The Decision Process

Mere naked advantage does not alone determine responses to the law's commands. Often a proposed new rule would in the view of its advocates clearly advantage its addressees, yet not induce the desired behaviour. The addressee's perception of his arena of choice differed from the draftsman's. The two assessments differed for several reasons. The role-occupant may have known of premiums and reward which the officials did not. Peasants knew of subtle peer pressures of which officials remained ignorant. Businessmen assessed the market quite differently than did law-makers who, assuming a particular market potential, reduced the tax burden to induce the entrepreneur to invest.[8] Corrupt officials estimated the probabilities of prosecution differently than law-makers.[9] In other cases, however, the role-occupant's refusal to comply with new rules made for his benefit seemed inexplicable, since he knew of the rule, had opportunity to comply, and the new rules, if followed, demonstrably advantaged him.

Choosing solves problems. New laws pose problems for people: whether or not to obey? How a person solves problems depends upon two factors: his system of problem-solving, and his guides for the unavoidable discretionary choices.

A. Ends-Means

Many people solve their problems by selecting ends and means. Their values identify the ends, more or less ranked. Faced by new law, problem-solving for each citizen becomes merely determining whether the means defined by the law will likely accomplish his personal goals. If not, he will probably disobey. (In the literature of deviance this became anomie theory[10]).

The ends-means system of decision-making maximizes the influence of the actor's values, usually culturally derived. Self-evidently, in conditions of change, these will probably oppose the implicit goals of the new rules. A law prescribing family planning may contradict acculturated notions of the desirable number of children. A law persuading peasants to join a co-operative may run afoul of traditions of individualistic economic decision-making.

Where a law's addressee follows ends-means, the bureaucrat must, inevitably, assume an authoritarian role. If the addressee's goals vary from those implicit in the law, the bureaucrat can only try to coerce or manipulate him into obedience. Manipulation may take the form of a bogus 'participation'. If a person must justify publicly his decision to obey a law, for example, it will more likely conform to law than if he decides secretly. Criminal law has long held that secrecy provides some evidence of consciousness of guilt. Despite a superficial resemblance to participation, forms requiring role-occupants to announce their obedience to law may become only a device to use group pressure to coerce.

B. Problem-Solving

Coerced by threats or promises, or manipulated to give verbal assent to new law but still disliking it, people will likely try without genuine compliance to avoid its sanctions or achieve its rewards.[11] Grudging compliance, evasion or withdrawal will not likely beget the creativity that development requires. Alternatively, the addressee of a new norm can be induced to examine his existential situation, to discover and test alternative explanations for it, and to determine whether the new law is an appropriate solution. If the law addresses a real trouble for the addressee, bases itself upon an adequate explanation, and provides a sensible solution for his difficulties he likely will conclude to obey.

Given a sensible law, problem-solving can nevertheless fail to induce obedience for many reasons. First, the role-occupant may act on the basis of ignorance or mistake, a defence at criminal law.[12] He may not realize the actual constraints and resources of his environment. A farmer who needs credit may pay exorbitant rates to a village money lender because he never learned about the State Agricultural Bank. A foreign investor may not consider a potentially rich mining area for investment because he never knew of its potential.

Second, problem-solving will fail if its addressee explains his troubles inadequately. All of us carry with us domain assumptions to explain particular events. If accurate information can substitute for unsubstantiated beliefs about disease, health programmes will progress. A peasant will more likely boil water from a suspect source if he understands that dysentary comes from germs and not a miasma.

Most explanations for particular troubles derive from larger scale perspectives or models of the world. All of us behave as amateur sociologists. We all have ideas about the structure of the world, and why it works.[13] Our world-view contains categories for classifying events, explanations for reality, and beliefs about the best way to solve troubles in view of these explanations.[14] Ordinarily, we never test our world-view. It serves merely to justify our past activity.[15] Accepted as true, however, it becomes the basis for action, and frequently leads to disobedience to law. A problem-solving methodology which tries to change behaviour must confront the role-occupant not only with accurate data, but also with alternative explanations to those drawn only from his own acculturation.

Third, a problem-solving method will fail if it does not provide some way to test alternative explanations against reality. The peasant who believes firmly that witchcraft causes crop failure will continue so to believe unless he confronts experience that falsifies it. Fourth, a problem-solving system will fail unless the role-occupant confronts alternative possible solutions, and can deliberate upon their probable consequences in the light of reliable data. Finally, such a system must fail if it does not adequately provide for praxis, or learning-through-doing. All of us have, at some point in our lives, knowingly violated the law. On occasion, we all cheat on taxes, or expense accounts, commit adultery, violate traffic laws, shoplift, keep the coin from the telephone when it erroneously returns it. Yet only a few break the law repeatedly and regularly. How officials treat delinquents helps define who will repeat, and who will not. The slum area boy stigmatized as a delinquent, harshly treated by the police, processed through a status-degradation ceremony (the sentencing) and sent to reform school, emerges from the experience with very different self-perceptions and social responses from the middle-class lad who for a similar offence receives a gentle warning not to repeat, and returns to the family bosom.[16] Similarly, agricultural extension agents in Africa frequently passed by 'unprogressive' peasants who in consequence continued ancient and generally unproductive methods of agriculture. Progressive farmers, by contrast, received credit, seed, fertilizer and information from officials. The former disobeyed policies looking towards improvement in agriculture, the other complied. Like slum and middle-class delinquents, the bureaucracy helped create the differences in the very process of enforcing the law.

What one learns from past behaviour also determines later choices. If I cheat on my taxes this year in a particular way, and succeed, I will likely try the same dodge next year. If I speed on a particular stretch of highway and get caught, I will probably attend to the speedometer when next driving there. Where law tries to induce changed behaviour, the same principle operates. The investor induced by investment statutes to build a plant in a country where he has not previously invested, will likely make further investment if successful. If a cash crop fails, a peasant will not likely soon try again. We learn through both personal and vicarious experience. If the first co-operative in an area fails, others learn to avoid co-operatives. If a new crop withers, not only the farmer who planted it but his neighbours learn that the crop seems a loser.

Our learning from experience depends in part on our technological

understanding. A peasant propagandized by the agricultural extension
agent to plant a new crop that fails, shuns the crop. A peasant taught
why the crop seems likely to prosper, and the conditions that will make
it grow, will learn from failure about how to improve his farming. Unless individuals analyse their experience, any setback will likely
preclude future attempts to comply. The rocky road of development
contains many setbacks.

Finally, success in obeying or disobeying a law may change the
individual's self-image. Village society frequently characterizes as
deviant a peasant who obeys a law looking to more 'modern' behaviour,
but officials will likely regard him as 'progressive', and deal with him on
that basis. In time, he may change his self-image into a 'modernizer',
and act to fulfil that image. In particular, he will likely associate more
and more with other modernizing types, forming a deviant modernizing
sub-culture.

Where a law aims at regulating or curtailing existing power (as when
government imposes new environmental regulations on manufacturers),
or seeks to redistribute wealth (as in a taxing statute), problem-solving
will likely teach the addressees only that the law does not advantage
them. Many, probably most laws in development, however, aim at
benefitting their addressees — for example, agricultural labour and co-
operative laws, and laws concerning women's rights. Obedience to such
laws will happen more often if the role-occupant discovers for himself
that obedience serves his advantage. Discovery requires a different
style of bureaucratic behaviour than the authoritarian one dictated by
an ends-means system of decision-making.[17] It requires participation.
Only a problem-solving methodology in which experts help provide
information, explanations and solutions, and in which addressees test
these as well as their own explanations and solutions against their own
experience, offers opportunity for genuine participation between
citizen and his government.

III. Values, Prizings and Other Subjective Factors

Whatever system of decision-making individuals adopt they must make
discretionary choices. Many subjective factors affect these choices. I
have already discussed the consequences of domain assumptions and
ideology; there remain anomie theory, the function of taste, role conflicts and role-self theory.

A. Anomie Theory

Anomie theory states that where internalized acculturated goals conflict

with the means that socially-approved and sanctioned norms permit,
an individual will probably disobey. It assumes conditions that plainly
do not exist in Africa: that a common, acculturated value-set provides
similar goals to practically everyone, and that the norms provide reasonable methods to achieve them for practically everyone, so that only a
peculiarly disadvantaged or abnormal person could become deviant.[18]

Disparities between goals and means may, however, explain some
disobedience in developmental conditions. In societies passing from
Status to Contract or Plan, from political dependence to independence,
the internalized goals of some citizens must conflict with the new rules.

Lionel Cliffe reported a striking example from colonial
Tanganyika.[19] The government introduced regulations to promote rural
change in the late 1940s. They increased in number and scope until
they became a veritable flood during the post-war period (1946-57).
The Native Authorities imposed these rules pursuant to their power to
make orders and rules 'for the peace, good order and welfare of the
native'.[20]

> There were orders on everything from 'improving bees wax and
> honey production in Central Province' to 'the control and eradica-
> tion of banana weevil' around Lake Victoria. Basically . . . they
> would be grouped into three categories: — those dealing with anti-
> erosion measures (compulsory tie-ridging and terracing, de-stocking,
> control of grazing, etc.); and of animal husbandary (cattle, famine
> crops such as cassava or groundnuts).[21]

Those compulsory measures generated a vigorous opposition. Some no
doubt came from 'the resistance . . . to change . . . based on the reluc-
tance to forsake a proven system for others which are less certain'.[22]
Some came from peasant wisdom, that accurately perceived the plans
of the agricolas as uneconomic, or as affected by social conditions
which they had not considered. For example, de-stocking among the
Wanyaturu of Singula, based on a fixed percentage reduction of everyone's cattle, bred resistance because it reinforced stratification. Some
opposition arose because 'the responsible persons had not been consulted'.

Nationalist goals frequently fired disobedience to imposed norms of
agricultural development. Anti-colonialists joined local tribal associations and the co-operative movement. After a long struggle, their
opposition ultimately succeeded under TANU leadership. By 1957 the
Director of Agriculture admitted defeat. 'The era of the big stick', he

said, 'is over.'[23] The acculturated goal of independence induced disobedience to colonial-imposed norms that for all their potential for improving agriculture implied continued African subservience to British rule.

B. Taste

Much modern social science and philosophy treats 'myths', 'perceptions', 'values', 'policy' and 'taste' as identical concepts, stating or implying individual prizings. While generally one need not so conceive their function in research or policy-making, tastes do supply ends or goals in choosing articles for immediate use and enjoyment.[24] These tastes may affect a person's decision to obey or disobey developmental rules or policies. For example, in an Indian village peasants did not adopt an improved wheat seed, capable of twice the yield of traditional seeds. Peasants simply did not like the new seeds as well as the old ones:

> The grains are indeed big . . . so big and tough that the women cannot grind them well in the old stone flour mills. Dough made from the new flour is difficult to knead and hard to bake into good bread. The new bread, which is all a poor farmer has to eat, does not taste like the old bread. [The cows and bullocks] do not like to eat the straw of the new wheat; they will die of hunger if we grow it. The straw is worthless, too, for thatching roofs. It does not even make a good fire.[25]

C. Role Conflicts: Internalized Norms

Role conflicts can emerge because the individual holds to internalized norms that contradict new law. Many African criminal cases occurred when the accused violated a rule of English criminal law because he adhered to a rule of customary law that he felt bound him. In *Rex* v. *Kimonirr*[26] (Kenya, 1916), for example, one Chesang faced charges of causing death by sorcery. Apprehended, pursuant to tribal custom the elders told him to hang himself. Custom required relatives to kill the witch. Chesang's brother, Kipkemai, therefore, gave him a rope which Chesang used to hang himself. An English judge found Kipkemai and five others guilty of the crime of abetting a suicide. The internalized norms to execute a witch of one's own family caused disobedience.

D. Role-Self Theory

'Role-self theory' also purports to account for deviance. To deal with the world, we must analyze and classify our surroundings. We perceive various objects as 'hoe', 'automobile' or 'building'. We classify persons into positions as 'teachers' or 'father' or 'Minister'. Culture creates these categories. We must also classify ourselves within one of these culturally acquired categories. The culture imposes some of these roles upon us; we each become a 'child' to our parents. But we select many of the most important roles ourselves. How others react to our choices mainly determines how and what roles we choose.

> We may lay claims to being a certain sort of person, but this claim must make sense in terms of the culture of those we are dealing with, and we must make those claims stick. To make the claim stick, we must validate it by meeting the cultural criteria of the role. We know we have done this when others, by their responses, indicate acceptance of us as valid specimens of the role . . .[27]

The role that we stake out may determine obedience to law. A girl perceives herself as 'feminine', and steals trinkets to support that style. A boy perceives himself as 'tough' or 'masculine', and steals to make good his claims.

> According to anomie theory, deviant behaviour is a way of coping with a problem of ends and means; of reducing the tension between cultural goals and an insufficiency of institutionalized means. Role-self theory . . . suggests another way of looking at deviance that is difficult to capture in the language of ends and means. It assumes an actor is trying to *tell* somebody something or trying to prove something. More fitting than the language of ends and means is the language of message and the *symbols* that convey it, or of claims and *evidence* . . . The goals we seek and the means we employ themselves express and validate the roles we claim. Where there is a disjunction between goals and means, businessmen may defraud their customers, professors plagiarize, ballplayers cheat. They covertly deviate from part of the role demands in order to fulfill another part.[28]

In every society, life-styles as well as specific economic roles support the values of dominant community groups. Most African traditional societies emphasized status as the principal element of authority. So did colonial society. Thus, many African administrators today perceive themselves as 'big men', with commensurate authority. Status-based authoritarianism easily results in behaviour by bureaucracy and politicians that violates norms looking for participatory decision-making.[29]

Conclusion: The Factor Affecting Choice

Reacting to the enlightenment model of rational man, freely and consciously choosing among alternative possible courses of action, nineteenth and twentieth-century social science substituted irrational man, caught in a web of values and attitudes. Neither works. Of course, values and attitudes help control choice and therefore channel behaviour, but so does reason. Our problem becomes a particular form of the questions of the age: the tensions between rational and irrational, reason and passion, ego and id, science and superstition.

Man makes choices about what he ought to do. He is a problem-solving animal. To understand how reason and unreason both affect behaviour, we must understand each of their contributions to problem-solving.

The theory of obedience and disobedience in Chapter Six purports to explain why people make their choices in the face of law. They must reach the point of choice. That requires a rule, communication and opportunity and capacity to obey. Then they must choose. Their choice depends on interest, perceptions and process. Unpacked, the theory holds that having reached the point of choice, a person will choose to obey a law looking to changed behaviour if:

1. Performance will likely yield a net reward for the role-occupant, including in the balance all the factors affecting choice, including
   a The premiums paid and penalties imposed by existing institutions for such behaviour,
   b. The manifest and latent consequences of official activity;
   c. The sanctions of antagonistic interest groups generally, including
      (i) The sanctions of antagonistic interest groups upon whom the role-occupant depends;
      (ii) The sanctions of disobedient reference groups;
      (iii) The sanctions of other members of the role-occupant's class.
2. The role-occupant will likely obey if he perceives that obedience will yield a net reward (that is, if his assessment of the constraints and resources of his environment matches the assessment the law-maker expected him to make), which depends upon:
   a. If the role-occupant uses a means-ends methodology for deciding whether or not to conform,
      (i) Whether his personal ends match those the law-maker expected him to hold;

(ii) whether his perceptions and weightings of the constraints and rewards of the environment match those the law-maker expected him to have; and

(iii) if he announces the decision to conform or not publicly, the announced decision (but not necessarily the consequent behaviour) will likely lean towards conformity;

(iv) whether the role-occupant has internalized any norm that he sees as so powerfully sanctioned as to outweigh the net gain he thinks he will otherwise receive from obedience to the new law; and

(v) whether his role-self image requires him to disobey the new law.

b. If the role-occupant uses a problem-solving methodology for deciding whether or not to conform,

(i) whether the difficulties the law addresses, the alternative explanations, the data, the alternative possible solutions, and the experience with those solutions match those the law-maker used in deciding to enact the law.

c. If the new law involves matters of immediate use and enjoyment, his personal tastes.

If law-makers propose that a law actually change behaviour — that is, they intend it to be more than symbolic — they must enquire upon all the issues affecting choice. Only so can they propose measures likely to induce obedience. In that sense, the propositions set forth here become, like all theory, no more, but no less, than an agenda for research. If followed, that agenda ought to make more likely accurate predictions about how a role-occupant will respond to the new rule, and hence increase the probability that the commands of law-makers will induce obedience.

In the view of many, that authoritarian proposition constitutes the evil core of social engineering, of planning and of law and development. In most existing legal orders, *they* make and administer laws for the rest of *us*. Before considering that objection, it is convenient first to consider the sorts of behaviour-inducing measures government has at its command. That is the subject of the following chapter.

Notes

1. D. Feldman, 'The Economics of Ideology: Some Problems of Achieving Rural Socialism in Tanzania', in C. Leys (ed.), *Politics and Change in Deve-*

loping Countries (Cambridge: Cambridge UP, 1969), pp. 85-112.

2. S. Quick, 'Aspects of Co-operative Development in Eastern Province. (Lusaka): Department of Government, University of Zambia, 1973) (cyclostyle).

3. A. Cohen, *Deviance and Control* (Englewood Cliffs: Prentice-Hall, 1966), pp: 10, 84.

4. G. Massell, 'Law as an Instrument of Revolutionary Change in a Traditional Milieu: The Case of Soviet Central Asia', *Law and Society Review*, 2, 179 (1968).

5. G.M. Sykes, *The Society of Captives: A Study of a Maximum Security Prison* (Princeton, N.J.: Princeton UP, 1958), p. 25; cf. M. Dalton, 'Conflict between Staff and Line Managerial Officers', *Am. Soc. Rev.*, 15, 342 (1950); S.M. Lipset, *Agrarian Socialism* (Berkeley: University of California Press, 1950), pp. 255-75.

6. V.T. Le Vine, *Political Corruption: The Ghana Case* (Stanford: Hoover Institute Press, 1975).

7. M. Field, *Search for Security: An Ethno-Psychiatric Study of Rural Ghana* (London: Faber, 1960).

8. See below, Chap. 15.

9. See below, Chap. 10.

10. Cohen, *Deviance and Control*, p. 76; R.K. Merton, *Social Theory and Social Structure*, rev. ed. (Glencoe, Ill.: Free Press, 1957), p. 146.

11. B.F. Skinner, *Beyond Freedom and Dignity* (N.Y.: Knopf, 1971), pp. 92-3.

12. See, e.g., Zambia: Penal Code, Sec. 10.

13. H.M. Johnson, *Sociology: A Systematic Introduction* (New York: Harcourt, Brace and World, 1960), p. 487.

14. See above, Chap. 4.

15. E.A. Hoebel, *The Law of Primitive Man: A Study in Comparative Legal Dynamics* (Cambridge: Harvard UP, 1964), p. 284.

16. See E. Rubington and M.S. Weinberg (eds.), *Deviance: The Interactionist Perspective*, 2nd. ed. (New York: Macmillan, 1973).

17. See below, Chap. 13.

18. Cohen, *Deviance and Control*. For criticism of anomie theory, see E. Lemert, *Social Problems and Social Control* (Englewood Cliffs, N.J.: Prentice-Hall, 1967), pp. 4-5; J. Blake and K. Davis, 'Norms, Values and Sanctions' in R. Paris (ed.), *Handbook of Modern Sociology* (Chicago: Rand, McNally, 1964), p. 456; M.B. Clinard (ed.), *Anomie and Deviant Behaviour* (Glencoe, Ill. The Free Press, 1964), pp. 12-14.

19. L. Cliffe, 'Nationalism and the Reaction to Enforced Agricultural Improvement during the Colonial Period' (Makerere: EASIR Papers, 1965).

20. Tanganyika: Native Authorities Ordinance, 1927, sec. 9(16).

21. Cliffe, 'Nationalism'.

22. H.K. Schneider, 'Economics of African Aboriginal Societies', in M. Herskowitz and Harvitz (eds.), *Economic Transition in Africa* (Evanston: Northwestern University Press, 1964), p. 53.

23. Lord Hailey, *Native Administration in the British African Territories*, Part I (London: HMSO, 1950).

24. J. Dewey, *Theory of Valuation* (Chicago: University of Chicago Press, 1939).

25. M. Marriott, 'Technological Change in Underdeveloped Rural Areas', *Ec. Dev. and Cultural Change*, 1, 261, 265-6 (1952).

26. 6 E.A.L.R. 159 (1916).

27. Cohen, *Deviance & Control*, p. 98.

28. Ibid.

29. See below, Chap. 16.

9 CONFORMITY-INDUCING MEASURES

After explaining existing behaviour, law-makers must use the legal order to restructure the arena of choice to influence role-occupants to behave in new and more desirable ways. Often law-makers assume that coercion alone can accomplish that objective. Myrdal argues that 'There is little hope in South Asia for rapid development without greater social discipline, which will not appear without general laws and regulations backed by compulsion.'[1] Here I discuss the inadequacy of such traditional sanctions in development and suggest an alternative schema.

I Concept of Conformity-Inducing Measures

A. The Traditional Definition of 'Sanctions'

Two core meanings pervade lawyers' uses of the word 'sanctions': Sanctions come from courts, and consist mainly of pains and penalties. Blackstone observed that 'with regard to the sanction of laws, or the evil that may attend the breach of public duties, it is observed, that human legislators have for the most part chosen to make the sanction of their laws rather vindicatory than remunatory, or to consist rather in punishments than in actual particular rewards'.[2] In jurisprudence the word ordinarily refers only to punishments for breach of a rule.[3] The core conception has both institutional and ideological sources. A truly autonomous legal system would clearly use courts to impose sanctions. During the nineteenth century hardly any other formal sanctioning institutions existed. Courts had virtually no capacity to order any except negative sanctions. They lacked power of the purse. They had no available administrative machinery except police, gaolers and sheriffs. Using these, they could only punish.[4] The traditional definition found nourishment in nineteenth-century beliefs. First, if law reflected custom, and custom reflected values, then the law too must reflect values. Punishment threats should induce the occasional, badly brought up deviant to behave properly. Second, analytical positivism defined law as a command. A command differed from 'other significations of desire by this peculiarity: that the party to whom it is directed is liable to evil from the other, in case he comply not with the desire.' Law in this sense *implied* punishment.[5]

This ideology created a sort of word fetishism. No rule became 'law' unsupported by sanctions, that is, by punishment. Therefore, every law needed related threats of punishment. So deeply ingrained was (and is) this notion, that policy-makers frequently left the question of sanctions to the Parliamentary Draftsman's discretion.[6] When Myrdal proposed coercion to cure 'soft' development, he succumbed to the same word fetishism. Punishment as a behaviour-inducing measure at best can effect only incremental change. It implies a particular model of social change.

I have already argued[7] that activity becomes institutionalised when society's various repetitive behaviour patterns serve up net rewards for the participants, taking each of their arenas of choice as unchangeable. In consequence, most people come to accept the existing normative system as right and proper. They do not need threats of sanction to obey.

Negative punishments can best enforce already institutionalized law. They function merely to nudge into conformity the occasional deviant. Arnold Rose hypothesized that 'the usual punitive sanctions of fine or imprisonment are likely to be more effective where the prevailing behaviour of the majority of the population is already in accord with the goals sought by the statute'.[8] Punishment therefore becomes the sanction governing elites and classes choose to maintain the *status quo*.

The contrary also seems true. Punitive sanctions probably will not change behaviour if deviance arises because the individual's institutional environment, legal sanctions aside, regularly rewards disobedient behaviour. Societies rarely have sufficient resources to impose the massive punishments required to induce radically changed behaviour by negative sanctions alone. Those sanctions instead will produce mainly evasion, antagonism or withdrawal.[9]

The laws concerning cash crops in Tanzania present an example. Practically every local District Council in Tanzania had a by-law, reflecting the late colonial policy, requiring farmers to grow cash crops. The North Mara District Council (Cultivation of Agricultural Land) By-Laws, 1966,[10] for example, required each farmer to cultivate at least two acres of cash crops. Since few Tanzanian farmers worked more than four acres, the Ordinance bore heavily on small peasants. It carried only negative sanctions (Shs. 500 fine, or six months imprisonment). Despite these harsh sanctions, the ordinances failed. If a market for cash crops flourished, farmers needed no ordinance to grow them. On the other hand, jailing farmers for failure to sow a cash crop that the soil could not support, or which had no market, became pointless and unenforceable. Economic institutions such as marketing facilities, seed and other technological inputs, and the availability of financing and credit determined whether farmers grew cash crops, not the law. The threat of criminal punishment could not coerce farmers to do what, without these supports, seemed quite mad.

Laws likely to induce development, however, address issues such as did these Tanzanian ordinances, rather than those of conventional rules, that usually only reinforce approved, established behaviour. Far from reinstitutionalizing custom, development looks to inducing new and unaccustomed ways of life. Development cannot succeed unless the state somehow induces role-occupants to comply with new rules; but that states a mere tautology. Development *is* new roles and new behaviour. Limiting available means, however to compulsion and coercion (as Myrdal seems to do), only guarantees either that the new rules will remain immured in the statute books, or that they will look only to incremental change.

B. *'Conformity-Inducing Measures'*

The sociological literature contains broader definitions of 'sanctions'. Schwartz and Selznick defined it as a court-imposed change in the life conditions of a role-occupant.[11] This definition, restricted to court action, omits all the other institutions through which the state might act to affect choice. Schwartz elsewhere proposed a different definition, suited to his study of sanctioning processes among Israeli kibbutz. He defined 'sanctions' as 'the administration of gain or loss to an actor. Sanction is *positive* when it results in gain for the sanctioned, and *negative* when it results in loss.'[12] This definition resonates with Skinnerian psychology, where operant conditioning serves the function that Schwartz assigns the word 'sanctions'.[13] It lacks sufficient breadth for our purposes. Disobedience can arise for reasons apart from the reward structure — failure of communication, want of opportunity, lack of capacity and so forth. To be useful, a definition of 'sanctions' must comprehend the entire range of potential legal solutions for all possible causes of disobedience. Moreover, officials frequently act to induce role-occupant behaviour defined only in policy, not in positive law. Imprisonment for non-payment supported the poll tax in colonial Kenya. Government imposed the tax, however, to compel Africans to work for expatriate firms in the export enclave. Focusing attention upon sanctions for failure to pay the tax too easily blinds one to the law's larger purpose. The meaningful questions about sanctions concern the interplay between what government expects from the law, and the activities it undertakes to get it.[14] Schwartz's definition obscures those questions.

Arens and Lasswell defined 'sanctions' as all measures to induce compliance with legal norms.[15] This is at once too broad and too narrow, for on its face it includes private sanctioning but excludes from consideration all prescriptions addressed to role occupants except formal law.

It seems better to abandon the word 'sanctions', and instead use 'conformity-inducing measures' to include the entire range of processes the state uses to induce obedience. It goes beyond the activity of judges and jailers, but excludes private responses to role-occupants' behaviour.

II. A Typology of Conformity-Inducing Measures

The measures the state undertakes in order to induce conformity invariably arise as solutions to emergent troubles. Like all solutions, they should address explanations for the trouble in question.

I have already proposed a theory to state the variables that determine obedience to law:[16] the rule and its communication, opportunity and capacity to obey or disobey, rewards and disrewards, problem-solving processes and perceptions, tastes, role-self images, ideology and other subjective factors. If the particular disobedience (or expected disobedience) at issue results from poor communication, the sensible remedy will ensure the law's communication to its addressees, not administer a whipping. If the role-occupant cannot comply for lack of skills, depositing him in a dungeon will not increase compliance. If the explanation for disobedience focuses on the processes by which role-occupants decide to obey, the state ought to reform those processes, not impose fines or imprisonment.

Our general model of law and development explains behaviour in part by the activity of state officials. Where the official responds directly to the activity of the role occupant by levying punishment or giving a reward, his activity becomes a 'direct measure'. To induce cash cropping one might punish those who refuse (as in the Tanzanian ordinances mentioned above), or reward those who do. Both are direct measures.

Most official measures to change the arena of individual choice do not aim directly at role-occupants, but at the various actors who comprise their social environments. Depending upon the reasons for disobedience, the solution for not growing cash crops might improve communications to the farmer, teach him appropriate techniques and skills, provide fertilizer, seed and credit, or ensure a market for his crop. I denote any conformity-inducing measure for these sorts as 'roundabout' measures.[17]

A third sort of conformity-inducing measure might be called 'educative measures'. The actor's choice does not depend merely on the environment, but also on a host of subjective factors. Government frequently attempts to induce compliance by education, moral suasion, propaganda and the like. If law-makers believe (as apparently they did in the Ivory Coast) that polygamy subverts development, one might outlaw it subject to various punishments.[18] A slower, but ultimately perhaps cheaper solution might require an educational and propaganda campaign to persuade people that polygamy is bad and monogamy good. Finally, the explanation for disobedience may lie in the individual's decision-making process. Changing these processes I shall call 'deliberative measures'; this chapter does not discuss them.

This catalogue reveals the narrowness of the traditional definition of sanction. Direct, roundabout, educative and deliberative measures can all affect the role-occupant's arena of choice. The traditional definition instead limits draftsmen to punishments. That confines the law-maker to incremental change. For development, that is too narrow by half.

Here I discuss direct, roundabout and a few educative measures.

III The Limits on the Use of Direct Measures

Each of these sorts of conformity-inducing measures has its own advantages and disadvantages, which constrain its utility in particular cases. Together, these constraints make up a significant component of the limits of the legal order's capacity to effect social change. Just as society limits the effectiveness of law by limiting its communication, so does society limit that effectiveness by limiting government's capacity to mount conformity-inducing measures. This section discusses the inherent limits of direct measures.

The Paradox of Punishment. Punishment follows disobedience. Its invocation confesses that in this case its threat failed to induce conforming behaviour. The inadequacy of punishment arises from this fact. We deal with the criminal today, but impose a punishment that has already proven itself inadequate. Classical theories of punishment admitted this failure, but punished anyway, either on mystical theories of retribution, or on equally mystical theories that punishing this individual would deter others by demonstrating that (in Holmes' phrase) the law will keep its promises.[19] Other theories admit the failure, and justify incarceration as providing opportunity for authorities to rehabilitate the criminal — a notion that assumes that crime mainly stems from wrong but alterable attitudes and values.

Unlike punishment, rewards do not confess their own failure, but celebrate their success. Every time a court sentences a criminal, it publicizes the law's weaknesses. Every time the state pays a reward, the payment advertises the advantages of obedience. Rewards may induce favourable responses. Punishments frequently only persuade role occupants to make greater efforts to conceal their disobedience.

Initiation of Interaction. With punishment, the state must ferret out offenders. The initiative lies with officials, not with role-occupants. With rewards, the complying role-occupant must initiate the sanctioning process by coming forward to claim the reward. This differential initiative has several consequences. In order to punish, the state must expend bureaucratic resources to uncover non-compliance. If only a few will disobey, this may make sense. If, however, the law produces a high rate of disobedience, policing the rule may drain bureaucratic resources, probably to no avail.[20] Bureaucrats must live in society, and they rarely enforce unpopular laws. On the other hand, where practically everyone obeys the rules, a reward system requires an unduly large bureaucracy to ferret out fraudulent claims. A bounty for killing predators is appropriate only because only a very few people usually claim the rewards. If the number of bounty claimants grew very large, the state might more cheaply punish those who did not hunt.

Development conditions usually create many disobedient persons. Rewards will therefore usually cost less to administer than punishments. This has special importance for countries with few trained bureaucrats. Moreover, where the law threatens to punish a great number of violators, sanctioning agents cannot enforce the law against every one. Whom they prosecute depends on official discretion.[21] Their power grows correspondingly. Prosecutors and police frequently use statutes forbidding fornication, adultery, social gambling and the like in the United States to harass political or other opponents.[22] Zambia's political leadership will be sorely tempted so to use the Leadership Code, which reaches a very great many people.[23]

Who initiates the bureaucrat-client relationship affects their apparent power over each other. By claiming a reward the role-occupant triggers bureaucratic activity. The role occupant, therefore, feels that he controls the administrator. With a punishment, the situation reverses. A collaborative relationship can exist only when power seems equally distributed. Obedience most easily develops in a collaborative relationship. Two-way communication also readily occurs in such a context.[24] Rewards encourage a collaborative relationship; punishments do not. How much rewards structure participation depends upon role-occupants appearing to control officials by demanding rewards. To the extent that a reward lies in the official's discretion, the role-occupant must petition for it, rather than demanding it from him. That of course undermines the collaborative relationship. Participation calls for entitlements, not discretionary grants.

Neither governments nor judges, however, will ordinarily make rewards a matter of duty to pay. Statutes which permit rewards typically make their payment highly discretionary.[25] Constitutions forbid the compulsory taking of property without compensation,[26] but rarely forbid the granting of tax or other benefits entirely in official discretion. The same courts that hold that a person has a 'right' not to suffer punishment entirely at official discretion, will label a reward as a 'privilege'.[27] Even procedural rights frequently hang on that distinction. Both constitutions and the rules of natural justice[28] extend a right to a fair hearing before government disadvantages a person. Where, however, government granted a reward (e.g. a licence to do business), judges have labelled it a privilege, and placed it outside both constitutional and common law protections.[29]

Inducement to Creativity. In general, punishments can easily sanction failure to perform to a set standard. They adjust poorly to varying levels of performance. Rewards, however, adapt easily to a sliding scale of performance. This fact, coupled with the initiative accorded the role-occupant by a system of rewards, makes drive, enthusiasm and creativity more likely under a reward than a punishment system.

Legitimacy. Punishments for breaching an innovatory rule appear to penalize role-occupants for pursuing what they see as their own interests. Rewards, on the other hand, appear to permit non-compliance, but to reward the particular role-occupant who elects to obey. Legitimacy demands that rulers appear to govern in the interests of the governed. When a new law demands conduct at odds with customary folkways, a reward system permits the governor to appear to conform to the folkways, while nevertheless using state power to induce change. The governor seems to act only when the role-occupant desires that he act. Rewards for compliance with innovatory laws do not threaten legitimacy; punishments do.

Punishment threatens legitimacy in another way. If government commands particular behaviour on pain of punishment, disobedience too easily becomes confounded with defiance. Government places its prestige at hazard. If government merely announces that it will reward desired behaviour, any failure of the law's addresses to claim the reward does not necessarily undercut legitimacy. Especially in Africa, where legitimacy became a scarce good, governments might well avoid confrontation.

Under development conditions, the state likely seeks to implement innovative, radical rules, although possessing scant reserves of either bureaucratic resources or legitimacy. Development demands creativity. A reward system seems typically to induce changed behaviour at lower costs than punishment.

IV The Costs and Benefits of Roundabout Measures

These measures operate directly upon one set of role-occupants to affect the behaviour of another set. If government desires to prevent political leaders from engaging in private business, it can enact a Leadership Code to prohibit them from so doing under threat of punishment. Or, it might adopt roundabout measures, such as nationalizing housing (thus destroying the most abundant opportunities to violate the Leadership Code), or prohibiting banks from extending credit to leaders. Roundabout measures usually serve to ensure obedience to some government policy unexpressed in formal law. Not seeing that direct measures functionally serve the same purposes as roundabout measures confuses much sanctioning theory. One can too easily ignore the issue, whether rules that directed bankers to issue credit only to co-operatives, for example, induced farmers to join co-operatives, and study only whether bankers obeyed the rule. The direct rule or regulation outdazzles the policy addressed to the farmers.

Conversely, every law that directs A to change his behaviour towards B also restructures the environment of B, and hence becomes a roundabout measure affecting B's behaviour. This principle explains many unanticipated consequences of laws.[30] In Soviet Central Asia during the 1920s, the new revolutionary government sought to free Moslem women from intolerable bondage, in part by inducing women to unveil. It supported this policy by direct and roundabout measures. The unveiled woman, however, restructured the environment of Moslem male. Many responded by casting the unveiled woman into the streets, where they eventually became prostitutes. Had a government policy favoured Moslem males casting off their women, requiring unveiling would have served as an appropriate roundabout measure.[31]

Self-evidently, only roundabout measures can succeed if disobedience results from poor communication or lack of opportunity or
capacity to comply. If peasants cannot grow rice because of insufficient
water, fining or imprisoning them will not do as well as cutting irrigation channels. Where the environment rewards disobedience, one must
choose between direct and roundabout measures. If peasants do not
claim rights under a land reform measure because landowners threaten
economic reprisals, the state can respond either by a bonus (a direct
measure), or suppress the intimidation (a roundabout measure). The
costs and benefits of roundabout measures in such cases depend on four
criteria: general effectiveness, drain on bureaucratic resources,
promoting participation and effect on legitimacy.

General Effectiveness. Once established, roundabout measures
operate to structure choice without the repetitive, continuing over-
sight of officials, that is, the change becomes institutionalized. So long
as the institutional matrix continues to reward disobedience rather than
compliance, the continuing effectiveness of innovatory rules depends
on what officials do. To institutionalize wanted behaviour, government
must use roundabout measures to change the arena of choice.

For example, the first attempts to induce the Tanzanian Masai to
join co-operatives provided water holes and dip tanks, which the Masai
greatly desired; these served as rewards for joining the co-operatives.
Government did not provide a ready market for meat, to draw the
Masai into the money economy. Although the Masai got their dip tanks
and water holes, the constraint and incentives of traditional Masai life
continued. They channelled Masai behaviour into traditional folkways.

Bureaucratic Resources. Roundabout measures, once institutionalized, exert their influence without continually spending bureaucratic
resources to reward or punish. To organize peasants into marketing co-
operatives, one might threaten penal sanctions if they do not join. On
the other hand, one might limit agricultural credit to co-operatives, pay
higher prices for co-operatively-produced goods, or supply transport
and fertilizer only through co-operatives. Such widescale change, of
course, involves heavy outlays. It usually seems less costly to enact a
statute supported by penalty or reward than to institute wide-scale
related changes in other institutions. Creating appropriate linkages
between different sorts of institutions lies at the core of development.
At this point, conformity-inducing measures meld with the larger problems of planning a viable, internally linked and integrated economy and

society. Such changes seriously burden administrative resources at the outset. A law supported only by direct measures, however, too often serves only symbolic purposes.[32]

Participation. Direct measures usually sharply narrow choice ('your money or your life'). Roundabout measures require the role-occupant to make continuous decisions about his own well-being. He must decide whether to embark upon cash farming, or to continue subsistence agriculture; whether to join a co-operative or to work in a manufacturing plant; whether to have unlimited offspring or to plan his contribution to the population explosion. If changed behaviour most easily becomes internalized and institutonalized when role-occupants make decisions for themselves, self-evidently, law-makers ought to select roundabout measures.

Legitimacy. For the same reasons, these measures do not threaten governmental legitimacy as does punishment. Government does not appear to command particular behaviour. The role-occupant makes his own decision.

Roundabout measures paradoxically can best solve development difficulties in the long run, but pose the most difficult short-term problems. They require more care and initially more bureaucratic resources to institute than direct sanctions. The agricultural ministry in Tanzania could more easily drill bore holes and dip tanks for the Masai than create a marketing organization for their cattle. In the long run, however, limiting conformity-inducing measures in that case to bore holes and dip tanks nearly sank the whole project.

V Educative Measures

For want of a better word, here 'educative measures' subsumes the most amorphous category of conformity-inducing measures. I exclude questions of general education (literacy and numeracy, the development of high-level manpower in general, and so forth), and skill-training (measures directed at want of capacity). I discuss here only the law itself as moral suasion, and ideology.

A. Moral Suasion

Political leaders everywhere try to persuade citizens to obey particular laws or policies. The general notions of obedience earlier advanced argue that moral suasion alone cannot ensure obedience to new law, because that requires communication, opportunity to conform, advan-

tage to the role-occupant and so forth.[33] All the exhortation in the
world will fail to persaude Eskimos to grow roses, any more than they
will do so under threat of the lash. Of the many sorts of moral suasion,
this section discusses only the very existence of the rule as persuasion
to obey.

How can the very existence of a law bring about a change in values
or attitudes? Obviously different rules have different consequences.
Laws prohibiting marijuana smoking in the United States did not
change community attitudes towards its use. Laws prohibiting adultery
have existed for centuries, but adultery remains a favourite indoor
sport. On the other hand, other rules, at first unpopular, in time came
to express popular attitudes. For example, white attitudes in the
southern United States towards school desegregation changed markedly
since the school desegregation decision of 1954.[34]

Three alternative points of view exist on this subject. One holds that
since law only reinstitutionalizes custom, it cannot have any independent socializing force.[35] At most, it can strengthen and support already
existing social attitudes.[36] On the other extreme, another view,
common among lawyers as well as sociologists, believes that the very
existence of law-in-the-books has an educative effect. Renée David
wrote a sophisticated 'ideal' Civil Code for Ethiopia, asserting that
while he knew that it would take many years for behaviour to conform
to the Code, Ethiopia needed a statement of the social ideal.[37] J.
Willard Hurst has repeated that law codifies and promulgates the
authoritative values of the community.[38] Soviet scholars made the same
assertion.[39] Too many unhappy examples exist, however, where the
promulgation of law did not result in acceptance by the population.
The Indian Constitution purportedly outlawed discrimination against
untouchables that has not significantly changed the values and attitudes
of most Indians. The United States Constitution asserted the equality
of persons before the law, without noticeable effect on white attitudes
for generations.

A third position lies between these two extremes. Law can change
values and attitudes only under some conditions. We must specify those
conditions. The literature contains little more than speculations, and I
have nothing more substantial to offer. In the first place, law will more
readily change attitudes where it first changes behaviour. Attitudes then
change to justify the new activity.[40] The income tax in the United
States has almost universal legitimacy although when introduced a voci-
ferous opposition attacked it bitterly. Behaviour towards untouchables
in India changed only marginally; likewise attitudes towards them. The

Ivory Coast did not enforce its statute outlawing polygamy; that the statute lies in the books has probably not changed attitudes towards polygamy. The books contained many statutes presumably making bribery and corruption criminal. Where unenforced, attitudes towards corruption did not change either. Although values and attitudes follow behaviour patterns, rather than precede them,[41] not every case of changed behaviour results in changed attitudes. Slaves did not all accept slavery.[42]

A variety of conditions affect the influence of behaviour upon attitudes and values. (1) The more legitimate a new rule under existing ideologies or attitudes,[43] the more likely the individual will build it into his value-set. (2) Addressees will not likely internalize a rule requiring its targets to act against their own interest. (3) If addressees see a rule as worthy of compliance, they will more likely internalize it. Its source must appear authoritative and prestigeful.[44] Both by their rhetoric and by their behaviour, law-makers and administrators must appear to take the law seriously.[45] (A law against corruption carries little weight when enforced by a corrupt policeman.) A respected reference group obeying the law may help. (Prestigious farmers in the area adopt a new agricultural programme.) It may help, too, to attach a serious sanction, demonstrating that the law-makers are serious about the law.[46] Finally, an authoritative communication channel through which the law comes may add an increment of legitimacy.

Scholars frequently argue that a rule will succeed in changing attitudes only if it concerns an area of life the role-occupant perceives as instrumental and not sacred. Rules concerning farming technology, for example, supposedly concern instrumental matters, but rules concerning sexual relationships, or the family, are frequently seen to intrude on the sacred. Keeting hypothesized that change will more likely occur in 'elective' areas of life.

> Instrumental techniques, elements of taste and self-expression, secondary group relations, and low-status position are apt to be highly malleable, for in these areas freedom, individualism and novelty are apt to be tolerated, even encouraged, and the range of acceptable alternatives may be rather broad. Conversely, conservatism and stability are apt to be found in those areas of human experience within a particular culture which are sharply crystallized, backed by tradition, enforced by sanctions, associated with prestige and status, overlaid with symbolism and ritual, saturated with strong emotions, and judged to be essential for the good citizen.[47]

Several examples seem consistent with Keeting's speculations. Throughout Africa, wherever farmers had a new cash crop, they changed technologies and land tenure patterns very quickly.[48] Efforts to change family patterns (e.g. attempts to impose monogamy on polygamous African societies) generally failed.[49]

Before accepting the proposition proposed, however, we need further data. African countries adopted many programmes to change agricultural patterns, but only some succeeded. In general, success attended adequate communications, sufficient resources, vigorously enforced measures to induce the desired behaviour, and participation in decision-making.[50] Programmes to change family patterns in Africa have never received analogous levels of resources or official commitment. None succeeded in changing behaviour. Whether concerning instrumental or sacred sectors, if behaviour does not change, the bare law-in-the-books will not likely change attitudes or values.

Finally, our assumption of the distinctions between governors and governed affects our beliefs about the educative consequences of law. If governors, and governed constitute necessarily disparate strata, then of course we must address the question of how the governors by mere enactment of a law change the values and attitudes of the governed. The question would not arise under a participatory system of social control. Genuine participation in deciding whether or not to enact a new rule would cause changed values and attitudes. Participation requires institutions that stress process over substance, and scientific method over all else. Given participation in such institutions; attitudes and values consonant with the scientific method will develop. If explanations serve as surrogates for values, then the process of problem-solving ought to bring subjective perceptions in accord with those that justify the new order.

If so, law-makers cannot rely heavily on the mere existence of law to educate in conditions of development. Those rules frequently sharply oppose the values, attitudes and myths associated with older patterns. Governments with fragile legitimacy cannot easily make law stipulating new behaviour appear to emanate from 'authoritative and prestigeful' sources. If the rule requires its addressees to subvert their own well-being, they will not likely adopt its teaching. Rules of law as educative instruments in themselves provide weak tools for change.

B. Ideology

Models of the world (i.e. ideologies) plainly help guide the discretionary choices that arise when people decide whether or not to obey a new law.

There are three available definitions. One perceives ideology as dogma, designed to trap its targets in its rhetoric;[51] another, as scientific hypothesis capable of subjecting otherwise inarticulated domain assumptions to empirical test;[52] a third, as scientific propositions paradoxically based on an act of will, not reason.[53] An ideology can fulfill a scientific function, but in the final analysis it must always rest upon an assertion of whose troubles matter.

Ideologies can, of course, motivate people to accomplish wonders. Ideologies, however, are not mere fungible rhetoric. In development, science, not dogmatics, will probably induce changed behaviour, for three reasons. Dogmatic ideologies present a unchangeable perception of reality. Unlike scientific ones, they cannot adjust to changing circumstances and new experience. Their adherents only slowly learn by doing. Second, dogmatic ideologies promote unthinking acceptance; scientific ones, problem-solving and creativity. Third, changed behaviour requires participation, a co-operative, problem-solving endeavour. Dogma wars with problem-solving.

Some varieties of socialist thought match the scientific mode. This element provides an alternative explanation for its attraction to the poor:

> . . . Socialism has a very special meaning for the new nations. It becomes the ethic for a system of political discipline emphasizing science — science for its own sake as a symbol of progress and as a form of political wisdom. In keeping with this aim, socialism offers a set of unified developmental goals that stress roles functional to modernization and the achievement of workmanlike, rational society in which people lend one another a helping hand because they feel themselves a part of a community effort towards industrialization . . .[54]

Future shock has become our special syndrome. Precisely because behaviour constantly changes, ideologies constantly change. Whether individuals adopt dogmatic or scientific explanations will determine whether they can adapt to future shock. Development implies continuous change.[55] Educative measures that teach a scientific ideology proceed slowly, but ultimately can become the foundation for the most efficacious and long-lasting sort of developmental measures.

VI A Catalogue of Conformity-Inducing Measures in Development

Conformity-inducing measures purport to solve problems. They must aim at the causes of disobedience. A catalogue of such measures must therefore rest on the explanation for disobedience earlier advances. The catalogue here limits itself to punishment, rewards and round-about measures.

1. The state through its agents can affect the arena of choice of role-occupant in four ways only:

   a. By direct measures: rewards or punishments imposed or awarded after the role-occupant disobeys or obeys;

   b. By roundabout measures: efforts to change the behaviour of others whose actions structure the role-occupant's arena of choice; and

   c. By educative measures: efforts to change the domain assumptions, perceptions of reality, role-self images, ideologies and prizings of role-occupants; and

   d. By deliberative measures: changing the processes of decision by role-occupants.

2. Punishments have the following costs and benefits in conditions of development:

   a. They occur after disobedience, and therefore advertise the in-efficiency of the law;

   b. With high rates of disobedience, they require many agents to police the rule; a low rate of disobedience correspondingly re-duces enforcement costs;

   c. With high rates of disobedience, officials have a correspondingly greater discretion as to when and against whom to impose punish-ments;

   d. They make the role-occupant dependent upon the bureaucrat;

   e. Where other factors reward disobedience, punishment induces efforts to evade, not obey;

   f. Punishments do not easily adjust to varying levels of performance, and therefore do not readily stimulate creativity and increased achievement;

   g. They tend to provoke confrontations with authority and there-fore undercut legitimacy.

3. Rewards have the following costs and benefits:

   a. They occur after obedience, and therefore advertise the efficacy of the law;

b. With high rates of obedience, they require correspondingly large resources to pay the rewards; a low rate of obedience correspondingly reduces enforcement costs.

c. With high rates of obedience, and limited resources, they increase discretion as to when and to whom to pay rewards;

d. If the payment of rewards does not rest on official discretion, it subordinates the bureaucrat to the complying role-occupant;

e. Where other factors reward disobedience, and the reward will not stimulate compliance, the role-occupant need not conceal his disobedience;

f. Rewards can readily adjust to varying levels of performance, and therefore induce creativity and increased achievement;

g. They enhance legitimacy.

4. Roundabout measures have the following costs and benefits:

a. Only roundabout measures can induce obedient behaviour where disobedience results from either (a) poor communication, (b) lack of opportunity or (c) capacity to obey.

b. Only roundabout measures can work where the state stipulates the desired activity of role-occupants as policy rather than in a formal norm.

c. The original cost of establishing roundabout measures will likely exceed that of equivalent direct measures; once established, they will likely cost less than direct measures;

d. Roundabout measures require role-occupants constantly to decide for themselves, whether or not to comply with a rule or policy without explicit threats by officials, and therefore they enhance participation;

e. As facilitative law, roundabout measures strengthen existing power relationships unless the state takes special measures to avoid that result;

f. Roundabout measures avoid confrontations between government and role-occupants, and hence maintain or increase legitimacy.

5. Therefore, measures likely induce obedience to law looking to radically new behaviour by role-occupants will match the following table ['+' means appropriate, '−' means inappropriate] :

Explanation for Disobedience (from Chap. 8 & 9)	Punishment	Reward	Roundabout	Remarks
Failure of communications	−	−	+	Improve communications.
Physical inability	−	−	−	
Inappropriate social place	−	−	+	Change social place; decrease opportunity to disobey.
Failure of others to supply necessary inputs	−	−	+	Ensure supply of inputs.
Incapacity of role-occupant	−	−	+	Provide necessary capacity.
Costs known to role-occupants outweigh benefits	+ / −	+ / −	+	Changing rewards and penalties offered by other institutions leads to institutionalization; rewards and punishments by officials do not. Punishment appropriate only with a small group of expected disobedient addressees.
Inaccurate individual assessment of actual costs and benefits	−	−	−	Use educative measures or change conditions of problem-solving.
Personal goals at variance with those implicit in law	− / +	+	+	As above. Punishments and rewards may work. Punishment appropriate only with a small group of expected disobedient addressees. Change reward structure of other institutions.
Law requires distasteful performance	− / +	+	+	As above.
Role-conflict arising from internalized norms	− / +	+	+	Educative measures may help. Participation in problem-solving the most helpful.
Inappropriate role-self image	− / +	+	+	As above.
Inaccurate domain assumptions	− / +	+	+	

This catalogue suggests three observations:

1. Punishments ('coercion') will work in surprisingly few situations. Usually they will work best to change the behaviour of a few people where law-makers cannot alter the institutional matrix to favour them. Frequently, this occurs when the law in question abolishes or reduces the powers and privileges of existing elites or ruling classes, such as land reform laws, the imposition of higher taxes, laws improving the status of women, or the expropriation or nationalization of property. In each case, the state must invoke coercion against the strata that the new laws disadvantage.

2. Educative measures plainly do not reach most causes of disobedience directly. Suasion to obedience alone will not induce conformity.

3. The range of possible behaviour-inducing measures grows once one includes roundabout measures. Rather than increased 'coercion' to remedy soft development, alternatives to *both* coercion and exhortation seem more likely to work.

Conclusion

I have tried in this and the two preceding chapters to explicate a general theory of how law influences behaviour. If the legal order can help relieve poverty and oppression, it must change the behaviour ultimately of individual citizens, but also of bureaucrats, judges, parastatal managers, policemen and legislators. Obviously, any development effort must first understand the uses and limits of political society's principal tool, the legal order.

Because African legal orders have authoritarian structures, their use to change behaviour rightly conjures up fears that law and development may only supply knowledge to enable elites to manipulate and coerce the mass more efficiently. The foregoing analysis demonstrates, however, that behaviour will not easily change except through participation by the role-occupants themselves in both law-making and implementing. Only they can provide information concerning their actual access to information about the law, their opportunity, capacity, interests, beliefs and perceptions, and their decision-making processes. Unless law-makers consult them, the law-makers will only by luck uncover the roots of the behaviour at issue. If law-makers do not, they will only by equally happy accident draft successful rules.

Successful law implementation also demands participation by the law's addressees. Communication of the new rule must involve a two-way, face-to-face situation. That demands participation. Role-occupants will not easily change perceptions, role self-images, or domain assumptions save in a problem-solving, participatory process. The more participatory and public their decision, the more likely they will choose to obey.

Now obviously some laws demand behaviour against individual interests. If a land reform law requires landowners to surrender their property, neither participation, roundabout measures, nor increased two-way interactions will make reform more palatable. Such laws require punishments or rewards, direct, rigorous sanctions to succeed.

Most necessary behavioural changes for development, however, lay their burden on those whom they should benefit. Peasants must learn new techniques; bureaucrats, development administration; workers, the ways of workers' councils. One can effect some of these changes through coercion. According to our analysis, however, surely these will more likely to lead to soft development than real change.

This analysis, therefore, *requires* participation. The usual justifications for participation of humanism, the value and dignity of the human personality, or for its own sake too easily fall before assertions that participation nevertheless moves too slowly, and inefficiently, and too readily excites mass demands that Government cannot satisfy. Punishment, however, may well produce quick results, frequently more so than participation. But, quick changes of behaviour that punishment creates rarely become institutionalized into new, lasting behaviour patterns. The legal order as an instrument of change requires participation not merely because of ethical imperatives, but rather because over the long pull no other way works.

To induce compliance through participation requires participatory deliberative processes. It requires changing how individuals decide whether or not to conform to new rules. The success of such deliberative measures depends upon careful fashioning of appropriate direct, roundabout and educative measures. Unless the state communicates its rules, unless the addressees have opportunity and capacity to comply, unless obedience is their interest and they perceive it so, suasion, ideology and participation alike will only persuade role-occupants that they are wise to disobey. Soft development does not arise because people are stupid. It arises because they are shrewd.

Notes
1. G. Myrdal, 'The "Soft State" in Underdeveloped Countries', *U.C.L.A. Rev.*, 15, 1118, 1125 (1969).

2. Sir W. Blackstone, *Commentaries on the Law of England* (Oxford, 1765), p. 56.
3. E.W. Patterson, *Jurisprudence: Men and Ideas of the Law* (Brooklyn: Foundation Press, 1953), pp. 159-70; R.M. MacIver, *Society – Its Structures and Change* (N.Y.: Long and Smith, 1933), pp. 248-52; J. Hall, 'Legal Sanctions', *Nat. L. Forum*, 6, 119 (1961): J. Austin, *The Province of Jurisprudence Determined*, H.L.A. Hart, ed. (N.Y.: Noonday Press, 1954), p. 18a.
4. See below, Chap. 12.
5. Austin, *Jurisprudence Determined*, pp. 13-14.
6. Notes on Legislative Drafting. Prepared for Use in the Attorney General's Chambers Dar es Salaam. (n.d.; no pub.) 23.
7. See above, Chap. 6.
8. A. Rose, 'Sociological Factors in the Effectiveness of Projected Legislative Remedies', *J. Legal Ed.*, 11, 470, 472 (1959).
9. B.F. Skinner, *Beyond Freedom and Dignity* (N.Y.: Knopf, 1971); see also H. Wheeler (ed.), *Beyond the Punitive Society – Operant Conditioning: Social and Political Aspects* (San Francisco: W.H. Freeman, 1973).
10. Tanzania: Northern Mara District Council (Cultivation of Land) By-Laws 1966 (Government Notice No. 32, 1/27/67).
11. R. Schwartz and J. Skolnick, 'Two Studies of Legal Stigma', *Social Problems*, 10, 133 (1962).
12. R. Schwartz, 'Social Factors in the Development of Legal Controls: A Case Study of Two Israeli Settlements', *Yale L.J.*, 63, 471 (1956).
13. See B.F. Skinner, *Science and Human Behaviour* (N.Y.: The Free Press, 1953), pp. 62-9.
14. H. Packer, 'Book Review', *University Chicago L. Rev.*, 29, 586 (1961).
15. R. Arens and H. Lasswell, *In Defence of Public Order: The Emerging Field of Sanction Law* (New York: Columbia University Press, 1959).
16. See above, Chap. 6.
17. I have borrowed the word 'roundabout' from R.A. Dahl and C.E. Lindblom, *Politics, Economics, and Welfare* (New York: Harper and Row, 1953).
18. R.J. Mundt, 'The Internalization of Law in a Developing Country: The Ivory Coast's Civil Code', *African L. Stud.*, 12, 60 (1975).
19. O.W. Holmes and H. Laski, *The Holmes-Laski Letters*, Howe, ed. (Cambridge Mass: Harvard University Press, 1953), p. 806.
20. Dahl and Lindblom, *Politics, Economics and Welfare*.
21. It is not a defence to a criminal charge that others are unpunished for the same offence. See e.g., *Oyler* v. *Bales*, 368 U.S. 448 (1962); *People* v. *Gray*, 254 Cal. App. 2d 256 (1967).
22. F. Remington and V. Rosenblum, 'The Criminal Law and the Legislative Process', *Ill. L. Forum*, 481, 493-4 (1960).
23. See below, Chap. 20.
24. See above, Chap. 7.
25. See e.g., Zambia: European Officers' Pension Ordinance, 1965; Zambia: Transferred Officers (Dependents) Pensions Ordinance, 1965; Kenya: Pensions Act, 1967.
26. See e.g., Ghana: Constitution, 1969, Chapter IV, Art. 18 (1) (c) (i); Zambia: Constitution, 1973 Part III, Sec. 18(1).
27. See, e.g., *Merchants Bank Ltd* v. *Federal Minister of Finance*, (1961) All N.L.R. 598 (Nigeria: Fed. Sup. Ct.); U.S. *ex rel. Knauff* v. *Shaughnessy*, 338 U.S. 537 (1950); *Bailey* v. *Richardson*, 182 F.2d 45, 55-59 (App. D.C. 1950) aff'd 341 U.S. 918 (1951).
28. A term of art in English administrative law. It requires that both sides be heard and that persons not be judges in their own case. See J.F. Garner,

Administrative Law, 3rd ed (London: Butterworth, 1970), p. 112.

29. *Merchants Bank* v. *Federal Minister of Finance* (1961) All N.L.R. 598 (F.S.C.).

30. Y. Dror, 'Law and Social Change', *Tulane L.R.*, 33, 787 (1959).

31. G. Massell, 'Law as an instrument of Revolutionary Change in a Traditional Milieu: The Case of Soviet Central Asia', *Law and Soc. Rev.*, 2, 179, 204-211 (1969).

32. J.M. Edelman, *The Symbolic Uses of Politics* (Urbana, Ill: University of Illinois Press, 1964).

33. See Chap. 6 and 16.

34. *Brown* v. *Board of Education*, 349 U.S. 294 (1954); see K. Clark, 'Desegregation: An Appraisal of the Evidence', *J. Soc. Issues*, 9, No. 4, p. 2 (1953).

35. L. Friedman, 'Legal Culture and Social Development', *Law and Society Review*, 4, 29 (1969).

36. See above, Chap. 4.

37. R. David, 'A Civil Code for Ethiopia', *Tulane L. Rev.*, 37, 187 (1963); See also G. Myrdal, *An American Dilemma: The Negro Problem and Modern Democracy* (N.Y.: Harper, 1944).

38. J.W. Hurst, *Law and Social Process in United States History* (N.Y.: Da Capo Press, 1972); J.W. Hurst, *Law and the Conditions of Freedom in Nineteenth-Century United States* (Madison: University of Wisconsin Press, 1956).

39. V. Chkhikvadze, *The State, Democracy and Legality in the USSR, Lenin's Ideas Today* (Moscow, Progress Publishers, 1972), p. 50; see G. Eorsi, 'Some Problems of Making the Law', *E.A.L.J.*, 3, 272 (1967).

40. E.A. Hoebel, *The Law of Primitive Man: A Study in Comparative Legal Dynamics* (Cambridge: Harvard University Press, 1964).

41. Ibid.; Skinner, *Science and Human Behaviour;* see J. Glendhill, 'The Reception of English Law in India', in W.B. Hamilton (ed.), *The Transfer of Institutions* (Durham, N.C.; Duke University Press, 1964).

42. H. Aptheker, *Negro Slave Revolts in the United States* (New York: International Publishers, 1968).

43. W. Evan, 'Law as an Instrument of Social Change', in A. Gouldner and S.M. Evans (eds.), *Applied Sociology* (New York: Free Press, 1965), pp. 285-9.

44. Ibid.

45. Ibid.

46. J. Andenaes, 'General Prevention', *J. Crim. L.C. and P.S.*, 43, 176 (1952).

47. F.M. Keesing, *Cultural Anthropology* (N.Y.: Holt Rinehart & Winston, 1962), pp. 353-4.

48. See e.g., P. Hill, *The Migrant Cocoa Farmers of Southern Ghana, A Study in Rural Capitalism* (Cambridge: Cambridge University Press, 1963).

49. Mundt, 'The Ivory Coast's Civil Code'.

50. See U. Lele, *The Design of Rural Development: Lessons from Africa* (Baltimore: Johns Hopkins University Press, 1975).

51. L. Dion, 'Political Ideology as a Tool of Functional Analysis in Socio-Political Dynamics: An Hypothesis', *Can. J. Ec. and Pol. Sci.*, 29, 47, 49 (1969); H.M. Johnson, *Sociology: A Systematic Introduction* (New York: Harcourt, Brace and World, 1960), p. 591; L. Binder, 'Ideology and Political Development', in M. Wiener (ed.), *Modernization, The Dynamics of Growth* (New York: Basic Books, 1964), p. 194.

52. D. Apter, *The Politics of Modernization* (Chicago: University of Chicago Press, 1965), p. 314.

53. See Chap. 3 above; see A.W. Gouldner, *The Coming Crisis of Western Sociology* (New York: Avon Books, 1970), p. 112.

54. Apter, *Politics of Modernization*, pp. 329-30.

55. S.P. Huntingdon, *Political Order in Changing Societies* (New Haven: Yale University Press, 1968).

10 HIGH-LEVEL BRIBERY: A CASE STUDY IN DISOBEDIENCE AND CONTROL

The usefulness of this theory of disobedience and conformity-inducing measures remains to be demonstrated. I attempt this by examining the question of high-level bribery.

I The Definition of the Troubled Situation

Corruption festers outside as well as within the developing world. Every edition of the *New York Times* reports some incident of corruption in the United States. The sorts of corruption, their explanations and consequences, however, vary with time and place. 'Corruption' has no single, commonly-accepted definition.[1] It includes bribery, extortion, speculation and nepotism of public officials. It seduces high-level officials (that is, members of the political elite: high civil servants, officials of parastatals and leading political figures), or low-level governmental employees. Each sort has its own explanations and results. High-level corruption affects development differently from low-level corruption. It involves actors with great power. High-level officials set the tone for government. A hot-handed Minister or Permanent Secretary likely has equally greedy subordinates. High-level corruption generates primitive accumulation of capital for political elites, and thereby facilitates the growth of a bureaucratic bourgeoisie.[2] This chapter deals only with high-level bribery, where a public official makes a public decision in consideration of money or other personal favours that others give him to influence the decision.[3]

Does high-level bribery pose a real trouble for the LDCs? The modern notion of bribery arises out of our property rules, which grant owners power to make decisions concerning it.[4] In an earlier era, public office was a property right. The lord of the manor governed the manor because he owned it, just as today a private corporation governs a company town because it owns it. Bribery had no relevance, for the owner of property might make decisions about it for any reason.

The earlier structures of colonial government followed this model. The Dutch East India Company for a time governed through a system under which officials did not receive a salary. They paid an annual fee to the Company for the prerogatives of office. The Company expected them to grab what they could.[5] In Africa, King Leopold's authority to rule the Congo came from his personal ownership. The chartered companies in East, Central and South Africa ruled because they owned the charters that authorized them to do so. If the British South Africa Company governed in Northern Rhodesia solely in consideration of private gain, it did not act corruptly; it profit-maximized.

The rise of bureaucratic government accompanied a formal divorce between office holding and property in the office.[6] The personal property interests of the office holder now lying outside the office, the office holder supposedly made decisions not in consideration of private advantage, but to serve public purposes.[7] For example, in Ghana during the Nkrumah regime, the collection officers of the Cocoa Marketing Board openly robbed the till, usually demanding and receiving 10 per cent of the farmer's crop as an illegal 'commission' for performing their public duty to buy the crop. After the 1966 *coup*, an investigating commission heard many suggestions that government delegate collections to private businesses.[8] These firms would profit from the collections just as the bureaucrats did from bribes. The bribes were illegal, but not the profits, although both involved farmers' payments to the collecting agency. The one involved public office, the other private property.

A set of sociological arguments attack this concept of bribery. In many LDCs, popular morality supposedly condones bribery.[9] In West African traditional society, most chiefs could assign plots of fallow land to farmers.[10] With his request, a peasant traditionally brought 'drinks', a small customary gift to the ruler. Some claim that the custom carried over into modern times, with civil servant as surrogate for chief. In traditional society, however, clear-cut bounds on gift giving and family obligations made corruption less likely.[11] 'Moreover, the deliberate exploitation of traditional practices and the rational calculation of the benefits to be derived are completely alien to customary social relationships.'[12] No doubt Ghanaians, like the rest of us, can distinguish between chief and civil servant. That after a *coup* every military leader cited corruption as a reason for overthrowing the previous regime evidences popular revulsion to it, whatever the traditional custom.

The sociological perception characterizes corruption as a problem of *deviance*, or violations of internalized norms. Our concern lies in *disobedience*, or violations of positive law. Positive law everywhere makes bribery illegal. Whether bribery poses serious difficulty for the LDCs raises another question. Myrdal argues that it does, because it introduces an element of irrationality into every development programme.[13] For example, in Ghana during the latter days of the Nkrumah regime, government decided to direct trade away from the hard-currency Western states towards barter arrangements with the socialist bloc. Endemic corruption infected the licensing scheme that controlled the import trade.[14] The Eastern European governments would not play along. Ultimately, corrupt ministry officials granted licences mainly to imports from the Western, private-enterprise, hard-currency states, taking as naught deliberate government policy.[15]

High-level bribery introduces irrationality because it transfers decision-making power from public officials to bribe-givers. Public officials should exercise power and discretion to benefit the public. They should, therefore, consider only the public interest. When they accept a bribe, they permit the private interests of the giver to control the decision. The bribe-giver, not the official, in effect decides. Bribery thus becomes part of the sociology of power.[16]

High-level bribery raises not merely a moral question, but also a policy issue: ought officials to abandon critical developmental decisions to bribe-givers, mainly expatriate businessmen? A wide array of American academics have argued that bribery promotes development because it thus transfers decision-making power.[17] No doubt, many of the development programmes subverted by bribery 'interfered' with market forces. Governments, however, rarely undertook them whimsically, but usually in desperation, to protect foreign exchange reserves against the ravages of falling commodity prices, to ensure new investment after waiting in vain for the private sector, to protect natural resources against private despoliation. To return decisions about such matters to the private sector through bribery allows the fox to guard the geese.

That bribery sometimes became a significant source of capital accumulation for bureaucrats and politicians also had its defenders. In Nigeria in 1964 the Federal Minister of Aviation, also Chairman of the state-owned Pools [lottery] Corporation, persuaded public lands authorities to lease him four industrially-zoned acres for 99 years at £1,000 per year. The next day he leased the same property to the Pools Corporation for £4,000 per year. A Nigerian newspaper defended him on the ground that Nigeria is a capitalist country, capitalism needs capitalists, capitalists need capital, and how else could a Nigerian accumulate capital?[18]

All of these economic arguments defend a policy bias that entrepreneurs can develop the Third World better than government.[19] Defending bribery on this ground assumes *sub silentio* the advantages of *laissez-faire*. In Africa, defending high-level bribery really defended

continued dependence upon the multinational corporations. Such
bribes in Africa frequently came from entrepreneurs looking for government favours. Since so few Africans had substantial capital, most entrepreneurial bribe-givers were foreigners. During the Nkrumah regime,
British and US firms with excellent reputations for honesty at home
actively bribed Ghanaian officials. Many American multinational corporations confessed that they bribed regularly. High-level bribery
became a principal mechanism for the continuation of external control
over internal decision-making despite political independence.[20]

II Legal Prohibitions

The former colonies entered the development period with penal codes
that defined bribery relatively narrowly. As it grew into a major
obstacle to development, the statutes broadened their scope. Today,
every country in the developing world owns a broad panoply of
statutes, frequently ambiguous, overlapping and vague, reaching every
sort of official bribery. I examine some of these statutes with respect to
the persons they cover, what acts they prohibit, mental element, proof
and sanctions.

A. Who is Covered

Coverage concerned two distinct issues. First, which state officers came
under the statute? Second, did it forbid giving as well as receiving
bribes?

1. *Which officials*? The principal disputed question concerned the
inclusion of parastatal officers. Penal statutes usually originated before
the post-independence flood of public corporations.[21] The formula
used in the East African Penal Codes, for example,[22] outlawed bribery
by or to 'any person . . . being employed in the public service.'[23] 'The
public service' did not include officers of parastatals.[24] They, however,
fell under another section, prohibiting kickbacks to employees anywhere.[25] The gists of the two crimes differed only marginally. Malawi
simply listed covered organizations in a Schedule, which changed from
time to time.[26] Tanzania's bribery statute since 1971 reached employees of the government, the East African Community and its institutions, local authorities, TANU and its affiliates, trade unions, and
public and private corporations in which one of these owned a majority
interest.[27]

2. *Corruptors as well as corruptees*? Most statutes reached those who
offered as well as those who received a bribe.[28] Even those jurisdic-

tions that did not expressly outlaw offering or giving one caught the bribe-giver as solicitor, aider or abettor.[29]

B. Actus Reus

Statutes often defined official bribery overbroadly.[30] Ghana defined it as 'bribery, willful oppression and extortion, or any other act contrary to the public order or prejudicial to the economic or financial interest of the Republic'.[31] This Act seemingly snared the driver of a government lorry who negligently smashed it.

C. The Mental Element

A requirement of specific criminal intent can cut down an overbroad statute's potential for mischief to the innocent.[32] Innocent action, otherwise within the apparent statutory ambit, will thus unlikely be trapped. Corruption statutes more frequently than not lacked even this minimal potential stumbling-block to conviction. The British Colonial Office Penal Code of the 1930s, widely in force throughout the Empire, covered only bribes received or given 'corruptly'. The Court of Appeals for Eastern Africa read this with its dictionary meaning: 'perverted from uprightness and fidelity in the discharge of a duty; influenced by bribery and the like; venal'.[33] So construed, the payment itself became proof of the state of mind. In Kenya, the statute created a rebuttable presumption that any person in public employment who received private money did so corruptly.[34]

D. Proof of Guilt

Some people argued that the law of evidence, the presumption of innocence, and the requirement of proof beyond reasonable doubt, shackled bribery prosecutions. In fact, corruption statutes frequently created presumptions adverse to the defence, or otherwise relaxed the requirements of criminal procedure favouring of the prosecution. One such device allowed as proof of bribe-taking evidence that the accused had assets unexplained by his legal sources of income.

The Home Secretary of India said in the debates leading to the passage of the Indian Prevention of Corruption Act, 1947, that its sec. 5

> . . . intended to deal with that kind of misdemeanour in which Government servants or public officers with no ostensible means of support or inadequate support are living obviously above their income and are in a position to invest in property which it appears

on the face of it to be impossible that they should have had the
money to acquire, or at any rate that they should have got those
resources honestly. It is particularly difficult to pin it down because
in cases of that kind the only thing that Government or the police
can find is that there is a man who has no ostensible sources which
can be accounted for as the basis of extravagant expenditures,
although no specific action can be alleged against him or proved in
the way of accepting a bribe or obtaining money by corrupt means;
and the object of this section is that it shall be possible for Government to detect and punish officers who have managed to evade
detection in that way.[35]

Section 5 of the Indian Act forbade 'habitually' accepting bribes. Proof
that the accused person, or any other person on his behalf, was 'in
possession, for which the accused person cannot satisfactorily account,
of pecuniary resources or property disproportionate to his known
sources of income . . . proved habitual corruption'. The accused could
rebut the presumptions by accounting for the assets. The statute both
reversed the presumption of innocence, and permitted conviction for
the unwritten crime of unexplained assets under a bribery indictment.
Similar provisions were found in some African Codes.[36] Some statutes
went even further. Ghana provided that the findings of a statutory
Commission of Enquiry, obtained under the loosest rules of evidence,
could become *prima facie* proof of corruption in any subsequent criminal trial. It thus allowed the prosecution to prove its case under the
vaguest procedural rules, but required the accused to disprove it under
the strict rules of criminal evidence.[37]

E. Sanctions

Every country had broad provisions to snare corrupt officials. They
differed most widely, however, in their statutory sanctions. Zambia
exemplified the wide disparity in maximum sentences. A conviction for
bribery and corruption by officials carried a maximum punishment of
three years.[38] A conviction under the secret commissions section[39] had
a maximum penalty of two years. If the secret commission dealt with a
transaction with government, a local authority 'or a public body having
the power to impose rates or entrusted with the expenditure of government funds or grants' the punishment might reach five years, although
the same act could also be bribery and corruption by an official (three
years). A member of a business corporation with majority government
ownership apparently would ordinarily incur only a two-year penalty.

Sanctions differed widely between jurisdictions. A misdemeanour in Zambia with a maximum penalty of five years in Kenya became a felony and subject to a shs. 10,000 fine and/or imprisonment for seven years. If the matter concerned a government contract it carried a maximum sentence of 10 years.[40] Some governments, obviously at their wit's end over corruption, adopted more draconian sanctions. In Tanzania, between 1963 and 1974, the Minimum Sentences Act required a *minimum* imprisonment of two years and twenty-four strokes of the cane.[41] Nkrumah's Ghana imposed a maximum sentence of twenty-five years.[42] Other non-African countries have imposed the death penalty.

III Explanations

How can one explain the widespread bribery of high-level officials in the face of this seemingly impregnable wall of legal prohibitions? To generate explanations, I look to the general theory of obedience advanced earlier. I assume officials knew that bribery is illegal.

A. High Public Officials: The Receivers of Bribes

1. *Opportunity to Obey.* Self-evidently, no individual official disobeys the law because he could not do otherwise. Why, however, did so many high officials in so many countries accept bribes? Vast opportunities to disobey ordinances outlawing widely desired gratifications inevitably breed disobedience, for example, laws against gambling, prostitution, marijuana or alcohol. Corruption, too, flourished in a rich feedbed. Lincoln Steffens gave a simple explanation for corruption in the United States: Given opportunity, he said, ordinary men will act corruptly.[43] 'Men steal when there is a lot of money lying around loose and no one is watching.'[44] Throughout the world, officials engaged in bribery when they had a limited amount of rich goodies to distribute, and potential recipients anxious to pay for them.

Development everywhere generated rules permitting government to dispense favours. India needed its Prevention of Corruption Act (1947) because:

> The scope for bribery and corruption of public servants has been enormously increased by war conditions and though the war is now over, opportunities for corrupt practices will remain for a considerable time to come. Contracts are being terminated; large amounts of Government surplus stores are being disposed of; there will for some years be shortages of various kinds requiring the impositions of con-

trols, and extensive schemes for post-war reconstruction, involving
the disbursement of very large sums of Government money, have
been and are being elaborated. All these activities offer wide scope
for corrupt practices and the seriousness of the evil and the possibility of its continuance or extension in the future are such as to
justify immediate and drastic action to stamp it out.[45]

What was true of India was true of Africa.

The statutes or legislative instruments creating power to distribute
governmental largesse and working rules of the applicable government
departments created the opportunities for bribery. Four conditions
predominated: broad and uncontinued discretion; minimal procedures
for accountability; secrecy; and the very existence of the private sector.

By granting very broad discretion to responsible officers or Ministers
in the authoritarian Colonial tradition, the law itself raised the port-
cullis to bribery. The Control of Goods Act of Zambia[46] permitted the
President to impose wholesale or retail price control 'whenever it
appears to him necessary or expedient'. Pursuant to this power, he
promulgated Regulations[47] that empowered the Minister to fix maximum and minimum prices for goods; to prohibit 'any person, any
specified person or any person of a specified class or group' to increase
prices for any commodity above the official ceiling; to fix 'the maximum, minimum or specified price of any commodity irrespective of the
cost to the seller', and to control the quality and quantity of goods
sold. Not a whistle limited this unbounded discretion. Speaking of
Southeast Asia, Myrdal observed that governmental policies to control
private enterprise became 'individualized and discretionary . . . Partly
out of necessity, but partly by prediliction and choice, government
policies become implemented less by general rules than detailed, individualized, discretionary, administrative choices . . . The wholesale
resort to discretionary administrative controls . . . increased the
demands on administration. Such controls breed corruption; the spread
of corruption, in turn, gives corrupt politicians and dishonest officials
a vested interest in retaining and increasing controls of this type.'[48]

Extensive discretion in parastatal management became the rule.
Executive officers and directors made large purchases and let substantial contracts without significant guidelines. A substantial number
seized the moment to exchange corporate favour for private gain.[49]
Procedures created further opportunities for bribery. These enabled
officials to award government favours without adequate study, reports
by trained staff, comments by interested parties, or public discussion.[50]

They allowed high officials to give favours with few requirements to account. That, too, enlarged discretion. In short, corruption did not (as many believe) necessarily reflect vast concentrations of governmental power. The contrary existed in Africa. It reflected the weakness of control by the centre over its agents.

Secrecy led to the same result. The British tradition of governmental secrecy, perhaps the most stringent in the world,[51] continued in her former colonies. Secrecy shielded decisions from scrutiny. Governmental secrecy drew reinforcement from the British tradition that held business affairs almost inviolate from government inquiry, let alone public exposure. In 1964, for example, no researcher could see the oil exploration licences issued by the Nigerian Government to private firms. Until the *coup* in Ghana in 1966, import licensing operated in deepest secrecy. The Zambia Pioneer Industries (Relief from Income Tax) Act, 1965, provided substantial income tax relief to any company that the Minister certified as a Pioneer Industry. The application for the certificate, however, had to remain secret 'except at the instance of such company'.[52] Finally, the very existence of the private sector offered extraordinary opportunities for high-level bribery. Given expatriate and local private businessmen in competition for government favours, and a private sector in which to invest ill-gotten gains, the itch of high-level bribery intensified.

Development through an authoritarian state structure generates unaccountable power. Africa crawled with opportunities for high-level bribes. The more opportunities to bribe, the more the bribery.

2. *Capacity to Obey.* Scholars sometimes argued that very low salaries induced corruption.[53] That did not explain high-level corruption, for political elites fell into the highest income class in Africa. Nor did the claims of the extended family on political elites explain bribery.[54] That might explain some nepotism in public affairs. It hardly explained official corruption that built legendary Swiss bank accounts in millions, and fur-lined luxury for the officials involved. Few high-level officials truly lacked capacity to resist bribery.

3. *Interest.* Bribery, of course, had enormous economic rewards. Other costs and benefits included:

a. *Political Rewards.* Politicians care about power as well as with money. Much high-level bribery, especially in West Africa, came about to provide funds for political purposes, just as did much corruption in

the United States. In most of Africa, the political parties originally
followed the British example, acting as private clubs whose managers
competed for political power. As private clubs, they received their funds
from private contributions. In theory, these came from party adherents.
In fact, of course, most political financing came from wealthy individuals
or business seeking political favours, in Africa as in the United States.
In parts of Africa, officials skimmed government contracts for that
purpose.

> The root of the matter is that political parties need money, and the
> small subscription from the average man is not available. The large
> subscription from the man of influence must, therefore, take its place
> and the accession of certain large sums to the party funds represents
> something not reprehensible, but notably self-sacrificial, on the part
> of those who are the channels of this communication. An unofficial
> percentage on a contract (and there are some big contracts), the
> compulsory purchase of land (i.e. condemnation under right of
> eminent domain) at unorthodox prices, a little wise direction in the
> development of real estate — these must not be too hastily
> condemned.[55]

The 'commission' on government contracts in Ghana became institutionalized. The party created a corporation, NADECO. The Cabinet
formally passed a resolution creaming off 10 per cent of every government contract to NADECO for Party financing.[56] (Although Ghana was
a *de facto* one-party state from about 1960 and a *de jure* one-party state
after 1964, it continued British forms of party financing.) In fact large
portions of the commissions stuck to private hands. Moreover, once the
miasma of corruption crept in, it overwhelmed most levels of government. Import licences went up for grabs; so did exchange control per-
missions, taxes, government land, and government contracts. Western
Nigeria had a similar history.[57] 'Commissions', originally finding excuses
as political financing, became a device to personally enrich members of
the political elite.

   b. *Criminal Sanctions.* The inducements of wealth and power weighed
in against bribery's potential costs. Existing criminal statutes threatened
enormous penalties. In making the cost-benefit calculus, however, high-
level officials inevitably discounted the amount of paper sanction by its
probability. Difficulties of detection, likelihood of prosecution and
lenient sentencing practice combined to make that very low.

Bribery cannot easily be uncovered. Like prostitution, gambling or drug offences, bribery has no specific victim. Lacking a victim, no individual called attention to the crime. No corpus delicti existed upon which a policeman might stumble. Nor did enforcement officials in the usual course vigorously expose bribery. Lower-level officials did not ordinarily police their political and administrative superiors. Even where the Constitution declared their posts independent of political control,[58] realities played hob with the legal fiction of prosecutorial independence. Finally, the draconian punishments set out in criminal statutes were rarely imposed. In 1973, Zambia convicted a former Permanent Secretary for receiving bribes to procure citizenship for Asian businessmen who feared measures requiring Zambian ownership of small enterprises. The crimes carried a maximum sentence of five years' imprisonment on each count, or twenty-five years in all. The official paid a fine of some $9,500 to avoid nine months in prison. The courts hit petty thieves harder.

Tap-on-the-wrist sentences for high-level corruption cases arose because of the punishment paradox. Penological theory holds that punishment has several purposes: general and special deterrence; the satisfaction of public feeling; restraint; and rehabilitation. When a 'respectable' person was convicted, these purposes frequently conflicted. In the case of the Permanent Secretary mentioned above, retribution and general deterrence spoke to a long prison term; a Permanent Secretary, however, obviously seems an excellent risk against recidivism. Special deterrence and requirements of rehabilitation, therefore, argued for no punishment at all. For the best of reasons, high status criminals everywhere receive gentle treatment.

c. *Reference Groups.* Departments or even whole Ministries tolerated and even encouraged bribery.[59] Chinua Achebe's great novel of Nigeria, *Things Fall Apart*, vividly portrayed the subculture of corruption. In many cases it became a taught disobedience.

If an individual's reference group fails to reinforce the law with informal sanctions for deviant behaviour the law loses a strong buttress.

We were all living in a country in West Africa where corruption was a very normal part of the scene and the assumption of corruption was part of everyone's equipment for his daily business.

Such a climate of corruption is in itself an important factor. There is a constant interaction between the willingness to pay bribes and the willingness of officials to receive them. People normally

behave in a way that the people they live with behave. In a society
with a high level of corruption, hardly any citizen can carry out his
business, avoid trouble with the government, and generally get
through life comfortably, without acquiescing to some extent at
least in the prevailing corruption.[60]

4. *Internalized Deviant Norms.* If society expect 'big men' to be
corrupt, they will in time believe that they can legitimately take bribes.
Krobo Edusei, a long-time Minister in Nkrumah's Ghana, spoke
passionately: 'The sweetness of the pudding is the eating thereof!'[61]

5. *Domain Assumptions.* Our unexamined domain assumptions derive
from the ambient culture. Some claimed that Third World politicians
held three domain assumptions that justified corruption. Many had
campaigned in the anti-colonial wars. They perceived government as
the very prize for which they fought. Having won, they thought themselves entitled to feast at its table.[62] Secondly, during the freedom
movment, they believed that government was 'theirs', not 'ours' and that
cheating expressed anti-colonialism. These cheating hearts beat on after
independence.[63] Thirdly, the 'idea of the national interest is weak
because the nation is new'.[64] Being new, its citizens and officials lacked
a strong sense of nationhood. They confused public with private
property. One cannot easily test these explanations. At any rate, they
can at best explain corruption by the first-generation independent elite.
Some corrupt officials today were children during the anti-colonialist
struggle.

6. *Anomie Theory.* Some say that in many of the new states get-rich-
quick became the dominating goal of the newly educated classes who
manned the senior posts of government. 'Politicians in West Africa do
not come from an established patrician class. Most of them are "new
men" and have therefore had no opportunity to develop standards
different from the rest of society . . .'[65] Myrdal writes that the exodus
of colonial officials 'left South Asia with few competent administrators
with the stricter Western mores [sic]'.[66]

This explanation, as so often with explanations from anomie theory,
fails for non-falsifiability. It purports to explain the self-aggrandize-
ment of elites in terms of acculturated goals of material enrichment.
The evidence of those goals becomes the very behaviour to be explained.

7. *Role-self Theory.* Many ministers and other officials lived on a

conspicuously opulent scale. Ministers in pre-*coup* Nigeria drove down the Marina in Lagos in Mercedes, followed by girl friends in a second Mercedes, and assorted body guards and hangers on in a third. A high official in a parastatal organization in Nkrumah's Ghana boasted of six Mercedes.[67] The 'big man' occupied a well-defined role not only in indigenous society[68] but in colonial society as well. The lowly assistant district officer in the Colonial Service had a small bungalow with a single bedroom; as a District Officer he might move to a two-bedroom house; by the time he became a Regional Commissioner he would have three bedrooms and a study. The Colonial Secretary had a mansion; and the Governor lived in the State House with innumerable rooms, a gaggle of flunkies and servants, and a huge motorcycle escort to clear the roads for the big man whenever he drove about. Some Africans learned from their former masters. They used their political position to gain the wealth necessary to act out the big man role.

8. *The Decision to Disobey.* The decision to disobey the law invariably occurred secretly, where the official needed to discuss the matter only with his corrupter. Officials negotiated government contracts privately rather than taking publicly bids. They made decisions to grant or reject an application for an import license privately. Social pressures against bribery had no chance to function.

B. Businessmen: The Givers of Bribes

Why did businessmen offer bribes, although often expatriate bribers had sterling reputations for probity in their own countries? For example, a general contracting firm with an excellent character in England obtained several large Ghana government contracts through bribery.[69] Assuming its behaviour in England warranted its reputation there, why the double standard?

High-level bribery inevitably followed a sort of Gresham's Law. Government favours (for example, import licenses) came in short supply. If one businessman paid a bribe, every businessman had to meet the competition or bow out. Once bribery began, the businessman believed he must bribe or perish; as he saw it, the public official used his power to extort payments from innocents. However, officials depended for bribes upon the class of businessmen. If no businessman bribed, bribery would disappear. Bribery like the tango required two partners.

This also occurred elsewhere. The United Kingdom proclaimed itself to enjoy a bribery-free public sector. How soon they forget! Before the middle of the nineteenth century, British public life was a cess pool.[70]

If the incidence of corruption lessened, some body with political clout must have demanded it, probably business itself.[71] Individual businessmen bribe because they see that it is in their interest. Plainly, however, bribery defeats the interests of entrepreneurs as a class, because it denies predictability. In this view, the relative level of corruption in different economies reflected mainly the relative cohesiveness of the entrepreneurial class in those countries.

The business community in every African polity differed from that in most developed countries. In the metropolitan countries, executives of long-enduring stable firms worked together in Chambers of Commerce, and played together in social clubs. In the LDCs, those ties hardly existed. In Zambia, for example, government contracts were awarded to Italian, British, American, West German, Japanese, Chinese, South African and Yugoslavian firms. In the UK, businessmen found their reference group among other English businessmen. Bribery defeated their collective interest. A briber violated group norms and would be sanctioned. Zambia had no similar reference group to maintain group probity.

Moreover, many firms doing business in Africa made racist assumptions that African officials inherently behaved dishonestly. Racist slanders abounded specifically on the honesty of African officials. These slanders became self-fulfilling prophecies. Once a businessman believed he must pay a bribe, he sometimes offered one. Once enough businessmen offered bribes some officials took the bait.

Finally, the acculturated goals and self-image of businessmen emphasized that their interest lay only in profits. English and American businessmen justified doing business in South Africa despite its *apartheid* policies, for example, on the ground that they cared only for profits, not politics and that so seemingly amoral a search for profits nevertheless did not lack its own morality. Businessmen took the same amoral attitudes with respect to bribing. A prominent New York law firm filled out a long check list before advising a client on entering a foreign market: taxes, import-export licensing, personnel localization laws, exchange control. The lawyer had to investigate the 'prevalence and amount of corruption'. Another researcher reported that prospective foreign investors tended to balance high tax rates against corruptibility in a perfectly amoral temper: bribery could cancel out paper taxes. US multinationals caught bribing officials around the world justified their shocking behaviour by invoking the maxim about copying the Romans.

IV Solutions

Pervasive, structural causes, conformity-inducing measures consisting only of punishments, and impotent enforcement mechanisms: no wonder that bribery sometimes overwhelmed African governments.

Solutions existed. None of them included any bold, over-arching spectacular that purported to eradicate bribery with a single statutory blow. The wide range of possible causes teaches that government must nibble at specific areas separately. Lessening high-level bribery in road construction contracts may differ from reducing it in school contracts, not to speak of import licensing, oil leasing or exchange control. Each has its own particular explanations and solutions. Here I merely suggest some general categories of possible solutions.

A. *Reduction in Opportunity*

One reason for high-level bribery lies in its ample opportunities. The solution for opportunity to commit crime lies in reducing the opportunity, a roundabout measure.[72] In Africa those opportunities arose from discretionary, secret, governmental favours to the private sector without institutional checks. Although market-oriented theorists frequently urged that course, one cannot abandon government intervention without abandoning development itself. Government favours will persist. Policy-makers must consider the probability of bribery when assessing the potential costs of any programme granting discretionary power to award them.

Overbroad discretion, however, need not persist. I discuss below ways to structure and make it accountable.[73] Committees can review contracts and their amendments, and publicize their findings. Many countries have Central Tenders Board to perform this function. Chartered accountants can devise better techniques for handling public and parastatal funds. Carefully selected clerks-of-the-works, quantity surveyors and inspection by independent architects and engineers may help prevent poor performance on building contracts.

All these are ameliorative. Structural change would reduce the size of the private sector, and reduce the authoritarianism that makes discretion possible. Transferring functions from the private to the public sector obviously raises whole new sets of problems, including sharp increases in opportunities for other sorts of corruption than bribery. The more funds that pass through the hands of officials, the more they can and probably will steal. The more power in lower-level bureaucrats to grant or withhold minor permits, the greater the potential for low-level extortion. The more employed by public enterprise, the greater the potential for nepotism. The same behaviours occur in the private sector, but they are not then labelled corruption. Employees steal from employers, minor clerks extort small bribes from customers, owners of business employ their relatives. Whether such activities will increase if enterprise moves into the public sector is problematical. That transfer, however, will necessarily reduce the incidence of high-level bribery.

B. *Economic and Other Interests of Officials*

1. *Direct Sanctions: Enforcement Institutions.* Most countries have a surfeit of criminal laws punishing bribery. The problem lies in detection and punishment.

Bribery has no particular victim to alert the police. The state must develop some device to persuade one of the two parties to the bribe to denounce the other. Standing offers of clemency and an informer's share might help. A number of countries have attempted to develop new investigative institutions for corruption. The Ombudsman and the procurators of the Eastern European states have become widely known.[74] Some police forces have special anti-corruption units. Without allocating resources to ferret out corruption, ordinary law-enforcement agencies will hardly make special efforts to do so. Most police forces have special traffic control units. Corruption control has at least as high a priority claim.

Amount of Punishment. Punishment alone will not reduce bribery. It fosters evasion, not compliance; it comes after the fact; it raises difficult enforcement problems. On the other hand, most high-level bribery occurs in a milieu in which officials calculate. Bribery is an instrumental activity, committed only rarely by people devoted to it as a way of life. For what they may be worth, direct negative measures obviously require vigorous enforcement.

The United States recently permitted a Vice-President to resign from office and pay a fine for tax evasion, rather than trying him for bribery. The Attorney-General, justifying the administrative decision not to prosecute, and to agree to a fine rather than a prison sentence, argued that the loss of office provided punishment enough. Americans could fairly infer that sufficiently high officials would never receive a prison sentence for bribery. If prosecutors adopt the Attorney-General's argument, the severe penalties supposedly attendant upon high-level bribery become merely theoretical. High-level bribery requires a statutory minimum sentence which a judge lacks discretion to reduce.

Andeneas has suggested that punishment serves not so much to deter

potential offenders, but to impress the citizenry with the seriousness of
the offence.[75] To rap a corrupt Permanent Secretary so lightly as did
the judge in the Zambian case earlier noted, may sensibly treat the particular human problem before the judge. It taught all Zambia, rightly or
wrongly, that government viewed bribery in high places as a mere
pecadillo.

2. *Roundabout Sanctions*. Officials accept bribes because they can
easily make use of their gains. Leadership Codes that prohibit political
leaders from owning income property,[76] increased egalitarianism in
living conditions, and dismantling of the private sector can reduce
incentives to high-level corruption. Plugging the leaks in foreign exchange procedures might also help. Since financing political parties has
so often caused corruption, some method for the public financing of
the political parties might help. One-party states can do that easily.
Even in the multi-party states, the costs of campaigning could become
a public expense. Campaign financing, as Americans know too well,
easily becomes the primrose path to bribery.

C. *Decision-Making*

The official accepts his bribe in secret. Publicizing the decisions
involved (a roundabout measure) might help. The chamber of horrors
of the Ghanaian import licence system appears to have rapidly improved after the 1966 *coup*, when authorities began publishing every
import license, and formulated standards for granting them. Ventila-
ting government contracts, too, might help, so that newspapers or dis-
appointed bidders could investigate them. The International Commission of Jurists said that 'To inspire confidence and to reduce the
possibility of maladministration especially in regard to capital investment in public development projects, it is recommended that full
accounts on such projects be the subject of independent and expert
examination, and that reports thereon be regularly submitted to the
legislature.'[77]

The principal institutional devices that maintained secrecy included
the Official Secrets Act and the General Orders of the Civil Service.[78]
Secrecy classifications, nominally in the interests of state security,
frequently cloak corruption the world around. High-level bribery, after
all, expresses the worst sort of authoritarianism, for the official who
takes a bribe on his own authority decides to negate public policy and
law. Secrecy stands ally to authoritarianism, constraining participation
and reducing corruption. A widespread subculture of corruption com-

plicated the issue. If an entire parastatal board was on the take, requiring the Board to make decisions rather than the General Manager alone would not likely reduce bribery, although it might affect the share-out.

The state must devise institutions requiring decisions with potentials for high-level bribery to be made in the presence of people outside the subculture of corruption, and requiring those decisions to be justified to them. How best to do that varies from case to case, depending on the strength of the party, and its relative freedom from corruption, the sorts of decisions involved, the potential for mass participation in the decision-making process, and the possibilities to require and publish justifications and their publication. If parastatal management must justify every high-level contract to its workers (presumably too numerous to share in any graft), perhaps bribery might decline.

D. Subjective Factors

Subjective variables lend themselves to control through direct measures, if at all, or change by educative and deliberative ones. Precisely because these prizings and ways of looking at things change slowly, strategy to reduce bribery in the short run must centre on the sorts of institutional changes I suggested above.

In the long run, high-level bribery can be eliminated by creating high-level leaders, possessed by an ideology which teaches that the cause of poverty and oppression lies in the institutions of the society itself. Elsewhere in this book I discuss institutions likely to promote development: ones looking towards greater egalitarianism between leaders and the mass, better feedback devices from the poor, a participatory style of work, and others. An institution works only when people obey the rules that define it. To install development institutions requires changing high-level behaviour. But officials, like all of us, learn through doing. Engaging in participatory egalitarian institutions must generate self-images of service to the mass, not personal aggrandizement. That consciousness will, I believe, internalize an ideology to make large-scale bribery impossible. That plan, it is said, has worked in the People's Republic of China.

E. Sanctions for the Payers of Bribes

To the extent that high-level bribery results from opportunity, reducing opportunity will constrain the payor as well as the recipient of bribes. Precisely because the expatriate entrepreneur is expatriate, however, the host government cannot easily restructure his environment to affect his choices regarding bribery.

Conclusion

Corruption is not unique to Africa, nor to the LDCs. Everywhere it has its own explanations. African countries emerged from a colonial past. They tried to meet the claims of development by buying it like so much soap powder from the private sector, especially from the great foreign corporations. Governments had enormous favours to dispense. But they had scant real powers. They had no institutional devices to make sensible decisions by regular, public, *institutionalized* processes. Instead, they relied upon the largely uncontrolled, secret, unaccountable discretion of officials. In such a seed bed, bribery thrived. Thus did the very processes of development through the private sector induce high level bribery, which in turn conspired to defeat development and foster dependency.

Following this explanation, the long-run solutions for bribery require radical institutional changes. Not development through a private sector, but through production controlled from the beginning in the public interest; not authoritarian decision-making, but participation; not official secrecy, but open decisions and public accountability: These are the indispensable minima to eradicate high-level bribery. Short of these, a number of specific reforms seem urgent, each aimed at particular situations. To the extent that high-level bribery has structural causes, however, any effective solution must address those causes. Throat lozenges rarely cure cancer.

A developing society with public ownership of the means of production, economic independence from the great multinational firms, and open, participatory decision-making must of course become both democratic and socialist. If the solution for high-level bribery lies in democratic socialism, its causes must lie in capitalism or at least, the particular form that capitalism takes in the developing world.

Notes

1. A.J. Heidenheimer (ed.), *Political Corruption: Readings in Comparative Analysis* (New York: Holt, Rinehart and Winston, 1970), pp. 4 *et seq.*
2. See below, Chap. 20.
3. Cf. Heidenheimer, *Political Corruption*, pp. 4 *et seq.*; J.C. Scott, *Comparative Political Corruption* (Englewood Cliffs, N.J.: Prentice-Hall, 1972), p. 4.
4. K. Renner, *The Institutions of Private Law and Their Social Functions*, O. Kahn-Freud, ed. and tr. (London: Routledge & Kegan Paul, 1949); W.J. Samuels, 'The Economy as a System of Power and its Legal Causes: the Legal Economics of Robert Lee Hale', *U. Miami L. Rev.*, 27, 261 (1973).

5. W.F. Wertheim, 'Sociological Aspects of Corruption in Southeast Asia', *Sociologica Neerlandica*, 1, 129 (1963), reprinted in Heidenheimer, *Political Corruption*, p. 298.

6. M. Weber, *The Theory of Social and Economic Organization*, T. Parsons, ed.; T. Parsons and A.M. Henderson, tr. (New York: Free Press, 1964), p. 336.

7. Heidenheimer, *Political Corruption*, pp. 9-10.

8. *Report of the Committee of Enquiry on the Local Purchasing of Cocoa* (Accra: Government Printer, 1966).

9. D. Apter, *Ghana in Transition*, 2nd. ed. (Princeton: Princeton University Press, 1972), p. 6; H.H. Werlin, 'The Roots of Corruption: The Ghanaian Case', *J. Mod. Af. St.*, 10, 247-53 (1972); Scott, *Comparative Political Corruption*, p. 10.

10. S.K.B. Asante, 'Interests in Land in the Customary Law of Ghana: A New Appraisal', *Yale L.J.*, 74, 848 (1965).

11. E. Mends, 'Traditional Values and Bribery and Corruption', *The Legion Observer*, 5, 13, 14 (1970).

12. Werlin, 'Roots of Corruption', p. 254.

13. G. Myrdal, *Asian Drama: An Inquiry into the Poverty of Nations* (New York, Pantheon, 1968), p. 1130.

14. *Report of the Commission of Enquiry into Irregularities and Malpractices in the Grant of Import Licenses* [The Ollenu Report] (Accra: Government Printer, 1967).

15. For other examples, see, generally, V.T. Le Vine, *Political Corruption: The Ghana Case* (Stanford: Hoover Institution Press, 1975).

16. H.A. Brasz, 'Some Notes on the Sociology of Corruption', *Sociologica Neerlandica*, 1, 111 (1967), in Heidenheimer, *Political Corruption*, p. 41.

17. N.H. Leff, 'Economic Development through Bureaucratic Corruption', *Am. Behavioural Scientist*, 8, 8 (1964); J.C. Scott, 'Corruption, Machine Politics and Social Change', *Am. Pol. Sci. Rev.*, 63, 1142 (1969) reprinted in Heidenheimer, *Political Corruption*, p. 549; D.H. Bayle, 'The Effects of Corruption in a Developing Nation', *Western Pol. Q.*, 19, 719 (1966), reprinted in Heidenheimer, p. 521; J. Veloso Abueva, 'The Contribution of Nepotism, Sports and Craft to Economic Development', *East-West Center Review*, 3, 45 (1966), reprinted in Heidenheimer, p. 531; J.S. Nye, 'Corruption and Political Development', *Am. Pol. Sci. R.*, 61, 417 (1967), reprinted in Heidenheimer, p. 567.

18. The incident is described in the *Nigerian Morning Post* for 21 February 1965, and following editions.

19. Werlin, 'Roots of Corruption', p. 250.

20. The phenomenon was also present in Southeast Asia. Myrdal, *Asian Drama*, p. 937.

21. See below, Chap. 14.

22. This Code is in force in Nigeria, Zambia, Malta, the Seychelles, Fiji and elsewhere, as well as the East African states, Malawi and Zambia. The Colonial Office drafted it in the early 1930s. See J.S. Read, 'Criminal Law in the Africa of Today and Tomorrow', *J.Af. L.*, 7, 5 (1963); O.E.C. Chirwa, 'The Prevention of Corruption by Legislation (The Tanzania Act of 1971)', *E.Afr. L.R.* 5, 225 (1972).

23. See, e.g. Zambia: Penal Code, Cap. 146, sec. 94.

24. Ibid. sec. 4.

25. Zambia: No. 41 of 1964, sec. 2.

26. Malawi Penal Code: Cap. 7.01, para 4.

27. Tanzania: Act 1 of 1970.

28. Zambia: supra n. 23, sec. 84(b).

29. *Moledina* v. *R.*, (1960) E.A. 778 (Uganda).

30. Zambia, Penal Code, sec. 94 (a) (anyone who 'asks, receives or obtains, or obtains, or agrees or attempts to receive or obtain, any property or benefit of any kind for himself or any other person, on account of anything already done or omitted to be done by him in the discharge of the duties of his office'); Uganda: Penal Code, Cap. 106, sec. 78(1) (An official 'who agrees or offers to permit his conduct in (his) employment to be influenced by the gift, promise or prospect of property or any benefit to be received by him, or by any other person, from any person whomsoever, or for any other reason. . .'.)

31. Ghana: Corrupt Practices (Prevention) Act, 1964 (Act 230), sec. 9.

32. Note, *Minn. L. Rev.*, 26, 661 (1942).

33. *A.G.* v. *Kajemba*, [1958] E.A. 503, 510.

34. Kenya: Prevention of Corruption Act, (No. 33 of 1956), sec. 7; see statement on the analogous Indian Prevention of Corruption Act by A.H. Potter, Home Secretary (India), 11 Council of State Debates No. 5, 180, 181, 189, 190, quoted in R.K. Soonvala, *A Treatise on Bribery and Corruption* (Bombay: Tripathi, 1964), p. 561.

35. Ibid.

36. See, e.g., Kenya: Prevention of Corruption Act, 1961 (No. 42 of 1961) sec. 17.

37. Ghana' Corrupt Practices (Prevention) Act., 1964. Malaya further stretched the rules of evidence by (1) statutorily reversing the rule, that a trier of fact cannot usually accept as true the uncorroborated evidence of an accomplice or co-conspirator; (2) depriving the accused persons of the privilege against self-incrimination in some circumstances (sec. 19); (3) protecting the secrecy of informers [sec. 20(1)]; (4) requiring banks to produce the accounts of suspected persons [sec. 23(1)]; and (5) extending the powers of the Public Prosecutor to require prospective witnesses to testify [sec. 25.]. Malaya has even appointed special courts, with relaxed rules of procedure. Pakistan provided for the appointment of special judges, with jurisdiction to hear corruption cases [Pakistan: Criminal Law Amendment Act, 1958 (Act 40 of 1958)].

38. Zambia: Penal Code, Cap. 146, secs. 94, 95, 96.

39. Ibid., secs. 384, 385.

40. Kenya, Prevention of Corruption Act.

41. Tanzania: Minimum Sentences Act, Act No. 29 of 1963.

42. Ghana: Corrupt Practices (Prevention) Act, 1974. By contrast, violation of the cocoa smuggling laws or the exchange control laws carried minimum penalties of twenty-five years.

43. A. Lincoln Steffens, *The Shame of the Cities* (N.Y.: McClure, Phillips, 1904).

44. J.Q. Wilson, 'Corruption: The Shame of the States', *The Public Interest*, 2, 23 (1966), reprinted in Heidenheimer, *Political Corruption*, p. 1965.

45. *Gazette of India*, 23 November 1946, Part V., p. 374, quoted in Soonvala, *Bribery and Corruption*, p. 5; Scott, *Comparative Political Corruption*, p. 12.

46. Zambia: cap. 690.

47. Zambia: The Control of Goods (Price Control) Regulations, 1965.

48. Myrdal, *Asian Drama*, pp. 1126, 1131.

49. See, e.g. Report of the Electricity Corporation of Nigeria Tribunal of Inquiry (Lagos: Government Printer, 1966), paras. 345-7; Report of the Tribunal of Inquiry into the Affairs of the Nigerian Railways Corporation (Lagos: Government Printer, 1967); Le Vine, *The Ghana Case.*

50. Le Vine, ibid., p. 90 *et seq.*

51. See below, Chap. 21.

52. Zambia: Pioneer Industries (Relief from Income Tax) Act, 1965 (No. 55 of

1965) sec. 10. The *Gazette* might publish that a certificate had been awarded.
53. Werlin, 'Roots of Corruption', p. 255.
54. Ibid.
55. R. Wraith and E. Simpkins, *Corruption in Developing Countries* (London: George Allen & Unwin, 1963), p. 13.
56. Le Vine, *The Ghana Case,* pp. 29-33; Report of the Commission to Enquire into Affairs of NADECO Limited (Accra: Government Printer, 1966).
57. Wraith and Simpkins, *Corruption in Developing Countries,* p. 20.
58. See below, Chap. 12.
59. Le Vine, *The Ghana Case,* pp. 53 *et seq*.: Scott, *Comparative Political Corruption.*
60. M. McMullen, 'A Theory of Corruption', *Sociological Review*, 9, 181 (1961), reprinted in Heidenheimer, *Political Corruption,* p. 317.
61. Quoted in Le Vine, *The Ghana Case,* frontispiece.
62. J.B. Moneiro, *Corruption: The Control of Maladministration* (Bombay: Monakatlas, 1966), Chap. III.
63. Werlin, 'Roots of Corruption', p. 255.
64. C. Leys, 'What is the Problem about Corruption?', *J. Mod. Af. St.,* 3, 215 (1965), reprinted in Heidenheimer, *Political Corruption,* p. 31.
65. McMullen, 'Theory of Corruption', p. 317.
66. Myrdal, *Asian Drama,* pp. 937-51.
67. Count by author in 1963.
68. M. Green, *Ibo Village Affairs* (London: Sidgwick and Jackson, 1958).
69. Le Vine, *The Ghana Case.*
70. Wraith and Simkins, *Corruption in Developing Countires.*
71. Cf. Scott, *Comparative Political Corruption,* pp. 28-9.
72. See above, Chap. 9.
73. See below, Chap. 13.
74. See, e.g., W. Gellhorn, *Ombudsmen and Others: Citizens' Protectors in Nine Countries* (Cambridge, Mass: Harvard U.P., 1961).
75. J. Andeneas, 'The General Preventive Effects of Punishment', *U. of Pa. L. Rev.,* 114, 949 (1966).
76. See below, Chap. 20.
77. International Commission of Jurists, *The Rule of Law and Human Rights* (Geneva: ICJ, 1966), p. 49.
78. See below, Chap. 21.

Part Four

THE IMPLEMENTATION OF DEVELOPMENT LAW

11 LAW AND THE ADMINISTRATION OF DEVELOPMENT: A THEORY*

Chapter 4's general model of law and development used implementation processes to explain whether and to what extent the legal order can change behaviour. Development, after all, mainly concerns changing behaviour. To accomplish this, governments apply conformity-inducing measures to role-occupants. That becomes the business of development administration.[1]

The myth of *laissez-faire* tells us that the administration's internal concerns consist only of law, order and collecting taxes. The market regulates the economy. Courts resolve conflicts within the economic system, and patrol the boundary between government and the citizen against bureaucratic poaching. Besides courts, the criminal justice system and civil service, no other governmental implementation institutions exist.

Self-evidently, this myth bore no resemblance to modern African reality. Courts had almost no relation to development (although they did settle disputes). The administration engaged in very different activities from maintaining law and order and collecting taxes, mainly, but not exclusively, concerning new economic activity.[2] An entirely new sector of governmental institutions concerned with implementation arose, the parastatals or government corporations. Neither courts, administration nor parastatals worked very well to stimulate development. Clouds of rhetoric, and some laws purporting to effect radical institutional transformation, but little actual change resulted (that is, soft development).

To explain this general failure, I must first characterize the sorts of decisions implementation institutions must make. I shall then present a general model of decision-making structures, and, finally a very general theory explaining the relative failure of the implementation institutions.

* Research on this and the following six chapters was done under National Science Foundation Grant NSF SOC75-16278. Anything stated here is of course the responsibility of the author and not of the National Science Foundation.

191

I The Decisions Required for Development

What we learn in school divides government into legislative, administrative and judicial functions. Law-makers create rules; the bureaucracy or a private individual asserts a breach; the courts decide guilt or innocence and assess punishment. Administration in this view 'is usually thought of as accepting goals from outside the system, as depending upon resources from other systems and being instructed in the use of means'.[3] Government packages these instructions about goals and means as rules. The administration must apply these rules, that is, they must enforce the laws. Administration, however, serves another function, problem-solving: '. . . developing goals within the system using resources over which the system has control, and being free in the use of means'.[4] In this function, the law-makers do not enact rules to guide the behaviour of the administration. Rather, they identify problems, and delegate authority to solve them to the administration.

Difficulties that government has long dealt with (for example, maintaining law and order) government long ago solved in ways that more or less satisfied the ruling elite. Rules define those solutions. The criminal law exemplifies such institutionalization. Incremental changes in the rules can deal with most emergent problems in such a sector. Of course, this frequently frustrates, for in time older solutions become inadequate, no matter how much the incremental tinkering. When that happens, the system reaches crisis, as with the criminal justice system in the United States today.

Notwithstanding the *laissez-faire* myth, when the African countries achieved independence their governments inherited institutionalized systems to deal with a wide range of problems, not only law, order and taxes, but economic, political and social issues as well. Now, however, they confronted a whole new set of difficulties, the demands for development. The existing rules could not deal with these new problems; indeed, in the broadest sense, the inherited colonial institutions constituted the core of the new difficulties. The nominal law-making organs (cabinet, Party and legislature) lacked the capacity to solve them.[5] They could only identify the difficulties at hand and turn them over to the bureaucrats to solve.

The United States' legal order underwent the same change. Federal judges increasingly tried to solve such problems as school integration, due process for prisoners, and the like, rather than applying fixed rules to neatly defined cases. The great administrative agencies of government, too, had to solve problems, and in the course of doing that, created necessary rules.[6]

As a result, the traditional allocation of policy-making to the legislature and implementation to the bureaucracy no longer applied.The
highest political authorities at most ordered the priorities of solving
problems. They left to the administrators the processes of analyzing
difficulties, devising solutions, implementing programmes and then
learning from those experiences. Determining policy in the traditional
sense of devising legislation that embodied specific programmes to
solve emergent difficulties passed from the supposed policy-makers to
the supposed implementers. Typically, in Africa formal legislation
merely defined a difficulty and empowered a minister to promulgate
subsidiary legislation towards its solution. The received implementation
machinery of the African states did not succeed in solving problems.
Decision-making machinery can never achieve universal application.
African implementing institutions lacked the capacity to meet the new
requirements of development.[7]

II Decision-Making Systems and the Range of Decisions

To explain why African implementation institutions could not make
developmental decisions, I must first suggest an analytical framework.
We can conceive that every decision-making system consists of inputs,
conversion processes, outputs and feedbacks:

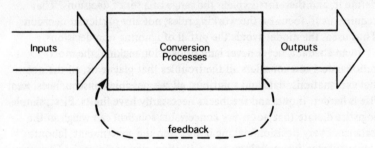

Inputs include the recruitment and socialization of decision-makers, the
troubled situations chosen for examination, candidate explanations,
data, proposals for solution, bodies of reliable knowledge and the
large-scale paradigms or ideologies (or 'values') that guide discretionary
choice in problem-solving. Conversion processes combine these materials
into decisions, or outputs. Feedback makes the output and its consequences an input to new decision-making, so that the system can learn
from what it does and, thus improve its subsequent decisions. The
decision or output purports to solve the problems identified by inputs
or feedbacks.

Decision-making systems in government always consist of many roles. Some participate in providing inputs, some in the conversion process, others, in feedback. As roles, they of course act in patterned ways, following formal rules or informal conventions, that define the range of inputs, conversion processes and feedbacks.

One can explain both organizational and human behaviour by asking two questions: what is the range of choice, and the choice within that range?[8] In this model, inputs and feedbacks define the range of choice, and conversion processes, the decision within them. When used to analyze individual decisions, however, too often the analyst takes as given the patterned behaviour of the several roles that comprise the system. He asks only why did the particular decision emerge from the inputs and feedbacks that the system generated? The model thus directs attention only to those matters that actually arise for decision, and the available range of choice. It does not analyze 'non-decisions'.[9] So used, the model remains inherently static. It accepts the existing structure of the system. It therefore cannot explain difficulties in terms of process or structure, upon which to ground institutional changes. It explains decisions mainly by the personal characteristics of the decision-makers.

Our interest primarily concerns structure and the working rules that define it, and therefore explain the range of a set of decisions. That requires us to focus on the working rules, not any particular decision. Thus used, the model avoids the pitfall of ignoring non-decisions.

In an abstract, never-never land of decision-making, the most rational decision considers all the troubles that plague us, all the potential explanations, data and solutions, all the possible consequences. Real life is harder. Inputs and feedbacks necessarily have limits. First, simple logistics dictate that not every conceivable solution can weigh in the balance. Every decision-making body, even the government, labours under substantive restraints. A constitution may prohibit the Congress from impairing the right of the people to carry arms. A corporate charter may limit decision-making power to manufacturing of cement. Second, every decision-making body follows repetitive behaviour patterns that define its processes. These rules of law or custom limit the activity of the various roles in the system, and consequently limit inputs and feedbacks. The limited range of input and feedback processes limit the range of potential outputs.

Conversion processes, too, have limits. First, every decision-maker carries a set of culturally-acquired values, that can be restated as a model of society. These values or models restrict the variables which

the decision-maker will consider. British decisions in African cases involving witchcraft excluded various factors that weighed with
Africans.[10] Since recruitment and socialization rules always limit the
people likely to become law-makers to those having a particular value-
set, these rules *pro tanto* preform the conversion processes and hence
the output. Second, the working rules of the conversion process also
constrain outputs. Requiring outputs to conform substantially to
existing law, for example, prohibits radical decisions. Rules that require written opinions limit decisions to those justifiable according to
prevailing morality. Collegial decisions may differ from individual
ones. In short, the grants of power and working rules necessarily constrain the range of inputs, feedbacks and the conversion processes, thus
limiting the range of potential outputs.

'Values', and the working rules of the system thus become functionally equivalent. They both perform the decision output, for they guide
the unavoidably discretionary choices of problem-solving. In this sense,
every decision-making process necessarily imposes its values on
decision-makers. No genuinely neutral decision-making process can
exist.

The procedural rules that define a decision-making structure always
constitute rules addressed to the various actors in the decision-making
structure. Rules of evidence, for example, address lawyers and judges
in the trial courts. The decision-making model described here refers to
working rules, because the way input, feedback and conversion processes affect behaviour depends upon how the various actors in fact behave.
How they behave relates to the formal procedural rules in the ways
defined by the general law and development model put forward in
Chapter 5. The two models thus combined explicate the relationship
between formal procedural rules and substantive output.

In designing decision-making structures, therefore, lawyers must
determine what sorts of inputs, conversion processes and feedbacks will
be likely to achieve rational decisions within the desired range of output, and then devise appropriate rules to induce behaviour that will
obtain them. *The rules that define the process of decision-making preform the range of substantive decisions.*

III A Theory of the Law of Development Administration

The misfit between the problem-solving tasks of the administration and
the existing norms that define its structure suggests an explanation for
its relative failures. In the *laissez-faire* model courts and administration
applied rules. That required responsibility and accountability to ensure

the administration's instrumental character. Discretion unconfined
embodies authoritarianism. Bureaucracy, inherently hierarchical, avoids
becoming dictatorial because it must conform to established rules.
Broad discretion insulates bureaucracy from accountability because
there no rule exists against which the reviewing authority can measure
performance.

In the colonial period, the bureaucracy was Janus-faced. To white
settlers it conformed to rules and the accountability requirement; where
discretion existed, white publics participated in decision-making. To
Africans, it exercised broad discretion free from rules, with no formal
participation by Africans. After Independence, the administration continued. In form hierarchical and compartmented, it could readily apply
rules, but could not solve problems easily or well. Yet the broad discretion the law gave to high bureaucrats continued. Now, however, they
had to solve new problems, and received new grants of yet more discretion. Whole areas of jurisdiction passed to the parastatals precisely
because law-makers thought that parastatals had the discretion and
power to be 'dynamic' and 'entrepreneurial' — that is, to solve problems.

In neither case did existing rules hold administrators to account. They
therefore used their discretion as administrators and managers usually
do everywhere, to maximize rewards and minimize strains for themselves
and their bureaucracies. They aggrandized themselves, or did favours
for friends and relatives, developing a 'bureaucratic bourgeoisie' (a
matter I address in Chapter 20). Rather than solving difficulties, they
more easily and profitably continued old ways of doing things, doing
nothing to induce change. Radical change threatens the existing holders
of power and privilege, who can best reward bureaucrats.

I put forward here a very general set of hypotheses to explain the
pervasive failure of African systems for the administration of development. I unpack this theory in the succeeding five chapters.

1. The working rules defining the inputs, conversion processes and
   feedbacks of a decision-making system preform the potential
   range of outputs.

2. Development requires problem-solving, not rule-applying.

3. Problem-solving institutions need wide discretion, to provide
   rewards, roundabout and educative conformity-inducing measures
   as well as punishments, and involve role-occupants in problem-
   solving processes.

4. Courts in Africa therefore only marginally related to development.

5. At Independence, the working rules that defined African systems to implement law (courts and the civil service) defined hierarchical, authoritarian, compartmented systems.

6. Substantive development law in Africa vested broad discretion in the civil service, and created the parastatal sector, whose managers also had broad discretion.

7. The received rules of administrative law, and the structure of the parastatals, contained only very weak controls over discretion.

8. Officials with broad discretion in authoritarian organizations usually use their discretion to maximize rewards and minimize strains upon themselves and their organization.

9. In Africa, the existing economic and political elite supplied most rewards and strains for the bureaucracy and parastatal managers.

10. Therefore bureaucrats and parastatal managers maximized rewards and minimized strains for themselves and their organizations by

    a. Aggrandizing themselves, their friends, associates and relatives, and

    b. Making incremental rather than radical changes in institutions, or no change at all.

Simply: *Authoritarian institutions whose managers have great discretion cannot generate decisions looking towards development.* Paternalism, as an authoritarian, discretion-soaked system, cannot work. 'Development from above' cannot work. When tried in Africa, it created soft development and the bureaucratic bourgeoisie.

Notes

1. F.W. Riggs, 'The Context of Development Administration' in F.W. Riggs (ed.), *Frontiers of Development Administration* (Durham: Duke University Press, 1970), pp. 72, 73.

2. A.L. Adu, *The Civil Service in Commonwealth Africa* (London: Allen and Unwin, 1969); W.C. Neale, 'The Economy and Development Administration', in Riggs, *Development Administration*, pp. 326, 327.

3. K.J. Rothwell, 'The Scope of Management and Administrative Problems in Development', in K.J. Rothwell (ed.), *Administrative Issues in Developing Economies* (Lexington: D.C. Heath, 1972), pp. 3-4.

4. Ibid., p. 4.

5. See below, Chap. 19.

6. J.W. Hurst, *The Growth of American Law: The Law Makers* (Boston: Little Brown & Co., 1950), pp. 406-11.

7. But cf. W.G. O'Donnell, 'Bridging the Public and Private Sectors of Development', in Rothwell, *Administrative Issues*, p. 39 ('The main responsibility for development lies with the managers of formal organizations in both the public and private sectors. Development depends basically upon the development of the individuals who comprise the system, and particularly upon its managerial resources.')

8. See above, Chap. 4.

9. P. Bachrach and M. Baratz, *Power and Poverty* (New York: Oxford University Press, 1970).

10. R.B. Seidman, 'Witch Murder and *Mens Rea*: A Problem of Society under Radical Social Change', *Mod. L. Rev.*, 28, 46 (1965).

12 COURTS AND DEVELOPMENT

Many lawyers and academics adopted Max Weber's legalism[1] as the appropriate model for developing societies.[2] That model celebrated courts as the core of the legal order.[3] The norms of most economic and social relationships supposedly arose in society. The legal order resolved disputes. Courts therefore became discontinuous with society. By applying universalistic norms that dealt equally with equals, by deciding issues pursuant to procedures tested in the long struggle for human freedom, summed up in the US Constitution's phrase Due Process, and by making the state itself subject to law, the independent legal order could achieve instrumental, developmental ends and simultaneously 'protect individual freedom, expand citizen participation in decision-making, enhance social equality, and increase the capacity of all citizens rationally to control events and shape social life'.[4] These dogmas elevated courts as *the* institution to accomplish all these desirable objectives.

Despite these theories, however, courts in independent Africa barely involved themselves in development. They mainly decided private disputes, and sanctioned inherited criminal and administrative rules.[5] Other institutions – bureaucracy, parastatals, the Party – implemented development rules.

Why did courts tend to abdicate despite a powerful legal ideology that extolled their importance? I first examine the position of courts in colonial Africa; second, the efforts made by the independent states to reform judicial systems; third, I attempt to explain the failure of courts as development institutions; and, finally, suggest a possible development role for courts.

I Courts in Colonial Africa

The colonial rulers transported English courts to Africa, pursuant to the notion of courts as the legal order's cutting edge. Notably, the common law's claim to a saving grace, the Rule of Law, never arrived.

The British included courts among the earliest institutions they introduced into Africa. Every Order-in-Council that established a government simultaneously established courts.[6] In the Gold Coast (now Ghana), English power established itself by progressively extending court jurisdiction.[7] Courts existed in the Gold Coast before they had law to apply. The reception clause in the Gold Coast stemmed from the local Attorney General requesting advice.[8] Courts preceded the substantive law in Africa as in England. As to Africans, the newly established 'English' courts dealt with matters analogous to those of Tudor Justices of the Peace. Those earlier magistrates concerned themselves not only with 'ordinary' crimes, but also with

> the conservation of highways, rivers and fortifications, employment regulations for apprentices, servants and labourers, unlawful hunting and games, tippling in alehouses, eating flesh at Lent, tile-making, selling of horses and harness by soldiers, possession of Papist symbols, Jesuits and Popish recusants, brawling in Church, attendance at church (compulsory, on pain of a shilling fine), 'Egyptians' or gypsies . . . price control of candles and earthenware, fuel, malt, corn and other commodities, plague-infested houses, pheasants and partridge, spawn of fish, watermen, claims to stolen horses, logwood, examinations in claims against the hundred for robbery, seditious meeting, regulations concerning sheriffs and bailiffs, taking bribes in the county court, and, of course, the perennial rogues, vagabonds and sturdy beggars.[9]

In colonial Africa, too, magistrates performed administrative functions. In the common law, the employment contract did not in principle differ from other contracts. If an employee breached, his employer could sue for damages. That did not help European employers, because Africans could rarely pay a money judgement. The employers demanded more stringent sanctions. They found a solution in the Master and Servant laws, enforced through the local magistracy. These laws made any breach of a labour contract by employees (read Africans) a crime. Under the Kenyan ordinance, for example,[10] an employee faced a fine up to five pounds or up to six months in prison for a wide range of offences: wilfully or while drunk doing 'any act tending to the immediate loss, damage or serious risk of any property' of the employer placed in his charge; refusing or omitting to do any lawful act required to be done for the safety of the employer's property; failing to report the loss or death of any animal; wilfully absenting himself from work; or refusing 'to obey any command of his employer or of any person lawfully placed by his employer in authority over him, which command it was his duty to obey'. Under the similar Northern Rhodesian ordinance, a prosecution charged that two Africans 'being farm labourers had each neglected to complete his allotted task of scything a section of standing wheat'.[11] They had completed 13/15th of the allotted task, but had then downed tools and refused to finish it. The Labour Office found that the task was not unreasonable, and the accused suffered convictions and fines. The criminal law sanctioned a breach of contract that elsewhere usually results only in discharge.

Courts enforced analogous rules of all sorts: agricultural regulation,[12] head taxes,[13] retail licensing laws.[14] The courts that directly dealt with Africans, like the Justices of the Peace in eighteenth-century England, far from being neutral, aloof arbiters, became the government's enforcers for many administrative regulations.[15]

If, for whatever reason, one does not question the substantive content of existing law, then the primary concern becomes either its elegance, or its abuse for particularist or parochial purposes. The Rule of Law, some claimed, prevented that abuse. Universalistic rules required equality before the Law. Easy and equal access to courts guaranteed their availability against public or private oppression. Judicial independence ensured that controversies would not be decided by politics, and that courts would police government itself.

Apologists for British imperialism, apparently sincerely, believed that the courts systems in Anglophonic Africa met these requirements. Lord Lugard wrote that 'nothing except education can compare in importance to the administration of justice in British colonies . . .'[16] Sir Kenneth Roberts-Wray positively gurgled. He persuaded himself that Africans as well as Englishmen saw in the reception of the British law and justice the greatest of their English legacies. They celebrated, he claimed, 'principally, no doubt, the fundamental principles, such as the rule of law, the independence of the judiciary, the writ of habeas corpus, freedom of speech and a fair trial for the accused person . . .'[17] Sir Kenneth celebrated courts of Africa as if they performed the same functions in Africa that they allegedly did in England.

They did not. In transforming the lower courts in Africa from ideal legalistic institutions into direct administrative instruments, the whole institution underwent a sea-change. None of Sir Kenneth's 'fundamental principles' regularly applied in colonial Africa to Africans. I discuss here (1) equality before the law; (2) access to the courts; (3) fair trial and the independence of the judiciary; and (4) the courts as guarantors of governmental regularity.

1. *Equality Before the Law.* We have earlier seen how Britain imposed a plural system of law upon its colonial subjects, and how that system buttressed a plural society. The British rulers devised a correspondingly dual system of courts.

A centralized court system mainly applying received English law and local statutory law existed from the very beginning of Crown rule. Every territory had inferior and appellate courts. At the bottom of this hierarchy sat the local magistrate, usually also the District Officer, his original jurisdiction mainly limited to the criminal law. Pursuant to the policy of Indirect Rule, there also existed a system of local or African courts, sometimes indigenous tribunals of chiefs or elders, sometimes manufactured by the British out of whole cloth[18] (the British did this particularly where they had trouble discerning any chief among the so-called acephalous peoples[19]). These local courts remained under British control, for in every case the local English magistrate had powers of review and supervision.

The local District Officer therefore became a key judicial and administrative officer. He judged most criminal cases; he reviewed civil and criminal native court judgements.

These several courts had jurisdiction over different people, and applied different law. The regular 'English' courts — i.e. the Magistrate's Court and the higher courts — tried all causes involving a non-African (with certain minor exceptions). The local (English) magistrate had original jurisdiction over crimes, whatever the race of the accused, except for a few customary offences. Higher courts controlled the magistrates by revision in minor crimes, and in serious cases, binding over to higher courts for trial. In these cases, the 'English' courts in the main applied the received 'English' and local statutory law. The local ('African') courts had original jurisdiction over civil actions between Africans, plus a very limited criminal jurisdiction, to which they applied customary law. (Exceptionally, Ugandan and Northern Nigerian 'African' courts had plenary criminal powers.) In some jurisdictions, mainly in West Africa, an appeal lay on points of customary law all the way to the Privy Council. In others, customary law followed its own appellate course, ending in an administrative decision.[20] Blacks, therefore, became generally subject to customary law and customary courts, whites, to English law and English courts. Africans regularly appeared before the higher 'English' courts in serious criminal matters. Whites were practically never tried in customary courts.

The built-in, structural inequities of the legal order in Africa ran against the grain of judges and lawyers. In *Kayela* v. *Botts*,[21] for example, the plaintiff, an African, had an altercation with the defendant, a white South African mineworker, during which the defendant called plaintiff a bastard. Plaintiff later approached defendant to ask why he had called him the name.

The defendant replied, 'Don't speak to me again or I will beat you.' The plaintiff said, 'Why will you beat me? Any European, even a small child, has a white skin and is my master. I am a black man, and I am not cheeky.' The defendant replied, 'A bastard like you I can kill. If I kill a person like you in Johannesburg, the payment is only £5.'

He thereupon struck and severely injured the plaintiff, who sued for damages.

The defence argued that the ordinary English rules of civil liability did not apply in an action by an African against a European. The Northern Rhodesian Order in Council, 1924, provided that the civil and criminal jurisdiction of the High Court would follow English law 'so far as circumstances admit', upon which phrase the defence based its claim. The Court summarily rejected the defence argument without lengthy discussion.

Colonial Service lawyers repeatedly urged the unification of the courts and law. As early as 1953, the Judicial Advisers' Conference reported:[22]

It is thought that the following propositions will meet with general acceptance:

a. In principle, any country should have one body of general law and one judicial system applicable equally to all persons.

b. Just as, with insignificant exceptions, that state of affairs (which represents complete integration) was achieved by Western countries centuries ago, so also it must be the ultimate objective in African territories.

c. No doubt in more backward areas this process will take a long time, but steps, however small, towards that objective should be taken as soon as conditions permit.

d. The development of the necessary conditions should be encouraged and the situation should be constantly under review.

Similar conferences made similar manifestos in 1955,[23] 1956,[24] and 1959.[25] Nothing came of them. The legal systems of colonial Africa continued to dispense 'justice' on ethnic criteria.

Despite official rhetoric, the white colonial populations opposed even formal equality before the law for Africans. A disturbance that took place in Northern Rhodesia in 1937 epitomized this opposition.[26]

That affair arose out of a minor assault case. An African was digging a ditch in Kitwe in the Copperbelt. A European seventeen-year-old, sitting round the corner, said to his companion, 'I bet the boys are sitting down.' He picked up a clod of earth, went round the corner, and, seeing the African sitting on the bank of the trench, threw the clod at him, swore, and kicked and hit him with his fist. A struggle then ensued, in which the African bit his tormentor's wrist. The African ran away, nursing a broken collar bone. The local magistrate tried and convicted the European for assult, sentencing him to four strokes of the cane.

The incident raised a storm on the Copperbelt. Over 400 whites held a mass meeting. A deputation visited the Governor, who designated the Acting Attorney General as a Commission of Enquiry. The Commission reported a series of incidents, of which the case in question was only the legendary straw. On many occasions, whites allegedly reported cases of insubordination or assault to the police, who failed to prosecute for lack of evidence. The local Police Inspector reported that 'Police Stations frequently receive notes from European householders saying, "This boy has refused to wash dishes, please give him a good hiding!" ' ('Of course' the police did not comply, he testified. However, 'If we do not give the native a talking to, this particular lady will have a grievance against the police. In order to satisfy everybody we do something which we are not entitled to do and this does no good even although we do it.'[27] Some Zambians today assert that in fact the Colonial police did on occasion beat Africans for employers.) A white housewife complained that a 'native had bumped into [her] when passing through the door. She says she pulled him up and told him to stand aside and let her pass out first. He was very disrespectful in his demeanour and insolent.' Her husband went into the yard and struck the African with his fists, and, the victim asserted, poked him with a stick and beat him with a golf club. The attacker was convicted and fined one pound.

The colonialists became outraged. A delegation told the Governor that the 'public' — i.e. the white, colonial public — 'have less faith in the Law Courts'.[28] Its spokesman said:

> If you tell a boy to do a thing and he will not do it you are liable to be assaulted for this by the native. If the man retaliates and tries to put the nigger in his place he is liable to be prosecuted by the Police and his job is jeopardized. Do you think this is correct, when the niggers know that they will be favored?

Things have come to a position in this country where the public
are losing faith in the courts and the Governor has been notified
of this – that if things are not altered there is only one alternative
to be taken and that is mob law and we absolutely object to mob
law in this country . . . We only ask one thing and that is fair British
justice.[29]

White settlers believed formal legal equality with Africans destroyed
their privileged position. In England, at the turn of the nineteenth
century, the middle classes used equality before the law as a weapon
against their class enemies. In Africa, the white population saw it as a
threat. Equality appeals to the disadvantaged, not to the elite.

The officials, however, at least rhetorically adhered to the ideal of
equality. Judges imbibe the Rule of Law in law school. Administrators
absorb an analogous bureaucratic culture. Second, the administration
had to consider the claims of English moral entrepreneurs such as
missionary groups, who could raise a small storm in the House of
Commons if the administration too openly discriminated against
Africans. Finally, every colonial administration sat on a tinderbox. The
ratio between Europeans and whites throughout Africa heavily weighed
against the Europeans. Colonial forces stood thin on the ground. Violence ever threatened. British officials supposed that in African eyes the
even-handed fairness of British justice legitimized the administration.
Socialization, moral pressure and claims for legitimacy combined to
persuade officials to declare support for the Rule of Law.

The local white settler population, however, could exert the most
pressure on the administrators, and unambiguously demanded white
supremacy. All over Africa, the administration responded as administrators everywhere do to contradictory claims. Law-implementation
shows less than law-making. The colonial administration maintained the
rhetoric and even some superficial forms of the rule of law, but actually
practised discrimination. To price killing a black by a white in
Johannesburg at five pounds exaggerated only a little.[30]

The greatest and least visible discrimination occurred in arrest, to
which white offenders sometimes seemed immune. In colonial Kenya
when settlers killed Africans, the police sometimes did not arrest the
offenders,[31] although they knew who had committed the crimes.
Elsewhere in Kenya, sanctions differentially applied to whites and to
blacks. In a 1907 Nairobi *cause célèbre,* the High Court revered a conviction of three Africans who allegedly had insulted some white women
(in Kikuyu, a language the women did not understand).[32] A settler

leader, Colonel Grogan, headed a posse, seized and bound the three
men, and flogged them before a large crowd in front of Nairobi Court
House, forcibly ejecting a senior police officer and a magistrate who
tried to interfere.[33] Grogan went to jail. (The administration accom-
modatingly permitted him to complete his 'hard labour' somewhat less
than onerously in an empty Government bungalow, where the Colonel
entertained his friends every evening, and higher courts reversed his
conviction.)[34]

2. *Access to Courts.* Relative access to courts measures access not only
to courts as dispute-settlers but also as rule-makers. Part of the conventional dogma of the Rule of Law requires that courts stand open at
everyman's knock. The rule guarantees access to both court functions.
In fact, of course, courts everywhere open only to those who have the
resources and sophistication to knock. In Africa during the colonial era,
three principal groups met the requirements: Asian businessmen in East
Africa, some whites in Central and South Africa, and wealthy cocoa
farmers in West Africa. The ordinary African, upon whom the weight
of colonial government most pressed, had no effective access.

The East African situation exemplifies the difficulty. A survey of the
reported opinions in the East African Court of Appeals for 1957
showed that about 84 per cent of the reported civil cases had an Asian
name in the title. In East Africa, Asians formed the small business
community, mainly retailing and wholesaling. They comprised, however, only about 2 per cent of the population. Practically no civil cases
involved Africans, although most criminal defendants had African
names.

When a class believes that its interests are not being advanced by
existing rules, they can seek incremental changes through judicial rule-
making. Land tenure rules in Ghana changed in this way after half a
century of litigation by cocoa farmers.[35] The Gold Coast permitted
appeals from the local courts system into the 'English' system. Cocoa
farming played hob with traditional notions of land tenure. Coffee trees
last fifty years. Traditional land tenure institutions, however, grew out
of shifting agriculture, not the cocoa industry, which it inhibited. For
example, Ghanaian customary law forbade the alienation of land without the consent of the local chief, whose power thus conflicted with
newly rich cocoa farmers. The customary law restriction brought appeal
upon appeal, demanding in effect that a rule change permit free alien-
ability. Over time, this occurred. Had the cocoa farmers had sufficient
legislative power, they could have produced the same result more

rapidly through legislation. The authoritarian nature of colonial government, however, prevented that. Stymied, the cocoa farmers turned to
the courts, successfully. But most Africans had about as much actual
access to the 'English' courts as do the poor to courts in the United States,
for much the same reasons.

3. *Fair Trial and Judicial Independence.* The Rule of Law implied a
healthy distrust of a policeman's suspicions. That he asserts that he
knows an accused is guilty of crime does not suffice for conviction.
Instead, the Rule of Law required proof 'beyond a reasonable doubt'
before an independent tribunal, rigorously enforced by procedures to
ensure a decision based on evidence, not bias. None of these conditions
existed in most African magistrate's courts, the principal colonial trial
courts. The sorts of crimes that these courts tried in the main involved
not traditional crimes, but criminalized forms of administrative rules.
Wearing their magistrate's hats, legally untrained District Officers sat
as judges.[36] As in an earlier era in England, 'the remarkable thing was
that so much government could be carried on through the forms of a
criminal trial'.[37]

These courts and the trials they conducted did not meet many
requirements of legalism. First, the magistrates, being untrained, did
not vigorously enforce procedural rules. In one Northern Rhodesian
case, a magistrate gave an obstinate witness ten cuts with a cane (and
reported that thereafter he became more tractable); in another, a
magistrate prosecuted and fined his own cook for contempt for 'serving
coffee cold to the Magistrate'; in a third, a magistrate charged a defendant with murder but convicted him of manslaughter 'because the
victim did not die'.[38]

Second, many jurisdictions forbade lawyers to appear before the
magistrates. In any event, only in extraordinary cases did Africans have
lawyers. Without lawyers, the adversary process fails, splendidly so
where great gulfs of ignorance divide defendants from court personnel,
process and even language. Finally, judges did not wear even the mask
of independence. The District Officer as administrative official prepared
the case for prosecution, then climbed behind the bench and heard it
as magistrate. For most of the colonial era, even appellate judges lacked
judicial independence, serving at the Crown's pleasure.[39] They obtained
formal independence only in 1954 in Ghana[40] and later elsewhere.[41]

Not accident nor want of manpower created the unprofessional,
dependent, courts that tried Africans, but deliberate policy. Chief Justice Speed of Nigeria opposed extending the right of counsel to

Africans, even in capital cases, holding that 'existing safeguards (including the power of transfer to the Supreme Court) were ample, and it
was the duty of the judge to watch the interests of the accused'.[42]
Lugard argued for the unity of administrative and judicial office. 'The
separation of functions', he said, 'would appear unnatural to the primitive African, since they are combined in his own rulers, and a system
which involved the delay caused by the reference, even in minor cases,
would be detested. Moreover, in a country recently brought under
administration, and in times of political difficulty, occasions must arise
when the strictly legal aspect must give way to expediency . . .'[43]
Expediency, not 'the strictly legal aspect', reigned everywhere.

Courts and trials thereby turned into mere forms for the imposition
of sentence, frequently harsh. In Kenya, the Chief Magistrate
repeatedly sent circulars to magistrates urging a reduction in flogging
sentences.[44] Local magistrates often imposed punishment illegally. In
1907 the Chief Justice of Kenya discovered that collectors (District
Officers) in many stations in Kenya kept 'shauri books', recording
sentences of flogging, imprisonment or fines outside regular cases. He
said that 'while the High Court fully realizes the difficulties experienced
by Collectors in dealing with wild natives in outlying stations' he could
not approve a system 'which in practice permits the Collector to disregard the laws or procedures in the Protectorate for the hearing and
recording of judicial cases, which laws have been devised to ensure
publicity and supervision for all cases dealt with by Magistrates . . .' He
concluded that 'the Collector as a Magistrate can only impose a fine as
the result of a conviction after judicial proceedings'.[45] Again, in a circular to magistrates in 1913, the Chief Justice complained that in many
hut tax cases, magistrates – i.e. the DCs – often made only single file,
charging any number of Africans together in one proceeding. That
improper practice 'may, in a crowd of twenty accused natives, act to
the prejudice of one or two who may have good reasons to urge in their
defence'.[46]

The subordination to administration also occurred in appellate
courts. Sekgome's Case upheld a detention order (a bill of attainder)
expressly on an administrative requirement, for in Bechuanaland a
few 'civilized men' had to maintain their rule over the vast mass of the
'semi-barbarous'.[47] In the Masai case,[48] the court ruled that the Masai,
although living under British law, paradoxically constituted a foreign
power. They could, therefore, make treaties with the Crown, subject
to the Act of State doctrine that a court would not enquire behind
the face of the treaty. In *Commissioner for Local Government* v.

Kaderbhai,[49] the Privy Council held that Government might burden with racial covenants public land in the Kenyan White Highlands it offered for sale, even though similar, private covenants in England could not survive challenge.[50] It justified the decision expressly on grounds of administrative convenience. Elsewhere, courts held that Africans had no notion of land ownership, and that therefore white men could at will take their land.[51]

4. *Control over Government. De facto* African lack of access to courts and want of judicial independence combined to make courts almost powerless to control governmental officials.[52]

Summary: Inequitable law, separate courts systems, differential de jure and de facto access, no lawyers, a confusion of administrative and judicial roles: for Africans, reality warred with the Rule of Law. Sir Donald Cameron, Governor of Nigeria, in 1933 stated that

> If the judgement of the court is to be a judgement of an officer experienced in the art of sifting and weighing evidence and is to be based solely on the evidence which has been laid before him in the case, it does not matter a great deal to me what he is called, administrative officer or magistrate, or what the court may be called: it is sufficient that the court is a judicial tribunal and the trial officer a judicial officer. But if the decision of the court may properly be swayed by political or other non-judicial considerations within the knowledge of the Administrative Officer and is therefore not to be based on the evidence which has been led, then, in my judgement, the court has ceased to be a judicial tribunal. Change the system of law, if you will, and punish the people by Administrative Officers exercising a kind of parental correction because the people are primitive; but remember always, pray, if you do so that you will thereby be depriving the natives of the protection of any judicial court and any judicial system of law.[53]

The dual system of law buttressed the dual economy and society. Administrative control, whatever its guise as a court system, let the Administration use coercion to maintain law and order as the imperial overlords defined it, and to bring about the social change desired by the Administration, mainly creating a labour force for European employers. So far as Africans were concerned, far from the Rule of Law, the court system of Africa became the rule of the District Officer. Courts, in British eyes, appropriately decided whether an

African had violated a rule, and imposed a coercive sanction if he had. No authoritarian government, however, can tolerate in such a key role a neutral decision-making body. The imperatives of authoritarianism coverted the English ideal-typical model of local trial courts from neutral institutions, judging between man and man, or man and government, into administrative arms. That did not happen because official opinion rejected the Rule of Law, but despite it. Ghai and McAuslan aptly stated the consequences:

> The role of public law in the colonial era, when looked at through the eyes of the colonized, provides one of the best examples there is of the operation of law as expounded by adherents of the Austinian theory of law. 'Orders backed by threats', 'the gunman situation writ large'; these phrases most adequately describe what is more usually but less accurately called the reception of the British common law. Law was second only to weapons of war in the establishment of colonial rule, and for the early settlers and officials there was little difference between the two; they were both useful implements to coerce the African . . . Africans were to be coerced into performing their required role in society, whether it was to work, to pay taxes, to live in a particular place or to move about the country, and thus the criminal law, and courts to enforce it, were in many respects the key institutions in native administration for they underpinned the whole approach of the colonial administrator . . . Europeans, on the other hand, were invited to, perhaps a more accurate description would be, were conceded as a result of their demands, a great degree of co-operation in the administration of law, whether in the field of government, in the Legislative and Executive Councils, in agrarian policies, or in the judicial system via the jury, a legally qualified judge, and the application to them of all the safeguards of an English criminal trial.[54]

II Court Reform in Independent Africa

With Independence, the lawyers initiated vast programmes to change the colonial court systems to resemble more closely the legalistic model. They made strenuous, and largely successful, efforts to reduce the pluralism of law and courts, to create judicial independence, to improve professionalism and accessibility. Lawyers justified these efforts in title of 'development'. Nevertheless, courts did not become important implementing agencies for development programmes. In 1966, for example, the Kenya primary courts decided over 50,000 civil and nearly 200,000

criminal cases. Almost all the civil cases involved customary law. A little
over 10 per cent of the criminal litigation concerned the Penal Code.
The remainder, a majority of the cases, involved administrative codes
mostly remaining from the colonial era: trespass, boundary markers,
markets licensing, taxation, stock movement, production or consumption of alcohol or narcotics, or non-compliance with the orders of
administrative personnel.[55] The most widespread developmental programme in Kenya, land registration and consolidation, for whose
implementation Kenya planned to spend 17 per cent of its agricultural
development budget, excluded courts. As guardians of the Constitution
courts in Africa seemed only slightly less irrelevant.[56] Despite the
mythology that placed courts at the very centre of the legal order they
remained peripheral to the processes of development. The next section
examines various programmes to reform the courts, and the succeeding
one, why they nevertheless remained marginal to development.

A. Court Reform

Courts in colonial times, lawyers repeated, did not match the ideal
required by the Rule of Law. Lawyers, both African and expatriate,
therefore tried to unify the law and the courts, foster judicial independence and develop the legal profession.

1. *Unification of Courts and Law.* The lawyers and political leaders of
independent Africa abhorred the discrimination inherent in dual court
systems and bodies of substantive law. Significantly, however, unification always stressed Western, not customary institutions. No doubt,
subjecting Europeans or African elites to customary courts and
customary law would work injustice on them. It becomes equally
unjust, however, to subject Africans acculturated to customary courts
and law to English process and law.

Court reform did not accidentally move away from customary law
and courts to English models, rather than vice versa. Customary law
appropriately serves a subsistence economy and society, English law, a
capitalist society with a high degree of specialization and exchange.
Since law ineluctably touched on economic matters, English law of
course conquered. Higher production required specialization and exchange, for which English law, not customary law, provided rules. The
movement also expressed a power conflict.[57] Political power always
seizes upon courts and the law as its instruments, both in feudal
England and tropical Africa. Substituting new, Western law for customary law undercut traditional power in favour of the 'modernizing'

centre; to replace chiefs and elders as judges undercut them in favour
of the Western-educated elite. Among the Kaguru people of Tanganyika
during colonialism, for example, 'the courts were the major political
institution . . . whereby those in authority maintained their power;
courts provided the only means whereby local leaders could coerce
strongly dissident elements without risking the disapproval of the
colonial administration which had allied itself with the traditional
status quo within the chiefdom.'[58] In Ghana, the chiefs asserted judicial
powers as an inherent aspect of their political power.[59] Changing
judges, like changing law, changes the locus of power. Courts and the
law did not, however, change completely. The substantive law everywhere remained bifurcated, although some states tried to formulate a
uniform 'customary' law.[60] Self-evidently, no state can create a uniform
law in a bifurcated society.[61]

Unified courts systems met with more success. The 1963 Conference
on Local Courts and Customary Law agreed that 'the ultimate objective
was for the local courts to become an integral part of an independent
judiciary of the State . . .'[62] That became an objective of policy in all
the Anglophonic African courts. Generally, the centre, not local authorities, appointed local court magistrates who had jurisdiction over everyone within their area without ethnic distinction,[63] subject to appeals
through the court hierarchy.

2. *Judicial Independence.* Despite general agreement among lawyers
of its desirability[64] they have not achieved full judicial independence
for all local court magistrates. Although it raised a minor storm in the
Kenyan Parliament, the Magistrate's Courts Act, 1967, permitted
District Commissioners and District Officers to serve as magistrates,
'clear evidence' that the modernization of the legal system in Kenya
stopped short of 'the full British conception of justice'. As in the
colonial period, 'it is to be tempered by the necessities of executive
power, notwithstanding that the arrangement gave rise to well-docu-
mented abuses of power in the past'.[65] Zambia, on the other hand,
represented the central tendency. After Independence 'the Judiciary
became responsible for the whole of the judicial work performed in
previous years by officers of the Provincial Administration exercising
magisterial powers'.[66]

3. *Lawyers.* Every expatriate who ever taught in African law schools,
it seems, felt compelled to write about African legal education.[67]
Every Anglophonic African country save the Gambia acquired its own law

faculty producing lawyers whose education probably equipped them better for practising in post-war London than for the professional roles that development required.[68]

B. Court Reform and Development

Despite these reforms, the courts in independent Africa could not help very much to solve the problems of development. The myths of legalism told African lawyers (and their British and American advisers) that if they conformed the court system to its legalistic ideal-type, they would at one blow achieve development, and also freedom, equality and participatory, rational control over social life.[69] They did change the court system radically. Nevertheless, most legislation concerned with development lay outside judicial consideration in fact, and frequently also in theory, such as laws concerning the affairs of parastatal bodies, housing authorities, credit programmes and so forth. Legislation concerned with new behaviour and likely to spark litigation frequently created new adjudicative institutions (land adjudication committees in Kenya,[70] mining arbitration boards in Zambia,[71] Rent Tribunals elsewhere[72]).

Experience thus falsified the propositions of legalism. Just as the buckling of a girder falsifies not only the engineering of the bridge, but, sometimes, the physics underpinning it, so failure of the reformed legal system to promote development falsified legalism's central hypotheses.

III Courts as Implementing Agencies in Social Change

Courts in Africa became irrelevant to development not because of their peculiar characteristics, but precisely because African lawyers mostly modelled them after the British pattern. That is to say, the inappropriateness of courts to development arose out of their very structure, another example of the non-transferability of law.

A. The Commingling of Dispute-Settlement and Norm-Enforcement

All society's dispute-settling mechanisms lie on a continuum between two ideal types. In one, the decision embodies compromise — what Laura Nader calls 'give a little, get a little'. In the other, one party wins and the other loses — 'winner take all'.[73] Common human experience teaches that the future relationship of parties to a dispute depends, to a degree, on their sense that its resolution treats them fairly. Where parties want to or must co-operate after the dispute, both must leave the settlement procedures without too great a sense of grievance. If, however, the parties need not live together thereafter, then the parties may continue their antagonism. Compromise resolves the disputes in the sense that it reduces continuing antagonism. Winner take all decides who wins, but it will not ameliorate antagonism.

For ongoing relationships, therefore, dispute-settling follows give a little, get a little. The world around, where people necessarily must continue to live in close contact after resolution of the dispute compromise becomes dispute-settlement's central principle.[74] Stewart Macauley demonstrated that businessmen do not bring law suits in the United States against customers whose trade they want to keep.[75] Married couples who want to stay married do not sue each other. They consult marriage counsellors, who look for compromises. Trade unions and employers regularly settle their disputes by arbitration.

On the other hand, a winner take all decision sanctions the breach of a norm; a compromise solution does not. The person who has breached a contract, but successfully compromises the claim, suffers less than full legal sanctions. The difference between give a little, get a little and winner take all embodies the difference between disputes-settlement as such, and norm-enforcement. These comprise two basic 'law jobs', to resolve disputes and to channel behaviour.[76]

Courts in the Western world therefore 'resolve' conflict only in a Pickwickian way. Instead of reconciling the parties, they declare one or the other the winner, and force the loser to swallow the decision. The official* dispute-settlement institutions of every Western, capitalist country, and of the LDCs which 'received' their law from these countries, relied mainly on 'winner take all', becoming primarily norm-sanctioning, not dispute-settlement institutions. Disputes triggered their processes, but they neither tried to nor succeeded in amicably resolving disputes.

How did courts acquire these seemingly incompatible functions? The middle classes made two principal claims upon the law. They wanted equitable and rational dispute-settlement institutions to ensure predictability. They wanted substantive law to favour themselves. Blocked from access to Parliament by rotten boroughs, aristocratic control and corruption,[77] like dispossessed classes elsewhere,[78] they thronged the courts. Those courts satisfied their dual demands. As winner take all

---

*Obviously, even in Western societies compromise settles most disputes. Where in case of failure to compromise a party must resort to a forum that decides on a winner take all basis, the parties will compromise on the basis of their estimate of probabilities in possible litigation *à l'outrance*.

institutions, they both ended disputes, and enforced rules through negative direct sanctions. In particular, the new middle classes wanted the state to protect their property interests, because of course public sentiment would only do so unreliably.

> One man may alienate the affection and love of another's wife, but neither the wife nor the seducer is clapped into jail. A man may undermine the authority of another, violate his obligations as a friend, lie and cheat, and misrepresent, all to his own advantage and all in flagrant violation of the other's role 'rights'. For the most part, all that the injured party can do is to call upon his friends to rally round, ask that onlookers observe the violation of the elementary decencies, and seek the unorganized protection of his immediate community. (In other words, the victim is in serious trouble.) In the normal course of role relationships, one man can destroy the life work of another and, in the process, violate the most sacred role obligations, yet he may at most be subject only to frowns, criticism, or loss of reputation. But heaven help him should he deliberately walk off with the other man's hat. The police apparatus would be mobilized, weapons inspected, warrants issued, jail keys turned.[79]

Moreover, not only does the law guard property rights, but it routinely invokes state power to do so. 'Normally, one does not bargain, negotiate, remonstrate or appeal to a thief; one calls the police.'[80]

Using courts to protect property demonstrates at once the importance of complicated economic rules in societies of specialization and exchange, and those societies' alienation and fragmentation. Diffuse public sanctions can work only in a relatively unified society that constitutes a genuine community, with deeply internalized norms. That courts and not the community at large administers sanctions arises because ruling elites, far from merely enacting law that 'reinstitutionalizes custom', impose most law upon the society and its members.

Parenthetically, I suggest that these propositions may have important consequences for legal theory. Much theory argues that law indeed merely reinstitutionalized custom. If courts enforce direct sanctions in part because society cannot sanction these norms in a general, diffuse and public manner (the hallmarks of a custom), then the law exceeds custom. If so the law must originate in the creative activity of law-makers. Unless we believe in schoolroom myths about governors as philosopher-kings, the self-interest of the law-makers and their allies must colour the law they write. At least in the main, governors *impose* law upon the governed. The very existence of courts as a sanctioning system contradicts the notion that law merely reflects custom.

B. The Consequences of the Use of Dispute-Settlement Processes for Sanctioning Functions

Confounding these two quite different court functions had many consequences. This section discusses in turn (1) inherent limits of courts as sanctioning agencies; (2) procedural problems; (3) incremental change; (4) the form of the laws; (5) overloading of the judicial system; and (6) want of expertise.

1. *Limits on Sanctions.* Roscoe Pound said that the law (i.e. the courts) 'secures interests by punishment, by prevention, by specific redress and substantial redress; and the wit of man has discovered no further possibilities for juridical action'.[81] Courts could do no other, not because the wit of man could not invent other ways to influence behaviour, but because courts institutionally could not apply other conformity-inducing measures. Rewards, roundabout sanctions and education usually required money, personnel and rule-making power. Courts did not have such resources or capacity because they intermingled dispute-resolution and norm-enforcement of a particular kind. In a stratified society, winner take all must govern property disputes, which punishment therefore typically sanctions. As argued in Chapter 9, direct, negative sanctions have little use in development.

2. *Rigid, Formal, Complex and Slow Procedures.* The world around courts seem rigid, formal, complex and slow, and therefore largely useless as sanctioning institutions in the development effort. These procedures flow from the peculiar functions of courts as they developed historically in England, the self-interests of lawyers, and the built-in dynamic of bureaucracy. In orthodox Western jurisprudence, the ideal-type court mainly settles disputes. Where a dispute arises from a claimed breach of law, a court must ascertain the facts. In the main, proof about matters of fact comes from the lips of observers. The verdict or judgement depends upon the trier of fact affirming these propositions. Whether or not the trier affirms these allegations depends upon his concluding that the statements of some witnesses rather than others are true. Common law courts have for centuries asserted that the credibility of witnesses can best be determined after cross-examination, and after observation of the witnesses' demeanour. The witnesses must therefore usually report their testimony in person to the trier of fact, and expose themselves to cross-examination, a time-consuming, slow

process.

Not every court trial is equally slow, complex or rigid. These characteristics develop only when courts try to determine conscientiously whether the defendant violated the rule. Many cases do that only cursorily. Small claims courts rarely undertake the painstaking investigation of a court dealing with very large sums. Cases involving only small sums rarely climb the full appellate ladder. Criminal matters concerning sophisticated and affluent defendants receive meticulous care, but those concerning the poor or the powerless, more casual treatment. Crimes with large possible penalties invoke more procedural strictness than parking offences. Courts always exercise the greatest care in civil trials with large property interests at stake, involving correspondingly important and powerful litigants. The rigidity, formality, slowness and complexity that critics often berate in judicial systems reflect the importance of the interests with which some courts deal. They are not faults, but the hallmarks of meticulous care. The procedures for dealing with important matters, however, became the standard. Only specifically enumerated exceptional cases (minor traffic offences, small claims, small probate matters, minor administrative rules, small criminal offences) used more casual procedures.

The professional self-interest of court personnel also led to these characteristics of judicial systems. Lawyers grew rich on the mysteries of litigation. Finally, courts had bureaucratic structures. As in all bureaucracies, rule-fetishism in time dominated their processes. The cumbersome process of courts made them all but useless in most development programmes.

3. *Incremental Change.* The confusion of dispute-settlement and sanctioning limited courts' competence as law-maker to incremental change. Precisely because courts purported to sanction existing laws, they denied themselves the explicit power to create new law. This I discuss below.[82]

4. *The Form of the Laws.* Legal rules performed many functions. One was to communicate expected behaviour to the role-occupant. When the rule used punishment as sanction, however, it divided behaviour subject to sanction from other behaviour. Draftsmen therefore used legalese in lieu of English[83] — a poor dialect to communicate the new norms of development.

5. *Overloading.* Every judicial system presently labours at the point of

overload or actually overloaded. Governments generally do not provide more judges and administrative personnel than they presently need. Courts serve as society's general, residual sanctioning system. In the developed countries, new statutes, or new judicially created laws occasionally overburden the courts. In the United States, for example, the widening legal basis for civil rights litigation seriously overloaded many federal district courts. Most new rules of law in the developed world instituted only incremental change. Obviously, in such circumstances, the courts did not confront enormous numbers of new cases. Where their load increased only marginally, courts coped. The contrary obtained with many rules that look towards developmental behaviour.

6. *Courts as General Sanctioning Systems and the Lack of Expertise.*
Many regulations imposed by a modern welfare state call for tribunals with highly specialized expertise. A court may have expertise about automobile accidents, but not about the construction of a giant steam generating plant. Specialized tribunals can enforce regulations controlling such construction better than courts, as with such subjects as radio and television broadcasting, labour relations and industrial safety statutes.

Institutions that can impose only punishments with rigid, complex and slow procedures, that can only institute incremental change, subject to rules in legalese, always at overload, and lacking expertise to deal with technical matters, will not implement many development rules. Those characterize at best, rule-applying institutions, not problem-solving ones. Development, however, required change-oriented, problem-solving institutions to induce new behaviour in a wide range of clients. The efforts of lawyers to ensure that the courts systems of Africa matched the ideal-type demanded by the Rule of Law missed the mark of development.

This perceived marginality of courts to development led many lawyers and non-lawyers alike to believe that law itself bore little relevance to development. Many defined 'law' as those rules that courts apply. So defining 'law', if one perceives courts as marginal to development, 'law' will seem equally impotent.

IV The Function of Courts in Developing Societies

The characteristics of courts that hobbled their utility in development arose out of their structure, which resulted from their mixed conflict-resolution and norm-enforcement functions. The characteristics of courts that place them at the centre of legalism and the Rule of Law —

judicial independence, universalistic rules, the exclusion of subjective values by judges through the use of legalistic reasoning — also arose from those dual functions.

Courts in modern Africa seemingly could perform some of the functions that jurisprudents celebrated. They might have protected human rights. They did not, save extraordinarily.[84] They might have policed administrative regularity. They did so only rarely.[85] Limited to winner take all, they even settled disputes poorly. All these functions needed new institutions appropriate to the problems of the emergent LDCs. Nevertheless courts performed important social control functions in transitional societies. In every society negative sanctions buttress a host of statutes, for example, the criminal law. A private sector's very existence excited disputed cases in contract, property and tort. Trials involving them frequently concerned difficult issues of fact. The reformed African courts reasonably well decided such disputes.

Second, precisely because legislation consists mainly of general rules, it can never provide for every possible contingency. Parties will contest the construction of the rules in new situations. Courts play a useful function in filling in the interstices of legislation. Courts in Tanzania might have done so in the *ujamaa* village programme.[86] A member of a village participated in the collective activities according to the village by-laws. After a time he resigned his membership and claimed his aliquot portion of the collective's earnings. The governing statute left vague the villager's rights in such circumstances. The case posed an issue, marginal to the overall programme, but demanding authoritative resolution. Only the courts would decide it. In Tanzania, the Chief Justice believed the issue involved political problems and informally deferred the case indefinitely, effectively closing the courthouse doors. The villager's impotence could not advance the programme, nor enhance government's legitimacy.

Third, every programme, even if it relies primarily upon roundabout sanctions, ultimately rests upon some direct sanction. A law that seeks to limit the economic activity of political elites may forbid bankers to extend credit to political leaders (a roundabout measure). That rule itself probably threatens criminal sanctions against the banker (a direct measure). Courts can usefully apply such 'last-stage' sanctions in development programmes.

Finally, courts in the common law systems have one unique characteristic: they at least nominally stand open to every citizen who conceives he has a cause. No matter what other institutions a government may fashion to settle disputes, control government illegality, protect human freedoms, sanction law-breakers, or generate interstitial rules, courts can resolve cases that otherwise lack a forum. Their generalist character, that disqualifies them from involvement in many developmental programmes, becomes an asset, the necessary condition of courts of last resort.

Other institutions can perform analogous functions. An Ombudsman or state procurator provides an avenue of appeal against claimed administrative irregularity. The Party can settle some minor disputes, as the ten house cell chairmen did in Tanzania. Inevitably, cases arise that have no specialized institution. Courts usefully open their doors to such residual cases. Especially when conditions change rapidly, the number of cases rises.

Courts cannot perform these functions without all the attributes of the rule of law. Judges must be independent. So far as they can, they must apply the law, not create it. When they must create new law, they should create incremental, not radical change. They must decide impartially. They must hear the parties by rules of evidence that permit wise and rational decisions about matters of fact. In short, they must behave like courts.

The efforts of African lawyers to remake courts from mere arms of the colonial administration into institutions matching the Rule of Law bore good results. Lawyers should not deceive themselves, however, that court and law reform exhausts their responsibility to adapt law to the demands of development.

Conclusion

Courts possess certain structural characteristics that arise from their dual functions of norm-sanctioning and dispute-settlement. These characteristics served the rising middle classes well during their early nineteenth-century assault on the citadels of aristocratic privilege, and entered legal ideology as part of the Rule of Law. Transferred to the colonies, however, the local courts performed few or none of the functions that myth ascribed to them. They became mere administrative instruments. Although reformed after independence, they remained without significant developmental functions. Structurally, they could not implement programmes to change behaviour or to solve new problems. The very characteristics which incapacitated courts from development, however, made them valuable residual institutions to which the individual might appeal when all other approaches to government fail.

Notes

1. See Chap. 4 above, n. 15 and articles cited.
2. D.M. Trubek and M. Galanter, 'Scholars in Self-Estrangement: Some Reflections on the Crisis in Law and Development Studies in the United States', *Wisc. L. Rev.*, 1062 (1974).
3. Ibid., p. 1072 ('. . . In a sense, the courts are the central institutions of the legal order.')
4. Ibid., p. 1063; see also D.M. Trubek, 'Toward a Social Theory of Law: An Essay on the Study of Law and Development', *Yale L. Rev.*, 82, 1 (1972).
5. See above, Chap. 2.
6. See e.g., The East Africa Order-in-Council, 1893; Barotzeland-North Western Rhodesia Order-in-Council, 1899.
7. G.E. Metcalfe, *MacLean of the Gold Coast: The Life and Times of George MacLean* (London: Oxford UP, 1962).
8. See p. 29 above.
9. C.K. Allen, *The Queen's Peace* (London: Stevens, 1953), pp. 139-40.
10. See above, Chap. 5.
11. *R.* v. *Kalana* [1945-48] L.R.N.R. 218 (1948).
12. *Musa* v. *R.*, E.A.P.L.R. 11 (1921) (Kenya: Disease of Animals Ordinance, 1906); Muu v. *R.*, [1951] E.A. 894 (Kenya: Movement of Maize No. 2 Order, 1953).
13. See above, Chap. 5; see e.g., In re Kakuiwa Gatanye, 8 E.A.P.L.R. 113 (1920) (Kenya: Native Hut and Poll Tax Ordinance, 1910).
14. See, e.g., Basutoland: Proclamation 72 of 1952.
15. Y.P. Ghai and J.P.W.B. McAuslan, *Public Law in Kenya* (London: Oxford UP, 1970).
16. F.D. Lugard, *The Dual Mandate in Tropical Africa*, (4th ed.) (Edinburgh: William Blackwood, 1929), p. 546.
17. R. Roberts-Wray, 'The Adaptation of Imported Law in Africa', *J. Af. Law*, 4, 66 (1960).
18. In Northern Rhodesia, for example, the Native Courts Ordinance of 1929 extended for the first time formal recognition to native courts. It provided that these courts '. . . shall consist of such chief, elder or council of elders in the area assigned to it as the Governor may direct'. Northern Rhodesia: Native Court Ordinance, No. 33 of 1929, sec. 3(2).
19. E.L. Hoover, C. Piper, and F.O. Spalding, 'The Evolution of the Zambian Courts System', *Zambian L.J.*, 2, 4, 12 (1970).
20. A.P. Munro, 'Land Law in Kenya', in T.W. Hutchinson (ed.), *Africa and Law: Developing Legal Systems in African Commonwealth Nations* (Madison: University of Wisconsin Press, 1968), p. 75.
21. 4 L.R.N.R. 183 (1947).
22. Judicial Adviser's Conference, Record, 9 J. Afr. Ad. (Supp.) Apr. 1957, p. 5, quoted in Hoover *et al.*, 'Zambian Courts System', p. 70.
23. Afrika Institut-Leiden, *The Future of Customary Law in Africa* (Leiden: Afrika Institut, 1956).
24. Judicial Advisers' Conference, 1957.
25. A. Allott, *Essays in African Law* (London: Butterworth's, 1960), see Hoover, *et al.*, 'Zambian Courts System'.
26. E.E. Jenkins, *Report of an Enquiry into the causes of a disturbance at Nkana on 4th and 5th November, 1937* (Lusaka: Government Printer 1937).
27. Ibid., p. 4.
28. Ibid., p. 9.
29. Ibid., pp. 11-14.
30. Compare *R.* v. *Malidisa*, (1961) 2 S.A. 377 with *R.* v. *Koning*, (1953) S.A.

220 and R. v. Metelerkamp, 1949 (4) S.A. 102.
31. N. Leys, Kenya (London: Leonard & Virginia Woolf, 1924).
32. Baili v. Kamao, 2 E.A.P.L.R. 39 (1907).
33. See Daily Mail (London), 15 March 1907; Times of East Africa (Nairobi), 6 April 1907.
34. Gray v. Rex, 2 E.A.P.L.R. 40 (1907).
35. S.K.B. Asante, 'Interests in Land in the Customary Law of Ghana: A New Appraisal' Yale L.J., 74, 848 (1965).
36. These courts have received only sparse study. Typically, scholars treated them as carbon copies of local magistrates' courts in England. In 1956 a resident magistrate in Northern Rhodesia, writing thirteen pages on the courts of that territory, covered nine pages on the local courts of England and only devoted one page specifically to the Northern Rhodesian courts. Kempton, Courts of Justice 9-2 (2d ed. 1956), cited in Hoover et al., 'Zambian Courts System', p. 50, n. 353.
37. J.P. Dawson, A History of Lay Judges (Cambridge, Mass.: Harvard UP, 1960), p. 140.
38. Hoover et al., 'Zambian Courts System', p. 50, n. 253.
39. Terrell v. Secretary of State for the Colonies [1953] Q.B. 482.
40. W.B. Harvey, Law and Social Change in Ghana (Princeton: Princeton UP, 1966), p. 216.
41. K. Roberts-Wray, 'The Independence of the Judiciary in Commonwealth Countries', in J.N.D. Anderson, Changing Law in Developing Countries (London: Allen and Unwin, 1963).
42. Lugard, Dual Mandate, p. 545.
43. Ibid., p. 539; see also Morris and J. Read, Uganda: The Development of its Laws and Constitution (London: Stevens, 1966), p. 43.
44. Circular to Magistrates No. 1 of 1905, 1 E.A.P.L.R. 156; Circular to Magistrates No. 6 of 1911, 4 E.A.P.L.R. xvi; Circular to Magistrates No. 1 of 1948, 23(2) K.L.R. 113.
45. Circular to Magistrates, No. 6 of 1907, E.A.P.L.R. 138.
46. Circular to Magistrates, No. 5, of 1913, 7 E.A.P.L.R. 172.
47. The King v. the Earl of Crewe (ex parte Sekgome), [1910] 2 K.B. 676.
48. See above, Chap. 5, n. 12.
49. 12 K.L.R. 12 (Kenya, 1930).
50. R.W. James, 'Implementing the Arusha Declaration – The Role of the Legal System' (University of Dar es Salaam, cyclostyle, 1972).
51. Gathome v. Murito, 9 E.A.P.L.R. 102 (1922); see also Re Southern Rhodesia [1919] A.C. 211.
52. See below, Chap. 13.
53. Nigeria, Legislative Council Address (Govt. Printer, Lagos, 1933), p. 25.
54. Y.P. Ghai and J.P.W. B. McAuslan, Public Law in Kenya (London: Oxford UP, 1970), pp. 506-7.
55. R. Abel, 'Case Method Research in the Customary Law of Wrongs in Kenya', E. Afr. L.J., 5, 247 (1969).
56. See below, Chap. 18.
57. L. Friedman, 'On Legal Development', Rutgers L. Rev., 24, 11 (1969).
58. T.O. Biedelman, 'Intertribal Tensions in Colonial Tanganyika', J. Afr. L., 10, 118; J. Afr. L., 11, 27, 39-40 (1966-7).
59. Harvey, Law and Social Change, pp. 198-9.
60. See E. Contran, 'Some Recent Developments in the Tanganyikan Judicial System', J. Afr. L., 6, 19, 26-28 (1962); M. Alliott, 'Problèmes de l'Unification des Droits Africains', J. Afr. L., 11, 86 (1967).
61. Hoover et al., 'Zambia Courts System', pp. 79-108.

62. *Report on the African Conference on Local Courts and Customary Law* (Dar es Salaam: Faculty of Law, University College, 1963).
63. See various Local Courts Acts, e.g., Kenya: The Magistrate's Courts Act (Cap. 10) §§3-7 (1967); Harvey, *Law and Social Change*, p. 215 *et seq.*; Abel, 'Wrongs in Kenya', pp. 260-83.
64. *Report on the African Conference on Local Courts and Customary Law* (Dar es Salaam: Faculty of Law, University College, 1963), p. 44.
65. Ghai and McAuslan, *Public Law in Kenya*, pp. 372-3.
66. *Zambia: Annual Report of the Judiciary and the Magistracy* (Lusaka: Gov't. Printer, 1964), p. 5.
67. J. Bainbridge, *The Study and Teaching of Law in Africa* (South Hackensack, N.J.: Rothman, 1972).
68. Ibid.
69. Trubek and Galanter, 'Scholars in Self-Estrangement'.
70. M.P.K. Sorrenson, *Land Reform in the Kikuyu Country* (London: Oxford University Press, 1967).
71. Zambia: The Minerals Act, 1969.
72. Uganda: The Rent Restriction Act, 1949 (Cap. 210) Sec. 4.
73. L. Nader, 'Styles of Court Procedure, "To Make the Balance" ', in L. Nader (ed.), *Law in Culture and Society* (Chicago: Aldine, 1969), pp. 69-74.
74. R.C. Abel, 'A Comparative Theory of Dispute Institutions in Society', *Law & Soc. Rev.*, 8, 217 (1973).
75. S. Macauley, 'Non-Contractual Relations in Business: A Preliminary Study', *Am. Soc. Rev.*, 28, 55 (1963).
76. L. Llewellyn and E.A. Hoebel, *The Cheyenne Way* (Norman, Okla.: U. of Okla. P., 1967), p. 20.
77. R. Wraith and E. Simpkins, *Corruption in Developing Countries* (London: Allen, 1963).
78. L.W. Pye, *Politics, Personality and Nation Building: Burma's Search for Identity* (New Haven: Yale UP, 1962), p. 104; Asante, 'Interests in Land'.
79. A.W. Gouldner, *The Coming Crisis of Western Sociology* (New York: Avon Books, 1970), pp. 306-7.
80. Ibid.
81. R. Pound, 'The Limits of Effective Legal Action', *A.B.A.J.*, 3, 55 (1917).
82. See below, Chap. 18.
83. See above, Chap. 7.
84. See below, Chap. 18.
85. See below, Chap. 13.
86. R.W. James, 'Implementing the Arusha Declaration – The Role of the Legal System' (University of Dar es Salaam, cyclostyle, 1972).

Courts lacked institutional capacity to implement development law. That task fell upon the administration. Two demands faced the civil service. Official activity must stay within boundaries the law defined ('the Rule of Law'). Simultaneously, bureaucrats must administer co-ordinated, creative and flexible programmes of development ('development administration'). The first requirement sought stability and predictability, the second, change and innovation. Together, the two became an African version of the universal paradox of the law: 'Law must be stable and yet it cannot stand still. Hence, all thinking about law has struggled to reconcile the conflicting demands of the need for stability and the need for change.'[1]

I The Dilemma of African Administration

By 1974, Africa had the worst of both worlds. Neither the Rule of Law nor development administration existed. I examine in turn traditional visions of bureaucracy and the Rule of Law; bureaucratic inability to solve developmental problems; and, last, the paradoxical African situation, which achieved neither change nor stability.

A. Traditional Bureaucracy and the Rule of Law

The myth of bureaucracy defines it as an instrument for implementing policy: infinitely flexible, nationalizing or denationalizing industry, running a postal system, an industrial corporation or a navy, administering foreign affairs and prisons. If so, the dilemma of African administration would disappear, for it could as easily administer development programmes as guarantee law and order.

The classical paradigm of bureaucracy followed Max Weber's ideal-type.[2]

(1) A continuous organization of official functions bound by rules.
(2) A specified sphere of competence.
(3) The organization of offices follows the principle of hierarchy; that is, each lower office is under the control and supervision of a higher one . . .
(4) The rules which regulate the conduct of an office may be techni-

cal rules or norms.

(5) ... The members of the administrative staff should be completely separated from ownership of the means of production or administration ...

(6) There is also a complete absence of appropriation of his official position by the incumbent ...

(7) Administrative acts, decisions and rules are formulated and recorded in writing ...[3]

Weber developed this ideal-type as part of his model of Western capitalist development. He assumed that Western European governments ruled in the interests of the capitalist class. They had to achieve the objectives of that class: instrumentality, predictability, equality before the law and authority. His model of bureaucracy, he thought, achieved these objectives.[4] It became instrumental by subjecting administrators to governing rules,[5] thus undercutting the feudal concept that the office holder might properly use his power for his personal advantage.[6] Because policy emerged as rules, official behaviour became predictable,[7] for the citizen could discover the rules that guided it.[8] Governance by rules led to 'the dominance of a spirit of formalistic impersonality, *"sine ira et studio"*, without hatred or passion ... The dominant norms are concepts of straight forward duty without regard to personal considerations. Everyone is subject to formal equality of treatment; that is, everyone in the same empirical situation ...'[9] A rising class always demands equality before the law.[10]

Lastly, the entrepreneurs needed an authoritarian government to dominate the lower orders. Weberian bureaucracy above all else became authoritarian.[11]

The propertyless masses especially are not served by a formal 'equality before the law' and 'a calculable' adjudication and administration, as demanded by 'bourgeois' interests.[12] Naturally, in their eyes, justice and administration should serve to compensate for their economic and social life — opportunities in the face of the propertied classes.[13]

Weber insisted that the rules defining power grant minimal discretion. ' "Equality before the law" and the demand for legal guarantees against arbitrariness require a formal and rational "objectivity" of administration, as opposed to the personally free discretion flowing from the "grace" of the old patrimonial domination.'[14] Rules do not control officials with unlimited discretion to act or not.

Before Weber lawyers developed similar notions under the rubric of
the Rule of Law. In 1885, Dicey wrote that law consisted of a body of
fixed and ascertainable rules. By the Rule of Law, he wrote, we

> mean . . . that no man is punishable or can be lawfully made to
> suffer in body or goods except for a distinct breach of law establi-
> shed in the ordinary legal manner before the ordinary courts of the
> land. In this sense the rule of law is contrasted with every system of
> government based on the exercise by persons in authority of wide,
> arbitrary or discretionary powers of constraint.[15]

The rules of administrative law became the principal instrument of the
legal order to control administration and implement the Rule of Law.[16]

Bureaucracy in this ideal form and the Rule of Law passed into the
common culture. African lawyers too came to believe that these concepts, where followed, ensured the infinite flexibility, perfect
obedience and superior efficiency of the administration and, also,
predictability and equality before the law.

B. Substantive Legitimacy and Development Administration

A counter-myth about bureaucracy opposed Weber's model. Bureaucracy had the characteristics of its vulgar usage: hidebound, conservative, snarled in red tape, unable to simultaneously chew gum and walk.
It could not change or develop itself, much less Ghana or Tanzania.
The bureaucratic ideal-type paid a price for legal-rational legitimacy:
rules bound it tightly. Through rules the bureaucratic structure supposedly ensured instrumentality, predictability and equal treatment.[17]

Control may produce certainty, but rarely creativity. Development
meant change, and required an administration to solve novel problems.
'Hierarchy and routinization are appropriate institutional characteristics of the classic governmental tasks of maintaining order, collecting
taxes and providing services', but 'flexibility and innovation are the
traits a bureaucracy needs to promote development'.[18]

The myth about bureaucracy extolled its infinite flexibility. African
law-makers responded to the demands of development by giving
bureaucrats great discretion, not by changing bureaucracy's structure. If
one believed the myth, the flexibility of bureaucracy enabled the Rule
of Law and development administration to operate harmoniously. The
discretion that development administration apparently needed, however, undermined the Rule of Law.[19]

A country might enjoy instrumentality, predictability and equality before the law, it seemed, but must therefore suffer authority, narrow discretion and compartmentalized, hierarchical decision-making. It might enjoy change, creativity and flexibility, and suffer discretion. One could not have both simultaneously. That became the 'deadlock' of development administration.[20]

In the event, broad discretion shot through development programmes.[21] In Kenya, '. . . in an attempt to increase the effectiveness of the administration, wider discretions are conferred upon officials by law, and these officials are prepared to take, and can get away with taking short-cuts'.[22] So everywhere: Dean Pound wrote that 'Almost all the problems of jurisprudence come down to a fundamental one of rule and discretion.'[23]

C. African Administration Between Two Stools

Bureaucracy or development administration? Rule of Law or discretion? Stability or change? Brake or accelerator? These antinomies posed seemingly insoluble dilemmas. By and large, Africa reached the worst of both worlds.

African administrations by 1974 suffered from particularism. Hyden said of the Kenyan Civil Service that

at present everyone pulls his own strings in order to get things done or settled in the civil service. There is often inconsistency in treatment, because both politicians and members of the public have come to realize that the quickest way of achieving results is often in contacting friends in the relevant ministry who can arrange that the matter is given preferential treatment.[24]

Despite their broad discretion, on the other hand, many complained that African bureaucracies were 'bureaucratic'. Compartmentalization reigned. The Zambian bureaucracy, for example, did not exemplify 'a unified and hierarchical body that is capable of pursuing a common policy. Rather, the administrative system is best characterized as a collection of departments enjoying a great deal of autonomy and only loosely tied to each other.'[25] National planning became an exercise in frustration.

Nor did African administrations win awards for creativity or experimentation. Robert Jackson asked 'whether this essentially bureaucratic system of administration [in Kenya] — with its sharp hierarchical structure, its preoccupation with defining and delimiting jurisdictional

area, its emphasis upon replicability within a framework of clearly
indicated rules and precedents — is entirely appropriate for present
development needs.'[26] He commented that in Kenya

> the most striking feature of government administration is . . . its
> rather rigid bureaucratic nature which is a contemporary legacy of
> the colonial past. The structure is well adapted to the quest for con-
> trol but was not fashioned with the aim of initiating and guiding
> development change . . . Bureaucratic administration requires and
> fashions leaders who tend to be preoccupied with procedure and
> routine and with correctly applying predetermined rules to every
> decision confronted. But development and social change generate
> novel problems and new situations for which pre-existing rules and
> decision-making precedents may offer no solution.[27]

Kenya's Ndegwa Commission summed up prevailing dissatisfaction with
existing administration there (and it might have spoken for all Africa):
What is required is that the administration

> must be highly change-oriented; it must reward initiative and experi-
> mentation; it must have a high concern for cost-effectiveness and a
> routine habit of evaluating all ongoing programs; it must be prepared
> to compromise between unified central control and the need for
> flexibility, variety and a degree of autonomy in field organizations
> charged with implementing policy; it must be extremely strong on
> action, time sequences, logistics and clearly defined goals; and at the
> same time it must retain a clear consciousness of its role as the ser-
> vant, not the master of the public, if its efforts to induce change are
> not to be self-defeating.[28]

African law-makers reasonably believed that despite broad grants of
discretion their administration would produce the regularity, predictability and equality of treatment promised by the Rule of Law. Africa
received from England the common law rules of administrative law.
Lawyers fondly believed those rules guaranteed the Rule of Law in
England;[29] why not in Africa? In fact, however, the rules of administrative law constituted a classic example of symbolic law — law-in-the-
books that hardly affected behaviour. It provided yet another example
of non-transferable law.

II The Failure of Administrative Law

A. *The Law Policing Administrative Behaviour*

The formal rules prescribing administrative behaviour in Africa, as in
England, fell into three groups. Statutes gave the several agencies
their missions, defined general powers and duties and sometimes
specified particular procedures. The General Orders of the administration, and innumerable regulations and subsidiary legislation stated
subordinate rules detailing specific matters: the form of hierarchy,
qualifications for office, spheres of competence of particular
officers, and so forth. Finally, a set of rules empowered courts to keep
officials within bounds and ensure they performed their duties. The
reception statute included only these last rules, for only they lay in the
common law. These rules of judicial control over administration enforced limits on power, controlled discretion, defined implementation.

1. *Rules Enforcing Limits on Power.* Substantive statutes grant power:
to run a post office, to build roads, to raise a defence force, to accomplish the myriad tasks of modern government. The Weberian model
required precise limits on each such grant of power.

The common law courts developed the *ultra vires* doctrine to enforce those limits: unless a public officer acts within the scope of his
statutory power, he has only the authority of an ordinary citizen.[30]
This central rule, a cornerstone of the British constitution, supposedly
simultaneously ensured an orderly administration, by enforcing the
statutory division of labour, citizen freedom from bureaucratic oppression, by preventing official over-reaching, and civil service instrumentality, by requiring that power be exercised only within legislatively-
established boundries. The *ultra vires* concept presupposed that substantive rules granted only limited power. 'Government under the rule
of law demands proper legal limits on the exercise of power. This does
not mean merely that acts of authority must be justified by law, for if
the law is wide enough it can justify a dictatorship based upon the
tyrannical but perfectly legal [sic] principle *quod principi placuit legis
habeat vigorem.*[31] The rule of law requires something further. Powers
must first be approved by Parliament, and must then be granted by
Parliament within definable limits.'[32] The English courts as a rule of
statutory construction therefore 'presumed that powers, even though
widely defined, have ascertainable limits, and that Parliament is unlikely to intend the executive to be the judge of the extent of its own
powers . . .[33]

In the United States, courts reached the same results, based on constitutional doctrines of the separation of powers.[34] In England, the
theory of parliamentary supremacy led to a different result. Courts
might not question an Act of Parliament, although they could construe it. English administrative law contained no concepts or principles
to enable courts to *require* Parliament to limit grants to power, so they
became adept at so construing statutes. Where Parliament unambiguously made a wide grant, however, a court could not diminish it.[35]

2. *Rules Patrolling Discretion.* If an official can determine whether to
act, or which course to adopt, he has discretion. Weberian bureaucracy
insists that he use that discretion only for public purposes. If he takes
private viewing considerations into account, he substitutes his personal
goals for public ones, a phenomenon that sociologists call goal substitution. Non-sociologists call some of those instances 'graft'. Goal substitution negates instrumentality.

English administrative law discovered two devices to reduce goal
substitution. The first required that substantive statutes specify the
considerations appropriately to be taken into consideration. The wider
the range of permissible considerations, the broader the discretion, and
the greater likelihood of goal substitution. A statute that defines
speeding as 'travelling over forty miles an hour' limits the discretion of
policemen, prosecutors and judges more than one which defines it as
'travelling at an unreasonable rate of speed considering weather conditions, amount of traffic, visibility, road conditions', and much more
than one which defines it as 'travelling at an excessive rate of speed'.

The English courts developed rules of statutory interpretation that
ensured that 'if it can be fairly implied that the powers were given for
some particular purpose, exercise for some other purpose will be
illegal'.[36] As with scope of power, however, so with scope of discretion: if Parliament plainly granted unlimited discretion, courts declared
that they lacked the power to structure it.[37]

Second, courts developed rules to ensure that administrators would
consider only matters relevant to public purposes. These rules required
administrators to consider all relevant facts, and to exclude private
viewing considerations. Rules of natural justice[38] required that there be
a fair hearing in quasi-judicial investigations.[39] These guaranteed that
those with the greatest interest, the parties, had opportunity to bring
relevant data to the administrators' attention. Other rules excluded
irrelevant data from consideration. Rules of evidence, however loosely
applied in administrative hearings, had a core of meaning. A whole

panoply of rules limited the facts appropriate to exercising discretion.[40] The United States, probably constitutionally required the tribunal to make findings of fact and conclusions of law.[41] English administrative law did not in general require those, although statutes frequently did so.[42] Such findings check the relevance of facts that the administrators consider. Finally, criteria that determine the minimum quantum of evidence for decision ensured that administrators decide on facts, not whimsy.[43]

The rules defining the exercise of discretionary power therefore mainly concerned procedure. Doctrinally they fed on the *ultra vires* rules: an agency that failed to follow prescribed procedures acted *ultra vires*. By controlling discretion, these procedural rules tamed bureaucratic power.

3. *Enforcement Institutions.* Without institutions to enforce these rules, they would be useless. England had such institutions. Internal bureaucratic controls based on the informal organization of the civil service, its internalized code and Old Boy homogeneity provided sanctions against corruption and manifest irregularity. Parliamentary questions and laying proposed delegated legislation on the table gave Parliament some control over ministerial rule-making. Private individuals whose toes the bureaucratic machinery had pinched could obtain judicial review. The most powerful public, and the public most likely to feel the pinch, the middle class, had lawyers and courts available. The rules themselves spoke in a middle-class rhetoric, striking a balance between 'private rights' and 'public interest'.

English administration did not in all respects, of course, comply with the Rule of Law. It contained discretionary powers that far exceeded what the US Constitution permitted. Subordinate legislation abounded, at Ministerial discretion,[44] with few or weak controls.[45] Only a very few, weak procedures could compel affirmative administration action.[46] As in most bureaucratic structures the niceties of the Rule of Law availed mainly to higher income and status groups, not to the lowly.[47] The rules of criminal justice, for example, which most affect the poor, wallowed in vagueness and imprecision.[48] Elites had excellent channels of communication with the administration.[49] They could afford lawyers to petition courts for them. The poor did not.

B. Administrative Law in Colonial Africa

The Colonial Service acted with reasonable regulatory and predictability, especially towards the white settler classes.[50] The Law of Non-

Transferability of Law teaches that the rules of administrative law that arguably contributed to legal-rational behaviour in England probably did not do so in Africa. In fact the received rules of administrative law hardly touched the behaviour of the Colonial Service. The Colonial Service did not pretend to act instrumentally. The policy that it implemented it also created. A gaggle of statutes, granting extraordinarily broad powers and discretions (much wider than those granted even in English statutes to the English administration), created its framework. For example, the common law requires that, before arresting a suspect for a felony, a policeman must have 'probable cause' to believe that the suspect committed the crime. In Africa, however, the standards became 'reasonable suspicion', whatever that is.[51]

Every level had broad discretion; that of the Governors, virtually no bounds. The East Africa Order in Council, 1902, gave the Commissioner power to 'make Ordinances for the administration of justice, the raising of revenue, and generally for the peace, good order and good government of all persons in East Africa'. The Ordinances issued under this grant delegated great discretion to lesser officials. The Wheat Industry Ordinance, 1952, in Kenya required a licence before adding machinery to a mill.[52] It created this standard for obtaining the licence: 'The Minister . . . after obtaining the advice of the Wheat Board, shall in his discretion either grant or refuse permission.' Northern Rhodesia provided that betting pools obtain a licence, and that

(1) The Governor in Council may in his discretion issue a licence to any person to promote a pool within the Territory. . .

(2) The Governor in Council may in his discretion attach conditions to any license issued under this section and without prejudice to the generality of the foregoing such conditions may require the payment to the Government by the licences of fees and other moneys.[53]

Precious few procedures in fact limited the exercise of these broad grants of discretion.[54] The breadth of these grants left little for a court to review. The Kenyan court denied an appeal from a Minister's refusal to permit petitioner to add machinery to his mill under the Kenyan Wheat Industry Ordinance:[55]

The Court is called upon to entertain appeals from an administrative authority upon questions with which it is that authority's particular province to be familiar. This, in itself, presents the Court with a difficult task. It is rendered none the less difficult by the absence of a guidance as to procedure, of any intimation of the matters to be considered and of any specific limitation on the scope of the appeal.[56]

Second, the African population rarely had lawyers to represent them. Only occasionally did Africans have either sufficient funds or knowledge to challenge administrative authority.[57]

Finally, most administrative controls over Africans came through the criminal law. What in England were administrative orders with civil penalties in Africa became crimes, tried before local magistrate. A Catch 22 developed, however, because the magistrate almost invariably also wore the hat of the local District Officer.[58]

The received rules of administrative law in this ambience of unrestricted discretion could not control administration. Legal-rational legitimacy rests upon the instrumentality of the bureaucracy. The Colonial Service was not an instrument of government, it *was* government. It achieved a kind of rationality of behaviour not because of its formal structure, but despite it. The rules of administrative law could not enforce the rules of a Weberian bureaucracy because none existed.

Our model of law and development emphasizes non-legal, societal constraints and rewards, contained in this case mainly in the recruitment and socialization systems, and in the reactions of other colonial servants. That group had its own ethos, the 'Code of the British Gentleman', that it enforced by heavy informal sanctions and rewards. That Code came from the public schools, created to develop a bureaucratic class for England. In the main, the Code embodied an ideology consistent with the Rule of Law. The Colonial Service, of course, had its own parochialisms. The Weberian ideal demands rigidly impersonal standards of judgement. The Colonial Service, on the other hand, had ascriptive criteria for judgement, preferring Christians before pagans, whites before blacks, Englishmen before lesser breeds, public school boys before grammar school boys, and the Old School Tie before all else. Competence, intelligence and initiative ranked low among the criteria for selecting recruits. An Oxford Blue may signify physical fitness, but it does not measure intelligence.[59] The public school code of behaviour led to a kind of legitimacy with the rest of officialdom. The Service's legitimacy with the settler population perhaps had another footing.

Practically every administrative law case in the appellate courts of colonial Africa concerned Asians,[60] but only a tiny number, Africans. East Africa reported very few cases of a white settler challenging

administrative action. Settlers did not confront the administration because it included them in its formal and informal structure. Asians
could not join white social circles, within which white settlers effectively influenced government. A quiet conversation over a sundowner
at the club resolved conflict more efficiently than litigation.

   Stevens v. *Moshi Water Board,*[61] a rare East African administrative
law case concerning an Englishman, involved a Water Board, with
powers to order the distribution of water for irrigation. The Board gave
A and B the right to run a water ditch across Stevens's land; Stevens
petitioned the Board for a revocation, which it granted. Instead of
appealing, A's brother visited the Governor. As a result, a new board
reconsidered the matter, and without taking evidence, decided that A
and B had 'not had a fair deal', and gave them half the water in the
stream and the right to reopen the furrow across Stevens's land. Instead
of appealing, Stevens, in his turn, scurried off to see the Governor, who
apparently threw up his hands and advised Stevens to sue.

   The great English firms with African branches had similar informal
ties with Government. Lugard[62] wrote that 'though the local representatives of commerce are assured of a sympathetic hearing and a full
investigation of any suggestions which they have to offer, the methods
of Crown Colony Government as applied to African dependencies
enable the principals of firms in England to carry their proposals direct
to the Colonial Office, and thus be somewhat indifferent to local
representation'. He complained bitterly that the Colonial Office in
London sometimes over-ruled local officials, presumably because of
intervention by commercial interests.[63]

   In time, the solidarity between the officials and the white settlers
and businessmen expressed itself in Industry Boards that managed the
economy,[64] the formal structure finally taking its pattern from the
informal. Government in the main acted in the interests of its white
constituency. The actual operation of colonial law and bureaucracy
affected the several classes in the population differently.

   The role of public law in the colonial era, when looked at through
   the eyes of the colonized, provides one of the best examples there
   is of the operation of law as expounded by adherents of the Austin-
   ian theory of law. 'Orders backed by threats', 'the gunman situation
   writ large' these phrases most adequately describe what is more
   usually but less accurately called the reception of the English
   common law. Law was second only to weapons of war in the establishment of colonial rule, and for the early settlers and officials there

was little difference between the two; they were both useful implements to coerce the African . . . Africans were to be coerced into
performing their required role in society, whether it was to work,
to pay taxes, to live in a particular place or to move about the
country, and thus the criminal law, and courts to enforce it, were
in many respects the key institutions in native administration for
they underpinned the whole approach of the colonial administrator . . . Europeans, on the other hand, were invited to, perhaps more
accurate description would be, were conceded as a result of their
demands, a great degree of co-operation in the administration of
law, whether in the field of government, in the Legislative and Executive Councils, in agrarian policies, or in the judicial system via the
jury, a legally qualified judge, and the application to them of all the
safeguards of an English criminal trial . . .

A matter of major significance for the development of public law
in Kenya is that the inequalities of the administration of law to
which the coercive and co-operative approaches gave rise was also
inherent in the introduction of the common law system into Kenya
. . . In the field of public law matters are made worse by the tradition of administrative disinclination to have discretion bound by
legal rules, and the complexity of the remedies available to control
the administration . . . Executive discretion unfettered by law was,
to some extent, controlled by political means as far as Europeans
were concerned through their system of co-operative administration,
but such a system did not apply to Africans for most of the colonial
period.[65]

As controls on colonial administration, courts and administrative law
were neither brake nor accelerator: they were mainly inoperative. The
Colonial Service departed Africa; its members one by one packed their
bags, sold their houses and automobiles, accepted the 'golden hand-
shake',[66] heard a Last Retreat played by the Police Bugle Corps (in
Lagos, as late as 1964, on the Yacht Club lawn, as the homewardbound
steamship departed the harbour in the sunset, the official standing at
salute on the fantail, and not a dry eye in the party) and turned their
faces towards the long-anticipated joys of gloomy weather, fog, flats
without heating, and the infinite delights of summer holidays in
Brighton. They left as a legacy neither formal or informal institutions
likely to induce conformity to the Rule of Law.

C. Administrative Law in Independent Africa

The new African states inherited colonial administrative law. I examine the rules of administrative law and their consequence.

1. *The Rules of Administrative Law.* The rules of administrative decision-making, secrecy, feedback and so forth that limit the range of decisions mainly to tension-management and incremental change I discuss
below.[67] Here I consider only rules to ensure bureaucratic accountability and instrumentality, particularly breadth of discretion and its
judicial control.

    Breadth of Discretion. The wide discretion of colonial law continued.
The Zambian statute and subsidiary legislation concerning price and
import controls, for example, remained in force in 1974.[68] The new
statutes of independent Africa continued colonial practice. Zambia's
Trades Licensing Ordinance, 1968, specified as a ground for denying
a trades licence that granting it would contravene 'the public interest'.[69]
The Tanzanian statute authorized the Price Controller to 'fix maximum
prices for the sale of goods', and prescribe the 'type of packing, weight,
size, quantity and the processing and ingredients of any goods manufactured' in the Republic, without specifying permissible grounds for
decision.[70] Under the Kenya Sisal Industry (Amendment) Act, 1965
the Sisal Board could in its discretion grant or refuse an application for
a license.[71] Preventive Detention Acts existed in almost every country.[72]
Every government retained the old Colonial right to deport without
hearing or stated reason.[73] 'Clearly, large delegations of function plus
small amounts of legislative guidance equals large numbers of discretionary decisions . . .'[74]
    Law-makers enacted these statutes despite their ritual homage to the
Rule of Law. The Notes on Legislative Drafting of the Tanzania Attorney-General[75] stated that discretionary powers 'require careful
watching. Whenever possible, the grounds upon which such a power . . .
may be exercised should be specified. If the discretion has to be large,
than it is desirable that there should be provisions for appeal (probably
to the Minister, or possibly to the President), though this is not always
acceptable as a matter of policy.' However, the Tanzanian Parliamentary Draftsman in 1970 said that he did not specify any grounds for the
exercise of a discretionary power to license tourist bureaux in a new
statute because the Minister would not tolerate any limitation on his
authority.[76]

2. *Formal Controls.* At Independence, only the courts exercised any
formal control over the administration. These remained beyond the

touch of most Africans. The rules defining the scope of judicial review, too, also still failed to control administrators. In *Matter of Sinioti*,[77] a Zambian case, petitioner complained that a Municipal Council denied him a trading licence. He belonged to the opposition party, the African National Congress. The secretary of the local United National Independence Party (the ruling party), had opposed licensing him specifically on political grounds. Council refused the licence, 'it being considered that the issue of such a licence would operate against the public interest'. The Court affirmed the denial of the licence. It found no actual bias, nor could it say, on the face of such vague and over-arching statutory discretion ('against the public interest'), that the Council had abused its discretion. (After the decision in the case, Sinioti abandoned ANC, joined UNIP – and received his licence.)

The Court need not have reached that result. It could have adopted the English canon of statutory construction that excludes considerations irrelevant to the statute's purposes. A Zambian court did precisely that in *Chilufa* v. *City Council of Kitwe*.[78] There the facts closely resembled *Siniotti's*. Petitioner, an ANC supporter, had a daily licence for a market stall. A small riot of UNIP supporters took place at the market. The UNIP-controlled Council thereupon terminated petitioner's trading licence, on the specific statutory ground that 'the issue of such licence is likely to cause nuisance or annoyance to persons residing, or occupying premises in the neighbourhood . . .'[79] The court reversed, citing English precedent. The Council had a duty to protect the petitioner's constitutional rights; the Council therefore improperly exercised its discretion. The Livingstone Council denied the market licence on indefinable grounds: 'against the public interest'. The court did not look beyond that vague phrase. The Kitwe Council denied it on a specified, rather narrow ground. The court held the specified ground improper. So long as statutes grant vague and imprecise powers, with discretion unstructured and broad a court can only with difficulty, if at all, ensure that administrators use their discretion for proper purposes.

Widespread use of formulae that excluded judicial review reinforced this trend. The Kenyan National Security Fund Act,[80] for example, provided:

> Without prejudice to any specific power conferred by any of the foregoing provisions of this Act, regulations may be made for facilitating the implementation of this Act . . . Any regulations made under this Act may make different provisions with respect to different cases or classes of, and for different purposes of this Act

may impose conditions and make exceptions and contain such incidental or supplementary provisions *as may appear to the Minister to be expedient* for the purpose of the regulations.[81]

A discretion to make rules so broad as to permit case by case discrimination, made judicial review in any event an empty ceremony. Nevertheless, the draftsman took no chances that the judiciary might hedge the Minister. The phrase 'as may appear to the Minister to be expedient' excludes judicial review.[82] In England, the Donoughmore Report of 1932,[83] recommended the exclusion of the analogous 'Henry VIII clause'. In Africa, draftsmen continued to include them. In such cases, 'the power to make subordinate·legislation is so widely drawn that it becomes impossible for the courts to apply the *ultra vires* doctrine to the delegated legislation made in pursuance thereof; Parliament has handed over its supreme power completely to the subordinate agency'.[84]

The specific exclusion of judicial control appeared particularly frequently in preventive detention statutes. Such acts typically made detention wholly discretionary, with judicial review excluded. The received administrative law purported to control an administration endowed with narrow grants of discretion, controlled by courts widely available to the affected public. The same rules transplanted to Africa, had no relevance, because neither of the necessary conditions for their use existed.

III Why Neither Development Administration nor Rule of Law?

To escape bureaucratic rigidity, African leaders endowed high officials with great discretion. With that discretion, supposedly they could use bureaucracy, that perfectly flexible, perfectly rational instrument of policy, to solve developmental problems. Nevertheless, they neither solved developmental problems very well, not did they behave with the regularity and predictability that the Rule of Law demanded.

Precisely because officials seemed to have such remarkable freedom of action, scholars facilely explained their failure by the rubric, that only good men make good government. The administrators somehow had personally failed. The circularity of that explanation gives us no nourishment.[85] Another common explanation fell afoul of the Law of Non-transferability. Administration did not work because the rules suffered fatal defects; scholars could find ideal rules in 'successful' administrations — that is, in the modernized nations. The solution would graft improvements onto the Weberian model: organization and management programmes, rules defining better filing systems, budgeting procedures, internal communications, promotion and pay schedules. If the administrators did not abide by them, the foreign experts prescribed harsher punishments, and returned to their home countries to write learned books about the hopelessness of it all.[86] The ecology school in opposition explained the failure of Weberian bureaucracy by its social surround.[87] If one accepts Weberian bureaucracy, however, then society itself becomes the independent variable, a singularly intractable one. Since administration should help change society, the ecology school too easily leads to a give-it-up conclusion: the relationship between administration and its social environment becomes another vicious circle of underdevelopment.

Another formulation would take society as it is, and explain administrative behaviour with bureaucratic rules and structure as the manipulable variables.[88] That formulation turned the question into a specific problem of the tension between law-in-the-books and law-in-action, between administrative rules and action. Why did the administrators not choose to follow the demands of either development administration or Rule of Law?

African public administration failed its developmental tasks for two reasons: it could not solve emergent problems, and it could impose only punishment as a conformity-inducing measure — i.e. it lacked capacity. Bureaucratic self-interest explains its failure to achieve the Rule of Law.

A. The Failure of Development Administration

1. *Bureaucratic Decision-Making.* Bureaucrats tend to enforce rules well, but solve emerging problems poorly. Their capacity to make decisions depends on how others supply them with inputs and feedbacks, and how the conversion processes work. In Africa, these adapted poorly to solve the constantly new, constantly emerging, constantly surprising problems of development. These problems had no obvious answers, only endless difficulties. Problem-solving requires continuous application, constantly perceiving and explaining difficulties, proposing solutions and then learning from their attempted implementation. Political authorities could only identify troubles, roughly order priorities and then turn the troubles over to the administration for solution. Parliament cannot readily decide how best to generate cash crops in Mongu. That requires a detailed analysis of the special constraints and resources of soil, water, marketing, roads and manpower, section by section and even farm by farm. Parliament could only require the administration to attend to the difficulty, and provide

resources for the task.[89] The bureaucracy in Africa, however, lay under the shadow of its colonial past. The Colonial Service dealt with problems of law and order, facing problems as they arose. It could not deal with problems of planning and induced change.

The political principle underpinning colonial administration lodged all authority in the Governor. Power radiated from him through the Colonial Secretary, and thence outwards to line officers in regions and districts, and to the departments, public works, health, agriculture.[90] The central decision-making system reflected this hierarchical power structure. Anything that required the Governor's decision became a minute paper, in fact 'the actual instrument by which policy of the Government is considered and orders of the Government are made'.[91]

A minute paper began in many ways: from letters or petitions or suggestions from below, or from above, by the Governor or by a despatch from the Secretary of State. Once a minute paper emerged, an assistant colonial secretary started it on its long journey through the bureaucracy: to a department head for comment and data, an appropriate district officer, the Attorney General for legal advice or for drafting a statute. In due course it returned to the secretariat together with supporting documents, sometimes an enormously bulky file. The Assistant Secretary wrote another minute, stating the alternatives and the pros and cons, together with his recommendation; the Colonial Secretary added his endorsement; the Governor finally decided. In addition to the consultation of the minute paper system, Commissions of Enquiry occasionally developed policy in a particular area. The history of colonial Africa relates many such commissions, on constitutional change, specific riots and social disorders, land policy, labour, prisons.[92]

A third system of institutionalized consultation comprised the various boards administering the several industries in East Africa, and the marketing boards of West Africa. There, of course, consultation became permanent and pervasive. The consultees in many cases had statutory power to make the decisions themselves.[93]

These decision-making systems continued after Independence. Planning emerged only fitfully to challenge them.[94] These three processes of decision-making had their built-in biasses: towards incremental change, towards punishment, and towards elite interests. Here I discuss the first two; the third I discuss in Chapter 20.

a. *Incremental Change.* Limited investigations, hierarchy, secrecy and compartmentalism led the civil service to confine their proposed solutions to incremental changes.

i. *The Collection of data.* Governments everywhere badly monitor
their own efforts. A 1972 policy paper for the Military Government of
the Mid-Western State of Nigeria stated that 'It is a common experience
that although the functions of senior officials with administrative
responsibilities comprise not only executing agreed policy but also
helping to originate new policies and modifying those existing, the
pressures of modern government make it difficult for officials with
departmental duties to find sufficient time to devote to policy or
procedural issues which require research, reflection and extensive
drafting.' The Military Governor there in 1969 established an Administrative Research and Support Division consisting of four officers drawn
from the Public Service — for a government spending $30,000,000 per
year. Even these four officers probably exceeded the formal research
capacity of most African governments. Minute papers, consultations
and commissions of enquiry in a sense monitored government's own
activity. Government's only other ongoing source of information lay
in the accumulated experience of senior officials.

These devices sharply restricted available data. Minute papers, consultations, and commissions of enquiry arose only in response to
systemic tensions. Bound by narrow terms of reference, the investiga-
tors hurried, and tended to record not carefully researched data but
their personal impressions of the situation. The intuitive impressions of
senior officials too often restated their domain assumptions unexamined. Every government tried programmes that failed, and then tried
the same programme again and again, because the officials involved
mistook antique mythologies for reliable knowledge.[95]

ii. *The Consequences of Hierarchy.* In the mythical blueprint of
government, the civil service implemented policies of political authorities. They supported the government of the day,[96] accepting the goals
it laid down, and implemented them. 'The business of a civil servant is
to do what he is told.'[97] In Africa, as elsewhere, hierarchy dominated
the bureaucracy.

Public administration studies teach that such bureaucracies mostly
limit their proposals to incremental change. Supporting the government
of the day confines bureaucracy to criticizing and suggesting improvements to existing programmes. Hierarchy and status differentials further
clog communications,[98] because the inferior fears rocking the boat, and
the superior wants to keep his distance lest closer relations increase his
subordinates' influence.[99] Where the superior controls rewards and
penalties, it is easier to get reports leading to rewards than to penalties.[100]

In any event, superiors deprecate inferiors' criticism; they do not have 'the big picture'.[101] Existing domain assumptions – and all organizations have their dogmas – filter out messages that contradict them.[102] Formal rules of communications, such as form sheets for monthly reports, create their own filters.

iii. *Secrecy.* At every level, the bureaucracy operated secretly and anonymously.[103] Secret decisions, without any need for public justification, maximized the influence of administrators' values and prejudices. Their domain assumptions built calluses impervious to fact.

iv. *Compartmentalism.* Public bureaucracies exist to accomplish some public task.[104] The structure subdivides the task into bits, and assigns one bit to each bureaucrat. In a single Zambian province, the Ministry of Rural Development alone had a Provincial Rural Development Officer, a Provincial Agricultural Officer, a Provincial Marketing Officer, a Provincial Co-operatives Officer, a Provincial Veterinary Officer, a Provincial and Regional Tsetse Control Officer, a Provincial Water Engineer and a Provincial Community Development Officer. In addition, many agricultural parastatal organizations had representatives there: the National Agricultural Marketing Board, the Cold Storage Board, the Agricultural Finance Company, the Dairy Produce Board, the Rural Development Corporation and its subsidiaries, the Provincial Co-operative Marketing Union Limited and the Tobacco Board.[105] This extraordinary compartmentalization frequently altogether filtered out messages which fell between jurisdictional lines; nobody saw the elephant whole, or could plan comprehensively among the bits and pieces.

Compartmentalism frequently bred departmental feuding.[106] In Zambia at one point the Ministry of Finance investigated how to increase taxes on the mining companies, while MINDECO, the mining parastatal, conducted research to lower taxes. Bureaucracy sometimes better than the state of nature exemplified a Hobbes war of each against each. Interdepartmental disputes too frequently led to compromise and incrementalism.

b. *Punishment orientation.* Bureaucratic punishment-orientation results from ideology and structure. Administrators see punishment as the only available conformity-inducing measure.[107] Administrators usually deal only with rules that they believe express custom. That suggests punitive sanctions. Hierarchical, authoritarian structures reinforce that notion. Higher authority does not exhort, plead or request; it orders. Orders by definition carry punitive sanctions. Officials frequently ignore rewards and roundabout measures.

A problem-solving, participatory process can serve to induce compliance with rules looking to changed behaviour. Participation is the
opposite of authority. African administrators possessed authoritarian
power. Allowing low-level actors to participate in decisions violated the
rules defining their roles.[108] In short, the very characteristics that
theoretically make bureaucracy a rational form of decision-making
— hierarchy — compartmentalism, rules, secrecy—denied developmental
objectives. Bureaucracy may tend the machine well. It does poorly
at changing it.

B. The Failure of the Rule of Law

Bureaucracy could not achieve much change. Simultaneously, the
administrators' self-interests constantly undermine the Rule of Law.
Organizations include more than roles. They include individuals, with
their own goals: advancement, money, leisure, ideology. The conflict
between individual goals and organizational goals frequently distorts
or displaces the organizational ones.[109] Sometimes this occurs because
the organization subdivides its goals into separate tasks. An Agricultural Officer demands water for irrigation; a Community Development
Officer, for domestic water supply. Since their rewards and careers
depend on their performance, they may fight and scheme to achieve
their particular objectives, disregarding the overall mission. In time,
each believes in the higher priority of his own job.

Other individual interests may lead to goal substitution. To avoid
excessive work, a hospital caterer may select a menu not for its nutri-
tion but its easy preparation. Road contracts may issue not out of need
for the road, but to secure a bribe for the contracting officer.

An hypothesis therefore emerges: *a bureaucrat will tend to exercise
his power and discretion to maximize rewards and minimize strains for
himself and his organization.*[110] He will do that, however, only if he has
choice — that is, discretion. Discretion thus conflicts with the notion of
instrumentality that underlies the Rule of Law.

Goal substitution increases with broader discretion, and conditions
offer the bureaucrat little resistance, where he has authority over
clients, or he can act in secret. The less the accountability, the greater
the potential for goal substitution. The broad discretion granted to
African bureaucrats in the title of development denied the objectives of
regularity and predictability of the Rule of Law, just as the hierarchy
and compartmentalism which underlies the Rule of Law denied the
objective of development administration.

Summary. One can now explain the simultaneous failure of African administration to solve the emergent problems of development and to achieve the objectives of the Rule of Law:

1. The task of inducing development in African required administrators to solve problems, rather than implement rules from political authorities.

2. Hierarchical, authoritarian, compartmented institutions limit outputs to incremental changes, and tend to be punishment-oriented.

3. African administrations were hierarchical, authoritarian and compartmented, and tended to be punishment-oriented.

4. Bureaucrats will tend to exercise their discretion to maximize rewards and minimize strains for themselves and the bureaucracy of which they are a part; this tendency increases to the extent that

   a. They have broad grants of discretion; and

   b. Subordinates and clients have little power to resist it; and

   c. Decision-making is secret.

5. In Africa,

   a. Officials had broad grants of discretion; and

   b. Subordinates and low-status clients had little power to resist; and

   c. Secrecy in administrative decision-making abounded.

Development must change behaviour by many people; behaviour changes most readily through participation; African administrations instead became authoritarian. Development requires problem-solving; problems come as a whole, not broken into bits; African administrations splintered themselves. Development requires much more than punishment as an obedience-inducing measure; African administrations used mainly punishment. Where African administrations dealt with matters that rules could routinize excessive grants of discretion defeated the Rule of Law. Where they dealt with emergent problems of development, hierarchy, authority and compartmentalization blocked their goal.[111] They fell between two stools.

'Development from above' must always so fail. Law, as a set of rules handed down from above and enforced through compartmented, authoritarian, punishment-oriented organizations, can at best haltingly induce social change.

IV Administrative Law in Developing Africa

In the main, African states have increasingly hived off development functions to parastatals.[112] Planning supposedly solved the difficulties of compartmentalization.[113] Decentralization, devolution and local participation aimed at authoritarianism;[114] on a national level, so did new institutions for feedback and control from below.[115] Many problems of regulation and administration remained. The remainder of this chapter discusses their solutions.

A. The Scope of Power and Discretion

One must first reduce discretionary administration. But the administration of course continues deep in developmental activities, arguably needing broad discretion. Many laws, some of them colonial relics, concern matters which surely need no broad discretion. Price control ordinances can identify standards for setting prices — out-of-pocket costs, depreciation, a stated amount of profit and so forth.[116] Market licensing ordinances do not need the catch-all phrase, 'against the public interest'. Statutes need grant no broader discretion than the matter at hand fairly requires.

The issue arose infrequently, perhaps because of over-exposure to English notions of parliamentary supremacy.[117] In *Awolowo* v. *Federal Minister of Internal Affairs*[118] a leading opposition politician retained an English QC, a member of the Nigerian bar, to defend him in a pending 'political' trial. The Minister refused his counsel permission to enter Nigeria. The Immigration Act provided that the Minister may, 'in his absolute discretion, prohibit the entry into Nigeria of any person, not being a native of Nigeria'.[119] The Court observed that the discretion had no limits: 'No condition is attached to the exercise of his power by the Minister, and the power is not expressly conditioned to be exercised if the recipient deems it to be in the public interest or in the interest of peace, order and good government.'[120] It held that since the statute conferred such unlimited power, the Minister could refuse entry without expressed reason. It doubted the relevance of malice 'in a case like the present where absolute discretionary power has been given the first defendant by Parliament'. Constitutionally Parliament could only legislate for the 'peace, order and good government of Nigeria'. The Court sustained a statute granting wider powers to the Minister than

Parliament had itself.[121]

1. *Structuring Discretion.* Courts, constitution or statute might require administrators periodically to promulgate guidelines for their discretion.[122] Ghana seemingly wrote this requirement into the short-lived Busia Constitution:

> 173. Where in this Constitution or in any other law discretionary power is vested in any person or authority
>
> (a) that discretionary power shall be deemed to imply a duty to be fair and candid;
>
> (b) the exercise of any such discretionary power shall not be arbitrary, capricious or biased, either by resentment, prejudice or personal dislike and shall be in accordance with due process of law; and
>
> (c) the person or authority, not being a Judge or other Judicial Officer in the exercise of his judicial functions, in whom the discretionary power is vested shall, by constitutional or statutory instrument, as the case may be, make and publish Regulations, not being inconsistent with any provision of this Constitution or that of any other law, which shall govern the exercise of that discretionary power.

The provision, however, received ambiguous treatment from the Ghanaian courts. In *Captan* v. *Minister for Home Affairs*[123] the court held that the revocation of a residence permit by the Minister, although plainly a discretionary act, fell outside the constitutional provision. The Court relied heavily upon British gossamer distinctions between 'quasi-adjudicative' and 'administrative' powers, asserting that the constitutional provision applied only to the former.[124]

Despite this additional discouraging example of slavish devotion to English precedents despite a written constitution, however, the Ghanaian experiment suggests a useful line of attack. Where political authorities can plainly define powers and so structure discretion, courts can require them to do so. That requirement serves another function. The act of formulating policies, plans and rules constitutes the act of decision.[125] To require them insists that government make planned decisions rather than muddle through. It aims at ensuring rationality, not harassing administrators.

2. *Implementing Guidelines to Discretion.* Even where an administrator

must exercise his discretion on the basis of enumerated criteria, how to ensure that the bureaucrat in fact acts on that basis? Requiring officials to justify their decisions might help. The tradition of judicial opinion-writing points in that direction. A delegate to the California Constitutional Convention in 1879, debating an article which required judges to give written opinions, put it nicely: 'Undoubtedly [the requirement] will . . . result in well-considered opinions, because they must come before the jurists of the country and be subjected to the severest criticism . . . It tends to purity and honesty in the administration of justice.'[126]

The state can require similar opinions of administrative officers. A Tanzanian statute[127] gave Regional Commissioners power to arrest a person whenever he 'has reason to believe that any person is likely to commit a breach of the peace or disturb the public tranquility, or do any act that may probably occasion a breach of the peace or disturb the public tranquility, and that such breach cannot be prevented otherwise than by detaining such person in custody'. A broader discretion could hardly exist. The Commissioner, however, must at the time of making or ordering the arrest 'record his reasons therefore in writing'.[128] The requirement of an opinion might restrain a Commissioner from making an arrest without a plausible factual basis for it.

Another, more limited technique emerged in the United States under the National Environmental Policy Act.[129] Every official who proposes any major construction must file a public Environmental Impact Statement.[130] Individual citizens may litigate the impact statement's sufficiency. The agency may proceed with its plan, even with an unfavourable environmental impact statement. The impact statement, however, at least insures the input of environmental data into the decision-making process. To that extent it structures discretion by ensuring the consideration of factors important to the law-makers.

B Enforcement Institutions

As controls over administrators, courts remained inaccessible to most citizens. Some African countries created Commissions of Enquiry to police bureaucracy. Almost every country had a Commission of Enquiry Act that permitted President or Prime Minister to create a special commission of enquiry to investigate specific charges. Most countries used these *ad hoc*. Three countries institutionalized them, thus perhaps providing a readily accessible forum to air of grievances against the bureaucracy. The constitutions of Ghana,[131] Zambia[132] and Tanzania[133] each established a permanent Commission of Enquiry.

Only the Tanzanian Commission had a considerable operating history.
The Presidential Commission on the Establishment of a Democratic
One-Party State first suggested it as a 'safeguard which the ordinary
citizen will have [against arbitrary behaviour of governmental officials]
which will not have the effect of limiting the actions of Government
and Party in a way which could hinder the task of nation-building'.[134]
The Act[135] empowered the Commission to investigate either on the
President's instruction, its own initiative, or citizen complaint, but not
to displace the courts in matters of ordinary administrative law.[136]
In fact, the Commission very frequently did precisely that.

Such a Commission can sanction bureaucratic violations of defined
duties. It, however, like the courts, cannot easily review a 'polycentric'
administrative decision.[137] In its first year, the Tanzanian Commission
adjudged a complaint against a Ministry as 'too general' and 'the Complainant having no personal interest'. Accepting only cases arising out
of a personal interest, of course, largely insulated from Commission
Review more generalized discretionary decisions. Most of the substantive complaints that the Commission investigated and dealt with
involved allegations of grossly *ultra vires* acts. In the first year, seventy-
six complained of illegal detention by various non-judicial officers;
109 involved threats and oppressions; 162 involved real property, a surprisingly high proportion involving officials' seizure of shambas and
houses without reason. Remarkably few cases challenged an officer's
discretion. Only sixty-one cases involved decisions not made, wrong or
unsatisfactory, un-executed or discriminatory. Of these, the Commission seemingly rejected all complaints that attacked decisions as wrong
or unsatisfactory, although it might have examined to see whether the
official took into account all he should have, or had considered
improper factors. Almost no complaints alleged what classical administrative law calls a violation of the rules of natural justice. Almost no
cases were involved under the rule that no man judge in his own case.
Only a very few cases involved a denial of a hearing. Instead, the Commission tended to decide cases on the merits when the decision seemed
grossly 'unreasonable'. For example, in one case,[138] the complainant
alleged that the Regional Commissioner had suspended his trading
licence without reasons. After investigation, the Commission discovered
that the RC had passed near an Asian's shop during a scuffle between
the shopkeeper's children and an African. The Commissioner enquired,
received rude answers from the Asian family, and concluded that they
had had no cause to beat the African. He ordered the suspension of the
shopkeeper's licence. The Permanent Commission of Enquiries found

the fight irrelevant to the trading licence, reported the matter to the President and the owner received back his licence.

The Tanzanian Commission became one of the most successful legal innovations in Africa, providing at once a channel to protect individual rights and, by ensuring integrity and competence in the bureaucracy, a buttress for governmental effectiveness.[139] It had, however, three structural weaknesses. Its statute limited its enforcement powers to reporting to the President any official who did not satisfactorily settle a complaint of the Commission. Most officials in fact did accommodate. Some claimed that the Commission needs power to institute court action against an obdurate administrator (as does the Swedish Ombudsman) or even to decide judgement in a case and enforce its judgement, as does the Soviet State Procurator.[140]

More deep-seated limitations arose out of the inbuilt relationship between the Commission and discretionary administrative activity. Any reviewing body may not 'second-guess' government. The Parliament lodges decision-making capacity with a particular agency. The reviewing body must refrain from substituting its discretion for the agency's. American courts resolved that problem by confining the scope of their review to ascertaining that 'some' evidence supports the decision made.[141]

Ultimately, the Commission only provided a less expensive, less formal and faster arena than the courts for citizen complaints. Nevertheless, even such a forum best served more sophisticated citizens. President Nyerere remarked that 'We must not forget that the Permanent Commission of Enquiry receives complaints only from the most literate, aware or energetic and courageous of our citizens . . .'[142] The Commission in any event could not solve the problems of development administration, for the Commission, like the courts, needed a rule-bound bureaucracy to regulate.

C. Improving the Rules of Administrative Law

English administrative law developed in a haphazard, unorganized, case-by-case way. A commentator remarked that 'the rules . . . became so obscure that it was an easy matter for the courts to over-rule administrative decisions of which they did not approve. Conversely, the courts could uphold any administrative action which they did approve regardless of whatever injustices had been committed.'[143] For example, a hearing ensures that decision-makers have as much relevant data as possible. Whether an administor must hear the parties, however, in English law depended upon a preliminary characterization of the proceeding as 'at least quasi-judicial', rather than 'quasi-legislative' or 'administrative'.[144] The line between the two so fades that the characterization becomes a conclusion, not a reason for the decision.[145]

The available procedures in administrative law cases at common law included the so-called prerogative writs, *mandamus, habeas corpus* and prohibition. They developed because in the eighteenth century, the Justices of the Peace, usually the local landowner, administered government in the British countryside. The higher courts in London controlled them somewhat through the prerogative writs. Their procedures became technical, overlapping and confused. The antique terminology has changed in some African countries,[146] but not the actual procedure.[147] Simpler remedies can be easily devised.

Finally, all administrative law problems start with a substantive statute that defines the powers of the administrators, and frequently, procedures. Courts might construe statutes to identify the considerations the administrator should take into account.

Courts have an important role to play as residuary control institutions. With administration, they might 'have a special role to play in curbing anomalies or aberrations which arise in policy implementation through overzealousness, misinterpretation of policy, lack of expertise, inefficiency, or, inevitably, bad faith. By so doing, not only would the courts guarantee their own future, but they would contribute significantly to the effectiveness of public administration.'[148]

D. Ideology

Discretion involves choosing among alternatives. Rules can structure it by directing the administrator to examine some data and to exclude others. Another device to ensure the proper use of discretion would match the administrators' models or paradigms of the world — i.e. their ideology — with the ideology of law-makers. Such paradigms direct attention to what counts and what does not, thereby structuring discretion.

Unfortunately, ideologies do not speak precisely or in detail; they constitute not dogmas but guides to action. As a result, equally ideologically committed administrators can decide discretionary matters differently. (Lionel Cliffe gives a remarkable example: '. . . the District Council which decided the most important step they could take to implement the policy of Socialism and Self Reliance in Tanzania was to become more self-reliant financially by cutting down on the practice of refunding school fees to the very poorest inhabitants!'[149]) Ideology can structure discretion but only when ideology advances beyond a vague statement of 'values' or very general goals ('freedom', or 'humanism') to specific propositions explaining the world. To rely on ideology as surrogate for rules so long as ideology remains vague and non-specific guarantees that neither the Rule of Law nor development occur.

Conclusion

Weberian bureaucracy and the Rule of Law assume hierarchical compartmentalized, authoritarian decision-making. They tame those tendencies towards goal substitution and arbitrariness that common human experience teaches is likely to occur in any such system. Power does tend to corrupt. By rules of administrative law, courts ensure that the law-in-action matches the law-in-the-books of Weberian bureaucracy. Rules defining in the narrowest possible terms how bureaucrats ought to act (that is, admitting of the least possible amount of discretion) constitute the core technique that the Rule of Law devised to tame the bureaucratic monster. Rules narrowly defining bureaucratic behaviour can only obtain when law-makers know quite concretely how they want the bureaucrats to behave. In conditions of development, nobody knew precisely how bureaucrats ought to behave. The problems came in torrents, the solutions by driblets. Law-makers at most could determine the priorities for problem solution. The administration must have sufficient options to experiment with alternative solutions, that is, broad discretion. Development administration warred with the Rule of Law.

The contrary also resulted. The authoritarian, hierarchical, compartmented organization of bureaucracy that Weber defined and the Rule of Law assumed, hobbled the solution of development problems, even when the bureaucrats had unlimited discretion. Problem-solving called for creativity, originality, drive, initiative. Bureaucracy's dead hand made these unlikely. Development administration required an overall view of the range of problems, to ensure that muddling through did not result in counter-productive, atomized 'solutions'. Compartmentalized bureaucracy could not easily take an overall view of anything. Development administration must simultaneously have broad discretion, but hold it accountable. No known device could do that very well. Development administration required changed behaviour by clients. That did not easily happen by giving orders from the top, enforced by punishment. Problem-solving required discussion, debate, experimentation, feedback, in short, participation. The Rule of Law implied a bureaucratic structure thoroughly dysfunctional to development. Small wonder that Africa fell between two stools.

Some ameliorative measures might help: grants of discretion no broader than actually required; insistence that bureaucrats state the rules or standards for the exercise of their discretion from time to time; improved rules of administrative law; ombudsmen; ideology. Mostly, however, African countries created entirely new institutions outside the received Ministerial, bureaucratic structure. They placed many new governmental functions in governmental ('parastatal') corporations (Chapter 14); they instituted economic planning, to take an overall look at development problems (Chapter 15); they tried new, participatory institutions (Chapters 16, 21). We turn now to these new institutions.

Notes

1. R. Pound, *Interpretations of Legal History* (N.Y.: Macmillan, 1923), p. 1.
2. J. LaPalombara, *Bureaucracy and Political Development* (Princeton: Princeton University Press, 1963), p. 11.
3. M. Weber, *The Theory of Social and Economic Organization*, A.M. Henderson and T. Parsons, tr.: T. Parsons, ed.; (New York: The Free Press, 1957), p. 344.
4. See, in general, F. Morstein Marx, *The Administration State: An Introduction to Bureaucracy* (Chicago: University of Chicago Press, 1957), pp. 183-93.
5. M.J. Esman, 'Administrative Doctrine and Developmental Needs', in E. P. Morgan (ed.), *The Administration of Change in Africa* (New York: Dunellen, 1974), pp. 5-6; F. Riggs, *Administration in Developing Countries: The Theory of Prismatic Society* (Boston: Houghton Mifflin, 1964), p. 7.
6. See above, Chap. 10.
7. Esman, 'Administrative Doctrine'.
8. H.L.A. Hart, *The Concept of Law* (Oxford: Clarendon Press, 1962).
9. Weber, *Social and Economic Organization*, p. 340.
10. B. Moore, Jr., *Social Origins of Dictatorship and Democracy: Lord and Peasant in the Making of the Modern World* (Harmondsworth: Penguin, 1966), p. 196.
11. C.J. Friedrich, 'Some Observations on Weber's Analysis of Bureaucracy', in R.K. Merton, A.P. Gray, B. Hockey and H.C. Selvin, *Reader in Bureaucracy* (New York: Free Press, 1952), pp. 31-2; L. Tiger, 'Bureaucracy and Charisma in Ghana', *J. Asian and Af. Studies,* 1-2, 13 n. 43 (1966-67).
12. *Pace* L.L. Fuller, *The Morality of Law* (New York: Fawcett Publications, 1964).
13. M. Weber, *From Max Weber, Essays in Sociology*, H.H. Gerth and C. Wright Mills, eds. (London: Oxford University Press, 1946), p. 221.
14. Ibid., p. 220.
15. A.V. Dicey, *Introduction to the Study of the Law of the Constitution* (London: Macmillan, 1959), p. 188; see F.S. von Hayek, *The Road to Serfdom* (Chicago: University of Chicago Press, 1944), p. 72.
16. H.W.R. Wade, *Administrative Law* (Oxford: Clarendon Press, 1967), p. 1; J.F. Garner, *Administrative Law*, 3rd ed. (London: Butterworths, 1970), p. 21.
17. B.B. Schaffer, 'The Deadlock in Development Administration' in C. Leys (ed.), *Politics and Change in Developing Countries: Studies in the Theory and Practice of Development* (Cambridge: University Press, 1969), p. 177.

18. D. Dresang, 'The Zambia Civil Service: A Study in Development Adminis- tration' (Ph.D. dissertation, UCLA, 1971), pp. xi, 277; see also C. Leys, 'Recruitment, Promotion and Training', in G. Hyden, R. Jackson and J. Okumu (eds.), *Development Administration: The Kenyan Experience* (Nairobi: Oxford University Press, 1970), p. 139; LaPalombara, *Bureaucracy*, p. 12.

19. Von Hayek, *Road to Serfdom*; Fuller, *Morality of Law*; Schaffer, 'Deadlock'.

20. Schaffer, ibid.

21. K. Nyerere, Address to Nat. Assembly, 3 June 1965, quoted in R.I. Martin, *Personal Freedom and the Law in Tanzania: A Study of Socialist State Administration* (Nairobi: Oxford University Press, 1974), p. 193.

22. Y.P. Ghai, and J.P.W.P. McAuslan, *Public Law and Political Change in Kenya* (Nairobi: Oxford University Press, 1970), p. 515.

23. R. Pound, *An Introduction to the Philosophy of Law* (New Haven: Yale University Press, 1922), p. 111.

24. G. Hyden, 'Social Structure, Bureaucracy and Development Administration In Kenya', *The African Review*, 1, 118 (1972); see also Tiger, 'Bureaucracy and Charisma', p. 20.

25. Dresang, 'Zambia Civil Service', p. 100.

26. R.M. Jackson, 'Administration and Development in Kenya: A Review of Problems Outstanding' in Hyden, Jackson and Okumu, *Development Administration*, p. 321.

27. Ibid., pp. 329-31.

28. Republic of Kenya, *Report of The Commission of Enquiry – Public Service Structure and Remuneration Commission* (Nairobi: Government Printer, 1971), p. 3.

29. Wade, *Administrative Law*, p. 1.

30. *Entrick* v. *Carrington*, 19 St. Tr. 1030 (1670).

31. 'The whim of the prince has the force of law.'

32. Wade, *Administrative Law*, p. 42.

33. Ibid., p. 64.

34. *Panama Sugar Refining* v. *US*, 293 U.S. 388 (1935).

35. Wade, *Administrative Law*, pp. 9-10.

36. Ibid., p. 64; *Associated Provincial Picture Houses* v. *Wednesbury Corporation* [1948] 1 K.B. 223; *Roberts* v. *Hopwood* [1925] A.C. 578.

37. *Liveridge* v. *Anderson* [1942] A.C. 206.

38. 'Natural justice' is a term of art in English administrative law, roughly ana- logous to the US concept of procedural due process of law.

39. *King* v. *Univ. of Cambridge*, 1 Str. 557 (1723); *Cooper* v. *Wandsworth Board of Works* (1863) 14 C.B. (N.S.). 180: *Board of Education* v. *Rice* (1911) A.C. 179.

40. *Municipal Council of Sydney* v. *Campbell* (1925) A.C. 338 (ulterior objects); *Westminster Corporation* v. *London & Northwestern Railway* (1905) A.C. 426 (mixed motives); *Smith* v. *East Elloe Rural District Council* (1956) A.C. 736 (*mala fides*); see Wade, *Administrative Law*, pp. 63 ff.; see S.A. de Smith, *Judicial Review of Administrative Action* (London: Stevens, 1959).

41. K.C. Davis, *Administrative Law* (St Paul: West Pub. Co., 1972), §.16.02, pp. 319-20.

42. Wade, *Administrative Law*, p. 197; M. Akehurst, 'Statements of Reasons for Judicial and Administrative Decisions', *Mod. L. Rev.*, 33, 154 (1970).

43. *American Thread Co.* v. *Joyce*, 108 L.T. 353 (H.L., 1913); *Smith* v. *General Motor Co.* (1911) A.C. 188; *Doggett* v. *Waterloo Taxicab Co.* [1910] 2 K.B. 336; *Cababe* v. *Walton-on-Thames U.D.C.* [1914] A.C. 102; *Porvell* v. *Minister of Pensions* [1946] 1 All E.R. 644.

44. J.F. Garner, 'Public Corporations in the United Kingdom', in W. Friedman and J.F. Garner (eds.), *Government Enterprise: A Comparative Study* (New York: Columbia University Press, 1970), p. 53.
45. Ibid.; see Committee on Ministers' Powers: Report, Cmd. 4060 (London: HMSO, 1936) (The Donoghmore Committee Report).
46. Wade, *Administrative Law*, pp. 14, 143.
47. A. Gouldner, 'Discussion of Industrial Sociology', *Am. Soc. Rev.*, 13, 396 (1948).
48. K.C. Davis, *Discretionary Justice: A Preliminary Inquiry* (Baton Rouge: Louisiana State University Press, 1969).
49. J.W. Grove, *Government and Industry* (London, Longmans, 1962), Chap. 5, reprinted in F.G. Castles, D.J. Murray and D.C. Potter (eds.), *Decisions, Organizations and Society* (Harmondsworth: Penguin, 1971), p. 254.
50. The Colonial Service, of course, had its occasional corruption scandal, usually hushed up with the misdemeanant bundled home. Older Africans tell tales of officers cheating on expense accounts that sound quite contemporary. As early as 1898, a prohibition on civil servants owning more than one house appeared in Uganda. The statement in the text however, so far as one can determine, appears substantially accurate.
51. Tanzania: Criminal Procedure Code (Cap. 20), Sec. 27.
52. Ibid., Sec. 9.
53. Northern Rhodesia: The Pools Ordinance, 1960 (Cap. 51).
54. R.B. Seidman, 'Administrative Law and Legitimacy in Anglophonic Africa: A Problem in the Reception of Foreign Law', *Law and Society Review*, 5, 161 (1970).
55. Tanzania: Criminal Procedure Code (Cap. 20), Sec. 9.
56. *Attorney-General of Kenya* v. *M.R. Shah, trading as Tanga Trading Corporation* [1959] E.A. 375.
57. Ghai and McAuslan, *Public Law*, p. 303.
58. See above, Chap. 12.
59. Whether the public school code did prevent cruelty by the colonial administrators on occasion may be doubted. The Chief Justices of Kenya for years had to remonstrate with local officials against excessive flogging of Africans (see Chap. 12). It would be interesting to know whether the atrocities committed during the Mau Mau emergency in that country were the acts only of settlers, or whether they were also perpetrated by the flower of British upper-class youth. See below, Chap. 16.
60. See below, Chap. 17.
61. *Tanganyika L. Reports*, 1 (R) (1972) 48.
62. F.D. Lugard, *The Dual Mandate in Tropical Africa*, Fourth ed. (Edinburgh: William Blackwood, 1929), p. 116.
63. Ibid., p. 159.
64. See above, Chap. 5.
65. Ghai and McAuslan, *Public Law*, pp. 506-8.
66. An extraordinarily high gratuity, paid by the newly-independent states, but demanded and obtained by England as part of the price of independence.
67. See below, Chap. 21.
68. See above, Chap. 2.
69. Zambia: Trades Licensing Ordinance, 1968, sec. 5.
70. Tanzania: Control of Prices Ordinance, 1951 (Cap. 309).
71. Kenya: Sisal Industry Act, 1965 (Cap. 341,§13(3)).
72. See, e.g., Kenya: Detention Camps Act, 1967 (Cap. 91).
73. See, e.g., Sierra Leone: Undesirable British Subjects Ordinance, 1939 (Cap. 87, 93).
74. Walter Dickey and F. Tsikato, 'A Look at Administrative Law in Ghana',

University of Ghana L.J., 9, 135 (1972) 159.

75. Tanzania, n.d., sec. 27 (cyclostyle).
76. Personal conversation with the author.
77. 1969 Selected Judgements of Zambia 54.
78. 1967 Selected Judgements of Zambia 66.
79. No. 41/1968, sec. 15(c).
80. Kenya: No. 28 of 1965.
81. Emphasis supplied.
82. *Institute of Patent Agents* v. *Lockwood* (1894) A.C. 347; see Garner, 'Public Corporations', p. 151.
83. Committee on Ministers' Powers.
84. Garner, 'Public Corporations', p. 150.
85. See Chap. 2.
86. J.R. Nellis, 'Is the Kenyan Bureaucracy Developmental? Political Considerations in Development Administration', *Af. Stud. Rev.*, 14, 389 (1971) 395; W. Ilchman, 'The Unproductive Study of Productivity', *Comparative Political Studies*, 1, 244 (1968).
87. F.W. Riggs, 'Relearning an Old Lesson: The Political Context of Development Administration', *Pub. Admin. Rev.*, 25 70 (1965); F. Heady, *Public Administration: A Comparative Perspective* (Englewood Cliffs, N.J.: Prentice-Hall, 1966), p. 101. Riggs argues that deliberate measures should be taken to restrict the expansion of bureaucracy.
88. G. Hyden, 'Introduction' in Hyden, Jackson, and Okumu, *Development Administration*, p. xiii.
89. These different kinds of tasks – rule-applying and problem-solving – were analogous to the categories proposed by Professor Fuller, between 'adjudicative' and 'polycentric' decisions. L. Fuller, 'Collective Bargaining and the Arbitrator', [1963] *Wis. L. Rev.*, 3. Adjudication is based upon a rule. It must be sufficiently specific that the decision-maker knows precisely which considerations are relevant, and which are not. Such a rule also makes it possible for the parties rationally to adduce evidence and argument addressed to the criteria declared relevant by the rule. A 'polycentric' decision, in Fuller's nomenclature, is one in which it appears impossible to formulate a clear rule for decision.

Consider the task that would face a court called upon by a coachless football team to assign positions to the players in a principled fashion. The difficulty in submitting this problem to adjudication is that, assuming the basis for assignment to be one of maximum benefit to the team as a whole, the decision regarding any one of the players cannot sensibly be made in isolation from the decisions with respect to the others. It is not possible to decide who should play quarterback, for example, and then decide separately who should play fullback, for the former decision will be influenced by the latter. And who plays end or center will be influenced by who plays quarterback and fullback (J. Henderson, 'Judicial Review of Manufacturers' Conscious Design Choices: The Limits of Adjudication', *Col. L. Rev.*, 73, 1531, 1537 [1973]).

The sorts of decisions that have to be made about development are mainly 'polycentric'. L. Fuller, *Morality of Law* (New Haven: Yale University Press, 1964), p. 186. The sharp dichotomy that Fuller attempts between polycentric and adjudicative decisions is not, however, the case: it is a continuum. When a judge must construe a statute or resolve ambiguities in a line of precedent, he necessarily formulates a new rule; and that is invariably a polycentric decision, by definition. See J. Stone, *Social Dimensions of Law and*

Justice (Holmes Beach, Florida: Wm. W. Gaunt & Sons, 1966), p. 708.·

90. A. Bertram, *The Colonial Service* (Cambridge: Cambridge University Press, 1930), p. 55.
91. Ibid., p. 52.
92. For an example, see *Meru Land Problem* (Dar es Salaam: Govt. Printer, 1952).
93. See Chap. 5.
94. See Chap. 15.
95. In Zambia in 1972, data for the consumer price index was drawn from elite retail stores in urban centers, not from slum or rural stores, whose prices were markedly higher.
96. A.L. Adu, *The Civil Service in Commonwealth Africa* (London: Allen and Unwin, 1969), p. 26.
97. Lord Welby, quoted in J.D. Kingsley, *Representative Bureaucracy* (New York: Antioch Press, 1944), p. 264.
98. H.A. Simon, D.W. Smithburg and V.A. Thompson, *Public Administration* (New York: Alfred A. Knopf, 1950), p. 236.
99. T. Caplow, *Principles of Organization* (New York: Harcourt, Brace and World, 1964), p. 96.
100. Simon *et al., Public Administration,* p. 240.
101. Ibid., p. 236.
102. Ibid., p. 233.
103. See below, Chap. 2.
104. A. Etzioni, *Modern Organizations* (Englewood Cliffs, New Jersey: Prentice-Hall, 1964), p. 3.
105. Republic of Zambia, *Report of the Working Party Appointed to Review the System of Decentralized Administration* (Lusaka: Cabinet Office, 1972), para. 7.13.
106. Ibid., p. 26.
107. See above, Chap. 9.
108. See below, Chap. 16.
109. Etzioni, *Modern Organizations*; R. Michels, *Political Parties,* E. and C. Paul, tr. (Glencoe, Indiana: The Free Press, 1915); R.K. Merton, *Social Theory and Social Structure* (Glencoe: The Free Press, 1957).
110. W.J. Chambliss, and R.B. Seidman, *Law, Order and Power* (Reading, Mass.: Addison-Wesley, 1971), p. 269; F. Riggs, *Administration in Developing Countries: The Theory of Prismatic Society* (Boston: Houghton Mifflin, 1964).
111. Nellis, 'Kenyan Bureaucracy'.
112. See Chap. 14.
113. See Chap. 15.
114. See Chap. 16.
115. See Chap. 21.
116. Compare the US price control law during the World War II periods and the Zambian or Tanzanian law. The US law was far more detailed and specific. United States: Emergency Price Control Act of 1942, 56 STAT. 23, *Pub. L.* 421 of 1942, §§ 2(a), (b), 3(a)-(c).
117. R.B. Seidman, 'Constitutional Parameters on Administrative Action in Nigeria', *Nigerian L. Rev.,* 2, 252 (1966).
118. 1962 L.L.R. 177.
119. Nigeria: Immigration Act, sec. 13.
120. 1962 L.L.R. 177, 179.
121. Seidman, 'Constitutional Parameters', see also Re Akoto [1961] Ghana L. R. 523.
122. K.C. Davis, *Discretionary Justice: A Preliminary Inquiry* (Baton Rouge:

Louisiana State University Press, 1969).

123. S.C. 16 January 1970: Constitutional S.C. 3/69 (1970) C.C. 35; see S.O. Gyandoh, Jr., 'Discretionary Powers in the Second Republic', *Univ. of Ghana L.J.,* 8, 98 (1971).

124. In a succeeding case, *People's Popular Party* v. *Attorney-General* (1971) 1 G.L.R. 138 (concerning the denial of a permit for a political parade) however, the court cast doubt on the earlier decision, stating that in *Captan* the court was of the opinion that the case did not involve discretionary powers.

125. Stone, *Social Dimensions of Law*, Chap. 14, *passim*.

126. The Debates and Proceedings of the Constitutional Convention of the State of California; quoted in M. Radin, 'The Requirement of Written Opinions', *Cal. Law Rev.,* 18, 486 (1930) 949.

127. The Regions and Regional Commissioners Act, 1962 (Cap. 461).

128. The statement was to be sent to a magistrate, to deal with the case under the Criminal Code.

129. United States: Pub. Law 91-190; 83 STAT. 852; (42 U.S.C.§§4321, 4331-4335, 4341-4347) (1969).

130. Ibid., § 4332.

131. Ghana: The Busia Constitution, 1969, arts. 165-68.

132. Zambia: The One Party Constitution, 1973, arts. 118-19.

133. Tanzania: The Interim Constitution, 1965, arts. 67-69.

134. Tanzania, *Report of the Presidential Commission on the Establishment of a Democratic One-Party State* (Dar es Salaam: Gov't. Printer, 1965), p. 32.

135. Tanzania: The Interim Constitution , 1965, art. 67.

136. Speech by the First Vice President introducing the Bill (Permanent Commission of Enquiry Act, 1966) National Assembly Debates, 22 Feb. 1966, tr. and quoted in Martin, *Personal Freedom*, p. 185.

137. See note 89.

138. No. 1059.

139. Y.P. Ghai, 'Ombudsman and Others', *East Af. J.,* 6, 34 (1969).

140. Martin, *Personal Freedom*, p. 213.

141. The precise language varies, United States: Administrative Procedure Act 60 STAT. 237 (1946) 5 U.S.C.A. § 1001 ("Substantial Guidance"); *see Hill Dry Goods Co., Inc,* v. *Industrial Commission*, 217 Wisc. 76, 258 N.W. 336 (1935); *Universal Camera* v. *N.L.R.B.*, 340 U.S. 474, 487-88 (1951).

142. Quoted in Martin, *Personal Freedom*, p. 181.

143. Ibid., p. 127.

144. Wade, *Administrative Law*, pp. at 139-46; Davis, *Administrative Law*, §§ 7.05-7.06, pp. 164-8.

145. Cf. K.C. Davis, 'The Requirement of a Trial-type Hearing', *Harv. L. Rev.,* 76, 193, 201-206 (1956).

146. See, e.g., Tanzania: Law Reform (Fatal Accidents and Miscellaneous Provisions) Ordinance, Cap. 360, s. 15, as amended by Act No. 55 of 1968, s. 2.

147. Martin, *Personal Freedom*, p. 130.

148. Ibid., p. 128.

149. L. Cliffe, 'Tanzania-Socialist Transformation and Party Development', in L. Cliffe and J. Saul (eds.), *Socialism in Tanzania: An Interdisciplinary Reader* (Nairobi: East African Publishing House, 1972), p. 266, reprinted from *Africa Rev.,* 1, 119 (1971).

14 THE LAW CREATING AND CONTROLLING PUBLIC ENTERPRISE

The world around, governments hived off particular functions into special, relatively 'autonomous' collectivities. Supplementing central and local bureaucracies, these became a 'third arm' of government.[1] Africa did not lag in creating these agencies. By sheer size, in most countries, they outstripped the Civil Service. In Tanzania in 1970, parastatals (i.e. government-controlled corporations) accounted for 24 per cent of total employment. In 1971 they accumulated 43 per cent of gross domestic capital formation.[2] In Zambia they accounted for an even larger share of each. In both countries, the parastatal sector employed far more people than did the Civil Service. In 1973 Nigeria had upwards of 250 parastatals; the Ministry of Agriculture in Kenya alone controlled 100; Uganda had 14 major corporations and one Development Corporation with 53 subsidiaries; Tanzania by 1975 had over 200.[3] Most were productive enterprises.

The creation of so large a public productive sector became a necessity because the new states so badly lacked equity capital, credit and entrepreneurial skills. New investment could not await private initiative. Many characterized the creation of so large a public productive sector as 'socialism'. On examination, it seemed ambiguous, really only the creation of a state capitalist sector that, like the still-large private sector, foreign enterprise frequently dominated.

State capitalism can move in either of two directions. It can become the vehicle for a political elite to become a new economic ruling class; or it can develop an economy which makes both production and distribution decisions in the interests of the mass. The direction in which the economies of Africa moved resulted in large part from the institutions defining the new public enterprises. The process began with the decision to place them outside the public service, and to adopt as models the British public or private corporation, with government as majority shareholder.

I The Decision to Place Enterprise in Corporations Outside the Civil Service Bureaucracy

Throughout colonial Africa, railroads, harbours and docks, post offices, telephone and telegraph systems did not function as specially created public corporations but as Departments of the Colonial Service. When colonial governments wanted to build roads, they did not create a special entity but called upon the Department of Works.

The departmental form fell into disuse. First, the British created the various marketing and industry boards that dominated the economies of Eastern and Southern Africa. Then came the era of development corporations, following World War II, culminating in a great wave of government enterprises, mainly but not entirely engaged in production.[4] All these new enterprises responded to the conditions of development: manifold pressing difficulties, and precious little information about how to solve them. The law-making authorities could only identify problems, assign priorities and delegate power and discretion for dealing with them. The Civil Service had a highly institutionalized, rigid, on-going organization defined in General Orders, Ministerial Directives, Civil Service Rules, budgeting processes, and a myriad of unwritten rituals and procedures. Rather than try to fit a new organization within it, frequently law-makers found it easier to create an entirely new organization outside its limits, endowing it with power and discretion to solve a particular problem.

Delegating broad discretionary power to new, independent entities, of course, created new power centres. It reopened a classical problem for government: how to delegate power and yet ensure its instrumental use? The ordinary business corporation shared this classical problem. The private corporation served to centralize management and control. Thousands of shareholders could not jointly manage a business enterprise. Instead, they elected a Board of Directors, which in turn appointed managers to carry on day-to-day executive and administrative tasks. In this way, business corporations also faced the problem: how to delegate power to directors and to management and yet ensure its exercise in the shareholders' interest? Supposedly, the business corporations found excellent solutions for the problem. The Swaziland Second National Development Plan 1973-77[5] declared that by purchasing a 50 per cent share ownership in various commercial and manufacturing enterprises, the National Industrial Development Corporation sought to establish 'a more balanced relationship between foreign and domestic ownership and control of modern enterprises . . .' If management of a business corporation faithfully promoted the interests of private shareholders, why should it not equally well promote the interests of government as shareholder?

Classical corporation law purported to ensure managerial accountability by elected Boards of Directors, the rules of *ultra vires* and the

profitability criterion. The directors represented shareholder interest
and determined policy. Management implemented policy under a vigi-
lant directoral eye. The rules of *ultra vires* limited the powers of corporate managers and directors to those that reasonably related to the
explicit powers of the corporate charter. The courts characterized
corporate directors and managers as fiduciaries for the shareholders.
Since shareholders had only profit-taking as a common objective, that
became the sole legitimate objective of corporate activity.[6] These
rules ensured management accountability to private shareholders; why
not to public ones?

Public enterprise, however, responded to two sets of imperatives.
It had to meet the need 'for a high degree of freedom, boldness and
enterprise in the management of undertakings of an industrial or
commercial character and . . . to escape from the caution and circum-
spection which is considered typical of government'.[7] At the same
time, profitability seemed too narrow a criterion, since government had
other, broader interests. The profitability criterion allegedly guaranteed
corporate efficiency; how to attain that while pursuing other, social
goals?

Britain reached a compromise solution by empowering the relevant
Minister to give policy directions 'of a general nature' to the directors,
but not to intervene in day-to-day operations. Hopefully, experience
and common sense would fix this vague line.[8]

The most important non-profit-making social factor for English
public corporations concerned pricing. In Britain, government corporations sprouted not on the economy's commanding heights, but in its
boggy fens – railroads, coal, steel – where new capital investment
seemed remote. Pricing, over which social and private objectives came
most sharply into conflict[9] led to directives to the public corporations
to keep prices at a level that would avoid losses, not maximize profits.
The provision of the Transport Act, 1962 was typical: 'Each of the
boards shall so conduct their business as to secure that their revenue
is not less than sufficient for making provision for the meeting of
charges properly chargeable to revenue, taking one year with another.'[10]
Supposedly, British public corporations achieved wild successes. The
Colonial Office exported their model all over the Empire, and the
newly independent states adopted it avidly.[11] 'As with most institutions
in developing Africa with roots in the colonial past, the structure of the
statutory corporations has been influenced to a greater extent by prevailing practice in the developed world, especially Britain, than by the
concrete features of the African setting.'[12]

The British model of the public corporation assumed that government had complete ownership. Africa, however, lacked capital and expertise. Most new enterprise drew capital and management from foreign investors. The ordinary private corporation form nicely adapted itself to a partnership between government and private investors. It had emerged, after all, to incorporate diverse investors into a working enterprise with unified management. Just as the public corporation became the typical form for the wholly state-owned enterprise, so the private corporation, invariably modeled on the British form, became the model for the state-private partnership. Together, they formed the parastatal sector.

II Parastatal Corporations and their Consequences: Investment, Productivity, the Bureaucratic Bourgeoisie

Public enterprise in most of Africa did not work very well, generating three principal complaints.

A. Public Corporations and the Investment Decision

1. *The Trouble: Growth (Sometimes) but No Development.* In almost all countries, the decision to make new investment mainly lay with specially created development corporations, or with the operating parastatals themselves. Neither produced investments likely to restructure the economy in desirable ways.

In Tanzania, two experienced commentators complained that 'decision-making in the field of industrial strategy remains premised on the shopping list approach', and that 'short-term opportunity and accident' dictated choice between projects.[13] Although Zambia created the Zambia Industrial Development Company as its principal instrument for industrial growth, '. . . Zambia's post-independence manufacturing industrial growth, while apparently exceptionally rapid, has not contributed much towards restructuring the economy. If anything, it has tended to perpetrate and even exaggerate the inherited dualism. The explanation for this distortion appears to lie in the adoption of an import-substitution policy, backed on the implicit assumption that the choice of projects is best left to existing "market forces" dominated by a narrow high-income group and giant multinational corporations. . .'[14] Value added by manufacturing in Zambia jumped from 48 million kwacha [KI = $US1.50 approximately] in 1965 to KI64.5 million in 1972, but this expanded manufacturing sector increasingly depended upon imported inputs. The composition of manufacturing did not change, with 40 per cent of value added in manufacturing in beverages and tobacco — hardly the key to future expansion of the economy. Between 1966 and 1969, fixed capital invested per employee doubled (thus decreasing employment in relation to investment). The geographical location of new manufacturing remained, as before Independence, along the urbanized line-of-rail.[15]

Ghana's story repeated the tale. Nkrumah reorganized the Industrial Development Corporation because it had concentrated on an ineffective programme to encourage small Ghanaian enterprise, rather than large industrial projects.[16] By 1960, an outside consultant said that its projects were '(1) usually small, (2) frequently irrelevant to any basic economic developmental goal, (3) sometimes unsuccessful as business enterprise, (4) occasionally involved in segments of the economy in which non-governmental businessmen are its competitors or could supplant it, and (5) sometimes continued after the IDC has completed its developmental purpose instead of being sold (to private interests) and proceeds used for development rather than administration'.[17]

Everywhere, government proposed making investments to restructure the economy, to accomplish increased specialization and exchange, employment and production, create poles of growth in the countryside and use local raw materials. It did not happen. Why?

2. *The Development of the Development Corporation.* Expectedly, operating parastatals, organized under the ordinary corporation law, made investments in part by profit criteria, and in part pursuant to managerial interests in advancement, power and privilege; so did private corporations. Social criteria seemed lost. Surprisingly, development corporations did not act very differently.

In most African countries, development corporations metamorphosized from a form of investment banking to facilitate economic growth through private enterprise, into the preferred instrument to develop a new, government-owned productive sector. They thus transformed themselves from a private sector infrastructural support into the principal institution for state capitalism. At the outset, the development corporations only supplied 'soft' equity capital and credit to private, mainly foreign, entrepreneurs[18] who initiated projects. The corporations chose projects to support on commercial grounds. In Tanganyika, the corporation's charter required it 'to facilitate the industrial and economic development of Tanganyika, and in particular . . . to promote, develop and manage and assist in the promotion, financing, development and management' of new and existing enterprises.[19]

These early corporations followed the model of the Commonwealth

Development Corporation. The Board of Directors had great independence, having as its only specific duty 'to use its best endeavours to
secure that its business as a whole is carried on at a net profit taking
one year with another'.[20] The relevant Minister, as in England, could
issue general directives to the corporation,[21] but rarely actually did so
anywhere. The corporation usually had to render accounts and a report to the legislature,[22] duties they frequently observed in the breach.

In their second phase, development corporations everywhere became
the major vehicle for governmental initiative in production investment.
In Ghana in 1961, government dissolved the Industrial Development
Corporation and the Ghana Holding Corporation, both modeled on the
Commonwealth Development Corporation. The state began vigorously
to purchase and create enterprises, with the state as majority or sole
shareholder.[23] Zambia followed after the Economic Reforms of 1968.[24]
INDECO's net group assets jumped from K35.5 million in 1968 to
K233 million in 1969. Its productive divisions employed about 45 per
cent of all manufacturing employees in Zambia.[25] Uganda seemed
headed on the same course following President Obote's Common Man's
Charter.[26] Tanzania made the NDC 'the government organization directed to participate in industrial enterprise',[27] and changed its charter to
require it not merely to 'facilitate' economic development, but to 'promote' it.[28]

3. *Why the Failure of the Development Corporations?* Despite the high
hopes and lofty rhetoric, usually socialist, that accompanied these
changes, in no country did the public investment match either hopes or
rhetoric. Rather than restructuring the economy, the development
corporations mostly invested in high visibility enterprises that increased
opportunities for management advancement, with avoiding loss years as
the over-riding limit. Their investments replicated the pattern of private
investment, while adding large dollops of irrationality. Even socialist
Tanzania provided no clear exception to the rule.[29]

Development corporations provided in the main archetypical examples of soft development, for reasons that fall under the general
explanation for disoebedience advanced above.[30]

  a. The ambiguity of the criteria for investment. Ambiguous or vague
norms permit the role-occupant's discretion to control behaviour.[31]
Everywhere, the development corporation's charters and statutes set
out thoroughly woolly investment criteria. In Zambia, the Second
National Development Plan defined INDECO's role as accumulating

profits from projects within the framework of the present high-income urban market, in order to invest these in industries designed to spread productive activities elsewhere.[32] The two goals contradicted each other. Which came first: the maximization of profits for future use, or investment now in the rural areas? (In fact, only 1.5 per cent of new industrial establishments in Zambia from independence to 1969 came in the rural area.[33])

Tanzania, too, had ambiguous investment criteria. Vague notions that investment should follow a plan presumably expressing social criteria[34] conflicted with profitability. The President stated that 'It is absolutely necessary that the new ... Corporation should have its own independent financial base to enable it to operate on a self-financing basis.'[35] In order to achieve this, he said, the corporation 'will be required to select its project participations in such a way as to have an overall surplus on all its investments'.[36] The Minister stated in the National Assembly that the reformed corporation would have to account for its performance and could not long rely on government subsidies.[37] The corporation's controlling statute therefore required the corporation to 'have regard to the economic and commercial merits of any undertaking it promotes, finances, develops, manages or assists', as well as 'the economic potentialities of Tanganyika as a whole', and should use 'its best endeavours to secure that its business as whole is carried on at a net profit taking one year with another'.[38]

The ambiguity between social and market criteria in investment policy resulted from an African variant of the British dilemma: how to use 'business principles' to operate a firm which also has social functions? In England, that social function mainly involved low prices. The statutory standard, avoiding losses taking one year with another, reasonably guided corporate policy. The day-to-day business of development corporations, however, concerned investment. National development policy and planning also focused on investment. Thus, the development corporation's policy became government's development policy. In effect, the basic directive in the corporate charter, to avoid losses taking one year with another, comprised all of government's instructions for development. Its insufficiency was pathetic.

As a result, governments gave the development corporations quite unrestricted discretion to determine investment. Tanzania tried to ensure the consideration of social as well as profit factors. In 1968, the president formally instructed the corporation that 'it is socialist investment which government wishes to see undertaken by NDC, not just any investment'.[39] That did little to clarify the investment criteria. The

Second Five-Year Plan mentioned the desirability of an industrial strategy, but failed to provide one, including instead a list of possible projects. In lieu of an industrial strategy, it laid down a set of considerations to control investment decisions, such as 'an increase in capital investment in the rural areas and in the *ujamaa* villages' and 'an increase in the export of manufactured goods'.[40]

The National Development Corporation tried to accommodate these new, but still vague criteria.[41] It defined three specific ones to be 'satisfied', and five to be 'considered'. Its primary criteria included (a) profitability, (b) national cost/benefit, and (c) foreign exchange effects. The five secondary criteria were (a) unemployment, (b) location, (c) industrial linkage, (d) budgetary impact and (e) investable surplus.[42]

This valiant attempt to introduce social criteria into decision-making failed. Loxley and Saul comment:

> In what way can primary criterion (a) be said to differ from secondary criterion (e) assuming NDC's objective to be NOT to maximize profit outflow overseas? What meaning can be attached to national cost/benefit if it is not commercial profitability adjusted for the social valuation of foreign exchange effects, employment, linkage, location and budgetary effects?[43]

In 1972, the General Manager of NDC said that

> If Party policy is defined in broad terms and if responsibility between the civil service and parastatals are indistinctly drawn, serious clashes over interpretation of Party policy will develop when practical cases are examined in the light of that policy . . . in several cases in the past we have been blamed for misinterpreting Government and Party policies.[44]

The perennial problem in structuring discretion by identifying a variety of criteria lies in their relative weighting.[45] Articulated criteria serve better than none at all, but, inevitably, the absence of a guide to relative importance leads to a 'great risk that these wider economic effects will only be appealed to in special cases where special interests are at play. Vague arguments of this kind may be used to back up bad projects.'[46] Investment policy seemed to defy any formulation to guide decision; only a detailed industrial strategy laid down in perspective and medium-term plans could do that. In its absence, the unconstrained discretion of corporate officials determined industrial investment. Actual invest-

ments resulted more from decision-making structure and the officials'
interests and subjective orientations than from the goals or policy of
political authorities.

   b. Opportunity and capacity. The development corporations could
not formulate or implement an industrial strategy to restructure the
economy. Usually, the responsible personnel did not even know of the
need for one. Even after the Arusha Declaration of 1967 (when
Tanzania unambiguously declared for socialism), government did not
formulate such a strategy.

   From its reorganization in 1964, government kept the development
corporation in Tanzania under its thumb. Six Ministers constituted a
majority of the Board of Directors, and the legislature gave the Minister
power to issue particular as well as general directions to it.[47] The parastatals should become 'instruments of execution — tools which must be
used by the policy-makers, and which must be at the command of the
responsible authorities'.[48]

   Government control without government policy, however, is boot-
less. In Tanzania, the Minister never directed the development corporation to do anything, general or specific.[49] In 1964, Tanzania had no
effective planning machinery.[50] Even if the Minister wanted to direct
the corporation's investments, he could not have done so. Government
plainly expected its dominance of the Board through the six Minister-
members to ensure compatability between investments and official
ideology. The six Tanzanian Ministers, however, had little influence on
development company investment policy. Themselves busy men, they
received papers for directors' meetings only shortly before the
meetings. The Board decided upon the Mwanza Textile Mill, the Sisal
Pulp Mill and the fertilizer factory — major Tanzanian industrial investments — after only a week's advance notice.[51]

   Potential foreign private investors initiated most of these projects,
hoping to obtain 51 per cent (or more) government financing. French
interests, for example, promoted the Mwanza Textile Mill. The staff
lacked sufficient time to consider issues other than the proposals'
economic viability. The proposals of the foreign investors, of course,
hinged mainly on prospective profits. This system of decision-making
ensured that market rather than social criteria would dominate investment policy.

   c. The interest of the managers. Many corporate investments lost
money. New skyscraping parastatal office buildings dominated every

African capital city just as the overblown office buildings of the great
multinational corporations dominated the skylines of American cities.
Other investments, too, garnered more glitter than profits. In Ghana
in 1965, an enormous sum, upwards of £7,000,000, went to construct
ten-storey high concrete silos to store cocoa. Supposedly, their design
followed that of grain silos. Cocoa is oily. The beans crush. Nobody
has ever dared use the silos to store cocoa, lest the beans at the bottom
become an oily, impregnable mass. In 1972 the silos still stood empty.
Parastatals built sugar refineries without ensuring the supply of sugar,
a tomato-tinning plant, without an adequate supply of tomatoes, a
plant to tin mangoes, without any market survey (the export demand
for mangoes did not seem overwhelming, and Ghanaians can easily
obtain the fresh fruit).[52] 'In many cases, no feasibility studies were
made and often even the most basic survey of potential markets and
raw material supplies was omitted. Political, rather than economic considerations appear often to have determined the siting of plants; much
of the construction was carried out without adequate Ghanaian participation or supervision.'[53]

Management everywhere has an interest in greater visibility, opportunities and power. At the same time, in Africa it had to avoid loss
years. A development corporation whose investments achieved both
high visibility and stayed out of the red would escape damaging criticism.[54] Maximizing profits became a low priority.

d. The perceptions of the managers. The actual decisions about investments came from either indigenous management or their expatriate
investment advisers. Most had Western training, and held Western
notions of investment appraisal, that emphasized profitability to the
exclusion of social criteria. In Zambia, in the early 1970s, the Kafue
Textile Mill expanded its capacity by about 50 per cent. Zambia produces cotton. Instead of installing facilities to produce cotton textiles,
providing inexpensive cloth for low-income consumers and backward
linkages for farmers, the mill installed machinery to produce synthetics
from imported components. The United Nations economist who advised the move justified it on the ground that 'the Zambian consumer'
– i.e. the high-income elite – demanded synthetics.[55]

Without any clear criteria for investment embodied in an industrial
strategy and a national plan, governments *de facto* left investments to
the discretion of the managers. Their interest often followed foreign
requests for government financing. Trained to emphasize market criteria, their personal career and other interests nevertheless induced

investment in high-visibility enterprises, and sometimes expansion for its own sake. Delegation of power without guidelines for its exercise always results in power-holders maximizing their subjective orientations. That proposition explains why African parastatals did not adopt a course of investments likely to produce development.

B. Productivity in the Individual State Enterprise

Africans constantly complained that parastatal enterprises were 'inefficient'. In Tanzania[56] and Zambia,[57] the development corporations overall showed a profit. The global figures hid many individual loss years behind a few successful subsidiaries.[58] Almost everywhere,[59] the parastatals frequently required subventions to rescue them from embarrassment.[60] Ghana became the archetype:

> By 1965-66, Ghana's public corporations had incurred deficits that amounted to 23.3 per cent of total government revenues. Several observers attributed such inefficiency to personnel redundancy, pervasive corruption, and a general deterioration of administrative co-ordination and planning . . . State enterprises employed more than twice as many clerical workers as similar size and type private-sector firms . . . When the Bibiani mine . . . ran out of ore in 1968, the Busia regime (1969-1972) still maintained its workers as of 1972 even though no gold was being produced. In 1966-1967, one factory reportedly expended 98.7 per cent of its total expenditures on salaries and only 2.3 per cent on raw materials; and in still another case, the State Fishing Corporation allegedly employed 435 personnel but had no fishing vessels, while the 37 employees in the accounts department found it hard to keep accounting records up to date.[61]

Even when government purchased an ongoing firm, retaining existing management (frequently connected with a multinational parent), costs sometimes rose abruptly. Costs per ton of copper extracted in Zambia's copper mines, for example, rose 20 per cent in the first year that it owned 51 per cent of the shares, although it made no change in operating management, nor did the rise in costs respond to a rise in the input prices. Nobody has ever explained the cost rise publicly. Tales of transfer price fiddles persisted, where foreign management purchased inputs from a related company overseas at grossly inflated prices.[62] Complaints arose about parastatal management inefficiency in Ghana,[63] Tanzania,[64] Uganda,[65] Nigeria[66] and Zambia.[67]

The British model in theory ensured business efficiency under
government policy control. Whatever the actual case in Britain, in Africa
that beneficent result eluded law-makers. Parastatals failed so often,
that one must search for systemic explanations.[68]

1. *The Scope of Discretion.* In the private corporation, the Board, the
ultra vires rule, and the profitability criterion supposedly limit managerial discretion. State corporations had mandates so broad that they
could justify almost any activity.[69] Specifically, the profitability criterion did not apply to every activity, for managers need only avoid
losses 'taking one year with another'. In effect, they had, in daily
operations as in investment, unlimited discretion.

2. *Opportunity and Capacity.* Just as in private enterprise, an originally
poor investment decision almost certainly limited future productivity.
In Ghana,

(a) The book value of the corporations is often well above the
current and economic value.

b) Excess capacity in relation to size of the domestic market is
common.

c) The short-term working capital position is often inadequate by
normal commercial criteria ...

d) The existing long-term indebtedness of the group [of the subsidiaries of the Ghana Industrial Holding Company, as of 1972]
involves very heavy servicing requirements.

e) The productive equipment of some corporations is not well suited
for sound commercial operation under local conditions ...[70]

3. *The Interests of Management.* Galbraith argued that management in a
private corporation had many interests besides profitability: more jobs,
power and perquisites.[71] So did managers of public corporations. In
the case of private corporations, management could not permit its profits to fall under a certain floor without endangering its position. If the
price of the shares too radically declined, takeover or shareholder revolt
threatened, management's own shares declined, and management
salaries grow smaller. In a private firm, management must at least 'satis-
fice'.

Most parastatals lacked these controls. No market for shares existed.

Private management compensation frequently depended on gross sales, not profit.[72] They often offset their losses on takeovers by the parastatal by gains to their parent transnational corporation (as in the case of purchases at an inflated price from the parent).[73] To local directors, only the possibility of criticism served to goad them to show any profit at all; for foreign management, only the remote threat of renegotiation of the management contract served as a limit. Social criteria, however much ignored in fact, always conveniently explained losses, for one could always blame the politicians.[74]

In a private corporation, in theory, management faced another constraint: unless they produced a profit, the Board of Directors might sack them. In the operating parastatals, although the Board theoretically had the same power, government held a majority of the shares, and a private firm held both a minority and a contract to provide operating management. These combined to make discharging management unlikely. There were several reasons for this. Part-time directors could not police management concerning profits any better than they could investment policy. The appointments to the board, not always of high quality, frequently became political pay-offs.[75] To avoid politics, East African governments sometimes appointed civil servants – in Tanzania, one civil servant sat on more than forty Boards at the same time.[76] Civil servants constituted the very group whose control government corporations aimed to avoid. In any event, the Board's position cramped their capacity to ride with a very tight rein. The success of the corporation supposedly depended on management. Inevitably, an alliance arose between directors and managers. The enemy, the nominal owner, government, threatened both. Parastatal boards parted with information about the workings of their corporations to their 'shareholder' (government) as reluctantly as did directors of American corporations to private shareholders. Rather than policing management in the interest of government, the directors frequently became management's first line in defence against it. In this they took advantage of traditions of civil service secrecy, reinforced by British notions about the inviolability of 'business privacy'. Together, these formed an impenetrable wall against 'outside' enquiry. 'Outside' frequently read 'any'.[77]

Without directorial control, management, as everywhere, sought to protect and enlarge its own interest. In African joint public-private corporations, that took a special form.

The organizational theory of private corporations holds that, however diverse, stockholders share an interest in maximizing profits. That provides a standard against which to measure management performance.

Respecting operations, profitability supposedly results from efficiency. In the joint public-private corporations of Africa, supposedly, private managers' substantial equity position guaranteed efficiency, for the greater the profits, the greater their return. That proved false, for frequently they had other, more pressing interests.

Choices frequently came even within the general rubric of 'economic' decisions. The interests of government and of the transnational sometimes differed over those choices. For example, a mining company might have to choose between extracting the richest ore immediately, even if doing so would make it very expensive to mine less desirable grades later on, or sacrificing quick return for long-run pay-off. What best suited government did not necessarily best suit its managers' transnational parent.

This problem, of course, particularly pressed where the operating parastatal might invest from its own reserves. The transnational frequently wanted quick recovery of cash, for reinvestment elsewhere, while government most desired reinvestment within the country.[78] In Zambia, they persuaded the Board actually to borrow from foreign sources at high interest rates to raise cash for dividend payments.

The issue arose as well over technology. Given equal costs, should the corporation adopt a labour-intensive or capital-intensive technology? The one maximizes employment; the other minimizes labour problems. Government and management sometimes had quite opposed interests in the matter. The Board of Directors usually lacked knowledge to protect government's interest in these choices. Without intimate engineering competence and knowledge of the state of ore bodies, for example, directors could not even recognize the existence of choice about ore extraction.

The provisions of some of the contracts between the managing agents and the corporation enhanced the difficulties of control. The agents sometimes bargained for, and obtained, the right to make all day-to-day decisions. In Zambia, the minority multinational directors of the great mining parastatals actually had a veto over *all* decisions of the Board they believed lacked commercial justification.[79]

C. The Emergence of a Dependent Ruling Class

These various parastatal corporations came into existence accompanied by rhetoric that directed them to restructure the several economies and in particular to substitute national economic control for foreign control. Management, however, usually came from a multinational corporation, perhaps with a few black faces as a down payment on

Africanization. The board usually had a majority of Africans. All these managers and directors had only marginal accountability. They dealt with corporate assets, determined the uses of the economic surplus — what proportion for new investment, for dividends, for managerial compensation and delights. The magnificent office buildings of the parastatals that dominated the African capital cities, the luxurious homes of the managers, complete with park-like grounds, swimming pools and high boundary walls topped with glass to protect them from thieves and robbers, and the elegant company automobiles, testified to their choices. Control of productive property carries with it power over corporate contracts and employment. Management and directors became the effective owners of the parastatals.

An economic class becomes a *ruling* class if it has great power over other people. Under capitalism, that power ordinarily comes from property and contract law. In the guise of rules concerning *things*, these laws delegate to the owners power over *people*. They control people because the state protects their ownership of things. The managers and directors of parastatals occupied the same position, although their power came from a different set of laws, that gave them power over things by virtue of the rules making them managers and directors of parastatal corporations. They became the owners of a new sort of property.

Most of the new directors, and even a few managers, had black faces. These new black entrants to the economic ruling class, however, had a peculiar dependency relationship to foreign firms. They had to favour them, or at least not rock the boat. They quickly discovered that their interests agreed with the interests of the multinationals. The expatriate managers became their allies, not their enemies. In most of Anglophonic Africa, the development of the parastatal sector, hailed by some and damned by others as a movement towards 'socialism', in fact developed not socialism, but a new ruling class allied to the expatriate firms. They became an important wing of the 'bureaucratic bourgeoisie', with little interest in radical structural change.

D. Summary: The Irrelevance of the Form of the Corporation

Whether in the form of the British public corporation, or an ordinary private one with government holding a majority of the shares, public enterprise did not achieve howling successes in Africa. Both forms came from the notion that the ordinary corporate devices to curb management would suffice: *ultra vires*, profitability criteria, the Board of Directors. Just as Berle and Means argued regarding publicly held companies in the United States, management and directors removed themselves from control by the nominal shareholders.[80] Just as Galbraith argued, those who controlled the technology, here the private foreign managers, controlled their nominal superiors.[81] Government embraced the corporation in despair over the rule-bound confines of bureaucracy. It gave their managers great discretion. Government must govern and not merely by delegating very broad tasks to separate entities. Delegated, unaccountable authority becomes authority not delegated, but divested.

Ambiguity from the outset characterized the parastatal sector. Any country that proposes to use law and state power to restructure its economy can attempt to do so either indirectly, through regulating the private sector, or directly, through state enterprises. Every African country tried both. The new state enterprises might serve to restructure the economy in the interests of the mass or become vehicles for the elite to consolidate and enlarge their power and privilege. In Africa, this latter course led to their allying with the foreign firms and using their power not to change things but to maintain the *status quo*.

Government needed decision-making institutions likely to solve the emergent problems of development. The private corporate form, at best, could only maximize shareholder profits – and modern scholarship casts doubt upon its efficacy even in that regard. The British public corporation worked haltingly in England, where it faced neither the problems of development policy, nor private partners and managers. Neither the public nor the public-private corporation in Africa served effectively to solve the difficulties that they attacked.

III New Decision-Making Structures in the Parastatal Sector[82]

A variety of responses to parastatal failures emerged, too many by half for me to discuss here in detail. Some tried to change managerial behaviour by new rules – for example, rules requiring financial accounts. Others attempted to improve the decision-making process, by improving inputs or otherwise. Others sought more drastic solutions, by removing particular decisions from managers. The most radical solution undercut the whole structure of discretion by creating new participatory institutions. I examine first institutions to improve business skills and financial accountability.

A. Business Skills and Financial Accountability

Some countries continued to assert the need for still greater managerial autonomy. The Guidelines for the Ghanaian Five-Year Development Plan,

1975-80, stated (as though nothing had happened in the preceding decade), that the short-term policy objectives were 'to promote industrial competition by allowing firms greater freedom in managerial and entrepreneurial decision-making'.[83] Other countries insisted that parastatals operate on a 'commercial basis',[84] or stipulated that the parastatal operate 'in the same way as other trade and commercial organizations'.[85] Some reiterated that government would not interfere in daily operations or that its principal function was to help parastatals become profitable.[86] Polities with such perspectives, however, still had to insist upon business skill and financial accountability.

The obvious first step became the improvement of directorial appointments. Surprisingly, little happened to improve selection processes. Ghana required that one member of the Board of Directors of the Ghana Industrial Holding Company have skills in finance, a second in commerce, including marketing, and third engineering or law.[87] Beyond that lone provision, however, African parastatal laws did little more than recite a dreary litany drawn from the British model, that directors not be bankrupts, convicted of felonies involving fraud or moral turpitude, and so forth.

Government generally made more efforts to localize management posts. Expectedly, nationals will manage in the interests of the country better than expatriates.[88] Countries tried to train the necessary personnel. Zambia, for example, initiated a School of Mines in the University. Management had to start training programmes and open administrative and executive posts to young Zambians. (This enterprise's success lagged, largely because old-line expatriate employees in the mining industry resisted in order to protect their parochial interests.)[89] Tanzania channelled university graduates into parastatals until localization in the parastatal sector equalled that in the Civil Service.[90] A National High Level Manpower Allocation Committee attempted to regulate high level manpower allocation to the parastatals.[91]

Almost every country tried to improve financial accountability. Most African countries by statute required parastatals to make annual financial accounting to government,[92] not with unvarying success. As always, governments first tried threatening harsh punishments, of course never actually imposed; the Ghanaian Bast Fibres Development Board Act provided for fines and imprisonment.[93]

All of these measures resonated easily with the power and privilege of the corporate directors and managers. Some countries sought to strengthen controls from above to deprive managers and directors of some of their power and discretion.

B. New Controls from Above

1. *Institutions to Provide Information.* In the received law, only the independent audit can provide information to shareholders free of managerial or directorial control. Tanzania has institutionalized the independent audit, by creating two new parastatal organizations to provide accountancy and legal services to the parastatals.[94] The Audit Corporation ensures that parastatal accounts conform to law. It also checks on compliance with existing parastatal directives and reports any deficiencies to the higher authorities in the development corporation. In addition, Tanzania nationalized the banking system. The parastatals must therefore bank with a government bank, which provides additional information about financial conditions.

2. *New Sectoral Controls.* To ensure parastatal obedience to ministerial policy directives, Tanzania and Uganda (before the end of the Obote regime) placed operating companies under the supervision of particular Ministers. Tanzania, for example, divided the NDC, hiving off the National Agricultural and Food Corporation and the Tanzania Tourist Corporations.[95] The NDC continued its supervision only over industrial development.

3. *Control of Parastatal Privileges.* Managers easily used their powers for personal aggrandizement. In Tanzania, the Presidential Standing Committee on Parastatal Organizations, initiated in 1967, froze parastatal salaries[96] and curtailed other perquisites such as housing and car allowances.[97] (A similar commission in Zambia recommended the *raising* of senior civil service salaries to the higher parastatal levels.)[98]

4. *Strengthening the Holding Company.* Most parastatals in Africa became subsidiaries of a development corporation. The development corporation thus played dual roles: investor and financier of new industry, and holding company of ongoing enterprises. To strengthen control, these holding companies established new roles and rules. In Tanzania, the Chairman of the National Development Corporation served as chairman of each group company. NDC department heads responsible for particular companies sat on their Boards of Directors. In some cases as well, NDC appointed its senior staff to the Boards.[99] It created a management information system to monitor the performance of its various departments. A new management executive committee regularly reviewed operating problems and current progress.[100]

Ghana undertook an analogous reorganization of GHIOC.[101]

5. *Withdrawing Power Over Investment.* Managers had their greatest
power and privilege when making investments. At least three countries
took steps to withdraw this power. Ghana created a capital investments
board.[102] Uganda required each parastatal to submit an annual investment plan, subject to government approval.[103] Zambia created an
Industrial Finance Company to control the lending activities of the
development corporation, a somewhat curious course.[104]

None of these measures to affect investment decision, however, held
much promise without institutions to generate an industrial development plan. Chapter 15 discusses these.

C. Control from Below: Workers' Councils in Tanzania

Controlling management becomes a problem because of management's
authoritative position. Without its authority, the question of the
control of discretion would not arise. A solution more far-reaching than
any of these looked to a participatory, not authoritarian workplace.
Worker self-interest in efficiency, it was argued, enhanced by bonus
schemes and ideological leadership, could be substituted for management interests in perquisites and personal advancement. Workers'
councils in Tanzania and Zambia,[105] however, although on superficial
examination directed to workers' participation, did not in fact produce
it.

Frequently, both management and employees support work councils.
Management sometimes explains low productivity on the ground that
workers without participation in decisions feel alienated from work.[106]
Employees frequently explain management decisions that disadvantage
workers by their exclusion from decision-making. Intriguingly, the
Tanzania movement towards workers' councils responded to management concerns, not workers'. That movement began in 1964, when the
statute creating the National Union of Tanzania Workers[107] (NUTA)
empowered its governing council to establish workers' committees in
factories, although the council hardly took advantage of the Act.[108]
The Arusha Declaration of 1967 proposed that the people own all
productive enterprise, but made no change in the actual institutions
of decision-making. President Nyerere in 1968 construed this from
management's viewpoint when he stated that 'communication of ideas
and information between workers and management and between
workers and workers can have the effect of improving the quantity and
quality of goods produced, provided that an atmosphere of common

endeavour and common responsibility is created', which required that top management regard workers as 'partners in a common enterprise'.[109] A series of meetings organized by NUTA and the Minister for Labour culminated in a 1970 Presidential Circular, which directed every parastatal to establish a workers' council.[110] Although enlarged, these councils had no more actual authority than the workers' committee of the 1964 legislation.[111] The same notions of participation in the interests of greater productivity, however, continued. In 1971, the President told the TANU national conference that

> We have gradually realized that public ownership of enterprises is not enough. These enterprises may be — and in most cases in Tanzania have been — managed well, and with the intention of serving the interests of the Tanzanian people. But they are still being managed for the people . . . Consequently, the people who are not in management positions in the public corporations, still do not feel that these corporations are theirs . . . the workers in the organizations frequently feel that they are working for 'them' and not for themselves.[112]

In consequence, the TANU guidelines (Mwongozo) of that year argued that in government and industry alike Tanzania inherited from the colonial era 'the habit in which one man gives the orders and the rest just obey them. If you do not involve the people, the result is to make them feel that a national institution is not theirs and subsequently workers adopt the habits of hired employees . . .'[113]

Given that ideology, of course the workers' councils that emerged did not in fact give workers any real decision-making power, but at most the illusions of participation. In any event, private ownership of a part of the parastatal enterprises would have made genuine worker participation difficult.[114] As a consequence, the workers' councils in Tanzania remained only advisory bodies, with the Boards of Directors retaining control. Their institutions and the Mwongozo reforms, however, had widespread consequences. A wave of strikes hit Tanzanian industry, as workers asserted the new powers they felt had been granted but inadequately realized. Government, TANU and NUTA combined to break these strikes.[115] Workers' Councils, which when created had such bright promise of restructuring decision-making in Tanzanian parastatals, seemed to have failed to do so.

Conclusion

How to explain the rapid creation of a whole new dimension of government in Africa, the parastatal sector, and its apparent inability to operate efficiently or carry out its mandate? This chapter proposes the following explanation:

1. Bureaucracies do not adapt to problem-solving as well as to rule applying; African polities had to devise institutions to solve problems.

2. The legal form that lawyers employ to meet new demands will likely come from the concepts and forms which they already know; in Africa, these included British forms of the public and private corporation.

3. Legal organizational forms impose limitations upon organizational behaviour, depending upon the social, political and economic milieu in which they function; the British form of the public or private corporation when it became the form of African public enterprise imposed no workable controls over managerial discretion.

4. Corporation managers, like other bureaucrats, tend to exercise their discretion to maximize rewards and minimize strains upon themselves and their corporations; in Africa, they did so by increasing their own compensation and perquisites, increasing total investment and output, increasing visibility, and corruption.

5. To the extent that managers of productive enterprise make decisions that in other systems private property owners make, they become a new propertied class; in Africa, the parastatal managers became a new propertied class.

6. To the extent that bureaucrats depend for their continuing power upon their bureaucratic inferiors, a *de facto* alliance arises between them against the nominal superiors of the bureaucracy as a whole; in Africa, a *de facto* alliance arose between expatriate firms acting as technicians and business managers of parastatal enterprises, and the African directors and managers.

7. To the extent that a polity imposes conditions of accountability on the managers of productive enterprise, it transforms them from a propertied class to functionaries in the service of the government; a few African states imposed some such conditions.

The issue involved the choice of political direction for the polity. The parastatal sector created a state capitalist economy. The direction that state capitalism would move – towards a new form of class domination, using state power to aggrandize the few, or towards assuring the welfare of the mass – depended more upon the institutional structures developed than the particular political rhetoric coming from the leadership.

African state enterprise spelled another moral. Jurisprudence and economics emphasize the concepts of property and ownership. We believe early on that whoever owns property controls its use. Karl Marx taught that the great contradiction of capitalism arose from the private ownership of the means of production against the social nature of production. In Africa, government formally 'owned' the state enterprises. The legal and institutional forms of the enterprises, however, strangely inverted the decision-making powers that in the private sector come with ownership. If ownership implies power to decide the uses of productive property, who 'owned' the parastatals, the state, local directors or multinational managements?

The concept of ownership may make sense when analyzing relationships between various private parties. It does not help, however, when the state itself becomes the 'owner'. Rather than using the concepts of property and ownership to analyze state enterprise, one must look to the institutions that structure the behaviour of various actors, and the decision-making power that dwells deep in their interstices. Examining these in the state enterprises of Africa teaches that their institutional and legal forms more than the prevalent public philosophy in fact determined the polities' socio-political choices.

Notes

1. J.F. Garner, 'Public Corporations in the United Kingdom', in W.G. Friedmann and J.F. Garner (eds), *Government Enterprise: A Comparative Study* (New York: Columbia University Press, 1970), p. 3.
2. J. Loxley and J.S. Saul, 'The Political Economy of the Parastatals', *E. Af. L. Rev.*, 5, 9, 9-10 (1972).
3. G. Hayden, 'Social Structures, Bureaucracy and Development Administration in Kenya', *The African Rev.*, 1, 118 (1972).
4. A.H. Rweyemanu lists seven functions of parastatals: (1) promotion of indigenous participation in commerce and industry; (2) price stabilization, particularly with reference to primary products in the agricultural sector; (3) provision of essential public services; (4) integration of the national economy through investments which do not attract private enterprise; (5) participation in projects involving international finance; (6) intervention to

avoid private monopolies; and (7) participation in profitable enterprises to increase government extraction of profits made in the economy. Quoted in G. Hyden, 'The Public Corporation in African Administrative Research' (Dar es Salaam, n.d.). This omits corporations whose function it is to ensure the nationalization of the economy in an effort to achieve centralized control over it – taking over the 'commanding heights', for example – and the nationalization of 'sick' industries, such as Ghana's gold fields or Tanzania's sisal plantations.

5. *Swaziland Second National Development Plan, 1973-77* (Mbabane: Swaziland Printing and Publishing Co., n.d.), p. 22.

6. See e.g., *Dodge v. Ford*, 204 Mich. 459, 170 N.W. 668 (1919).

7. W. Robson, *Nationalized Industry and Public Ownership* (Toronto: University of Toronto Press, 1960), p. 4; E.S. Mason, 'The Roles of Government in Economic Development', *Am. Ec. Rev., Papers and Proceedings* (Mav, 1960), 637; R.K. Jain, *Management of State Enterprises in India* (New York: Paragon, 1967), p. 44.

8. Robson, *Nationalized Industry*.

9. C.D. Drake, 'The Public Corporation as an Organ of Government Policy', in Friedmann and Garner, *Government Enterprise*, p. 26.

10. UK: Transport Act, 1968, sec. 18.

11. 43 Parl. Deb. H.C. (5th Ser.) 2018 (1947), quoted in R. Pozen, *The British Public Corporation in Ghana: Legal Transfers in the Third World* (New Haven: J.S.D. dissertation, Yale Law School, 1973), p. 18; Lord Hailey, *African Survey,* revised 1956 (London: Oxford University Press, 1957), pp. 1325-7, quoted in Pozen, p. 19.

12. E.A. Botchway, 'Operational Autonomy and Public Accountability in Statutory Corporations: A Case Study of Ghana's Development Experience and a Blueprint for Reform', *Ga. J. Int'l. and Comp. L.*, 3, 55, 56 (1973).

13. Loxley and Saul, 'Political Economy of the Parastatals', pp. 12-13.

14. A. Seidman, 'Import Substitution in Zambia', *J. Mod. Af. Studies*, 12, 631 (1974).

15. Ibid.

16. Pozen, *Legal Transfers in the Third World*.

17. G.H. Whitman, Inc., *The Ghana Report* (New York: G.H. Whitman, Inc., International Economic Consultants, 111 Broadway, 1959), p. 26; quoted in A. Seidman, *Planning for Development in Sub-Saharan Africa* (New York: Praeger, 1974), p. 142. The Tanganyikan experience was too brief to permit any generalization about the sorts of investments made. The Minister who introduced the new Bill which changed the structure of the Development Corporation stated only that the old form was insufficient because of 'the lack of clarity of a clearly defined framework of action . . . A corporation to be successful must be run in a business-like manner' and that it did not have 'an assured base of finance of its own'.

18. Tanzania: Arthur D. Little, Inc., *Tanganyika Industrial Development* (1961); International Bank of Reconstruction and Development, *The Economic Development of Tanganyika* (Baltimore: Johns Hopkins Press, 1961), pp. 241-4; Ghana: Pozen, *Legal Transfers in the Third World*, p. 25; see L.C. McQuade, 'The Development Corporation in Africa', *Am. J. Comp. L.*, 10, 188 (1961); see Tanganyika Parliamentary Debates (Hansard) National Assembly Official Report, First Session (Second Meeting) (Dar es Salaam: Govt. Printer, 1962) 26 (5 June 1962); Ghana: R.C. Pozen, 'Public Corporations in Ghana: A Case Study of Legal Importation', *Wisconsin L. Rev.*, 243 (1971); Uganda: L.C. McQuade, above.

19. Tanganyika National Development Corporation Act, 1962 (cap. 468), sec. 4(1).

20. Ibid., sec. 4(2).
21. Ibid., sec. 5(1); see Hansard, National Assembly Official Report, p. 30.
22. Tanzania: National Development Corporation Act, 1972 (Cap. 478).
23. Zambia: Industrial Development and Agriculture Ordinances (Repeal) Act, 1961; see National Assembly Debates, 286-92 (Nov. 3, 1961), in Pozen, *Legal Transfers in the Third World*, p. 30.
24. See generally, B. DeGray Fortman, *After Mulungushi* (Nairobi: East Af. Pub. House, 1969); C. Elliot (ed.), *Constraints on the Economic Development of Zambia* (Nairobi: Oxford University Press, 1971).
25. A. Seidman, 'The Need for a Long-Term Industrial Strategy for Zambia', in A. Seidman (ed.), *National Welfare and Natural Resources: The Case of Copper* (New York: Praeger, 1975), pp. 359, 369.
26. *The Common Man's Charter* (Entebbe: Govt. Printer, 1970).
27. Tanzania: Presidential Circular No. 5 of 1964.
28. Tanzania: Industrial Development Corporation (Amendment) Act, 1964, sec. 4.
29. R.H. Green, 'Law and Economic Planning in Africa: Some Preliminary Notes With Special Reference to Public Enterprise' (cyclostyle; n.d.), p. 5.
30. See Chap. 11.
31. Ibid.
32. *Zambia: Second National Development Plan* (Lusaka: Govt. Printer, 1971).
33. A. Seidman, 'Import Substitution', p. 634.
34. K.E. Svendsen, 'Decision-Making in the National Development Corporation', ERB (Restricted) Paper 68.4 (Dar es Salaam: Economic Research Bureau, University College, 1968), reprinted in L. Cliffe and J. Saul (eds.), *Socialism in Tanzania* (Dar es Salaam: East African Publishing House, 1973), pp. 89, 90; see J. Rweyemanu, *Underdevelopment and Industrialization in Tanzania: A Study of Perverse Industrial Development* (Nairobi: Oxford University Press, 1973), p. 177.
35. Presidential Circular No. 5 of 1964.
36. Ibid.
37. Tanganyika Parliamentary Debates (Hansard), 7th Meeting (Dar es Salaam: Govt. Printer, 1963), p. 68.
38. Tanzania: Industrial Development Corporation (Amendment) Act, 1964.
39. Quoted in Svenden, 'Decision-Making in the NDC', p. 90.
40. *Tanzania, Second Five-Year Plan For Economic and Social Developments (1969-74)* (Dar es Salaam: Govt. Printer, 1962).
41. B. Mramba and B. Mwansasu, 'Management for Socialist Development in Tanzania', *The African Rev.*, 1, 37 (1972).
42. Ibid.
43. Loxley and Saul, 'Political Economy of the Parastatals', p. 20.
44. Quoted in ibid., p. 18.
45. E. Penrose, 'Some Problems of Policy in the Management of the Parastatal Sector in Tanzania: A Comment', *African Rev.*, 1, 50 (1972).
46. Svenden, 'Decision-Making in the NDC', p. 92.
47. Tanzania: Industrial Development Corporation (Amendment) Act, 1964.
48. Rweyemanu, *Underdevelopment*, p. 177; Tanzania: Presidential Circular No. 2 of 1969; TANU: *TANU.s Guidelines to Safeguard, Consolidate and Further the African Revolution* (Dar es Salaam: Govt. Printer, 1971), Art. 11.
49. Green, 'Law and Economic Planning'.
50. R.C. Pratt, 'The Administration of Planning in a Newly Independent State: The Tanzanian Experience 1963-66', *J. Comm. Pol. Studies*, 5, 38 (1967).
51. Svendsen, 'Decision-Making in the NDC', pp. 94-5.
52. Pozen, *Legal Transfers in the Third World*.

53. L.E. Grayson, 'A Conglomerate in Africa: Public-Sector Manufacturing Enterprises in Ghana, 1962-1971', *Af. St. Rev.*, 16, 315, 316 (1973).

54. B. Kehinde, 'The Politics and Administration of Public Corporations in Nigeria', in A. Adedeji (ed.), *Nigerian Administration and its Political Setting* (London: Hutchinson Educational, 1968), p. 96.

55. Conversation with the author, Lusaka, 1972.

56. Loxley and Saul, 'Political Economy of the Parastatals'.

57. A. Seidman, 'Import Substitution', p. 615.

58. See Nat'l. Ins. Corp. of Tanzania, Ltd., *The Insurance Industry in Tanzania* (Dar es Salaam, Gov't. Printer, 1972).

59. This statement is true of government corporations in Britain and in the United States, where the postal system, now a federal public corporation, has always required subvention; so has Amtrak, the government railroad corporation.

60. Ghana: National Assembly Debates, 10 (13 January 1965), quoted in Pozen, *Legal Transfers in the Third World*, Chap. 1, n. 99; United Nations, *Report of the United Nations Mission in the Re-Organization of the State Enterprise Secretariat in Ghana* (Cyclostyle, 1966); Zambia: K.K. Kaunda, Mulungushi Speech, *Zambia Daily Mail* (Lusaka, 1 July 1975).

61. C. Cottingham, *Contemporary African Bureaucracy: Political Elites, Bureaucratic Recruitment, and Administrative Performance* (Morristown, N.J.: General Learning Press, 1974), p. 11.

62. Rweyemanu, *Underdevelopment*, p. 138.

63. Grayson, 'Conglomerate in Africa'.

64. Loxley and Saul, 'Political Economy of the Parastatals'.

65. G. Glentworth and M. Wozei, 'The Role of Public Corporations in National Development in Uganda: Case Studies of the Uganda Development Corporation and the Uganda Electricity Board' *The African Rev.*, 1, 54 (1972).

66. M.E. Blunt, 'State Enterprise in Nigeria and Ghana: The End of an Era?', *Afr. Affairs*, 69, 27 (1970).

67. T. Ocran, 'The National Agriculture Marketing Board of Zambia' (Ph.D. Dissertation, University of Wisconsin, 1971).

68. Kehinde, 'Public Corporations in Nigeria'.

69. See, e.g., Ghana: Bast Fibres Development Board Act, 1970 (Act 376), sec. 2(1) (g).

70. Grayson, 'Conglomerate in Africa', p. 316.

71. J.K. Galbraith, *The New Industrial State* (Boston: Houghton, Mifflin, 1967).

72. V.N. Carvalho, 'The Control of Managing Agents in Tanzania Parastatal Organizations with Special Reference to the National Development Corporation', *Eastern Af. L. Rev.*, 5, 89 (1972), see M. Bostock and C. Harvey, *Economic Independence and Zambian Copper: A Case Study of Foreign Investment* (New York: Praeger, 1972).

73. Cf. United States: Treas. Reg. 1.482 – 2 (b) (7) (4) (4,5) (1976); T.C. 6998; 1919-1 C.B. 144, 145-46.

74. Carvalho, 'Control of Managing Agents', p. 94.

75. Kehinde, 'Public Corporations in Nigeria', p. 95; R.B. Turkson, Ministerial Control of Public Corporations in Ghana', *University of Ghana L.R.*, 11, 83 (1974); Ghana: *Report of the Committee of Enquiry into the State Furniture and Joinery Corporation* (Accra: Govt. Printer, 1968); Ghana, *Report of the Committee of Enquiry into the Manner of the Operation of the State Distilleries Corporation* (Accra: Govt. Printer, 1968).

76. Carvalho, 'Control of Managing Agents', p. 95.

77. I.G. Shivji, 'From the Analysis of Forms to the Exposition of Substance: The Tasks of a Lawyer-Intellectual', *E. Af. L. Rev.*, 5, 1, 5 (1972).

78. Bostock and Harvey, *Zambian Copper.*
79. Ibid.
80. A.A.Berle and G.C. Means, *The Modern Corporation and Private Property* (New York: Harcourt, Brace and World, 1932).
81. Galbraith, *New Industrial State.*
82. This section is based upon a working paper prepared by Richard Bourgeois.
83. Ghana, *Guidelines for the Five-Year Development Plan, 1975-80* (Accra: Govt. Printer, 1975), p. 18.
84. Uganda, *Uganda's Plan III: Third Five-Year Development Plan: 1971/2-1975/2* (Entebbe: Govt. Printer, 1972), pp. 133-4.
85. S. Graba, 'Problems Relating to Management and Control of Public Corporations in Ghana', *Greenhill J. of Adm.,* 1, 100, 103 (1974).
86. Sierra Leone: *Ministry of Development and Economic Planning, Central Planning Unit, National Development Plan 1974/75-1978/9 (Freetown:* Govt. Printer, 1974), pp. 118-19; see also *Budget Speech Delivered by the Honourable C.A. Kamara-Taylor* (Freetown: Govt. Printer, 1972), p. 15.
87. Ghana: Ghana Industrial Holding Company Decree, Para 1(7); see Graba, 'Problems', p. 103.
88. 'Socialist Management Means Full Power to Workers', *Jenga,* 10 (Dar es Salaam) 46 (1971).
89. M. Buraway, *The Color of Class* (Lusaka: Institute for African Studies, University of Zambia, 1972).
90. Mramba and Mwasasu 'Management', p. 38.
91. Ibid., pp. 40-41.
92. See, e.g., Tanzania: Public Corporations Act, 1969; Uganda: The Produce Marketing Board Act, 1968, sec 3(8) (Act 2 of 1968); Kenya: Maize and Produce Board Act, 1966, (Cap. 320, sec. 20, and Cap. 338, sec 33); Irrigation Act, 1966, sec. 23 (National Irrigation Board); Sierra Leone: The Electricity Corporation Act, 1969, sec. 25; Malawi: Malawi Broadcasting Corporation Act, 1964, sec. 18 (Cap. 20:01).
93. Ghana: Bast Fibres Development Board Act, 1970, sec 12(1).
94. Tanzania: Tanzania Audit Corporation Act, 1968.
95. Tanzania: Public Corporation Act, 1969.
96. Mramba and Mwasasu, 'Management', pp. 38-9.
97. See, T. Szentes, *Economic Policy and Implementation Problems in Tanzania: A Case Study* (Budapest: Center for Afro-Asian Research of the Hungarian Academy of Sciences, 1970), p. 14.
98. Zambia: The Commissioner appointed to Review the Grade Structure of the Civil Service, Report of the Salary Scales of the Civil Service, the Teaching Service, The Zambia Police, the Prisons Service, the Salary Scales and Wages of non-Civil Service (Industrial Employees of the Government) and the Pay Scales and Conditions of Service of the Zambian Defense Force (Lusaka: Gov't. Printer, 1966).
99. Mramba and Mwasasu, 'Management', p. 32.
100. Ibid., p. 33.
101. Graba, 'Problems'.
102. Ghana: *Outline of Ghana Investment Policy* (Accra: Govt. Printer, n.d.), p. 1.
103. *Uganda's Plan III,* pp. 143-4.
104. Industrial Finance Co. Ltd., *In the Forefront of Zambia's Economic Reforms: A Businessman's Guide* (Lusaka: Govt. Printer, 1973), pp. 2-3.
105. See, R. Bottomley and A. Quimby, 'Work Councils and Industrial Relations in Zambia', in J. Fry (ed.), *The Labour Market in Zambia* (forthcoming).
106. See below, Chap. 16.
107. Tanzania: NUTA Establishment Act, 1964.

108. K.F. Ileti, 'Post-Mwongozo Workers' Disputes in Tanzania: Two Case Studies', *E. Af. L.J.*, 7, 157 (1974).
109. Quoted in ibid., p. 159.
110. Presidential Circular No. 1 of 1970.
111. Ileti, 'Post-Mwongozo Workers' Disputes'.
112. Quoted in B.P. Mramba, 'Organizational Theory and the Tanzanian Concept of Workers' Participation', *Taamuli No. 1*, p. 27 (1972).
113. TANU: 'The TANU Guidelines' (Mwongozo wa TANU), *The Nationalist* (Dar es Salaam), 22 February 1971; also in *Mbioni*, 8 (Dar es Salaam) 4 (1971); 1 Mazungumo (Michigan), 59 (1971), paras. 13-15.
114. Mramba, 'Organizational Theory'.
115. Illeti, 'Post-Mwongozo Workers' Disputes'; P.B. Mihyo, 'Labour Unrest and the Quest for Workers' Control in Tanzania: Three Case Studies', *E. Af. L., Rev.*, 7, 1(1974). President Nyerere said about these strikes that '. . . they say that Mwongozo makes the worker strike. But we are in an unequal society, how can you expect that workers will not go on strike? They will sit down and we will say, do you understand what inequality means? We must have a society where this is expected, where if you like, we experience the birth of socialism. We accept this . . .' Quoted in Mihyo, p. 1.

THE LAW OF PLANNING

The rhetoric and ideology of economic (or development) planning pervaded Africa as it did all the developing world.[1] It originally sought to reduce compartmentalism in government[2] and ensure compatibility between ministerial programmes.[3] Planning left no ministry 'free to act as an undisciplined entrepreneur, promoting funds and projects to maximize the status of the ministry. Instead, all must accept the discipline of planning.'[4] 'Planning' in this sense coincided with the new ideology of colonial development that seized the Colonial Office after 1946.[5] Development mainly meant economic development, and that led planners to consider issues of increased production.[6]

At independence, productive enterprise lay almost exclusively in the private sector.[7] The market ordinarily regulated the economy. 'Planning' subsumed, therefore, every governmental action that affected economic behaviour.[8] Unlike Eastern European plans, African plans did not prescribe specific economic interactions.[9] Instead, they set targets for economic growth. If these merely matched what the economy would achieve in any event, however, they remained merely epiphenomenal and trivial. Development plans led to changed behaviour, or they did nothing. To induce such behaviour, 'every [planned] target must be accompanied by policies and measures which have been designed specifically to fulfill it — otherwise, it becomes only a forecast or a projection'.[10] The planning function thus included not merely harmonizing ministerial sectoral plans, but the design and recommendation of 'policies, instruments of policy, and other measures and machinery required to mobilize financial, material and human resources for implementing development plans'.[11] Implementing these policies was, of course, primarily the function of ministries and parastatal organizations.[12]

The legal order intersected the planning function at two points. First, all the planned policies and programmes operated through the legal order. Secondly, the legal order structured planning processes and institutions themselves, and thereby became a variable that explained the sorts of plans that emerged.[13]

I discuss first, the pervasive difficulty, that planning epitomized 'soft' development. I then propose some explanations. The first set of explanations concerns the failure of implementation. The second addresses the paradox that the planners repeatedly drafted plans that did not get

285

implemented.

I The Failure of Planning

By and large, planning in Africa worked poorly. Plans remained on
paper. Governments abandoned one third of the national plans before
their term;[14] practically all of them underwent major revisions during
their course. No plan achieved even its public sector investment targets, in most cases inducing only 70 per cent to 80 per cent of planned
expenditures.[15] Administrative and infra-structural projects came closer
to their planned targets than productive enterprise.[16] Bessanov concluded after a comprehensive survey of all African plans that 'generally
only a few of the planned projects are really implemented', and even
those usually suffered serious delays.[17] Moreover, government accomplished many non-planned projects; plan distortion, of course, constituted a kind of implementation failure.[18] Projects exceeded their
planned costs. Every plan experienced serious shortfalls in outside
financing.

Plans for private investment led to even more dismal results. Except
for oil-rich Nigeria, nowhere did they come very close to the total
planned amounts and everywhere they missed badly their sectoral
allocations.[19] A Nigerian economist remarked in despair that 'there is
little discernible relation between what is contained in a Plan and what
in fact gets done'.[20]

In time the planners set two targets for their public and private
investment programmes. The Lesotho Second Five-Year Plan, for
example, first stated a public investment target of R111.6 million, but
then declared an alternative one: 'delays and programme adjustments
which are difficult to anticipate will combine to reduce the likely total
capital expenditure to less than 100% of the total planned . . . [I]t has
been assumed that there will be slippage − of the order of 25 to 30% −
so that actual capital expenditures of the public sector will be about
R80 million rather than . . . R111.6 million . . .'[21] The Second Nigerian
Plan achieved only 67 per cent of its planned targets. Of this, the Third
Plan said, 'This must be regarded as a satisfactory [sic!] performance . . .'[22] The Third Plan planned ₦32 billion,[23] but expected no
more than ₦20 billion actual investment. The difference, in a sense,
measured government's 'will to develop' − or lack of it.[24]

Not only in Africa, but world-wide (at least in the non-socialist
LDCs) planning was notable mainly for its lack of implementation.[25]
That is to say, the legal order failed to carry out its task to ensure the
behaviour prescribed. I first examine this phenomenon, especially with

respect to private productive investment.

II Plan Implementation and the Legal Order

Plans that failed of implementation failed to induce desired behaviour. They exemplified soft development. Explaining why African development plans failed in one sense addresses the task of this entire book. Here I provide two much more limited explanations.

A. *Contract*

The perspective of Contract explained poverty by low levels of capital, natural resources and technology and population problems. It assumed that only private entrepreneurs normally engaged in productive activity, although occasionally government might supply financing. It treated institutional arrangements mainly as a 'black box' except as they inter-fered with private entrepreneurial activity.[26] This perspective concept-ualized planning as an ends-means process. The policy-makers advised the planners, all economists, about desired output levels for goods and services. Based on historical experience in the particular economy planners could specify the investment level required to produce the specified output level. That assumed that the 'black box' would work as it had in the past.

In this view, changing the input mix of capital, population, natural resources and technology required that the ministries and other imple-menting organizations devise and carry out appropriate means. Minis-tries had to make the public sector investments that the plan specified. In the productive, private sector, ministries had to find appropriate legal devices or 'policies'[27] to induce private entrepreneurs, mainly foreign, to invest: tax incentives, tariffs, trade licensing, Pioneer Indus-try statutes, subsidies, development corporations, credit controls and others. If these devices did not stimulate the desired investment, government might create parastatals to fill the gap.

The planners know that the economic inputs had tight limits, but they assumed that they had, as it were, an unlimited supply of law — that the existing infinitely flexible legal order could induce any desired behaviours by any addressees. The planners regarded law as business-men too often regarded clean air and water, as an unlimited free good.

Given that assumption, the plans' shortfalls resulted from either a failure of political will, or technical imperfections in planning or imple-menting agencies. Either the politicians did not really want to accom-plish the plans, and planning played no more than a symbolic function,[28] or a host of technical deficiencies made successful planning impossible: manpower weaknesses; insufficient economic models; weaknesses in the organization of the planning unit itself; insufficient statistics, especially the data base to derive the historical relationship between investment and income (the capital-output ratio); lack of coordination between budgetary and planning processes; insufficiency of capital for investment; general incompetence and corruption; and unforeseen and unforeseeable exogenous factors, such as catastrophic declines in the prices of exports, drought or political instability.[29] Given that enormous range of explanations, planning's failure excited little suprise. Curiously, however, the planners nevertheless soldiered on.[30]

B. An Institutionalist Explanation

Alternative explanations treated the failure of plan implementation as a case of soft development. Soft development in general arose because the existing legal order could not perform its tasks in the social, political and economic conditions of underdevelopment. Far from a free good in unlimited supply, the legal order became a very limited, very expensive, critical element in implementing policies necessary for successful plans.

I have already examined some difficulties in implementing development programmes: insufficient courts; inappropriate bureaucracy; unaccountable parastatals. Here I examine two limited issues: first, plan indiscipline in the public sector itself, and second, implementation in the private sector.

1. *Implementation in the Public Sector.* Ideal-typical planning implicitly or explicitly followed a military model, with the Cabinet as High Command, planners, the General Staff, and bureaucracy, the line officers.[31] That model nicely fitted the colonial legal order, adding only the planning board as General Staff. It did not work for many reasons.

Not a single formal law or regulation in all Anglophonic Africa required anyone, even ministries or parastatals, to obey the plan. A development plan 'authorizes nothing. Even public expenditures are authorized not by the Plan but by the Annual Budget.'[32] The Third Nigerian Plan went the furthest. It threatened that the degree of plan fulfilment by each Ministry or parastatal would become the principal criterion of efficiency of the organization and its top personnel[33] — at least a veiled threat of sanctions for non-fulfilment. No other plan went beyond exhortation, begging the people the plan addressed to abide by it. By contrast, in the socialist countries of the world, the legislatures usually voted on the plans, giving them the force and legitimacy of law.[34] Without an explicit rule, locating the plan machinery in the President or Prime Minister's office might indicate that the plan had a force superior to other Ministerial programmes.[35] Even this did not happen in many countries, that made the planning organization a mere section in a Ministry of Development or of Finance.[36] The plan might have acquired an additional increment of authority if the planning commission had constitutional status. Only the (now suspended) Lesotho Independence Constitution contained such a provision.[37]

The plan by its own force might have induced compliance. I have earlier tried to define the circumstances when the mere existence of a rule likely will make its addressees obey.[38] None of these conditions existed with respect to any African plan, except perhaps in Tanzania. The notion of planning as a set of constraints on decision-making (as opposed to predictions of behaviour) had no place in the Western capitalist tradition in which most African elites grew up.[39] The plan frequently exhorted ministries and parastatals and private actors to behave in ways that visibly opposed their own interests. Unprecedented and novel planning commissions did not receive respect, nor did legislatures by enactment legitimize their plans (Tanzania enacted a statute making the entire National Assembly the Planning Commission, not, however, to enact plans, but to advise government on planning).

The government, frequently the Cabinet itself, often ignored the plan. 'Thus, for example, several months after the publication of the [first Tanzanian] Plan, the Minister of External Affairs . . . was able with little difficulty to secure Government agreement to a significant increase in the number of Tanzanian embassies overseas and to a raiding of other Ministries to staff them.'[40] In many countries nobody, respected or otherwise, obeyed the plan. Despite efforts in a few places, the plans did not come out of a participatory process. Rather, they arose from recommendations of a few expatriates, who bound them between hard covers, and presented them to government. No wonder the plans failed to induce obedience by their mere existence!

Second, governments and their constitutive agencies lacked the structural capacity to implement development plans. They built roads more readily than factories, because the Ministry of Public Works existed with long experience in building roads, but no government department had experience in building factories.[41] Communication between departments barely existed.[42] Most governments had no or poor feedback mechanisms, and never learned the extent of plan compliance early enough to take corrective measures.[43] In the federal states, ethnic and regional competition frequently set at naught the planners' resource allocations.[44] Elsewhere, compartmentalism within government bureaucracies set one department at the other's throats in fierce competition. Their shoot-outs sometimes killed the plans in the crossfire.

Tanzania created a Directorate of Development and Planning in the Office of the President, and appointed to it three Ministers of State for Development and planning, all of cabinet rank. The government endowed it with extensive powers of infra-governmental supervision and control and the responsibility 'of ensuring that appropriate steps are taken by all Ministries concerned to conform with these policies and to obtain these objectives [of the Plan]'.[45] Despite this seemingly high-powered control mechanism, various ministries asserted and sometimes made good their independent policies. The Treasury objected to the projected rate of growth and tax proposals; the Ministry of Education, to the plan's educational programmes; Agriculture, to the planned strategy of rural development. Some ministries never submitted their proposals to the planners, who therefore invented some of their own. The Cabinet accepted them but they broke on the rocks of ministerial non-co-operation.[46] R.H. Green concluded that

> One point which has become clear in the introduction of planning in states which were formerly British colonies is that the British administrative and institutional structure is inherently unsatisfactory for development-centered government. The dominance of the Treasury has consistently led to an emphasis on budgetary and relatively short-run financing problems, and often to a preference for cutting capital rather than recurrent estimates. Ministers with considerable autonomy in preparing their own estimates have regarded the plan figures — especially the recurrent totals — as optional advice. The division of ministerial functions into compartments such as law, order, social welfare, and infrastructure, has hampered effective control over the productive sector. The *ad hoc* creation of state corporations which are not subject to any very clear or effective control in their productive operations has further weakened co-ordination.[47]

Moreover, bureaucracy could apply rules, not act as entrepreneur. Development planning must search out new opportunities, ascertain their feasibility and proceed to take the risks that unavoidably accompany problem-solving. Bureaucracy nowhere accomplished that task very well.[48]

Scholars sometimes characterized non-epiphenomenal planned economies as 'command' ecomonies.[49] The words conjured a quasi-military model. That very model, however, ultimately defeated planning. Planning, like development itself, could not merely identify ends and then implement them; it had to solve emergent problems coherently. Structures that carried out orders laid down by a High Command rarely solved problems successfully.

2. *Influencing the Private Sector.* Planning a mixed economy requires government to influence the behaviour of private decision-makers. The state does this continuously, if not always self-consciously, through the legal order. Contract and property in all their ramifications, for example, always form part of the arena of choice for entrepreneurs.

Given that fundamental structure of the legal order, the processes of planning included efforts to change the behaviour of private actors in many ways:[50] increasing the number of local entrepreneurs and high-level employees;[51] controlling prices and incomes;[52] increasing agricultural productivity (usually not foodstuffs but export crops);[53] reducing the drain of foreign exchange, both by direct controls[54] and through limiting imports;[55] increasing employment opportunities in the countryside;[56] stimulating savings;[57] increasing productive investment. To achieve these objectives in the private sector, governments tried different techniques, none of them very successfully. I examine here three different policies to induce private investment: Increasing savings, building physical infrastructure and protecting 'pioneer industry'.

a. *Increasing savings.* Development economists frequently argued that savings became investment; and that new investment multiplied by an historically-determined factor (the marginal capital-output ratio), equalled increased gross income. That is;

$$\text{if } S = \text{savings}$$
$$I = \text{investment}$$
$$k = \text{marginal capital output ratio}$$
$$Y = \text{increase in income,}$$

$$\text{then} \quad S = I$$
$$kI = Y$$

Planners built their predictions of planned increased income upon these relationships.

It never worked. Dr Abdel Meguib explained this by rewriting these equations in a different form, emphasizing the assumptions on which they rested:

> Given: (1) 'perfect' financial institutions to mobilize savings, (2) no limitations on entrepreneurship whether public or private, (3) availability of evaluated and profitable projects, (4) availability of foreign exchanges to obtain the foreign content of investments,

$$S \text{ --- } I$$

> (5) the right climate for investments, encompassing price, wage and tax structure, (6) . . . etc.

> AND

> Given: (1) the 'right' choice of investment projects, (2) knowledgeable procurement of capital goods, (3) successful choice and application of technical processes, (4) sufficiency of infrastructural services, and

$$I \text{ --- } Y$$

> (5) watchful follow-up on progress of capital formation, (6) marketing outlets at home and abroad, (7) . . . etc.[58]

That is to say, laws requiring forced savings did not work because the necessary institutions for them did not exist.

b. Economic Infrastructure. The most popular Western prescription for development held that if the state provided adequate infrastructure — roads, water, communications, railroads, ports and docks, schools and public health facilities — then private enterprise would rush to invest.[59] Like the notion that increased savings would readily yield increased income, this also depended on a host of assumptions about the existing economy: that there actually existed private entrepreneurs with capital, appropriate financial institutions, labourers possessing necessary skills, appropriate prices, wages and taxes, effective demand for the product, and only small gaps between the various elements in the production and marketing chains. (Private enterprise may provide transport from farmers to an existing rice mill, but will not, merely because a new road has opened, likely provide rice mill, storage, wholesale and retail facilities, credit, agricultural inputs and transport.) Building infrastructure may generate productive investment but only if a whole set of other institutions also exist. If they do, the proposed investment will amount only to incremental change.

   c. Inducing private foreign investment. Every country sought to induce foreign private investment, most believing that success in that effort was the key to further development. Almost everywhere that effort fell far below expectations. Between 1970 and 1974, Kenya realized only 5.29 per cent of its planned foreign investment,[60] Tanzania in 1971-75, 13.55 per cent.[61] Only countries with a fortuitous mineral discovery, such as oil, reached their planned targets.[62] What foreign investment took place usually focused in sectors peripheral to economic development, such as beer, cigarettes and hotels, usually located in urban areas.[63]

   Every country* enacted laws extending advantages to new foreign investment. These laws usually provided that if certain conditions were met, government would grant a certificate as a 'pioneer company'. The earlier statutes gave pioneer status to any new investment.[64] Increasingly, the requirements became more stringent. After 1971, Nigeria defined a pioneer industry as one not existing in Nigeria on a scale to match the country's needs, and with good growth prospects.[65] Each industry could have 'pioneer companies', depending upon the amount of value added locally, or the product line.[66] Ghana had four criteria for favoured investment: (1) using Ghanaian natural resources; (2) cutting imports and raising exports; (3) creating high employment and training; and (4) using fully and expanding resources and labour.[67]

   The various countries competed to shower goodies on approved investors. Tax holidays of varying length sprouted;[68] so did accelerated depreciation plans,[69] exemptions from export duties[70] and guarantees against expropriation, sometimes combined with arbitration provisions for compulsory acquisition.[71] Kenya provided discretionary protections against competition, such as favourable tariffs, licences and quotas.[72] The Kenya Trade Dispute Act, 1965, outlawed strikes against a protected industry. All these incentives, seemingly too good to refuse, failed to

* The following section is based on a working paper by Tom Russell.

induce enough new investment, for two reasons. First, world-wide
demand exceeded by far available private capital, even of the multinational corporations. The various countries competed ruinously —
Lesotho actually advertised 'the longest tax holiday in the world'. A
race like that has more losers than winners. Second, the LDCs
generally lost the race to the already developed countries. US investments went mainly to Canada, Western Europe, South Africa and the
lucky ones with oil.[73] New investment follows potential profit, enhanced managerial prestige and opportunities, or good managerial
living. By and large, poverty-ridden African states offered investors
only weak internal markets, low external economies, unstable government, and managerial amenities that did not challenge those of London
or Paris.[74] Investors hardly fell over themselves to invest in such un-
promising locales, whatever the offered tax advantages.

Savings programmes, infrastructural development and investment
incentives exemplified the policies that governments adopted to implement development plans. In each case, the rule or policy directed
capitalists to invest in particular sectors. Because the investors owned
their capital, usually outside the jurisdiction, governments could not
order them to invest or be punished. Law-makers instead tried these
different roundabout measures,[75] to change the investors' arenas of
choice. But the other constraints and resources that affected choice
(for example, the economic institutions that determined return to
investors), conspired to make the African countries unattractive investment locales, whatever the infrastructure or tax incentives.

What investment occurred ordinarily exploited precisely those
characteristics that identified the country as underdeveloped: producing raw materials for export, paying inhumanely low wage rates,
internally, satisfying elite demands, and not producing for the poor,
using imported components, with little local value-added, capital-
intensive, and located in the urban centres. Even that capital came in
driblets.

I can summarize this explanation for the failure of government
policies to induce private investment:

1. The decisions of private entrepreneurs tend to maximise their
   rewards and minimize their strains and losses within their arenas
   of choice.

2. Government cannot ordinarily by direct measures induce private entrepreneurs to invest if the investors' arenas of choice do not give them opportunity or capacity to do so, or if investment does not enhance their perceived interest as defined by those arenas.

3. Governments cannot by changing only a small part of the complex of institutions that make up investors' arenas of choice (taxes, roads, etc.) significantly change private investment decisions.

The development of a vigorous private sector, therefore, required re-structuring an entire range of new institutions, affecting credit, market-ing, storage, processing and manufacturing, and so forth. Paradoxically all these new institutions required new public enterprises: banks, mar-keting boards, railroads, cold storage boards, maize mills, fertilizer plants, agriculture implement factories . . . the list was endless. Suc-cessful implementation of plans even for the private sector required the rapid enlargement of the public sector. Without a vigorous state capital-ism, even the private sector withered.[76] Everywhere, state capitalism flourished. State capitalism holds two possibilities. It can move towards an authoritarian, stratified society ruled by the bureaucratic bourgeoisie, or towards increased participation and socialism. The latter needs deliberate planning. As the public sector grows, those who control it, unless themselves controlled, will of course use it to enlarge their own power and privilege. The new public sector, unless planned, will respond to the 'tyranny of the market', not to the demands of the poor and dispossessed that development purports to meet.

Planning for democratic, egalitarian development required using state power and the legal order to create and to direct the public sector. Successful new resource allocations needed various actors to undertake new production; that in turn needed appropriate behaviour from many new organisations. The planners, as General Staff, had to advise what new institutions to create, and how to induce the new desired be-haviour.[77] Without such new institutions and behaviour, plans could only die unrealized. How and why planners repeatedly produced un-workable plans I discuss next.

III The Structure and Process of Plan Formulation

In such a difficult enterprise as development, the failure of any partic-

ular plan would startle nobody. Strangely, however, that happened in
case after case, without the planning agencies directly addressing the
reasons for their failure. Instead, all over the non-socialist world 'plans
almost always provide detailed information about *what* is to be achieved, but not about *how* to go about securing development objectives
or targets, or about *who* in government or elsewhere should be responsible for carrying out the required tasks'.[78] To explain the behaviour of
the planners, I ask the questions of the earlier model: rule and communication, opportunity, capacity, interest.

Rule and Communication. Planners had guidelines at best vague, but
usually non-existent. None very clearly articulated their prescribed
tasks. Their instructions told them only to prepare a plan, and sometimes not even that. The Uganda Planning Commission Act, 1963[79]
only directed the Commission 'to plan and advise the Cabinet on
the planning of (i) the economic and social development of Uganda;
and (ii) the effective and efficient utilization of the resources of Uganda
in order to attain the maximum rate of growth of output.' In Swaziland, even more vaguely, the Department of Planning and Statistics
should 'advise Government on development and to prepare and follow
up the implementation of programmes of agreed projects . . . and to
provide overall policy direction and central advisory and administrative services to departmental programmes.'[80] Its job description said not
a word about planning's responsibility to prepare the plan. Every
government only told its planners to act as its General Staff for development. The sort of plan – epiphenomenal or directive, long term or
short, specific or general, public sector shopping list or detailed statement of economic linkages – lay in the planners' discretion.

Despite this broad discretion, African development plans resembled
each other amazingly. The earliest only listed ministerial projects.[81]
By the late 1960s, however, a standard Table of Contents emerged:

(1) Current economic conditions.
(2) Government objectives.
(3) Proposed public expenditures.
(4) Likely developments in the private sector.
(5) An economic forecast relying on a capital-output ratio, excused
     by the phrase, 'it seems reasonable to assume . . . '
(6) Government policies.
(7) Lists of projects by sector or ministry.[82]

Why the remarkable similarity of African development plans? Particularly why did the planners not plan institutional changes, on which all their planning for new resource allocation depended on that?[83]

The planners chose within their perceived range of constraints and resources. I examine in turn their opportunities, capacities, interests and perceptions.

Opportunity. In most countries, especially after the regime held power for some time, no doubt planners who tried to change institutions radically would not long survive. Changing institutions radically changes power relationships radically. Political elites will likely institute radical institutional change only when their interests oppose the economic ruling class. But, I believe, in most African states that condition obtained at Independence.[84] Why did the planners even then not propose institutional change?

Capacity. What planners do relates, somewhat confusedly, to their intellectual processes and justifications. The first involves behaviour,[85] the second, intellectual analysis, the third, persuasion. For example, the Lesotho Second Five-Year Plan solemnly recited four 'national aims': 'Economic growth, social justice, maximum domestic employment, economic independence'.[86] Thirteen 'specific objectives' followed, attempting 'to ensure that the nation's resources are utilized effectively in the attainment of its broad aims . . .'[87] These included an 'increase of 46% in total output', 'encouragement of private investment in industry', 'localization of most of the posts now held by expatriates . . .' and so forth. On its face, it seemed that the planners deduced these 'specific objectives' from the broader national purposes. It actually happened the other way around. The individual ministries submitted their shopping lists. From those proposals that gained Planning Commission approval, the Commission itself induced the 'specific objectives'. Such general national purposes easily subsumed any ministerial programme. The plan's justification – that is, its claim that logical necessity related ends and means – little resembled either the intellectual or behavioural processes that actually produced the plan.

Lawyers' concerns with planning institutions lay in the formal and working rules that defined input, conversion and feedback systems and therefore defined the sorts of plans planners could produce. Formal rules hardly existed, so we must focus instead on conventions and actual practice.

a. *Input and feedback processes*. Everywhere planners claimed that

they simultaneously planned 'from above' and 'from below'.[88] The former meant canvassing the political leadership for its goals or objectives,
the latter, canvassing ministries, localities, parastatal organizations and
the private sector for their projects and programmes.

Politicians (or planners for them) everywhere stated extremely
vague political objectives. Similar statements floated from country to
country, all very like the Lesotho objectives. Goals so vacuous as to sub-
sume every programme cannot in practice serve as the logical source of
any. The specific projects and programmes the various operating agencies put forward, not national goals, determined the sorts of plans that
emerged. Planners insisted that the key to good planning lay in a shelf-
full of projects.[89] These original inputs left their indelible stamp upon
the entire planning process. The planners might harmonize the several
programmes, or amend them somewhat, but the first submissions dominated the final outcomes. Sectoral or ministerial programmes filled
several input functions. They identified difficulties for the plan to
address; they implied explanations; they proposed solututions. They
based all of this upon ministerial perceptions of reality, ideologies and
'values'.

In many, probably most countries, plans have not greatly changed
since the early 'shopping lists'. In Lesotho, about one year before the
First National Plan's scheduled expiration, the planners circulated the
ministries, requesting proposals for the next five-year plan. (Some did
not comply; for these, the planners simply invented programmes.) After
harmonizing proposals, and balancing their costs against projected
government revenues, the Commission stitched them together to make
the Second Five-Year Plan.

The shopping lists reflected the bureaucracy. Its hierarchical, com-
partmental structure produced mainly incremental, tension-management proposals.[90] Its top-heavy concentration of the 'bureaucratic
bourgeoisie'[91] produced projects to favour that class. Nigeria's most
vigorous programme in 1975 enabled wealthy locals to buy shares in
existing enterprise.[92] Everywhere, male-dominated ministries produced
anti-feminist programmes. Land reform in Kenya, for example, lodged a
fee simple title in the owner, almost always a man. In fact, women
worked the land. Fee simple ownership in part supposedly ensured the
land's availability as security for loans. Under customary law, women
who actually worked the land had recognized rights in it. The conversion to a fee simple in the men wiped these out. The men could now
sell their land, or borrow on its security, to the detriment of the women
who won their livings from it.[93] Predictably, the bureaucrats, practically

all of whom of course were men, failed completely to perceive this injustice.

Almost every country tried to broaden plan inputs, usually by obtaining proposals from the private sector, especially from foreign private business. Botswana created a National Economic Advisory Council to represent these entrepreneurs and advise government.[94] Elsewhere, specialized industry boards performed the same function.[95] In Nigeria, a broader planning base arose almost accidentally from the subdivision of four huge regions into twenty smaller ones. Each region submitted its programme, thus spreading planned development projects throughout the country, creating potential poles of growth in the hinterland.[96]

Personnel, a second important set of inputs, comprised mainly expatriates on short-term contracts, usually British or American economists. The plans inevitably reflected their training and backgrounds. Sometimes an individual planner perceived the necessity of restructuring institutions. The introduction to the 1964-70 Kenya Plan, signed by President Kenyatta, declared that 'we plan . . . to establish new economic institutions and modify old ones . . . developing new concepts of economic organization'. The plan itself stated that 'institutions must exist or be created for regulating their use . . .'[97] The theme repeated itself in the next plan.[98] These plans, however, contained no details of the institutional changes required. Economists deal with resources allocation, not institutions, and the planners had no expertise available to plan institutional transformations.

Planning theories constituted a third sort of input. These came entirely from the planners; the choice of planner determined the theory that would underlay the plan. The monochrome of African development plans reflected the monochrome of the planning community that produced them.

A fourth set of inputs concerned the occasional implementation policies that the plans stated. These, like the projects, came mainly from the operating ministries. They suffered from the same perceptions, and bolstered rather than undercut existing institutions.[99]

b. *Conversion processes.* Conversion processes here refer to processes putting together these inputs to produce the plan documents. Typically, one cannot discover very much about the actual mental processes involved. The written plans did not describe those mental processes, any more than did academic prescriptions for planning. The former justified the plans, the latter theorized about their construction. Neither described the behaviour that resulted in the plan documents.

Justifications and theories, however, influence decision-making processes. No matter how a decision actually arises, if decision-makers cannot justify it in the accepted way, they will usually discard it. Theory
filters the feedbacks and inputs — difficulties, explanations, proposals
for solutions — the planners will actually consider.

African plans hardly tried to justify their proposals. They described
the state of the economy, but practically never attempted to explain it.
They stated the ends of governments, and then directly set out the
planned targets.[100] Without any real justification for their decisions,
African planners could easily conceal their actual conversion processes,
which they did. They never revealed how much of the plan came from
detailed calculation and hard data, and how much from fudge. They
never spelled out whether or how specific programmes and projects
related to overall goals, or even to each other, whether rigorously vetted
for viability, or resulting from parochial pressure. Plans therefore never
had explicit justifications. They rested on the power of government. A
General Staff need not justify proposals so long as the High Command
accepts them as their own. Development planning based itself on ends-
means, not problem-solving.[101] That methodology ultimately rests not
on reason but on power. The planners did not provide justifications because they saw no reason to do so, and their theory told them that ends
could never have any. African plans *assumed* that government could
implement whatever they planned. They rested on a very weak reed.

c. *The interests of the planners.* Most planners flew into Africa as
birds of passage from the developed world, and expected to return
there. Nobody has published a study of the development planning
profession in Africa; I can offer only impressions. Many planners, very
young, had recently graduated from a British or American University.
Senior planners frequently came from those same Universities, with a
scattering from Eastern Europe. In any event, the planners' careers did
not depend upon their clients, but on the planning profession. Often,
senior planners could appoint to universities, and recommend to the
United Nations or the World Bank, or to other planning commissions.
Planners planned not merely to meet the requirements of the African
governments, but those of the community of planners. The criteria of
the Harvard Development Advisory Service probably influenced Nigerian
or Ugandan plans as much as the particular needs of those countries.

d. *The perceptions of the planners.* Everything conspired to permit
the planners themselves to define what sorts of plan they would

produce: the norms addressed to them, the capacities of the planning institutions, their own interests. What was the planners' ideology?

State economic planning began in the Soviet Union. It did not use planning, however, to change institutions, but to define economic interchanges and investments. Standard Soviet doctrine first changed institutions, and then planned.[102] Economic planning in Western countries began much later, with France as the model. There, planning became mainly indicative and epiphenomenal. If everyone knew where they would likely go in any case, they would tread the way more firmly.

The colonial experience resembled neither of these except in name. Colonial planning did not plan for production, but only for infrastructure. When planners considered the problems of development planning, they therefore had precious little experience to draw upon. Inevitably, Western planning theory reflected Contract explanations of underdevelopment, taking institutions as 'black boxes'. As economists, the planners assumed that planning meant allocating resources, not planning institutional changes, as to which they claimed no expertise. Inevitably, development planning mainly produced macro-models, public sector expenditure programmes and 'policies', only small adjustments to the range of choice of economic actors. It did not produce co-ordinated, specific, detailed plans for institutional change. But, development *is* institutional change; and so the planners shot very wide of the mark.

Conclusion

Planners in Africa repeatedly wrote plans that government did not and could not implement. The plan targets, whether public or private, required for their implementation vast institutional changes. The planning rules and institutions did not, however, either require or induce the planners to plan such changes. Instead, they gave the planners broad discretion to determine what to plan. Inputs necessarily came from the existing hierarchical, authoritarian government structure, that constrained the range of potential change to incremental movement. The planners' need to satisfy their fellow planners as well as their own training led them to follow current planning wisdom. They planned for resource allocation, and did not consider institutional change.

Development requires changed institutions. Planners could not produce implementable plans for resource allocation unless they planned the necessary accompanying institutional changes. The law defining planning, by leaving the sort of plan to the planners' discretion, under the circumstances ensured that planning would come to exemplify soft development.

Available resources obviously limit possible change. The task of development planning involves planning for change, not operating a steady-state economy. Planning for change must therefore include planning the increases in the stock of available resources for changing. The new institutions necessary to accomplish new resource allocations became critical. Planners cannot sensibly set new resource allocations targets unless they consider what institutions exist or can be created to bring them about — that is, unless they plan the new institutions required.

It has been said that planning has a tendency to gobble up all governmental decisions, and that perhaps if planning includes everything it becomes nothing. The aphorism reads backwards. Unless planning *includes* institutional change, it becomes nothing.

Notes

1. G. Myrdal, *Asian Drama: An Inquiry into the Poverty of Nations* (New York: Pantheon, 1968), p. 711.
2. See, e.g., E. Williams, 'The Purpose of Planning', in M. Faber and D. Seers, *The Crisis in Planning* (London: Chatto and Windus, 1972), pp. 39, 43; *Kenya: Development Plan, 1964-70* (Nairobi: Gov't. Printer, 1964), pp. 3-4.
3. W.A. Lewis, *Development Planning: The Essentials of Economic Policy* (New York: Harper & Row, 1966), Chap. 1; see, e.g., *Kenya: Colony and Protectorate of Kenya, The Development Programmes 1960/63* (Sessional Paper No. 4 of 1959/60) (Nairobi: Gov't. Printer, 1960).
4. *Kenya: Development Plan, 1964-70*, p. 2; see also *Botswana: National Development Plan, 1970-75* (Gaborone: Gov't. Printer, 1970), Introduction.
5. See Chap. 2.
6. Lewis, *Development Planning*, Chap. 1; A. Waterston, *Development Planning: Lessons of Experience* (Baltimore: Johns Hopkins Press, 1965), Chap. III; A. Seidman, *Planning for Development in Sub-Saharan Africa* (New York: Praeger, 1974), pp. 81 *et seq.*
7. D. Seers, 'The Prevalence of Pseudo-planning', in M. Faber and D. Seers, *Crisis in Planning*, pp. 19, 30; A. Seidman, *Planning for Development*, p. 84.
8. R. Bicanic, *Problems of Planning, East and West* (The Hague: Mouton, 1967), p. 19.
9. E. Dean, *Plan Implementation in Nigeria, 1962-1966* (Ibadan: Oxford University Press, 1972), p. 29.
10. Waterston, *Development Planning*, p. 336; see P.J.D. Wiles, 'Economic activation, planning and the social order', in B.M. Gross (ed.), *Action Under Planning: The guidance of economic development* (New York: McGraw-Hill, 1967), pp. 138, 147; G. Beneviste, 'Towards a Sociology of National Development Planning', *J. Dev. Areas*, 3, 27, 30 (1968).
11. Ibid., p. 436; see Bicanic, *Problems of Planning*, p. 58.
12. *Kenya: Development Plan for the Period 1965/66 to 1969/70* (Nairobi: Gov't. Printer, 1966), p. 2.
13. But cf. Y. Dror, 'Planning and Law', in C.J. Friedrich and S.E. Harris (eds.),

Public Policy (Cambridge, Mass.: Grad. School of Public Admin., 1963) (Law serves as (i) a restraint on planning, (ii) an instrument to accomplish planning, and (iii) within planning institutions which perform quasi-legal functions.)

14. S.A. Bessanov, *Economic Planning for the Developing Countries of Africa* (Budapest: Institute of World Economics of the Hungarian Academy of Sciences, 1974), p. 26.
15. Ibid., p. 40.
16. Ibid., p. 41. For Nigeria, see Dean, *Plan Implementation*, p. 87.
17. Bessanov, *Economic Planning*, p. 41.
18. Dean, *Plan Implementation*, p. 143.
19. Bessanov, *Economic Planning*, p. 46.
20. A. Adedji, 'Economic Planning in Theory and Practice', *Nigerian J. Ec. and Soc. Stud.*, 1, 16 (1966).
21. *Lesotho: The Second Five Year Plan, 1976* (Maseru: Gov't Printer, 1976), para. 3.14 (R1 – $US1.20 +).
22. *Nigeria: Third National Development Plan 1976-80* (Lagos: Central Planning Office, Federal Ministry of Economic Development, 1975), p. 13.
23. ₦1 = $US 1.25 +.
24. Waterton, *Development Planning*, p. 345.
25. Ibid., p. 293; O.B. Forrest, *Financing Development Plans in West Africa* (Cambridge, Mass.: MIT Center for International Studies, 1965), p. 6.
26. See above, Chap. 3; see P. Samuelson, *Economics: An Introductory Analysis*, 10th ed. (New York: McGraw-Hill, 1968), Chap. 38.
27. Waterston, *Development Planning*, p. 336; J. Tinbergen, *Development Planning*, (London: Weidenfeld and Nicholson, 1967), pp. 167 *et seq.*
28. Waterston, *Development Planning*; D. Seers, 'Pseudo-Planning'.
29. Bessanov, *Economic Planning*; Waterston, *Development Planning*, pp. 293 *et seq*; Dean, *Plan Implementation*.
30. C. Leys, 'A New Conception of Planning', in Faber and Seers, *Crisis in Planning*, p. 56.
31. Ibid., p. 63.
32. Lewis, *Development Planning*, p. 19.
33. Nigeria, *Third National Development Plan*.
34. Waterston, *Development Planning*, p. 118.
35. Ibid., Chap. 9; Botswana, *National Development Plan*, p. 9; Botswana, *National Development Plan*, p. 11. Analogous solutions were used in many countries.
36. For example, in Kenya.
37. Lesotho: *The Lesotho Independence Order, 1966: Schedule to the Order* [The Constitution of Lesotho], sec. 90.
38. See Chap. 9.
39. See Bicanic, *Problems of Planning*.
40. R.C. Pratt, 'The Administration of Economic Planning in a Newly Independent State: The Tanzanian Experience 1963-66', *J. Comm. Stud.*, 5, 38, 51 (1967), reprinted in 2 L. Cliffe and J. Saul, *Socialism in Tanzania: An Interdisciplinary Reader* (Nairobi: East Af. Pub. House, 1972), pp. 11, 19.
41. Dean, *Plan Implementation*, p. 153.
42. Ibid., p. 18.
43. Ibid., p. 48.
44. Ibid., pp. 52 ff.
45. Quoted in ibid., p. 14.
46. Ibid., p. 16.
47. R.H. Green, 'Four African Development Plans: Ghana, Kenya, Nigeria and

Tanzania', *J. Mod. Af. Stud.*, 3, 272-73 (1965); see Bicanic, *Problems of Planning*, p. 47. On the dominance of the Minister of Finance in Nigeria, see Dean, *Plan Implementation*, pp. 45 *et seq.*

48. A.R. Abdel Maguib, 'The Methodology of Comprehensive Planning', in 1 Faber and Seers, *Crisis in Planning*, p. 117.
49. See Wiles, 'Economic Activation', pp. 171-2.
50. See Bicanic, *Problems of Planning*, pp. 58 *et seq.*
51. Ibid., p. 63.
52. Ibid., p. 61.
53. Ibid., p. 59.
54. Ibid.
55. Ibid., p. 60.
56. Ibid., p. 62.
57. Ibid., p. 63.
58. Abdel Maghuib, 'Methodology', pp. 116-17.
59. Waterston, *Development Planning*, Chap. 9.
60. Kenya: *On Economic Prospects and Policies* (Nairobi: Gov't. Printer, 1975).
61. Tanzania: *The Economic Survey* (Dar es Salaam: Gov't. Printer, 1975).
62. Africa: *Economic Growth Trends* (US Agency for Int'l. Dev., 1971).
63. *Report of the Second Meeting of the Follow-up Committee on Industrialization in Africa, Addis Ababa* (Addis Ababa: UN, 1975).
64. See, e.g., *Nigeria: Handbook of Commerce and Industry*, 5th ed. (Lagos, 1962).
65. Nigeria: Industrial Development (Income Tax Relief) Decree, 1971 (No. 22 of 1971), sec. 1.
66. Ibid., sec. 3.
67. Ghana: Capital Investments Act, 1963, sec. 5; see also Tanzania: Foreign Investments Protection Act, 1963 (Cap. 533, No. 40 of 1963); Kenya: Foreign Investments Protection Act, 1964 (Cap. 518 No. 35 of 1964) sec. 3(1); Uganda: Foreign Investments Protection Act, 1964 (Cap. 518: No. 17 of 1964).
68. Nigeria, supra. n. 63, sec. 10 (three years, plus an additional two years in discretion of Minister of Finance); Ghana: Capital Investments Act, 1963 sec. 10(1) (one to ten years in discretion of Minister).
69. See, e.g., Nigeria: Income Tax (Amendment) Act, 1958; East Africa: Income Tax Act, 1958; Lesotho: Pioneer Industries Encouragement Act, 1969, secs. 7, 15, 17.
70. See, e.g., Nigeria: Industrial Development (Import Duties Relief) Act, 1957 (Cap. 86); Ghana, supra n. 66, sec. 14; East Africa: Customs Management Act, 1952: Liberia: Investment Incentive Code, 1966.
71. See, e.g., Nigeria: Republican Constitution, 1963, pars. 31(1) (a) (b), (4) Kenya: Constitutions, sec. 75(1), (2) (guarantees against appropriation); Convention on the Settlement of Investment Disputes between States and Nationals of Other States (Text in 60 Am. J. Int'l. L. 892 (1966)); Ghana: Capital Investment Decree, 1973, sec. 11; International Center for Settlement of Investment Disputes (Enforcement of Awards) Decree, 1973, 1967 (No. 49 of 1967) (arbitration provisions).
72. See, e.g., Treaty between Federal Republic of Germany and Kenya concerning the Encouragement of Investments, signed 4 December 1964.
73. Waterston, *Development Planning*, Chap. 9.
74. A.N. Hakam, 'The Motivation to Invest and the Locational Pattern of Foreign Private Industrial Investments in Nigeria', *Nigerian J. Ec. and Soc. Stud.*, 8, 49 (1966); Deepak Lal, *Appraising Foreign Investment in Developing Countries* (London: Heinemann Educational P., 1975), pp. 19 *et seq.*; G.L. Reuber, *Private Foreign Investment in Development* (Oxford: Oxford

University Press, 1973), Chapter 4.

75. See Chap. 9.
76. The outer limit of the tendency were recommendations that the state develop new industries and then spin them off to private investors. See, e.g., W. A. Lewis, *Industrial Development Corporation (Ghana) — Report of the Economic Adviser*, par. 38 (Memo., 1958), cited in R. Pozen, 'Public Corporations in Ghana: A case study in legal importation', *Wisc. L. Rev.*, 802, 816 (1972).
77. Bicanic, *Problems of Planning*, p. 33.
78. Waterston, *Development Planning*, p. 337.
79. Cap. 320, Act. 35 of 1963, sec. 4.
80. Swaziland: *Recurrent Estimates of Public Expenditure for the Financial Year 1975/1977* (Mbabane: Gov't. Printer, 1975), p. 46.
81. See Nigeria: *Ministry of Economic Development, National Development Plan 1963-68* (Lagos: Gov't. Printer, 1962), p. 6; Waterston, *Development Planning*, Chap. 5.
82. Lewis, *Development Planning*, p. 13.
83. Cf. D.S. Paauw, *Development Strategies in Open Dualistic Economies* (Washington: National Planning Ass'n., 1970).
84. See Chap. 17 below.
85. C. Leys, 'The Analysis of Planning', in C. Leys (ed.), *Politics and Change in Developing Countries: Studies in the Theory and Practice of Development* (Cambridge: University Press, 1969).
86. Lesotho, *Second Five Year Plan*, p. 20.
87. Ibid., p. 21.
88. Waterston, *Development Planning*, Chap. 6.
89. Lewis, *Development Planning*, Chap. 1.
90. See Chap. 14 above.
91. See Chap. 20 below.
92. Nigeria, *Third National Development Plan.*
93. *Second Overall Evaluation of the Special Rural Development Program, Institute of Development Studies Occasional Paper No. 12* (Nairobi University of Nairobi, 1975) Chap. 14.
94. Botswana, *National Development Plan*, para. 2.6.
95. Nigeria, see n. 22; Lesotho, see n. 21; Kenya, see n. 2.
96. Nigeria, ibid.
97. Kenya, see *Development Plan*, pp. 1, 2.
98. Kenya, see *Development Plan*, pp. ix-xii.
99. Waterston, *Development Planning*, p. 336.
100. See Tinbergen, *Development Planning*, Chap. 11.
101. See Chap. 3 above.
102. Bessanov, *Economic Planning*; Bicanic, *Problems of Planning*, p. 15.

16 DECENTRALIZATION, PARTICIPATION AND THE LAW OF DEVELOPMENT ADMINISTRATION

To some, it seemed that poverty and oppression demanded contradictory solutions. Increased production required a high degree of specialization and exchange and an hierarchical, compartmentalized bureaucracy.[1] Elites at the centre would drag a dull, inert, fatalistic, backward peasantry into modernity.[2] Dull, inert, etc. peasantries could not participate in that process. Social justice, participation and fair shares seemed at war with increased productivity, efficiency and output.[3] Huntingdon argued that participation increases expectations, creating unfulfillable demands that lead to a breakdown of stability and order.[4] How then to coerce, manipulate, co-opt, deceive and bribe the lower orders into modernity? Some called for 'discipline', 'duty', 'obedience';[5] others would manipulate instead of coerce. Unless the worker felt important, he would not produce efficiently. Since the worker in fact could not make high-level decisions, governments should create a phantom participation.[6] Seventeen leading US academics stated in 1967: 'The problem remains one of increasing the feeling of participation without necessarily increasing the local input into decision-making.'[7]

These claims for coercion and manipulation for change warred with contemporary knowledge about administration,[8] learning theory,[9] social work,[10] community development[11] and the new field that studies 'change agents'.[12] Authoritarian systems weaken spontaneity and creativity.[13] 'For simple tasks under static conditions, an autocratic centralized structure . . . is quicker, neater and more efficient. But for adaptability to changing conditions, for "rapid acceptance of a new idea", for "flexibility in dealing with novel problems, generally high moral and loyalty . . . the more egalitarian or decentralized type seems to work better".'[14] Development requires massive re-education. Re-education requires a participatory environment.

The analysis of the preceding chapters sits easily with these modern views. In conditions of development, consciously changed behaviour will not easily occur without participation:

1. Effective communication requires two-way, usually face-to-face discussion, in which one actor cannot coercively distort the relationship.[15]

2. The law-maker can most easily discover the role-occupants' arenas of choice by including them in the law-making process.

3. A role occupant will more likely obey a law if he discovers for himself the explanation for the difficulty, and the appropriateness of the new rule of behaviour to solve the original dilemma.[16] 'Clearly, if the people decide that a project is a good idea (either through participation in policy-making or discussion of the problem) or are informed about it in a way that engenders support, the costs [of inducing changed behaviour] are lower and the likelihood of success greater.'[17]

4. Participation in problem-solving can change domain assumptions, role-self images, ideology and the like.[18]

5. The problem of discretion disappears if participation determines outcomes. Discretion implies power to make decisions affecting others.[19] Participation destroys hierarchy and thus discretionary power.

6. Participation also destroys compartmentalism. Compartmentalism depends upon hierarchy,[20] participation's opposite.

Participation, in this view, went beyond a mere 'value'.[21] Only it could really effect the changed behaviour that constitutes development.[22] This capsized the argument of the modernization school. Soft development arose not from too much participation, but too little.

The claims of participation always hung in uneasy balance with the claims of central direction and planning. Local participation cannot build trunk roads, great steel plants or lorry factories. Participation cannot develop even locally unless the centre supplies expertise and material resources. At the same time, government needs participation to excite local enthusiasm and creativity. Development needs both leadership and participation.[23]

A host of officials supposedly provided local level leadership: ministerial representatives such as District Officers, agricultural extension officers, and department heads; community development personnel; local government officials; in some countries, party cadres. Together they formed the 'development front'.[24] I deal here with the success of the development front in increasing local level participation.

In our era, those favouring participation coursed with the hounds.[25] Participation, however, had little commonly agreed content.[26] Development demanded that law-makers and law-implementers communicate laws effectively, discover role-occupants' opportunities, capacities, interests and perceptions, induce obedience and change conceptual patterns in a centralized state with national planning. I mean by 'participation' those problem-solving processes involving bureaucrats and clients likely to accomplish these tasks.[27] What formal rules will induce official behaviour appropriate to such participatory institutions? Our own bureaucratic culture so programmes us that the radically different official behaviour required to induce change sometimes escapes us. Two scenarios both from Zambia may serve to illustrate this.[28]

The people of Luombwa, in Serenje District in Zambia, get their supplies and travel to markets and government centres over a wooden bridge. In November 1964, the Secretary to the Rural Council reported the bridge's poor condition. The Public Works Officer, six months later, expressed concern. The Secretary of the Rural Council thereupon informed the District Secretary, who then had funds for bridge maintenance. Two days later the District Local Government Officer told the Secretary of the Rural Council that the Council would soon take over the bridge maintenance and that the Council should therefore go ahead with the repair. The Secretary then told the Public Works Officer to supervise work on the bridge. Meanwhile, in June 1965, the District Secretary sent out a Land Rover to inspect the bridge. He found some work already underway. Annoyed, he curtly rebuked the Council Secretary for wasting his time. Over the next two years the bridge deteriorated. The District Development Committee therefore requested funds to rebuild it from the Provincial Development Committee. In October, the Committee released K1401,* with more funds for two other bridges. The rural council, however, could only work on one of the three bridges. At the end of the year, the grant for Luombwa Bridge lapsed.

The rural council then approached the District Governor (a political rather than an administrative officer), to obtain funds from the provincial block bote. In the meantime, the Army threw up a temporary Bailey bridge nearby, apparently because political conflict required the police to have easy access to a neighbouring area. The District Development Committee recommended transferring the Bailey bridge to Luombwa, thus cutting off the neighbouring area. Nothing happened, however; the recommendation got lost between the Ministry of Power, Transport and Works and the Ministry of Defence.

*K1 = US $1.50.

In May 1969, the District Governor, having failed to obtain either funds or a Bailey bridge, decided on self-help. The Provincial Roads Engineer advised how to make the bridge temporarily safe for light vehicles. On May 28, the District Governor circulated all Heads of Departments and local councillors, instructing them to come with members of their staff and the public on 4 June with tools. The work proceeded as planned. Six months later, however, the Head Teacher of a nearby school warned the District Secretary that the bridge had a bad crack, that two pillars had collapsed and the rest wobbled. The letter came to the Secretary of the Rural Council, with instructions to inspect and report on the bridge before the rainy season set in. Nothing much happened. In October 1970, the Head Teacher wrote that the crack grew worse, and all the pillars had collapsed. The District Secretary forwarded the letter to the Secretary of the Rural Council, who wrote to the Head Teacher that the Public Works Officer would again inspect the bridge. At Christmas, the bridge washed away, isolating the transriverine areas.

In February, 1971, the District Secretary wrote to the Permanent Secretary in Lusaka urgently asking for funds to build at least a temporary bridge over the Luombwa River. All the people beyond the bridge, including two schools and a co-operative, had no access route to receive mealie meal, and famine threatened. The Permanent Secretary replied that he had no funds but would include K60,000 in the 1972 estimates for a permanent bridge.

Meanwhile, since a new bridge had replaced the Bailey bridge, officials decided to try to obtain it for temporary use. The District Development Committee instructed the Chairman of the Rural Council, the District Secretary and one other member to get it. The Provincial Roads Officer told the delegation on 4 August 1971, that only the Provincial Roads Engineer in Lusaka could authorize the transfer of the bridge, and that government had earmarked it for the Lusaka area. The District Secretary then wrote the Provincial Roads Engineer, and the delegation trekked to Lusaka. On 3 September, the Provincial Roads Engineer advised the District Secretary that government had promised the Bailey bridge to the Chinese, then constructing the TANZAM Railway. As of October 1971, the matter hung in balance, since the Chinese had no immediate need of the bridge. The transriverine settlement remained stranded.

Our second scenario also comes from Serenje. Nalubi Village had thirty families who supported themselves by fishing, while many of the men worked at the mines as migrants. They had a women's club and a

Community Development Officer in a neighbouring village. Many villagers supported Jehovah's Witnesses, with whom the government, following colonial tradition, dealt very sternly.

In 1964, the Community Development Officer and his assistant visited the women's club. They told the women that 'the Government was not against them,' and explained that the department assisted local self-help projects. The women began to make bricks for a clubhouse, and planned to improve their houses. In 1965, the Community Development Assistant planned two projects: a community hall and building a new house for each village family. The community hall would provide a village meeting-place, with rooms to store food and equipment, and a bedroom for visitors. A communal garden would raise necessary funds. The committee sparked further efforts and still more bricks. The Community Development Officer forwarded applications for grants-in-aid to the rural council, and the villagers also raised funds privately. By the end of June, they had produced more than 15,000 bricks. The Provincial Community Development Officer authorized K320 for the thirty-two houses of the Group Housing Scheme, and K110 for the Community Hall. In November, the Community Development Officer obtained the help of an Agricultural Assistant, who advised the cultivation of maize and beans, immediate uprooting of trees and a tractor. The people stumped the four acres immediately but could not obtain a tractor. Finally, a local villager, who had a tractor for his own plot, surrendered its use to the community. Visits from higher officials (the District Co-operative Officer, the Junior Minister for Agriculture and the local Member of Parliament) encouraged the people to form a co-operative and to stump 150 acres for a communal farm.

From September 1965 on, the group busily built the community hall. The rural council and the Community Development Officer provided tools to cut forest timber for the hall. The villagers, however did not know how to use the tools, and ultimately employed a local timber cutter from a nearby village. In September, 1966, the hall officially opened.

During 1967, the group concentrated on making more bricks and raising funds, about K100. Then the whole group built the walls of the houses, one by one. Another grant-in-aid from the rural council brought the doors and windows, and the locally-raised money, corrugated iron for roofs. The housing scheme ended in October 1963, but additional village housing starts continued. Men retiring from the mines commonly reimbursed the rural council, through the Community Development Officer, for the necessary supplies.

Obviously, these two scenarios do not 'prove' anything. They do illustrate, however, different official styles in organizing local developmental efforts. As I discussed in Chapter 13, the received administrative law can at most prevent excesses of power under the first model. What sort of administrative law would induce the behaviour of the second?

Africa had rich experience seeking 'participation', variously defined. In the main, this quest failed. I first examine its history and then try to explain its failures.

I   The Failure to Induce Participation*

In 1946, Whitehall discovered the 'winds of change', and participation entered its rhetoric. Decentralized aministration already existed; the institutions of local government and community development followed. Despite its rhetoric, however, the colonial government did not seek mass participation, but both to co-opt the new educated Africans and to legitimize British rule. Its participatory rules exemplified 'symbolic' law, enacted not to accomplish its ostensible objectives, but to throw dust in the public's eyes.[29]

A. The Effort and The Failure to Induce Participation

1. The Colonial Experience. Africans faced a highly decentralised Colonial Service,[30] a child of necessity. Weak, all but non-existent communications systems made it imperative. Before about 1947, however, it did not pretend to African participation, for everything frankly depended upon the discretion of the 'man on the spot'.

a. The beginnings. The new rhetoric of colonial development followed the 1946 Labour Party victory. In the same year, a select Parliamentary Committee reported that

Planning should start with the colonial peoples themselves, their needs and potentialities . . . Rapid and effective progress requires the introduction of methods of communal development in water supply, agriculture hygiene, domestic living, cultural values, self-help and democratic organization . . . A large-scale advance in agriculture means reaching into every village, forming farmers' groups and agricultural societies, demonstrating new techniques on farmers' holdings, promoting co-operation and providing

*This section is based in part on working papers by Richard Nelson, Richard Bourgeois and Richard Hawkes.

fertilizers, improved tools and cattle . . . Once the leaven is stirred
which will release the potentialities of the people themselves, the
tasks of individual administrators will become not more but less
formidable.[31]

Coercion did not work. Local governments had to enlist community-
mindedness and self-discipline.[32] Planned development required the
'co-operation of the local people, and that co-operation can best be
secured through the leadership of local authorities'.[33]

Behind that rhetoric lay more hard-nosed considerations. The Colonial Service faced a new class of educated men. Lord Lugard had earlier
dismissed them as 'lacking in integrity, self-control and discipline, and
without respect for authority of any kind'.[34] The British could no
longer ignore them. A Preparatory Paper for a 1947 Colonial Office
conference held that 'it is from these new classes that the political
leaders . . . in the future are most likely to be drawn . . . It is especially important that we reach a full understanding with the small class
of highly educated Africans who have most power to do harm if they
are against us or to do good if we can secure their co-operation.'[35]
The working group, concurring, said that if allowed to become embit-
tered, this small class could endanger 'good race relations'.[36] ('Good
race relations' became a code term meaning continued British political
and economic presence after self-government.[37])

b. Local government. The way to enlist African co-operation in
development and to defuse the revolutionary potential of this new
educated class lay in combining local government and community
development. A century before, Earl Grey had proposed local government for British Guiana as 'the best training that a population can hope
for the right usage of a larger measure of political power'.[38] In 1865,
Sir Benjamin Pine similarly recommended it for the West Coast of
Africa,[39] as did Lord Lugard.[40]

In 1947, a famous despatch from the Colonial Secretary endorsed
a new version of this old Whitehall nostrum:

Since I took office . . . I have been considering some of the basic
problems of African administration . . . since our success in handling these problems, and the extent to which we can secure the
active co-operation of the Africans themselves, may well determine
the measure of our achievement in the programmes of political,
social and economic advancement on which we have now embarked.

I believe that the key to success lies in the development of an efficient and democratic and local government. I wish to emphasize the words efficient, democratic and local . . . because they seem to me to contain the kernel of the whole matter: *Local* because the system of government must be close to the common people; *efficient* because it must be capable of managing the local services in a way which will help raise the standard of living; and *democratic* because it must not only find a place for a growing class of educated men, but at the same time command the respect and support of the mass of the people.[41]

Following that despatch, every African government introduced new forms of local government, always more or less following the British model, with scant adaptation to Africa.[42] Eastern Nigeria, like Britain, used the county as the unit for local government, although Nigeria had no counties.[43]

British local government on a small scale imitated its national institutions. Elected officials served part-time and without pay. In fact, a paid professional staff, headed by the Clerk (usually a lawyer), governed. The councillors, through committees, nominally overlooked professional staff.[44] Under this system, in Britain most councillors came from the more or less leisured local gentry and middle class.[45] Local government in Africa never became efficient.[46] Since everyone had to work the fields, few villagers could serve as unpaid councillors, except young men who used the posts for illicit income, not dedicated public service.[47] Professional staff hardly existed.[48] Local government did ensure that the 'new men' took charge,[49] but these included mostly local, minimally educated businessmen, not the highly educated modernizers whom the programme sought.[50] Frequently, they snuggled up cozily to the local traditional leadership.[51] Rather than mass participation in local affairs, 'those who consulted together and made the decisions were the local elite, who were often the main beneficiaries of those decisions'.[52]

c. *Community development.* The Colonial Office through community development tried to enlist the co-operation of the local masses[53] as a necessary complement to local government for the educated elite.[54] It had the goal of 'giving people the inspiration, and evoking from them the hard work, to better the world for themselves'.[55]

Community development always suffered ambiguity. At the outset, the colonial administration used it to control the 'ignorant and illiterate population' whose 'unsatisfied appetites' made them an easy target for 'subversive propaganda',[56] a device for obtaining the 'confidence' of people in government,[57] that only 'intensified' the administration's regular paternalistic efforts[58] to persuade local communities to co-operate with government in inexpensive betterment schemes.[59]

Community development as a legitimizing device had its heyday in Kenya during Mau-Mau, seeking to enlighten Africans 'on the benefits which British and European development brought to Kenya.'[60] One 'satisfactory development' in Central Province in 1953 led to 'the institution of home guard posts and the concentration of villages around them, which is a form of community development'[61]. At the notorious Athi River Camp for Mau- Mau detainees, the Community Development Department directed rehabilitation. It first classified detainees into 'co-operators' and 'non-co-operators', a task that a screening committee of 'loyal' Kikuyu accomplished, trained 'by experience to probe the truth, and the result of examination, which varies in length according to the individual, is usually a confession'[62] They 'encouraged' co-operators to proclaim their conversion to the entire camp, after which re-education began. They heard 'in clear language of the vast benefits brought by the British government in Kenya, and not least to its Kikuyu inhabitants'. The 1954 Report stated that 'prior to making a clean breast of their Mau-Mau associations', the detainees appeared usually 'secretive, sullen and unhealthy . . . with dull skin and narrowed eyes. Once they have gotten the poison out of their system then confidence and candour increase,. they are ready to laugh and their physical health is obviously improved'[63].

Despite its origins, community development held the potential to encourage genuine local participation. Many community development workers had a social work background. They became committed to their clients, not to the authorities. They emphasized that the initiative for change must come from the people themselves.[64] For some workers, however, that meant individual, not social development.[65] For others, it did not even mean development but conservatism: traditional values, attitudes, social structures[66] and leadership.[67]

Nevertheless, the dynamic of enlisting group co-operation led some community development workers toward genuine mass participation. The initiative, they held, had to come from the community itself.[68] 'It is axiomatic that the 'recipient's interests and desires must be observed, and that any form of dogmatic instruction and imposition from above should be avoided wherever possible. . .'[69] 'An instruction which takes shape as a genuine group decision is not resented, and is often obeyed with a new alacrity and energy. When people plan the service they shall give, they may give better service than their superiors would dare to demand. Moreover, initiative in the rank and file grows with the experience of such participation.'[70]

Participation can become truly revolutionary. It requires a power shift from the governors (government, elites, ruling classes) to the governed. Paralleling the United States' short-lived poverty programmes giving the poor 'maximum feasible participation',[71] the African establishment confronted the inherently radical strain in community development.

Summary. The basic British strategy to deal with the winds of change in Africa appeared in a statement by the New Kenya Group, a 1950's political movement among some Kenyan settlers: 'The only solution, in our view, is vigorously to tackle the basic problem of low living standards, so that there may rapidly emerge from the poorer majority people having similar interests and similar ideals, to those (whites) economically more advanced.'[72] Local government would provide a political vehicle for these emerging wealthier classes. Community development would legitimize British rule with the mass.

The local population nevertheless continued to salute the British District Officer as he made his rounds through the villages, immaculate in white shorts, knee length socks and spotless shirt. Agricultural development used the big stick. Colonial government ineluctably remained authoritarian.

2. Independence and After. The newly independent governments continued participatory rhetoric, and accordingly tinkered with the received institutions. The new innovations, in the main, however, failed to bring about the participation they said they wanted.

a. National administration: Centralization and decentralization. A variety of forces initially influenced every government to centralize its authority:[73] conflict between rural traditional authorities and the new men at the centre; ethnic particularism;[74] desperately scarce trained manpower.[75] Concentration, however, bred its own ills. Local morale suffered from impotence. Central ministries stressed daily operations, not policy formulation. The capital suffered increased urban growth as the most qualified officers congregated at the centre.[76] Communications channels clogged, and decisions piled up.[77]

Deconcentration inevitably followed, accompanied once again by the
rhetoric of participation. A Zambian commission claimed that decentral-
isation sought to secure popular participation in the decision-making
process '. . . not only at the level of the central parliamentary process,
but down to the very grassroots of the society itself.'[78]

Decentralization occurred in different ways. Kenyan local leadership
lay with civil servants, Zambian and Tanzanian, with political officials.
Even where nominally political, as in Zambia, however, frequently
civil servants in fact exercised local power.[79] Everywhere, decentralization created opportunities for local participation. In Zambia, the
District Governors had the specific duty to provide 'effective leadership for the local people, encouraging their participation in advancing
their own welfare.'[80] In Tanzania, President Nyerere cautioned that
decentralization did not mean 'a transfer of a rigid and bureaucratic
system from Dar es Salaam to lower levels.'[81] Decentralization did not,
however, lead to participation. Kenya returned to the colonial system
of district officers.[82] They met the people mainly in *barazas*, or public
meetings. In Vihiga, a division in Western Kenya with a population of
close to 300,000, in the early 1970s, 280 *barazas* took place each
week.[83] A District Officer in Mbere said that these *barazas* served 'to
remind people of government policies' and 'to inform people what
government wants.'[84] Two observers concluded that

> the Mbere District Officer is an experienced officer possessing a
> strong belief in the efficacy of administrative exhortation and
> control. He exudes a confident conviction that Government, and
> especially the Provincial Administration, have but to select, state
> and explain a policy and the people will automatically follow —
> a belief shared at least by the officers of other departments.[85]

The chiefs and sub-chiefs became local brokers, who took national
government demands from the DO and translated them into local
terms. After 1967, the local people no longer elected the chiefs.

> The chief explains government policies at these barazas . . . Appeals
> are made for loyalty to the nation and to the President. Govern-
> ment plans are noted. Pleas are made for the payment of taxes
> and contributions to self-help schemes. The barazas frequently are
> tax-collecting devices. Police check tax receipts during them and
> not-so-voluntary contributions to self-help schemes are collected
> . . . The baraza still has an aura of the colonially enforced meeting.

A policeman stands by the chief with his baton. The symbol of order and control, the chief, becomes the explainer of Government actions . . .[86]

b. *Local government.* As independence neared, British justifications for local government changed. Now, instead of an institution to co-opt the newly educated Africans, it became a Lockean device to maintain local democracy against centralized autocracy. With a fine disregard for history, the chairman of the 1961 Cambridge Conference on Local Government said that the Colonial Office had introduced it into Africa both to bring about greater efficiency, and because 'Africa's national leaders demanded English-style local government and would have no other, while their overlords could think of no better school for mass education in democracy . . . And when independence came, the local authorities would stand guardians of local individual liberty against the hand of absolutism at the top.'[87] Alternatively, local government might become a transmission belt for government policy.[88] That perception of local government's functions followed the 'development front' model.

Whatever the perception, local governments in Africa did not work very well.[89] Inefficient, they failed to educate Africans for democracy,[90] and sometimes became quite unrepresentative. In Kenya, for example, a statute required that councillors be literate,[91] thus limiting political activity to the educated. Some countries, in fact, appointed the councillors.[92] In 1968, under pressure of national politics the Kenya Government cancelled local government elections on the ground that opposition petitions had procedural defects. For want of opposition, every councillor in the country won re-election.

One common response to weak local government reduced central government contributions to local councils. Ghana, in 1959-60, spent 1.4 per cent of the national budget for local government; in 1966, less than 1 per cent. The Second National Plan linked social welfare expenditures and community development to local government.[93] The Seven-Year Plan, following, looked to community development for less than 20 per cent of such investment.[94] In Tanzania, after a local council in 1968 smothered thirteen imprisoned tax defaulters in an airless cell, government withdrew local taxing power from local councils. This removed 80 per cent of their revenue sources.[95] In 1973, Tanzania formally abolished local councils and replaced them with District Development Corporations.[96] In Kenya, shortfalls in anticipated Council revenues required constantly increasing government subsidies.[97] In 1965, the Provincial Administration took over the collection of personal tax. In 1968, the central government all but took over local government affairs.[98] Of the funds allotted to local government, the Kenyan government paid only miniscule amounts to the rural areas; in 1965, for example, about one-third went to Nairobi alone.[99]

Along with central government subvention went central government control over local affairs. The Kenyan Permanent Secretary in the President's Office put it bluntly: 'Huge amounts of money are paid by the Central Government to the Councils as grants. It would be unfair if the Government were expected to give the grants to the Councils and have no means of ensuring that the money is used for the purpose for which grants are given.'[100] In Zambia, a government commission stated in 1972 that the Ministry of Local Government and Housing 'keeps a tight rein on local government initiative and the system is a standing illustration of the principle that he who pays the piper calls the tune'.[101]

Some governments created new structures for local development efforts, the hierarchy of Village, Ward District and Provincial Development Committees.[102] These began during colonialism as local administrative committees to alleviate compartmentalism in the colonial service. Zambia, Tanzania and Kenya later used them for the development functions in which they saw local government failing. The Village Productivity Committees in Zambia, the lowest of several Development Committee levels, had the duty 'to plan the growth and development of a village . . .'[103] Local administrators sat *ex officio* on District and Provincial Development Committees. In Mongu in Western Zambia, for example, the Provincial Development Committee in 1972 drew a majority of its active membership from local representatives of the central government ministries. They acted as 'the main organs of coordination and communication in relation to development on the local level'. In Zambia, the District and Provincial Development Committees never had any statutory basis, but arose from administrative instructions in 1965 as part of plan implementation.[104] Each Provincial Development Committee originally received a fund 'to enable it to overcome unforeseen bottlenecks in the execution of approved programmes of development that are not the responsibility of any single ministry or cannot easily be solved by normal procedures or through local authority action'.[10] Those funds later disappeared when the Ministry of Finance concluded that they were not being used for their intended purposes.[106] The Provincial Development Committees grew in almost direct proportion as their financial powers dwindled. Some eighty members crowded a meeting of the Central Province Development Committee in 1974.[107] Officials commonly judged them a failure.[108] Zambian District Development Committees also withered, and Village and Ward Committees hardly existed on the ground. One District Governor commented, 'The local people . . . are not there'[109] They had no power, no money, no staff.

Tanzania at first supplied no exception. Thoden van Velzen reported a Village Development Committee meeting in Tanzania in May 1967.[110] The Chairman began by thanking all the important people (the officials) for coming to show them the true path to a better life. The Village Executive Officer and a TANU Ward chairman castigated the people for laziness, and other officers exhorted them to work harder and to pay their tax. The Community Development Officer (of all people) said, 'I am not a kind and polite man: I am cruel! If I see that government orders are not obeyed I will know where to find you and how to punish you. I do not care if you hate me, for it is only important that the orders of the government are fulfilled. . . . I have a strong medicine for this job, we will give it to all lazy people.' He announced that people would thereafter have to work every Saturday on a road construction project.

Decentralization and devolution made participation theoretically possible. These Kenyan and Tanzanian officials presumably could have structured a participatory rather than an authoritarian situation. To a degree, they had discretion to generate participation, but did not.

B. Explanations for the Failure to Achieve Participation

Decentralization, devolution to local government, the Development Committees and community development all created opportunities for participation. They chopped decisions into bits, small enough for a face-to-face group to digest. Why did local level bureaucrats fail to induce citizen participation?

1. *Communication of the Policy and Rules.* Both before and after independence, bureaucrats repeatedly heard of their obligation to induce 'participation'. The policy, however, had no detailed rules that defined it. In the main bureaucrats learned that 'participation' could manipulate the local population to win their 'co-operation'.

Tanzania's rhetoric alone suggested a concept of participation that came closer to our definition. President Nyerere meant by partici-pation decision-making by peasants and workers. *Ujamaa* villagers must truly make their own decisions.[111] Leadership

does not imply control, any more than it implies bullying or intimidating people. A good leader will explain, teach and inspire. In an ujamaa village, he will do more: he will lead by doing. He is in front of the people showing them what can be done, guiding them, and encouraging them. But he is with them. You do not lead people by being so far in front or so theoretical in your teaching that the people cannot see what you are doing or saying. You do not lead people by yapping at their heels like a dog herding cattle.'[112]

TANU, Tanzania's ruling party, embodied these prescriptions in its 1971 guidelines:

The truth is that we have not only inherited a colonial government-al structure but have also adopted colonial working habits and leadership methods. For example, we have inherited in the government, industries and other institutions the habit in which one man gives the orders and the rest just obey them. . . .

There must be a deliberate effort to build equality between leaders and those they lead. For a Tanzanian leader it must be forbidden to be arrogant, extravagent, contemptuous and oppressive. . . .

For people who have been slaves or have been oppressed, ex-ploited and disregarded by colonialism or capitalism, 'development' means 'liberation'. Any action that gives them more say in deter-mining their affairs and running their lives is one of development, even if it does not offer them better health or more bread. Any action that reduces their say in determining their affairs or running their lives is not progressive and retards them even if the action brings them better health and more bread.

The duty of our Party is not to encourage people to implement plans which have been decided upon by a few experts and leaders. The obligation of our Party is to ensure that the leaders and experts implement the plans that have been agreed upon by the people themselves . . . It is not correct for leaders and experts to usurp the people's right to decide on an issue just because they have the expertise.[113]

Even in Tanzania, however, the vagueness persisted. How could 'the people' agree upon plans? That required detailed procedural rules and institutions, which did not exist.

Community development sometimes became an exception. Com-munity development training manuals had detailed instructions about

encouraging local initiative: learn the local community, its structure
and culture. Encourage people to come forward. Participate in the work
yourself. Look for groups, not individuals. Suggest projects that reward
communities for participating in them, rather than those that add to the
prestige of the local bureaucracy. Win over the local power structure to
support the project.[114] The successes of community development, as in
the second scenario above, argue that some of these rules come from
valid experience.

2. *Capacity*. Absent detailed rules, role-occupants, of course, generally follow their socialized norms, or pursue their self-interest. In Africa, the training and style of the bureaucrats, the structures of local decision-making,
and the available resources made participation a losing proposition.

a. *Training and Style*. Leadership for a participatory group differs
from authoritarian leadership. Their British teachers taught African
bureaucrats to follow their example. British Colonial servants maintained a vast gulf between Africans and themselves. They lived in
different quarters; Lord Lugard prescribed a gap of 440 yards between
the 'native quarter' and the Cantonments or European district.[115]
Officials' spotless white uniforms demonstrated that *they* did no
manual work. They spoke mainly to chiefs and headmen. Their education, their language, their style of life set them apart from their African
clients. Independence changed bureaucratic skin colour, but little else.

Participation does not easily take place between people from
different worlds. An assessment of the Tanzania Government's Village
Settlement programme, an important feature of its first Five-Year Plan,
argued that the poor morale of the villagers in these schemes came
largely from the gulf between the villagers and the (usually expatriate)
staff in income, living style, education and language, and from aloof and
authoritarian staff behaviour.[116]

b. *The Institutional Structures of the 'Development Front'*. The structures did not make participation likely. I discuss the local agencies of central
government; local government; co-operatives; and development committees.

(i). *Local agencies of central government*. Local-level ministerial
agents did not account to local people, but to their bureaucratic superiors.
In Kenya, the Provincial Administration reported directly to the
President,[117] serving as his 'primary agent for exerting political control
throughout Kenya'.[118] The provincial administration officers collected
taxes on behalf of local authorities, and chaired local land boards, loan

boards, agricultural committees, licensing committees, self-help committees.[119] Accountable only to bureaucratic superiors, they readily
adopted a paternalistic style towards inferiors.

In those countries that made the local representatives of the central
government political roles, the chain of their responsibilities became
more blurred. In Zambia, their advancement depended upon their party
superiors at the centre.[120] In Tanzania, Regional Commissioners put
their developmental efforts into visible and dramatic projects to enhance their reputations.[121] The career and reward structure of the central administration and of the political party discouraged local administrators from promoting local participation.

(ii). *Local government.* Western constitutional law relies on periodic
elections to ensure local-level accountability. Periodic elections, however, do not ensure participation for development purposes. President
Kaunda said in the introduction to his party's 1974 election manifesto,
that the adoption of One-Party Participatory Democracy the year
before 'means that we have moved away from representative democracy
in which people are asked every three or five years to choose their Local
Government or Parliamentary representatives to a system which involved
people's active participation in decision-making at all levels and at all
times'.[122] President Nyerere said in 1972 that 'The purpose of the Arusha
Declaration and Mwongozo [the TANU Guidelines] was to give people
power over their own lives and their own development. We have made
great progress in seizing power from the hands of capitalists and traditiona
lists, but we must face the fact that, to the mass of the people, power
is still something wielded by others, even if on their own behalf.'[123]

British-style local government could not achieve these high aims. It
lodged power not with elected representatives but with the professional
staff. Even the elected representatives did not participate very much in
the business of governing.[124]

Although most African local government systems on paper opened
these elected roles to everyone, individuals within any community have
varying advantages. Few women won places on local government councils anywhere in Africa. The men who did usually either had more
money or more Westernized education than most, or already held
traditional power.[125] It exemplified the proposition that the most powerful will seize the advantages facilitative law offers.

(iii). *Co-operatives.* The co-operative in its many forms became a
stock institution.

Throughout South Asia, agricultural policy is oriented toward land

and tenancy reform in the interest of the small peasants and sometimes the landless . . . Co-operation is then relied upon to combine
the benefits of decentralization and of economies of scale . . .

The effort to build up co-operatives and at the same time institute
and strengthen local self-government is what in the region is called
'democratic planning' . . . The operative ideal is to improve the
conditions of life and work for individual small-scale entrepreneurs;
it is not a desire to bring their enterprises under state ownership
and management.'[126]

Kenya asserted co-operative rural development as a national objective.[127]
Tanzania's principal development programme aimed at building *ujamaa*
(co-operative) villages.

A long history of African co-operatives reached back into the colonial
era, mainly marketing co-operatives, some very large – the Victorian
Federation of Co-operative Unions in Tanzania by 1964 became the
largest East African enterprise. Central government gazed at them with
greedy eyes, both for their surpluses[128] and because they seemed a
channel for penetrating the countryside.

As usual, colonial co-operative law aped the British. African statutes
incorporated the Rochdale principle of 'one man, one vote'.[129] Equality
in formal voting assumes equality among voters. In practice, authority
patterns, wealth and privilege mocked the egalitarian principle.[130]
In Tanzania, in Mwanza Region, 'some progressive farmers (i.e. the
wealthier ones) were willing to formally establish *ujamaa* (co-operative)
villages . . . so as to ensure their access to credit and inputs . . .'[131]
Myrdal concluded his study of co-operatives in South Asia by stating:

Unfortunately, the notion that co-operation will have an equalising
effect is bound to turn out to be an illusion. While land reform and
tenancy legislation are, at least in their intent, devices for producing
fundamental alterations in property rights and economic obligations,
the 'co-operative' approach fails to incorporate a frontal attack in
the existing inegalitarian power structure. Indeed, it aims at
improving conditions without disturbing that structure and represents, in fact, an evasion of the equality issue . . . If, as is ordinarily the case, only the higher strata in the villages can avail themselves of the advantages offered by co-operative institutions – and
profit from the government subsidies given for their development –
the net effect is to create more, not less, inequality. This will hold
true even when the announced purpose is to aid the disadvantaged

strata.[132]

As with local government, the prevailing regime of facilitative law contributed to elite domination of co-operatives. 'The fight for maintaining both the economic benefits and social prestige of the upper strata has taken place, first of all, in the field of winning the new and key positions and posts.'[133] After securing these, the elite used them to maintain their power and privilege. Co-operative law, a form of facilitative law, became a device not for co-operation but for aggrandizing power.

(iv). *Development committees.* The development committee structure induced neither much development nor much participation. Zambian development committees built schools, roads, clinics and waterworks but not productive enterprise. Development came to mean schools, roads clinics and water supplies. Zambia had long-existing and competent Ministries and departments of education, public works, health and water. Each had a local presence. Development committees easily found a government organization to build a road or a clinic, but not to develop a rice mill or abattoir. Nor did the development committees induce participation. Dominated by civil servants, much more highly educated and more articulate than their local counterparts, they at best harmonized the many local-level agencies' programmes, provided a meeting place for local-level bureaucrats and the elite, but not a forum for local-level mass participation.

c. *Resources.* Participation in local development cannot occur unless the participants share control of scarce material resources, manpower and knowledge. Africa had a limited local fisc. Localities had ordinarily three sources of income: local taxes, usually very small; their various petty business ventures; and — largest and most important — subsidies from the central government. The power of the purse put central government, not the local institution, in charge. In any event, local government fell short in manpower. Engineers, accountants, lawyers, medical officers, educators: desperately few, they flocked to the centre with its amenities and power. A medical assistant in rural Zambia in 1972 complained that he could not buy enough food locally to feed himself and his family, and available food came dearly. 'Either you get your protein from dried caterpillars and bukoko or you pay through the nose for Great Wall bully beef from China.'[134]

Participation in development, no quilting party, requires knowledge, information and skill. Expertise generates power. Delegating decision-making authority to a collectivity frequently delegates decision-making not to the membership but to the experts. Cliffe and Cunningham examined the history of villagization in Tanzania.[135] Government initiated most co-operatives or other local organizations and appointed a bureaucrat or a technical expert to manage them. In the supervised settlement schemes internal relations 'corresponded more to a landlord-tenant relationship than to a co-operative'.[136] Although each scheme had its village development committee, the committees could mainly only advise; the manager decided. In fact, this usually expatriate (i.e. white, European) officer had 'control over all aspects of scheme life . . . Small wonder that the attitude of participants corresponds more to that of paid labourers . . . We have in fact heard of instances where the settlers in pilot schemes referred to themselves as *Watumwa wa Serikali* (slaves of the government).'[137]

3. *Interest.* Governments built participation in part to curb administrative discretion. Administrative discretion implied that some administrators made decisions affecting other people. If the people concerned shared the decision-making, that limited the bureaucrat's authority.[138] Bureaucrats did not usually voluntarily surrender power, nor did local councillors or development committees.

Bureaucrats like others will act to win rewards from those who dole them out. If the upper echelons of the bureaucracy desire to 'pacify' the Mau-Mau more than to encourage local participation, community development officers took their cues. Important officials disagreed even with the rhetoric of participation.[139] Their subordinates would not likely see much profit in inducing it.

The local power elite also structured the interests of local bureaucrats and elected officials. They had and used their resources to influence administrators and politicians. Thoden van Velzen analyzed this for an administrative district in Southern Tanzania.[140] Two elites became especially powerful: the salaried central government, representatives of the central government, and the wealthier farmers. The former formed a closely knit, mutually supportive reference group whose future careers and immediate rewards depended upon each other. In income, education, costume, language and housing they lived a world apart from ordinary peasants. Both their collective and individual interests lay in maintaining their power and privilege, not in encouraging participation. The governing elite coalesced with the wealthier farmers. These farmers had economic favours for officials. They gave gardens to *every* official in the region resident for more than two years. They lived as well as the staff. In the eyes of authorities and peasants alike, they exemplified development, proof positive of the effectiveness of official efforts.

The wealthier farmers became patrons for smaller peasants, who in turn supported their patrons for leadership roles. Some government programmes explicitly required the official to favour the 'progressive' farmer. The officials chose the 'natural' leaders for positions of prominence in local committees and institutions. One village filled 17 of 28 official posts occupied by villagers by farmers drawn from the wealthiest 20 per cent; another drew 7 out of 15. These relationships committed the staff and wealthy farmers to the *status quo*. They sat on top of the local heap. It opposed their interest to disturb it. The existing ways of doing things gave them power and privilege. They were not likely to choose participatory modes that threatened their position.

4. *Ideologies, Values and Other Internal Factors.* The received model of the administrator portrayed a 'big man' barking orders. In 1963, we went with a Community Development Officer to see a self-help school building project in Northern Ghana. The official, from the South, did not speak the local language, but used an interpreter. When we arrived, the villagers had not yet started the day's work. He sent his interpreter to fetch the chief, who came on the run and saluted. After berating him severely, the official fined the village a shilling per head for not being at work when he arrived with a University visitor. The official labelled the farmers as 'backward' and 'primitive'. When a group of villagers arrived and began to make mud bricks, the official in his spotless white uniform did not participate. He shouted at them, through a translator, of course.

We all assume that institutions exist of necessity. Officials and their African clients met always as superiors and inferiors. Superiors gave orders and took advice from bureaucratic subordinates, but they did not let mere clients participate at all. Additionally, African administrators stepped into the shoes of white officials, who rarely doubted their superiority to their black clients. African administrators easily believed that they could give orders because they *were* superior.

5. *The Forms of Decision.* The processes of role-occupants' behavioural choice helps determine the decision. Administrators in Africa usually decided about admitting clients into participation privately or in the company of their peers. The former maximized their acculturated behavioural notions; the latter reinforced them. Community development workers sometimes differed. They held training sessions and met at conferences discussing participation.[141] Such community development workers moved from the bureaucratic to the cadre model.

Summary

Participation failed in Africa not because of the people involved, but because of the sorts of institutions that structured their behaviour. The colonial designers of African participatory institutions did not want participation, but its simulation, thus ensuring the colonial service its immense power. Continuing those institutions after independence meant that all the participatory rhetoric died a-borning.

II From Bureaucrat to Cadre

The received administrative law assumed an authoritarian, hierarchical and compartmentalized administrative structure. What sorts of rules might structure participatory administration? What administrative law could serve development administration? To some, the question seems silly. An officer with long experience in West Africa, both before and after decolonialization, asked how law related to community development.

> So far as I know, there is no 'law' about it. Activities that depend so much on insight, on personal identification and on stimulating initiative cannot be regulated by law. . . . Even today . . . we do not find a Community Development Law in the same way that we find a Local Government Law or a Trade Union Law. We find instead that a number of laws — notably those of local government and education — lay upon Departments or local authorities the duty or the power to do a hundred and one things that will bring about 'the betterment of the people'; if legal authority for community development is necessary it will be found in such laws; but its real purpose is to translate these many and beneficent laws into reality, principally by helping people to translate them into reality themselves. It was always a weakness of the British in Africa that they thought they had solved a problem by passing a law about it; but who could possibly *enforce* a law about self-help?[142]

That perception placed the blame for the failure of participation not upon the bureaucrats and officials who were supposed to stimulate it, but upon the 'backward peasants.'[143]

Here I deal with the rules which control administrative behaviour. What sorts of rules might induce officials to build participation? I discuss the rules that define the conditions for such behaviour; the rules of participatory interaction between officials and citizenry; and the structure of local-level institutions.

328   The Law of Development Administration

A. Rules Defining the Conditions of Participation

1. *Communication.* Communication raises both substantive and procedural issues. Substantively, law-makers must articulate detailed rules of how officeholders should behave.[144] TANU in 1971 recognized this when it required the Party to provide guidelines on 'work methods and attitudes, and decision-making.'[145]

A second communications issue deals with process. Merely broadcasting rules will not likely reach their specific targets, nor, if they do, change their behaviour. New rules requiring bureaucratic change will not likely succeed unless government ensures that they reach officials in a participatory context. Tanzania instituted seminars for officials to discuss the requirements of participation.[146] Eastern Nigeria had a Community Development training school, through which more than 3,000 officials had passed by 1964.[147]

2. *Training.* Self-evidently, participation will more likely succeed if officials have specific training. Community Development provided that for many years.

3. *Living Style.* Rules can ensure that bureaucrats live on the same level as their clients, and participate in the breadwork. How to recruit for so spartan a career? So long as the private or parastatal sectors offer high salaries, power and perquisites, and highly educated young people can choose their vocations, the public service must offer competitive rewards. But participation requires that bureaucrats and their clients live closely together. A polity can have bureaucrats living on a level high enough to resist the siren allures of the private sector, or participation, but not both. In practice, a polity can have a participatory bureaucracy or a substantial private sector, but not both.

4. *Resources.* Local governments must have the authority and capacity to raise revenue or the central government must subsidize them. Human resources do not come so easily. African local units usually had few career incentives to attract high-level manpower. The Working Party on Decentralization in Zambia recommended that local government employees join the Civil Service, with consequent expanded career option,[148] thus attracting better local-level personnel, but, unless guarded against, at the cost of local control.

5. *Control over Resources and Discipline.* Participation implies a transfer of power from the bureaucrat to the participating group. That

power includes control over resources and over discipline. Group control over resources limits the usable technology. The lower the technical training of the people who control property, and the higher the technology, the more capital at risk. Everywhere in Africa, one heard tales of farmers who used government-provided tractors as much for joy-riding as for plowing. Participation imposed different parameters upon technological choice than efficiency.[149]

6. *Interest.* Unless rewards and penalties to bureaucrats make it serve their interest to encourage local-level participation, they will not likely do so. New civil service rules relating successful participation to promotion and rewards would help, but never issued.

Government must also eliminate the rewards that local elites paid to officials. A rule forbidding gifts might help. Making the career of the official depend on local approval would help more — a matter to which I return later.

7. *The Decision to Adopt a Participatory Style.* Role-occupants are more likely to adopt new rules if they are led through a problem-solving process, and so bureaucrats will more likely change their style of work if they, too, undergo such a process. That requires participatory institutions within the bureaucracy itself. Rather than higher authorities evaluating local-level bureaucrats on the visible results of their performance (physical completion of buildings and roads and the collection of taxes), superiors must observe their style in dealing with the local population and constantly discuss with them the practical problems of participation.

B. Rules Defining Participatory Processes

Every deliberative or adjudicative assembly has rules of membership, competence and procedure. Robert's Rules of Order, for example, assume a deliberative assembly with articulate, literate participants appropriately reaching decisions on the basis of majority interests; it aims at ascertaining the weight of bias. A participatory assembly probably must operate on the basis of democratic consensus,[150] not majority rule; it seeks not the mobilization of bias, but the most feasible solutions to existential problems.

In the United States, most adults know the elements of Robert's Rules. If they attend a Parent and Teacher Association meeting, a social club, a union or a professional organization, they know something of the rules of procedure, what the group can and cannot do. They do not know the appropriate working rules for a participatory assembly, that seeks not majority but consensus.

The most difficult rules to articulate define the appropriate processes at the point of decision. Existing administrative law subsumes most of these under the notion of fair hearing. Two concepts of fair hearing exist in the law. One concerns settling disputes: an adjudicator determines a conflict between two parties. The other concerns formulating rules, as when a local zoning board holds a public hearing upon proposed zoning changes. That notion, too, contains the concept of an adjudicator, for whom the hearing provides inputs for decision. The common law requires a fair hearing only in the first case,[151] although many statutes require a hearing of the second sort.[152] When people whom the proposed new rule involves will not decide its content, they can at most provide inputs to decision: data, theories, arguments. The conversion process, the act of decision, rests with the adjudicators. If one of the adjudicators has a secret interest or information which may sway his vote, he must at least declare it. But where the targets of new rules decide upon them, what function does disclosure serve?

Groups reach decisions by vote, compromise or problem-solving.[153] Voting and compromise alike assume that group decisions properly reflect mobilized bias. In such systems, individuals, of course, vote their tastes, interests or values. Problem-solving, on the contrary, assumes that with a common perspective or ideology, consensus will emerge from data and experience. Such a case may require disclosure of interest or secret information. Problem-solving requires experts to contribute technical information and ideas, and to teach a problem-solving methodology. In what sense does a Ph.D. in agronomy participate with an unlettered peasant to determine the best sort of fertilizer to use? Considerable experience in other contexts fortunately teaches how experts and clients can participate. That becomes the central problem in education. Teachers conduct either authoritarian or participatory classrooms, and educationists have studied the subject extensively.[154]

Many rules determine input processes: defining jurisdiction (Power over what subjects, individuals and territory? What rights for dissenters?), rights and obligations to participate (Who may speak and vote? Who must do so?), relevance and evidence (Hearsay? Opinion? Who decides?). Participatory administration must promulgate appropriate rules about input and conversion processes (Voting? By majority, or some larger number? Are individual explanations of votes required?). Without such rules, participation becomes an empty catchphrase.

C. The Institutions of the Development Front

Decentralization alone obviously will not create local participation; neither will rules that define participatory meetings. Participation also needs local-level institutions that ensure central government inputs; maximize local participation; and resolve the inevitable resulting tensions. Self-evidently, no single prescription can solve these three problems throughout Africa. The particular constraints and resources of each situation require individual assessment. At most, I can make only a few quite general suggestions.

One candidate for local government is always the existing indigenous one.[155] Everywhere, some sort of local community ties people together. Sometimes it frustrates development, for example, where a powerful local chief coercively exploits the local populace. In other cases, however, the existing local structure may encourage mass participation.

Most cases, however, require a new structure. The standard response to the issues both of hierarchical control and compartmentalism in the civil service has moved towards a prefectural system, like the 1971 Tanzanian solution.[156] District officials received authority not merely to 'co-ordinate' the activities of local ministerial representatives, but actually to control their activities. They reported to him, and became subject to his requirements. Prefectorial system may solve problems of compartmentalism. Under it, however, the careers of central administration representatives, however, still lay within their own ministries. Inevitably, they must seek to please not their local clients so much as their bureaucratic superiors.

Every country moved to institutionalize local inputs into the development process. After the virtual demise of British-style local government, most nations used development committees, co-operatives and the Party.

If development committees consisted only of civil servants, they responded only to the problems of compartmentalism, not those of local participation. With elected representatives, the form suffered from the same difficulties of any elected local government: Elections guaranteed at most periodic accountability, not popular participation in decision-making. Without carefully-designed nominating procedures, nominations fell to the powerful and the privileged. The same frequently occurred in co-operatives.

One response elsewhere structured all local level institutions to ensure mass representation (therefore denying it to the local elite). That required quotas on the principal boards of local government bodies, guaranteeing a particular number of places for women, or limiting the number of educated people.[157]

A more radical solution lay in the Party organization. Tanzania alone relied upon the Party as the principal unifying and participatory local-level agency. It relied most on the Ten House Cell system, whose leaders served as well on higher-level committees such as the Ward (formerly the Village) Development Committee.[158]

The potential for using the Party to ensure local participation in development depended upon its actual organization and activity. In theory, the CPP in Ghana under President Nkrumah filled the same function as TANU; so did Zambia's UNIP. The Party could bring about development only if, given opportunity, every local group can produce its own leadership. That will not result if the Party itself becomes authoritarian and bureaucratic. In Ghana, the CPP first became hierarchic, then bureaucratic, and finally moribund.[159] I discuss these processes with respect to TANU and UNIP in Chapter 21.

Finally, how to resolve the inherent tensions between bureaucracy and participation, the demands of the centre and the locality? Obviously, one useful device localizes decision-making in joint central-local committees. Supposedly, the development committees had this task.[160] The Party, too, might serve such a function. Another such device that Tanzania attempted involved budgeting through the Regional Development Fund.[161] Local Development Committees initiated projects that, however, required approval by the relevant Regional Development Committees, which central government representatives dominated. Given a genuinely representative Local Development Committee the system required central government and local consensus on particular development projects.

Prior to 1969, administrative and technical considerations mainly from the central government side dominated the choice of projects. In 1969, however, central government directives emphasized that *ujamaa* villages receive most Regional Development Fund projects. These co-operatives permitted increased peasant participation in decision-making. As a result, observers reported a 'drastic' change. Resources began to flow directly to the peasants participating in *ujamaa* villages, with consequent increases in their participation and control over their own lives.

On the bottom line, however, lay the question, Who shall have final power in case of irreconcilable dispute between locals and the representatives of the centre? In terms of final decision, the question becomes fatuous. Of course, the centre will prove more powerful than the local area and will not likely surrender that ultimate power.

But who shall have power over local officials? I conclude with that question.

Conclusion: From Participation to Countervailing Power

Governments can specify in rules the various conditions likely to induce a participatory style by bureaucrats and elected officials. Some of these rules can easily merge into the General Rules of the Civil Service. Legislation can prescribe the forms of local government and of the Party, formulating rules to prescribe bureaucratic behaviour at the point of contact with the client may prove more difficult but no doubt impossible. But how to ensure that the bureaucrat or elected officer in the end follows the pattern not of the British DC with his swagger stick and helmet, but that of the community development worker in old clothes actually making bricks alongside his clients? How does the bureaucrat become the cadre?

The obvious solution lodges the power of discharge or recall of local officials *with the clients*. Civil servants in Britain theoretically serve at the pleasure of their Minister, in Africa, subject to the Public Service Commission. If they served at the pleasure of the local group our earlier rules might possibly work. Constitutions guarantee recall referenda for elected officials elsewhere in the world.

Another possibility would place the recall decision with the local Party organization. That requires several conditions for success. The Party must exist in a meaningful sense, sufficiently separate from government so that it does not risk its reputation and legitimacy whenever it criticizes, or else it cannot police government. It must have sufficient close and real connections with the mass to organize it for Party policies – perhaps against the bureaucracy itself. It must have few internal bureaucratic tendencies so that it can recognize bureaucratic behaviour. No Party in Anglophonic Africa had many of these characteristics, although Tanzania might be headed in that direction. No Anglophonic African country could likely generate truly participatory social change. That seems unlikely without a cadre of leaders, in agreement on the methodologies of decision-making, general development programmes, and a participatory style of work.

Development needs participation. Without it, changed behaviour is unlikely – and development requires changed behaviour by many people. To induce participation, bureaucracy must adopt a participatory style. That requires decentralized decision-making; communicating rules of participation to bureaucrats; new training programmes; changes in income of officials and their living styles; allocating resources to local-level institutions, lodging with them control over both resources and discipline; recruiting more personnel, and therefore new career and reward patterns for bureaucrats; participatory controls by superiors over lower-level administrators; detailed rules concerning the inter-actions between bureaucrats and citizenry; new local-level institutions ensuring at once adequate central and local inputs, and their harmoniza-tion; the development of a local indigenous Party structure not tied to the state machinery; and a sharp reduction in the private sector's power to attract young, well-educated people.

Participation will not develop through marginal tinkering with existing institutions. Ultimately, the legal order must create new local organizations with power of decision over as many aspects of local affairs as possible. Development requires radical changes in social institutions, that is to say, radical changes in power relationships. The national legal order determines and supports those institutions and re-lationships. Local-level participation works by empowering local people to change their own societies. To do that, the legal order must empower them to confront their own local power holders. Paradoxi-cally, that means that the legal order must create countervailing power to the national legal order itself. Apparently, the revolutionary govern-ment in Ethiopia at one point attempted that through peasant commit-tees to bring about land reforms.[162] The *ujamaa* village movement in Tanzania, too, had that potential, although its moment may have passed.[163] Even after a political elite representing the mass of the popu-lation takes power, it stands in constant danger of co-option by existing institutions.[164] More or less autonomous organizations of the people can mobilize popular support to ensure that the leadership remains accountable and undertakes progressive change. In that sense, the struggle always continues.

This problem, of course, expresses the paradox that underlies the very phrase, Law and Development. 'Law' remained as received — static, hierarchical, compartmented, authoritarian. 'Development' means change. It required dynamism, participation, democratic planning. On its face, it seemed quite mad to think that the governing elite would surrender its control over the legal order and the state to favour of the mass. I address that final paradox in the remainder of this volume.

Notes

1. R. Aron, *Progress and Disillusion: The Dialectics of Modern Society* (London: Pall Mall, 1968), p. 4; S.N. Eisenstadt, *The Political System of Empires* (New York: Free Press, 1963).
2. W. Schramm, 'Communication and Change', in D. Lerner (ed.), *Communication and Change in the Developing Countries* (Honolulu: The East-West Center Press, 1967), pp. 5, 16.
3. F.W. Riggs, 'The Dialects of Development Conflict', *Comp. Pol. Studies*, 1, 199 (1968).
4. S.P. Huntingdon, *Political Order in Changing Societies* (New Haven: Yale University Press, 1968).
5. See, e.g., K. Kaunda, in *Zambia Daily Mail* (Lusaka), 1 July 1975.
6. McGregor, *The Human Side of Enterprise* (New York: McGraw Hill, 1960), p. 125.
7. 'Local Development in Africa', Report of a Conference held at the Foreign Service Institute, Department of State, D.C., July 1967, p. 5, quoted in J.R. Finucane, *Rural Development and Bureaucracy in Tanzania* (Uppsala: Institute of African Studies 1974), p. 15. Included in the group making the statement were Ashford, Bienen, Brokensha, Fallers, Foltz, Kilby, Kilson, W. Arthur Lewis, Norman Miller and Zolberg.
8. D.R. Kingdon, *Matrix Organization: Managing Information Technologies* (London: Tavistock, 1973).
9. K. Lewin, *Forces Behind Food Habits and Methods of Change* (Washington D.C.: National Research Council, 1943).
10. R. Lippit, J. Watson, B. Westley, *Planned Change* (New York: Harcourt, Brace and World, 1958).
11. S.D. Alinsky, *Reveille for Radicals* (Chicago: University of Chicago Press, 1946); R.D. DuBois, *Neighbors in Action: A Manual for Local Leaders in Inter-group Relations* (New York: Harper, 1950).
12. W.G. Bennis, K.D. Benne, and R. Chin (eds.), *The Planning of Change* (New York: Holt, Rinehart and Winston, 1961).
13. V.A. Thompson, *Modern Organization* (New York: Alfred A. Knopf, 1964), p. 181.
14. W.G. Bennis, *Beyond Bureaucracy: Essays on the Development and Evolution of Human Organization* [formerly titled *Changing Organizations* (New York: McGraw Hill, 1966), pp. 19-20; see also K. Lewin, *Resolving Social Conflicts* (New York: Harper, 1948), p. 65.
15. See Chap. 8; see J. Zorn, 'Co-operation or Control: The Public Service in a Developing Nation', *Melanesian Law Journal*, 3, 40 (1975).
16. See Chap. 8, 9 above.
17. F.M. Heyward, 'Political Participation and Its Role in Development: Some Observations Drawn from the African Context', *J. Dev. Areas*, 7, 591 (1973) 607.
18. See Chap. 9 above; see United Nations, *Popular Participation in Decision-Making for Development* (New York: United Nations, Sales No. E. 75. IV. 10, 1975), p. 17.
19. See Chap. 13 above.
20. Ibid.
21. See Declaration of Social Progress and Development (UN General Assembly Resolution 2542 (XXIV) of 11 December 1969).
22. J.K. Nyerere, *Freedom and Development* (Dar es Salaam: Oxford University Press, 1973), p. 60; F.G. Burke, in *Proceedings of the Conference on African Local Government Since Independence* (Lincoln, Pa: Institute of African

Government, Department of Political Science, Lincoln University, 1966), p. 41.

23. Nyerere, *Freedom and Development*.

24. L. Cliffe, 'Tanzania – Socialist Transformation and Party Development', in L. Cliffe and J. Saul (eds.), *Socialism in Tanzania: An Interdisciplinary Reader* (Nairobi: East African Publishing House, 1972), p. 266, reprinted from *Africa Rev.*, 1, 302 (1971).

25. See, e.g., United Nations, *Popular Participation*; United Nations, *Popular Participation in Development: Emerging Trends in Community Development* New York: United Nations, Sales No. E. 71. IV. 2, 1971); United Nations Research Institute for Social Development, *Rural Institutions as Agents of Planned Change* (Geneva, 1969-72); ILO, *Participation of Workers in Decisions Within Undertakings* (Geneva: ILO Labour-Management Relations Series No. 33, 1969).

26. Heyward, 'Political Participation'; United Nations, *Popular Participation*, n. 4.

27. This definition is close to what Etzioni calls 'active' participation. A. Etzioni, *The Active Society* (New York: Free Press, 1968); see United Nations, *Popular Participation*.

28. Research Project on Administration for Rural Development, Case Studies in Development: Luombwa Bridge. Nalubi Village, Pilot Agricultural Mechanisation Scheme (PAMS) (Lusaka: National Institute of Public Administration, Cyclostyle, 1972). I have borrowed the idea of contrasting scenarios from J. Zorn, 'Co-operation or Control'.

29. M. Edelman, *The Symbolic Uses of Politics* (Urbana: University of Illinois Press, 1964).

30. F. Lugard, *The Dual Mandate in British Tropical Africa*, 1st ed. (London: Frank Cass, 1962), p. 96.

31. Quoted in A. Creech-Jones [Secretary of State for the Colonies], Opening Address, in Colonial Office, Summer Conference on African Administration, 2nd Session . . . 1948: The Encouragement of Initiative in African Society (African No. 1174 Not for Publication), p. 17.

32. J. Griffiths, Opening Address, in Colonial Office, Summer Conference on African Administration: 4th Session . . . 1951: African Local Government (African No. 1128 Not for Publication), p. 14.

33. A. Creech-Jones, in a speech in 1947; quoted in L.G. Cowan, *Local Government in West Africa* (New York: Columbia University Press, 1958), p. 63.

34. Lugard, *Dual Mandate*, pp. 428-9; see also pp. 79 *et. seq.*

35. Colonial Office Summer School on African Administration, First Session . . . 1947: African Local Government (African No. 1173 CONFIDENTIAL) (London: HMSO p. 125.

36. Ibid., p. 135.

37. But see e.g., U.K. Hicks, *Development from Below: Local Government and Finance in Developing Countries of the Commonwealth* (Oxford: Clarendon Press, 1961); J. Robinson in Cambridge University Overseas Studies Committee, Summer Conference on Local Government in Africa (Cambridge, 1961), pp. 5 *et seq.*

38. Quoted in B.K. Lucas, 'The Dilemma of Local Government in Africa', in K. Robinson and F. Madden (eds.), *Essays in Imperial Government Presented to Margery Perham* (Oxford: Basil Blackwood, 1963), p. 193.

39. Ibid,

40. Lugard, *Dual Mandate*, pp. 85 *et seq.*

41. Creech-Jones, See n. 33.

42. C.A.G. Wallis,'The British Form of Local Government Finds New Adherents',

J.A.A., 4, 68 (1952); Lucas, 'Local Government in Africa'.

43. Nigeria: Eastern Region Local Government Law, 1955 (No. 26 of 1955) 312.

44. S. and B. Webb, *English Local Government: Statutory Authorities for Special Purposes* (London: Longmans, Green, 1922), pp. 453-7.

45. Ibid., pp. 467, 478.

46. Nor in UK: W. Robson, *Nationalized Industry and Public Ownership* (Toronto: University of Toronto Press, 1960).

47. J. Watson, 'The Official in Local Government in the Colonies', *J.A.A.*, 5, 11 (1954): L.P. Mair, 'Representative Local Government as a Problem in Social Change', *J.A.A.*, 10, 11 (1958); R.S. Jordan, *Government and Power in West Africa* (New York: Africana, 1969); 'Local Government in Africa'; M.N. Evans, 'Local Government in the African Areas of Kenya', *J.A.A.*, 7, 123 (1955).

48. Lucas, 'Local Government in Africa'; F.A. Montague and F.H. Page-Jones, 'Some Difficulties in the Democratization of Native Authorities in Tanganyika', *J.A.A.*, 3, 21 (1951); W. Peters, 'Tradition and Change in the Saltpond Sub District of the Gold Coast Colony', *J.A.A.*, 6, 5 (1954).

49. R.S. Burles, 'The Katengo [Barotseland] Council Elections', *J.A.A.*, 4, 14 (1952).

50. Ibid. and see sources cited supra n. 47.

51. H.G. Graham-Jolly, 'The Program of Local Government in Nyasaland', *J.A.A.*, 7, 188 (1955); Ministry for Local Government, Northern Region, Nigeria, 'A Review of the State of Development of the Native Authority System in the Northern Region of Nigeria on the First of January, 1955', *J.A.A.*, 7, 77 (1955).

52. Jordan, *Government and Power*, p. 168.

53. Quoted in T.R. Batten, *Communities and Their Development: An Introductory Study with Special Reference to the Tropics* (London: Oxford University Press, 1957), p. 1.

54. P. du Sautoy, *Community Development in Ghana* (London: Oxford University Press, 1958), p. 22.

55. Ibid., p. 31.

56. Ibid., p. 14.

57. *Kenya: Community Development Organization, Annual Report – 1951* (Nairobi: Government Printers, 1951), pp. 1, 4, 11.

58. Du Sautoy, *Community Development*, p. 11.

59. *Kenya: Report of the Dept. of Community Development* (Nairobi: Gov't. Printer, 1950), p. 1; R.E. Wraith, 'Community Development in Nigeria', *J. Local Administration Overseas*, 3, 92 (1964); T.G. Askwith, *Progress through Self-Help: Principles and Practice in Community Development* (Nairobi: Eagle Press, 1960).

60. See Kenya, *Annual Report; Report of the Dept. of Community Development*, p. 32.

61. Report of the Dept. of Community Development, p. 2.

62. Ibid., p. 3.

63. Kenya, *Report of the Department of Community Development*, p. 23.

64. Du Sautoy, *Community Development*; C. King, *Working with People in Community Action: An International Casebook* (New York: Association Press, 1965), *passim*; Colonial Office, supra n. 31 at 73 *et seq.*

65. Colonial Office, see note 31, p. 25.

66. Ibid., p. 32.

67. C.W. Kindelsperger, *Community Development and Community Organization: An International Workshop* (New York: National Association of Social

Workers, 1961), p. 16.
68. Du Sautoy, *Community Development*; King, *Working with People in Community Action.*
69. Colonial Office, see note 31, p. 87.
70. Ibid., p. 73.
71. P. Marris and M. Rein, *Dilemmas of Social Reform: Poverty and Community Action in the US* (New York: Atherton, 1961); L.J. Cary (ed.), *Community Development as a Process* (Columbia, Mo.: University of Mo. Press, 1970), p. 96.
72. C. Leys, 'Recruitment, Promotion and Training', in G. Hyden, R. Jackson and J. Okumu (eds.), *Development Administration: The Kenyan Experience* (Nairobi: Oxford University Press, 1970), p. 126.
73. D. Dresang, 'The Zambia Civil Service: A Study in Development Administration' (Ph.D. dissertation, UCLA, 1971), p. 202.
74. R. Wraith, *Local Administration in West Africa* (New York: Africana Publishing, 1972), p. 44.
75. D. Conyers, 'Organization for Development – Tanzania', *J. of Administration Overseas*, 13, 438 (1974) 443.
76. *Ghana, Report of the Commission on the Structure and Remuneration of the Public Services in Ghana 1967* [The Mills-Odoi Commission Report] (Accra: Government Printer, 1967), pp. 2-3.
77. Finucane, *Rural Development*, pp. 176-7.
78. *Zambia, Report of the Working Party Appointed to Review the System of Decentralised Administration* (Lusaka: Cabinet Office, 1972), para. 3.5: see also Ghana, *Report of the Commission on the Structure and Remuneration of the Public Services in Ghana 1967* [The Mills-Odoi Commission Report] (Accra: Government Printer, 1967), pp. 2-3; P. Collins, 'The Working of Tanzania's Rural Development Fund: A Problem in Decentralization' in A. H. Rweyemamu and B.V. Mwansasu (eds.), *Planning in Tanzania: Background to Decentralization* (Nairobi: East African Literature Bureau, 1974); Kenya, Memorandum by The Office of the President presented by the Permanent Secretary to the Commission on Local Government, May, 1966 (mimeo), in C. Gertzel, M. Goldschmitt and E. Rothchild (eds.), *Government and Politics in Kenya: A Nation-Building Text* (Nairobi: East African Publishing House, 1969), p. 366.
79. Dresang, 'Zambia Civil Service'; see Chap. 21, below.
80. Zambia: Cabinet Office Circular No. 24 of 1970, 1 May 1970.
81. J. Nyerere, 'Decentralization', in J. Nyerere, *Freedom and Development* (Dar es Salaam: Oxford University Press, 1973), pp. 344, 346.
82. H. Bienen, *Kenya, The Politics of Participation and Control* (Princeton: Princeton University Press, 1974), p. 393; T. Mulusa, 'Central Government and Local Authorities', in Hyden, Jackson and Okumu, *Development Administration*, p. 233.
83. Bienen, ibid., pp. 40, 41.
84. D. Brokensha and J. Nellis, 'Administration in Kenya, A Study of Mbere', *J. Admin. Overseas*, 13, 510 (1974) 517.
85. Ibid., p. 517.
86. Bienen, *Kenya*, p. 41.
87. Burke, *Proceedings*, p. 5.
88. F.G. Burke, 'Research in African Local Government: Past Trends and an Emerging Approach', *Can. J. Af. St.*, 3, 79 (1969), 79.
89. Cambridge University Overseas Studies Committee, Summer Conference on Local Government in Africa (Cambridge, 1961); Speck, in *Proceedings of the Conference on African Local Government Since Independence*, p. 3; H.B. Schiffer, 'Local Administration and National Development: Fragmen-

tation and Centralization in Ghana', *Can. J. Af. St.*, 4, 57 (1970).
90. Speck, *Proceedings*, p. 7.
91. Kenya: Local Government Ordinance, 1948 (Cap. 140).
92. It was a requirement not rigorously observed. S. Humes, 'The Role of Local Government in Economic Development in Africa', *J. Admin. Overseas*, 12, 21 (1973).
93. *Ghana: Second Development Plan, 1959-64* (Accra: Gov't. Printer: 1959), pp. 32-3.
94. *Ghana: The Seven Year Plan: A Brief Outline* (Accra, n.d.), p. 29; all as quoted in Schiffer, 'Local Administration'.
95. Finucane, *Rural Development*, p. 57.
96. Ibid.
97. *Kenya, Report of Local Government Commission of Inquiry, 1966* (Nairobi: Government Printer, 1967), pp. 32-6.
98. Ministry of Local Government, Circular 45/67, August 4, 1967; quoted in Gertzel, Goldschmitt and Rothschild, *Government and Politics in Kenya*, p. 416.
99. T. Mulusa, 'Central Government and Local Authorities', in Hyden, Jackson and Okumu, *Development Administration*.
100. G.K. Kariithi, Address at a Seminar on Local Government at the Kenya Institute of Administration, 6 Dec. 1967 (Mimeo), reprinted in Gertzel, Goldschmitt and Rothschild, *Government and Politician Kenya*, p. 43.
101. Zambia, *Report . . . Decentralized Administration*, para. 8, 10; and see K.J. Davey, 'Local Bureaucrats and Politicians in East Africa', *J. of Admin. Overseas*, 10, 268 (1971); S. Humes, 'The Role of Local Government'.
102. See, e.g. Zambia: The Registration and Development of Villages Act, 1971 (No. 30 of 1971).
103. Zambia: Registration and Development of Villages Act, 1971 (No. 30 of 1971). First Schedule, Sec. 8.
104. Zambia, *Report . . . Decentralized Administration*, p. 87.
105. *Zambia, First National Development Plan, 1966-70* (Lusaka: Government Printer, 1966), p. 18.
106. Zambia, *Report . . . Decentralized Administration*, p. 88.
107. Ibid., p. 89.
108. Ibid., p. 90.
109. Ibid., p. 91.
110. Thoden van Velzen, 'Staff, Kulaks, and Peasants', in Cliffe and Saul, *Socialism in Tanzania*, pp. 138, 137.
111. Nyerere, *Freedom and Development*, p. 8.
112. Ibid., p. 9.
113. Tanzania: 'The TANU Guidelines (Mwongozo wa TANU)', *The Nationalist* (Dar es Salaam) 22 Feb. 1971; also in 8 Mbioni (Dar es Salaam) 4 (1971); I Mazungumzo (Michigan) 59 (1971).
114. See, e.g., Batten, *Communities and their Development*; Du Sautoy, *Community Development*; King, *Working with People*; Kindelsperger, *Community Development*.
115. Lugard, *Dual Mandates*, p. 148.
116. L. Cliffe and G. Cunningham 'Ideology, Organization and the Settlement Experience in Tanzania', in Cliffe and Saul, *Socialism in Tanzania*, p. 53; see also R. Apthorpe, *Rural Co-operatives and Planned Change in Africa* (Geneva: UN Research Institute for Social Development, 1972).
117. Kenya, Memorandum by the Office of the President presented by the Permanent Secretary to the Commission on Local Government, May, 1966 (mimeo), in Gertzel, Goldschmitt and Rothschild, *Government & Politics in Kenya*, p. 209.
118. Bienen, *Kenya*, p. 36.

119. Ibid., p. 37.
120. Dresang, 'The Zambia Civil Service'.
121. Cliffe, 'Tanzania', p. 207.
122. K. Kaunda, 'Message from the President', in UNIP, *National Policies for the Next Decade, 1974-1981* (Lusaka: Government Printer, 1974).
123. Nyerere, *Freedom and Development*.
124. S. and B. Webb, *The Development of English Local Government: 1689-1835* (London: Oxford University Press, 1963), p. 112.
125. G. Hunter, *The New Societies of Tropical Africa* (London: Oxford University Press, 1962).
126. G. Myrdal, *Asian Drama: An Inquiry into the Poverty of Nations* (New York: Pantheon, 1968); Hunter, ibid., p. 274.
127. Kenya: 'African Socialism and Its Application to Planning in Kenya', *Sessional Paper No. 10* (Nairobi: Government Printer, 1965).
128. Finucane, *Rural Development*, p. 59.
129. Zambia: Cooperative Societies Ordinance, 1948 (Cap. 217, § 24).
130. M. Kideri and M.C. Simpson 'Co-operatives and Agricultural Development in the Sudan', *J. Mod. Af. Studies*, 6, 509, 514 n (1968); R. Golebrowski, 'Social and Economic Changes in a Delta Village in the Period 1952-1966', *Africana Bulletin*, 14, 69, 86-87 (1971).
131. Finucane, *Rural Development*, p. 68.
132. Myrdal, *Asian Drama*, p. 1334.
133. R. Golebrowski, 'Social and Economic Changes', p. 85.
134. NIPA, 'Visit to Chepepo and Mukbwe Wards', in C. Gertzel (ed.), *The Political Process in Zambia: Documents and Readings* (Lusaka: University of Zambia, 1973), p. 271.
135. Cliffe and Cunningham, 'Ideology'.
136. Ibid., p. 126.
137. Ibid.
138. United Nations, *Popular Participation*, p. 25.
139. R. Hewman, 'African Leadership in Transition – An Outline', *J.A.A.*, 8, 117 (1956) 117.
140. Thoden van Velzen, 'Staff, Kulaks and Peasants', pp. 153-79.
141. See, e.g., St Clair Drake and T.P. Omari (eds.), *Social Work in West Africa* (Accra: Dep't of Social Welfare and Community Development, 1963).
142. R.E. Wraith, 'Community Development in Nigeria', *J. Local Admin. Overseas*, 3, 92 (1964) 96.
143. See, e g., M. Zinkin, *Development for Free Asia* (London: Catto and Windus, 1956), p. 64.
144. L. Cliffe and J. Saul, 'The District Development Front in Tanzania', in Cliffe and Saul, *Socialism in Tanzania*, 302, 323.
145. See note 113.
146. L. Cliffe, 'Tanzania – Socialist Transformation and Party Development', in Cliffe and Saul, *Socialism in Tanzania*, pp. 266, 274.
147. R.E. Wraith, 'Community Development'.
148. Zambia, see note 78, p. 104.
149. M.R. Mujwahuzi, 'Is Popular Participation a Viable Alternative: The Case of Rural Water Supply in Tanzania?' (MS, 1975).
150. R.B. Raup *et al.*, *The Improvement of Practical Intelligence* (New York: Harper, 1950), pp. 25, 34.
151. K.C. Davis, *Administrative Law Text* (St Paul: West, 1972), p. 157.
152. See, e.g., Mass. Gen. Laws Ann., ch. 404, 6.
153. Raup, *et al.*, *Practical Intelligence*, p. 23.
154. Ibid.
155. This point has been made frequently in conversation by Professor Raymond Penn.

156. Finucane, *Rural Development*, p. 175.
157. K. Chlao, *Agricultural Production in Communist China, 1949-1965* (Madison: University of Wisconsin Press, 1970), p. 57.
158. Tanzania: Act No. 6 of 1969.
159. D. Austin, *Politics in Ghana, 1946-1960* (London: Oxford University Press, 1964); S.K.B. Asante, 'Law and Society in Ghana', *Wisc. L. Rev.,* 1113, 1118 (1966).
160. Finucane, *Rural Development*, p. 93.
161. Collins, 'The Working of Tanzania's Rural Development Fund'.
162. M. Ottaway, 'Social Classes and Corporate Interest in the Ethiopian Revolution', *J. Mod. Af. St.,* 14, 469, 480 (1976).
163. See, e.g., J. Boesen, *Report on Ujamaa Villages in a Tanzanian Region* (Copenhagen: Institute of Development Research, 1974).
164. See Chap. 20 below.

Part Five

LAW-MAKING INSTITUTIONS

17 LAW AND STAGNATION IN AFRICA: THE FAILURE OF THE LAW-MAKERS

Still, Africa stagnated. The rich and powerful grew fat, and the poor died young. New governments produced clouds of radical rhetoric, but attended to the rich and powerful, not the poor. Explanations for their failure abounded: insufficient trained manpower, physical and financial resources, adverse international power configurations, the CIA, and many more. Nevertheless, the law-makers had some choice. The world ever changes, ever containing a few potential alternative development strategies. State activity determines which a polity will follow. That countries with seemingly equal resources developed so differently (China and India, Sweden and Greece, the United States and Mexico) evidenced the potential for choice. Why did most African governments only marginally alleviate poverty and oppression?

Philip P. Heck wrote that 'the fundamental truth is that each command of the law determines a conflict of interests; it originates in a struggle between opposing interests, and represents as it were the resultant of these opposing forces . . . It operates in a world full of competing interests, and, therefore, always works at the expense of some interests. This holds true without exception.'[1] Choosing what law to retain or introduce means favouring this or that group or strata.

Government differs from the state. The state consists of the institutions within which its employees function: courts, legislatures, bureaucracies, parastatals, armies, police, gaols. At any given time it embodies a particular legal order. Through that legal order, it bolsters a particular socio-economic system, and therefore the system's allocations of power and privilege. The state includes government, which consists of actors with formal policy-making powers, (Ministers, Parliaments and Supreme Military Councils). A revolutionary government by definition comes to power in opposition to the existing state-supported system and classes. The day after the revolution, the new government rules through a state that supports its enemies. The African revolutions needed to change the legal order and the state to help those that the new governments claimed to represent. When African law-makers left the law pretty much the same, they inevitably favoured the beneficiaries of imperial law, mainly foreign entrepreneurs and white colonialists.

Every constitution today asserts in rolling periods that law-makers should govern in 'the people's' interests, as one man, one vote, implies. They grandiloquently assert the great democratic liberties — free speech, free press, freedom from arbitrary power. By not changing institutions, African law-makers failed in their constitutional obligations.

Some plead despair: perhaps choice existed at independence, but soon the political elite became a 'bureaucratic bourgeoisie,' the new ruling class. Ruling classes rarely initiate radical change to favour the mass. Therefore, this book talks of pie in the sky.

Of course whenever the political elite allies with the economic rulers, it does not initiate much change. But they did not ally themselves at Independence. Black rulers seated themselves in the thrones of power over the resistance of the white rulers, while asserting an intense desire for rapid change to promote popular interests. I cannot conceive Nkrumah and Kenyatta, Kaunda and Obote and Azikwe as hypocrites.[2]

By and large, however, they failed in their stated aims. Failing, they created the conditions which today make radical change under the present leadership in most Anglophonic African countries doubtful. Yet in time, whether by peaceful succession, military *coup* or revolution, new leaders arise without ties to the ruling class. Then the questions of this book will once again demand answers. Unless the new leadership then acts differently than the first generation, history will repeat itself.

We must learn from experience. Why did the bright promises of Independence fade? What might law-makers do to prevent the quick squelching of revolutionary ardour? Why did African law-makers default on their pledges of development? I discuss this almost pervasive failure of law-makers in these concluding chapters. Here I examine alternative explanations for failure.

I Why The Lawmakers Failed

Africa relapsed into a nineteenth-century plague. Society, man's creation, seemed beyond control.

The early nineteenth century saw the mass enter politics. It promised government in the interests of the majority, but simultaneously developed large-scale organization, bureaucracy and narrowed decision-making bases. Bureaucracy betrayed the bright democratic promise. Eighteenth-century thinkers 'worked on a series of assumptions: that a society such as the American and its form of government by the state were bound together inseparably; that both could be made more perfect; and hence that the progress of society and progress of the state were one and the same ... Eighteenth-century optimism was based on legislative reform, conscious political judgement, and action. Revolution was the servant of the legislature and the legislature was the servant of the people.'[3] The nineteenth and twentieth centuries overwhelmed that sanguine temper. The world man created defied man's control.

The Western post-war era began in the spirit of a new Enlightenment. Conscious man, technically competent, and shed of ideology, would solve all emergent social problems by pragmatic social engineering. The United Nations, its specialized agencies, and the aid programme of the developed nations, would instantly eliminate underdevelopment. Vietnam stands a monument to the failure of tension-managers and power brokers in the United States; poverty, frustration and stagnation attest their failure elsewhere.

Both Marxist and elitist theory purported to explain why democratic man lost control of his own creature, the seemingly democratic state. Marxism's key variable became the class struggle. The 'essence' of law lies in 'the expression of the will of specific, politically dominant classes.'[4] They control the state, 'an organization of the authority of the dominant machine', with whose aid 'the exploiter classes in exploiter society crush and oppress the toiling masses. In its activity, the state — realizing the will of the dominant class to which authority belongs — defends and guarantees the interests of that class.' It achieves these ends through law, 'binding rules of conduct (chiefly in the form of legislation) established by the dominant class, which assures observance thereof by the entire force of its apparatus of constraint: the state'.[5] Addressing the bourgeoisie, the Communist Manifesto shouted loud and clear: 'Your law is merely the will of your class, erected into legislation — a will whose content is defined by the material conditions of the existence of your class.' In Africa, law failed the masses precisely because it expressed the will and hence secured the interests of their oppressors. The Marxist explanation advocated a revolutionary solution: Replace the government of the economic ruling class by a government of the working class. Elitist explanations arose quite explicitly to counter that revolutionary demand.[6] Elitist theory alternatively explained 'democratic' governments' failure to rule in the interest of the mass.[7] An elite, a small group of people with power to decide, rather than an economic class, inevitably control things. The elite of course runs the government in its own interests, not those of the mass.

Marx's ultimate solution, communism, would eliminate classes. The elitists in effect told Marx that his solution solved nothing. The mass cannot run governments. All states inevitably have governors and governed. Modern man lives in societies with presidents, prime ministers, princes, potentates and popes, admirals and generals, Senates,

Congresses and Parliaments. Michels put it uncompromisingly: 'It is organization which gives birth to the dominion of the elected over the electors, of the mandatories over the mandators, of the delegates over the delegators. Who says organization, says oligarchy.'[8] In any bureaucratically organized society, a few governors inevitably control the many. Governors infrequently become saints, kings rarely philosophers. They use power in their own interests, not those of the mass. The more the state plans, the more powerful become the planners.[9] Social engineering begets power, and power tends to corrupt. Social engineering through law, like law generally, must favour some and not others. Governors inevitably use power to aggrandize themselves.[10]

The yea-sayers then devised various theories that celebrated elite domination. Democracy worked not despite elites, but because of them. Pareto argued that elites monopolized competence. Elites circulated, the able displacing the incompetent so any person might join the golden circle. Electoral democracy forced elites to serve the masses or else face displacement. Marx characterized history as class struggle, Pareto as the graveyard of aristocracies.

The American pluralists advanced an alternative model. No elite has *general* power; each separate elite, business, political, military, social and so forth, has its discrete sphere of influence and interest. Competition for resources and power limits the power of each.[11] Marxism begat an ideology of revolution, elitism, an ideology for pluralist democracy.[12]

In Africa, independence seemingly recreated nineteenth-century Europe: sudden mass entry into politics, and centralized governmental bureaucracy. That contradiction elicited both Marxist and elitist analyses of the African circumstance. Some understand Marxist and elite theories not as explanations but ideal-types. So perceived, Marxism seemingly predicts that political governors will always comprise an economic ruling class. Elitist theory does not demand this unity. Academics spent inordinate amounts of print debating whether African polities had a ruling class or an elite.[13]

In this, the elitists clearly had the edge. The colonial masters constituted a ruling class. They manned the controls of both economy and government. At independence, however, expatriates remained masters of the economy, while black Africans held political power. Very few blacks had yet entered the economic ruling class. The new rulers obviously did not represent a non-existent black capitalist class, nor did they represent the imperialists whom they had just displaced. If Marxism as ideal type required a unity of interest between political and economic rulers, Africa did not measure up. Elite theory, however, accommodated the situation.

The characteristics of the mass, too, seemingly matched elite theory. It perceives an 'atomized' mass, whose members cannot organize themselves for concerted political action. Instead, each person lives his own private life, tending his own row of cabbages. His life touches only his family, neighbours and workmates. Such narrow confines blind the individual's view of public affairs. Unlike the elite, he lacks a vantage point over the social system. 'The members of the mass are caught in their own milieu in which it finds itself and creates a new environment. Only the elite in the command posts of society gains an overall view . . . The man in the mass . . . has no prospects of his own; he fulfills the routines that exist.'[14] That seemingly described the African condition.

The question, whether Africa matched elitist or Marxist ideal-types, only plagues some academics. The pain of Africa needs explanations and solutions. It, not ideal-types, commands our attention. Explaining and solving the troubles of the population requires that we solve problems and so use and test grand theory. Marxism and elite theory in this view become not dogmas but alternative potential guides to action.

The British transferred political control to a small group of Africans but still commanded economic affairs. Why did the new African governors do so little to induce institutional change in favour of the mass? I suggest six alternative explanations. Different varieties of elite theory inspire the first three. The next two arise from crude versions of Marxism. Finally, I suggest an institutionalist version that uses the concept of the political elite, but then suggests why African political elites and the economic ruling class finally lay together.

1. *Social Engineering and Oligarchy.* Elites inevitably use power to their own advantage. Society can best defend itself by forbidding them to engage in social engineering at all, organizing the economy instead through facilitative law and the free market.[15]

2. *'Good Men Make Good Government'.* Elites will inevitably govern. One can only ensure that they include good men, and insulate them from the hurly-burly.[16]

3. *The Bargaining Model.* Laws emerge from a 'complex chain of group bargains,' made between various elites. Every law thus reflects the relative power of various interest groups within the system.[17]

4. *The Values of the Law-Makers.* Government lacks the will to achieve

mass development, whatever its rhetoric. Progressive governments have progressive values, reactionary governments, reactionary values. Since African governments do not seek radical change, they must have re-actionary values. That analysis instructs us only to find law-makers with new values — that is, good men. It defies falsification, because it asserts that the leaders had secret 'values' or ideologies that varied from their public statements. One cannot publicly falsify an explanation by secret data.

5. *The Social Background of Decision-Makers.* Elites drawn from peasant or working-class backgrounds will have the values of the mass. Elites drawn from chiefly or entrepreneurial classes will have values and attitudes that favour those classes. Expatriates favour expatriates, Africans favour Africans. Their backgrounds explain elite values and therefore behaviour. This only explains elite behaviour within their existing arenas of choice. It does not enquire about the existing instit-utions. Any adequate explanation must of course include the system of recruitment to political office as one, but not the sole variable.

II The Institutionalist Explanation

An alternative explanation draws upon our general law and develop-ment model.[18] It accepts that some social roles concentrate dispro-portionate law-making power. It argues that the behaviour of law-makers, like that of other role-occupants, depends upon their arenas of choice, and their reasons for choosing within those options. Following the model of Chapter 4, I here examine (1) formal legal controls; (2) non-legal constraints and resources; and (3) ideologies, domain assumptions and other subjective factors.

A. *Formal Legal Controls on the Behaviour of Law-Makers*

Law-makers possess uniquely broad *de jure* discretion. Hans Kelsen built this proposition into his hierarchy of norms.[19] The Grundnorm (or Constitution) prescribes very general rules for the conduct of law-makers; these become more specific through the actions of legislature, ministries and agencies, courts and tribunals, and ultimately sheriffs, police, bailiffs and jailors.

The British tradition of Parliamentary supremacy expressed the ultimate constitutional ambiguity. An English judge once said that Parliament can do no wrong, although it can act very foolishly. In this tradition, the law-maker violated no law if he, like a bump on a log, did nothing. Every African constitution continued this tradition.

Zambia's provided that 'the legislative power of the Republic shall vest in the Parliament of Zambia which shall consist of the President and a National Assembly.'[20] With minor exceptions, it did not require Parliament to enact any laws. Like its British model, the Zambian Parliament might constitutionally ignore development problems. That constitution did, however, constrain Parliament's power, since it could act only 'subject to the provisions of this Constitution'. Without a requirement of affirmative legislative action formal judicial controls did not reach Parliamentary inaction. In any event, judicial sanctions only marginally affected law-making or law applying. I discuss these in Chapter 18.

B. Capacity To Effect Change

Despite the absence of formal constitutional norms requiring the leadership to institute change, the dominant constitutional theme required government to rule in the majority's interests. Law-makers in Africa of course knew their duty and had opportunities to comply. They lacked capacity to conform in three respects.

1. *Decision-Making Institutions and the Range of Choice.* A special set of institutions affects the choices of law-makers. Problem-solving requires discretionary choices.[21] Decision-making systems aim at solving problems. Their structure and processes necessarily exclude part of the total range of potential issues, explanations, solutions and data. They therefore define the decision-makers range of choices.[22] African law-making institutions tended to limit law-makers to incremental change. I unpack this proposition in Chapter 19.

2. *Resources: Men, Material, Knowledge.* Resources of course limit desired change: people (especially high level manpower), funds and knowledge never come in sufficient quantity. Everywhere, African governments frontally assaulted the first two. Universities sprang up like grass in the early rains.[23] (But did students ever learn much that aided development?) I do not here pursue the question of education, nor how African states tried to recapture and redeploy the economic surplus.[24] In Chapter 21 I briefly discuss new knowledge-generating institutions.

3. *Feedback Institutions: Access and Scope.* How government learns about its own performance (feedback circuits) helps to explain whom government favours in its law-making and enforcing activities. These

circuits determine whose troubles, whose perception of the data, whose explanations and whose proposed solutions government will consider, and hence whom government favours. Formal rules define some of these circuits, such as Parliament and the civil service. Others exist informally, for example, officials' chitchat over sundowners at the Club. They all provide information for making decisions. Perhaps more than any other single factor, they determine to whose demands and interests a government will respond. Chapter 21 considers the African case.

C. The Interests of the Law-Makers

Precisely because formal African constitutional commands controlled law-makers only weakly, the constraints and rewards of their institutional environments did so the more strongly. Many of these institutions offered direct incentives of money and power. People do not act without motivation. Law-makers too need motivation to either act affirmatively or do nothing (of course also a way of action). Every contemporary economic system grants power and privilege to some, while denying it to others. Any systemic change inevitably affects the power structure. A political elite will change the economic system, therefore, only to the extent that it has the will to change the economic power structure. Law-makers' motivations depend partly upon economic, political and social rewards. If the economic ruling class supplies those rewards, or the economic interests of political elites coincide with those of the economic ruling class, political elites and the economic ruling class ally. Only rarely do such allies commit hari-kari.

The Law of the Reproduction of Institutions teaches that ignoring institutions probably perpetuates them, and with them the existing power structure. Therefore, *a political elite will not likely change economic institutions unless their perceived interests contradict the interests of the economic ruling class.* Law will not produce development if political governors ally with economic generals. Chapter 20 examines the economic interests of political elites.

D. Ideologies

A fourth variable in decision lies in the law-makers' ideologies (or explanations of the world, or grand theories). Ideology alone never successfully explains decisions, for other constraints always press too vigorously. Ideologies, however, clearly filter law-makers' choices. They of course usually relate to the economic and other interests of law-makers and their constituencies, for only occasionally does anyone profess a grand theory that opposes his self-interests. Grand theories explain the world. Some explain underdevelopment in terms of existing social, political and economic institutions. Others accept those institutions. Governors who do not explain poverty and oppression by existing institutions will not likely try to change them radically, whatever their claimed devotion to the poor and oppressed.

I do not discuss here the question of the best ideologies for development,[25] but only now how political recruitment systems inevitably favour one or another stratum. Classes and groups have definable interests. Because interest relates to ideology, class and group correlate somewhat with ideology. When African recruitment processes selected leaders from particular classes or groups, they to that extent selected the ideologies that controlled decisions and thus prejudiced the range of potential decisions. Chapters 19 and 21 discuss recruitment.

Conclusion

I now explain the failure of law-makers in Africa:

1. A political elite will change existing social, political and economic structures to bring about development favouring the mass if:

   a. Formal, sanctioned prescriptions require them to effect such change; and

   b. The decision-making institutions can actually generate decisions for such change; and

   c. The political elite has sufficient resources of manpower, material and knowledge to accomplish such change, and

   d. The feedback institutions give access and transmit messages from strata or classes favourable to such change; and

   e. The perceived interests of the political elite contradict the interests of those who hold economic power; and

   f. The ideologies of the political elite identify existing institutions as the causes of underdevelopment.

2. Few formal prescriptions that defined affirmative behaviour by law-makers existed in African constitutions; nor did Africa have many effective formal legal controls over the law-makers' behaviour.

3. Decision-making institutions in Africa had structures that led to incremental, not radical institutional change.

4. Resources of manpower, material and knowledge for the purposes of development remained very low.

5. African feedback channels mostly transmitted messages favourable to the maintenance of the *status quo.*

6. The perceived interests of African law-makers motivated them to retain the *status quo* with only incremental changes.

7. African political recruitment systems selected political leaders whose ideologies did not explain underdevelopment in institutional terms.

This explanation argues that the realities of decision-making and representation explain law-making better than paper constitutions. Constitutional norms relate to activity as do ordinary laws. Our explanation, if valid, should work for military as well as constitutional regimes.

African elites took power within particular institutional contexts, which limited their options to those that resonated harmoniously with the existing economic and social order. The decision-making systems of any social system limit choice to actions that will likely maintain the machine, not redesign it. Within existing decision-making systems the new African elites made rational choices. They thus usually maintained the machine, instead of changing it. That reinforced the existing economic ruling classes, still mainly white and foreign. The state in Africa did not constitute the conscious executive committee of the bourgeoisie; it merely behaved like one. I can therefore propose a more general explanation for the failure of law-makers almost everywhere to change things, whatever their rhetoric:

1. The institutions of any ongoing society more or less integrate with and support each other; that is what makes a social system a *system.*

2. The decision-making sub-system of government more or less integrates with the rest of society.

3. The decision-making sub-system of government will therefore generate decisions that support other societal institutions.

4. A change in role-occupants, *ceteris paribus,* does not change the behaviour of the role, and hence does not change how the decision-making institution works.

Law-makers in Africa at independence did not consciously serve the interests of expatriate economic elites. Many sincerely advocated 'development', and grew dismayed at their own failure to achieve it. That failure need not have occurred. Man creates his institutions, and he can amend them. Lenin put it apocalyptically: the Revolution must first smash the old state machinery. Some agree because they suspect the allegiances of the old bureaucracy. The old machinery plainly needs radical change, but not necessarily for that reason. Development needs decision-making structures that can induce rapid, fundamental change. The problem lies in the decision-making institutions, not merely the decision-makers.

To remodel society, rather than accept the constraints imposed by its present structure, however, elites must know that institutions structure choice, and that law can within limits change institutions. Development requires an ideology that so advises law-makers. The particular perspectives of individual leaders or cadres can change the course of events. Individuals do matter. Good men do not necessarily make good governments, but leadership ideologies do affect political choice. How else to explain why Tanzania, Kenya and Uganda, with independence of the same cloth, in only a decade look so different?

Notes

1. P. Heck, 'Interessinjurisprudenz in Recht und Staat in Geschichste und Gegenwart' (1933), reprinted and translated as 'The Jurisprudence of Interests', in M.M. Schoch (ed. and tr.), *The Jurisprudence of Interests: Selected Writing of Max Rumelin et al.* (Cambridge, Mass: Harvard University Press, 1948), pp. 29, 34.
2. But cf. F. Fanon, *The Wretched of the Earth*, C. Farrington, tr.: (New York: Grove, 1963), p. 128.
3. L. Krader, *Formation of the State* (Englewood Cliffs, N.J.: Prentice-Hall, 1968), p. 2.
4. O.S. Ioffe and M.D. Shargorodskii, 'The Significance of General Definitions in the Stating of Problems of Law and Socialist Legality', translated in *Soviet Law and Government* 2, 3 (1963).
5. S.A. Golunskil and M.S. Strogovich, 'Theory of the State and Law in Soviet Legal Philosophy', in H.W. Babb (tr.), *Soviet Legal Philosophy* (Cambridge, Mass: Harvard University Press, 1951), p. 366.
6. H.S. Hughes, *Consciousness and Society: The Reorientation of European Social Thought, 1890-1930* (New York: Knopf, 1958)
7. G. Parry, *Political Elites* (London: George Allen and Unwin, 1969); T. Bottomore, *Elites and Society* (London: Watts, 1964).
8. R. Michels, *Political Parties: A Sociological Study of the Oligarchical Tendencies of Modern Democracy*, E. and C. Paul, tr. (Glencoe, Ill.: Free Press, 1915), p. 401.
9. J. Stone, *Social Dimensions of Law and Justice* (Stanford: Stanford University Press, 1966), pp. 761, 766.

10. F.A. von Hayek, *The Road to Serfdom* (Chicago: University of Chicago Press, 1944).
11. R.A. Dahl, *A Preface to Democratic Theory* (Chicago: University of Chicago Press, 1956).
12. Parry, *Political Elites*, p. 25.
13. See, e.g., P.C. Lloyd, *The New Elites of Tropical Africa* (London: Oxford University Press, 1966).
14. Parry, *Political Elites*, p. 54.
15. See Chap. 5.
16. See Chap. 2.
17. See L. Friedman and J. Ladinsky, 'Social Change and the Law of Industrial Accidents', *Col. L. Rev.*, 67, 50, 72 (1967).
18. See Chap. 4 above.
19. H. Kelsen, *General Theory of Law and State*, A. Wedberg, tr. (New York: Russell, 1961).
20. Zambia: Independence Constitution, Art. 57.
21. See Chap. 3.
22. See Chap. 11.
23. See Chap. 2.
24. A. Seidman, *Planning in Sub-Saharan Africa* (New York: Praeger, 1974); A. Seidman (ed.), *Natural Resources and National Welfare: The Case of Copper* (New York: Praeger, 1975).
25. But see above, Chap. 3.

18 JUDICIAL CONTROL AND FUNDAMENTAL FREEDOMS*

The government of independent Africa took office under constitutions that colonial civil servants wrote. The draftsmen profoundly distrusted the new African politicians. To control the new men, the Colonial Service invoked two contradictory principles. First, they knew that the actual business of governing falls not to elected politicians but to bureaucrats and judges. They created constitutional institutions that so far as possible insulated bureaucratic and judicial appointments from political influence. Second, they relied upon the paraphernalia of eighteenth century constitutional theory, especially free elections and fundamental human rights. In this chapter, I examine the appellate courts in their role as 'sentinels of liberty'.[1]

Orthodox Western constitutional theory feared government itself. It made the judiciary chief protector of liberty against government encroachment. Courts do better as brakes than accelerators of government,[2] a function that implies that that government governs best that least governs. Africa needed accelerators more than brakes, and some feared that judicially implemented fundamental freedoms would intolerably clog state initiatives. Fundamental freedoms, however, actually perform indispensable functions for social change. A free citizenry tells government about the consequences of its programmes; they supply it with new ideas beyond the imagination of Party or bureaucracy; they keep the government aware of public sentiments.

Most African constitutions made the judiciary responsible for protecting fundamental freedoms.[3] That protection rested on two bases: prosecutorial and judicial independence, and a zealous defence of freedom.

I Independent Prosecutors and Judges

To ensure that courts would ride herd on the politicians, the colonial constitution-makers insulated prosecutors and judges from political interference and lodged their appointment with expatriate officials. They failed, however, to protect fundamental freedoms.

*I am indebted to Professor B. O. Nwabueze for comments on an earlier draft.

A. The Director of Public Prosecutions

The British Director of Public Prosecutions (DPP), like other common law public prosecutors, enjoys the broadest discretion of any public official.[4] The DPP will likely prosecute official malefactors only if free of political pressures. In the United States, the difference in prosecutorial vigour between the regular Justice Department officials and the Special Prosecutors in the Watergate crimes evidenced that prosecutors there sometimes succumbed to political pressures. In Africa, too, they succumbed despite constitutionally guaranteed independence.

The Zambia Independence Constitution, for example, specifically provided for a DPP. He had unlimited power to institute criminal proceedings against any person, in any civil court 'in which he considers it desirable to do so,' explicitly free of external control,[5] save judicial.[6] The DPP became a public office,[7] for which the independent Public Service Commission, not the political authorities, had powers of appointment and removal.[8] Like judges, the government could remove the DPP from office only for reaching age sixty, incompetence or misbehaviour.[9] A special tribunal of three judges or ex-judges had to try the question of removal. In Zambia at Independence, only non-Africans qualified.[10] Analogous provisions graced almost all the independent constitutions.

Widespread corruption and the absence of prosecutions against high-level officials demonstrated the failure of the constitutional scheme for the DPP.[11] The DPP did not institute a single prosecution for the massive election scandals in the Nigerian 1964 election,[12] nor for the abuse of preventive detention in Ghana by low-level officials[13], nor for the torture of political prisoners repeatedly charged against police in Uganda, Kenya and Zambia. Nowhere did the independent DPP fully perform his anticipated constitutional function. Formal independence does not isolate an official from society. Prosecutors want to become judges, or perhaps ministers. Almost never would they prosecute the very politicians who appointed and would hopefully promote them.

B The Independent Judiciary

No more autonomous a legal system exists than one which judges government itself. To achieve that, the independence constitutions created a formally independent judiciary.

During all but the last years of the colonial regime, the judges had no judicial independence, but held office at the Crown's pleasure.[14] (In Britain, by contrast, only both Houses of Parliament could remove a judge.) The African Constitutions drawn up at independence went beyond both the English and the colonial positions. Uganda could appoint a puisne judge only on the recommendation of an independent, constitutionally-defined Judicial Service Commission. It could only remove him for incapacity or misbehaviour, after hearings before an investigating judicial tribunal and the Privy Council.[15] Usually, only former judges could serve on the Judicial Service Commission – at Independence, usually only whites. Typically, the Chief Justice became Chairman.[16] Constitutions invariably prescribed the Commission's absolute independence.[17] In Zambia, only the President could remove a commissioner during the commissioner's term of office, and then only for incapacity or misbehaviour.[18] The judiciary with such awesome independence consisted mainly of British judges. The few African judges had British training and, usually, experience in the Colonial Judicial Service.

These elaborate provisions for a formally independent judiciary mainly continued in subsequent constitutions. Variations usually increased presidential appointing power.[19] Procedures for removal remained, save in Ghana and Malawi,[20] as did the term of judicial appointment.[21] In fact, remarkably little overt political tampering with the judicial process occurred. B.O. Nwabueze, after an exhaustive review, concluded that 'with but a few aberrations, the affirmation of faith in the independence of the judiciary by Commonwealth African presidents has been matched by their action. Except in Ghana under Nkrumah, there has been no attempt to employ the courts as an instrument in the power struggle. Nor has the colonial conception of the courts as a machinery for the enforcement of policy based upon "an over-riding necessity for the preservation of good government" been continued.'[22] In constitutional cases, at least, politicians had precious little need to intervene. The judges in Africa supinely upheld laws against constitutional challenge.

II The Judicial Review of Legislation

In Westminster itself, parliamentary supremacy and an unwritten constitution denied judicial power to declare legislation unconstitutional. Once written, however, the Westminster model implied very different judicial powers. Parliamentary supremacy bowed to the constitution. The courts had final authority, for after enactment any constitutional challenge to the law fell before the courts.[23] Such cases always search the reality of judicial independence. The 'fundamental human rights' provisions sought to protect fair trials, free speech and press and freedoms from slavery, arbitrary arrest and unreasonable search and seizure.[24] Historically, the political process forged these rights; without exception, they arose in political trials. A challenge to a law on these grounds challenged government at its most sensitive nerve-end, its capacity to stay in power.

Constitutional review of legislation arises in one of two contexts. In one, plaintiff claims that the action of the administration lies within the scope of a particular statute, but that the statute on its face or as construed violates constitutional standards. In the other, he claims that although the statute may not generally violate the constitution, this particular action does. Only the first involves judicial control over lawmakers; in the second case, the judiciary controls the executive. Here I discuss only the former, and hence deal only with constitutional review of statutes on their face or as construed.

A. Judicial Response to Claims of Unconstitutionality

In African civil liberties cases that presented any real choice within the constitutional language, courts almost invariably favoured the governmental action. Only where the constitutional language permitted no choice did the judges uphold the claim for freedom. But with individual property rights, courts usually invalidated governmental action. I first examine the various fundamental human rights provisions.

1. *The Constitutional Provisions.* The fundamental rights provisions of the African constitutions found their prototype in the 1960 Nigerian Constitution.[25] Some of these rights admitted no exceptions. For example, the Zambian Constitution provided that 'No person shall be held in slavery or servitude.'[26] A court called upon to construe such provision need only determine whether the particular facts involved 'slavery' or 'servitude'.

Other human rights provisions seemed more ambiguous. Most contained derogation clauses. The provisions first broadly protected the right. A succeeding section then derogated from it by defining circumstances in which government might deny that right. For example, although the Zambian Constitution provided that 'No person shall be required to perform forced labour,'[27] the succeeding section immediately emasculated the first. This second section provided that the expression 'forced labour' excluded labour required by a court's sentence, a prisoner's 'reasonably necessary' labour for hygiene or prison maintenance, labour of a member of a 'disciplined force' in his duties, labour during war or emergency, and 'any labour reasonably required as part of reasonable and normal communal or other civic obligations'. Self-evidently, judges construing 'forced labour' might range far wider than with 'slavery' or 'servitude'.

The derogation clauses became most ambiguous with protections of private property and from unlawful searches and seizures, freedom of conscience, freedom of expression, and freedom from discrimination. The freedom of expression provision in the Zambian Constitution began with a grand declaration:

> 22(1) Except with his own consent, no person shall be hindered in the enjoyment of his freedom of expression, that is to say, freedom to hold opinions without interference, freedom to receive ideas and information without interference . . . and freedom from interference with his correspondence.

That broad grant immediately shrivelled:

> 22(2) Nothing contained in or done under the authority of any law shall be held to be inconsistent with or in contravention to this section to the extent that the law in question makes provision −; (a) that is reasonably required in the interests of defence, public safety, public order, public morality, or public health . . . and except so far as that provision or, as may be, the thing done under the authority thereof is shown not to be reasonably justifiable in a democratic society.

Since one could easily hang any law restricting freedom of expression on one of the hooks of defence, 'public safety, public order, public morality or public health', the issue always turned on the phrase, 'reasonably justifiable in a democratic society'. This became a leitmotif in the five human freedoms provisions earlier mentioned.

2. *Judicial Response to Constitutional Challenges.* Relatively few African cases tested these provisions. In general, when the constitution limited the scope of construction, courts voided statutes that plainly violated it. For example, in *Ubingira* v. *Uganda*,[28] the court summarily held that a statute[29] empowering the Minister to send individuals into exile within Uganda violated a constitutional provision[30] permitting internal deportations only of 'persons generally or a class of persons'. In Kenya, the Supreme Court[31] denied that a 'court' included a magistrate at his discretion imposing collective punishment without hearing each individual defendant,[32] where the constitution forbade any compulsory taking of

property without compensation except on orders of a 'court'.

Cases involving the derogation clauses almost uniformly went for the government. The Nigerian court sustained a left-over colonial sedition statute that prohibited any statement that subjected government to discredit or ridicule, regardless of its truth or falsity, or its effect on public order. The court justified the statute on the ground that a democratic society could take reasonable precautions to preserve public order,[33] relying on the 'dangerous tendency' test long since discarded in the United States.[34]

In *Ross-Spencer* v. *Master of the High Court*,[35] a Swaziland statute,[36] also a colonial legacy, empowered a court to administer and distribute by customary law the intestate of any unmarried person who himself or whose parent belonged to an African sub-equatorial 'aboriginal race of tribe'. The Constitution contained the usual guarantee against discrimination, which it defined as

> different treatment to different persons attributable wholly or
> mainly to their respective descriptions by race, tribe, place of origin,
> colour or creed whereby persons of one such description are subjec-
> ted to disabilities or restrictions to which persons of another such
> description are not made subject, or are accorded privileges or advan-
> tages which are not accorded to persons of another such description.[37]

The court sustained the statute, holding the discrimination 'reasonably justified in a democratic society'[38] under Swaziland conditions.

Courts, however, invariably protected substantial property rights. In Nigeria, they blocked compulsory acquisitions;[39] in Kenya, they protected Asians' trade and market stall licences.[40] The list did not stretch far because few people litigated constitutional cases. When they did, courts gave patterned responses. If the constitution plainly covered the case, courts enforced the constitution. When courts had to construe constitutional language, they found against claims of freedom and for claims of property.

B. Explanations

The literature provides three alternative explanations for judicial decision-making: positivist, political science and process or realist. The positivist model holds that 'a judge decides his cases by the somewhat mechanical application of legal rules which he finds *established* in the legal system. They are, in this sense, *binding* on him completely apart from his own judgement as to their fitness for his purpose.'[41] This legalistic[42] model explains appellate court decisions by the notion of the law as a seamless web, within which judges decide cases that involve seemingly ambiguous or non-existent law through 'higher order' principles logicially derived from the corpus of the law itself.[43]

In contrast, both the political science and process models hold that judges can never decide cases involving ambiguous law by resorting only to the law itself.[44] Rules, like the words which compromise them, have a core meaning and a penumbra. Reasonable men can agree that the statute subsumes some states of affairs ('core meaning'), but will disagree about others (the 'penumbra'). I denote cases involving the core meaning, 'clear' cases, and ones involving the penumbra, 'trouble' cases. Judges in trouble cases must determine whether the statute or other rule in question covers the particular case. In such cases at least two alternative constructions of the words seem plausible. The court cannot avoid choice between them and to that extent must legislate. It determines not what the law is (about that reasonable men differ) but what it ought to be.

Why did judges in Africa almost always decide trouble cases concerning fundamental freedoms for government? The rules of law cannot provide an answer, for in such cases by definition they produced only ambiguity and hence required choice.

The political science model explains that judges choose as they do through their personal 'values'. Glendon Schubert states that

one can understand and explain — at least, on a first level of initial apprehension — everything about judicial decision-making on the basis of attitudinal similarities and differences in the decision-making group . . . Both legal norms and legal facts are viewed as functions of attitudes towards the public policy issues in a case . . . Why do judges differ in their attitudes? Judges differ in their attitudes because they have come to accept some beliefs, and reject others, as the result of their life-experience. What a judge believes depends upon his religious and ethnic affiliations; his wife; his economic security and his social status; the kind of education he has received, both formally and informally, and the kind of legal career he has followed before becoming a judge. His affiliations, marital and socio-economic status, education and career will in turn by largely influenced by where he was born, to whom, and when . . . There is still a third level of possible analysis. Why and how does it matter where a judge was born to whom and when? Why and how, in other words, are judicial attributes determine by cultural differences? . . . The analysis of cultural differences, in both

primitive and complex political systems, is directed towards an
attempt to understand and explain how and why different judges
come to have different attributes.[45]

This explanation disturbs lawyers who fondly believe in governments of
laws not men, and therefore that the judge's values should not control
the decision. Happily, Schubert's explanation fails, for at least three
reasons. Sometimes judges make decisions opposed to their ostensible
value-sets. For example, racist, district court judges in the southern
United States sometimes judged favourably to desegregation. Second,
it asks only, Why do judges choose as they do within the constraints
and resources of their environment? but not, Why those constraints and
resources? Finally, it becomes circular, since the evidence of the values
that explain decisions becomes the decisions themselves.[46]

C. Appellate Courts as Decision-Making Systems

A third explanation considers appellate courts as decision-making
systems whose procedures define the inputs, conversion processes and
feedbacks that in turn limit the range of potential decision.[47]

1. *Inputs. a. Selecting issues.* Courts cannot function as 'sentinels of
liberty' unless cases before them raise constitutional issues. Surprisingly,
very few constitutional law cases appear in the African law reports,
because of the adversary system.

Courts in Africa, as in other common law systems, depended upon
litigants to raise issues before them. They had no independent super-
visory power, and until some litigant brought an action, they could do
nothing to protect fundamental freedoms no matter how egregious the
infringement. Only private litigants brought constitutional law cases.
The government, of course, never attacked itself, nor did the purportedly independent African DPPs.

Private litigation costs money. Few Africans had the money to employ competent counsel. In the United States, only wealthy private
litigants or clients of some private association of moral entrepreneurs,
the NAACP or the American Civil Liberties Union, for example, typically raise constitutional issues. Such associations hardly existed in
Africa. Even so, most petititoners in freedom of expression cases had
support from opposition political groups.[48]

b. Permissible construction of the constitution. In statutory and
constitutional construction alike, the over-riding prescription to judges,

H.L.A. Hart's most important rule of recognition,[49] the core of Dean Pound's 'taught law', commands judges, where they can, to apply existing law. When competent speakers of the language must agree that a particular set of facts falls under the language of a law judges *must* apply it as written.

Every African case that upheld a claim for freedom in Africa fell under this rule. For example, the Nigerian constitution contained the usual *nulla poena sine lege** provision: 'No person shall be convicted of a criminal offence unless that offence is defined, and the penalty therefore is prescribed, in a written law',[50] without any derogation clause. The Nigerian court easily reversed a criminal conviction for violating unwritten customary law.[51]

In *Ross-Spencer,*[52] the Swaziland case, the statute based discriminatory treatment on ethnic origins. In the derogation clause, the constitution provided that the prohibition against discrimination did not apply if the alleged discrimination 'was reasonably justifiable in a democratic society'. The appellant in effect urged the court to construe the provision as though it contained a further clause: 'and a discrimination based on ethnic origin cannot find reasonable justification in a democratic society if the discrimination concerns the probate of estates as between classes or groups of people living under different social or economic systems'. The court held the contrary; vagueness of the constitutional provision opened wide the door to construction, permitting counsel and court to devise alternative constructions.

c. Rules of evidence. Sound decisions about what the law ought to be must rest upon accurate knowledge about society[53] and the probable consequences of the rule at issue. The data that enter decision-making control *pro tanta* the ultimate decision. The kind of evidence a trial court ordinarily hears concerns only the question, whether a claimed set of historical events actually occurred. Did the defendant run down the plaintiff on the Great East Road at 12.30 on January 17? Did the brakes of the defendant's car work properly? Did he keep a good look-out? Did the plaintiff fracture his right tibia?

Long judicial experience developed rules to ensure that the trier of fact consider only data related to these narrow questions. They excluded hearsay, opinion and irrelevant matter. In deciding what the law ought to be, however, the relevant data for a legislative committee goes beyond courtroom evidence, including statistics describing tenden-

---

* No punishment without law.

cies in the society, sogiological and political analyses, and other 'legislative facts'. The rules of evidence discourage the use of these legislative
facts in trials. For example, a lawyer cannot easily present survey data
based upon the hearsay statements of many informants and enumera-
tors.

The political science model of the judicial process argues that judges
decide on their values, not data. Those values, however, operate upon
the judge's view of the case. In *Ross-Spencer*, the court justified its
decision that the statute at issue did not discriminate on racial grounds
by defining Swaziland society:

> The population of Swaziland comprises two classes of people, one
> living under a more sophisticated European system, with a fully
> developed concept of the individual ownership of property and the
> right to dispose of it after death; the other living under tribal cus-
> toms, in which the basic system of property is that it belongs to the
> family and not to the individual members of the family and is not
> transmitted by will . . . To this may be added that, unlike the
> urbanized parts of the population, the Swazis in tribal areas mainly
> live on the produce of their cattle and ploughing fields and their
> farming is not conducted on a cash basis but is subsistence
> farming . . .
>
> The difference between these two systems is the basis of the
> differentiation contained in s. 72 (now 68) of the Administration
> of Estates Proclamation.[54]

The court assumed that race defined these two economic classes, which
justified the statute's racial discrimination. In fact, of course, by 1977
race no longer separated those who lived under 'European' and under
'tribal' customs. Some Swazis had university educations, serving as
ministers, permanent secretaries, lawyers, doctors, teachers and university lecturers. If the rules of evidence exclude the information that
judges need, inevitably they fall back upon their acculturated perceptions, domain assumptions and values.

Lawyers and judges in the United States devised a few rather
awkward devices to supply courts with necessary social and economic
data. The 'Brandeis Brief', the most common, summarized social data
about the matters in issue for the appellate court.[55] No lawyer even
attempted such a brief in Africa.

d. *Personnel.* The Colonial Service had only one formal requirement for a judge: Membership in either the United Kingdom or the Irish Bar. In fact, judicial appointment required some service on the colonial legal staff. The independence constitutions perpetuated these requirements. A Justice of Appeal or a High Court justice in Zambia, for example, must have either (a) held high judicial office, or (b) seven years' eligibility as advocate or solicitor in some part of the Commonwealth or in the Irish Republic, or (c) eligibility as solicitor and seven years' experience as Resident Magistrate or lawyer in the Colonial Service.[56] At Independence, no Africans in East and Central Africa could meet these standards for either the High Court or the Court of Appeals of any country. (In West Africa, a few did; all had served in the colonial legal systems.) A statute relaxed these rules in 1969; thereafter three Zambians became judges in Zambia. Consider, for example, three of the serving judges of the East African Court of Appeals in 1970: Sir Charles Newbold, the President: born in New York of British parents, educated in Barbados and at Oxford and Gray's Inn. Formerly Legal Secretary for the East African High Court; justice and Vice President of the Court of Appeal; member of the Legislative Assembly of Kenya for thirteen years immediately prior to independence and through the Mau-Mau period. Mr Justice Eric J.E. Law: born in Burma, educated at Wrekin College, at Cambridge and the Middle Temple. Crown Counsel in Nyasaland; Resident Magistrate, Tanganyika; judge, Zanzibar; and judge, Tanganyika. Mr Justice John Farley Spry: educated at Perse School Cambridge and at Cambridge University. Sometime Assistant Registrar of Titles and Conveyances in Uganda, Chief Inspector of Land Registration in Palestine; Registrar General of Tanganyika, of Kenya, and again of Tanganyika; member, Legal Service Commission; and Puisne Judge of the High Court of Tanganyika. Between them, they had sixty-four years of service in the colonial administration before independence.[57]

The colonial judicial officers came from the same class and social backgrounds as most Colonial Service Officers: 'good' family, public school, Oxbridge. One cannot reliably predict from the antecedents of a particular individual his probable world-view or ideology. (Friedrich Engels, the co-founder of Marxism and a passionate socialist, owned a prosperous Birmingham factory and rode to the hounds regularly on Thursdays.) But the political science model rightly holds that most members of a class or group follow ideologies consistent with their interests. Persons deeply socialized into a particular bureaucracy acquire that bureaucracy's convictions. Judges socialized into the Colonial Service and the Colonial Judicial Service tended towards the

Service's authoritarian ideals, and its injunction to support the government of the day.

Most appellate judges in Africa received their education in England, and joined the Bar there.[58] Analytical positivism dominated English legal education. In English universities, as late as the 1950s

> Legal philosophy continued to be concerned primarily with the linguistic problems involved in the analysis of doctrinal issues; books about precedent and evidence still tended to be collections of rules about precedence and evidence. The same was true for statutory interpretation. There was little attempt to discover the fundamental bases of precedent, evidence or statutory interpretation or the role they played in the legal process . . . International law was still generally taught independently from international relations and diplomatic history. Constitutional law was still divorced from politics and political science; and administrative lawyers still regarded themselves as having little concern with the problems of the civil service or public administration. Meanwhile, in widely studied subjects like tort and contract, there was still remarkably little research in practical problems — whether it was scope of arbitration, the development of commercial practices, the growth of contract outside the courts, or the impact of insurance on the law of torts.[59]

In England, 'the majority of law teachers appear[ed] not to regard it as their task to go outside the traditional doctrinal frame work used by English judges in rationalizing their decisions'.[60] Judges educated only in the Inns of Court had, if anything, even a narrower training. Their education ensured the narrowest sort of legalistic law-finding.

Judges' private interests obviously affect their decisions. Judicial independence purports to insulate judges from such incentives. Trial judges, however, always hope for advancement to a higher bench. Even appellate judges have their own reference groups, whose reactions inevitably affect their decisions. Robert Martin puts it sharply:

> We must also ask whether the whole concept of the independent judiciary is illusory. Judges are members of the ruling class by birth or assimilation (regardless of what that class may be) and hired employees of the State who depend ultimately on the coercive power of the executive for the enforcement of their decisions. To disregard these conditions in an attempt to be totally independent would be meaningless.[61]

The political elite in Africa included the judges. Their interests favoured the *status quo*. Paper guarantees of judicial independence failed to transform them into vigorous civil libertarians. After independence, expatriate judges had particular disabilities, increasing their sensitivity to the political winds. The judiciary everywhere, as the most fragile branch of government, depends upon popular approbation. As Stalin supposedly said of the Pope, judges do not command many divisions.

Expatriate judges in Africa knew the tenuousness of their power. An expatriate member of the East African Court of Appeals, defending that court's legalistic opinions, said that to address policy questions openly would lead to the withdrawal of jurisdiction over politically sensitive cases.[62]

2. *Conversion Processes.* Nobody knows much about how judges decide cases. We know a good deal about their justifications, for appellate judges typically write opinions. Courts write opinions mainly for other judges and lawyers, to persuade them that the decision fits within prevailing justification rules. A common law judge who like the ancients appealed to the Oracle at Delphi would become a laughing stock.[63]

Justifications can control decision-making. A judge must be a fool if he cannot justify his decision pursuant to prevailing rules. Opinions require the judge to justify his conclusion, and so constrain his decision-making. They define the conversion processes of appellate courts.

a. *Opinion styles in Africa.* One can distinguish three periods of opinion writing in Britain and the United States. The first, which Karl Llewellyn called the Grand Style, ended in the latter half of the nineteenth century. In cases of first impression, judges employed frank appeals to policy. In the celebrated case of *Priestly* v. *Fowler*,[64] Lord Abinger said, 'It is admitted that there is no precedent for the present action . . . We are therefore to decide the question upon general principles, and in so doing we are at liberty to look at the consequences of a decision the one way or the other.'

The Formal Style replaced such candid policy statements with legalistic justifications. Formal opinions resolved coherencies by reasoning only from legal cases and statutes, not social data. Opinion styles in East Africa followed this pattern.[65] The first period lasted until the 1920s and after. Terse opinions rarely cited extensive authority; many disputes really involved 'clear case' matters, where the appellate court corrected an obvious error by the local magistrate. For example, in *Re A Reference* (1915)[66] the admissibility into evidence of an unstamped promissory note fell for decision. The court had to construe ambiguous language both in section 35 of the Indian Stamp Act and in the Secretary of State's Order applying that Act to East Africa. In 1904, Judge Hamilton had decided in favour of admissibility, saying only that 'any instrument to which the first provision of section 35 applies may be admitted into evidence on payment of the duty with or without penalty as the Court thinks fit in the circumstances of the case.[67] He did not attempt to justify his decision. Eleven years later, the same judge, deciding the same question, came to precisely the opposite answer: 'Now, it is clear that the first provision to section 35 does not apply to promissory notes, for a promissory note is expressly made an exception to the proviso. The law on this point appears, I regret to say, to have been incorrectly stated by myself so far back as 1904 . . .'[68] Only that the law suffered ambiguity became clear. Yet Judge Hamilton justified neither his earlier decision nor its reversal. This extraordinary absence of justification probably reflects two factors. First, East Africa lacked adequate law-books. Second, lay District officers served as magistrates,[69] who rarely questioned the decision of professional appellate judges. The early opinions needed only to announce the law, not to justify decisions to lower courts and lawyers.

Increasing sophistication of opinions after 1930 probably reflects the changing composition of the judiciary and the Bar. The 1950s brought more lawyers, more legally qualified Resident Magistrates and better libraries. The earlier brief opinions gave way to the Formal Style.

In the United States, but not in England, a third sort of opinion the Realist Style, emerged in the 1930s. Influenced by American legal realism, judges addressed policy issues frankly, as for example, in the desegregation cases.[70]

Independence in Africa created a new situation. A President of the East African Court of Appeals wrote that a 'blind adherence to precedent' when circumstances changed 'and the needs of the community [were] vastly different' could do harm that outweighed any enhanced certainty in the law. 'When a precedent has outlived its usefulness, [it is better] to say so and the community [will] have the benefit of a clear-cut change in principle, of a decision based on modern requirements or based on a sounder logic . . .'[71] That a precedent no longer met 'modern requirements' required considering its social consequences and justifications in similarly candid terms.

The new situation therefore demanded a return to policy-oriented justifications. In a period of rapid social, political and economic change

African states required what Weber called substantively rational law-making, not legalism. Planned development required rules that consciously sought to meet substantive demands. Only then could justifications of opinions match the imperatives of modern Africa. The Formal Style leaves the social utility of decisions to chance. Resting on the fallacy of the law as a gapless web, forbidding explicit judicial policy choice even in troublesome cases, the Formal Style inevitably balances opinions on Holmes's inarticulate premise, arising from the personal, undisclosed predilictions of the deciding judge. Formal Style opinions do not force the judge to articulate his domain assumptions and therefore confront them. The more ambiguous the rule, the wider the scope for policy choice. Constitutional norms contain more ambiguities by far than most law. In constitutional decisions, the Formal Style permits the widest play for the judge's personal 'values' or biases. Despite the cloud of chop-logic in Formal Style opinions, they readily mask decisions expressing the judge's sentiments, not reason.

b. The Style of Justification in Constitutional Cases. The principal technical adviser in drafting the Ghanaian 1960 Constitution defined the 'formal principles governing Ghana's republican constitution':

1. It is a mechanism, and all its operative provisions are intended to have the precise effect indicated by the words used — no more and no less.

2. It is drafted on the assumption that the words used have a fixed and definite meaning and not a shifting or uncertain meaning; that they mean what they say and not what people would like them to mean; and that if they prove unsuitable they will be altered formally by Parliament and not twisted into new meaning by 'interpretation'.

3. It leaves no powers unallocated; those not reserved to the people are exercisable by the authorities established by it . . .

4. It assumes that legitimate inferences will be drawn by the reader, but that he will not transgress the rules of logic — as by drawing an inference from one provision which is inconsistent with the express words of another provision.

5. It needs to be read as a whole and with care.[72]

These rules summarized the Formal Style of justification. That style has both virtues and faults. In clear cases, where reasonable men could not dispute the meaning of words, the Formal Style requires judges to enforce the law as it plainly reads.[73] The clearly untrue assumption that words always have only one meaning, with sharp boundaries, however, blinds the search for ambiguity. Insensitive to ambiguity, courts too often decide cases as if ambiguous language had only one possible meaning.

For example, in a Kenyan case[74] the police compelled the accused to testify under the Exchange Control Ordinance. They prosecuted, using his own earlier testimony to convict him. He appealed on the ground that the provision violated the Kenyan constitutional provision that 'No person who is tried for a criminal offence shall be compelled to give evidence at his trial'. He lost. The plain meaning of the constitutional provision only prohibits compelling the accused to testify *at his trial*. Any compulsion against the accused occurred at the Exchange Control hearings. The word 'trial', however, might include the proceedings for compelling the evidence as well as the courtroom proceedings[75] — an alternative construction the court never mentioned. The court thus decided on far-reaching policy, seemingly unaware that it did so. Policy-making in ignorance that one makes policy only accidentally makes good policy.

Re Akoto[76] also reflects the disastrous consequences of Formal Style justifications in constitutional cases. There, the Ghanaian court upheld the constitutionality of the Preventive Detention Act. Petitioner relied in part upon Article 13 of the Constitution, requiring the President upon assumption of office to declare his adherence to the propositions:

That freedom and justice should be honoured and maintained . . .

That no person should suffer discrimination on grounds of . . . political belief.

That subject to such restrictions as may be necessary for preserving public order, morality or health, no person shall be deprived of freedom of religion, of speech, of the right to move and assemble without hindrance or of the right of access to courts of law.

The Chief Justice justified his decision on linguistic grounds:

It will be observed that Article 13(1) is in the form of a personal declaration by the President and is in no way part of the general law of Ghana. In other parts of the Constitution where a duty is imposed the word 'shall' is used but throughout the declaration the word used is 'should'. In our view the declaration merely represents the goal which every President must pledge himself to attempt to achieve. It does not represent a legal requirement which can be enforced by the courts.[77]

The Court therefore rather surprisingly concluded that an article of the Ghanaian Constitution did not form part of the law of Ghana. It ignored alternative possibilities, for example, to create out of Article 13 a presumption that the President would adhere to his oath, and by construction to conform the statute to the Constitution.

The Formal Style demonstrated its vacuity when construing the sybilline phrase, 'reasonably justifiable in a democratic society'. *Patel* v. *Attorney-General*[78] attacked a Zambian Exchange Control Regulation[79] that empowered an authorized officer who reasonably suspected that a postal article contained contraband to seize it without warrant. An officer seized some packets containing illegally-exported Zambian currency. On trial, accused objected that their admission into evidence violated a constitutional prohibition against unlawful searches and seizures. That constitutional provision contained the usual derogation clause, 'reasonably justifiable in a democratic society'. Plainly, the phrase's ambiguity required a judge to determine policy: What scope for freedom from search and seizure did a 'democratic' society require? In *Patel*, the judge quoted disapprovingly Humpty Dumpty in *Through the Looking Glass*: 'When I use a word . . . it means just what I choose it to mean — neither more or less.' He then combed the dictionary to define the word 'democracy' as 'government by the people'. He cited one Indian and two American cases emphasizing that a free government requires freedom of speech and press but added that 'all this is, however, subject to the security of the state (see *American Communications* v. *Douds*),[80] so that some degree of control is permissible in the interests of security but only so far as is reasonably necessary for that purpose.' He cited *Entick* v. *Carrington*[81] for the proposition that general search warrants conflicted with democracy, and so also a warrantless search. He then referred to the American cases that distinguished between a search of premises and of vehicles, and between a search for ordinary criminal purposes and a search for contraband. He then analogized a parcel in the mails, and a moving vehicle, both of which move. On this basis, he held Regulation 35 'justifiable in a democratic society' without regard to the importance of private communications in a democracy.

Obviously, an equally 'logical' argument could reach an opposite conclusion. Why the judge came to the one conclusion and not the other does not appear in the decision, despite its great length. The Formal Style maximized the space for the judge's personal values to roam.

Conclusion

Decisions in African constitutional cases find their explanations in the following salient features of the decision-making system. First, constitutional cases depend upon the initiative of private litigants or the DPP. That initiative emerged only fitfully, confronting the courts with constitutional issues only rarely. Second, derogation clauses arguably justified almost any law. Third, the legalistic Formal Style system of justification prevented the courts from openly addressing policy issues, and therefore permitted them to choose upon their personal, subjective, unexamined 'values'. Fourth, the rules of evidence precluded their consideration of 'legislative facts'. Finally, their constitutional decisions reflected the decision-making system: in clear cases judges adhered to the literal language of the constitution; in cases with room for discretionary choice, their value sets led them to find for the government in civil liberties cases and for the private property owner in individual property rights cases. No clearer parallel to the Supreme Court of the United States during the period prior to the great Court revolution of 1937 could exist.

The constitutional arrangements of the independent African countries held that the courts should stand as 'sentinels of liberty'. This idea necessarily failed, not (as is frequently assumed) because of inadequate judicial independence, or because African politicians perverted the judicial process. Rather, it died because of the institutional structure of African appellate courts.

Notes

1. A. Grove, 'The Sentinels of Liberty? The Nigerian Judiciary and Human Rights', *J. Af. L.*, 7, 152 (1963).
2. See Chap. 13.
3. Ghana, Tanzania, and Malawi did not include specific human rights provisions in their independence constitutions.
4. K. Davis, *Discretionary Justice: A Preliminary Inquiry* (Baton Rouge: Louisiana State University Press, 1969), pp. 188 *et seq.*; see *Brack* v. *Wells*, 184 Md. 86, 90, 40 A.2d 319, 321 (1944); R. Jackson, *The Machinery of Justice in England* (Cambridge: Cambridge University Press, 1972), pp. 136-49.

5. Zambia: The Independence Constitution, art. 53 (1964).
6. Ibid., art. 125(10) Any case that the DPP believed involved 'general considerations of public policy' he should bring to the attention of the Attorney-General and abide his instructions. Ibid., art. 53(b). The constitution declared the AG in turn free of any authority (Ibid., art. 52(4)) except judicial. Ibid., art. 125(10).
7. Ibid., art. 53(1).
8. Ibid., art. 114(3).
9. Ibid., art. 118(2).
10. With the appointment of three Zambians to high judicial office in 1970-72, this changed.
11. See Chap. 10.
12. See M. Vickers, 'Background to Breakdown in Nigeria: The Federal Elections of 1964-65', *Afr. Q.*, 7, 106 (1967); P. Rake, 'Nigeria After the Elections: What Happened', *Afr. Today*, 12, 5 (1965); D G. Anglin, 'Brinksmanship in Nigeria: The Federal Elections of 1964-65', *Int'l J.*, 20, 173 (1965). The author personally observed many of these violations.
13. S.K.B. Asante, 'Law and Society in Ghana', *Wisc. L. Rev.*, 1113, 1115 (1966), reprinted in T.W Hutchinson (ed.), *Africa and the Law* (Madison: University of Wisconsin Press, 1968); W.B. Harvey, 'Post Nkrumah Ghana: The Legal Profile of a Coup', *Wisc. L. Rev.*, 1096, 1103-07 (1966), reprinted in ibid.
14. *Terrell* v. *Sec'y of State for the Colonies*, 2 Q.B. 482 (1953). Despite the absence of formal guarantees of judicial independence, the colonial regulations provided that any proposal to dismiss a judge had to be referred to the judicial committee of the Privy Council.
15. Uganda: The Independence Constitution, art. 92 (1962); see Nigeria: The Independence Constitution, arts. 106, 117; Sierra Leone: (Constitution) Order-In-Council, 2d Schedule; Ghana: The Independence Constitution, art. 41(3); see generally T.O. Elias, *Ghana and Sierra Leone: The Development of Their Laws and Constitutions* (London: Stevens, 1962), p. 136. Later constitutions omitted appeal to the Privy Council. Kenya: The Independence Constitution, art. 173; Malawi: The Independence Constitution, art. 77.
16. Zambia: The Independence Constitution, art. 100. Expatriate judges were, however, frequently on contract with a six-month termination clause.
17. Ibid., art. 104(4).
18. Ibid., art. 104(2c)
19. Ghana: The Republican Constitution, art. 44(1) (1960) (Presidential appointment power); Tanzania; The Interim Constitution, art. 57(2) (1965) (Presidential, after consultation with Chief Justice); Malawi: Proposals for a Republican Constitution 12 (1966) (Presidential, after consultation with the Judicial Service Commission); Nigeria: The Republican Constitution art. 112(1) (1962) (by Prime Minister).
20. B.O. Nwabueze, *Parliamentary and Presidential Constitutions in Africa* (forthcoming); Ghana: The Republican Constitution, art. 45(3) (as amended by the Constitution Amendment Act, 1964, s.6) (Presidential power to remove judges at will); Malawi, Proposals for a Republican Constitution (proceeding before National Assembly).
21. Nwabueze, *Parliamentary and Presidential*. The six-month termination clause for expatriate judges has never been invoked in Africa.
22. Ibid.; but see Y.P. Ghai and J.P.B.W. McAuslan, *Public Law and Political Change in Kenya: A Study of the Legal Framework from Colonial Times to the Present* (Nairobi: Oxford University Press, 1970).

23. There were no 'constitutional' courts, as in West Germany and Italy.
24. Zambia: The Independence Constitution, Chap. III (1964).
25. T. Franck, *Comparative Constitutional Process* (Dobbs Ferry, N.Y.: Oceana, 1968), p. 6.
26. Zambia 'Independence Constitution', art. 16(1).
27. Ibid., art. 16(2).
28. [1966] E.A. 306 (U).
29. Uganda: Deportation Ordinance (Cap. 46).
30. Uganda: The Independence Constitution, art. 28(3) (c) (1962).
31. *Muhuri v. Serebi Ole Hampei*, S.C. Kenya Cir. 1021/64.
32. Kenya: Stock and Produce Theft Act, c. 355, s. 15(1) (c).
33. *Obi v. DPP* [1961] All N.L.R. 458.
34. *Schenck v. United States*, 249 U.S. 47 (1919).
35. Swaziland: Civ. App. No. 1 of 1971, dated 17 April 1972; see A. Aguda, 'Discriminatory Statutory Provisions and Fundamental Rights Provisions of the Constitutions of Botswana, Lesotho and Swaziland', *S.A.L.J.*, 89, 299 (1973).
36. Swaziland: Independence Constitution, art. 15(3).
37. Ibid., art. 15(3).
38. Ibid., art. 15(4).
39. *Lakanmi v. Att'y Gen.* (West Nigeria) SC 58/59 of 14 April 1970.
40. E.g. *Shah Vershi v. Transport Licensing Board* [1970] E.A. 631.
41. P. Weiler, 'Two Models of Judicial Decision-Making', *Can. Bar. Rev.*, 46, 406, 409 (1968).
42. D.M. Trubek, 'Max Weber on Law and the Rise of Capitalism', *Wisc. L. Rev.*, 720, 736-39 (1972).
43. Ibid., pp. 730-51; see also Chap. 2 above.
44. See generally W.J. Chambliss and R.B Seidman, *Law, Order and Power* (Reading, Mass: Addison Wesley, 1971), p. 120; R.B. Seidman, 'The Judicial Process Reconsidered in the Light of Role-Theory', *Mod. L. Rev.*, 32, 516 (1969).
45. G. Schubert (ed.), *Judicial Behaviour: A Reader in Theory and Research* (Chicago: Rand, McNally, 1964).
46. See above, Chap. 2.
47. See above, Chap. 11.
48. *Obi v. DPP*.
49. H.L.A. Hart, *The Concept of Law* (Cambridge: Clarendon Press, 1962).
50. Nigeria: The Federal Constitution, art. 22(10) (1963).
51. *Aoko v. Fagbemi*, 1961 All N.L.R. 400.
52. Swaziland, see note 35 above.
53. O. Holmes, *The Common Law* (Boston: Little, Brown, 1881), p. 1.
54. Swaziland, see note 35 above.
55. See generally C. Auerbach, L. Garrison, J. Hurst and S. Mermin, *The Legal Process* (San Francisco: 1961), pp. 99-130; C. Vose, 'The National Consumer's Council and the Brandeis Brief', *Midwest J. of Pol. Sci.*, 1, 267 (1957); C. Wyzanski, 'A Trial Judge's Freedom and Responsibility', *Harv. L. Rev.*, 65, 1281 (1952).
56. Zambia: The Independence Constitution, art. 99(C).
57. *Who's Who In Kenya, 1963-65* (n.d.); Kenya: *1966 Staff List* (Nairobi: Government Printer, 1966).
58. In Botswana, Lesotho and Swaziland, they tended to be educated in South Africa.
59. B. Abel-Smith and R. Stevens, *Lawyers and the Courts: A Sociological Study of the English Legal System: 1750-1965* (Cambridge, Mass.: Harvard Uni-

versity Press, 1967), p. 372.
60. Ibid., p. 368.
61. R. Martin, *Personal Freedom and the Law: A Study of Socialist State Administration* p. 55 (Nairobi: Oxford University Press, 1974).
62. In conversation with the author, December 1969, Dar es Salaam.
63. Chambliss and Seidman, *Law, Order and Power*, p. 118.
64. 3 Mees. & Wels. 1 (Exchequer, 1837).
65. R.B. Seidman, 'The Style of Appellate Opinions in East Africa: A Comment', *E. Afr. L. Rev.*, 3, 189-201 (1970).
66. *E. Afr. L. Rev.*, 6, 45 (1915).
67. *Kanji* v. *Admin. Perez Din, E. Afr. L. Rev.*, 1, 61 (1904).
68. *E. Afr. L. Rev.*, 6, 45 (1915).
69. See Chap. 13.
70. *Brown* v. *Board of Education*, 347 U.S. 483 (1954).
71. Sir C. Newbold, 'The Values of Precedents Arising from Cases Decided in East Africa as Compared with those Decided in England', *E. Afr. L. Rev.*, 2, 1, 9 (1969).
72. F. Bennion, *Constitutional Law of Ghana* (London: Butterworth, 1962), p. 111; see S. Gyandeh, 'Principles of Judicial Interpretation of the Republican Constitution of Ghana', *Univ. of Ghana L.J*, 3, 33 (1968).
73. See Hart, *The Concept of Law*.
74. *Republic* v. *El Mann*, 1969 E.A. 357, 360 (High Court, Kenya).
75. See *Miranda* v. *Arizona*, 384 U.S. 486, 86 S. Ct. 1602, 16 L. ed. 2d 694.
76. [1961] *Ghana L.R.* 523.
77. Ibid., p. 533.
78. Selected Judgements, Zambia, No. 33 of 1968, 111.
79. Zambia: Exchange Control Regulations, 1965. Sec. 35.
80. 340 U.S. 268 (1951).
81. *St. Tr.*, 19, 1030 (1695).

19 CONSTITUTIONAL LAW FOR DEVELOPMENT

One reason for the failure of African law-makers to induce development, lay in the weaknesses of their central decision-making institutions. Constitutions purport to define those institutions. This chapter examines African constitutions as charters of decision-making, and begins by proposing a methodology of constitutional law.

I The Inbuilt Bias of Constitutional Arrangements

Two different lenses for studying constitutions yield equally different images. The classical view sees the state as an impartial framework for social struggle. Our secondary school civics textbooks explain that the people elect legislatures, who enact laws; the neutral, perfectly flexible civil service and the executive implement them. Constitutions must restrain the momentary political victors from destroying the supposed neutrality of the system. Constitutions limit power.[1] In the words of Professor de Smith,

> I am very willing to concede that constitutionalism is practised in a country where the government is genuinely accountable to an entity or organ distinct from itself, where elections are freely held on a wide franchise at frequent intervals, where political groups are free to organize and to campaign in between as well as immediately before elections with a view to presenting themselves as an alternative government, and where there are effective legal guarantees of basic civil liberties enforced by an independent judiciary; and I am not easily persuaded to identify constitutionalism in a country where any of these conditions are lacking. These are, I think, modest standards.[2]

The state represents the consensus of all of us,[3] a neutral framework peaceably to contain social strife.

A contrary view, the anti-classical, argues that constitutions ineluctably embody value choices. Karl Loewenstein writes:

> We have not yet begun to investigate the ontological causality between the form of government a constitution endorses and the socio-economic structure of the society to which it is applied.

378

The inquiry is hampered by still existing residues of the naive optimism of the eighteenth century that a functionally well-constructed constitution can adjust peacefully to any power conflict. That much can be learned from the crude materialism of the Soviet-orbit constitutions; viz that a definitely chosen socio-economic pattern requires a commensurate institutionalization of the power situation. The Communists realized that not every constitution can accommodate any form of a specific constitutional order. The concept that the constitution, confined to the jurisdictional determination of authority, can be 'neutral' and 'objective' toward the power process is as much a by-product of liberal relativism as is the concept that the written constitution itself is a child of liberal rationalism. In the light of our — admittedly limited — historical experience, it seems likely that an inner congruity exists between constitutional form and substance.[4]

The anti-classical perspective, far from viewing the state as neutral, understands it as the most powerful weapon of social control, which the politically victorious class brandishes in its own interest.[5] The state has inherent biases;[6] so too, the legal order. Rules of constitutional law, like other norms, must favour some and not others. Constitutions organize comprehensive decision-making structures; their input, conversion and feed-back procedures preform the potential range of outputs. The relationship between process and output expresses the 'ontological causality' between constitution and society.

Constitutional law, like other laws, prescribes behaviour. The actual behaviour that it induces defines the decision-making structure. African constitutions created institutions that could not make laws likely to induce change. Their failure falsified the classical propositions about how constitutions do and should work.

II Constraints on Input Functions

Constitutions purport to solve the problems their authors perceive. The early bourgeois constitutions freed burgeoning private enterprise from the tyrannies of feudalism and mercantalism. They therefore mainly limited governmental power. The constitutions of the new socialist states, by contrast, assumed the state's primary obligation to organize the economy. The bourgeois constitutions resonated in Contract, the socialist ones, in Plan.

Whitehall wrote the African constitutions. The triumphant nationalists had to accept them as a condition for independence.[7] They

embodied Whitehall's solutions for African problems, as mediated by
their acculturated perceptions of constitutional law. The British thought
that the independence constitutions should restrain the new educated
Africans that the Colonial Service had earlier tried to shunt off into
local government,[8] but who now would plainly become the central
movers and shakers. As early as 1929, the Commission on a Closer Union
of the Dependencies in Eastern and Central Africa said that

> Experience has taught mankind that a man however just and honour-
> able, ought not to be made a judge in his own cause. An unconscious
> bias tends to deflect his judgement . . . That one part of the commun-
> ity should govern the whole, or that one class should make laws for
> another, was declared by Pericles more than two thousand years ago
> to be a form of tyranny. The foundation and only sure defence of
> freedom, a principle for which more than any other the British
> Empire stands, lie in a proper balance of interests and powers in the
> States.[9]

The amazing assertion that the British Empire stood for the principle of
freedom rested on the common justification for all authoritarian government: precisely because it represented no interests, it could more fairly
represent all. The Colonial Service assumed that African politicians would
use their new power selfishly. Sir Arthur Burns feared that independence would make 'democracy' a facade for the exploitation of the masses.[10]

At the same time, most British officials knew they had to co-opt the
new men. Sir Michael Bundell, a leader of 'moderate' white Kenyan
opinion, wrote:

> The only possible policy was a liberal one which attracted the best
> of the new African thought which was now coming to the fore,
> allied with measures which created a wider economic sphere for the
> African generally . . . As African political thought becomes more
> experienced in the actual practice of government, there will be a
> regrouping on economic lines if democracy continues in Kenya; one
> party will be socialist and revolutionary in concept, looking to the
> landless and lower paid workers for support, while the other will
> increasingly be a progressive evolutionary alliance of property owners
> and 'haves' as distinct from the 'have-nots'.[11]

How to give the new African politicians a stake in the power structure, without giving them real power? The answer came in the Westminster-style constitution. The constitutions which crowned the African Athenes as they sprang fully clothed from Britannia's brow all purported to follow Britain's unwritten one. Ceremonial head of state; prime minister accountable to parliament; cabinet solidarity; independent civil service; elections – the constitutions only missed requiring judges and barristers to wear wigs, and in practice they did *that* too.

All the African constitutions smoothed the paths to political authority for the new African elite, and simultaneously imposed explicit and implicit constraints that limited their actual power, thus ensuring rule not by elected officials, but by the Civil Service.

A. Recruitment Processes

In most parliamentary democracies, the mass paradoxically governs itself by periodically electing its governors.[12] The myth states that anyone can run for office. Reality, of course, denies the myth. Electoral processes and qualifications for office in fact prejudice nominations and elections. I discuss some of these in Chapter 21; here we examine only two of the relevant provisions of the independence constitutions[13] which ensured that the new educated elite had central power but limited their power by reinforcing traditional, rural authorities.

1 *Eligibility for Parliament.* In countries with no common language, what could be more sensible than requiring fluency in English for election to the legislature? Almost all the independence constitutions had such a requirement.[14] Effectively, they limited membership in parliament to the new educated men (and, since ministers had to be members of parliament,[15] membership in government as well). Only the Republican Constitutions of Ghana and Tanzania removed this restriction.[16] In Republican Ghana, however, the removal remained rhetorical. There, the Elections Act, 1959,[17] probably unconstitutionally retained the English language requirement.

2. *Federalism and Traditional Elites.* The only specifically African problem that the independence constitutions addressed concerned ethnic and regional pluralism. Wherever the departing British saw this as a threat, the constitution institutionalized diversity through federalism.[18] Federal constitutions inevitably buttressed the hegemony of traditional regional elites. History and constitution conspired to ensure that educated, modernizing elites took power at the centre. The federal structure could not contain the resulting conflict.

Every African polity chose quickly to transform the Westminster to a republican model, if only to exorcise the ghosts of colonialism. Mr Kofi Baako, then Minister of Information in Ghana, said that 'when we talk of a republic, it is not because we do not like the Queen, or because we do not like monarchy, but because people feel that an independent African State like Ghana should have a leader they can see.'[19]

In changing to a republican constitution, every country additionally amended it. Nigeria and Uganda[20] merely changed the head of state's title. Traditional authorities still ruled in the regions, modernizing elites at the centre. Both countries exploded. In Nigeria, the first *coup* ended in counter *coup* triggered by the threat of a unitary state.[21] In Uganda, President Obote integrated Buganda into a new unitary state by force; the Kabaka fled into exile.[22]

The Ghanaian experience differed.[23] The independence Constitution partially conceded traditionalists' demands for federalization, and the government created regional assemblies.[24] The regional opposition for some curious reason boycotted the regional elections, giving government a majority to abolish the regional assemblies,[25] and then to end consultation with the Houses of Chiefs.[26] The Republican Constitution of 1964 drove the last nail in the coffin. Article Four declared that 'Ghana is a sovereign unitary Republic'. Kenya followed the Ghanaian pattern.

B. Limitations on Input Functions

Although the constitutions ensured that educated elites would seem to take control, they limited the new politicians' power by constraining the available inputs for political leaders. I discuss federalism, property rights, the elaboration of roles and the dominance of the civil service.

1. *Federalism and the Limits of Power.* Dividing power dilutes it. Federalism did so in some of the Independence constitutions. It required that 'widespread innovation or experimentation in social and economic policy would tend to wait until the effectuation of a sufficient national consensus'.[27] In Kenya federalism designedly frustrated change. The agreement which preceded the Constitution[28] recited that 'there should be the maximum possible decentralization of the powers of Government to effective authorities capable of a life and significance of their own, entrenched in the constitution and drawing their being and power from the constitution and not from the Central Government'. A KANU[29] member described how it worked: 'It militated against effective government at the Centre . . . It prevented the

co-ordination of that national effort when it was most important that development be planned on a nationwide scale'.[30] Federalism in Kenya died; in 1965 the Republican Constitution replaced the original independence version.

In Nigeria, federalism limited development mainly by splitting planning power between the centre and the regions. Land tenure, which often limited African economic development, lay exclusively within regional power.[31] Even higher education defied planning; universities proliferated as each region insisted upon its own. Federalism obstructed planning in any shape, especially if government desired to control the 'commanding heights'.[32]

2. *Guarantees of Property Rights.* Property and contract define the economy and its power relationships. Constitutions must explicitly or implicitly deal with them. The constitution of South Vietnam (1967), for example, expressly recognized 'the right of private property', and required that the state accompany expropriation by 'speedy' compensation at the current market level.[33] The constitution of North Vietnam provided as the 'main forms' of property 'state ownership . . . cooperative ownership . . . ownership by individual working people, and ownership by national capitalists'.[34] It specifically prohibited 'the use of private property to disrupt the economic life of society, or to undermine the economic plan of the State'.[35]

In the classical tradition the African constitutions purported to accommodate any sort of economic system. They said nothing about property relationships. Invariably, however, they protected private property from social revolutionaries. Article 18 of the Zambian Independence Constitution prohibited any compulsory taking of property except on 'prompt payment of adequate compensation', with an absolute right to court or other review of compensation and the legality of taking, and an equally absolute right to currency convertability. Such a provision limited nationalization, and barred expropriation.

Plan as a jural postulate ultimately required government ownership and operation of principal productive enterprises. Government, therefore, needed power to expropriate property, either without compensation or by paying compensation in long-term, low interest bonds. The proviso hindered socialism.

3. *The Elaboration of Roles.* When government wants to accomplish a task, it defines appropriate positions by rules, and then ensures that role-occupants perform. If government seriously wants to provide

medical services for a particular area, it hires a Medical Officer, defines his task, and directs others to provide necessary funds, buildings and support services. Every constitution specifies roles to carry out particular tasks. By defining such roles, African constitutions ensured that decisions about their concerns would occur. Conversely, by not defining other possible roles, they prevented other decisions from arising; they remained 'non-decisions'.[36]

African constitutions squarely addressed the problems of the British government in the nineteenth century. The table of contents of the Independence Constitution of Nigeria, for example, included: (1) The Federation and its Territories, (2) Citizenship, (3) Fundamental Rights, (4) The Governor-General, (5) Parliament, (6) Executive Powers, (7) Courts, (8) Police, (9) Finance, (10) The Public Service and (11) Miscellaneous provisions. The constitution ignored even the limited welfare state concerns of the late nineteenth century. The Ghanaian Republican Constitution made the President the 'fount of honour', so that he could create Earls and Barons, Dames and Ladies, Orders of Merit and (who knows?) Orders of Empire. It failed to mention development planning.

These constitutions prescribed many specific roles. The Zambian Constitution created an Attorney General,[37] a Director of Public Prosecutions,[38] an Electoral Commission,[39] a Judicial Service Committee[40] and an Auditor General,[41] as well as such familiar positions as President, members of the legislature and so forth. Many constitutions provided for a prisons service[42] and a police force.[43] None of them, however, structured roles to deal specifically with development. In particular, none mentioned economic planning. Constitutions outside the common law tradition commonly did so. The 1971 Constitution of the United Arab Republic, for example, provided that the Council of Ministers could prepare 'the general plan of the State'.[44] The Constitution of the People's Republic of China gave the National People's Congress the duty to approve national economic plans,[45] and the State Council the obligation to implement them.[46]

Why this silence on development? I suggest two explanations: dogmas of 'flexibility' and acculturated constitutional orthodoxies. The classical perspective demands a constitution that can accommodate any government policy. That requires flexibility. Two leading academic lawyers in Tanzania wrote:

It is desirable that the main characteristic of the present Constitution — that of flexibility — be retained in any future Constitution.

By flexibility we mean the number of situations in which either no rule at all is provided, or the rule that is provided can only be made to work with the addition of conventions and understandings growing amongst whose function it is to govern the country and make the Constitution work. We believe that this is an eminently desirable feature of the Constitution and one that will be most necessary to incorporate in the new Constitution, where the situations dealt with by the rules may be novel, and may require a period of adjustment before they are working satisfactorily.[47]

Obviously, constitutions cannot specify institutional arrangements so precisely that every law must amend the constitution. Successful planning, however, requires fundamental realignments of governmental power. A constitution should above all allocate power.

Constitutional orthodoxies also limited the creativity of the British framers. They knew and revered their own British constitution. The Westminster model effectively bounded governmental activity; of course it did not specify development roles. Rather, African constitutions laboured to guarantee that development issues would fall by default. In consequence,

[it] should . . . be noted that the Westminster model, or any unsubstantially altered version of it, does not address itself to social revolutionary conditions and to the needs for changes in that direction. In the Anglo-Saxon tradition, it tends to leave certain sectors of society, such as the economy, as far as possible outside the area of constitutional arrangement . . . Most important, it does not directly address itself to the roots and principal features of the social and political control-structure, such as points from the formal-legal system, placing them beyond the reach of social-revolutionary elements so long as those elements can be compelled to play the game by the established rules.[48]

After independence African constitution-makers developed four novel institutions to meet elite perceptions of pressing African needs; the *de jure* one-party state;[49] new electoral systems;[50] leadership codes;[51] and Permanent Commissions of Enquiry.[52] Planning's continuing exclusion from African constitutions despite its pervasive practice, reflected the African constitution-makers' preoccupation with nineteenth- and even eighteenth-century models.

4. *The Civil Service.* In British mythology, the Civil Service silently, anonymously and impersonally implements Parliament's laws and, within those laws, the Cabinet's policies. It purportedly gives similarly impersonal and impartial expert advice to the ministers, and supplies them with necessary data for drafting new laws.

That, of course, hardly describes the Colonial Service, the lineal antecedent of every African civil service. In Colonial Africa, the service governed. It formulated policy and then implemented it. The independent constitutions ensured that the Civil Service would continue that tradition. Throughout Africa, most legislation originated within the civil service. They applied the rules daily; they learned of the troubles, and evolved their own explanations and solutions for them. These became the principal inputs for legislation. For example, every idea about the Tanzanian Range Management Development Act[53] came from the civil service, or its advisers.

Many factors constrained ideas that the civil service developed. Its system of decision-making,[54] its differential access to information,[55] its relative openness to different strata for a feedback channel[56] limited its proposals to incremental change. So did the interests of its members[57] and their perceptions of the world.[58] The independent constitutions gave actual law-making power not to the new and feared African politicians but to the civil service. In addition, constitutional provisions ensured British control over the civil service for so long as possible.

a. The Independent Civil Service. The relationship between the government and the civil service in the Independence constitutions capsized the nominal British convention of Parliamentary supremacy over the civil service. In Africa, the civil service functioned apart from government, rather than serving it.

The British neutral, non-partisan, civil service served well when Westminster governments only differed marginally within the same set of values. American experience, particularly during the New Deal, however, demonstrated that great reform movements require high-level administrators with a passionate commitment to the programmes they implement.[59] At Independence, British officials filled most senior posts in most African civil services. They had served long years in the colonial service. Few had strong commitments to development.

> The Civil [Colonial] Service was . . . geared to the rather negative
> policy of preventing trouble and bringing the Pax Britannica to all
> the dependent territories overseas. It was not until comparatively

recently concerned with economic and social development as a major objective of administration ... Economic activities were mainly in the hands of private trading companies from overseas — usually British ... The central administration had no positive policy towards the promotion of these enterprises except to create the conditions under which private enterprise could flourish, and to intervene where necessary to ensure fair play to the unsophisticated peoples of the territories.[60]

Traditional theory accepts the lack of the bureaucrats' personal commitment, but assumes they will obey the leadership or else the leadership will sack them. In Africa, however, government lacked that power.

In Africa, as in England, traditional anonymity insulated the civil service from partisan interference. Individual civil servants never signed public documents. Nobody publicly knew who made particular decisions. That arguably protected civil servants from political interferences with their supposedly 'neutral' functions. Correlatively, in Britain, the minister became responsible for every act of his civil servants. In the House of Commons in 1954, Herbert Morrison said: '[t]here can be no doubt that a Minister of the Crown is responsible for all the acts of his civil servants — and all the absence of acts required. He is responsible for every stamp stuck on an envelope ... There can be no question whatever the Ministers are responsible for everything their officers do ...'[61] In Constitutional theory, ministerial power to dismiss a civil servant at will enforced this responsibility.[62] Lord Kilmuir, then the Home Secretary, said: '[t]he position of a civil servant is that he is wholly and directly responsible to his Minister. It is worth stating again that he holds his office 'at pleasure' and can be dismissed at any time by the Minister and that power is none the less real because it is seldom used.[63]

That did not hold in Africa. Independent Public Service Commissions stood between minister and civil servant. The Zambian President could 'appoint persons to hold or to act in any office in the public service ... to exercise disciplinary control over persons holding or acting in such offices and to remove such persons from office.[64] What the Constitution gave, however, it immediately snatched away: the Public Service Commission, not the President, exercised these powers. The President instead appointed the Commission.[65] Only the President could remove a Commissioner before the end of his seven-year term and only for incapacity or misbehaviour.[66] The President might give the Public Service Commission 'such general directions with respect to the exercise of the functions of the Commission ... as the President may consider necessary and the Commission . . . shall comply with those directions'.[67] With that exception, ' . . . the Public Service Commission shall not be subject to the direction or control of any other person or authority in the exercise of its functions under this Constitution'.[68]

The Constitution took this formula from the British rule that defined the relationship between public corporations and the relevant ministry. This rule supposedly insulated public corporations from 'politics'. In Africa, it insulated the civil service from control by elected officials. Without even knowledge of who within the service made particular acts or decisions, the elected branch depended upon the civil service.

b. The Decision-making Process within the Bureaucracy. I earlier discussed the decision-making process within the bureaucracy,[69] stating that its authoritarian, hierarchical, rule-bound, compartmented character better adapted it to tending the machine than changing it. 'The choice of public decision-making styles is a factor in growth. Style is affected by organizational structure . . . Where there is a high degree of uncertainty in the relation between the goals of a program and the technology available, the structure ought to be innovatory rather than adaptive.'[70] The structure of African bureaucracies reinforced an adaptive rather than an innovative decision-making style. Consequently, mainly suggestions for adaptive, not innovatory laws entered the law-making process.

African governments committed to radical social change, but not more conservative governments, inevitably suspected the good faith of such bureaucracies. The Republican Constitutions of Nigeria, Kenya, Uganda, Zambia and Sierra Leone that followed the Independence Constitutions retained the independent civil service commission. The Republican Constitutions in Ghana and Tanzania abolished them. Both countries altogether dropped the British convention of an impartial civil service, and encouraged civil servants to join the Party.

Summary. African constitutions imposed sharp limits on inputs to law-making. Federalism restricted central power; so did explicit guarantees of property rights. The roles they defined ignored development. The civil service escaped political control, and could not propose deep-seated institutional change. African constitutions by design or serendipity constrained the input function to data and proposals for incremental change.

III Conversion Processes

Conversion processes combine inputs into decision. Particular conversion processes inevitably exclude some sorts of outcomes, and favour others. I argue here (1) that its procedures in the African context seriously weakened Parliament's nominal control over law-making, thus leaving most decisions to the executive; and, (2) that the Executive depended on the civil service. This strange reversal of constitutional roles arose out of the very imperatives of development.

A. Parliament

Throughout Africa, Parliament did not in fact decide about law. In Ghana, under Nkrumah, Parliament enacted laws that others drafted. 'Members usually pass bills which are submitted to them without a division, and their comments tend to be confined to the effects which such bills might have upon their own positions within the party.'[71] In Nigeria under the federal constitution prior to the 1966 military *coup* the Prime Minister saw the House 'as an institution which permits the minor elements in politics to achieve a sense of importance and blow off a little steam, but no more'.[72] In Tanzania, 'Members of Parliament certainly "rubber stamp" many important measures', although on rare occasions they resisted governmental initiatives.[73]

The speed with which bills whipped through Parliament demonstrated its impotence. The Zambian State Security Act, 1969, that sharply narrowed individual civil liberties, had its first reading on 15 October 1969, and its second reading and enactment on 17 October. The Federal Parliament of Nigeria discussed bills for an average of two hours each.[74] In Tanzania, from October 1960 to December 1964, 121 out of 334 bills passed under a Certificate of Urgency, obviating even the otherwise required twenty-one clear days between publication in the *Gazette* and first reading.[75] The majority of cases involved no real urgency.[76]

The diminishing role of African Parliaments paralleled their Western counterparts. In England, Parliament only rarely made a genuine decision, usually when government had only a thin majority.

In the modern era [in Great Britain] the legislation enacted by Parliament is almost entirely a Government product. The ministers of the Crown, who form the Government, are invariably members of the Commons or the Lords. The remaining members of the majority party in the House of Commons, the 'Government back-benchers', are subject to party discipline imposed by party whips, which in practice is sufficient to ensure the passage of Government-sponsored legislation in the House of Commons . . . The Government's power over the legislative process is such that a bill has little chance of reaching the statute book unless it is one introduced by the Government.[77]

Everything conspired to ensure Parliamentary impotence in Africa. I discuss here first its explanation and, second, the transition from the Westminster to the Presidential model.

1. Structural Impotence. Parliamentary impotence resulted from its interests and its procedures. Legislatures everywhere assert their power over the executive only when their interests clash. In England, Parliament rarely challenged an executive whose continuation in office determined the tenure of the majority party. In the one-party African states, party loyalty made the entire Parliament dependent on the executive. Genuine debate came only when back-benchers fought Government.

Government had additional influence over many MPs. Everywhere the executive appointed some members, usually between 15 and 20 per cent of the House, supposedly to represent women, chiefs and other special groups. Secondly, in a Parliamentary system, a minister must hold a Parliamentary seat. In the middle of 1966, for example, ministers comprised 39 per cent of Kenya's House of Representatives.[78] The procedures of the several African legislatures furthered their impotence. These aped British conventions. They gazetted bills a stipulated period before introduction, usually twenty-one clear days, after which the first reading introduced the bill without debate. Shortly thereafter, on the second reading, the Members debated the policy or 'principle' of the bill. Later, at the so-called committee stage, the House considered the bill in detail, followed by a third reading and vote. A distinction between ends and means underlay this procedure. Policy dealt with ends; the second reading dealt with those. The means involved technical matters; that occupied the Committee stage. Since Parliament made policy and the civil service devised means, the second stage became crucial for Parliament. Only the executive normally brought legislation before the House.

In their legislative function, parliaments in these [Anglophonic African] countries have been executive rubber stamps. No important piece of legislation desired by the executive has been refused: indeed, such legislation has been enacted not infrequently with unseemly haste. Moreover, legislative initiative has rested almost entirely with the executive. There have been very few examples of private members' bills introduced in parliament, and no such bill has been enacted.[79]

Parliament on the second reading celebrated legislative enactment, it did not deliberate it. Without legislative committees, staff or provisions for public hearings, African Parliaments could not investigate or analyze very well. Only the civil service had intimate knowledge of the situation. Since most bills originated in the civil service, its data always supported the proposed legislation. As a result, like the human appendix, Parliament had little clear function. It might become a feedback system, for their constituencies to communicate with party and government. I discuss this potential feedback function of Parliament below.[80]

2. From Parliamentary to the Presidential Model. The Westminster constitutions enabled Parliament to remove the executive by denying it a vote of confidence. The ceremonial Head of State, usually the Crown-appointed Governor-General, selected a government that would likely command a Parliamentary majority. African governments without exception quickly shed themselves of the Queen and her representatives.

Ceremonial Head of State. The British convention gives the monarch a nominal residual power in selecting a new government. The Westminster export model gave the governor-general a larger role. In Nigeria and Sierra Leone, for example, the governor-general could remove a prime minister whom he believed no longer commanded the confidence of a majority in the House. In Nigeria, he could dissolve Parliament on his own motion when the office of prime minister was vacant, and he believed that no successor with majority support would emerge within a reasonable time. The English Crown had far less power.[81]

Radical groups feared the head of state's power to block change; conservative ones valued it for the same reason. In Nigeria, the Republican Constitution hardly changed more than the ceremonial head of state's title. Uganda amended the Independence constitution, severing the imperial tie, making the President ceremonial head of state, with, however, carefully circumscribed powers.[82] Ghana's and Tanzania's Republican Constitutions abolished the ceremonial head of state altogether.

The Presidential Model. Historically, classes desiring to limit governmental initiative supported separation of powers. It arose originally as middle-class ideology to oppose despotic, mercantilist European governments. In England it only divided the judiciary from parliament (at whose pleasure the Executive served). In the United States it formed a tripartite division, between legislative, judicial and executive. The executive, the President, had tenure independent of the legislature.[83] In Africa, the 'Presidential model' constitution made the executive's tenure independent of Parliament.

It seemed curious that both Ghana and Tanzania justified the Presidential form because 'countries in a hurry' needed increased executive power,[84] considering their legislatures' actual impotence. Their adoption of it stemmed from the political leadership's distrust of the legislature. In Ghana, the Republican Constitution [85] even gave Dr Nkrumah the power to legislate by decree. Instead, both emphasized the Party. Nkrumah reiterated that 'Ghana is the CPP[86] and the CPP is Ghana'. In Tanzania President Nyerere built TANU,[87] as an 'all-embracing union, a national movement'.[88]

African countries probably abandoned the Westminster model for the Presidential model largely because the training of constitutional lawyers focused on the paper document. Textbooks detailed the advantages and disadvantages of Presidential and Parliamentary systems. They virtually ignored Soviet-style constitutions and the constitutional role of a Planning Commission. They emphasized formal protections against government, not the realities of decision-making. Lawyers debated the merits of a ceremonial head of state, although no governor-general in Africa ever independently selected a government nor, given political realities, would he. They detailed presidential versus parliamentary forms, as though the legislature really had the independent power the constitutions prescribed, but ignored relationships between Party and Executive, and Executive and Civil Service. The problem of presidential versus parliamentary constitution in Africa arose not out of life, but out of constitutional theory.

B. *The Executive and Law-Making*

The executive manipulated Parliament, but could hardly escape the civil service. This arose because of the decision-making process, and the executive branch's structure.

1. Decision-Making Processes. In the late colonial era, formal decision-making authority lay in the Governor-in-Council, subject to Whitehall's veto. An Assistant Secretary proposed new legislation, putting the issues and alternatives. In due course the Governor, with the Legislative Council's advice, decided the matter. With new policy, the Governor requested Royal Assent, thus giving the Colonial Office opportunity to veto. The Royal Assent gave relevant English publics a voice in colonial legislation.

The legislative process in independent Africa followed an analogous path. In Zambia,[89] for example, ideas for new legislation arose almost invariably in the ministries. After the Attorney-General decided that the proposal involved a matter of policy, not mere 'tidying up', the Minister submitted a memorandum to the Cabinet[90] with a brief description of the bill and its purpose, a statement of its urgency, complexity and whether it would create controversy or not. If the Cabinet approved, the Ministry sent detailed drafting instructions to the Solicitor-General.[91] The Parliamentary Draftsman then drafted the bill, and sent it to the Ministry for scrutiny. After further consultations, if necessary, the Cabinet's Legislation Committee received the final draft, and a detailed statement of the bill's purposes. That statement was 'essential if the Legislation Committee is to check the Bill to ensure that the intention has in fact been achieved'.[92] If any member so desired the Cabinet again considered the bill, together with a new memorandum that 'set out in detail the policy issue on which the matter was referred back to the Cabinet'. After final approval, the bill went to Parliament, which performed the rituals of enactment. The Cabinet, not Parliament, in fact decided what legislation to enact. What institutional constraints and resources channelled its choices?

2. The Organization of the Executive Branch. In the parliamentary blueprint, the cabinet makes policy decisions with the technical advice of senior civil servants. Each Cabinet Minister at once sits in Cabinet and also heads an arm of the civil service, so that Cabinet and civil service can easily communicate. A Cabinet Minister's responsibility for each department institutionalizes executive control over the bureaucracy. Cabinet government maximizes the civil service's influence in lawmaking.

> One important feature of the procedural rules relating to the Cabinet [in Tanganyika on Independence] was the opportunity they provided for the senior civil service to exert an influence. The preparation of cabinet papers relating to items on the agenda of the cabinet, treasury comments upon the financial implications of proposals being made to the Cabinet and even the mere fact that prior notice is required of items to be raised at Cabinet meetings, gave the civil service the

opportunity to submit ministerial ideas to close scrutiny.[93]

Always at his Minister's elbow stood a senior civil servant, at Independence mainly British Colonial Service relicts.[94]

Without Party responsibility for policy, electoral democracy becomes a sham. In England, cabinet solidarity supposedly guaranteed that responsibility. Lord Salisbury said that 'for all that passes in Cabinet each member of it who does not resign is absolutely and irrevocably responsible, and he has no right afterwards to say that he agreed in one case to a compromise, while in another he was persuaded by his colleagues'.[95] It combined with ministerial responsibility to ensure that the governing party would and must take responsibility for government policy and action. The African independence constitutions embalmed cabinet solidarity.

Party responsibility makes sense when the party controls government, and government controls the civil service. For that system to work the minister must have power to sack civil servants. African constitutions deprived him of that ultimate control. Consequently, the civil service controlled the politicians. Government, bound by principles of cabinet solidarity and ministerial responsibility, had to take responsibility for what the civil service did, but could do precious little to control it.

Summary. The decision-making processes and structures in African independence constitutions in reality made supreme not Parliament or the executive, but the civil service. The Colonial Service tried to give African politicians, the 'new men', apparent but not real power. They created roles for themselves as advisers, controllers and elder statesmen, with *de jure* or *de facto* qualifications that at the outset no African likely could meet. Governor-generals, judges, Judicial Service Commission, senior civil servants, Auditor-Generals, Attorney-Generals, Directors of Public Prosecutions, Army generals, Public Service Commission, Commissioner-Generals of Police, Speakers of the House: at Independence, former colonial servants occupied almost all of these and tutored their successors. The independence constitutions explicitly insulated many of them from political control. Holding those posts, who cared about the nominal African governors?

Besides creating key control posts for British officials, they created central institutions that made radical change unlikely. Inputs included only proposals for incremental change. Conversion processes maximized civil service influence. The decision-making institutions upon which

African political leaders depended could not institute radical change. The weakness largely lay in the decision-making structures, not merely in the 'values' of the political leaders.

Constitutions purport to solve problems. No single constitutional model can solve everyone's problems. Constitutions define decision-making systems, structuring them to preform the range of decisions. Concerning development issues, African constitutions ensured that law-makers could not even propose radical institutional change, let along enact or implement it.

IV Law-Making and the Civil Service: Attempted Solutions

African governments seldom tried to revise the basic received law-making institutions. They variously tried to solve the principal issue, the relationship between civil service and government.

The Westminster constitutions promised to avert what happened in Africa. They supposedly guaranteed that the elected African governments would determine policy, and the civil service implement it. The African experience stood that myth on its head, and demonstrated what now seems self-evident: to grant anonymity, secrecy and independence to senior bureaucrats ensures their dominance over elected politicians. African governments tried a series of devices to reverse that dominance.

They first tried to make cabinet government operate as the blueprint supposed it would. President Nyerere's first circular as Chief Minister, in October 1960, argued that 'political parties, and therefore members of the Legislative Council, can certainly play their part in ensuring a good public reception of Government's policies, but I repeat that the responsibility of carrying out government policies lies with the civil service.'[96] He did not try to build a strong presidential office. 'The conclusion is inescapable. Nyerere wanted to undermine neither the position of his Ministers nor the role of the Cabinet.'[97] Cabinet government of the ideal-type cannot meet demands for radical change; it makes the civil service too strong.

A second response led to the Presidential constitutions. Those failed because they blamed the failure of development on the legislators, not on the structure of decision-making.

A third response put new projects in parastatal organizations rather than the civil service. Governments believed, quite erroneously, that their 'ownership' of the parastatals gave them real control.[98]

A fourth response strengthened the decision-making capacity of the President's office, particularly under Nkrumah in Ghana, and Kaunda in Zambia. In both countries, the President had great initial charisma, and demanded extensive institutional change. In Ghana, the governing Convention People's Party by 1960 withered to a dry husk. Its direct beneficiaries kept it alive, Party bureaucrats and functionaries, Regional Commissioners and Members of Parliament. It lost contact with the mass, and fell prey to internal factionalism and jockeying for power and privilege.[99] By 1973, the Zambia ruling party, UNIP, seemed cut from the same bolt. In both countries, the President began to rely not on Party, but upon foreign 'experts'. These advisers all lay outside the constitutional scheme. Nobody has studied their internal organization, or their precise relationships with the President. The nature of the advisers reflected at the outset the personal style of each President: expatriate radicals (or pseudo-radicals) in Ghana, expatriate missionaries in Zambia.

A fifth response, in Tanzania and Zambia, counterpoised the Party to the civil service. Each constitution made the Party supreme. The Zambian Constitution (1973) provided that in case of disagreement between Cabinet and the Party's National Executive Committee, the latter should prevail.[100] The Cabinet changed from policy-making to policy-implementing. That gave the Cabinet the same role that the senior civil service had in the Westminster blueprint.

Finally, some countries had open war that the civil service sometimes won. Some African *coups* (the Ghanaian *coup* of 1966 that ousted President Nkrumah, for example) involved the senior civil service as much as the military and police. Commonly, after a military *coup* the civil service formally took over policy-making, with the former Permanent Secretary replacing the former Minister.

Nobody in Africa discovered a sure cure for the domination of the civil service in decision-making. Its solution plainly required restructuring the bureaucracy, so that it lost the hierarchical compartmented character that underlay its adaptive orientation. It required building new channels of communication between the masses and the lawmakers, so as to change the sorts of inputs that led to decision-making. Africa needed constitutions that attacked the problems not of nineteenth-century Britain, but of twentieth-century Africa.

Conclusion

African constitutional law developed few novelties. The constitutions created only incremental changes, based on limited models of other Commonwealth constitutions and the US constitution, and textbooks that focused myopically and ethnocentrically upon Britain and the

United States. Practically everywhere, the received systems ensured control by educated 'modernizers', and (in the early independent years at least) expatriate advisers, and the elimination of traditional elites. Jitendra Mohan's observations about Ghana under Nkrumah generally applied to all Africa.

Transfer of power was viewed not in terms of its democratization, but of its Africanization. The system of colonial administration was designed to exclude as much as possible both traditional and modern elements of democracy. The distant objective of self-government meant no more than that the system would finally be administered by Africans.[101]

The Colonial Service had remarkable success in implementing its plan for the transfer of power. First its British hold-overs, and then the 'good men' it trained dominated most African civil services. Insulated from political control, they, not elected officials, dominated law-making. The radical structural changes required for development could hardly begin until the leadership transformed their very systems of decision-making. That could only happen if the political leadership understood its necessity. They would not likely do so as long as their lawyers stared bemused at nineteenth-century British and United States models, instead of confronting directly African constitutional issues.

Notes

1. B.O. Nwabueze, *Constitutionalism in the Emergent States* (London: C. Hurst, 1973).
2. S.A. de Smith, 'Constitutionalism in the Commonwealth Today', *Malayan L.J.*, 4, 205, 205-206 (1962); see W. Andrews (ed.), *Constitutions and Constitutionalism* (New York: Van Nostrand Reinhold, 1961), pp. 9-14.
3. Compare R.K. Merton, *Social Theory and Social Structure* (Glencoe, Ill.: Free Press, 1952) with G.W. Lenski, *Power and Privilege: A Theory of Social Stratification* (New York: McGraw-Hill, 1966); see Wagner, 'Types of Socio-logical Theory', *Am. Soc. Rev.*, 28, 735 (1963); A. Auerbach, L. Garrison, W. Hurst and S. Mermin, *The Legal Process* (San Francisco: Chandler, 1961), pp. 600-602.
4. K. Lowenstein, 'Reflections on the Value of Constitutions in Our Revolutionary Age', in A. Zurcher (ed.), *Constitutions and Constitutional Trends Since World War II* (Westport, Conn.: Greenwood, 1951), pp. 191, 224; see also C. Friedrich, 'Some Reflections on Constitutionalism in the Developing World', in H. Spiro (ed.), *Patterns of Development: Five Comparisons* (Englewood Cliffs, N.J.: Prentice-Hall, 1967), p. 9.
5. V.I. Lenin, *State and Revolution: Marxist Teaching about the Theory of the State and the Tasks of the Proletariat in the Revolution* (New York:

International, 1932).

6. I. Kovacs, *New Elements in the Evolution of Socialist Constitutions* (Budapest: Akademiai Kiado, 1968).

7. But see, L.C.B. Gower, *Independent Africa: The Challenge to the Legal Profession* (Cambridge: Harvard University Press, 1967), p. 16.

8. See Chap. 16.

9. *Report of the Commission on Closer Union of the Dependencies in Eastern and Central Africa* (London: HMSO, 1929), Cmd. 3234.

10. A. Burns, *In Defence of Colonies: British Colonial Territories in International Affairs* (London: George Allen and Unwin, 1957), p. 80.

11. M. Blundell, *So Rough a Wind, The Kenya Memoirs of Sir Michael Blundell,* (London: Weidenfeld and Nicholson, 1964), p. 263.

12. A. Schumpeter, *Capitalism, Socialism and Democracy,* 4th ed. (London: Allen and Unwin, 1954), p. 269.

13. Whether these consequences were intended by the British is irrelevant for our purposes. Compare H. Bretton, *Power and Stability in Nigeria: The Politics of Decolonialization* (New York: Praeger, 1962) and R. Fitch and M. Oppenheimer, 'Ghana: End of an Illusion', *Monthly Rev.,* 18, 1, 11-13 (1966), with S.A. de Smith, 'Westminster's Export Models', *J. Comm. Pol. Stud.,* 1, 2 (1961).

14. See, e.g., Ghana: The Independence Constitution, Art. 27 (1957); Tanganyika: The Independence Constitution, Arts, 13, 19 (1964); Kenya: The Independence Constitution, Art. 40(1) (b) (1963); Nigeria: The Constitution of the Federation of Nigeria, Art. 254 (1960) (Parliament to conduct business in English).

15. Nigeria: The Federal Constitution, Art. 81(5) (1960); Kenya, The Independence Constitution, Art. 75 (3) (1963).

16. Ghana: The Republican Constitution, Art. 20 (1960); Tanzania: The Republican Constitution, Art. 24 (1964).

17. Act 78 of 1959.

18. See, K. Friedrich, 'Federalism and Opposition', *Government & Opposition,* 1, 286, 288 (1966); B.O. Nwabueze, *Constitutional Law of the Nigerian Republic* (London: Butterworths, 1964); O. Awolowo, *The Autobiography of Chief Obafemi Awolowo* (Cambridge: Cambridge University Press, 1960), p. 163; A. Richards, 'Constitutional Problems in Uganda', *Pol. Q.* 33, 360, 362-63 (1962); Y.P. Ghai, 'Independence and Safeguards in Kenya', *E. Afr. L.J.,* 3, 177 (1967); C. Ogwurike, 'The Aims of Nigerian Federalism', *Nigerian L.J.,* 2, 194 (1965).

19. Quoted in W. Daniels, *The Common Law in West Africa* (London: Butterworth 1964), p. 219; see H.O. Davies, 'The Legal and Constitutional Problems of Independence', in P. Judd, *African Independence* (New York: Dell, 1962), p. 328.

20. See Constitution of Uganda Act (First Amendment) (No. 61 of 1963); see H. Morris and J. Read, *Uganda: The Development of its Laws and Constitution* (London: Stevens, 1966).

21. R. Sklar, 'Nigerian Politics in Perspective', *Government & Opposition,* 2, 526 (1967).

22. G.F. Engholm and A. Mazrui, 'Violent Constitutionalim in Uganda', *Government and Opposition,* 2, 585 (1967).

23. See W.B. Harvey, *Law and Social Change in Ghana* (Princeton: New Jersey: Princeton University Press, 1965), Chap. 3, from which this discussion largely stems.

24. Ghana: The Regional Assemblies Act (No. 25 of 1958). Their roles were merely advisory.

25. Harvey, *Law and Social Change,* pp. 145-6.

26. Ghana: Constitution (Repeal of Restrictions) Act (No. 38 of 1958); The Houses of Chiefs Act (No. 20 of 1953).
27. E. McWhinney, *Comparative Federalism: States' Rights and National Power* (Toronto: Toronto University Press, 1965), p. 7.
28. *Report of the Kenyan Constitutional Conference, 1961* (London: HMSO 1962), Cmnd. 1700, p. 17.
29. Kenya African National Union.
30. B. Njonjo, 'Recent constitutional changes in Kenya', *E. Africa L.J.*, 1, 98 (1965). A member of KADU [Kenya African Democratic Union] wrote: 'The desire for rapid economic advancement, the economic and other objectives of the majority party, pan-Africanism, African unity, etc., have all had an effect, but a negative one, on our recent constitutional development, in that all these have driven people to think more of communal safeguards and the individual rights instead of, as expected, giving more power to the central figure in the nationalist movement. For many are aware that under the guise of rapid economic development a lot can be done to deny communities and individuals the rightful liberties and freedoms due them. This attitude may make it difficult in the future for the federal government to implement certain measures desirable for economic well-being of the people.' [P.K.H. Okondo, 'Kenya's new constitution', in *The Constitutions and Administrative Institutions of the New States* (Report of the 33rd Incidi Study Session held in Palermo from 23 to 27 September 1963, Institut International des Civilisations Differentes, Bruxelles, 1965) hereinafter cited as INCIDI)], 103, 112.
31. Nigeria: The Federal Constitution, The Legislative Lists (The Schedule) (1960).
32. See Chap. 4.
33. A. Blaustein and G. Flanz, *Constitutions of the Countries of the World* (Dobbs Ferry, New York: Oceans Publications, 1971), Art. 19.
34. Ibid., Art. 11.
35. Ibid., Art. 17.
36. P. Bachrach and M. Baratz, *Power and Poverty* (New York: Oxford University Press, 1970).
37. Zambia: Independence Constitution (1964), Art. 52.
38. Ibid., Art. 53.
39. Ibid., Art. 67.
40. Ibid., Art. 104.
41. Ibid., Art. 113.
42. See, e.g., Ghana: The Republican Constitution (1962), Arts. 146-148.
43. See, e.g., Nigeria: The Federal Constitution (1963), Arts. 105-110.
44. United Arab Republic: Constitution (1971), Art. 156(f).
45. Ibid., Art. 27(9); see Blaustein and Flanz, *Constitutions*, vol. III.
46. Ibid., Art. 49(7).
47. Y.P. Ghai and J.P. McAuslan, 'Constitutional Proposals for a One-Party State in Tanzania', *E Af. L.J.*, 1, 124 (1965).
48. Bretton, *Power and Stability*.
49. See below, Chap. 21.
50. Ibid.
51. See below, Chap. 20.
52. See below, Chap. 21.
53. See above, Chap. 1.
54. See above, Chap. 13.
55. See below, Chap. 21.
56. Ibid.
57. See below, Chap. 20.

58. See above, Chap. 2.
59. J.W. Hurst, *The Growth of American Law: The Law-Makers* (Boston: Little Brown, 1950), p. 422.
60. A.L. Adu, *The Civil Service in the New African States* (New York: Praeger, 19 15; see R.L. Harris, 'The Role of the Civil Servant in West Africa', *Pub. Admin. Rev.*, 25, 308 (1965).
61. Quoted in G. Bring, *Reap the Whirlwind: An Account of Kwame Nkrumah's Ghana from 1950 to 1966* (London: Macgibbon & Kee, 1968), p. 189.
62. *Dunn* v. *Queen* (1896) 1 Q.B. 116; *Bainbridge* v. *Postmaster General* (1906) 1 K.B 178.
63. Quoted in B. Ging, *Reap the Whirlwind*, p. 189.
64. Zambian Constitution (1964) Art. 115(1). There were a few exceptions. Ibid., Art. 115(3), 116(2) and 115(5).
65. Ibid., Art. 114(1)
66. Ibid., Art. 114(5).
67. Ibid., Art. 114(9).
68. Ibid., Art. 114(11).
69. See Chaps. 13, 15.
70. B.B. Schaffer, 'The Deadlock in Development Administration' in C. Leys (ed.), *Politics and Change in Developing Countries: Studies in the Theory and Practice of Development* (London: Cambridge University Press, 1969), p. 210.
71. J.M Lee, 'Parliament in Republican Ghana', *Parliamentary Affairs*, 16, 376 (1964).
72. J.P. Mackintosh, 'The Nigerian Federal Parliament', *Pub. L.*, 333, 351, (1963).
73. W Tordoff, 'Parliament in Tanzania', *J. Comm. Pol. Studies*, 4, 85 (1966).
74. Mackintosh, 'Nigerian Federal Parliament'.
75. Tordoff, 'Parliament in Tanzania', p. 88.
76. Ibid., p. 91.
77. See generally, E.C. Bellquist, 'Congressionalism and Parliamentarism', *NUEA Manual*, 27, 13 (1953), reprinted in H. Wahlke and J. Eulau (eds.), *Legislative Behavior: A Reader in Theory and Research* (Glencoe, Ill: The Free Press, 1959) 35.
78. N.M. Stultz, 'Parliaments in Former British Black Africa', *J. of Developing Areas*, 2, 479 (1968).
79. Ibid.
80. See below, Chap. 21.
81. de Smith, 'Westminster's Export Models'.
82. M.K. Mwendwa, 'Constitutional Contrasts in the East African Territories', in *E. Afr. L. Today*, 1 (ICLO Supp. Pub. No. 12, 1966).
83. See Robson, 'The Transplanting of Political Institutions and Ideas', *Pol. Q.*, 35, 407 (1964).
84. Government of Tanganyika: *Proposals of the Tanganyika Government for a Republic* (Gov. Paper No. 1, 1962 (Dar es Salaam: Government Printer, 1962), p. 3; see de Smith, 'Westminster's Export Models'.
85. Ghana: The Republican Constitution (1962), Art. 555.
86. Convention People's Party.
87. Tanganyika African National Union.
88. J.K. Nyerere, *Democracy and the Party System* (Dar es Salaam: Gov't. Printer, 1963)
89. Zambia: Cabinet Office Circular No. 72 of 1969.
90. Ibid., Sec. 4.
91. Ibid., Sec. 5.

92. Ibid., Sec. 8.
93. C. Pratt, 'The Cabinet and Presidential Leadership in Tanzania, 1960-1966',
    in 1 L. Cliffe and J. Saul (eds.), *Socialism in Tanzania: An Interdisciplinary
    Reader* (Nairobi: East African Publishing House, 1972), reprinted from M.
    Lofchie (ed.), *The State of the Nations: Constraints on Development in
    Independent Africa* (Berkeley: University of California, 1971), p. 232.
94. Ibid.
95. Quoted in A. Keith, *The British Cabinet System,* 2nd ed. (Gibbs, ed.)
    (London: Stevens, 1954), p. 92.
96. Quoted in Pratt, 'Cabinet and Presidential Leadership in Tanzania', p. 226.
97. Ibid., p. 228.
98. See above, Chap. 14.
99. D. Austin, *Politics in Ghana, 1946-1960* (London: Oxford University Press,
    1964), p. 418.
100. Zambia: The One-Party Constitution (1973).
101. J. Mohan, 'Nkrumah and Nkrumahism', *The Socialist Register*, 1967, 191,
     192.

20 HOW THE LEGAL ORDER DEVELOPED A BUREAUCRATIC BOURGEOISIE

Chapter 17's explanation for Africa's stagnation argued that the political elite allied itself to the economic ruling class and therefore avoided radical change. I examine here the alliance between these two groups, its explanation and various solutions.

I The Interpenetration of Political Elites and the Economic Ruling Class

The political elite, like other role-occupants, chose to maximize the benefits and rewards of their environment as they perceived it. Throughout Africa, they acquired property and received incomes as high as those of white managers and officials. Expatriates, however, remained the captains of the private sector. This section traces (1) the movement of political elites into the economic sphere; (2) the cohesiveness of the educated elite; (3) their private use of public resources; (4) the consequences for decision-making; and (5) their relationships with expatriate firms.

A. Political Elites and Wealth

The rich in Africa comprised a tiny fraction of the population. In Kenya in 1962 only one-half of 1 per cent of African taxpayers had incomes over £400.[1] Most highest black income earners served as senior civil servants and politicians. 'The prominent position of the civil servant in Kenya is a fact. He is seen as a man of status, considerable power and some wealth.'[2] In Uganda in 1965 only 5,000 people earned over £300 annually. In Western Nigeria 'the farmer usually pays tax on an assessed income of £50; the unskilled labourer earns £75 a year and the most skilled artisan nearly £300. The holder of a West African School Certificate . . . will expect to start earning £240 as a clerk or teacher. The university graduate, however, commences at £750, with a ceiling at £3,000; in addition, he is given a loan to buy a car and a monthly allowance to run it; he may, if in the higher ranks, occupy a part-furnished government home, paying one-twelfth of his income (rent of a privately-owned house would take between a quarter and a fifth of his income).'[3] At independence, black university graduates hardly existed. Zambia in 1965 had only 150 for a population of about 4,500,000.

High-income Africans concentrated among the political elite. Towards the end of Empire rapid advancement came to Africans in the Colonial Service. The British created the salary structure of the service to attract Europeans to Africa. It became 'an integral part of the colonial hegemony and a reflection of the "white man's burden" '.[4] This salary structure continued into independence. Zambian 1974 Civil Service salaries had ratios of one to twenty-seven (if one included officers of parastatals, 1:50). Top parastatal officers received $27,750 plus allowances; the lowest employees, $25 per year. Successful politicians also received high salaries. West African legislators in the 1960s received £1,000 per annum, and in addition could pursue their own businesses or professions. Ministers received as much as £3,000.[5]

By 1975, the higher civil service across Africa had land and investments. No longer exclusively a salariat, it approximated a true rentier class. In Nigeria in the early 1960s, many members of the political elite acquired land for petrol stations. The Northern Nigerian Government in 1965 actually had to prohibit civil servants from owning more than one such plot. Kenyan and Zambian civil servants and politicians purchased large settler farms, often with generous bank or government credits. One senior civil service officer in an African country supposedly owned the largest fleet of taxicabs as well as a large commercial farm.

The politicians' hot hands itched even more than the civil servants'. In Nigeria, Chief Festus Okoto-Eboh, the Federal Minister of Finance, owned among other enterprises the only plastic shoe factory in the country. (He imposed a stiff tariff to protect his own infant industry.) In Ghana, the head of the national co-operative organization owned five commercial farms. In Malawi, the President supposedly owned an 80 per cent shareholding of Press Trade Ltd, an octopus-like holding company with enterprises in retail trade, tobacco and transport. Government singularly favoured these companies in grants of trading licences, and the national bank showered them with credits.

The list multiplied endlessly. Two examples from Kenya symbolized the commercial success of some politicians. Hosep Mwangi Kariuki served as Lower House Member for Aberdares, Kenya's National Youth Leader, chairman of the Betting Control and Licensing Board, member of the board of governors of Egerton College, director of Allsopp's East African Breweries, and owned 1,000 acres of farmland, a bookshop, and shares in sisal and coffee, a racing stable and a newspaper[6]. Maside Muliro became MP for Kitale East, Chairman of the Maize and Produce Board, owner of two farms and most of the Kitale Transportation Company.[7]

Most civil servant and politician property owners, however, did not themselves become entrepreneurs. Rather, they invested in speculative

real estate.[8] Northern Nigerian civil servants owned petrol stations but
did not operate them. They used their position as civil servants to
acquire land. They leased it for long terms to oil companies, who built
and operated the petrol stations. The civil servants and politicians who
acquired land in Kenya and Zambia became absentee landlords. Okumu
writes:

> The national elite in Kenya . . . has little serious involvement in
> industrial or farming enterprise. Although it has moved into the
> immediately lucrative purchasing of houses, its precarious financial
> position and its indebtedness forces it to accept managerial positions
> in locally based foreign enterprises which give it little power, if any,
> over the activity of these enterprises. This is a condition which applies
> not only to senior civil servants and politicians but to the new middle
> class as a whole. These are some of the conditions which led Franz
> Fanon to the conclusion that post-independence Africa failed to
> establish a true African middle class, that 'there is only a sort of
> greedy caste, avid and voracious, with the mind of a huckster, only
> too glad to accept the dividends that the former colonial hands out
> to it'. This get-rich-quick middle class shows itself incapable of great
> ideas or of inventiveness.[9]

B. Cohesiveness of Educated Elites

All across Africa, education identified almost all high-income Africans.
In 1960 in Ghana, Nigeria, Kenya, Uganda and Tanganyika, legislators
had educational backgrounds as follows: primary school, 335;
secondary, 103; teachers' training, 204; higher technical or professional
training, 98; graduate, 134; unknown, 18. Their occupations revealed as
much: teachers, 290; traders or businessmen, 147; lawyers, 46; civil
servants, 215; professions, 53; farmers, 29; village or local chief, 12;
clerical and co-operatives, 34; miscellaneous, 37.[10] Sixty-one per cent
had educations above primary school, where the majority of the population suffered illiteracy. Only 4 per cent worked in village occupations
such as farming, although most people lived in the villages.

The educated elites in Africa developed a remarkable cohesiveness.
All the Old Boys came from the same schools: Achimota in Ghana,
King's College in Nigeria, Tabora Boy's in Tanzania, and graduated from
the same universities: London, Legon, Ibadan, Makerere. They married
each other's sisters, drank at the same clubs and met at the same parties.
In West Africa, many came from a few large families that acquired
wealth or education a generation or more before Independence. In

Achimota School in Ghana, during the early 1960s, one-third of the students comprised children of Old Achimotans, the children of educated elites.[11] They chose their friends from others in the same status.[12]

C. Use of Public Resources

These elites drew a disproportionate share of government resources. Even egalitarian Tanzania biased health care and education towards the urban rich. Curative services received 75-80 per cent of the recurrent health budget, while preventive services received about 5 per cent. The wealthy can prevent disease for themselves. They need curative services. The few large hospitals served the urban population – and the elite lived in cities. Muhimbili Hospital in Dar es Salaam received 16 per cent of the curative budget in a city containing 2 per cent of the total population. The cost of building two new regional, urban hospitals could have built nearly 200 rural health centres and clinics, enough to give the country its entire basic complement. The *recurrent* costs of the three large hospitals in Tanzania could provide forty new health centres a year, more than twice the number the Five-Year Plans projected. [13]

Government also skewed the allocation of educational resources. In 1967, Tanzania made Swahili the language of instruction throughout the primary school system, except in a few 'English' schools, mainly for expatriates. Remarkably, many children of African leaders found their way into these schools.[14] In Nkrumah's Ghana, children of professionals had 140 times the chance of entering secondary school as those of semi- and unskilled workers.[15] By 1975 the governors in Africa had become an 'elite of education'.[16] The same held true for other government services. The police patrolled the elite areas of every African city better than the slums. Those areas had better roads, better public transport, better electricity and water supply, more of everything the government dispensed. In Lusaka, Zambia's capital, government employed a remarkable bit of legal legerdemain. More than half the population of Lusaka, all Africans, lived in dreadful urban slums or 'squatter compounds'. The legal position of their miserable shacks lay in impenetrable shambles. The government therefore labelled the squatters 'illegal'. Obviously, government should not extend public services to 'illegal' occupants. Expatriates conveniently occupied most of the 'legal' homes. By 1973 Lusaka provided municipal services to almost all whites but only a few blacks.

D. Consequences for Law-Making

The political elites retreated from change-oriented decisions to support the *status quo* for many reasons.

The radically skewed income distribution pattern warped the economics of every African country:

> The importance of the issue is hard to exaggerate, for it is precisely this aspect of the colonial legacy which lays the basis of what has rightly come to be known as neo-colonial development. Politically these huge differentials [of income] lead directly to class formation and conflicts of interests which impair the ability of the nascent elites to take seriously the need for development with social justice. Economically, it provides the hook from which to hang all of neo-classical economics, and from there all else follows logically. Because this economics considers as the only legitimate demand, demand that is backed by money or 'effective demand', it immediately legitimizes the existing income structure and supports the building of an economic structure which serves the elite, or any outside or foreign agency with money, for resources are channelled to those with 'effective demand'. Non-industrialized economies built on such demand patterns have a high demand for foreign consumer goods and this encourages their dependence on exports and foreign technology, expertise and capital.[17]

Second, the departing Colonial Service carefully educated the most senior African civil servants and some political leaders[18] into its perception of appropriate governmental concerns: law, order and collecting taxes. Radical change violated their domain assumptions. Third, their social position inclined them to the problems of the rich, not the poor. They had new money. 'The parvenu who still seeks to prove that he belongs to the upper class must do so by socializing with others who evidently do belong and thus tends to be reluctant to risk his insecure social standing by being seen with middle-class associates'.[19] Relatively wealthy African elites usually maintained an extraordinary social distance between themselves and lower class Africans. Their upbringing reinforced that distance. 'Separated from their homes during the long years of secondary and university education, most of the African elites have become divorced from their land.'[20] They lived in the administrative centres, particularly the national capital. The gulf between them and the mass yawned deep and wide.

The cohesiveness of the governing elites and their social contacts reinforced their self-interest. Informal communications channels frequently outweigh formal ones.[21] The man he drinks beer with at the club frequently influences an administrator or politician more than formal messages through official channels. Every person has a reference group whose approval and support he seeks. The members of the reference group usually have informal access to each other and to each other's communication channels. Wealthy Africans increasingly coalesced into an aristocracy.

E. The Influence of Foreign Firms

Economic mastery remained with the foreign firms in the export enclaves. They held as clients the new elite. The great foreign enterprises awarded lucrative and high-status managerial posts, dealerships, exclusive agencies and memberships on Boards of Directors.[22] Foreign banks gave credit. Inevitably, Africans seeking economic advancement accommodated foreign enterprise. To decorate their public image, expatriate firms quickly added African executives, usually as public relations or personnel officers.[23] Nyerere, at least, was suspicious:

> When we were struggling for independence, how many of us did the capitalists invite to become directors? How many of us were able to borrow money to build houses for renting out? How many of us were lent money to buy large shambas [farms] on which it is necessary to employ labour? If we have acquired those things since independence most of us have done so because the capitalists want to involve us in their system of exploitation so that we shall become defenders of that system. The fact that this question is asked shows that this technique has had some success.[24]

In their accommodation, they developed social ties. At the formerly all-white Lusaka Club, one could see an occasional black Permanent Secretary playing golf with an otherwise expatriate foursome. In an interview Mr Kariuki, the Kenyan MP, remarked on his ownership of a race horse (he was the first African in Kenya to own one) and his membership in the appropriate club. 'In fact', he said, 'when I am with people like Lord Delemere and Sir Ferdinand and Sir Charles Markham, I feel quite happy — we exchange ideas.'[25] In the Ikoyi Club in Lagos, the Dar es Salaam Yacht Club, the Lusaka Club, all the former outposts of white colonial rule, a few very wealthy, educated Africans mingled with the wealthy, predominantly white membership.

Colin Leys concluded his important article on Kenya elites by remarking on the difference between the African middle class and the petit-bourgeoisie of Marx's day: 'First, in Kenya, they were *in* political power and likely to remain so; although they needed an alliance with other groups, it was difficult to envisage any regime which did not substantially represent them. Second, because of this, and because foreign (i.e. large-scale) capital was seen as indispensable, they were ready to accommodate themselves to it and in a position to insist on reciprocity. The result of these two factors was: (a) a very rapid extension of the system of monopoly and political control to the sectors of the economy the African petty-bourgeoisie was entering; and (b) a system of alliances with foreign capital . . . It was a case of "if you can't beat 'em join 'em" and joining them was on the whole made easy and reasonably rewarding.'[26]

In the event, personal economic interests reconciled political elite with the economic ruling class. They perched on top of the pyramid. They lived the good life: cars, opulent houses, clients and retainers, whirling social life, jet-set travel, the accoutrements of power – they had them all. Their social distance from the mass stretched a vast gulf. No such political elite could remain revolutionary. Their interest in change at most led them to Africanize remaining expatriate power. A perceived necessity for continuing foreign exchange limited even that.[27] By 1975, in most countries they had become a 'bureaucratic bourgeoisie',[28] with strong alliances with foreign enterprise, and a vested interest in slowing change, not accelerating it.

II Why Did A Bureaucratic Bourgeoisie Develop?

Elite theory argues that elites do not reach eminence by serendipity but because of their extraordinary abilities.[29] President Kaunda of Zambia advanced another explanation. Political office depends upon continued electoral support. 'It is this insecurity of political jobs, together with the very human desire to secure one's future and that of one's children, together with dependents, which leads a good number of leaders in political life to think of extra activities in the social and financial world.'[30] Kaunda 'proves' that leaders strive for security because they entered the private sector – precisely the trouble he tries to explain. Civil servants, with the most secure jobs in Africa, engage in the same activities as elected officials, a fact undercutting Kaunda's explanation.

The new African elite did not become a bureaucratic bourgeoisie because of their inherent nature but because of their roles and the range of choice within those roles.[31] The legal order itself gave them power.

I have already discussed three causes for the rise of the bureaucratic bourgeoisie: the growth of the parastatal sector,[32] excess discretionary authority in the civil service[33] and corruption.[34] In addition, the legal regime offered them extraordinary opportunities to join the economic ruling class. Two different opportunities thus opened: investment in the private sector and vast discretionary control over men and resources. Their interests as administrators harmonized with those of the economic ruling class. The two tendencies reinforced each other.

A. Opportunity and Capacity For Private Investment

The socio-economic environment of independent Africa provided the new elite ample opportunities to invest in the private sector because they had: (1) high income, (2) a supportive legal regime, (3) easy credit, (4) Africanization policies and (5) high education.

1. High Incomes. The political elite had the highest incomes among Africans. They had savings to invest. Their incomes ensured easy credit. Corruption sometimes increased their wealth, occasionally beyond belief. Excess capital stimulated the investment itch.

Most African countries had no formal incomes policies.[35] Instead, contract, reflecting market power, determined salaries. Historically high civil service salaries,[36] politicians' power to set their own salaries, and the scarcity of educated personnel for the private sector all drove up their salaries.

2. The Legal Regime of the Private Sector. The common law permits anyone to invest in the private sector, through universalistic rules of contract and property.[37] The rules of real property particularly (a favourite investment for a class that cannot pursue business interests full-time) permit anyone with capital to acquire speculative or income-producing property. Kenya and Nigeria created stock exchanges,[38] encouraging persons with accumulated capital to invest without devoting their full energies to business pursuits. The law thus structured a private sector and permitted the political elite to enter it.

Most countries had only a few rules specifically limiting private economic activity by the political elite. Those constrained the Civil Service more than politicians. The General Orders prohibited only moonlighting and conflicts of interest. In Zambia, an officer might not take an outside job without approval[39] even while on leave.[40] He might not engage 'in trade or in any commercial or agricultural undertaking', although his wife might.[41] He could purchase only a single residential plot without specific permission of the Permanent Secretary (Establishments) on the certification by the officer's own Permanent Secretary that 'in his opinion the purchase of the land will not bring the officer's private affairs into real or apparent conflict with his public duties'.[42]

Civil servants might buy local stocks or shares, but they 'must remember that [their] personal interests as . . . speculative shareholder[s] may not coincide with the interests of [their] general position as . . . civil servant[s], leading to allegations of conflict between private interest and public responsibility.' A civil servant must, therefore, report all such shareholding to the Permanent Secretary (Establishments) who might direct the officer to sell the shares.[43] These rules only attacked conflicts of interest, not the creation of a bureaucratic bourgeoisie. The General Orders proclaimed these rules 'especially important in the case of officers occupying senior posts in the Civil Service, particularly those whose duties include the negotiation of contracts, or the acceptance or rejection of tenders for services, construction and supplies, and those who have or may be considered by the public to have advance information which would help them to profit financially from speculation in stocks and shares'.[44] Embodying British conventions, these regulations made African civil servants rentiers, not entrepreneurs. Civil servants in most countries did not play as visible a role in the private sector as the politicians. A civil servant occasionally resigned to enter a parastatal or private corporation at a higher salary, but Ministers or MPs almost never did so.

Kenya removed even these restrictions on civil servants' business activities. Rather than give civil servants a substantial pay increase, the Ndwega Commission recommended that government give them permission to 'take their opportunities like other citizens'.[45] Government immediately adopted the recommendations.

Minimal rules restricted legislators in their business activities. Parliamentary Standing Orders prohibited Members from voting in matters affecting their personal interest, or, sometimes, merely required them to declare their interest before debating an issue. The Zambian rule excluded from even this latter requirement ' . . . any interest which a Member may have in common with the public generally or with any class or section thereof'.[46] A new tax bill might affect an MP who owned a business. His personal interest might well warp his vote, but this interest fell outside the limiting rules.[47] MPs did not work as such full-time, so most also worked elsewhere.

3. Access to Credit. The credit rules particularly favoured the political elite. To a US trained lawyer, the banking laws of Africa seemed notably vague. In the absence of specified rules, banks in Africa granted credit pursuant to ordinary contract law. Bankers sought above all else sound credit risks. Without property for security, people with high, regular salaries seemed the best risks. The political elite best met this requirement. They easily obtained credit for real estate ventures. 'Investment in building land and house property is . . . one of the main outlets for savings, especially, for instance, in Nigeria and Ghana where salaried elites are able to obtain loans from government corporations. In the former a modern house might well yield a return of fifteen per cent per annum of the cost of the building - an amount which well exceeds the mortgage payment.'[48] Kenya borrowed a large sum from the United Kingdom to buy out white settler farms. It lent this money to good credit risks to purchase the farms. The good credit risks of course, comprised mainly civil servants and politicians.[49] President Kaunda of Zambia said that leaders buy and develop land 'because of our ability to borrow money from banks . . . because of our position as leaders'.[50]

4. Africanization Policies. African governments actively encouraged black Africans to enter economic sectors of the economy that expatriates or colonials formerly monopolized. [51] In colonial Ghana, for example, Lebanese dominated part of the import and wholesale trade. A 1970 ordinance required that Africans own all wholesale and retail businesses doing less that ₵500,000* per year.[52] The political elite seized the advantage. Uganda deported Asians, creating opportunities for those with only a little capital to acquire going businesses. The political elite acquired many such Asian businesses.

5. Educational Qualifications. In general, Western education identified both the political elite and African entrepreneurs.[53] That education equipped them to operate within complex institutions, raise a bank loan, to thread the bureaucracy to find the right person to get a land grant, an import licence or taxicab permit. Thus, the legal order itself gave them opportunities for aggrandizement, which they seized. In so doing, they accordingly allied with the economic ruling class.

B. Development Programmes and the New Property

The ownership of productive property gives the owner the power to command others.[54] Delegating control over others in economic

---

* ₵ = Ghanaian cedis.

affairs in effect makes the power holder the 'owner'.

The African political elite did little to change the fundamental structure of the colonial economies, but they did something. Development
programmes proliferated. Most had hierarchical organization, lodged
power with upper echelons, and great discretion with that power and
few constraints. Broad discretion had two consequences. It often bred
corruption, inflating the already high incomes of the political elite.
In the absence of outright corruption, elite cohesion ensured favours to
old schoolmates, relatives and political allies. In either case, discretionary power aggrandized the political elite.

Three examples illustrate how the system worked. Nigeria land law
made government land of most of Victoria Island, the poshest suburb
in Lagos. It gave the Minister discretionary power to allot it, usually
freely or at a token rent. Many civil servants and MPs obtained land
from the Minister, rented it against house plans, with ten or more years
paid in advance and with the advance rent paid to a builder to construct
the house. The lucky civil servant or MP became the owner of a substantial property with literally no cost to himself.

In colonial East and Central Africa, a highly discretionary licensing
system prevented Asians and Africans from competing with European
firms. After independence, it created monopolies or oligopolies for a
favoured few. For example, in Kenya a colonial licensing system for
road transport effectively excluded Africans from the transport industry
on main roads. A regulation enacted after independence gave the Road
Transport Board power to discriminate against non-citizens. A combin-
ation of circumstances in 1968 made it profitable to transport oil from
the coast to the interior by road instead of by rail. The Board issued only
a few licences, but they went to 'some very prominent people'. For
three years they had an oligopoly in the profitable trade.[55]

Kenya established the Industrial and Commercial Development
Corporation in 1955 to succour flagging expatriate industries during the
Mau-Mau Emergency. In 1967, it capitalized ICDC Investment Company
at £100,000 to buy shares in profitable companies and to sell its own
shares to African citizens. 'By 1970, 59% of its shares had been bought
by some 1,900 Africans . . . The share register read like a roll-call of
the Kikuyu middle class, who held over 95% of the shares sold to
individuals.' The government then loaned ICDC Investment an additional £100,000 in 1970 'for expanding its portfolio' thus increasing
the shareholders' profits at no cost or risk to them.[56]

Only private entrepreneurs in the export enclave could use most of
the goodies which the new political elite dispensed: import licences,

exchange control permits, government credits, pioneer tax advantages, government contracts for construction or supply. The very class that could gain the most from the exercise of elite discretion could handsomely reward the bureaucrats. The economic ruling class, frequently expatriate firms, did so. They had a bundle to give away: directorships, credit, dealerships, legal retainers, bribes. A symbiotic relationship between political elites and the capitalists arose, paralleling that of private-government joint ventures.[57]

Our theory collapses into a set of propositions:

1. Where laws and institutions create and support a private sector, and the political elite have high incomes, access to credit and education, and Africanization programmes encourage them to enter the private sector, they will invest in the private sector.

2. Where new development programmes rely on either parastatals, or the civil service, and give unstructured, unreviewable discretionary power to their managers and directors, exercisable in secret, their managers and directors will tend to use their power to maximize rewards and minimize strains for themselves and their bureaucracy.

3. In most African polities, the private sector, especially the great expatriate firms, offered the greatest rewards and threatened the greatest strains to bureaucrats.

I suggest, more succinctly, a general hypothesis: *state control over the economy through hierarchical structures with great discretion lodged in the political elite within an economy with a relatively strong private sector will likely result in an alliance between the political elite and the economic ruling class.*

It exemplified the Marxist hypothesis that every system of economy germinates the seeds of its own demise. Capitalism requires a working class that in time will overthrow capitalism. In the same way, African development efforts involved various sorts of development programmes and enterprise. In Africa, these very efforts fostered an alliance between political elite and economic ruling class. The interests of the political elite came to lie in stagnation, not development. In each case, the state by the legal order created a new class with the potential to destroy the very order that created it.

Western states developed systems of property and contract law that created the capitalist system — and the industrial proletariat. In Africa, too, the state structured the economy — and bred a new class, the bureaucratic bourgeoisie, that rapidly lost any will for radical structural change.

III Institutional Constraints on the Formation of a Bureaucratic Bourgeoisie

The bureaucratic bourgeoisie arose because African political elites used the legal order as they did. They might have used it differently. I have earlier suggested some alternative legal forms: better controls over para-statal managers and directors; a participatory instead of an authoritarian bureaucratic structure; controls over corruption. Reduction in secrecy and better feedback channels might also help.[58] Here I discuss only devices to prevent the political elite from entering the private sector.

Traditional theories assume that officials become biased and greedy. Civil service and parliamentary rules supposedly prevent private interest from controlling public decision, with civil service rules going further to prevent even the appearance of conflict of interest. More radical social models perceive the problem not as merely one of personal, but of class interest. Capital formation by the political elite likely develops interests congruent with the economic ruling class. The political elite will then usually favour these common interests. Inevitably, they will support existing capitalist institutions, rather than changing them. A Leadership Code does not require law-makers to choose the socialist path, but its absence can never do so.

These different models produced different solutions. Three African states — Ghana, Tanzania and Zambia — introduced Leadership Codes. Tanzania went further and reduced the opportunities for private investment.

A. The Leadership Codes

1. Content. Ghana's Leadership Code focused upon the first of the two troubles, Tanzania's upon the second. Zambia moved from the first to the more radical perception during the formulation process.

a. Ghana. Cutting the ties between the Ghanaian political elite and the economic ruling class aborted. President Nkrumah spoke on this subject only in the famous Dawn Broadcast of 8 April 1961, saying that 'any Party Member of Parliament who wishes to be a business-

man can do so but he should give up his seat in Parliament . . . This
tendency [to enter the private sector] is working to alienate the support
of the masses and to bring the National Assembly into isolation.'[59] The
President's Office ruled that party members should not own more than
two houses of a combined value of £20,000, more than two motor cars,
or additional land worth more than £500.[60] The rules did not prohibit
leaders from entering trade, holding more than one government job, or
investing in the private sector but aimed mainly at ostentatious living
by party members. They did not affect civil servants directly, since the
General Orders already contained analogous provisions. Nkrumah's
ideology produced this limited reach for the Ghanaian code. Despite
his 'socialist' rhetoric, Nkrumah saw a 'classless' Africa.[61] His explanation for Africa's poverty focused on evil foreigners, neo-colonialists
and imperialists and blinded him to the role of the Ghanaian elite. He
therefore worried about elite legitimacy but not about its alliance with
the economic ruling class, about flaunting wealth but not about class
interests. After 1962, Nkrumah rapidly lost his popular support for
many reasons: the fall in cocoa prices, economic chaos, preventive
detention, haphazard economic planning, corruption.[62] He believed he
had to surround himself with personal loyalists, many already corrupt.
He took no vigorous steps to implement the Dawn Broadcast.[63]

b. Tanzania. The Arusha Declaration (1967) took a forthright stand
against class formation: A truly socialist state 'does not have two classes
of people: a lower class consisting of people who work for their living
and an upper class consisting of those who live on other people's
labour. In a true Socialist State no person exploits another, but everybody who is able to work does so and gets a fair income for his labour,
and incomes do not differ substantially.'[64] 'Peasants and workers'
must in fact as well as theory lead a socialist state. Such leaders 'should
never live on another's labour, neither should [they] have capitalistic
tendencies . . . Socialism is an ideology and it is difficult for leaders to
implement it if they do not believe in it.'[65] Nyerere had warned of
the possibilities as early as 1962:

As nationalism becomes successful, the chances of Europeans and
the Asians maintaining a permanent privileged position in our
countries will tend to diminish. But the chances of the educated
Africans to become a new privileged class will multiply. Yet this
will not be so obvious while the Europeans and Asians are so
strikingly wealthier than the Africans. The would-be African ex-

ploiter can masquerade as a great social reformer by concentrating the attack on European and Asian privilege. Before we know where we are, what is now an essentially dying-out privileged class will have been replaced by a permanently privileged class of educated Africans.[66]

The Arusha Declaration therefore went beyond conflicts of interest or ostentatious living. It contained standards for leadership that undermined the alliance between political elite and economic ruling class.

1. Every TANU and Government leader must be either a peasant or a worker, and should in no way be associated with the practices either of Capitalism or Feudalism.

2. No TANU or Government leader should hold shares in any Company.

3. No TANU or Government leader should hold directorships in any privately-owned enterprises.

4. No TANU or Government leader should receive two or more salaries.

5. No TANU or Government leader should own houses which he rents to others.

6. For the purposes of this Resolution the term 'leader' should comprise the following: Members of the TANU National Executive Committee; Ministers, Members of Parliament, Senior Officials of organizations affiliated to TANU, senior officials of parastatal organizations, all those appointed or elected under any clause of the TANU Constitution, councillors, and civil servants in high and middle cadres. (In this context 'leader' means a man, or a man and his wife; a woman; or a woman and her husband.)

Elite pressures apparently led to four significant changes that appeared in the implementing legislation.[67] First, that legislation changed the dual salary provisions to allow both a leader and his spouse to receive a salary.[68] Second, it defined income from a trust or *waqf* (the Islamic analogue to a trust) as a 'salary'[69] thus permitting a leader to transfer income-producing property or shares in trust for a spouse without other income. Third, it defined the word 'salary' so that a leader might receive income from more than one source, so long as the total did not exceed

An MP's salary.[70] Finally, 'salary' excluded income from contract payments. A lawyer MP, for example, could continue to receive legal fees in addition to his MPs salary.[71] The Leadership Code did not seriously threaten the means of any leader with a reasonably stable marriage. At best, it warned young people that the path to great wealth no longer lay in politics.

C. Zambia. Zambia's Code on paper progressed from the Ghanaian to the Tanzanian models. The President first proposed a Code in 1970. A number of provisions from the Tanzanian Code seemingly reduced participation by Party leaders or senior public servants in the private sector. The rules forbade them, for example, from associating in any way with the practices of capitalism and other forms of exploitation; from receiving more than one salary; from participating in business, either as an individual entrepreneur, shareholder or director. A Party leader 'must choose either to remain in the Party or Government leadership, or retire to engage in other pursuits in industry, business or farming'. On the other hand, leaders could become landlords, except 'whilst living in a Government house'. President Kaunda justified applying the Code to 'leaders' and 'senior public servants' because 'all these people handle, in one way or another, state secrets which they can take advantage of in pursuit of their own interests at the expense of their fellow men who are not privileged to know Government policy'.[72]

The 1970 proposal was never beyond talk. The question arose again in 1972. The Report of the National Commission on the Establishment of a One-Party Participatory Democracy in Zambia[73] clearly identified the problems as corruption and legitimacy.[74] The proposed Code stated:

(b) No leader who is in full-time employment and receiving a salary from *party or public funds* shall take a paid employment which would, in all, entitle him to two or more salaries *from party or public funds:*

(d) No leader . . . shall let a house owned by him *whilst living in a house belonging to the state.* Party, local authority or any other authority or employer where such authority or employer receives public funds or funds appropriated by Parliament [emphasis supplied] .

Leaders must not own businesses, but could hold managerial or profes-

sional posts in the private sector while receiving a salary from public or
Party funds.

In its White Paper on the Commission Report, the government only
remarked that the proposed Leadership Code required more study. The
1972 One-Party Constitution accordingly provided for a Leadership
Code Committee to promulgate the Leadership Code, curiously without
requiring formal approval by Parliament, Cabinet or Party.

In 1973, the Leadership Code Committee went beyond its predecessors. It forbade any leader from engaging in any business, trade or
profession, or receiving any remuneration, gain or profit, except the
salary of his office; from owning more than one plot of land, (connected
with his dwelling house, and not to exceed ten hectares); or from
renting out that house (unless transferred). It excepted only interest
on bank deposits, on Zambian Government bonds, and income from
personal labour on a personal plot of land.[75]

The coverage of the 1973 Code, however, enormously (and un-
accountably) expanded. Until the Code saw print, the public assumed
it would apply only to senior personnel. The Committee's Code
reached 'all civil servants' (apparently even the sweepers in the
ministries), all members of the police force and the defence forces,
every university employee and all parastatal employees. (In Zambia,
this latter category included some 40,000 low-paid copper miners, for
the state had a 51 per cent shareholding in the mining companies.) It
reached every spouse and child of all these 'leaders'. Miners earning
some $90 per month with no political or executive responsibilities
hardly qualified as members of the political elite. They comprised
many of the 200,000 people to whom Zambia's leadership code
included – with their families, probably one-quarter of Zambia's
population. For most of its subjects, the Committee's Leadership Code
required job-sharing, rather than preventing the alliance of political and
economic elites.

2. *Enforcement.* A leadership code became an obvious candidate for
soft development. The codes prescribed vastly changed leadership
behaviour at great personal cost. How to enforce them?

Zambia chose a course typical of 'soft' development: sweeping laws,
paper dragons of negative sanctions, and a cloud of moral suasion. The
1973 Zambian Code required a once-only affidavit, filed either within
three months after enactment or the leader taking his post. It failed to
provide for checking the accuracy of the affidavits filed, understandably
in view of the over 200,000 affidavits it required. For violation, the

Code threatened only dismissal and suspension from the Party. Negative
sanctions to rules susceptible of widespread disobedience cost a great
deal to enforce.[76] Rewards for non-compliance ran high, the avenues for
successful avoidance or evasion opened wider. The Code gave yet
another weapon to the top leadership to beat dissent. Negative sanctions
for common misbehaviour create discretionary power to impose them
selectively. Inevitably, power-holders exercise discretion to serve themselves. A Code provision that permitted the President in his discretion
to relieve any leader of its burden reinforced this prediction.

The same negative sanctions supported Tanzania's Leadership Code
as Zambia's: removal from office and suspension from the party. The
code, however, applied to many fewer people. The Tanzanian Code
therefore required annual affidavits rather than the Zambian once-only
affidavit. Published research has not studied the Tanzanian Code's
effectiveness. As of 1972, only two MPs had resigned or suffered ouster
under it. Over a quarter of District and Town Councillors resigned
rather than comply, perhaps because councillors receive no pay.[77] So
porous a Code, however, could not long prevent elite enrichment.
Tanzania, however, introduced a variety of roundabout measures to
prevent the growth of a bureaucratic bourgeoisie.

B. Roundabout Measures in Tanzania

In addition to the Leadership Code, Tanzania aimed two principal
strategies in support of its aims. It reduced both elite income (hence
available investment funds) and the size of the private sector (hence
investment opportunities). In 1966, President Nyerere cut his Ministers'
salaries by 20 per cent and other officials' salaries by somewhat smaller
amounts. By 1974, Civil Service incomes spread only from 1:18, much
less than other African countries. Parastatal organizations followed the
same scale. Government withdrew car allowances from ministers and
forbade high officials government car loans.[78] Withdrawing these perquisites reduced some incomes by 50 per cent.[79] Taxation and pricing
policies reduced liquidity in the upper income groups. Loans for private
housing had a limit of Shs/75,000 (US $11,000). Government prohibited
the importation of all private automobiles except Volkswagens and
Volvos. The Mercedes Benz, the symbol of the new elite (sometimes
called 'waBenzi' or 'people of the Benz') became a thing of the past.
Opportunities in the private sector sharply narrowed. Parastatals took
over most expatriate firms. Their pay schedules conformed to the
national incomes policy, and the Leadership Code applied to their
managers. Parastatals in the agricultural wholesale trade and import-

export trade, formerly lush grounds for private profit, reduced speculation. Most important, in 1970, the state expropriated all private rental
housing in Tanzania, thus at a stroke removing the single most popular
investment opportunity for the newly rich.[80] Tanzania did not
vigorously Africanize the private sector, as did most other African
countries. Because Tanzania had nationalized the banking system, it
directly controlled credit. It was doubtful that a leader would approach
a nationalized bank for a loan that obviously financed an illegal investment.

Conclusion

Alliances between political elite and economic ruling class did not arise
by blind chance. The state made certain choices about law and state
power, many of them genuinely to induce development. Many factors
channelled those choices: ideology, resources and existing institutions.
As a result, the very development programmes that the state undertook
entangled the political elite with the economic ruling class and created
relationships that blocked further development.

The new alliance between political elite and economic ruling class
arose because African political elites were not so much evil as human.
Growing up in an acquisitive milieu, acting within legal institutions that
encouraged get-rich-quick, African elites typically did not resemble
angels. The bureaucratic bourgeoisie did not arise because of the political
elite's value-sets or attitudes, but because of their institutional environment. The solution therefore lay in better designing African institutions.
Some leadership codes tried to prevent the alliance between political
leaders and economic rulers because the private sector and its captains
too readily co-opted the political governors. Without a private sector,
governments would need no leadership code. A leadership code could
not work, however, on negative sanctions and exhortation alone.
Roundabout measures removing the bases for elite entrepreneurial
activity seemed required. Tanzania's course suggested a possible route,
although its success remained doubtful.

Notes

1. Republic of Kenya, *Development Plan 1966-70* (Nairobi: Government
   Printer, 1966), p. 28; in general, see ILO, *Employment, Incomes and
   Equality, A Strategy for Increasing Productive Employment in Kenya*
   (Geneva: ILO, 1972).
2. J. Okumu, 'The Socio-Political Setting', in G. Hyden, R. Jackson and J.

Okumu (eds.), *Development Administration: The Kenya Experience* (Nairobi: Oxford University Press, 1970), p. 25.

3. P.C. Lloyd, *The New Elites of Tropical Africa* (London: Oxford University Press, 1966), p. 11.
4. Okumu, 'Socio-Political Setting', p. 37.
5. Lloyd, *New Elites,* p. 11.
6. Quoted in C. Gertzel, M. Goldschmitt and D. Rothschild (eds.), *Government and Politics in Kenya: A Nation-Building Text* (Nairobi: East African Publishing House, 1969), p. 78.
7. Ibid.
8. Lloyd, *New Elites*, p. 5.
9. Okumu, 'Socio-Political Setting', p. 40.
10. G. Hunter, *The New Societies of Tropical Africa* (London: Oxford University Press, 1962), p. 285 .
11. Rough count by Jonathan Seidman, then a student at Achimota, in 1964.
12. Lloyd, *New Elites,* p. 38.
13. M. Segall, 'The Politics of Health in Tanzania', in J.F. Rweyemanu, J. Loxley, J. Wicken and C. Nyirabu, *Towards Socialist Planning* (Dar es Salaam: Tanzania Pub. House, 1972), p. 149.
14. A. Van de Laar, 'Growth and Income Distribution in Tanzania Since Independence', in L. Cliffe and J. Saul (eds.), *Socialism in Tanzania* (Nairobi: East African Publishing House, 1972), p. 106.
15. Lloyd, *New Elites,* p. 25; see P. Foster, *Education and Social Change in Ghana* (London: Routledge and Kegan Paul, 1965); cf. R. Clignet and P. Foster, *The Fortunate Few: A Study of Secondary Schools and Students in the Ivory Coast* (Evanston: Northwestern University Press, 1966).
16. A. Ardener, 'The Notion of the Elite: A Review Article', *Af. Affairs,* 66, 64 (1967).
17. H. Bienefeld, *Tanzania: Party Transformations and Economic Development* (Princeton: Princeton University Press, 1967), p. 181.
18. R. B. Seidman, 'Administrative Law and Legitimacy in Anglo-Phonic Africa: A Problem in the reception of Foreign Law', *Law and Society Review,* 5, 161 (1970); see Chap. 2.
19. P.M. Blau, *Exchange and Power in Social Life* (New York: Wiley, 1967), p. 139, quoted in M. Buraway, *The Color of Class* (Lusaka: Institute for African Studies, University of Zambia, 1972), p. 63.
20. Lloyd, *New Elites,* p. 9.
21. H.A. Simon, D.W. Smithburg and V.A. Thompson, *Public Administration* (New York: Alfred A. Knopf, 1950), p. 226.
22. C. Leys, 'The Limits of African Capitalism: The Formation of the Monopolistic Petty Bourgeoisie in Kenya' (Cyclostyle; n.d.).
23. Lloyd, *New Elites,* p. 8; Buraway, *Color of Class.*
24. J. Nyerere, *Arusha Declaration, Answers to Questions* (Dar es Salaam: Government Printer, 1967), p. 7.
25. Quoted in Gertzel *et al., Government and politics in Kenya,* p. 82.
26. Leys, 'Limits of African Capitalism'.
27. Buraway, *Color of Class.*
28. R. Dumont, *False Start in Africa* (London: Deutsch, 1966); see also R. Wraith and E. Simpkins, *Corruption in Developing Countries* (London: Routledge and Kegan Paul, 1963) (a 'gentry').
29. See generally G. Parry, *Political Elites* (London: George Allen and Unwin, 1969); T. Bottomore, *Elites and Society* (London: Watts, 1964); see above, Chap. 19.
30. K.D. Kaunda, 'Address on the Occasion of the Opening of the National

Council, 1st December, 1972' in *A Nation of Equals — The Kabwe Declaration: Address to the National Council on the United Independence Party at the Hindu Hall, Kabwe, 1-3 December 1972* (Lusaka: Government Printer, n.d.).

31. Cf. C. Wright Mills, *The Power Elite* (New York: Oxford University Press, 1965).
32. See above, Chap. 14.
33. See above, Chap. 15.
34. See above, Chap. 10.
35. Those that did tended to limit their strictures to wage-earners. See e.g. ILO, *UNDP Tax, Report to the Government of the United Republic of Tanzania on Wages, Incomes and Prices Policy* (Dar es Salaam: Government Printer, 1967) (Government Paper No. 3 of 1967); see generally A. Seidman, *Planning Development in Sub-Saharan Africa* (New York: Praeger, 1974).
36. Dumont, *False Start*.
37. S. Picciotto, 'The International Firm, International Law and the Nation-State', *E.A.L. Rev.*, 6, 1, 3 (1973); see above, Chap. 5.
38. Note, 'Securities Marketing and Stock Exchanges in Black Africa', *Col. L. Rev.*, 62, 892 (1967).
39. *General Orders, Issued by the Permanent Secretary [Zambia]* (Lusaka: Government Printer, 1966) General Order 63(a).
40. Ibid., General Order 63(b).
41. Ibid., General Order 62.
42. Ibid., General Order 61.
43. Ibid., General Order 60(a).
44. Ibid., General Order 60(b).
45. Republic of Kenya, *Report of the Commission of Inquiry — Public Service Structure and Remuneration Commission* (Nairobi: Government Printer, 1971), p. 14.
46. Republic of Zambia, *National Assembly Standing Orders* (Lusaka: Government Printer, 1967), Sec. 5(2).
47. L. Cliffe, 'Personal or Class Interest: Tanzania's Leadership Conditions', in L. Cliffe and Saul, *Socialism and Tanzania*, p. 254.
48. Lloyd, *New Elites*, p. 9.
49. Republic of Kenya, *Report . . .*, pp. 13-15.
50. Kaunda, 'Address'.
51. A.A. Beveridge, 'Economic Independence, Indigenization and the African Businessman: Some Effects of Zambia's Economic Reforms', *Af. Stud. Rev.*, 27, 447 (1975); J.C. deWilde, *The Development of African Private Enterprise* (Washington, D.C.: IBRD, 1971).
52. Ghana: Ghanaian Business (Promotion) Act, 1970 (Act 334) 11-15, 19.
53. A.A. Beveridge, 'African Businessmen in Zambia: Their Origins, Growth and Impact' (Department of Economics, University of Zambia, mimeo, 1973).
54. K. Renner, *The Institutions of Private Law and Their Social Functions*, O. Kahn-Freund, ed. and tr. (London, 1949); see above Chap. 5.
55. Leys, 'Limits of African Capitalism'.
56. Ibid.
57. See above, Chap. 14.
58. See below, Chap. 21.
59. D. Austin, *Politics in Ghana, 1946-1960* (London: Oxford University Press, 1964), p. 403.
60. Ibid., p. 405.
61. K. Nkrumah, *Consciencism* (London: Heinemann, 1965).

62. For a brilliant novelistic picture of the loss of legitimacy, see K. Armah, *The Beautiful Ones Are Not Yet Born* (Boston: Houghton-Mifflin, 1968).

63. K. Nkrumah, *Dark Days in Ghana* (London: Pasaf, 1968).

64. The *Arusha Declaration and TANU's Policy on Socialism and Self-Reliance* (Dar es Salaam: Publicity Section, TANU, 1967), p. 3.

65. Ibid., p. 4.

66. J. Nyerere, 'Speech on Receiving an Honorary Degree at Makerere', *Africa Report*, May 1963, p. 9.

67. The Interim Constitution of Tanzania (Amendment) (No. 2) Act, 1967 (Act No. 40 of 1967).

68. Ibid., Sec. 27(d).

69. Ibid., Sec. 12(a) (10).

70. Ibid., Sec. 12(b).

71. Ibid., Sec. 12. See generally, B. Rahim, 'Legislative Implementation of the Arusha Declaration', *East Af. L.J.*, 4, 183 (1968).

72. K.D. Kaunda, *Take Up The Challenge, Speeches made by His Excellency the President Dr. K.D. Kaunda to the UNIP National Council, Mulungushi Hall, Lusaka, 7-16 November 1970* (Lusaka: Zambia Information Services, 1970), p. 52.

73. *Report of the National Commission on the Establishment of a One-Party Participatory Democracy in Zambia* (Lusaka: Government Printer, 1972), pp. 54 *et seq.*

74. The Leadership Code 'would eliminate corruption among leaders, ensure and maintain a high standard of discipline and portray an unquestionable recitude as well as a high sense of duty and responsibility. Thus their public image would be protected from unnecessary attacks and insinuations.' Ibid.

75. The Leadership Code, published in full in the *Zambia Daily Mail*, 26 Oct. 1973, p. 6.

76. See above, Chap. 9.

77. L. Cliffe and J. Saul (eds.), *Socialism in Tanzania: An Interdisciplinary Reader* (Nairobi: East African Publishing House, 1972), p. 254; see also B. Rahim, 'Legislative Implementation'.

78. Van de Laar, 'Growth and Income Distribution', p. 114.

79. Ibid.

80. The Acquisition of Buildings Act, 1971; see R.B. Martin, *Personal Freedom and the Law in Tanzania* (Nairobi: Oxford University Press, 1974).

21 WHOM DOES GOVERNMENT REPRESENT? INFLUENCE, REPRESENTATION, PARTICIPATION AND LAW-MAKING

An hierarchical legal order inevitably generates a powerful elite preoccupied with its own interests. Mass participation seemed the obvious solution. Although every African government agreed rhetorically, most seemed to aid the rich and powerful, not the poor and oppressed. Participation in small groups seemed possible.[1] Institutions for mass participation on national questions, however, seemed unlikely. For example, TANU declared that its leaders and experts should implement plans 'that have been agreed upon by the people'.[2] What institutions could possibly realize that bold declaration?

The complex nature of political decisions provides an answer. National decisions 'can rarely, if ever, be described in terms of a single, once and for all act. Instead a "decision" on any major policy must be seen as the outcome of an accumulation of smaller "decisions" in which many people have taken part . . .'[3] Because complex systems, not individuals, make national level political decisions the working rules that define their inputs, conversion processes and feedbacks explain their range of outputs.[4] They determine what problems the system will address, that is, *whose* difficulties, explanations, data and proposals for solution it will consider. These working rules determine who has influence, and therefore, whose interests the outcome will likely favour.

No polity has devised very useful institutions for direct mass participation in national conversion processes. Referenda and public opinion polls become expensive, clumsy and manipulable, and depend on the level of mass information. Mass participation in national level questions can at most supply inputs and feedbacks to the system. Most Western constitutions formally limit mass participation to the very narrow input function of representative elections. Joseph Schumpeter defined democracy as 'that institutional arrangement for arriving at political decisions in which individuals acquire the power to decide by means of a competitive struggle for the people's vote'.[5] If political democracy kept its promises, African governments would represent the impoverished majority. Instead, in practice they largely ignored it.

A course of decision that favours a particular group or class must result partially from the inputs and feedbacks the governors hear.

Influence, ensuring that governors understand and attend to one's problems,[6] therefore, depends upon access to feedback and input processes. A government represents those who influence it. Influence never distributes itself equally. Governments must have input and feedback processes.[7] Decision-makers, however, cannot consider everything. Input and feedback processes therefore select the messages they will accept, from whom they will accept them, and how they will transmit whose messages. Thus, these processes must advantage some and disadvantage others. Particularly strata and groups have varying influence with government, which therefore represents them differently. Governments cannot act 'neutrally'.

I attempt to relate different input and feedback processes to the likelihood of real development. I then examine African bureaucracy, Parliament and Party as principal input and feedback channels in light of this theory.

I A Theory of Input and Feedback Related to Development

Input and feedback channels discriminate in the sorts of messages they accept; the publics they hear and the relative amounts of information these publics possess; and how they aggregate information for decision-makers.

A. *Kinds of Inputs and Feedbacks Accepted*

We can distinguish three sorts of input and feedback channels:[8] goal-seeking or negative, goal-changing or learning, and consciousness or self-awareness. A governmental agency monitors one of its programmes. As it learns that the programme is failing, it corrects to reach the selected goal (negative feedback). The electorate votes the former opposition into power with a new party platform. The elections signal new goals to the governors (goal-changing or learning feedback). A convention, after examining the existing constitution proposes changes to amend the state's fundamental power relationships (consciousness, or 'self-awareness' feedback). Self-evidently, the broader an input or feedback channel's scope, the greater the influence of those with access. The scope of feedback also determines the possible rate of induced change.

Every situation can have a variety of outcomes. Complicated situations have great potential for unforeseen consequences, and hence in such situations, government needs quick, broad-reaching feedback.[9] Governments seeking development become organizations in flux,[10] in the midst of the most complex, difficult, unknown, rapidly changing state of affairs in all the world. Without a broad scope of inputs and feedback circuits, government can only attempt incremental change.

The sorts of messages the system will transmit differently affects the interests of various publics. A system which permits only negative feedback favours publics who agree with existing programmes. A system which permits messages complaining about governmental structure, (consciousness or self-awareness feedback) favours more radical publics. The one can trigger only incremental, the other revolutionary change.

B. Access

Access to any particular input or feedback system determines which public it will advantage. A law school dean whose door opens easily to senior faculty, but not to students, will decide on information from faculty, not students. Faculty and student perceptions of difficulties, their explanations and solutions, often vary. Those who may see the dean control his decisions. A minister whose door opens to expatriate chairmen or managing directors of foreign enterprise but not to the leaders of trade unions, and less to individual peasants, will probably act accordingly. Access partially defines influence.

In general, lower bureaucratic levels gather primary data. Higher levels deal with aggregated data, explanations and solutions. Higher levels of access mean greater influence. A petitioner who can see the Permanent Secretary of the Ministry of Agriculture likely has greater influence than one who sees a lowly *bwana shamba* (agricultural extension officer).

C. Information

Without information, governors cannot make sensible decisions.[11] Since access incorporates one into decision-making, access requires information. The rules that define opportunity and capacity to acquire information help to explain influence.

D. The Aggregation of Information

Bits of information only ineffectually affect decision. Policy-makers require problem definitions, explanations and solutions ('options'), and the aggregated data or 'legislative facts' on which these rest.[12] An input and feedback circuit's capacity to convert raw information into more usable forms measures its effectivness.

Summary: A Theory of Influence

I propose an explanation for the tendency of African governments, despite populist or socialist rhetoric, to favour the rich and powerful:

1. The range of inputs and feedbacks that governors received performs the range of decisions.

2. Therefore, governors make decisions that advantage those publics whose messages they receive as inputs and feedbacks.

3. a. 'Influence' means the opportunity and capacity to obtain governmental decisions that favour one's interests.

   b. Governors 'represent' a particular public when they make decisions that favour its interests; that is, governors represent publics who influence them.

4. The sorts of messages governors receive as inputs and feedbacks depend on:

   a. The messages input and feedback institutions accept and transmit, and

   b. The changes those institutions make in those messages while transmitting them to the governors.

5. The relative influence of a particular public therefore depends upon whether input and feedback institutions will transmit messages that favour its interests, and make only favourable changes in them.

6. Whether such institutions transmit messages that favour any particular public depends upon:

   a. That public's ability to acquire relevant information;

   b. Its access to input and feedback institutions;

   c. The sorts of messages those institutions accept and transmit; and

   d. Those institutions'capacity to process messages into usable forms for law-making.

7. In independent Africa,

   a. Government kept many of its activities secret, and

   b. Access to input and feedback institutions lay mainly with the political elite and the economic ruling class; and

      c. These institutions rejected or filtered out all but negative
         feedback; and

      d. These institutions had very weak aggregational capacity.

    8. Therefore, African governments tended to represent the elite and
       the economic ruling class.

Obviously, the elite and the economic ruling class always have access,
if only through a myriad of social contacts at work, club and home. Any
access of the poor always comes through mass movements (strikes,
demonstrations), or through formal institutions. I examine here only
three formal input and feedback institutions; the civil service bureaucracy; Parliament; and the Party.[13] I assess these institutions against
four criteria: the messages they transmitted; access; ability to acquire
information; and aggregational capacity. Together they indicate which
publics had influence, and therefore whom the African governors
represented.

II The Civil Service as Feedback Channel

The balance of power between bureaucracy on the one hand, and
Parliament, Party and the executive on the other, capsized the classic
myths.[14] The bureaucracy all but monopolized inputs and feedbacks to
law-makers. Generally,

> Cabinet ministers can hope to control the activities of their bureau-
> cracy through reports from clients of government departments or
> sympathetic party followers. The minister, however, is at the mercy
> of his subordinates in situations in which the public at large is not
> aware of government activities. In such situations, civil servants who
> do not agree with, or do not understand the purposes of the govern-
> ment, are able to modify policy without much fear of detection. Max
> Weber has pointed out that the absolute dictator is often completely
> in the power of his bureaucracy, since, unlike the democratic ruler,
> he has no means of discovering whether his policies are being en-
> forced. Weber suggested that the bureaucracy is less powerful in a
> democracy, for the governing politicians will be kept informed by the
> public. This suggestion is only half-truth, for the public can be aware
> of only a part of the government's activities. The areas of government
> work that are hidden from the eyes of the public are often closed to
> the cabinet minister as well.[15]

I earlier discussed four institutions which shape the civil service: the independent civil service Commission, the convention of anonymity,[16] the internal communication channels[17] and capacity to aggregate information.[18] Here I discuss only secrecy, the kinds of messages the bureaucracy transmits, and access.

A. Secrecy

Axiomatically, participation depends upon knowledge. James Madison wrote: 'Knowledge will forever govern ignorance. And a people who mean to be their own governors must arm themselves with the power knowledge gives. A popular government without popular information, or the means of obtaining it, is but a prologue to a farce or tragedy, or perhaps both.'[19]

Policy-makers need three sorts of information: specific descriptions; legislative facts; and reliable knowledge, propositions that either explain reality, or propose and weight solutions. African bureaucracies collected all three. Their capacity to collect and aggregate information, and to exclude others from that process or its products, in part explained their power. In Anglophonic Africa, official secrecy blacked out all sorts of information. In 1973 Zambia proposed to create Intensive Development Zones to focus rural development.[20] Government formulated the IDZ plans in Stygian secrecy. Nobody, not researchers, reporters, even local officials in the targeted areas, could discover these plans, although one advance publicity blurb emphasized participation in planning as the key to a successful IDZ programme! No Zambian non-bureaucrat had any influence in the process.

Again: officials of Tanzania's Ministry of Economic Affairs and Development Planning early in 1969 submitted the Second National Development Plan to the Cabinet, the Party's National Executive Committee and the National Conference of TANU. Government published it only at the last stage. By that time, of course, any critique came too late. Only planners (mostly expatriate) and Tanzania's political elite influenced the process.[21]

The secrecy rule applied as well to historical matters. As did all the former English colonies, Nkrumah's Ghana forbade researchers from examining archival documents more recent than fifty years. (When Britain reduced its secrecy period to thirty years, all the Anglophonic African countries obediently followed suit.) As late as 1965, Ghana forbade research into colonial archives after 1915. Learning from experience, the only path to rational government, becomes impossible when one can only learn from experience fifty years out of date.

1. Origins and Causes. Scholars have advanced historical, class, socio-logical and psychological explanations for British governmental secrecy, Historically, office-holders 'owned' their office, and hence information gathered in connection with it.[22] Senior civil servants insisted upon secrecy to save their jobs.[23] Strict secrecy rules permitted overly cautious civil servants to stamp everything 'secret'.[24] Surely the thirst for power explains much governmental secrecy.[25] Like anonymity, secrecy represents 'one of the greatest strategic triumphs of the bureau-cracy'; 'a method of exercising power without being required to pay the costs of error'.[26] It ensures that political leaders will give extra weight to bureaucratic advice, since civil servants alone have 'the facts'. Secrecy becomes a device for reversing the blue print of political sup-remacy over the civil service.

The Colonial Service, of course, ruled as authoritarian government, naked and unashamed. It maintained perfect inscrutability, if only to protect itself from African nationalists.[27]

2. The Institutions of Secrecy. The General Orders for the Civil Service and the Official Secrets Acts defined official secrecy. I examine Zambia as a case study.

General Orders. A thick booklet of General Orders governed em-ployment conditions in every African civil service. Zambia's stated:

> It is an offence under the Official Secrets Ordinance for any officer
> to disclose, except to an authorized person or in the course of his
> duty, any matter or information which he has obtained or to which
> he has had access on account of his official position. This pro-
> hibition relates to disclosure in any manner, either orally or in
> writing, and whether by publication in the Press or in book form.
> It applies to all officers not only during the period of their service
> with Government but also after they had left that service.[28]

Literally, it made the location of the toilets in the Ministry an official secret. (Actually, it went beyond the draconian Official Secrets Act.) Other sections limited the articles an officer might publish,[29] press communications,[30] and empowered his Permanent Secretary to censor an officer's lectures and books.[31]

Official Secrets. The Official Secrets Acts in Africa sprang from the 1911 Act of the United Kingdom[32] and its 1920 revision.[33] Britain recently reduced its broad reach. Africa did the opposite as changes in the Zambian statute from its origins[34] to 1974[35] demonstrated.

These Acts had two related thrusts: against espionage, and to prevent leaks of confidential information. Originally, the espionage sections prohibited making any sketch or note that was 'calculated' or 'might' be or was 'intended' to be 'directly or indirectly useful to any enemy',[36] for a purpose 'prejudicial to the safety or interests of the State'. The 'known character' of the accused, however, might prove the mental element.[37] If a person communicated with a foreign agent, the statute presumed a wrongful purpose; and if he visited the address of a foreign agent, the law presumed communication.[38] In 1967 this was expanded[39] to forbid any person who had taken the Security Oath[40] to reveal to any unauthorized person any information that he learned in his employment.[41] Only a few people in unusually sensitive executive positions, however, took the oath.[42] A 1969 revision extended these provisions to every government officer,[43] who could now commit the crime by telling anyone anything directly or indirectly 'useful' to a 'foreign power' or a 'disaffected person'.[44]

The second thrust of the Official Secrets Acts tried to plug official information leaks. The Northern Rhodesia Ordinance outlawed only disclosing matters clearly related to security.[45] In 1967, Zambia expanded this to include 'any classified matter'.[46] It defined 'classified matter', however, as any information or document 'which under any system of security from time to time in use by the Government . . . is not to be disclosed to the public and of which the disclosure to the public would be prejudicial to the security, safety, or interests of the Republic'.[47] The latter branch of this definition provided for judicial review of classification, for in a prosecution the state had to prove the necessity of classifying the material.[48] The Attorney General, introducing the 1969 revision, complained only that a court could review a security classification. 'Needless to say', he asserted, 'under the Bill the Government, and the Government alone, will decide what is to be classified matter.' The 1969 Act therefore redefined 'classified matter' as 'any information or thing declared to be classified by an authorized officer'.[49] The new Act removed the defence 'for the accused person to prove that when he communicated the matter he did not know and could not reasonably have known that it was classified matter'.[50]

Finally, penalties were inflated. Under the Northern Rhodesian Ordinance, espionage carried a maximum penalty of seven years, and leaking official secrets, two years. These expanded in 1967 to fourteen years, and again in 1969 to twenty-five years for espionage, and twenty years for leaking classified matter. The web became·complete. It cloaked everything against disclosure. A civil servant might not even legally disclose without authority to another civil servant. Legislators, ministers and Party personnel had no right to learn anything in the bureaucracy's possession. The State Security Act, and the General Orders which exceeded it, prevented the first condition of popular participation: knowledge. Zambia's political leadership call Zambia a 'participatory democracy'.

B. The Civil Service As A Negative Feedback Channel

The civil service constituted the principal input channel for law-making. Its routine problems, its hierarchical communications and the administrator's acculturated perceptions limited message flow mainly to negative feedback. The civil service had two tasks. It implemented existing programmes. 'It is in the day-to-day application of a law that its inadequacies are to be perceived and the daily rub of the administrative mill that ideas for reform are burnished.'[51] Its structure admitted negative feedback of the narrowest sort. Development, however, required the civil service to deal with emergent problems, radically different from those that concerned existing programmes.[52] Its structure did not adapt for the sorts of inputs and feedbacks that problem solving required.[53]

Few civil services organized very well even collecting information about existing programmes. 'Development administration has the self-regulatory features of closed loop control, that is, there are clear and strong feedback circuits, whereas the traditional government administration is of the open loop variety, that is, the control feedback characteristics are weak or lacking and purposeful development action therefore is hard to achieve.'[54] Of all institutions, governments (and universities) probably do the poorest self-monitoring.

Finally, the self-images of bureaucrats limited their messages upwards to negative feedback. Every civil service descended from the Colonial Service. The most senior civil servants continued from the colonial period. Their conventions, styles of work, habits of mind and even the General Orders remained mainly the same from the heyday of the Crown. The structural bias of bureaucracy and the received colonial working rules and attitudes limited the messages it transmitted to ones that bolstered the *status quo*. Information and messages that might threaten it rarely entered the system; if so, they rarely reached formal decision-making levels. African bureaucracy transmitted only negative feedback.

C. Access To The System

The civil service, uniquely in Africa, both gathered and processed information. Access measured influence. High civil servants, of course, had the easiest access, and formed their own constituency. Civil servants' interests no more than their ideologies led them to demand radical change. Other elite members, too, had easy access to the civil service. The expatriate manager of a mining company could easily see a Permanent Secretary or a Minister, or the President himself. In any high administrative post,

> the time available for communication is short, and . . . choices must be made as to its allocation. Among the whole range of people and groups upon whom the individual administrator and his organizations are dependent, the administrator will have to pick out the ones with the most important influence and seek information about them. Among this group of influential units with which the administrator communicates, he may select a much smaller group of the most influential individuals, with whom he seeks to establish personal and intimate contract.[55]

One's world-view identified 'important' or 'influential' people. Most civil servants held the managers of large enterprises more important than workers or peasants. Likewise, high bureaucrats readily opened their doors to organization leaders: trade unions, co-operatives, the Chamber of Commerce. In Africa, unincorporated interest group associations hardly existed among the peasantry, and little more among the urban working class.

The information, claims and demands of the 'small' men enter most hierarchical feedback systems at the very lowest, 'grass-roots' level. In Africa, the nerve ends of the system lay with the assistant District Officer, the *bwana shamba*, the assistant labour or co-operative officer or price inspector. Since those officers acted authoritatively,[56] their clients had no influence, at least until they erupted violently. The bureaucratic structure ensured elite influence and mass impotence.

D. Solutions

The power of the civil service in Africa derived from its anonymity, job security, control over information and close personal and professional ties with the executive.[57] Its conservative influence in decision-making derived in part from its negative feedback structure, and its limits on access. Governments tried various devices to reduce the civil service's pervasive conservative influence. Here I discuss only two: policy-oriented research institutes, and freedom of information.

1. Increasing Research Capacity. Research institutes grew like weeds. Usually, although not invariably, these had university homes, all supposedly to engage in policy research. They responded to felt needs for additional decision-making information. Their success was mixed. The 1962-68 Nigerian National Development Plan described the Nigerian Institute of Social and Economic Research (NISER) as
as

> the major National Institute of Applied Research on Nigerian development problems. The Institute will concentrate its attention upon long-range problems of the Nigerian economy with particular reference to the National Plans. It is intended that . . . its research program shall be prepared in close consultation with [the national] government.

At least one state complained that NISER limited its area of interest to social and economic problems, while the state government's most pressing needs were for research on 'administration, local government and legal responses to emergent problems there arising'. Moreover.

> for historical reasons, NISER has largely concerned itself with academic approaches to the problems of development. Such research is of course extremely important, but it is not the sort of research required by administrators faced with practical problems. For this, practical solutions capable of being translated into laws and regulations and ultimately into programs of governmental activity are required.[58]

The latter complaint echoed widely. The Economic Research Bureau in Dar es Salaam became a striking exception. It consistently produced papers that affected government decision-making processes. Its success probably lay in its communication channels with government. The Director of the Bureau had an office in the Planning Commission, and attended Planning Commission functions. Other institutes lacked such institutionalized communication channels.

Proposals in the Midwestern State of Nigeria in 1972 and in Lesotho in 1973 wanted to locate the Bureau in the national university to ensure genuinely critical research. To avoid the inevitable tendency of academics to produce for their academic peers, however, they demanded strong communication links between Bureau and Government. The Lesotho proposal placed most Permanent Secretaries on the governing council and required the director to consult each Permanent Secretary regularly, report on ongoing research, organize annual seminars on research for senior administrative officers, and arrange the secondment of regular line administrative officers to the Research Bureau.

2. Freedom of Information. A Canadian author wrote that Commonwealth countries

> are steeped in the monarchical tradition and its undesirable implications for bureaucracy. They have not yet succeeded in throwing off the old legal theory that civil servants are servants of the King rather than of the public, that the King can do no wrong, and that, by the process of what one might call 'virtue by association' civil servants can never — well, hardly ever — do wrong. Formerly officials acted on behalf of the King, and the old hierarchical myth would even have us believe that when they acted it was really the King who was acting. Hence they had to remain anonymous and their actions secret. These ideas are obviously out of tune with modern democratic government, and we must ask ourselves whether the reasons we now give to defend anonymity and secrecy are not mere rationalisations, whether in reality these characteristics of bureaucracy in the Commonwealth are not preserved mainly for the convenience of the Government in power. For they place serious difficulties in the way of the public's legitimate access to information, its 'right to know', in a democracy.[59]

Some non-Commonwealth countries reportedly ventilated government. The Swedish Constitution provided that citizens should have free access to official documents, 'subject to only such restrictions as are demanded out of consideration for the maintenance of privacy, security of person, decency and morality'.[60] Sometimes reporters read ministerial mail before the Minister had even seen it! The United States also had a freedom of information statute,[61] as did several states.[62] These laws made most government documents and information publicly available. They forbade classification of documents as secret merely because some public official deemed it desirable 'in the public interest'.[63]

The fundamental rights provisions of African constitutions arguably also did so. Art. 22(1) of the Zambian Constitution, for example,

provided in part that ' . . . no person shall be hindered in the enjoyment
of his freedom of expression, that is to say . . . freedom to receive ideas
and information without interference, freedom to communicate ideas
and information without interference (whether the communication be
to the public generally or to any person or class of persons) . . .' The
derogation clause immediately following provided that no law violated
this section, to the extent that the law 'imposes restrictions upon public
officers', except so far as the law in question or the thing done under
its authority 'is shown not to be reasonably justifiable in a democratic
society'. Minimally, the Constitution permitted any person to challenge
a particular classification on the ground that it was not 'reasonably
justifiable in a democratic society'. Under this reading of the Constitution, the 1969 revision of the Zambian Official Secrets Act violated it.

Lawyers might have used constitutional freedom of information
guarantees to attack aspects of the Official Secrets Act. It was clearly
not 'reasonably necessary in a democratic society' to threaten with long
years of imprisonment every public official, no matter how lowly, if
he disclosed anything he learned in the course of his public office.
Other 'democratic' countries managed to get on without draping
government in impenetrable secrecy.

III Parliament

Parliament played a minimal role as decision-maker, the Westminster
blueprint notwithstanding. It had potential, however, as a feedback
system. President Nyerere said it could 'act as a bridge . . . between
people and government for the transmission of ideas' and 'keep government devoted to the people's interest by intelligent criticism'.[64] In
most of Africa, however, Parliament poorly played even that role. I
examine in turn its ability to acquire information; the sorts of messages it accepted and transmitted; access; and the aggregation of information

A. Opportunity to Acquire Information .

In both debate and question, Members of Parliament have everywhere
articulated only parochial demands and considerations.

> Ministers and assistant ministers have at their disposal the resources
> of the bureaucracy, but the ordinary M.P. lacks these. In the absence
> of external and independent sources of opinion and information
> such as might be provided by lobbyists (which are practically non-
> existent in Africa), the ordinary M.P. . . . seems most often obliged

. . .'to exercise his own judgment, supported by whatever meagre supply of facts he can discover for himself'.[65]

Thus, 'demands articulated are often specific in content, unaggregated, and rooted in the local circumstances of the member's constituency'.[66]

Members did not have any right to receive information from the civil service. In Zambia the Price Controller refused permission to the presidentially-appointed Chairman of the Price Control Board, an MP, to examine records in his office, on the ground that the General Orders and Official Secrets Act forbade it. Nor did legislative bodies in Africa organize themselves to develop information. The legislator could himself discover very little. Most information came from those constituents to whom he talked.

B. Parliament: A Negative Feedback Channel

Parliaments in the civics textbook make laws. The rules formally permitted legislators to do so, having ample opportunity to criticize and debate policy. The African milieu, however, closed these seemingly open feedback systems. This section examines restrictions on Parliamentary debate, governmental indifference to Parliament, and the structure of the Parliamentary Question.

1. Restrictions on Parliamentary Debate. The common law protects free Parliamentary debate. Members have immunity from civil or criminal liability for what they say in Parliament.[67] Africa, however, bred serious and pervasive *de facto* limitations. In the first place, Cabinet solidarity prohibited Cabinet members from criticizing government. In practice, this extended to all ministers. African legislatures remained relatively small; many MPs also served in government. In Kenya in 1966 for example, 39 per cent also acted as ministers and assistant ministers.[68] These Members thus could not criticize. Government also had controls over back-benchers. British back-benchers only occasionally broke Party ranks to criticize government measures. In Africa, too, their own tenure depended upon government's survival. In public debate they defended government, or kept their silence. They criticized, if at all, before debate at a parliamentary Party Caucus. Finally, preventive detention in most African states posed an overhanging threat. Strict *de facto* limitations replaced *de jure* freedom of debate.

2. Governmental Indifference to Parliament. Parliament in England had three functions: law-maker, keeper of the purse, and watchman over government. The Speaker of the Kenyan Parliament once said that the latter consists of

> the right and indeed the duty of Parliament, to whom Government is answerable, to seek explanations from Government, and to criticize and advise Government, in the exercise of its executive authority. That does not mean that Parliament controls the executive authority of Government. The government of the day has complete executive authority in the management of the affairs of the country, subject only to the laws made by Parliament and its financial control, and heeds the criticism of Parliament as much or as little as it thinks fit. But, in the end, Government depends on the support of a majority in Parliament. So, if Government is too heedless of the criticism, or inadequate explanation is made in its answers to Parliament, it may find one day that it governs no more.[69]

Government in Africa, however, did not hear Parliamentary Questions very well, or listen to Parliamentary debate very attentively.

In Africa as in England, MPs at a scheduled time asked ministers about particular matters. Ordinarily, the questions carried implied criticisms. African governmental responses suggested thick callouses to that criticism. In Britain, answers to Parliamentary Questions have first claim on the time of civil servants.[70] In Federal Nigeria, by contrast Parliamentary Secretaries frequently refused to answer supplementaries,[71] making it impossible for an MP to press a point. From October 1960 to December 1964, in Tanganyika, of 1,651 questions in the Parliamentary Order Book, 286 received no answers at all. Nor did African governments hear much parliamentary debate. I have already described how bills travelled through Parliament.[72] By the first reading, the Ministries had silently and secretly discussed the proposal and submitted a Memorandum for the Cabinet to debate; the Parliamentary Draftsman wrote the bill, which the civil service and (in some cases) the Cabinet criticized — all secretly. Parliament only received the bill after government, civil service and Party had committed themselves to it. They saw Parliament no longer as a voice to heed, but a hurdle to jump.

Even civilian African governments did not depend on parliament for much of anything. The executive often stopped listening at the very moment that parliamentary questioning and debate began. Even if Parliamentary questions searched governmental conduct, even if debate did not ordinarily celebrate government wisdom, perspicacity, patriotism and wisdom, no matter; government did not attend. Parliament's questions and debate remained non-inputs.

3. *Parliamentary Questions.* African Parliamentary Questions followed the British model. Through it, Parliament supposedly exercised its 'critical function' as the Grand Inquest of the nation. 'There is no more valuable safeguard against maladministration, no more effective method of bringing the searchlight of criticism to bear on the action or inaction of the executive government and its subordinates.'[73] The Parliamentary Question in fact, however, served only as limited negative feedback. In England, 'immediately the Question strays on to wider issues involving general policy matters and issues of political concern, then little, if anything, of practical significance can be achieved'.[74] Parliamentary Standing Orders everywhere limited questions to a narrow range. The Zambian Orders provided that 'Questions shall be put only to Ministers and then only relative to public affairs with which they are officially connected, proceedings pending in the Assembly, or any matter of administration for which they are responsible'.[75]

The questions in Zambia's Parliament during 1969 suggests this narrow range. A slight majority concerned the progress of specific intrastructural projects: the tarring of the Chingola-Solwezi road, the building of a health clinic at Mbabala Island, Samfya. More than half the remainder obviously responded to the complaint of some constituent: why the recent dismissals in the Department of Public Works? Will redundant employees of the Ministry of Rural Development get other jobs? Why has Petauke District received so few commercial loans? Some remaining questions requested information: When will the new edition of the Revised Laws issue? A few suggested administrative action: Does the Ministry plan to provide first aid boxes for schools not near clinics? Would Government bring government hostels under the supervision of the Hotel Board? A very few raised issues of new policy: What has Government done to combat rising crime rates? What will it do about squatter compounds? Even if government had been listening to Zambian Parliamentary questions, it would not have heard very much.

C. Access

Access to Parliament means access to its Members. Some people had informal access to their Member. The developing alliance between political and economic elites gave businessmen easy access. Most people's access lay to him in his capacity as a Member. His continued tenure depended upon the particular election system. That itself determined access. Election to Zambia's Parliament depended upon

Party nomination, which in turn depended on support from local political leaders and other influentials. Members usually, therefore, responded mainly to their claims and demands.

The Parliamentary questions reflected this pattern of access. About half the questions demanded that a local area receive its shares of the infrastructural cake. These questions sought to soothe the complaints of local political leaders, who needed to win more goodies from the centre. Complaints from co-operative leaders stimulated a few questions: What criteria does government use for making loans to co-operatives? Why did a particular co-operative close? How many co-operatives did government register in a particular period? Some questions came from elite aspirants (How many students did the University of Zambia admit?) or government employees (Do the courts have enough court reporters? Why did a particular department lay off employees?) Still others obviously came from local business interests: What criteria determined commercial loans? Did the minister intend to reduce poultry feed prices to commercial chicken farmers? Only a few very reflected complaints from the disadvantaged: Why did the stores not stock roller meal (a cheap food staple)? (A white nominated member with no electoral constituency asked this.) Why did the aged and handicapped in Solwezi get no government assistance? The questions suggested that in Zambia in 1969 local political leaders, local commercial and business interests, co-operatives and trade union leaders, and local employees of the central government had access to MPs. The poor apparently had no meaningful access to Parliament, mainly a consequence of the election system in force.

D. The Aggregation Function

Debate in African parliaments included almost no legislative facts. Second hearings ordinarily only paid homage to the leadership. Members almost never discussed the sorts of aggregated data, explanations or proposals for solution that is the stuff of meaningful participation in law-making. They could hardly have done so, for no institutions provided that data. In the US Congress each Senator or Representative had an extensive staff at government expense. The Library of Congress had a special section to research problems for Members. Legislative committees with substantial professional staffs held hearings, collected information on their own initiative, aggregated data and developed explanations and solutions. Private lobbyists stood ready to serve.[76]

None of these institutions existed in Africa. The Presidential Commission on the Democratic One-Party State in Tanzania said: 'debates [are] lifeless and superficial . . . legislation has been passed without challenge to basic principles or careful examination of detailed principles'.[77] It proposed standing committees to examine proposed legislation in detail.

Four possible reforms suggest themselves. In the first place, one ought to admit Parliament's role as a ceremonial rubber stamp for legislative decisions. A one-party state and perhaps any Parliamentary system makes that inevitable. Parliamentary processes might change, however, to strengthen it as a feedback channel. The Zambian National Commission on the Establishment of a One-Party Democracy in Zambia noted 'the present practice whereby the freedom of speech of Members of Parliamen was controlled by the dictates of party discipline and parliamentary caucus decisions'. They advocated abandoning the caucus, and that Members (but not ministers) freely criticize government policy.[78] Government accepted this although it did not write it into the new Constitution.[79]

Second, if the timing of Parliament's debate on Bills preceded rather than following final Cabinet approval, it might have some impact. If the Cabinet decides on new law, later debate becomes futile.

Third, Parliament must have capacity to aggregate information through a committee system. Most African Standing Orders provided for committees, but in fact had none. Without committees and staff, Parliament could provide only negative feedback. Tanzania created a series of standing committees.[80] Reducing civil service secrecy would make existing information available to Parliament.

Finally, new institutions could direct Members' attention to the concerns of the poor as well as of local elites, such as the genuinely innovative Tanzanian system of one-party elections (Zambia's 1974 Constitution embodies analogous provisions). The Party nominated two candidates, who competed for election. In 1965, the first election under the new scheme, only twenty-one of fifty candidates and Members won re-election.[81] The

criterion of 'keeping in touch', an important factor in the voters' valuation of their former representatives, was probably seen not just as a matter of paying visits, but also connected with his habits and his ability still to identify with the people from whom he had sprung. Those who were proud and aloof, who found it difficult to associate with the ordinary man, were judged harshly, as were those who adopted the symbols of a different way of life too conspicuously — the large cars, living in European-type hotels.[82]

Many new Tanzanian MPs came from the elite, but also included

> significant numbers of farmers, clerks, and primary teachers who do
> not represent an economic or social *elite*. Moreover, apart from the
> peasant farmers, there are few who are self-employed or who have
> business interests. Thus, in contrast to any other states the parliamen-
> tary membership does not consist mainly of an emerging African
> bourgeoisie; rather its composition represents a fairly broad range of
> social and political interests in Tanzanian society.[83]

The Zambian Commission recommended that government provide local
offices for all Members.[84] The state might require Members periodically
to tour their constituencies, and hold local public conferences. The
Permanent Commission of Enquiries in Tanzania did this successfully.[85]
African constitutions might include recall provisions. Tanzania tried some
of these devices.

> Predictably these changes have created a National Assembly which
> is a more vocal instrument and which scrutinizes executive actions
> more fully than was formerly the case. Parliament now meets for
> twice as long each year; the number of Parliamentary Questions has
> increased fourfold. Government proposals or past actions are now
> challenged on occasions; government Motions have even been
> defeated or withdrawn, Ministers and their departments are criticized,
> and a watchful eye is kept on Government expenditure.[86]

IV The Party

Most African political parties declined. Military regimes had none. In
most other Anglophonic countries, by 1974 parties did not participate
meaningfully in government. Lesotho and Swaziland had no parties.
KANU (Kenya) had wound down. In Malawi, the Party seemed to consist of vigilantes for political leaders. Almost nowhere could it serve as
a significant feedback circuit. Africa became a continent not of one-
party states, but no-party states.

In Zambia and Tanzania, however, the Party remained alive and
kicking. Each became *de jure* one-party states, and appended the Party
Constitution to the national Constitution. This section addresses the
relationships between their Party organization and governmental output.

Western scholars' explanations for the failure of most African one-
party states played changes on elite theory. Without opposition, elites
follow their own interests. A one-party state becomes a contradiction

in terms:

> To become a 'party' to something always means identification with
> one group and differentiation from another. Every party in its essence
> signifies *partnership* in a particular organization and *separation* from
> others by a specific program.

> Such an initial description, to be sure, indicates that the very defi-
> nition of party presupposes a democratic climate and hence makes it
> a misnomer in every dictatorship. A one-party system (i.e. *party
> unique*) is a contradiction in itself.[87]

That explanation had its day: 'It is generally recognized that governments and methods of controlling them exist without formal opposition
parties — as in a one-party state'.[88] The explanation for this seeming
failure of control cannot come from etymological derivations or Western Parliamentary models. It must base itself upon the reality of the
one-party regimes.

A variety of alternative explanations arose. One merely restated the
difficulty: the Party faded before bureaucratic power. Tanzania[89] and
Zambia[90] demoted government from policy-maker to implementation
agency for Party policies. Zambia asserted that 'The Party shall be
supreme and members of the Central Committee shall take precedence
over members of the Cabinet'.[91] The Party constitution but not the
national one provided that in event of conflict, the Central Committee's
decision should over-ride Cabinet's.[92] All these assertions implied that
the conflict between Party and civil service arose from their relative
power relationships. That, of course, comprised the problem.

Other explanations arose. Modernizers saw the Party as aiding
modernizing elites to mobilize the inert, fatalistic, uneducated mass
into development.[93] The political apparatus, however, never touched
very many people.[94] Moreover, as the parties that had mobilized people
against the British began to rule, 'the party became largely an agency of
governmental bureaucracy, or, at the expense of its rank and file, in
certain cases a mere extension of the personality of a strong president
or prime minister'.[95] The mobilization theories assumed that the
leadership continued dedicated to the mass. Why normally hard-headed
and cynical political scientists assumed that African elites, uniquely
in world history, would remain selfless and devoted, defies analysis.

Instead of assuming that the Party really represented 'the people'
one ought to examine whom the Party really represented, and why.

One explanation applied the pluralist, bargaining model to internal Party processes.[96] That explanation had the same weaknesses as the bargaining model generally.[97] The Party's influence over government simultaneously defined the Party and explained government policy. That influence depended on the Party as feedback channel rather than as 'mobilizer of the masses'.

Both the Tanzanian and Zambian Presidents argued that their respective political parties should communicate upwards to government, as well as downwards to the people. Nyerere saw TANU as 'a two-way, all-weather road, along which the purposes, plans, and problems of the Government can travel to the people at the same time as ideas, desires, and misunderstandings of the people can travel direct to the Government'.[98] Kaunda said: 'The objectives of Humanism must be to increase participation and at the same time mobilization for development'.[99] Here I compare and contrast TANU and UNIP as feedback channels.

Very little published research examined the actual operations of the two parties. This section, therefore, examines only their respective constitutions, both extremely vague. For example, 1973 UNIP Constitution provided that 'the Constituency Committee may, in consultation with the Regional Committee, suspend a branch, section, or a village committee'.[100] It did not enumerate the grounds or procedure for such a suspension. Nothing reveals whether or how the Party used its suspension powers.

A. The Messages Transmitted

1. Party Objectives. Both Party constitutions began by declaring broad developmental objectives: raising standards of living, enhancing individual dignity and respect, and so forth.[101] UNIP expressly included mobilizing the people 'To organize and maintain in the country and in elected bodies support for the Party', and 'to give effect to the principles approved from time to time by appropriate organs of the Party'.[102] TANU did not speak of enforcing Party policy and firing up popular support for government, but of policing government. Of its twelve formulated objectives, nine began with the words 'to see that the Government . . . '. The TANU guidelines of 1971 reinforced that position.[103]

2. Member's Rights to Criticize. Every system of course accepts and transmits messages that celebrate the system. The test of the Party as input and feedback channel for the poor lay in the scope individual members have to criticize Party, government, policies and officials. A Party that primarily mobilized people to implement directives from above tolerated less criticism than a Party that tried to ensure that government does what 'the people' want. The UNIP Constitution required a Party member 'to be loyal to the Party, to accept and uphold the agreed principles and policies and to correctly carry them out and to observe Party discipline'.[104] He must never criticize the Party publicly, and 'report alleged shortcomings to the appropriate committee of the Party to which the reported member will be entitled to answer the allegations in person'.[105] He could 'criticize any shortcomings in the Party at Party meetings where there are due reasons and grounds', and 'to request the Party committee at all levels up to and including the Central Committee to consider any questions or petitions'.[106] However, he could not violate any provision of the [Party] Constitution — for example, to criticize the Party without 'due reasons and grounds', act disrespectfully to any Party official at any Party meeting[107] or publish 'orally or in writing', anything that Central Committee or National Council adjudged 'an attack on the Party or an attack on a member or official of the Party in relation to the discharge of his functions as a member or official of the Party'.[108]

TANU imposed different obligations. Formally, a member needed only subscribe to TANU's beliefs, aims and objectives in the Constitution,[109] and take the Member's Pledge[110] to serve country and people, strive to eliminate poverty, disease, ignorance and corruption, and serve TANU as a 'faithful member'. The Constitution imposed no other limits upon criticism. Only the National Conference could expel a member.[111] The Conference appointed a Disciplinary Committee to investigate allegations of improper conduct, and report them to the National Executive Committee.[112]

3. *The Transmission of Messages.* A message transmission belt can change a message's content in at least two ways: it can filter it out entirely, or amend its contents. The UNIP constitution filtered messages at constituency, National Central Committee and National Council levels. The constituency chairman, the key elected regional official, could 'rule out any proceedings which he may consider not in the interests of the Party'.[113] The President of the Party (also the Republic's President)[114] could 'exercise discretion in regard to items for discussion by the Central Committee or the National Council and may, after explanation to the appropriate body, delete any item from the agenda of a meeting'.[115] Nobody would likely say anything against the

the interests or preconceptions of either his constituency chairman or the President.

The Central Committee's appointees,[116] the District Governors, also had power to block or distort feedback. Originally, they ostensibly provided Party watchdogs over the civil service. President Kaunda expressed 'disgust' at their 'apathy, sheer lack of initiative and indiscipline'.[117] The new appointees briefly acted with unforeseen militancy, so a Cabinet Office Circular[118] confined them to politics. The UNIP constitution made the District Governor chairman *ex officio* of the Regional Committee, with 'overall responsibility' for Party units in the region (i.e. Branch and Constituency units). He presided over meetings of the Regional Council and Regional Annual Conference. Despite his title, he played a political, not a governmental role. The District Governors controlled the weekly agendas that each branch, constituency and region prepared, setting out the activity planned for the week. 'The regional office can at any time totally supersede the agenda of the branch offices . . . The regional secretary was observed inserting items into the branch agenda, or otherwise usurping control over it . . . This strongly suggests that the distribution of power is hierarchical in UNIP, with power concentrated in the regional office.'[119]

The TANU Constitution also allocated power between appointed and elected officials. It formally limited appointed officials' power over policy. In TANU, Branch, District, Regional and National Conferences formulated policy. The Branch Annual Conference could 'discuss such matters of local competence as it seems fit and to make recommendations thereon to the Annual District Conference'.[120] Analogous provisions protected free discussion at annual conferences of District, Region and Nation.[121]

4. *Recruitment to Leadership Posts.* Election and appointment procedures determine upward communication. In UNIP, an annual secret ballot of the members elected branch officials.[122] The Constituency Annual Conference triennally chose constituency officials.[123] The General Conference every five years, elected the Central Committee of twenty members plus the President. Any member of the Party could run for the Central Committee, but the incumbent Central Committee, prior to the General Meeting, could 'agree on the candidates the Central Committee will support . . . and . . . regard shall be had to the merit of the candidates and the need of getting all parts of the country represented in the Central Committee of the Party as far as possible'.[124] Delegates to the General Conference included all members of the

National Council, and up to 600 delegates from each Province.

Ultimate policy-making in UNIP lay with the National Council, that met twice a year. It consisted mainly of members that the Central Committee selected directly or indirectly, for example, the heads of Zambian missions abroad, and the executive officers at national head-quarters. Members of Parliament belonged, but the National Council had to approve their candidacy as MPs. They too thus indirectly depen-ded upon the Central Committee for their tenure.

The National Council purported to ensure 'democracy' in UNIP. Aside from its selection process, it structually could not make policy. It had several hundred members. Its meetings lasted only a long weekend, and prepared speeches by the President and other functionaries con-sumed much of that. Inevitably, like any large deliberative assembly, the leadership manipulated the National Council. Once the National Council adopted a position, however, Party members had to support it. Since all MPs belonged to the Party, a National Council resolution about pending legislation ensured a Parliamentary rubber stamp.

UNIP's formal structure, therefore, on paper relied on elected officials, who presumably represented their constituents. The consti-tution's many controls exploded that proposition. In fact, the pattern of mobility

> suggests that the opportunities for advancement open to local branch leaders strongly motivate them to accept the viewpoints articulated by their political superiors . . . Given the control by the party hier-archy over the selection of personnel, lower party officials seek to impress upon their superiors their fitness for promotion. As part of this process, they acquire many of the attitudes and viewpoints of their superior officers.[125]

The 1965 TANU Constitution, by contrast, provided highly centralized control over the Party's daily operation, but left policy formulation to elected representatives. At each level, the centre appointed a Secretary; above the District level, the President himself did so.[126] Each Secretary served as chief executive officer of the appropriate level, overseeing routine Party administration.[127] The policy-making Annual Conferences at various levels drew mainly elected delegates from constituent units, local MPs, and area Secretaries and other appointed officials. In each case, however, appointed officials expressly had no vote at the appropriate Annual Conference. Even members of the National Execu-tive Committee (whom the President appointed) could serve as delegates to the National Conference, but not vote.

The difference between these constitutions seemed clear. The UNIP constitution allowed Party officials, especially appointed District Governors, to filter out messages from below. It ensured leadership domination. Tanzania, on the contrary, repeatedly excluded appointed officials from voting on policy.

These formal constitutional provisions, of course, do not describe what actually happened. They only prescribed what ought to happen, and only in very broad terms. Nor did the TANU constitution address the question of daily feedback. Unfortunately, no recent published research discussed the actual operation of the party as feedback mechanism.[128] The prescribed relationships themselves, however, do suggest that since UNIP had almost as bureaucratic a structure as the civil service, it likely became subject tothe same inhibitions on upward feedback. Regional Governors would likely conform to the centre's desires. Constituency and Branch chairmen would likely control debate to please higher officials, not their constituents. Like the civil service, UNIP seemed to provide mainly negative feedback, unable to generate new goals or critiques of Party of government. TANU, on the other hand, had a far more open formal communications structure to suggest new goals or even new ways to organize affairs.

B. Access To The Party And Capacity To Acquire Information

Three factors determined access to the Party: informal access to officials; formal qualifications for membership; and 'grass-roots'. Party structure. On the first, little available information existed. Casual observation suggested that the highest officials in UNIP moved in elite circles of senior civil servants, Ministers, MPs and parastatal managers.

1. Party Membership. Both UNIP and TANU proclaimed themselves 'mass' parties. Supposedly anyone might join who satisfied relatively simple membership requirements.

Both Party constitutions appended themselves to the national constitution. TANU's constituted a formal Schedule to it.[129] UNIP's became 'annexed hereto for information'.[130] The draftsmen of Zambia's Constitution apparently believed that not making the Party Constitution a *formal* Schedule prevented it from conferring enforceable rights.[131]

2. Structure at the Grass Roots. The Party's nerve ends lay at the interface between it and the general public. That interface determined how well the Party gathered information about popular needs and demands. Research produced little about the actual local UNIP activity, however, while a relatively rich literature existed concerning the TANU ten-house cell.[132] Even those who envisaged the Party in Africa as a two-way communication channel conceded that it also mobilized. If that mobilization became authoritarian, it necessarily interfered with feedback just as authoritarian bureaucratic work habits tended to limit the civil service's information about their client's responses. On the other hand, the absence of mobilization cut the Party off from its most useful source of information. As anyone else , it could only learn through doing, but that required a non-authoritarian mobilization function. If the Party only ships busloads of complaisant party workers to cheer visiting dignitaries, its local officials may win kudos, but do not learn much about making policy to help the poor.

UNIP's constitution defined its smallest unit as Section Committes in urban areas and Village Committees in rural areas, which Branch officials supposedly supervised.[132] In fact, few Section Committees existed. In the local UNIP branch, officials (frequently local shop-keepers or small businessmen) usually constituted the active membership. In the squatter and mine compounds of the line-of-rail cities, local UNIP branches exercised great power to settle disputes[133] and allocate land. The style of work at the branch level became highly authoritarian. UNIP officials invited complaints and communications from the populace, and in some places, regularly toured their areas. Those conversations had to dampen any complaints:

> Peculiar to the Party [as opposed to the Mineworkers' Union in the same area] , however, is the practice of turning occasions for upward communication into occasions for the downward trans-mittal of political information and points of view. When a person comes to the Party, he is interrogated. He is asked for his party card. He is asked for the names of his section officials. If his complaint has a 'political element', as in the case of market prices, he is queried about government policy toward the matter . . . In this manner, the occasion for upward communications becomes an occasion for impressing knowledge of the party's structure and viewpoints upon the township resident.[134]

That process likely transformed the 'occasion for upward communication' into its opposite.

The TANU ten-house cell formed its basic unit.[135] Each cell included not only TANU members but all the residents of ten houses. Each cell elected a leader who also attended the Branch Annual Conference.[136] The Publicity Secretary of TANU wrote in 1965 that the cell system ought to (1) provide two-way communication between people and government; (2) make leaders readily available to ordinary people; (3) obtain information about economic and social development; and (4) increase security.[137]

The actual jobs of the cell leaders did not invariably match their descriptions. Everywhere, the leaders spent much time settling disputes within the cell.[138] They checked on security, especially along the troubled Mozambique border.[139] The cell leaders appeared less effective in communication and mobilization[140] apparently because of the communications structure between cell leaders and branch, and the recruitment of cell leaders. Levine writes:

> In most instances it appears that the links between cell and Branch are rudimentary, sometimes non-existent. The formal organization has been set up, but is rarely activated. Geography is an important factor here. The cell leaders often live far away from the Branch. They do not receive any travel allowance, or compensation for work time lost. In many of the rural areas roads are in bad condition, impassable in the wet season, and no transport is available. An equally real factor, though, is the lack of an effective working relationship between the Branch officials and the cell leaders. The cell leaders should act as a kind of catalyst in a continuous dialogue between the people and their representatives higher up the organizational ladder. But too often the Branch officials concentrate on relationships at the Branch and District level, and the cell leaders confine their attention to their cell members, both at the expense of their relations with each other.[141]

Without direct communication, cell leaders apparently mobilized their cell members for development only spasmodically. Weak as the system of communication down became, however, channels upwards grew even less well institutionalized.[142] 'As long as . . . the majority of cell leaders continue to work on their own, they will remain in a position where, however, influential they are in the community as arbitrators and peacekeepers, they will not be fulfilling their functions as mobilizers of the people and as links in the communication chain between Party and Government on the one hand, and the people on the other.'[143]

The system of recruitment widened the gap between centre and cell. Ideally, cell leaders should come from younger, literate, progressive elements. In fact, most drew on older, traditional or wealthier groups. The cell leader required authority. If under local custom he could impose fines, control land or irrigation rights, or because of education, age or wealth, he commanded respect, he could more readily settle disputes and give leadership.[144] Leaders from the elite do not usually advocate the interests of the poor.

Summary. The constitutions of UNIP and TANU defined different feedback channels. UNIP's seemed more authoritarian and hierarchical. Scanty evidence suggested that in fact it barely reached the grass roots, but like the CPP in Ghana,[145] became increasingly an organization of officials following orders. TANU, by contrast, attempted to reach the citizenry, and involved them both in mobilization and upward communication. UNIP seemed at best a negative feedback channel, hardly more open than the civil service itself, with access limited to Party officials. TANU seemingly had at least a potential for meaningful general access.

V New Input and Feedback Institutions

Whom a government represents depends upon to whom it listens, a function of input and feedback instutions. Only the elite had much influence in most African countries. Government listened mainly to the civil service, which had no structural capacity to listen to the mass or transmit their messages. Parliament floundered in irrelevance and the Party in bureaucracy. Government represented the elite partly because no institutionalized channels of communication to it from anyone else existed.

If government takes seriously its populist rhetoric, it must force new input and feedback institutions from the mass. The Party seemed the most likely vehicle, as Tanzania perhaps illustrated. Alternative devices existed, especially co-operatives and trade unions. In Nkrumah's Ghana, the Party included co-operative, trade union and student movements as 'integral wings'. In Tanzania, the National Union of Tanganyika Workers, the Co-operative Union of Tanganyika, and the Tanganyika African Parents Association affiliated with TANU. The effectiveness of such affiliation depended upon the openness of internal communication channels, the institutionalized character of Party contracts, and how much the leadership of the affiliated organizations continued to rely for their tenure on their constituencies rather than the Party leadership.

In Africa, none of these reached very deeply into the peasantry.

Tanzania experimented with *ujamaa* (co-operative) villages. If *ujamaa* villages involved the peasantry in development and the ten-house cell system touched their lives, peasant input and feedback messages might reach the centre.

Exotic participatory institutions may suggest new paths for Africa, for example public referenda or the use of public opinion polls. The Chinese, of course, tried the most interesting experiments. They built an entire system for making public policy around the 'mass line':

> In all practical work of the Party, all correct leadership is necessarily from the masses to the masses. This means: Take the ideas of the masses (scattered and unsystematic ideas) and concentrate them (through study turn them into concentrated and systematic ideas); then go to the masses and propagate and explain these ideas until the masses embrace them as their own, hold fast to them and translate them into action, and test the correctness of these ideas from the masses and once again go to the masses so that the ideas are persevered in and carried through. And so on, over and over again in an endless spiral, with the ideas becoming more correct, more vital and richer each time.[146]

This became

> the process by which the politically conscious leadership puts itself in direct contact with the inarticulate, largely illiterate and politically underdeveloped mass of the local community, learns from the members of that community what are their aspirations, their sense of possibilities, their doubts and problems; sums up these ideas in terms of the wider experience and responsibilities and of the theory of the leadership; returns them to the masses in an articulate form, and poses new questions; with the agreement of the majority, puts the consequent decisions into practice, and studies the results in the same terms.[147]

The mass line required detailed investigation of the citizenry's actions and concerns. It involved many different sorts of investigations. Michael Oksenberg described an investigation of a fishing village off Hong Kong by a group of fifteen higher-level cadres. The fishermen had some discretion in the kinds of fish they caught, and the state wanted to set prices to encourage the fishermen to catch certain varieties, and to market them in China, not Hong Kong. The cadres stayed in the village

for a month, worked on the fishing boats daily, talked constantly to the
villagers as well as their leaders, and ate and boarded with common folk.
They made daily notes, analyzed their information, and finally submitted a report.[144]

Other Chinese institutions included the nationally organized campaign, accompanied by a peasant mobilization.

An essential element of Chinese propaganda techniques was that
they demanded discussion within the organizational context of the
'small group'. Virtually everyone was a member of at least one unit,
whether based on factory, school, office, or place of residence,
through which he was in regular contact with a cadre. The cadre's
job [included] . . . making them declare their opinions in front of
their peers . . . Where a basic-level cadre was faced with wide-spread
opposition to a given policy, he could either recommend to his
superiors that it be modified or he could appeal for support . . .
from higher echelons . . . It was common practice to try new policies
on a local basis in order to test their efficiency before launching the
them 'with great fanfare' throughout the country.[147]

The Chinese gave peasants and workers direct control over elite careers.
University candidates had to work in an enterprise or co-operative for
two years, and win their work-mates' approval for admission to the University.[147] Members of the elite had to return to manual labour frequently, usually at least annually. 'The idea is that [bureaucrats] should
learn to respect and understand the vast majority of Chinese people who
do manual labour, break down their own attitudes of white-collar
supremacy, and become more physically fit through labour.'[148] Local
public meetings criticized officials directly.

Obviously none of these institutions can move directly to Africa.
The Law of Non-transferability of Law teaches that they will not
likely work in Africa exactly as they do in China. They might, however,
provide sources for ideas about institutions of popular participation.
Oksenberg wrote:

I describe investigation work . . . primarily because of a conversation with an earnest local cadre in a bus bounding along a dirt
road in rural Honan. I had inquired: 'What do I have to understand
in order to comprehend why you think China is a democracy? What
do you have instead of elections?' He replied: 'Investigation work.
You must understand investigation work.' [He added that infor-

mation acquired in investigation work] are then aggregated — 'concentrated' was his word — at each level and passed up. For this reason he believed the highest levels represented the distilled wisdom of the masses. Proper investigation work enable the higher levels to know about local conditions . . . In sum, investigation work and the reporting of it are the heart of the 'mass line' process.[149]

Conclusion

Elite members can always find a hearing with other members of the elite, formally or informally. Unless government consciously forges institutions to listen to the problems of the poor, and propose and test explanations and solutions to generate useful knowledge and information, government, whatever its rhetoric, will favour the elite, not the mass. In Africa, the formal institutions of feedback, civil service, Parliament and the Party mainly accepted and transmitted negative feedback from the elite. Like African political institutions, and those that bred a bureaucratic bourgeoisie, feedback institutions hindered development in favour of the mass. The vast gulf between radical rhetoric and conservative, incremental change grew not out of the duplicity or insincerity of the leadership, but African institutions of law-making.

Notes

1. See above, Chap. 16; see generally United Nations, *Participation in Decision-Making for Development* (New York: United Nations), Sales No. E.75.IV.10.
2. See above, Chap. 16.
3. G. Parry (ed.), *Participation in Politics* (Manchester: Manchester University Press, 1972), p. 6.
4. See above, Chap. 11.
5. J.A. Schumpeter, *Capitalism, Socialism and Democracy,* 4th ed. (London: Allen and Unwin, 1954), p. 296.
6. R.A. Dahl, 'The Concept of Power', *Behavioural Sciences,* 2, 201 (1957); cf. P. Bachrach and M. Baratz, *Power and Poverty* (New York: Oxford University Press, 1970).
7. R.A. Rosenthal and R.S. Weiss, 'Problems of Organizational Feedback' in R.A. Baker (ed.), *Social Indicators* (Cambridge, Mass.: MIT Press, 1966), p. 304.
8. K.W. Deutsch, 'Social Mobilization and Political Development', *Am. Pol. Sci. Rev.,* 55, 493 (1961); see also W. Buckley, *Sociology and Modern Systems Theory* (Englewood Cliffs: Prentice-Hall, 1967), p. 56.
9. P.T. Bauer and B.S. Yamey, *The Economics of Underdeveloped Countries* (London: James Nisbet, 1957), p. 181.
10. Rosenthal and Weiss, 'Organizational Feedback'.
11. H.L. Wilensky, *Organizational Intelligence: Knowledge and Policy in*

Government and Industry (New York: Basic Books, 1967).

12. G. Almond and W. Powell, *Comparative Politics: A Developmental Approach* (Boston: Little, Brown, 1966), p. 98.
13. I omit discussion of press, radio, co-operatives, trade unions and other private feedback channels for lack of space, not importance.
14. M.F. Lofchie, 'Representative Government, Bureaucracy, and Political Development: The African Case', *J. Dev. Areas*, 2, 37 (1967) reprinted in M.E. Doro and N.M. Stulz (eds.), *Governing Black Africa: Perspectives on New States* (Englewood Cliffs, N.J.: Prentice-Hall, 1970), p. 278.
15. S.M. Lipset, *Agrarian Socialism* (Berkeley: University of California Press, 1950), pp. 255-72. See O. Odinga, *Not Yet Uhuru* (London: Heinemann, 1967), p. 247. ('The Civil Service, I found, could frustrate the best plans of the best intentioned government. Given a chance, top civil servants can direct a minister, not the other way about. An inexperienced, naive, or unconscientious minister can be committed to a policy in flat contradiction to the overall policy of his government . . .')
16. See above, Chap. 20.
17. See above, Chap. 13.
18. Ibid.
19. Quoted in E. Campbell, 'Public Access to Government Documents', *Aus. L.J.*, 41, 73 (1967) 74.
20. Zambia's urban, industrial, and export-oriented activities centered around the railroad line that led to the copper mines. Commercial farming and urban development clustered tightly around the line-of-rail.
21. K.E. Svendsen, 'The Present State of Economic Planning in Tanzania', in A.H. Rwayemanu (ed.), *Nation-Building in Tanzania* (Nairobi: East Africa Publishing House, 1970), p. 85.
22. A.J. Heidenheimer (ed.), *Political Corruption: Readings in Comparative Analysis* (New York: Holt, Rinehart and Winston, 1970), p. 11, quoting M. Weber, *Economy and Society* (New York: Bedminster Press, 1968), p. 1086.
23. V. Subramaniam, 'The Research Scholar and the Administrator', *Pub. Adm.*, (Sydney) 20, 364 (1961).
24. Campbell, 'Public Access'.
25. M. Weber, *The Theory of Social and Economic Organization*, A.M. Henderson and T. Parsons, tr., T. Parsons, ed. (New York: The Free Press, 1947), p. 399.
26. W.S. Sayre, 'Bureaucracies: Some Contrasts in Systems', *Indian Pub. Admin.*, 10, 219, 352 (1964).
27. Cf. R. Braibanti, *Research on the Bureaucracy of Pakistan: A Critique of Sources, Conditions and Issues, with appended documents* (Durham, N.C.: Duke University Press, 1966), pp. 58, 62. ('. . . any government . . . might prefer not to face the irresponsible distortions which "impassioned" public discussion engendered among poorly educated but articulate persons.')
28. Zambia: *General Orders, Issued by the Permanent Secretary (Establishments)* (Lusaka: Government Printer, 1966), par. 68.
29. Ibid., par. 64(a).
30. Art. 64(b); see also Arts. 64(c), (e).
31. Art. 65(a).
32. 1 & 2 Geo. 5, c. 28.
33. 10 & 11 Geo. 5, c. 75.
34. Northern Rhodesia: Official Secrets Ordinance, 1914, Cap. 38.
35. Zambia: State Security Act (1969), (Cap. 110).
36. Northern Rhodesia, supra n. 34, sec. 4(1) (Cap. 38).
37. Sec. 4(2).
38. Secs. 7; 4(2).

39. Zambia: Official Secrets Act, 1967 (No. 12 of 1967).
40. Zambia: Security Oaths Act (Cap. 68).
41. Sec. 4(1).
42. Zambia: Hansard No. 8 (1966) 96.
43. Zambia: State Security Act, 1969, Sec. 4(1) (Zambia).
44. Sec. 3(b) and (c). A 'Disaffected person' meant one likely to engage in subversion.
45. Sec. 5(1).
46. Sec. 3(1).
47. Sec. 2.
48. There was no discussion in the Assembly of any part of this Act. The Vice-President asserted that it was introduced to bring the legislation 'up to date, and . . . does not involve any change in the principles governing the protection of official information and defense installations'. (Zambia: Hansard No. 8 1966, pp. 95-6.) It was introduced on 13 December, very briefly discussed at second reading the following day, rushed through the Committee stage without discussion the following day, and enacted five days thereafter.
49. Sec. 2(1).
50. Sec. 5(2).
51. J.D. Kingsley, *Representative Bureaucracy* (New York: Antioch Press, 1944), p. 270.
52. See above, Chap. 12.
53. See above, Chap. 13.
54. S.M. Katz, 'A Systems Approach to Development Administration' in F.W. Riggs *Frontiers of Development Administration* (Durham, N.C.: Duke University Press, 1971), p. 121.
55. D.K. Leonard, 'Communications and Deconcentration', in G. Hyden, R. Jackson and J. Okumu (eds.), *Development Administration: The Kenyan Experience* (Nairobi: Oxford University Press, 1970), p. 93.
56. See above, Chap. 16.
57. That the civil service had a near monopoly of highly educated people is an important additional source of power.
58. Quoted from a report on the establishment of a local research institute submitted by an *ad hoc* Committee of Permenent Secretaries in the Mid-western State of Nigeria, 1972.
59. D.C. Rowat (ed.), *The Ombudsman: Citizen's Defender*, 2nd ed. (Toronto: University of Toronto Press, 1968), p. 290.
60. Quoted in Campbell, 'Public Access'.
61. 5 USC § 552 (Supp. V, 1975).
62. See, e.g., N.Y. Pub. Off. Law   85-99 (McKinney, Supp. 1975-76).
63. See, e.g., 5 USC § 552 (a) (2).
64. J.K. Nyerere, *Address at the Opening of The National Assembly after the General Election* (Dar es Salaam: Ministry of Information and Tourism, 1965).
65. N.M. Stultz, 'Parliaments in Former British Black America', *J. of Developing Areas*, 2, 479 (1968), reprinted in Doro and Stultz, *Governing Black Africa*, p. 152.
66. Ibid.
67. 36(1) Eng. & Emp. Digest, tit. Parl. VII,§ 5(2) (London: Butterworth, 1976).
68. Stultz, 'Parliaments', p. 154.
69. Mr Speaker Slade in Republic of Kenya, *Official Report, House of Representatives* (Nairobi: Government Printer, 1964), cols. 2267-8, quoted in C. Gertzel, M. Goldschmitt and D. Rothschild (eds.), *Government and Politics*

in Kenya: A Nation-Building Text (Nairobi: East African Publishing House, 1969), p. 196.
70. N. Johnson, 'Parliamentary Questions and the Conduct of Administration', *Pub. Admin.,* 39 139 (1961).
71. J.P. Mackintosh, 'The Nigerian Federal Parliament', *Public Law,* 342 (1963).
72. See above, Chap. 21.
73. F.A. Ogg, *English Government and Politics,* 2nd ed. (London: Macmillan, 1936), p. 456.
74. Johnson, 'Parliamentary-Questions'.
75. Zambia: *National Assembly Standing Orders* (Lusaka: Government Printers, 1967): Order 27(1).
76. See, generally, D.N. Berman, *In Congress Assembled: Legislative Process in the National Government* (New York: Macmillan, 1964).
77. Tanzania: *Report of the Presidential Commission on the Establishment of a Democratic One-Party State* (Dar es Salaam: Government Printer, 1965).
78. Zambia: *Report of the Working Party Appointed to Review the System of Decentralized Administration* (Lusaka: Cabinet Office, 1972), p. 8.
79. Art. 87 merely repeats the provision of the Independence Constitution that members shall be free to speak on any issue.
80. L. Cliffe, 'Democracy in the One-Party State: The Tanzanian Experience', in 2 L. Cliffe and J. Saul (eds.), *Socialism in Tanzania: An Interdisciplinary Reader* (Nairobi: East African Publishing House, 1972), p. 244.
81. Ibid., p. 243.
82. L. Cliffe (ed.), *One Party Democracy* (Nairobi: Oxford University Press, 1967), pp. 304-5.
83. Ibid., p. 335.
84. Zambia: *Report . . .,* p. 20.
85. *Annual Reports of Permanent Commission of Enquiries* (Dar es Salaam: Government Printers, 1969, 1970, 1971).
86. Cliffe, 'Democracy in a One-Party State', pp. 244-5.
87. S. Neumann, quoted in D. Apter, *The Politics of Modernization* (University of Chicago Press, Chicago, 1965), p. 181.
88. J.P. W.B. McAuslan and Y.P. Ghai, 'Constitutional Innovation and Political Stability in Tanzania: A Preliminary Assessment', *J. Mod. Af. Studies,* 4, 479 (1966).
89. TANU Guidelines (Mwongozo wa TANU), *The Nationalist* (Dar es Salaam), 22 Feb. 1971, p. 1.
90. Zambia: *Report of the National Commission on the Establishment of a One-Party Participatory Democracy in Zambia* (Lusaka: Government Printer, 1972).
91. Ibid.
92. UNIP Constitution, Art. 12(3).
93. J.S. Coleman and C. Rosberg, *Political Parties and National Integration in Tropical Africa* (Berkeley: University of California 1965); D. Apter, *The Political Kingdom in Uganda* (Princeton, New Jersey: Princeton University, 1961), pp. 22-4.
94. H. Bienen, 'The Ruling Party in the African One-Party State: TANU in Tanzania', *J. Comn. Pol. Studies,* 5, 214 (1966), reprinted in Doro and Stultz, *Governing Black Africa,* pp. 69-71.
95. R.I. Rothberg, 'Modern African Studies: Problem and Prospects', *World Politics,* 18, 571 (1966).
96. J.J. Wjatr and A. Przeworski, 'Control Without Opposition', *Government and Opposition,* 1, 227 (1966).
97. See above, Chap. 5.
98. J. Nyerere, *Arusha Declaration, Answer to Questions* (Dar es Salaam:

Government Printer, 1967), p. 158.

99. K.D. Kaunda, 'Address on the Occasion of the Opening of the National Council, 1st December, 1972' in 'A Nation of Equals' — The Kabwe Declaration: Addresses to the National Council of The United Independence Party at The Hindu Hall, Kabwe, 1-3 December 1972 (No publication data in pamphlet).

100. Art. 23(7).

101. UNIP Constitution (1973) Art. 4; TANU Constitution, Preamble.

102. Art. 4(j) and (k).

103. Tanzania, quoted in Chap. 16, p.

104. Art. 6(1) (f).

105. Art. 6(1) (h).

106. Art. 6(2) (b) and (d).

107. Standing Orders Art. 5(2).

108. Ibid.

109. Art. III (a) (1).

110. Art. V(E).

111. Art. IV(E) (2).

112. Art. IV(E) (6).

113. Art. 24(1) (b).

114. Art. 8(6).

115. Art. 14(d).

116. Art. 20(3).

117. Zambia News, 17 November 1968, quoted in D. Dresang, 'Entrepreneurialism and Development Administration in Zambia', *The African Rev.*, 1, 101 (1972).

118. Cabinet Officer Circular No. 13 of 1969, quoted in ibid., pp. 102-3.

119. R. H. Bates, *Unions, Parties and Political Development: A Study of Mineworkers in Zambia* (New Haven: Yale, 1971), pp. 180-1.

120. Art. IV(B) (5).

121. Arts. IV(C) (2), IV(D) (3).

122. Art. 26(2).

123. Art. 23(4).

124. Art. 8.

125. Bates, *Unions, Parties,* pp. 173-7.

126. Art. IV.

127. Art. IV(B) (2), IV(C) (2), IV(D) (2).

128. H. Bienen, *Tanzania: Party Transformation and Economic Development* (Princeton: Princeton University Press, Rev. Ed. 1970) is the most recent study.

129. Art. 3(4).

130. Art. 4(2).

131. They seemed in error, either on constitutional grounds, cf. *Marsh* v. *Alabama*, 326 US 501 (1946) or on common law grounds protecting against discrimination or arbitrary action towards non-members of 'private' organizations that in fact wield great economic or quasi-governmental power; see, generally, *Harvard L. Rev.*, 76, 683; *Yale L.J.*, 74, 1313; *Mod. L. Rev.*, 30, 389; *Russell* v. *Duke of Norfolk* (1949), 1 All E.R. 109 (C.A.), esp. Lord Denning's opinion.

132. Art. 28(6).

133. Bates, supra n. 119 at 184.

134. Ibid.

135. Art. IV(A) (1).

136. Art. IV(A) (3).

137. W.A. Kleruu, *Mashina ya TANU, TANU Cells* (Research Department TANU Headquarters, Dar es Salaam, 1966).
138. N. Njohole, 'Building Party Cells in Tanzania', in J.H. Procter (ed.), *The Cell System of The Tanganyikan National Union* (Dar es Salaam: Tanzania Publishing House, 1971), p. 1; K. Levine, 'The TANU Ten-House Cell System' in 1 Cliffe and Saul, *Socialism in Tanzania*, p. 333.
139. Levine, ibid.
140. Ibid.
141. Ibid., p. 334.
142. J. O'Barr, 'Cell Leaders in Tanzania', *Af. Studies Rev.*, 15, 437 (1972).
143. Levine, 'TANU Ten-House Cell System', p. 334.
144. Ibid., p. 322.
145. D. Austin, *Politics in Ghana, 1946-1960* (London: Oxford University Press, 1964).
146. J. Gardner, 'Political Participation and Chinese Communism', in G. Parry (ed.), *Participation in Politics* (Manchester: Manchester UP, 1972), 218.
147. Ibid.
148. M. Okensberg, 'Methods of Communication within the Chinese Bureaucracy', 57 *The China Quarterly* 1 (1974).
149. Id. at 28.

Part Six

CONCLUSION

22 A GENERAL THEORY OF THE STATE, LAW AND DEVELOPMENT

Law and development studies what Gunnar Myrdal called 'soft' development. The golden promises of African independence proved false. Instead of excitedly planning for development, serious men contemplated international triage — choosing among whole peoples, which to save and let die. Governments in all the poor countries made stirring statements about development, and tried to use the legal order to achieve it — and failed. Poverty and oppression continued. Why did the legal order fail?

Scholars, I believe, ought to explain that failure and thereby generate knowledge about the uses and limits of the legal order to induce development. I have tried to state some of the propositions that I think constitute such knowledge: tentative, tested at best impressionistically, problematical and always subject to falsification. This chapter puts those propositions together into a first approximation of a general theory of law and development.

A. How Law Affects Behaviour

1. Society consists of individuals and collectivities that choose within the constraints and resources of their physical and social environment as they perceive them (their 'arenas of choice').

2. In any society, particular sets of individuals and collectivities have roughly similar arenas of choice, and therefore tend to behave regularly over time. 'Institutions' means such regular patterns of behaviour.

3. 'The legal order' means the set of rules and policies that the state promulgates, together with the activities of state employees. A 'law' means such a rule.

4. 'Role-occupant' means an individual or collectivity to whom the state addresses a rule or policy.

5. Role occupants will likely consciously conform their behaviour to a rule or policy requiring changed patterns of behaviour under the following conditions:

   a. The rule or policy states how they should behave;

    b. They learn of the rule through a two-way communication channel;

    c. They have opportunity and capacity to obey;

    d. It serves their interest to obey;

    e. They perceive that it serves their interest to obey; and

    f. They decide whether to obey in a public, participatory, problem-solving process.

6. The state can intentionally change regular patterns of behaviour of role occupants by changing the role-occupants' arenas of choice.

7. Except by chance, the state can formulate and promulgate a law that induces the behaviour it prescribes only if:

    a. It communicates the rule in a two-way communication channel;

    b. It knows of and accounts for the role-occupants' arena of choice; and

    c. It institutionalizes public, participatory, problem-solving processes within which role occupants decide whether to obey.

8. Therefore, the legal order can change role-occupants' regular behaviour most readily if the role-occupants have a participatory relationship with law-makers.

B. The State and the Legal Order

1. In any given society, various sets of individuals and collectivities have broadly similar economic interests ('strata').

2. Every law or state policy, and every activity of state employees affects various strata differently, advantaging some and disadvantaging others.

3. In countries seeking to develop, a legal order always exists that necessary advantages or disadvantages particular strata.

4. The various strata constantly contend to control the state, to introduce or to maintain a legal order to their own advantage.

5. The legal order advantages particular strata by three devices:

    a. By laws, policies and official activity that directly benefit some strata, and deprive others;

b. By laws, policies and official activity that delegate to some strata and not to others authority to make particular decisions; and

c. By endowing officials with discretionary power, which they ineluctably use to advantage some strata and to disadvantage others.

6. Officials exercise discretion by choosing within their arenas of choice to maximize rewards and minimize strains for themselves and their organizations.

7. Usually, strata with power and privilege can better maximize rewards and minimize tensions for officials.

8. Therefore, officials usually exercise their discretion in favour of those strata with power and privilege.

C. The State Structure

1. Input, conversion, and feedback processes that prescribe the behaviour of various individuals and collectivities define all decision-making institutions.

2. The range of inputs, conversion processes and feedbacks preform the range of outputs ('decisions').

3. The state forms a decision-making structure whose processes of inputs, conversion and feedback ('the state structure') the legal order defines, and whose decisions concern the legal order.

4. The state's range of decisions therefore depends on the state structure.

5. Since the legal order necessarily advantages some strata and disadvantages others, by preforming its decisions concerning the legal order, the state structure necessarily advantages some strata and disadvantages others.

6. Therefore, the structure of the state and the legal order contain ineluctable biases for some strata and against others; it cannot act neutrally.

D. The Legal Order in Africa Just Before Independence

1. In Africa just before independence, the legal order so structured

the arenas of choice of various strata that they followed repetitive behaviour patterns, which in turn constituted the then prevailing social, political and economic system.

2. The prevailing institutions created and reinforced the economic advantage of foreign firms and their managers and owners, mass poverty, political rule by a small elite, national dependency on the metropolitan countries, and the hinterland's dependency on the export enclave.

3. The legal order did so by direct benefits to the strata controlling the economy ('the economic ruling class'), giving decision-making power to that class directly or through facilitative law, and giving high state officials ('the political elite') great discretion, which they exercised to favour the economic ruling class.

4. The implementing institutions included mainly courts and bureaucracy:

   a. Courts apply laws to particular cases, and have capacity to institute only incremental change.

   b. Bureaucracy becomes hierarchical, compartmented and authoritarian; it can best apply rules to cases; bureaucracy therefore can readily institute only incremental change, and cannot readily solve emergent problems that require radical solutions.

5. A government represents the strata that influence it, that is, those with whom it has strong input and feedback circuits; in colonial Africa, government had strong input and feedback circuits with officials, foreign entrepreneurs and white settlers, but only weak circuits with Africans.

6. The formal legal order allowed the political elite to enter the private sector as entrepreneurs and rentiers; informal social norms, career patterns and other factors affecting choice prevented such entry.

E. The Conditions of Development

1. 'Development' means the processes by which the state acting through the legal order seeks to solve the problems of the poor, poverty and oppression.

2. The existing legal orders in Africa supported the conditions for

poverty and oppression.

3. Problem-solving requires identifying and explaining difficulties, and solutions for them; solving the problems of poverty and oppression required a new legal order, not applying existing rules through existing institutions.

4. In a society of unequals a political elite allied with the economic ruling class will not likely try radically to change the existing legal order to advantage the poor and the oppressed; development requires that the political elites not ally themselves with the economic ruling class.

5. A political elite whose ideology instructs them that men, not institutions, make good government will not likely seek social change through the legal order; development also requires that the political elite have an ideology that instructs them to use the legal order to change institutions.

6. Authoritarian, hierarchical, compartmented institutions can only apply existing rules to perpetuate the *status quo*, but not solve emergent problems; development further requires organizing the state structure to solve problems.

7. A government will enact or continue that legal order which favours the individuals and strata with the strongest channels of communication to it; development further requires such channels between the poor and the political elite.

8. Development lastly requires institutions to husband or acquire knowledge, manpower, capital and arms.

F. *The Legal Order Since Independence*

1. At Independence, the interests of the political elite in practically every African policy opposed those of the economic ruling class.

2. Perhaps excepting Tanzania, none of the political elites in Anglophonic independent Africa had an ideology that economic, social and political change requires change in economic, social and political institutions, and that such institutional change requires changes in the legal order.

3. Perhaps excepting Tanzania, political elites in Africa largely retained courts and bureaucracy as they existed at Independence.

4. Every African government lodged many development programmes

in parastatal corporations; those corporations gave great power and discretion to their managers.

5. Every African government created planning institutions, whose plans required implementation by existing institutions, and did not plan to change institutions.

6. Every African government attempted to institutionalize local participatory institutions in an institutional environment that fostered not participation but authoritarianism.

7. Perhaps excepting Tanzania, political elites in Africa largely retained input and feedback circuits between themselves, other members of the political elite, and the economic ruling class, and did not create new input and feedback circuits between themselves and the mass.

8. Perhaps excepting Tanzania, political elites in Africa largely retained as it existed at Independence a formal legal order that provided opportunities for the political elite to enter the private sector as entrepreneurs and rentiers; no informal social norms, career patterns or other factors prevented such entry.

9. Despite great changes in the formal institutions of law-making, effective law-making power remained mainly in hierarchical, authoritarian and compartmented bureaucracies.

10. The political elites in Africa retained the broad discretion of many colonial statutes, and gave themselves broad discretion in a wide range of development programmes.

11. Perhaps excepting Tanzania, the political elites of Africa used their power and privilege to purchase entry into the private sector.

12. Because foreign firms dominated the economic order, and because the public positions and private prosperity of the political elites depended upon the continued existence and success of those firms, the political elites of Africa, perhaps excepting Tanzania, in time became dependent allies of the foreign firms.

13. Perhaps excepting Tanzania, therefore, the legal order in Africa since Independence thus advantaged the political elites and the foreign firms, and did not affect development.

G. Soft Development

1. The political rhetoric of every African political elite at Independence and since advocated development.

2. Perhaps excepting Tanzania, the legal order since independence prevented the African states from accomplishing development.

We can further condense this explanation. Marx compactly summarized his explanation for the capitalist system by pointing to the contradiction between the private ownership of the means of production, and the social nature of production. That explanation plainly suggests public ownership as a solution. The elite theorists told Marx, in effect, that his solution solved nothing. Public ownership requires organization which, they said, inevitably generates elites. The African experience at first glance tended to confirm the elitist objection. Development paradoxically created elites out of programmes that tried to raise the mass. They endowed administrators with broad and quite uncontrolled discretion; they created parastatals in which managers realistically need not account to their government shareholders; they created governments that did not serve parliament and bureaucracies that did not serve government. At the same time, these programmes did not effect much change in favour of the dispossessed. Development required change; change required participation; but development programmes ran from the top down. Development required unitary, not compartmentalized decision-making to solve emergent problems; African administration became fragmented. Development required communication channels to the poor; very few such channels existed in Africa.

Development, in short, raised anew the great challenge to law and the state: who governs the governors? The great institutions of Western democracy, the Rule of Law, judicial control over the administration, electoral democracy, the separation of powers, fundamental freedoms, responded to that agonized question. However well these worked in the West (and there are volumes telling us that they were frequently frauds), in Africa they did not and could not function as they advertised. Attempts to utilize them there bred anew an alliance between the political elite and economic ruling class, bringing not development but stagnation.[1]

This explanation argues that the authoritarian structure of the legal order limited its effectiveness in inducing change. It becomes a brief hypothesis: *soft development results inevitably from the contradiction between an authoritarian legal order and the participatory imperatives of development.* In Africa that contradiction prevented the legal order from changing much behaviour; discretion reigned supreme; corruption gnawed away; and the political elite, once revolutionary, tamely supported social, economic and political systems so much like the preceding era that they deserved the name neo-colonialism.

This explanation resonates easily with Marxism. In the nineteenth century the legal order used private property as the principal device to delegate authority over economic affairs to entrepreneurs. They used their power in their personal interest although their decisions had widespread social consequences. In twentieth-century Africa, the legal order delegated command to a bureaucratic bourgeoisie that worked hand-in-glove with multinational corporations. The institutions of private property constituted only one form of that delegation. Other laws endowed the political elite with command over resources affecting the whole society, but exercisable *de facto* in their own interest. Those laws, better than legalisms concerning title, explained soft development. How the state delegated that power involved form, not substance.

That hypothesis explains the failure of popular early theories of modernization.[2] They shared a common domain assumption: the elite consisted of 'modernizers', the mass remained 'backward'. The failure of paternalistic, top-down attempts at development buried those theories in the wreckage of the Development Decade. They ignored the limits of the legal order's authoritarian, hierarchical, compartmented structure.

That hypothesis also explains the failure of conventional 'trickle-down' theories of economic development.[3] Those theories assumed that economic incentives explain all behaviour, and therefore treated institutions as 'black boxes'. They failed because they falsely explained behaviour. To ignore institutions insulates both them and the *status quo* they embody from directed change.

Bertrand Russell epitomized the problems of most governments when he posed a famous paradox:

> . . . the problem of government is two-fold. From the point of view of the government, the problem is to secure acquiescence from the governed; from the point of view of the governed, the problem is to make the government take account, not only of its own interests, but also of the interests of those over which it has power.[4]

In conditions of development, government requires acquiescence to change behaviour; the mass requires accountability by government to ensure that it attends to their problems.

Almost everyone today agreed that participation encourages the governed's acquiescence. But, some argue, participation excites demands for more than government can give;[5] others contend that those demands will likely express traditional or parochial attitudes. The centre must therefore insulate itself from popular demands, and austerely soldier on. That proposal begs the questions raised by the second branch of Russell's paradox. How to ensure government in the interests of the mass? How to govern the governors themselves?

The question arises because of the legal order's inherent authoritarianism. Two possible responses exist. One, control from above, relies on the Rule of Law to control the political elite, without, however, changing the legal order's authoritarianism. That denies the participation necessary to induce changed behaviour. The other, control from below, resonates easily with the participation that development requires.

To propose participation in general terms, however, of course produces only a muddle. We must carefully consider particular situations, and formulate rules that define participation in both local and national institutions. Participatory societies must begin with existing reality. Law and development as a professional subject does not draw utopian blueprints, but answers the urgent question, what do we do *now*? Some people, when they decide what to have for dinner, first select a menu, consult a cookbook for the ingredients, and then purchase them at the market. Others look around the kitchen and ask, 'What do we have in the refrigerator?' Governments cannot purchase development at a supermarket. Of course they must fashion policy out of materials at hand.

At first glance, that seemingly poses another circular dilemma of development: to change things, things must first change. How to use what the refrigerator presently holds? How to use an authoritarian legal order to forge a participatory society?

So long as the political elite and the economic ruling class remain allies, obviously development will stagnate. That condition does not, however, last forever. In the history of every country, whether by war, revolution, or peaceful succession, revolutionary moments shatter that alliance. Such moments loom big with change. They occurred at African independence. In 1977, in some countries — Mozambique, Angola, Tanzania, perhaps Zambia — although opportunities for change seemed to dissolve daily, those moments still lived. They will occur repeatedly in every African country. At such moments, progressive regimes must utilize existing tools to induce development. They require detailed knowledge about the limits of law in social engineering. They must

Full popular participation

vigorously and rapidly restructure law-implementing and law-making institutions to solve the difficulties of authoritarianism. That is, they must use the legal order to transform the legal order, state power to transform the state. In the long run, they must erase differences between mass and elite. Russell's paradox, like the model of Chapter 4, presupposes a gulf between law-makers and the rest of us. Greater mass participation in decisions works to fill that gulf. In China the Committee of Concerned Asian Scholars found this 'most startling fact': that 'there is no division into things "political" and "non-political" . . . Everyone is a politician and no one is only a leader.'[6] That course finally must obliterate the line between governors and governed. The mass will then no longer remain, as elite theory supposes,[7] 'caught in their own milieux', nor will it occur that 'only the elite in the command posts of society gains an overall view'. If development requires participation, people in society must transform themselves.

Such a transformation demands not merely development, but liberation. Denis Goulet writes that 'Liberation implies the suppression of elitism by a populace which assumes control over its own change processes.'[8] People cannot liberate themselves until they take an overall view of their condition. When the mass see whole social institutions free of myth, prejudice, stereotype and illusion, their competence over affairs increases, and greater participation becomes possible.

Fortunately, people learn through doing. Institutional changes come first. The more the mass participates in crucial decisions, the more they liberate themselves; the more they liberate themselves, the more they escape the hedges and blank walls, to live on the mountain heights from which alone they can see society whole. The more they see society whole, the more they can contribute meaningfully to decision-making. By the same token, full popular participation requires the end of law as we know it: a system of norms that the Sovereign promulgates and the State enforces. Law in that sense will end because the sharp boundary between sovereign and subjects will disappear. I cannot suggest an alternative model for understanding legal processes in such conditions. Just as a fish cannot imagine living out of water, so do I, and all of us, fixate on a society with distinct rulers and subjects.

Africa, however, will not soon require such understandings. Development must begin with reality, not dreams. It begins with disease and hunger and early death and oppression and cruelty, and an authoritarian legal order hardly fit to induce radical change. A government not totally allied with those now deriving out of misery their power and privilege, however, *can* devise ways to initiate the processes of change.

It requires knowledge of the uses and limits of the legal order. Social scientists concerned with development must study the state and the law.

Lawyers, despite their purported expertise in 'the Law', have no more of this knowledge than social scientists. That knowledge, like all knowledge, arises not out of contemplating the infinite but out of doing: out of life, procedures, the disciplined study of experience. As lawyers, we do not learn how rules influence behaviour by examining merely the rules themselves. Law-in-the-books tells only part of the story. If we lawyers can meaningfully contribute to development, we must emerge from libraries and dusty tomes to study behaviour, the law-in-action as well as the law-in-the-books. Lawyers and the legal order can help alleviate poverty and misery only when lawyers themselves participate in development. That calls for concern, for engagement, for commitment — in short, a passion simultaneously for knowledge and for justice.

All the world has for long ages borne the burden of authoritarian legal orders and state structures. These expressed the inequitable societies of which they were a part, in which lords and ladies lived on the misery of serfs, nabobs and gentry, on agricultural labourers, capitalist robber barons, on impoverished immigrants, transnational corporate managers and shareholders, on the Third World's poverty. Those who owned the world ran it, and devised and kept in force legal orders designed to maintain their power, not to change things. The legal order has powerful ideological and mythical supports, that we all come to believe. So long as we are bound by them, for so long will we support the authoritarianism that lies at the heart of soft development. A passion for both knowledge and justice must seize not only lawyers, but all the actors in the drama. Only then will the poor likely become emancipated from poverty and oppression, and come to enjoy the benefits of both law and development.

Notes

1. The theory of Western 'democratic' constitutions is that the electoral process makes it possible for other publics than the rich and powerful to provide rewards and punishments for politicians.
2. See, e.g. D. Apter, *The Politics of Modernization* (Chicago: University of Chicago Press, 1965); G. Almond and W. Powell, *Comparative Politics: A Developmental Approach* (Boston: Little, Brown, 1966); J.H. Boeke, *Economies and Economic Policy of Dual Societies* (New York: Institute of Pacific Relations, 1965); R. Braibanti, *Research on the Bureaucracy of Pakistan: A*

Critique of Sources, Conditions and Issues, with appended documents (Durham, N.C.: Duke University Press, 1966); H. Bretton, *Power and Stability in Nigeria* (New York: Praeger, 1966); J.S. Coleman and C. Rosberg, *Political Parties and National Integration in Tropical Africa* (Berkeley: University of California Press, 1965); S.P. Huntingdon, *Political Order in Changing Societies* (New Haven: Yale University Press 1968); L.W. Pye, *Politics, Personality and Nation Building: Burma's Search for Identity* (New Haven: Yale University Press, 1962); F.W. Riggs, 'The Sala-Model: An Ecological Approach to the Study of Comparative Administration', *Philippine Journal of Public Administration*, 6, 3 (1962), reprinted in A.J. Heidenheimer (ed.), *Political Corruption: Readings in Comparative Analysis* (New York: Holt, Rinehart and Winston, 1970); D.M. Trubek, 'Toward a Social Theory of Law: An Essay on the Study of Law and Development', *Yale L.J.*, 82, 1 (1972); M. Weiner, (ed.), *Modernization: The Dynamics of Growth* (New York: Basic Books, 1966); E. Shils, 'Political Development in the New States', *Comparative Studies in Society and History*, 11 (Morton, The Hague, 1969).

3. See above, Chap. 3.
4. B. Russell, *Power, A New Social Analysis* (New York: Norton, 1958), pp. 197-8.
5. See above, Chap. 16,
6. Committee of Concerned Asian Scholars, *China Inside the People's Republic* (New York: Briton Books, 1972), p. 50.
7. See above, Chap. 18.
8. D. Goulet, *The Cruel Choice: A New Concept in the Theory of Development* (New York: Atheneum, 1973), p. xv.

INDEX

administration *see* development
administration; bureaucracy;
Colonial Service; civil service
administrative law: African 235
et seq.; discretion and 230;
enforcement institutions 230;
failure in Africa, generally 229;
improvements in 249; participation and 327 *et seq.*; power,
limits on 229, 245; ultra vires
doctrine 229
Africanization, and bureaucratic
bourgeoisie 411
agriculture: enforcement of
regulations, by courts 140; land
adjudication tribunals, in Kenya
213; obedience to regulations 140
analytical positivism *see* jurisprudence
anomie: bribery, high-level, as
explanation for 178; development,
as creating 100-1; decision to obey
and 139
arena of choice, defined 71
Arusha Declaration 322, 415-17
Austin, John 72
Azikwe, N. 346

banking law 411
bargaining model of society 349
behaviour: influenced by law 35, 73
et seq.; institutionalization of,
defined 100; law as influencing 35
Botswana: National Economic
Advisory Council 299
bribery, high level: aid to development 168-70; criminal sanctions
for 177-8; defined 167; elections
and 75-6; explanations for 173-9;
givers of bribes 179-80; history of
167-8; legal provisions 170-3;
political parties and 175; solutions
for 181-5; United Kingdom and
179-80
bureaucracy: communication and 125;
explanation for failure of 195-6,
238 *et seq.*; generally 224 *et seq.*;
goal substitution in 243; planning
and 298; political control over
395-6; rate of change and 240-1;
Rule of Law and 224-6;

see also civil service, Colonial
Service; development administration.
bureaucratic bourgeoisie: alliance
with local elite, 325; corruption
411-13; development programmes
and 411-13; discretion 243, 412;
education and 405; explanation
for 408; institutional constraints
on development of 414-20;
Kenya 404; loans to 411; multinational corporations and 407-8;
municipal services and 405;
planning and 238; public corporations and 266-7, 271 *et seq.*;
secrecy 429; Zambia 227; *see
also* class; elite
businessmen: education and 411;
high level bribery and 179-80;
see also multinational corporations

calculation: anomie and 100; law,
deciding whether to obey 99-100
cabinet 393-4
cadres 307
capacity: element of arena of choice
101-2
categories *see* vocabulary
change: rate of, and bureaucracy
240-1; rate of, and courts 217
choice: as model of man in society 34;
decision-making systems 194;
elements of 70, 101 *et seq.*; law,
deciding whether to obey 100
civil liberties *see* fundamental
human rights
civil service: access to 433; anonymity of 387; communications,
power and 125; communication
system 118, 219, 319; constitutions and 386-7; control over
ministers 428; feedback channel
428; general orders 409-10, 415, 430;
investments in private sector 409-10;
Public Service Commission 387;
research capacity 434-5; secrecy
in 429-32; *see also* administration;
bureaucracy; development
administration
class: as element in arena of choice
135; economic ruling class,

474